THE ENGLISH TRADITION

Modern Studies in English History

EDITED BY

Norman F. Cantor

AND

Michael S. Werthman

VOLUME II

SINCE 1714

The Macmillan Company · *New York*
Collier-Macmillan Limited · *London*

© Copyright, The Macmillan Company, 1967

All rights reserved. No part of this book may be reproduced or transmitted in any form or by any means, electronic or mechanical, including photocopying, recording or by any information storage and retrieval system, without permission in writing from the Publisher.

Second Printing, 1968

Library of Congress catalog card number: 67-17857

The Macmillan Company, New York
Collier-Macmillan Canada, Ltd., Toronto, Ontario

Printed in the United States of America

ACKNOWLEDGMENTS

The editors wish to express their gratitude to the following publishers and individuals for permission to quote selections from the works designated.

George Allen & Unwin Ltd., London: W. L. Burn, *The Age of Equipoise.*
Ann Elmo Agency, Inc., New York: George Dangerfield, *The Strange Death of Liberal England, 1910-1914.*
The Beaverbrook Foundations, London: Lord Beaverbrook, *Decline and Fall of Lloyd George.*
Ernest Benn Limited, London: Élie Halévy, *England in 1815.*
The Bobbs-Merrill Company, Inc., Indianapolis: Lord David Cecil, *Melbourne.*
Herbert Butterfield: Herbert Butterfield, *George III, Lord North and the People, 1779-1780.*
Cambridge University Press, New York: O. MacDonagh, "The 19th Century Revolution in Government, A Reappraisal," *Historical Journal*, I (1958); H. Parris, "The 19th Century Revolution in Government; A Reappraisal Reappraised," *Historical Journal*, III (1960); P. Deane and W. A. Cole, *British Economic Growth, 1688-1959*; H. J. Habakkuk, *American and British Technology in the 19th Century.*
Chatto & Windus Ltd., London: Raymond Williams, *The Long Revolution.*
By permission of the Clarendon Press, Oxford: Lucy S. Sutherland, *East India Company in Eighteenth Century Politics*; N. Sykes, "The Church," in A. S. Turberville, ed., *Johnson's England*, Vol. I; George Rudé, *Wilkes and Liberty*; D. E. Butler, *The Electoral System in Britain Since 1918*, 2nd ed.; Henry Pelling, *The Origins of the Labour Party.*
Columbia University Press, New York: Mary Mack, *Jeremy Bentham*; Raymond Williams, *The Long Revolution.*
Constable and Company Limited, London: Lord David Cecil, *Melbourne.*
Curtis Brown Ltd., London: J. H. Plumb, *Sir Robert Walpole*, Vol. II.
George Dangerfield: George Dangerfield, *The Strange Death of Liberal England, 1910-1914.*
E. P. Dutton & Co., Inc., New York: Philip Magnus, *Gladstone: A Biography.*
Victor Gollancz, Ltd., London: E. P. Thompson, *The Making of the English Working Class.*
Hamish Hamilton Ltd., London: A. J. P. Taylor, *Englishmen and Others*; L. B. Namier, *Crossroads of Power.*
Harvard University Press, Cambridge, Mass.: G. Kitson Clark, *The Making of Victorian England*; Eugene Black, *The Association.*
Heinemann Educational Books Ltd., London: Mary Mack, *Jeremy Bentham*; R. T. McKenzie, *British Political Parties: The Distribution of Power Within the Conservative and Labour Parties*, rev. ed.
Houghton Mifflin Company, Boston: J. H. Plumb, *Sir Robert Walpole*, Vol. II.
Alfred A. Knopf, Inc.—Random House, Inc., New York: S. H. Beer, *British Politics in the Collectivist Age*; E. P. Thompson, *The Making of the English Working Class.*
Longmans, Green & Co. Limited, London: G. M. Trevelyan, *The Peace of the Protestant Succession*, Vol. III of *England Under Queen Anne*; Vincent Harlow, *The Founding of the Second British Empire*; H. J. Hanham, *Elections and Party Man-*

agement; Richard Pares, *A West-India Fortune*; Norman Gash, *Politics in the Age of Peel*; S. J. Checkland, *The Rise of Industrial Society in England, 1815–1885*.

MacGibbon and Kee, Ltd., London: George Dangerfield, *The Strange Death of Liberal England, 1910–1914*.

By permission of Macmillan & Co. Ltd., London, The Macmillan Company of Canada Limited, and St. Martin's Press, Inc.: Asa Briggs, *Chartist Studies;* Roy Harrod, *The Life of John Maynard Keynes*; E. H. Phelps-Brown, *The Growth of British Industrial Relations;* J. W. Wheeler-Bennett, *Munich: Prologue to Tragedy*.

The Macmillan Company, New York: L. B. Namier, *Crossroads of Power*; Barbara Tuchman, *The Guns of August*.

Meredith Press, New York: Lord Beaverbrook, *The Decline and Fall of Lloyd George*.

Methuen & Co. Ltd., London: G. Kitson Clark, *The Making of Victorian England*; A. R. Humphreys, *The Augustan World*.

John Murray Ltd., London: Philip Magnus, *Gladstone: A Biography*.

Lady Namier: L. B. Namier, *Crossroads of Power*.

W. W. Norton & Company, Inc., New York: W. L. Burn, *The Age of Equipoise*.

J. H. Plumb: J. H. Plumb, *Sir Robert Walpole*, Vol. II.

Oxford University Press, London: under the auspices of the Royal Institute of International Affairs, W. K. Hancock, *Problems of Nationality, 1918–1936*, Vol. I of *Survey of British Commonwealth Affairs*.

Pantheon Books, New York: E. P. Thompson, *The Making of the English Working Class*.

A. D. Peters & Co., London: Herbert Butterfield, *George III, Lord North and the People, 1779–1780*.

Frederick A. Praeger, Inc., Publishers, New York: R. T. McKenzie, *British Political Parties: The Distribution of Power Within the Conservative and Labour Parties*, rev. ed.

G. P. Putnam's Sons, New York: George Dangerfield, *The Strange Death of Liberal England, 1910–1914*.

St. Martin's Press, Inc., New York: S. J. Checkland, *The Rise of Industrial Society in England, 1815–1885*.

Stevens & Sons Limited, London: J. P. Mackintosh, *The British Cabinet*.

Barbara W. Tuchman: Barbara Tuchman, *The Guns of August*.

University of Toronto Press, Toronto: J. P. Mackintosh, *The British Cabinet*.

John Wiley & Sons, Inc., New York: A. P. Thornton, *Doctrines of Imperialism*.

Yale University Press, New Haven: W. E. Houghton, *The Victorian Frame of Mind, 1830–1870*.

INTRODUCTION

THE HISTORIAN's main task is always to justify the past to the present, to explain to educated contemporaries how the present society and culture came to be. For nineteenth-century English historians this was not a hard task to fulfill. Because the Victorian historians were all members of the upper middle class elite, the range of contemporary experience whose creation they had to account for was very narrow; it involved parliamentary and cabinet government, the common law, Protestantism, commercial and industrial enterprise, and imperial supremacy. The making of this distinctive English tradition was explained in a heavily organic, teleological, and deterministic frame of reference: out of pristine Germanic communal institutions grew the great oak of English liberties whose beneficent boughs sheltered a national religion and provided freedom for economic progress.

With each passing decade of the twentieth century this view of the English past seemed less convincing, relevant, and persuasive, and by the 1960s it had collapsed in a shambles. The organic assumptions were thrown away along with other remains of Victorian intellectual baggage. The present condition of English society appeared disappointing, difficult, and even desperate, and therefore it was contemporary failure as well as success which had to be shown to be grounded in the past. Finally, the thought-world and experience of professional historians has greatly broadened out beyond that of the small upper middle class Victorian elite, as scholars of diverse backgrounds (not only petty bourgeois British but even Central European, French, and American) have come to the fore as interpreters of the English past and have sought to find historical foundations for a contemporary ambiance that encompasses war, bureaucracy, secularism, economic decline, loss of empire, class struggle, increased democracy, and mass pop culture.

The purpose of this book is to offer carefully edited representative selections from important work done by twentieth-century historians in relating their vibrant and unstable world to the English past. These historians have in recent decades reconstructed the whole shape of English history. They have sought to give meaning to the exhilarating and exhausting conflicts of the present by extending the traditions of the past far beyond their narrow, genteel Victorian confines. They have demonstrated that political, administrative, and legal life is carried on within the context of intellectual, religious, and economic realities. They have discovered and illuminated an English tradition of power and class contentions, social inertia and violent change, bureaucratic control and centrifugal localism, philosophy and science, radical religious and political commitments, greed and exploitation, as well as idealistic, sensible devotion to great leaders and noble causes. The English tradition is no longer simply liberty, nonconformity, and prosperity; it has become as heterogeneous, variable, paradoxical, and complex as later twentieth-century English society and culture themselves.

N. F. C.
M. S. W.

CONTENTS

Part I: 1714–1815

1. The Legacy of the Hanoverian Settlement — 2
   G. M. Trevelyan
2. Sir Robert Walpole as the King's Minister — 10
   J. H. Plumb
3. The Political Influence of the East India Company — 16
   Lucy S. Sutherland
4. The Early Georgian Cabinet — 23
   J. P. Mackintosh
5. The Structure of Mid–Eighteenth-Century Government and Politics — 29
   L. B. Namier
6. The Hanoverian Church — 38
   Norman Sykes
7. Reason and Feeling in the Eighteenth Century — 54
   A. R. Humphreys
8. The Planter Aristocracy — 64
   Richard Pares
9. Economic Growth in the Eighteenth Century — 75
   P. Deane and W. A. Cole
10. The Political Tragedy of George III — 85
    Herbert Butterfield
11. The Social Ingredients of the Wilkite Movement — 90
    George Rudé
12. The First Reform Movement — 100
    Eugene C. Black
13. The Crisis of the Empire — 105
    Vincent Harlow

14 The Apotheosis of the Whig Aristocracy   111
    DAVID CECIL

15 Bentham and the Old Regime   118
    MARY MACK

16 The Heritage of Wesley   125
    ÉLIE HALÉVY

17 The Forming of Working Class Consciousness   136
    E. P. THOMPSON

PART II: 1815–1906

18 The Debate on the First Reform Bill   144
    NORMAN GASH

19 The Essentials of Chartism   163
    ASA BRIGGS

20 From Empire to Commonwealth   179
    W. K. HANCOCK

21 The Victorian Middle Class   190
    S. J. CHECKLAND

22 Individualism and Collectivism in Mid-Victorian
    England   201
    W. L. BURN

23 The Victorian Mind   215
    W. E. HOUGHTON

24 The Social History of Nineteenth-Century Education 228
    RAYMOND WILLIAMS

25 Benthamite Doctrine and the Victorian State   235
    O. MACDONAGH AND H. PARRIS

26 Gladstone as a Christian Statesman   243
    PHILIP MAGNUS

27 Palmerston and Disraeli   248
    A. J. P. TAYLOR

28	County Politics in the Age of Disraeli and Gladstone H. J. HANHAM	258
29	The Social Foundations of Late Victorian Politics G. KITSON CLARK	264
30	The White Man's Burden A. P. THORNTON	284
31	Entrepreneurial Decline in the Late Nineteenth Century H. J. HABAKKUK	293
32	The Formation of the Labour Party HENRY PELLING	299

PART III: 1906 TO THE PRESENT

33	The Labour and Welfare Policies of the Liberal Government, 1906–1914 E. H. PHELPS-BROWN	308
34	Rupert Brooke—Symbol of an Age GEORGE DANGERFIELD	321
35	August 1914 BARBARA TUCHMAN	330
36	Lloyd George in War and Peace LORD BEAVERBROOK	343
37	John Maynard Keynes and the Bloomsbury Group ROY HARROD	348
38	A Judgment on Munich J. W. WHEELER-BENNETT	362
39	The Party Structure in the Twentieth Century ROBERT MCKENZIE	366
40	The Labour Party as a Political Institution S. H. BEER	376
41	Electoral Sociology D. E. BUTLER	388

PART I
1714-1815

I

THE LEGACY OF THE HANOVERIAN SETTLEMENT

G. M. Trevelyan

The Master of Trinity College, Cambridge, George Macaulay Trevelyan was through the first half of the twentieth century the highly effective spokesman for the whig-liberal interpretation of modern English history, a view so forcefully expounded in the Victorian era by his great-uncle, T. B. Macaulay. Trevelyan believed that the Glorious Revolution of 1689 and the Hanoverian Settlement of 1714 were the foundation of England's modern greatness and glory. While he was by no means blind to the greed, corruption, and squalid power conflicts that prevailed in Whig circles, he nevertheless regarded the Whig party as something more than a group of aristocratic factions. He saw in the history of the Whig aristocracy a continuous thread of devotion to liberty and the rule of law that provided the indispensable foundation for Britain's rise to economic, imperial, and military power in the eighteenth and nineteenth centuries. Trevelyan, like his great-uncle, was a wonderfully prolific writer and a master of a clear and compelling style that allowed him to communicate his ideas to a very wide lay audience. The following selection shows some of Trevelyan's high narrative art and presents his general view of early Georgian government.

ALL THE WORLD was hurrying to St. James's Palace, on foot, in chairs, or by coach-and-six. Power and fashion, Whig and Tory, all the Lords and Commoners who were left in London during the recess, thronged that morning to greet the rising sun of Hanover, and bask, if possible, in its beams.

But it was also a 'Sabbath morn,' and in the sober City, before the news had been told, vast congregations of business men and their employees had gathered in the Dissenting places of worship, in an agony of fear and hope. For it was the day on which, by statute, the Schism Act came into force, to destroy their schools and usher in, as they believed, another age of persecution—unless the Queen should die. Their friend Bishop

---

FROM G. M. Trevelyan, *The Peace of the Protestant Succession*, Vol. III of *England Under Queen Anne* (London: Longmans, Green & Co., Limited, 1934, 1946), pp. 310–321. By permission of the publisher.

Burnet, gone westward early in the morning to hunt for news, had agreed to send a message, if the great change took place, to Mr. Bradbury, the Independent minister of Fetter Lane. As the preacher began his sermon, he looked up from the pulpit to the gallery, and saw a man push his way to the front and drop a handkerchief into the body of the hall. It was the Bishop's signal. Bradbury broke off his discourse to announce to his hearers that no longer Queen Anne but King George was their liege sovereign. The sea of upturned, anxious faces was transformed in a moment by the action of joy, and at the bidding of the preacher they rolled out a psalm of thanksgiving to the God who had delivered them once more. They all knew now that the Schism Act was born dead; that their persecutors would be hurled from power, and that they and their children would be allowed to live as freemen, the most loyal of all the subjects of King George.

While these humbler folk were rejoicing, 'the great' were busy at St. James's. Bothmar and Kreienberg, the Hanoverian Ministers, were summoned to be present. Time was needed to draw up the proper form in which to proclaim the new King, and while this was being done in one room, in another the important work was in process of naming and swearing in the Regents or 'Lords Justices,' who were to bear rule in the island till George in person should arrive. Under the Regency Act they were to consist of seven great officers of state, and eighteen more persons named by the Successor. Three sealed documents, each containing the list of his choice, were solemnly opened, one after the other, and found to correspond. They revealed a few Hanoverian Tories and a goodly number of moderate Whigs, but neither Somers, Sunderland nor Wharton: George was not in the pocket of the Junto.

Bolingbroke, as mere 'Secretary,' was not one of the *ex officio* Regents and he had not been named by King George. His day was over. But Archbishop Tenison, in whom the High Church Queen had never confided and who had during the Tory regime retired from all the Councils of State, came over from Lambeth Palace to take a leading part in that day of triumph for the tolerant and moderate principles which in his thought were proper to the Church of England.

The other Privy Councillors treated with regal ceremony those Regents who were present among them, and messengers were sent off to those who were at their country homes to bid them come up to town and rule the land.

Meanwhile the Proclamation had been prepared, and was eagerly signed not only by the Regents and Privy Councillors but by many Lords, Bishops, Members of the Lower House, and officials such as Sir Christopher Wren, Surveyor General. A hundred and twenty-seven names in all were appended to the Proclamation, of which perhaps half were Tory, including not only the Hanoverian Tories but Bolingbroke, Wyndham and Ormonde. It was a national act.

These formalities had taken up the morning hours, but between one and two o'clock the patience of the vast crowd waiting in front of St.

James's Palace met its reward. They saw appear first the Regents, then the Privy Councillors, the Lord Mayor, and the throng of nobles and gentlemen who had signed the Proclamation. The kettledrums rattled and the trumpets spoke; every man present bared his head; and the Herald read the Proclamation:

We therefore, the Lords Spiritual and Temporal of the Realm, being here assisted with those of Her Late Majesty's Privy Council, with numbers of other principal gentlemen of quality, with the Lord Mayor, Aldermen and Citizens of London, do now hereby with one full voice and consent of tongue and heart, publish and proclaim that the High and Mighty Prince George Elector of Brunswick Lunenburg is now by the death of our late sovereign of Happy Memory, become our only lawful and rightful liege Lord, George, by the Grace of God King of Great Britain, France and Ireland.

When he ended with the words 'God save the King,' a great and joyful shout went up, spreading in waves up St. James's Street, through the Mall and along the Strand. Again the kettle-drums and trumpets sounded, and far away the batteries of the Tower told the City and the river that George was King.

The night was a night of cheering crowds, illuminations and bonfires in all the streets of London. There was ample space in the great squares where the nobility had their mansions, and each magnate had his bonfire kindled by his servants before his door. One of the largest was Bolingbroke's, before his house in Golden Square, which caused much amusement to the Hanoverian and Harleian Tories, was observed that their enemies, so 'rampant' a few days ago after Oxford's dismissal, 'began to turn upon their heel very quickly.' Oxford, elated at his rival's downfall, broke again into execrable and ungrammatical verse, writing on August 18 to his friend Dartmouth:

> And for those who did conspire
> For to bring in James Esquire
> Now hope to be saved by their own Bonfire.
> Doctors agree they are never the higher.
>   Teste Jonathan.

The late Lord Treasurer, helped by 'Jonathan' Swift, had already persuaded himself that he for one had never been in favour of 'James Esquire.' Possibly he never had been at heart, but in that case the Abbé Gaultier and his young correspondent in Lorraine had been the more deceived.

Bolingbroke kept up his spirits bravely for awhile. Two days after the Queen's death he wrote to Swift:

The Earl of Oxford was removed on Tuesday; the queen died on Sunday. What a world is this and how does fortune banter us.... I have lost all by the death of the queen by my spirit; and I protest to you I feel that increase upon me. The Whigs are a pack of Jacobites; that shall be the cry in a month if you please.

So wrote the 'man of Mercury.' Swift replied with greater insight into the situation:

> Your machine of four years modelling is dashed to pieces in a moment; and, as well by the choice of Regents as by their proceedings, I do not find there is any intention of managing you in the least.

Indeed there was no desire to keep terms with Bolingbroke. The Regents treated him not as a power to be propitiated but as a culprit to be examined, and before the end of the month he was curtly dismissed from the Secretaryship, before ever the King reached England. And when at last George arrived he gave the coldest reception not only to Bolingbroke but to Oxford. The hangers-on of the late Ministry were soon in distress. Lady Masham was a private person once more. And Mrs. Manley, the libeller, wrote a begging letter to Oxford on August 30:

> I have nothing but a starving scene before me, Lord Marlborough and all his accomplices justly enraged against me. Nothing saved out of the wreck.

Meanwhile the Marlboroughs returned from exile. They had decided to come home before they knew that the Queen was dangerously ill. But they had chosen the right moment. On the evening of the day of the Queen's death they arrived at Dover to meet the news, and were received at their landing with every sign of popular enthusiasm. On August 4 they made triumphal entry, side by side in their glass coach, over London Bridge and through the City to Marlborough House, 'amid the acclamations of the people as if he had won another battle at Hochstet.' Before them rode an improvised escort of 'two hundred horsemen three in a row,' with a company of London train-bands marching behind, through shouting crowds, though hooting was mingled with the cheers.

George had offended Marlborough by failing to name him as one of the Regents, but the first document he signed in Hanover as King of England, only five days after the Queen's death, made the Duke once more Captain-General. Even Bothmar, lately suspicious of his loyalty, wrote on that day, 'He will be of great service if the Pretender makes any attempt.' He was again England's magnificent arm of defence, but his political influence was never revived in the counsels of State. For if he was no longer a Tory, neither was he a Whig, and the Whigs were now supreme. In old age and with failing powers, he enjoyed the domestic leisure and happiness at Blenheim for which he had so often sighed in years gone by, when writing his letters home to Sarah from the field.

The King had seen no reason to make haste to England. There was no danger to his throne. Not a mouse had stirred against him in England, in Ireland or in Scotland. When Anne died, Bolingbroke, Ormonde and other Jacobites told Ilberville that at all costs civil war must be avoided, that at present they were loyal to King George and that the French King must accept the situation. Louis XIV, who had no wish for another war, acknowledged the fact of the Protestant Succession and repulsed the attempt of the Pretender to come to Paris and embroil France and England. Berwick, the ablest Jacobite, was besieging Barcelona a fortnight away from news. Nothing was anywhere attempted on James's behalf. Queen Anne had left no will; only a mysterious packet of papers was found, with directions upon it in her handwriting that it should be burnt unopened, as it duly was by the Regents in Bothmar's presence. Some have surmised that it contained her brother's appeals to her, to which she had not responded as he hoped; but there is in fact no evidence save the merest rumour as to what the packet contained.

And so, having set his German affairs well in order, and said a slow and sorrowful farewell to beloved Hanover, promising often to come back, the elderly German gentleman proceeded by leisurely stages towards his new inheritance. It was not till September 18 that he landed at Greenwich, where he was received in state by a loyal nobility and people. It was not so dramatic an affair as Charles II's landing at Dover or Napoleon's return from Elba, but, alone of the great dynasties of Europe, his race has continued ever since to occupy the throne without losing possession even for a day. Our country is still ruled by King George under the terms of the Act of Settlement.

The Whig hegemony that continued for forty years, as a result of the happenings during the four last years of Queen Anne, was caused by the divided state of the Tory party and its uncertain loyalty to the throne. The first two Georges had no choice but to take Whig servants and had therefore to accept their terms. They could not, like William and Anne, play off one party against the other, and for that reason the independent political power of the Crown still further declined. When Bolingbroke and Ormonde, alarmed and provoked by their impeachment, fled to France and joined the Pretender in 1715, when Wyndham plotted in vain to raise Western England, and when Scotland was actually rent by an evenly contested Civil War, it was made more than ever impossible for George I or his son after him to look with favour on the Tories. His subjects, too, craved for quiet and an end to the long round of civil wars and persecutions of a century past. If the Whigs could give men security they could be permitted to bear rule, riding the country on a light rein. Most of the Hanoverian Tories or their children became Whigs of one kind or another. The Tories who still followed Wyndham in Parliament, dwindled to a mere group. And Bolingbroke, in spite of his speedy and complete renunciation of Jacobitism after six months' experience as the Pretender's Secretary, was never admitted back into the House of Lords. All he could do was to turn pamphleteer and preach the 'moderate' doctrine of his old rival Oxford, as his own new philosophy of 'the Patriot King' above all party divisions.

When Bolingbroke fled to France, Oxford, with the cool courage that was the finer part of his phlegmatic nature, remained to stand his trial. Fortunately the French archives were not available to the prosecution; and the House of Lords, always at this period a moderator of party heats, acquitted him as it had acquitted Somers sixteen years before. In so doing, it served England well, for the use of impeachments against fallen statesmen is unsuited to a constitutional regime. In civilized society men cannot be expected to serve their country with ropes round their necks.

The outstanding fact in political history under the first two Georges is the abeyance of the Tory party as an effective force in Parliament. The two-party system did not die but it slept. There were always avowed Tories in Parliament, but they were not numerous enough either to take over the government when a change was needed, or to act alone as an Opposition. They usually worked with that section of the Whigs who happened to be opposed to the Whig Government of the day. Since there was no rival party which the Whig aristocracy as a whole had cause to fear, it grew negligent of public opinion, and relied more and more on perfecting the corrupt machinery of elections, instead of appealing on points of principle to the electorate. Where there are no effective Tories there can be no proper Whigs. As the struggle for power ceased to be political it became personal, a scuffle of the rival 'great houses' for the power to distribute the good things of Church and State.

The question in Parliament from 1715 to 1760 was not whether 'the Whigs' should be turned out, but only which Whigs should be turned out and which Whigs should take their place. The principles for which the party had stood in old days, such as Toleration of Dissenters and the limitation of the Power of the Crown, were no longer in the forefront of controversy, largely because they had been realized and had become an essential part of the political structure of the land, and partly because they were forgotten amid the personal rivalries of 'the great.' In the last years of this regime, the elder Pitt appealed to the country over the heads of the degenerate Whig oligarchy of the day, and in the great crisis of the Seven Years War revived the old popular spirit of Whig nationalism, in a call to Britons to defend their religion, liberties and commerce against the House of Bourbon. Neither Walpole as Prime Minister nor Newcastle after him had made any such appeal.

The Jacobite danger was the real strength of the Whigs. Neither the King nor the electors would turn the Whigs out to bring in James. Even Bolingbroke had learnt by his brief personal experience at the Pretender's Court that to make him King would be to make Roman Catholic priests once again the directors of royal policy. To restore such a regime would merely lead to another Revolution. The existence of the dynastic question which had ruined the Tories in 1714, continued to divide and distract them, and to render them suspect to powerful classes who would otherwise have been on their side.

Security and liberty were obtained under the Hanoverian Constitution, because, under Walpole, the Whigs became, what they had not always been, the 'moderate men.' At bottom their famous 'moderation' was due to the fact that they were a minority in the island; they were normally the weaker party, holding office by the accident of the dynastic question and the division of the Tories on that supreme issue.

Before the Industrial Revolution, England was still mainly agricultural. Therefore the squires and the rural clergy were more powerful, when united and aroused as in 1710, than the Dissenters and the business and professional classes who had rallied round the Whigs and the House of Hanover in 1715. If the Whigs were wise, they would never injure the interests or alarm the prejudices of the clergy and squires. The Whigs could monopolize power, if only they would leave the Tory classes alone. Walpole, as he grew older, fully grasped this principle, and acted upon it for many years as Prime Minister, with complete success. His motto was *quieta non movere*, 'Let sleeping dogs lie.'

In ecclesiastical affairs great care was taken not to give cause for another cry of 'Church in Danger.' Through the help of the able manager, Bishop Gibson—himself an actively loyal Hanoverian but not a Low Churchman—the Whig Ministers brought about an understanding between the House of Hanover and the Established Church. That was the true basis of Eighteenth Century peace and stability in England.

In pursuance of this 'moderate' policy in matters ecclesiastical, the Occasional Conformity and Schism Acts of Anne's reign were repealed in George I's reign, but no further concession was made to the Dissenters. The Test and Corporation Acts were left untouched. Those Nonconformists who refused to qualify by taking the sacrament according to the rites of the Established Church, were still excluded from municipal and State office.

Owing to the moderation of the Whigs in doing no more for their Nonconformist clients and nothing more to provoke the clergy, there was no repetition of the popular outcry of 'Church in Danger' that had done the Whigs such harm in the days of Dr. Sacheverell. The growing spirit of Latitudinarianism, characteristic of the educated classes in the Eighteenth Century, helped Whig statecraft gently to lay the spirit of High Church enthusiasm.

So the Whig attempt to come to terms with the Church was successful under the first two Georges, far beyond what could have seemed possible in the fervid days of William and Anne. Nor was the Whig policy of 'moderation' confined to the religious field. The Tory squires were left unprovoked. Many of them were placed on the Bench as Justices of the Peace. Fielding in *Tom Jones* represents Squire Western as a magistrate. He had been placed on the Bench by those Whig Lords and 'Hanover rats,' of whom he said 'I hate the very name of themmum'; he had no thought of joining the Pretender in 1745. So too, academic liberties were rigidly respected by the Government, who never interfered with the extreme Toryism of Oxford.

After long generations of trouble, persecution and hatred, England had at last won through to a period of domestic peace and individual freedom. It was not a period of avowed idealism; it was not a period of legislative reform. But neither idealism nor reform is the whole of life for men or nations. The vigour and initiative of Englishmen, at home and overseas, in all branches of human effort and intellect, were the admiration of Eighteenth Century Europe. The greatness of England in the Hanoverian epoch was made by men acting freely in a free community, with little help indeed from Church or State, but with no hindrance. The great art of letting your neighbour alone, even if he thinks differently from you, was learnt by Englishmen under Walpole, at a time when the lesson was still a strange one elsewhere. Some European countries have not learnt it to this day or are rapidly unlearning it again. The manners and customs of English political and ecclesiastical controversy were softened between 1715 and 1760, and this change left a lasting mark on life and politics.

It has been calculated that there were about seventy 'great Whig families,' who, under the early Hanoverian Kings, formed the Government and led the Opposition. Each of these great families usually had its titular head snugly in the Upper House, while its heirs and cadets sat for family boroughs and made their reputations in the faction fighting in St. Stephen's Chapel.

This is the system which Disraeli termed 'the Venetian Oligarchy.' An oligarchy in some sense it was; but it was the very opposite of Venetian. The methods of the rulers of Venice were despotism, inquisition, enforced silence, and secret political justice. But the 'Whig Oligarchy' was submissive to the rule of law, and the English laws gave to the Executive no power to suppress speech or writing that attacked the Government. Unless the Law Court found a critic of Government guilty of sedition, Ministers could do nothing to silence him. The Law Court, not the Government, decided what was libel, blasphemy or sedition. And the Judges were independent of the Executive, and the Juries were often hostile.

The highly civilized conception of law as a power superior to the will of the rulers was strong among the Eighteenth Century English. The Law of England had triumphed in the great battle with the Stuart Kings; the idea of the rule of law—as propounded by Coke and Selden—had been victorious on the field of Naseby; had been muddled away by the quarrels and outraged by the violence of its Puritan champions; had been restored in 1660, imperilled in the later years of Charles II, destroyed by James II, but had finally triumphed at the Revolution. The King had then been made definitely subject to the law. The prerogative that claimed to be above the law had been killed dead. The Whig oligarchy, after 1714, made use of the powers of the Crown as defined by the Revolution of 1688. But those powers so defined were closely limited. The irremovable judges could no more be removed by the Whig nobles than by the King.

Modern criticism of this regime and its mentality is not that it interfered too much, like a 'Venetian Oligarchy,' but that it interfered too little, allowing law to grow antiquated and out of date, while society was being reborn by industrial change. Not tyranny but an exaggerated conservatism was the weakness of the Walpoles and of the Pelhams after him. *Quieta non movere* is not the motto of a Reformer, but neither is it the motto of a Tyrant.

The specific work of the early Eighteenth Century in England, on the line down which it was launched by the events of Anne's reign, was the establishment of the rule of law, and that law a law of liberty. On that solid foundation the reforms of succeeding epochs have been based.

If England between the Revolution and the death of George II had not established the rule of the law of freedom, the England of the Nineteenth Century would have proceeded along the path of change by methods of violence, instead of by Parliamentary modification of the law. The establishment of liberty was not the result of the complete triumph of any one party in the State. It was the result of the balance of political parties and religious sects, compelled to tolerate one another, until toleration became a habit of the national mind. Even the long Whig supremacy that was the outcome and sequel of the reign of Anne, was conditional on a vigilant maintenance of institutions in Church and State that were specially dear to the Tories, and a constant respect for the latent power of political opponents, who were fellow subjects and brother Englishmen.

2

SIR ROBERT WALPOLE AS THE KING'S MINISTER

J. H. Plumb

A student of G. M. Trevelyan and also obviously under the influence of the work of L. B. Namier, J. H. Plumb has with his definitive biography of Sir Robert Walpole made a contribution of the greatest importance to early eighteenth-century English political history. Plumb is completely free from any tendency to soften and sentimentalize the Whig oligarchs and their dependents, but his work is also marked by a deep sensitivity to the limitations of what can be achieved in public life and a very sharp eye for the nuances of personality. The following general view of Walpole in power, taken from the second volume of Plumb's biography, reveals all of these characteristics and demonstrates in a few pages why Plumb stands in the front rank of twentieth-century English historians.

FROM J. H. Plumb, *Sir Robert Walpole* (London: Cresset Press Limited, 1960), II, 325-333. By permission of Houghton Mifflin Company and Curtis Brown Ltd.

THE YEARS 1733 and 1734 form the watershed of Sir Robert Walpole's career: yet the slope towards defeat and retirement was so gentle that few of his contemporaries perceived it. To his royal masters, to the members of the cabinet, to his family and friends, to the public at large, and even to the opposition, his authority after the election of 1734 seemed as great as ever. In the Court, in the cabinet and in the Commons he was still the master, still 'the Great Man'. Yet this moment in his career is more appropriate than any other for assessing the influence which his twelve years of power had had not only on the affairs of his country but also on his own nature. His favour with the King and Queen had never stood higher; he had shown that he could manage them even against their natural sympathies, for he had brought them to accept a policy in foreign affairs, a field which they regarded as peculiarly their own, that conflicted with all that they had been taught to believe and cherish. In domestic arrangements at Court, his word was law. The King had dismissed, for his sake, old friends of a lifetime and taken into his confidence servants whom he despised. There was hardly a place of profit under the Crown or in the Church, the Army, or the Navy that could be disposed of without prior consultation with him. His interference in elections was as constant and as authoritative as his disposal of patronage. He dominated his cabinet with more ease than he dominated the Commons. In twelve years of government he had suffered one check and one check only—the Excise crisis—for the fiasco of Wood's halfpence had no influence on his political position in England. His control of the financial affairs of the nation was, apart from the methods of taxation, absolute, and he ruled his Treasury with an efficiency unmatched throughout the eighteenth century. These things were more obvious to Walpole than to us. He had pursued power and found it; he had enriched the nation by fostering commerce, by efficiency of management, by low taxation; he had kept the King on the throne. These were the avowed objects of his political life and he had achieved them.

He took most pride in establishing the Hanoverian succession and defeating Jacobitism. His great speech on the Septennial Bill makes this clear enough; and the alarms, excursions and even rebellions of the Jacobites were dealt with so easily and the solemn succession of Georges seems in retrospect so inevitable that Walpole's constant preoccupation with the dangers of faction, ferment, public criticism and disorder, because of the opportunities they gave for the Jacobites to exploit them, appears like one of those common delusions of men of power, who conjure up phantoms of public danger in order to suppress criticism. And this element is not entirely lacking. When Walpole sees the hidden hand of Jacobitism in the spontaneous criticisms which excise engendered, he becomes the dupe of his own obsessions. Yet his preoccupation with Jacobitism cannot be written off as a convenient bogy with which to secure the destruction of tories and to stifle public agitation. He had in his own lifetime witnessed one rebellion and two attempted invasions, and uncovered a widespread plot. The flight of James II was one of the most vivid recollections of his early childhood. He had grown to manhood as the civil wars of Ireland and Scotland had brought fresh strife and bloodshed and almost ruin to the nation. These were the actualities upon which his fears were grounded. They were kept alive by the monstrous rumours, lies and grains of truth that his elaborate espionage system revealed. In Brussels, Calais, Boulogne, Paris, Rome, Walpole placed his spies and agents. His correspondence teems with as much rumour and conjecture as the vast mass of the Stuart papers themselves. For the Jacobites the flicker of dissatisfaction in a politician spelt a promise of a return to his Stuart allegiance; for Walpole, the unguarded action of the son of a tory on the Grand Tour hinted of conspiracy and plot. An atmosphere such as this fostered that inclination to deceive, to betray, to undermine, which threads the lives of all who seek power; minor betrayals abounded and suspicion festered as men smeared each other's reputations. The money which Walpole spent, the time which he consumed, the secret meetings which he contrived, all demonstrate, however, that this world of lies, rumour and suspicion was a real world of fear to Walpole himself. The need to circumvent Jacobitism was one of the fundamental principles that guided Walpole's decisions in domestic and foreign affairs. And the invasion of 1745, after his death, showed clearly enough that exaggerated as this fear of invasion might be, it was never groundless. Walpole was completely committed to the service of the Georges, upon whose survival, he maintained, depended both the whig party and whig principles.

All the arts of his political management were therefore directed to the maintenance of the Hanoverian succession. The more men who were tied to the Court, the greater the strength of the dynasty. The means Walpole employed were not simple and they have been misunderstood. By strict attention to all appointments at Court, in the Church, in the Army and in the Navy, by the same rigorous supervision of all officers in the counties and boroughs, Walpole set about achieving a loyal establishment. Such was the rigorous nature of his selection that by 1734 there was scarcely a tory bishop, general, admiral, or deputy-lieutenant to be found in the land and tory courtiers never cast a shadow on a Drawing Room. For better or for worse the toryism that had flourished so vigorously in Queen Anne's day was by 1730 without political significance. There were no converts and constant defections; it had become the creed of squireens, Oxford-bred parsons and a few families dedicated to their ancestral past. In the whig triumph patronage had played its part as Walpole intended it to do. There was never enough, but what there was paid whig dividends. Aristocratic and gentle families were taught to look to the Court and to the politicians for their economic and social advancement. What was intended to secure stability through loyalty rapidly became a scramble for place, in which personal vendettas, greed, ambition and devotion to principles became hopelessly mixed. These things were, perhaps, the inevitable consequences of an aristocratic and oligarchic society yet the slide into factional politics with all their tragic consequences, was undoubtedly made quicker and easier by the methods which Walpole employed. Few can doubt that ambition to enjoy the social prestige and financial fruits which came with a place in the establishment, helped to give stability to the regime: nevertheless it was not in itself sufficient.

There were men who prided themselves on independence of spirit, others who were intractable or incalculable friends and enemies by fits and starts, men who cared little for the drudgery of politics and lacked sufficient influence or estate to secure rewards without work. There were a large number who were uncommitted, but inclined to accept authority so long as it was in the hands of their neighbours and friends. Upon these men Walpole used his persuasive arts, and his cunning lay not so much in parliamentary rhetoric or dazzling oratory as in facts, figures and clarity, with an adroit use of all the advantages in parliamentary procedure that ministerial power gave him. Unless he was really ill his attendance in the Commons was exceptionally assiduous; he intervened in most debates, displaying an astonishingly detailed knowledge of the whole range of affairs, domestic or foreign. This ability to dominate the Commons, to defeat the attacks of the opposition, week after week and year after year, was one of his principal duties as the first servant of the King. Naturally this had made him responsive—not to the clamours of the opposition—but to the ideas and opinions of those who supported him with little hope of reward.

The authority which Walpole acquired in the Commons was derived not only from his favour with the King, the disposal of his patronage, his skill in debate and the adjustment of policy to back-bench sentiment, but also from the authority which comes to a first-class administrator, the fruits of whose work are there for all to see. Walpole governed well; the financial system of the country worked better in his hands than ever again in this century; customs, excise, land-tax, ran quite efficiently; relations with the Bank of England and the great chartered companies were exceptionally smooth; interest rates fell; government stock maintained its price. A great deal of this was due to economic causes over which Walpole exercised no control; much also was due to that tireless attention to detail that sent him hurrying through the wintry gloom to the Treasury to be at his desk before eight o'clock in the morning. Walpole's energy was directed to making the machine work. He was not averse to innovation. Regular issues of Treasury bills, payment of interest on a daily rate —these show his shrewd grasp of detail and his willingness to accept innovation. Yet his long rule at the Treasury was not marked by any radical reforms. No antiquated office was abolished, no cumbersome procedure reformed; he preferred to keep every office in being so long as it could be used to further the stability of ministry. Efficiency within the old framework of government was all that Walpole desired to achieve. And this he accomplished. And yet paradoxically he was as responsible for the inefficiency of the administration which followed his as for the efficiency of his own. Deeply rooted in Walpole was the belief that men had a prescriptive right to rewards from the institution they served. It was as natural to him to establish generations of Popples in the Board of Trade and Cardonnels in the Salt Office as to give places for life to his own children. Loyalty, the prescriptive right of birth, weighed more with him in the end than efficiency.

An excellent administrative ability, an outstanding parliamentary skill, the unshakable favour of the King, these factors gave Walpole an eminence in English life unparalleled since Burleigh. They brought crowds of sycophants to his door; dukes and duchesses begged his favours; bishops waited for his commands; such constant attention, such constant sycophancy, did not leave his character unmarked. He grew impatient of criticism, regarded with hostility men of strong will who would not accept his yoke, bullied weaker characters with a coarseness and brutality that shocked. Naturally he did not relish formal or semi-formal meetings by which his authority appeared to be diminished and preferred to work through private interviews with individuals or secret discussions with his tried and loyal supporters. He quoted with approval George I's dislike of large cabinets and agreed with him that no good ever came of them. He preferred the closet to the cabinet except when others appeared to have more of the King's sympathies than his own; then he favoured a small, 'efficient' cabinet in which he could be sure of a majority. And, of course, he found it difficult to brook rivals; his career is littered with the broken careers of gifted men who crossed his path—Pulteney, Carteret, Townshend, Chesterfield, Cobham—and apart from Hardwicke, a man of massive moral integrity and great intelligence, and one or two others, he surrounded himself with faint replicas of himself or fools and flatterers. At least, by 1734 he had come to that and it is a measure of how power had hardened his character.

All that he does and says in the early thirties argues a growing inflexibility of temperament, a greediness to grasp and exercise power; the anxiety lessens, and the future is contemplated less than the present. As a young man his contemporaries spoke of his gaiety, of his ebullient life, of the warmth and spontaneity of his nature. Some of this he never lost. Although he could be the most affable of men, quick to respond even to his defeated enemies, this should not blind us to the essentially ruthless nature of his political actions. Where he differed from many great men who have wielded political power as great as his, is this: he did not require the death or even exile of men who had vainly crossed his path. Their complete political impotence was all he desired. Nor did great power make him secretive or remote or grossly suspicious of his close friends. He went on giving the same trust and loyalty to his brother, to Hardwicke, to Pelham, even to Newcastle, that he had always shown towards them. He was available to all from field marshals to ensigns, admirals to midshipmen, archbishops to curates, princes to merchants, so long as they were prepared to wait patiently in the throng that daily besieged his doors. And to his colleagues, and to the Court, he remained open-hearted, generous almost to a fault, retaining his delight in ostentatious display, in gargantuan meals and vast potations; his coarseness, his love of a lecherous sally, grew rather than diminished with the years, so that even Queen Caroline, no prude herself, had to rebuke him for his language before the princesses. His frankness, his lack of all pretentiousness, were nevertheless tinged with vulgarity, with a gross enjoyment, with almost a delight in stimulating the envy of men.

Certainly that envy was stirred, more profoundly, more publicly than is the common lot of great men of state. He was hated more for being himself than for his conduct of affairs. Not only was his power resented; and his royal favour loathed; his whole manner of life bred detestation wherever he went. He paraded his wealth with ever greater ostentation. He bought pictures at reckless prices, wallowed in the extravagance of Houghton, deluged his myriad guests with rare food and costly wine; his huge ungainly figure sparkled with diamonds and flashed with satin. And he gloried in his power, spoke roughly if not ungenerously of others, and let the whole world know that he was master. Such a way of life invited criticism on a personal level. All the opposition Press revelled in portraying the grossness of Walpole's life; ballads were sung of his ill-gotten wealth; obscene caricatures illustrated his relations with the Queen; bitter pamphlets laid bare the graft, the corruption, the favouritism of his regime. The Chelsea Monarch, Bob of Lynn, The Quack Triumphant; year in, year out the gutter Press squirted its filth over his reputation. His friends did little better; the institutions by which he governed worse. The Court was corrupt, his ministers feather-witted, his Treasury a swindle, his Parliament bought, the Church a political trade. He was the dupe of France, of Spain, of the Dutch. His sole aim in life was to amass gold and aggrandize his family. Day after day, week after week, month after month, year after year through the two decades of his ministry this twisted and malicious criticism never ceased: and embedded in the heart of the sludge was a grain of truth, enough indeed for this uncontrolled propaganda to carry with it a certain conviction. The good that he did—the stability, the peace, the prosperity, were taken for granted—the evil magnified to phantom proportions.

Public life and the institutions of government were thereby brought into dispute: by 1734 Parliament had lost much of the respect it had enjoyed in the early years of the century; an ever franker acceptance of the greedier side of human nature strengthened self-seeking, weakened altruism and vulgarized politics, until critical issues of state became a matter of personal vendetta. In 1734, this had not yet gone so far as it was to go at the time of the War of American Independence, but each year that Walpole remained in power lowered the standards of public life, for the vituperation and criticism were as responsible as the long years of power for hardening his nature and coarsening his response to life.

By 1734, his life, his attitudes, his methods had been clamped into an iron mould; the years had hardened and coarsened the fibres of his personality; and as his vision narrowed into a desire to retain power for its own sake, as intolerance of criticism grew, as the fluid, sensitive feeling of the realities of men and politics were smeared by success and calloused by power, so too did Nemesis creep upon him. Time no longer favoured him; the dashing young sprigs in the Commons—the hooting patriot boys—calculated his age and drank to the future. No longer could he regard the years ahead as a time of promise or fulfilment; the unfolded years were his consolation and delight. The future would bring the death of friends, the decline of powers, age, sickness and defeat.

3

THE POLITICAL INFLUENCE OF THE EAST INDIA COMPANY

Lucy S. Sutherland

A close alliance and active cooperation between the royal ministers and the merchants and bankers of the City of London was a prime constituent of the Whig political order under the first two Georges. One of the salient aspects of this interdependence of businessmen and politicians, to the benefit of both sides, is here carefully assessed by Oxford scholar L. S. Sutherland, with emphasis on the role played by the "nabobs" of the East India Company.

THE RAPID transition which took place in the political scene from the bitter dissensions of the last years of Anne's reign to the stable if inert political system of Hanoverian England is one of the most striking changes in English history. Its deep-seated causes are no doubt to be sought in the good sense and absence of rancour of the English landed and commercial classes in a society both prosperous and expansionist. It was also due to the skill and determination shown by a few men, in particular Robert Walpole and his successor Henry Pelham, in consolidating and manipulating political power under the curious conditions of their time.

FROM Lucy S. Sutherland, *East India Company in Eighteenth Century Politics* (Oxford: The Clarendon Press, 1952), pp. 18–27. By permission of the Clarendon Press, Oxford.

The political system which Walpole built up and his successors maintained was founded on four bases: the confidence of the Crown; the solidarity of interest of a knot of important Whig families who often inaccurately described themselves as the 'Revolution' families; a coordinated use of public and private patronage managed with economy to achieve directly or indirectly the requisite parliamentary majorities; and the support of a strong financial interest in the City of London. The use of the power thus gained was almost entirely negative. As David Hume said in one of his essays: 'We are ... to look upon all the vast apparatus of our Government as having ultimately no other object or purpose but the distribution of justice or, in other words, the support of the twelve judges.' In fact to maintain the machinery of law and order at home; to keep up (however inefficiently) the strength of the armed forces so that they would not prove wholly inadequate to the demands made upon them by the balance of power in Europe and the pressure for expansion in the areas of colonial conflict; and to be able to lay hands on financial resources sufficient for these purposes—these may be said to sum up the public obligations of a government of the time. It was with these limited public obligations in mind (as well as a wide variety of private obligations to individuals which might frequently prove more obtrusive) that the machine was constructed. In this machine, which, apart from occasional checks, ran with reasonable smoothness until the death of Henry Pelham in 1754, and did not wholly break down till the fall of the Duke of Newcastle in 1762, the East India Company was a cog and quite an important one.

In the first place, even in this period, there was always a small body of members of Parliament with East Indian interests. Several of the twenty-four directors usually had seats, attracted thither, like other prominent merchants, by the prospect of government contracts and other profitable rewards for support of government. Some of these were men of great influence in the City and in close touch with the Government on all matters concerning its relations with that body. The Company's stock ledgers also show a number of other Members of Parliament to be large holders of stock and therefore likely to react with the directors on matters concerning the Company. The East India interest in Parliament was not at this time so strong either as it had been during the struggles of the 'Old' and 'New' Companies in the preceding century, or as it was to be when the enriched Company's servants sought seats in the House and the Company's affairs once again became the object of parliamentary scrutiny. It was far less strongly represented than the West India interest or the more loosely articulated but numerous body of persons with interest, direct or indirect, in the trade with the American colonies. Nevertheless, the Government did not disdain its parliamentary alliance, and the support of the Company had one special advantage in that it widened the scope of ministerial patronage. As the *Craftsman* pointed out, the directors had in their bestowal 'several Governments of much greater value than any in his Majesty's gift' and they appointed to a great number of minor positions at home and abroad. The recipients of this patronage were for the most part those serving or connected with the Company. The day had not yet come when the fame of the 'Nabobs'' riches made a writership or a commission in the East Indies the goal of the younger sons of England and Scotland, and the senior posts a haven for the jackals of great men seeking to recoup their own and their patrons' fortunes. Still, public men were already aware of the openings that existed for the relatives of some of their lesser supporters, and ministers were already exploiting their connexions with the Company to this end.

In the second place the East India Company, with its wide commercial connexions, was clearly an important element in the politics of the City of London, not only when it came to Parliamentary elections but in those of the City government in which, in view of the unique importance of the City, the Government often thought it necessary to concern themselves. The reasons for this arose from the necessity of combating the activities of opposition as well as from the needs of government itself. Though the existing party structure had dissolved with the collapse of the Tory party, the elements of an opposition to the triumphant group of Whigs in power soon began to become apparent. In addition to the scattered bands of Tories left in permanent opposition, there were from time to time groups of 'rebel Whigs' who broke off from the ruling connexion and declared hostilities against it. So complete was the collapse of the old party divisions that there was nothing to prevent these two types of opposition from fusing into a common 'Country party' opposition to administration, and this from time to time they did. As early as 1716 a startled Jacobite agent noted the disappearance of all real party divisions. Reporting the debate on the Septennial Act he said:

> The most remarkable thing was that the Tories talked like old Whigs and Republicans, against monarchy and ministers, etc. and the Whigs magnified the advantages of unlimited absolute power and prerogative, vilified the mob, ridiculed the people and exalted the Crown.

It was this fact that made possible united oppositions such as that in which Bolingbroke joined with Pulteney and Carteret in their assault on Walpole. Such oppositions—weaker or stronger according to the age of the reigning king, the relationships between prominent political personalities and the appearance of good popular issues—could normally aim at no more than the reversion of power in a future reign or the chance to force on the ministry a few of its leaders. In the clamour of unsuccessful war it could, however, even drive a government from power.

The strength of such an opposition must lie in the support of something of the nature of public opinion both within and outside the House. As Edmund Burke remarked later, 'we know that all opposition is absolutely crippled, if it can obtain no kind of support without doors'. Such a public opinion was found among the independent country gentlemen and among the lesser merchants of London and a few of the bigger outports, and these very different interests found themselves in consequence from time to time joined in a curious alliance. The watchwords of this oddly assorted coalition were derived from the Whig traditions of the past; demands for a place or pensions bill, for the return to triennial (or even to annual) Parliaments, and for the abolition of the standing army; and, unreal as those issues were, they had sufficient hold on contemporary imagination to embarrass a government, particularly if brought forward just before a General Election. The real issues by which, whenever this opposition grew formidable, they wooed public opinion were, however, of a different kind; the opposition to the Excise Bill in 1733, complaints of the weight of the Land Tax or, the only really effective rallying point, discontent at failure in the waging of war. Among the factors which predisposed a considerable section of the London merchant classes to hostility to government, particularly during war, was their jealousy of the small class of rich merchants and financiers and of the 'monied Companies' on account of their privileged position in government finance. It was said of Robert Walpole that 'He is hated by the city of London because he never did anything for the trading part of it, nor aimed at any interest of theirs but a corrupt influence over the directors and governors of the great moneyed companies.'

The City of London was thus a battleground in eighteenth-century politics. The Government needed and obtained the support of the monied interest there, the rich merchants who might act as contractors or subscribe government loans and the great corporations on which national credit depended. The Opposition sought the support of their enemies, 'neither the top nor the bottom', as one of their leaders called them. The position of the three Companies and the methods of Treasury finance at the time gave a real unity to this monied interest which was the object of so much suspicion and envy from their fellow citizens. Though by law no director of one of the Companies could serve on the Court of the others, the three Corporations were on close and friendly terms. The East India Company had, it is true, watched with some suspicion the rise of the South Sea Company and had protected itself against the compulsory engrafting of some of its stock after the collapse of the Bubble, but its negotiations with the unfortunate Company were quite friendly and their later relations easy. With the Bank of England its relations were closer, since the latter was its banker and had come to be the supplier of the short-term credit necessary for the smooth flow of its trade between its sales. It also provided much of the silver bullion which at this time was exported to the East. The three Companies co-operated in their dealings with the Government when their common interests were involved. Together they consulted about protesting against the imposition of duties on the transfer of stock: one after another they waited on new First Lords of the Treasury when they came into office, and they formed the centre of the *bloc* of state creditors who frustrated the attempt to reduce the interest on the National Debt under Walpole in 1737, and who had to be bought off by concessions when Pelham succeeded in carrying out his conversion operation in 1749. It was an indication of those close relations that the East India Company permitted directors and ex-directors of the Bank and the South Sea Company to share the privileges of its own directors at the Company's regular sales.

The Company was thus of political significance to the Government in the City as part of the ministerialist monied interest there which clashed with an anti-ministerialist popular interest both in Parliamentary and City elections. Its main significance, however, in the governmental machine lay outside the realm of party politics and in that part of public finance. Eighteenth-century governments depended for their fiscal requirements partly on a system of taxation which was from the modern point of view both rigid and unproductive and partly on credit raised in the form of short- and long-term loans. For obtaining this credit they depended on the growing London money market, with the Bank of England rising to a central position in it, and (in the case of long-term loans) on the power of the London market to mobilize the funds of the *rentier* class not only of the British Isles but also, at least in some degree, of various continental countries, particularly the Dutch. This power gave particular strength to Great Britain in the great wars of the century. The East India Company was a factor in the arrangements for both short- and long-term credits.

The Company's influence on the short-term credit arrangements was exercised indirectly. As Sir John Clapham has shown, governments were throughout this period coming increasingly to rely on the Bank of England to provide their short-term credit needs. No longer was there question, as in 1698, of the East India Company being pressed to subscribe money for the 'circulation' of Exchequer Bills, and the advances made by prominent individuals as advances on the Land Tax were being gradually eliminated. The influence of the Company arose from the fact that it was itself a big issuer of short-term credit instruments in its India Bonds, the total issue of which had greatly increased since the union of the Companies until in 1744 the maximum was raised to £6,000,000. These bonds had become by convention negotiable on the market, were in convenient denominations, and became so popular that it was argued that 'money will always be borrowed at a lower rate on those bonds than in any other way'.

The rate at which the Company could raise money on bond varied with the prosperity of its trade but also with the general state of public credit. In 1711 the directors instructed their Committee of Treasury to consider means for bringing their bonds 'into better reputation'. They then bore interest at 6 per cent. By 1715 it had been reduced to 5 per cent., and by 1718 to 4 per cent. In 1719, during the speculative boom of the Bubble they had to pay 5 per cent. and it was not till 1724 that they were able in view of 'the present situation of the Company's affairs and the general credit of the nation' to reduce it to 4 per cent. After two further fluctuations an attempt was made in 1732 to reduce it to 3 per cent. on the initiative of a body of shareholders anxious to avoid a reduction in the Company's dividend at a time of trade depression. The attempt failed but a reduction to 3½ per cent. was finally achieved and this rate remained constant until 1746, a year of great credit difficulties on account of the Jacobite rebellion and the war with France, when the directors were forced to raise it to 4 per cent. When peace came and Pelham began to plan the great conversion of the National Debt from which the 3 per cent. Consols emerged, it is significant that the first step he took was to get one of his most trusted financial advisers, the Jewish jobber, Samson Gideon, to organize in 1749 a successful subscription for the reduction of the interest on India Bonds to 3 per cent., the lowest level they had ever achieved.

In the raising of the long-term funded loans the Company exercised a similar indirect influence (since its stock was, with that of the Bank and the South Sea Company, the only stock other than government securities always quoted on the market) but also a more direct one. The Government no longer depended for its loans on direct contributions from the great Corporations, though it still extorted them on such occasions as the renewal of their charters. Subscriptions from the monied public had come to predominate and by 1749 only some 26 per cent. of the 4 per cent. annuities were made up of loans from the three monied Companies. Nevertheless their position on the market put them still at the centre of public credit and the method employed by the Treasury in raising their loans emphasized the fact. The normal Treasury procedure when floating a loan at this period was what was known as the 'closed subscription' and had as its aim the procuring of a body of subscribers of sufficient financial strength to keep up the price of the stock when it came on the market as soon as the first instalments of payments were made. They began by asking for applications from individuals with whom the Treasury was in touch. It was understood that each applicant spoke for a considerable body of would-be subscribers as well as himself; certain of them represented the foreign capitalists, particularly the Dutch, who were beginning to constitute an important element in the body of public creditors; prominent merchants and government contractors, often themselves Members of Parliament, had the names of a number of members (particularly of government supporters) on their lists, and other special interests, such as that of the Jewish financiers, might be included. While these proposals were being formulated there was a period of active discussion behind the scenes between the Treasury and the more prominent of the applicants; then a meeting was convened to settle the terms. Contemporary references confirm the accuracy of Lord North's description in 1781 of what happened at such a meeting:

> The rule of the meeting was to convene all the monied men who had made applications and offers and to convene the heads of all the great public Companies who usually assisted the Government with money, but who never made any applications previous to that meeting; by these gentlemen so collected the terms were settled and it was always usual to expect that the gentlemen who were present were to take up a pretty considerable share of the loan among them.

The list was in fact nearly always over-subscribed and, after the terms of the loan had been passed by Parliament, the final list of subscribers was drawn up by the Treasury, usually with the advice of some City supporter. Among the subscribers there appeared, not the names of the Companies in their corporate capacity, but those of their directors, with considerable sums against them. When a list of applicants has survived, as well as the list of those on whose behalf they made successful application, the position of the Companies becomes clear. In 1759–60, for instance, when what was then the large sum of £8,000,000 was to be borrowed there stands before the names of the nineteen private applicants, 'Mr. Burrell for the Bank of England £466,000, Mr. Bristow for the South Sea Company £330,000, Mr. Godfrey for the East India Company £200,000.'

The East India Company thus maintained, in the more favourable conditions of Hanoverian England, its traditional policy of alliance with the Government of the day; its direct and indirect contribution to the establishment of public credit was one of its chief claims to government favour. As the directors boasted in 1720 they could 'by several instances, and some very late ones, make it evident that they had been as zealous as any of their fellow subjects to support the publick credit'.

They were wise to foster their connexion with government and fortunate in that financial considerations strengthened the case for supporting them, for the tide was running strongly against both monopolies and the joint stock organization in trade, and in favour of unrestricted commercial enterprise. The hostility shown by Adam Smith towards the Company in his famous *Wealth of Nations* followed a line of criticism that had never died out since the seventeenth century, and the Bubble Act of 1720 had effectively checked the development of this form of organization. The East India Company had the further disadvantages that its imports were regarded with suspicion by powerful groups of British manufacturers and that, until the sixties, it was a considerable exporter of bullion. As late as 1754 an attempt was made in the City to get up a petition against it on this count. The stability of the Government they were allied with, however, preserved them from any serious danger from an Opposition who might take up the case of their opponents, while the freedom from serious internal faction which their good sense and moderation had ensured, enabled them to present a united front to any attack.

4
THE EARLY GEORGIAN CABINET
J. P. Mackintosh

The Scottish political scientist John Mackintosh, in his book The British Cabinet, *judiciously summarized the results of twentieth-century scholarship on the subject, which has aimed to free itself from the anachronistic preconceptions of Victorian constitutional historians. The following selection is a precise and vivid account of the nature of the cabinet under the first two Hanoverian rulers.*

THE NEW King was advised by his envoy in London, Bothmer, to appoint his Cabinet as soon as possible, and the first meeting took place on October 8, 1714, nine days after George had landed in Britain. In the next two years the King (accompanied by the Prince of Wales) continued to summon and preside over Cabinet meetings at the royal palace while the Lords of the Committee met as before in Whitehall. When George went to Hanover in the summer of 1716 he left the Prince of Wales, with whom his relations were already strained, as Guardian of the Realm and Lieutenant. In this capacity the Prince called a Cabinet every Thursday to consider business which had often been the subject of discussion and provisional decision at an earlier meeting of the Lords of the Committee. In some cases, new issues were considered by the Cabinet and referred to the Lords.

A week after the King returned in early 1717 he held a Cabinet and there were further meetings in the summer at Hampton Court, but Bonet reported that "this custom is no longer adhered to in London, except, of course when a definite day is arranged for a Cabinet meeting." Meetings became irregular and the King's attendance infrequent and by the end of 1717 the Cabinet was being held in Whitehall without George being present. The royal withdrawal was never complete. George I called a meeting in March 1718 and may have attended once in 1721. The Austrian ambassador, Count Kinsky, reported some conferences between George II and his ministers in 1733 which might have been Cabinets. Certainly the King presided once in 1745 and perhaps on two other

---

FROM J. P. Mackintosh, *The British Cabinet* (London: Stevens & Sons Limited, and Toronto: University of Toronto Press, 1962), pp. 47–55. By permission of the publishers.

occasions, while George III made three appearances (in 1779, 1781 and 1784), but for practical purposes after 1717 the Cabinet ceased to be a body meeting with the King.

The reasons for this change have not been pinpointed but a number of motives are fairly evident. The old explanation that George's inability to speak English led to the withdrawal has been abandoned since the problem of communication had evidently been overcome for the best part of three years after George's accession. The chief reason was that George's personality altered the situation. He was both ignorant of English affairs and stupid and could never be at ease presiding over a wide-ranging discussion among ten or twelve Cabinet ministers. Like many stupid men he was suspicious and preferred to lean on his German advisers and mistresses and perhaps on one or two Englishmen. The politicians, for their part, sensing this situation, preferred to consult with the King in private and not at the Cabinet where misunderstandings and animosities could so rapidly arise and flourish. An added motive was that if the King attended it was difficult to deny the Prince of Wales the right to attend and to preside as Regent in the King's absence. George and his son had not been on good terms in 1716 and the reports which reached Hanover of the Prince's activity in politics and popularity stung George till he was convinced that there was an attempt to discredit him and form a rival centre of attraction. Even after the partial reconciliation in 1719 the Prince was neither made Regent nor nominated as one of the Lords Justices on George's subsequent visits to Hanover. Finally, the King did have certain very definite desires in foreign policy and while the Cabinet infuriated him with its reluctance to enter into hostilities against Russia in 1716, he (like his German advisers and mistresses) found individual ministers much more pliable in personal interviews.

Thus a complex of motives led George to formulate his dissatisfaction with the Cabinet system as it had operated under Queen Anne in a withdrawal from its meetings. There was no reason why this should have been permanent and George II might well have decided to return to the practice of the early years of his father's reign. However the personal factors remained fairly constant for over twenty years. George II disliked the full Cabinets and Sir Robert Walpole in 1725 declared that "no good ever came from them." The original ejection of Walpole and Townshend from the Ministry in 1717 had taken place largely because Sunderland and Stanhope had the ear of the King in Hanover, and Walpole's chief problem after he was taken back into the Cabinet in 1721 was not finance or the opposition in Parliament but the credit that the Sunderland group in the Cabinet still enjoyed with George I. Whether Walpole's opponent was Sunderland or Carteret, the solution was to prevent him bidding for royal favour. The task of holding the approval of George I and his intimates, or George II and Queen Caroline, could be simplified by keeping the number of close advisers at a minimum.

The diary of Lord King gives a good picture of the working of the Cabinet between 1725 and 1730, and the details can be picked up after

1739 in the Newcastle papers supplemented for two years by Hervey's memoirs and Admiral Norris's diary.

In the first place, the King decided on the composition of the ministry and a list of Cabinet Council posts was filled. The offices which carried Cabinet rank were fairly definite. The Archbishop of Canterbury was automatically a member, and still attended on occasion. The Lord President, Lord Chancellor, Lord Privy Seal, Lord Steward, Lord Chamberlain, the Groom of the Stole, Lord Treasurer, the Lord Lieutenant of Ireland, the Master of the Ordnance, the First Lord of Admiralty and the two Secretaries of State were almost certain to be members. Other posts that could carry Cabinet rank were the Master of the Horse, the Keeper of the Great Seal of Scotland, a third Secretary of State, the Chancellor of the Exchequer and very occasionally the Lord Chief Justice. It was possible to be a member of the Cabinet without holding any office and in some cases minor appointments carrying no real duties were considered suitable (including such unlikely ones as Constable of the Tower and Warden of the Isle of Wight). The Cabinet Council was formally nominated as the Lords Justices of the Regency on the King's regular visits abroad.

What had been known as the Lords of the Committee was referred to as "the Select Lords" or "Lords whom the King principally intrusts with his affairs," and again the members were specifically nominated, as when George II, on his accession, said he "would not let it (a treaty with the Duke of Wolfenbuttel) be communicated to the whole Cabinet but would take the first three of the lay lords, viz., the Chancellor, the President, the Privy Seal, the two Secretaries and Sir Robert Walpole, the Chancellor of the Exchequer."

The King also decided what items were to be submitted to the Select Lords. There was clearly no right to give collective advice and in the 1730s no obligation on the Crown to adopt recommendations that were not acceptable. Many matters were settled by the King acting with his German councillors or the one Secretary who accompanied him to Hanover. In 1725 George sent over a treaty to have the Great Seal affixed and when the Chancellor asked Lord Somerset whether this should not have first been submitted to the Regency, he was told that it was an absurd idea because the King had already agreed to and signed the treaty. In the same year when danger was apprehended from Spain, the King instructed that the matter be laid before the Select Lords. The King also gave instructions when the full Cabinet was to be summoned, though this became more automatic during the regencies and on occasion the Lords, having given their opinion, suggested that a matter should or should not be laid before the full Cabinet.

Out of these arrangements arose the distinction made in the 1750s and 1760s between posts with or without the circulation of papers. Almost all information of importance originated in the form of despatches to the two Secretaries and the first Lord of the Admiralty. If the King placed a matter before the inner Cabinet, he asked these ministers to read all the relevant papers to the members and in time this meant that on most matters, they were kept regularly informed. But all such questions were not put before the full or outer Cabinet and it only heard those letters or reports which were necessary in order to understand the proposals submitted. In 1740 Lord Harrington, who was the Secretary in attendance on George II in Hanover, wrote to approve of Newcastle's action in putting certain questions before the Lord Chancellor, the Lord President, Sir Robert Walpole (with, of course, Newcastle present) and said they should

continue to meet and confer upon all points of importance that may occur, as also upon the instructions you will from time to time receive from hence, and it is His Majesty's pleasure that you should communicate to them the letters I shall write to your Grace by his consent and those which you shall receive from the King's ministers abroad, and that you shall settle always previously amongst yourselves which of those dispatches may be proper to be laid before the Lords Justices and prepare such heads of business as are to be considered by their Excellencies.

Lord Hardwicke, writing to the Duke of Bedford in 1748 says

I observe by your billet that your Grace makes a very proper distinction between such papers as are proper to be read at the meeting of the Lords Justices and such as are not: from whence I took the hint of perusing them with that view, and beg leave to submit it to your consideration, whether those letters and papers which I have separated, by tying them together with red tape, should for the present at least be read there or not; for they all make some mention of those points which the King has directed should be particularly considered by such of his servants as are consulted on the most secret affairs.

It is clear, then, that the withdrawal of the King led to a marked decline in the power of the Cabinet. This was only to be expected. The smaller "working parties" under William III or Lords of the Committee under Anne had always included "those more trusted and employed than others." These men occupying the senior offices, better informed and more active in government, were only kept subordinate to the Cabinet by the fact that the presence of the Crown enabled the larger body to alter and revise and issue the definitive orders. When the King was no longer present this superiority came to an end in practice, though the Cabinet (especially as the Regency) still carried more formal authority.

Again Lord King's diary reveals how the inner Cabinet became the directing body. When the Crown wanted advice on an important matter, it was referred to the Select Lords. Walpole would dine with one or two colleagues or call at their offices and thrash out the problem. Then there would be a meeting of the inner Cabinet and the King informed of the consensus of opinion. On many occasions this concluded the matter, but if the King had asked for specific directions to be prepared for commanders or for foreign ambassadors or if a public announcement was required, then heads of business would be drawn up and a Cabinet summoned. At the meeting letters would be read explaining the problem and it was, on most occasions, to be expected that in the discussion the views of the Select Lords would become those of the Cabinet. Agreement having been reached, advice was tendered in the traditional form that "their lordships are humbly of opinion that..." It was by no means certain in the 1730s and 1740s that the King would accept the advice, and this is why the most important discussions then took place in the closet as Walpole, Carteret or Newcastle sought the agreement of George II.

It has often been argued that the chief effect of the King's quitting the Cabinet was to produce a Prime Minister in the person of the politician who was asked to preside. This is, however, purely a theoretical supposition and has no basis in practice. Who took the chair at the full Cabinet was not a matter of any importance. The order of business at the inner Cabinet is nowhere explicitly described, and while at various times some ministers clearly carried more weight than others the question of formal precedence does not seem to have been of any importance. The determining factors were that the Crown both chose its principal ministers, and decided what matters should be submitted to them in any collective capacity. Each minister was responsible for his own department and would resent any suggestion that the King was taking advice on departmental matters from other individuals. Parliament likewise understood the idea that it could criticise a minister for his departmental failings and was on guard lest this responsibility should be obscured by a premier or "sole minister" as Pitt called Carteret in 1743. Thus the development of the post of Prime Minister was hampered by the fact that in many ways the King was his own Prime Minister, and by opposition from the other members of the Cabinet and from the Commons.

The relations between the King and his ministers are well brought out by the process of forming an administration. This was not always carried out by the individual who was likely to be most prominent, as all the King needed was a trusted negotiator. Even when the ministry was in office it was not always clear who was the leading member. In 1721 and 1722 Walpole and Sunderland were in equal competition for power, and though Newcastle and Pelham and later Newcastle and the elder Pitt co-operated it was open to argument as to who was the senior partner. Finally, when a leading minister fell from power this did not mean the end of the government. Even when Walpole resigned in 1742, only three Cabinet posts changed hands.

Until the early years of George III there were three senses in which it was possible to describe a Cabinet member as Prime Minister. The first, and by far the most important, was that he was strongest in the closet. Walpole's claim to the title depends chiefly on the fact that from 1727 to 1739 George II, prompted by Queen Caroline, reposed complete trust in him. The second sense, which derives directly from the first, was that a strong minister could carry a number of his supporters into office with him, and, if gaining power, could in time exclude more and more of his opponents—this being probably the most evident feature of Walpole's ascendancy. Finally the term might be used to designate the minister on whose ability the government rested, sometimes in the prosecution of a war, but more often in the management of Parliament. It was because this latter task was of such importance, and because getting money bills through Parliament was a major part of the work that the minister most likely to be described as the premier usually held the post of First Lord of the Treasury.

Despite the firm view that responsibility was owed only by individual ministers to the King and to Parliament, a slight suggestion of joint responsibility was beginning to develop simply because it was evident that some policies were the work of a group of ministers in the inner Cabinet. The Duke of Argyle, discussing events in 1721, declared that, though he had been commander-in-chief and a member of the Cabinet, he had never seen Admiral Vernon's instructions because he was not of what he described as "the ministers' council." When Pitt told Newcastle in 1755 that "if it was expected that he should take an *active part* in support of measures, he must be enabled to do it, which he could not think the calling him to the Cabinet Council would, in any degree, do... he could not, and would not, take an *active part* in the House of Commons without he had an *office of advice* as well as of *execution*," he was simply saying that he would not take a share of responsibility unless he was a member of the inner Cabinet. Ministers on occasion asked for their dissent to be recorded on the minute in which the advice of the full Cabinet was conveyed to the King. More often they indicated their disapproval by ceasing to attend Cabinet meetings. All this was merely a recognition of the fact that a ministry had, on the whole, to present a united front in Parliament and that a degree of joint responsibility was involved. No modern doctrine of collective responsibility could arise while the Cabinet was not chosen by a Prime Minister on the basis of political principle, but members owed their places individually to a monarch who played a large part in determining policy.

5

THE STRUCTURE OF MID–EIGHTEENTH-CENTURY GOVERNMENT AND POLITICS

L. B. Namier

Along with Frederick Maitland and R. H. Tawney, Sir Lewis Bernstein Namier was the most influential twentieth-century interpreter of the English past. A Polish Jewish emigré to England just before the First World War, a businessman and Zionist leader in the 1920's and early 1930's before becoming a professor at Manchester and then London, Namier took as his special field of study the House of Commons in the 1750's and 1760's. His Structure of Politics at the Accession of George III, *published in 1929, is a truly seminal work. The first important writer on English history to have a high regard for Freudian theory, Namier had no illusion that the public professions of politicians were identical with their ultimate motives and intentions. He believed that the theoretical pronouncements made by eighteenth-century politicians, particularly by the Whig critics of George III, were merely a facade behind which operated the real forces of eighteenth-century political life, namely, aristocratic leadership, oligarchic factions, and family connections. Namier's consistent view of eighteenth-century history, his mastery of the source material, and his apparently unsentimental and realistic way of looking at politics made his approach powerfully attractive to the new generation of scholars of the late '30's and '40's. Namier inspired and directed a whole generation of English historians, not only those students working on the Hanoverian era but also researchers in other centuries of English history as well, to undertake extremely detailed biographical studies of M.P.s and ministers, to trace the network of personal and factional connections and interests that underlay the contours of ideology and party, and to reveal the wide gap between moral affirmation and actual conduct in public life. The following selection, taken from Namier's 1934 Ford Lectures at Oxford, presents his general thesis on the nature of Hanoverian government and politics at about the year 1760.*

REPRINTED by permission of The Macmillan Company from *Crossroads of Power* by L. B. Namier (New York: The Macmillan Company, 1962), pp. 78, 87–93, 113–117. Copyright © 1962 by Lady Namier. By permission of Hamish Hamilton, Ltd., Publishers.

IN 1760 the King of Great Britain was the actual head of the Executive, as the President of the United States is today; he was expected to take an active part in Government, and, by universal agreement, had the right to choose his Ministers. This was the constitutional theory consciously held by contemporaries, and usually acted upon in practice.

What then was the nature of that contest which took place in the early years of George III's reign, and in which the extent of the Royal power is supposed to have been at issue? A deliberate and persistent attempt was alleged to have been made by the King to stretch his authority beyond its established limits, and the outcry was raised that the standard of prerogative had been hoisted once more in Great Britain; this was answered by countercries of oligarchical confederacies formed to enslave the Crown; and the two cries seemed to bear each other out in creating the semblance of a clash of principles. But neither charge was ever formulated in clear constitutional terms, still less was it substantiated; there, a void remained—subsequently to be filled by conceptions belonging to a later age. And I ask myself: can we find in the first ten years of George III's reign a real, fundamental difference of ideas concerning the nature and extent of the Royal power; or was the dispute a logical outcome of an inherently incongruous arrangement, aggravated by personal factors and fortuitous circumstances? ...

There is no doubt that in theory, about 1760, the right of the King to choose his ministers stood uncontested; but in practice disagreement about this choice lay at the basis of all the political conflicts of the period —with the cries of independency on the one hand and of prerogative and oligarchic faction on the other—and pointed to a fundamental ill-adjustment in the constitutional machinery.... I propose to ... prove that the right of the King to choose his ministers at that time was more than a current assumption, or a constitutional convention, and that it was both inherent in the political situation of that time and its inevitable logical result—much as the limitation of the powers of the Crown in that choice a hundred or a hundred and fifty years later was again no constitutional convention but the logical outcome of a new situation. Here I should like to join issue with Dicey on a matter of terminology which is of far-reaching importance. In his book on the *Law of the Constitution* he regrets that certain maxims (the conditions of tenure of office by ministers being one of them) 'must be called conventional', for the word 'suggests a notion of insignificance or unreality'. For my own part I object to the word 'convention' even because of its more fundamental meaning: it might imply that these maxims are the result of an understanding, an agreement which, as a rule, the contracting parties are free to shape according to their own choice. In reality, the basic power of the King to choose his ministers in 1760, and his basic duty to accept them from Parliament in 1910, was, and is, the inevitable outcome of a situation which no single individual could control.

What then was it that in time placed the Prime Minister at the head of the executive in this country? It was the evolving system of big, closely knit and well-disciplined parties, a system that clearly singles out men, or a group, able to command a majority in the House of Commons. If there were a multitude of small parties in the House, as there is for instance in France, or were the allegiance of members to their party uncertain, the Crown as the one fixed element in Government would regain considerable latitude in the choice of the Prime Minister.

What then is it that exercises the greatest constraining force on the Member and binds him to his party? In other words what is the main factor in party discipline? It is dependence of the Member on his party for his seat in Parliament, and—viewed from this angle—it is indifferent whether his success is due to the goodwill of his constituents or to the strength of the party machine. The more the Members depend for their seats on the party organization and its leaders, the greater the inner coherence of the party and the strength of its leaders against all and sundry.

But so long as politics were local in character, there could be no real party discipline. Members sat in their own right or else on the influence of private patrons; and, most important of all, so long as the Crown, through a system of patronage, controlled the disposal of certain posts, it exercised considerable influence both in elections and in the House.

About 1760, even in the freest constituencies, politics still bore a local character to a remarkable degree. In my book *The Structure of Politics*, I have given numerous examples of it, and here I shall only illustrate the matter with one telling example: in 1774, in the populous free constituency of Newcastle-upon-Tyne, the question of the right to graze cows on the castle leas played a greater part in the election of Members to Parliament than the entire, colossal, problem of America.

But most important of all at that time was the influence exercised by the Crown. From it, only Members sitting for private or pocket boroughs, or boroughs practically devoid of voters, could be wholly free. Research into the matter shows that the number of seats really controlled by the Treasury, or other government departments, was relatively small; but that the cost to a private patron of cultivating an interest in an average borough would have been almost prohibitive without access to government patronage. Thus beside the patronage handed out directly to Members in the form of places and favours to themselves and their relatives, the Crown also had a hold over them through the preferments it conferred on their constituencies. Though the Crown's control of Members was far less complete or wide than the hold of parties is over individual Members today (because of the party-trained electorate) it still was the largest electoral influence in the eighteenth-century House of Commons. And from this situation there was no escape, and could be none so long as appointments to the Civil Service were not removed altogether from the sphere of politics and submitted to definite rules and competitive examinations. Furthermore, so long as a certain limited number of people could determine elections even in large constituencies, there had to be a controlling electoral influence at the centre (in the Treasury) and the question only was who exercised it, the King or his ministers. Fundamentally the position was this; had a set of ministers obtained exclusive control of that electoral influence, they would indeed have become kings. Whereas if the King was to hold the balance between the parties, or factions, in Parliament he was bound to have the choice of ministers. And should he have wished to attach himself absolutely to one individual or minister, and delegate his own power to that individual, the cry of 'Favourite' was bound to go up from all the other, thwarted, aspirants. In the case of Lord Bute it did so.

Originally—and not in England alone—the King was head of the executive, and his ministers were his tools and servants bound to carry out his policy, as ministers in the United States are to this day bound to carry out the policy of the President. The legislature, under those conditions, was like an audience watching the performance of actors with enough approval or disapproval to influence—and even direct—the performance up to a point, but without playing an active part in it. The next development was reached when the English realized that the work of governing was easier if the servants of the Crown were chosen from among the leading members of the legislature. But since the legislature was divided into parties or factions, a curious—indeed, a paradoxical—position arose; the system functioned best when one side was definitely tainted with disloyalty to the Crown—in the first half of the eighteenth century, if they were either Jacobites or adhered to the undutiful heir to the throne. For then the King was induced to work with the chiefs of one party, and did so more or less harmoniously. But as the parties became extinct, the position grew inherently more difficult; until, about 1760, almost all men in both Houses were, as far as loyalty to the Crown was concerned, fit to enter the King's service. And from then on, there was something inherently illogical in the King constituting himself—as he was bound to do so long as he had the choice of ministers—the chief of the 'ins' as against the 'outs'. This is not to say that there was no friction between the King and his ministers. A certain amount of it there always was, and the King's desire to choose his ministers from among the best men of any party was not based on high principles alone. Thus, at the very time when Bute was preaching 'strict union' to Grenville, Egremont his brother-in-law, and Halifax his friend, letters were passing between Bute and the King on the desirability of avoiding too strong a union among them. 'Nothing can be more true', wrote George III to Bute about 17 March 1763, 'than my dear friend's sentiments with regard to having men not too much ally'd in the active posts of Government that my independency may be preserved.' Still, the opposite factor must not be overlooked either—the desire of the King not to constitute himself the chief of one party in the State was much more congruous with the fundamental conception of royalty than the acceptance of a party by him when he was contributing considerably, even in Parliament, to their securing a majority. It is when thus regarded that the constitutional and Parliamentary position in Great Britain about 1760 appears to contain the inherent contradiction I have spoken of. And you will concede that it was bound to continue until both the King and the Civil Servants were taken out of party politics.

When the discovery of the system of party government is hailed by 'Whig' historians as a great achievement of eighteenth-century Britain, insufficient regard is usually paid to the contradictory position in which that system was bound to place the King. Personalities (the King, Bute, and Pitt) did add considerably to the confusion and difficulties of the first ten years of George III's reign; but the fact remains that while George III never really transgressed the limits of authority set for him by the constitutional customs of the time, he came over and again into conflict with the leading statesmen or with political factions. Yet those conflicts of the period which seem to be about the constitution itself, should really be described as the result of inevitable maladjustments in the constitutional machinery; and during the period of transition from purely Royal to purely Parliamentary government, these maladjustments were inevitable.

A somewhat similar position can be seen in France under the July Monarchy when Louis Philippe tried to uphold the French tradition of a strong and independent executive coupled with a Parliamentary system copied from Great Britain. And the French, with their genius for definition, coined during that period a number of fine terms closely applicable to the problems of George III's early years. Prerogative they called *pouvoir personel*, corruption—*conquête individuelle* and for them the whole doctrine of the position of the King turned on whether Theirs's definition—*le roi règne et ne gouverne pas* should be accepted or not. Guizot passionately denied the theory, and asserted that the throne was not an empty chair and that the King was *un être intelligent et libre*. As for the King's advisers, he considered it their task to mediate between the King and Parliament, and to establish harmony between them by obtaining the King's consent for the policy which they thought it their duty to defend before Parliament. In other words they were to form a buckle between the legislature and the prominent head of the executive, a buckle which, even at the best of times, was bound to bear much strain; and it was always with a view to gaining the ready acquiescence of Parliament and the public that a wise King was to choose his ministers. Chatham, too, once gave a definition of the Cabinet as it should be constructed. He wished 'to see the best of all parties in Employment, that that was the only means of carrying on affairs with any degree of utility'. And Walpole's rhetorical question to the Duke of Richmond, about the desirability of everybody depending on King Rockingham and no one on King George, echoed in its own way the theory that the Cabinet should be a compromise between a party, or group, in Parliament and the Crown. Curious expressions on the part that a popular minister could play are to be found in a correspondence between Henry Fox and a small dependant of his, John Luke Nicholl (they are among the Holland House MSS.). On 19 October, Fox wrote to Nicholl criticizing

Pitt's famous letter to the City, in which he explained his resignation on the ground that he had no longer been allowed to 'guide' the policy of the country. 'Surely Mr. Pitt's letter can do him no service', wrote Henry Fox, '... sole Prime Minister used to be thought an abomination in a free country.' To which Nicholl replied,

These are surely the most extravagant times my little reading or experience ever knew. Mr. P. the man best fitted for them—Hanover; Continental German measures; and a prime sole Minister, were formerly held in horror and the promoters in detestation. But *he* was the Prime Minister of the people not the Sovreign—and thereby enabled to do more for the latter, than all the most abandon'd Court Ministers since the Conquest ever could or dared attempt to do....

Note how this letter also points to another disturbing element in the situation. Pitt was a Prime Minister neither of the Sovereign nor of the Parliament, but of the people and therefore, at the height of his power, carried out with ease for the King measures that no other minister could have achieved.

Let us now look at the relations between the ministers and the King from another angle. Once he had placed them in office and if he continued to support them, their tenure was practically unlimited, unless they were overthrown by some national disaster. Such relative permanency produced, naturally enough, a form of disloyalty, innocuous yet personally galling: I have in mind the gathering of an opposition round the Prince of Wales which was based on the conflict between fathers and sons, typical in the House of Hanover, and which was bound in its turn to embitter that family conflict. Clearly, if the support of the King was sufficient to keep more or less well-chosen ministers in office, the chances of the 'outs' to come in were meagre until the King's death. And yet if he dismissed his ministers without some obvious and overwhelming reasons, or without the ministers themselves giving up their offices in despair at their own incapacity to cope with a situation, he could not but give the impression of being whimsical or even arbitrary, and was certain to create enemies for himself. In fact, in the early years of George III's reign, the unsteadiness of the Parliamentary situation was aggravated by there being no Prince of Wales capable of leading an opposition to the Sovereign. And so Bute, and the legend which soon gathered round him, and the whole problem of the so-called 'King's friends', became the chief disturbing elements, and endured for the first ten years of the reign.

What then were the restrictions on the King's choice of ministers? In the first place they resulted from the material—its availability. When on 1 November 1760 Devonshire urged Bute to have management for Pitt as administration would be impossible without him, Bute replied,

'My Lord, I would not for the world the King should hear such language, he would not bear it for a moment.'
I answered 'not bear it! He must bear it. Every King must make use of human instruments to attain human ends or his affairs will go to ruin.'

Furthermore, the men who could be simultaneously placed in office were to some extent already in the habit of working together or, to put it in eighteenth-century language, were grouped in factions; and the King as a rule had to accept this fact. Lastly—a very important point—the number of men fit to hold office was by no means great, which is proved, for instance, by the failure of the Newcastle-Rockingham group to form an administration in May 1765, or to carry on effectively in 1766. These failures point a significant difference between the 1760s and our own time. A great statesman requires much the same qualities today as he then did, though these qualities will, possibly, express themselves somewhat differently; but from the middling rank and the working ministers much more was then required than is now. Today, for their political work in Parliament, ministers can call on the help of a party system which efficiently eases the running of the machinery of government. Then, not even the worst corruption could have achieved anything like such easing. Equally, in the administrative work of the departments, working ministers now enjoy the support of a highly trained Civil Service. Such assistance was almost entirely lacking to the eighteenth-century minister. The junior lords at the various boards and one or two secretaries in each department (frequently themselves sitting in the House of Commons) composed between them what might be called the first-division staff, and the burden on them, and the ministers they served, was heavy indeed. I have been through the correspondence of Lord Sandwich as Secretary of State—it is preserved at Hinchinbrooke, in the Record Office, and in the Stowe Papers in the British Museum—and there is hardly a draft which is not in the handwriting of Sandwich's under-secretary, Richard Phelps, or of Sandwich himself.

It is almost inconceivable with what trifles not only the Under-Secretary but ministers and even the King had to deal personally all the while. Small wonder that the choice of ministers open to the Crown was never great. . . .

The original functions of the House of Commons were primarily financial; therefore the Treasury was the department with which the House was more immediately concerned. The connexion continued, and in a certain sense continues to this day. Further, though various Government offices like the Admiralty and the Post Office, had their own patronage, the greatest amount of Government patronage centred in the Treasury. And once the principle was accepted that the First Lord of the Treasury should have the management of the House of Commons, the patronage of other departments under the Crown—in so far as it could be used for electoral purposes—came to be subordinated to the Treasury. But this was not achieved without considerable resistance from the other ministers. The one branch of the services which the Hanoverians, with their predilection for soldiering, managed, to some extent, to keep out of the hands of their chief ministers was the Army. And a constant grievance of Newcastle, even more than of Sir Robert Walpole, was George II's refusal to allow either of them to subordinate the interests of the Army to Parliamentary considerations. It was in his double character of guardian of the national finance and maker and manager of the House of Commons that the First Lord of the Treasury came to be looked upon, more often than not, as the first man in the Cabinet.

In these circumstances, it was logical that the First Lord of the Treasury should be in the Commons. Sometimes the fact is stressed that between 1721 and 1801 there were about twice as many First Lords of the Treasury in the Upper House as in the Commons. But consider how long peers held the Treasury, rather than how often they were appointed to it. While Sir Robert Walpole held it for twenty-one years, his successor, Lord Wilmington, only did so for something over a year; Pelham held it for eleven years, till his death in 1754, but the Duke of Newcastle spent two most uncomfortable years casting about for a deputy in the Commons, and then gave up the attempt. During the next four years Devonshire and Newcastle were mere figureheads for Pitt. Bute held the Treasury for one year. George Grenville, though at first considered hopelessly weak, steadily gained strength in the House, and succumbed only at the third attempt of the King to overthrow him. Lord Rockingham spent one uneasy year at the Treasury; and even the mighty name and shadow of Chatham could not secure the smooth working of government after he had gone to the House of Lords. But when, in 1770, Lord North, another Commoner, was placed at the head of the Treasury, it required the disasters of the American Revolution to overthrow him; and even so he had a twelve-years' run. Next, three peers, Rockingham—who died after a few months—Shelburne, and the Duke of Portland, carried on for a joint twenty months; while their successor William Pitt lasted seventeen years.

Even allotting to the peers the four years when Pitt—rather than Devonshire or Newcastle—was the first minister, during the period 1721–1801 the average life of administrations presided over by peers ran into about as many months as that of Commoners ran into years.

Whenever the First Lord of the Treasury was in the House of Commons, he was also Chancellor of the Exchequer. To this there is not one exception during that period. And in official reports he is often described as Chancellor of the Exchequer, and not by his higher title of First Lord of the Treasury. But whenever the First Lord of the Treasury was in the Upper House, there had to be a Chancellor of the Exchequer to represent the Treasury in the Commons. However, as the First Lord of the Treasury still took an active part in the financial work of the Treasury, the Chancellor of the Exchequer was something of an Under-Secretary to him. Yet, since the Chancellor of the Exchequer, when there was one in the Commons, naturally was the chief representative of the Treasury in the House, he ranked far above the other ministers. Nonetheless, he was not as a rule deemed of Cabinet rank. Even when a man of the political standing of Charles Townshend had, in 1766, been browbeaten by Chatham into accepting the office, he 'was not called to the Cabinet'; and only managed to worm himself in a few months later. The Duke of Grafton wrote in his *Autobiography*, 'On the night preceding Lord

Chatham's first journey to Bath, Mr. Charles Townshend was, for the first time, summoned to the Cabinet.' His successor Lord North was included in it not as Chancellor of the Exchequer, but rather as leader of the House of Commons.

During the eighty years from 1721 to 1801, whenever the First Lord of the Treasury was in the Commons, both Secretaries of State were in the Lords; but whenever the First Lord of the Treasury was in the Upper House, one Secretary of State was in the Commons—with very few exceptions, and none of these lasting for more than a few months. Since the other two of the 'Big Five' who completed the core of the efficient Cabinet —the Lord Chancellor and the Lord President of the Council—were invariably peers, it seldom happened that more than one minister of first rank sat in the Commons. For even when the First Lord of the Admiralty or the Commander-in-Chief happened to be Commoners and were included in the efficient Cabinet—like Ligonier, Granby, Saunders, or Hawke—such a minister's function in the Cabinet and in the House was that of an expert rather than of a politician.

A Secretary of State who was in the Commons had, therefore, always an obvious claim to the leadership of the House. But could the leadership of the House be separated from its management, and hence from patronage, the lubricant of that management? Here we touch one of the great inherent difficulties in the position of a Prime Minister who was a peer. Foreign Affairs and the Army were always considered to some extent the special personal domain of the King, and it was an accepted rule that the Secretaries of State could directly discuss questions of foreign policy with the King. But the position of the First Lord of the Treasury, with regard to the King, was based on his management of the House of Commons—as understood by Newcastle, 'home affairs'. Were the First Lord to cede this management to the Secretary of State, he would have been left with nothing but revenue business.

In 1754, Newcastle offered Fox the Secretaryship of State but without the management of the House of Commons, and Fox refused. When a year later they came to an understanding, Newcastle still tried to have the circular letters, summoning Members of Parliament to the opening of the session, sent out by his Chancellor of the Exchequer, H. B. Legge, rather than by Fox. With Pitt, in 1757, a peculiar *modus vivendi* was established, Newcastle being the 'minister of men', in charge of patronage, while Pitt was the 'minister of measures'—the leader in the House of Commons and master in the Cabinet. Still, judging by the bitter remarks which Pitt threw out to James West when, in November 1757, he was asked for orders concerning the circular letters, he was perhaps not quite so happy in that position as is sometimes supposed; and this may have been the reason why in 1765 he insisted on having Temple at the Treasury. In fact during this period, hardly a case can be quoted of a truly happy partnership between a First Lord of the Treasury in the Upper House, and a Secretary of State leading the Commons. It was while Bute was at the Treasury and George Grenville led the Commons, as Secretary of State in the summer of 1762, that the first rift in their relations occurred—Grenville being rather reluctant to do on Bute's behalf work in the Commons in which he excelled later, when doing it for himself. Even the mild and indolent Rockingham seems to have had his jealousies, towards Conway; and to have tried to work through Dowdeswell, his Chancellor of the Exchequer, in order to retain the management of the House while in the Treasury. Horace Walpole, when trying in the spring of 1767 to persuade Conway to take the Treasury, said

He could not be Minister of the House of Commons without power; had Lord Rockingham imparted any to him before?

and added that he himself

would propose nothing so ridiculous as Rockingham and Dowdeswell over again.

The limit of absurdity was, however, reached in the first year of Chatham's administration when, on certain important measures, the two Cabinet ministers in the Commons—Conway, Secretary of State, and Townshend, Chancellor of the Exchequer—opposed Government measures which had to be carried through in the House by men of second rank, such as Jeremiah Dyson Commissioner of Trade, and Thomas Bradshaw Secretary to the Treasury.

In 1770, with Lord North First Minister in the House of Commons, normality was once more reached. And Horace Walpole thus summed up the general sense of relief,

It was obvious how much weight the personal presence of the first minister in the House of Commons carried with it.

6

THE HANOVERIAN CHURCH

Norman Sykes

Zealous Victorian church reformers held such a low opinion of the clerical establishment in the eighteenth century that it has been necessary for twentieth-century scholars to undertake an unpreju-

---

FROM Norman Sykes, "The Church," in A. S. Turberville, ed., *Johnson's England* (Oxford: The Clarendon Press, 1933, 1952), I, 16–38. By permission of the Clarendon Press, Oxford.

diced and dispassionate re-examination of the institutions and personalities that prevailed in the Church of England in the era of Whig hegemony. The most valuable studies in this direction have been made by Norman Sykes, who in the following selection summarizes his conclusions on the ecclesiastical conditions in the Hanoverian era. Sykes' investigation reveals that the eighteenth-century churchmen were not particularly disposed to moral depravity but that in other areas of public life, as well as in politics, society's expectations of the standards of public conduct altered radically between the eighteenth and the nineteenth centuries.

In TRUTH the Hanoverian Church was both reformed and unreformed; for the Reformation which had remodelled its doctrine and liturgy had effected comparatively few changes in its internal administration.

The episcopate itself was not only the keystone of the ecclesiastical constitution but the best illustration of the character of the establishment of Georgian England. Traditionally the English bishop was a royal counsellor in matters of state, upon occasion holding offices of state, no less than a prelate of the Church. Even as late as the beginning of the eighteenth century, during the early years of Johnson's life, Bishop John Robinson of Bristol was accredited as British plenipotentiary at Utrecht; and the reward of his diplomatic services there took the form in the ecclesiastical sphere of translation to the rich see of London and in the political of his appointment as Lord Privy Seal in the Administration of Oxford. The elevation of a divine to secular office was an exception at this date, but the political influence of prelates had suffered a change of form rather than of principle since the Reformation. The eighteenth century indeed witnessed a development in the parliamentary importance of the episcopate which provoked much criticism, especially of the method of its recruitment. 'No man, for instance, can now be made a bishop for his learning and piety,' complained Johnson on Good Friday 1775; 'his only chance for promotion is his being connected with somebody who has parliamentary interest.' Nor did learning seem a surer passport to preferment. 'Few bishops are now made for their learning,' observed the Doctor upon another occasion; 'to be a bishop, a man must be learned in a learned age, factious in a factious age, but always of eminence. Warburton is an exception, though his learning alone did not raise him... Pope introduced him to Allen, Allen married him to his niece; so by Allen's interest and his own, he was made a bishop.' It would be as incorrect to interpret the sentiments of Johnson as implying that Georgian bishops were eminent for factiousness alone, as to infer that piety and learning were unrepresented among their virtues; but the growth of the organization of political parties, which seemed to him the quality of a factious age, introduced important modifications in the relations of the episcopate to the Crown and to its ministers of state.

The political consequences of the Revolution settlement led to a considerable appreciation of the power of Parliament, and, combined with the stabilization of the parties of Whig and Tory, necessarily affected the position of the bench. In particular the establishment of the custom of homogeneous party Administrations resulted in the virtual appropriation of the ecclesiastical patronage of the Crown by the political leaders, and the consequent nomination to the episcopate of divines of their own allegiance, whether Whig or Tory. Imperceptibly the bishops became the friends and allies of the rival Whig and Tory ministers rather than direct counsellors of the ruling prince. In this capacity they not infrequently employed their talents, both of voice and pen, in support of their own party, so that it seemed natural to Lord Shelburne, in nominating Dr. Richard Watson in 1782 to the see of Llandaff, to express 'to the duke of Grafton his expectation that he [Watson] would occasionally write a pamphlet for their administration'. Within the House of Lords itself the control of a solid phalanx of twenty-six votes of the episcopal bench was of obvious importance to ministers to whom the art of parliamentary management was an essential element of statecraft. The acme of episcopal loyalty was enjoyed by Sir Robert Walpole in 1733 when in two critical divisions in the Upper House on May 24 and June 1 of that year he was saved from defeat by the fact that 'out of the twenty-six bishops, twenty-five were present or voted by proxy, of which twenty-four were for the court'; a result, the moral of which was pressed home in a popular ballad bidding him to

> Consider the church is your rock of defence,
> Your South Sea escape in your memory cherish,
> When sinking, you cry'd, 'Help, lords, or I perish'.

The close alliance between the episcopate and the Ministry provoked much criticism, which proceeded generally from opponents who, like Johnson, believed that Whiggism 'as a mere party distinction under Walpole and the Pelhams, was no better that the politics of stock-jobbers and the religion of infidels'. But the only solution of the problem, that of depriving the bishops of their seats in Parliament, was repudiated with equal indignation by the critics, as by Johnson himself in his reply to Sir Adam Ferguson: 'Who is more proper for having the dignity of a peer than a bishop, provided a bishop be what he ought to be; and if improper bishops be made, that is not the fault of the bishops, but of those who make them.'

Another circumstance which cemented the alliance between prelates and ministers was the great inequality in revenue of the several sees. A list of the ecclesiastical dignities in the gift of the Crown with their estimated annual value, drawn up for George III about 1762, revealed a wide disparity between such sees as Canterbury with £7,000, York with £4,500, Durham with £6,000, and Winchester with £5,000 a year, and those of Bristol with £450, Oxford and Llandaff with £500 each. When Secker became bishop of Bristol in 1735 he computed the revenues to be 'no more than £360 a year, out of which he was to pay £27 a year tenths, and maintain a steward, so that the true profits were but £300 per annum, and there was £900 to be paid in first fruits'. Twenty-five years later Bishop Newton complained that its net profits were still only £300; yet the expenses of living in London for the greater part of the year in attendance upon the Court and Parliament, together with the maintenance of a sufficient hospitality in both the capital and the diocese, were the same for all bishops whether rich or poor. Accordingly, the prelates of Bristol or Oxford were compensated by the addition of other Church preferment to eke out the scanty substance of their sees; for example, both Butler and Newton at Bristol held the deanery of St. Paul's *in commendam*, whilst that of Westminster was joined generally to the see of Rochester. Occasional protests were raised against this practice of episcopal commendams, but the protesters, as in the case of Bishop Watson of Llandaff, earned no gratitude from either Ministers of State or Primates to whom they urged the adoption of schemes for equalizing the revenues of bishoprics and for raising the value of the benefices of the inferior clergy at the expense of cathedral dignities. Even to their holders, commendams were but a temporary expedient, and the prelates of 'the little bishoprics' hoped always for translation to a lucrative see, a desire which naturally ensured their loyalty to the Administration which had appointed them and to which they looked for further rewards of service. There can be no doubt that the expectation of translation to a rich diocese curtailed the independence of many bishops; for the prediction of Bishop Watson on his own nomination to Llandaff that 'he had hitherto followed and would continue to follow his own judgement in all public transactions, that all parties understood this, and it was probable that he might continue to be bishop of Llandaff as long as he lived', indicated the fate which he anticipated as the result of his sturdy individualism. His elevation, indeed, had been more the effect of accident than design on his part, for having written against 'the supporters of the American war because he thought that war not only to be inexpedient but unjust', he happened thereby 'to please a party and they made him a bishop', only to leave him in distant Wales for the remaining thirty-three years of his life. The degree of political fidelity expected of clerics promoted by a party minister found apt illustration in the nomination of Dr. Zachary Pearce by Sir Robert Walpole to the deanery of Winchester in 1739. Hitherto Pearce had been accounted a friend of Walpole's rival, Pulteney, who therefore released him from the political consequences of that friendship by declaring to him:

> Dr. Pearce, though you may think that others besides Sir Robert have contributed to get you this dignity, yet you may depend upon it, that he is all in all and that you owe it entirely to his goodwill towards you. And therefore as I am now so engaged in opposition to him, it may happen that some who are of our party, may, if there should be any opposition for members of parliament at Winchester, prevail upon me to desire you to act there in assistance of some friend of ours: and Sir Robert at the same time may ask your assistance in the election for a friend of his own against the one whom we recommend. I tell

you therefore beforehand that if you comply with my request rather than with Sir Robert's, to whom you are so very much obliged, I shall have the worse opinion of you.

In an essay contributed to *The Spectator* of March 24, 1710/11, Addison, lamenting the overcrowding of the clerical profession, observed that

we may divide the clergy into generals, field officers, and subalterns. Among the first we may reckon bishops, deans, and archdeacons. Among the second are doctors of divinity, prebendaries, and all that wear scarfs. The rest are comprehended under the subalterns. As for the first class, our constitution prevents it from any redundancy of incumbents, notwithstanding competitors are numberless. Upon a strict calculation it is found that there has been a great exceeding of late years in the second division, several brevets having been granted for the converting of subalterns into scarf-officers. As for the subalterns, they are not to be numbered.

The cleavage between the positions of the higher and lower clergy thus noted by Addison, and particularly the sharp contrast between the plurality of preferments enjoyed by the former and the poverty of the latter, continued throughout the age of Johnson. From the Reformation to the nineteenth century the practice of pluralism was regulated by the statute of 21 Henry VIII, c. 13, entitled *Spiritual Persons abridged from having Pluralities of Livings*. The Act, having laid down the general rule that no person possessing a benefice with cure of souls of the value of £8 or above should be suffered to hold any other benefice with cure, proceeded to recite a long list of exceptions to this rule, embracing the chaplains of all peers, temporal and spiritual, and divers other persons there specified. To cathedral dignities, being benefices without cure of souls, the statute of course did not apply; and since the number of chaplains allowed to the several ranks of the peerage varied from the six of dukes and archbishops to the single chaplain allotted to the Lord Chief Justice and to the Warden of the Cinque Ports, the number of preferments necessary to satisfy the dignity of the nobility was very considerable. It was indeed a point of honour on the part of noblemen to secure a proper reward for their spiritual attendants, and the profession of Orders was regarded further as a fit sphere for the talents of the younger sons of noble families who might hope to find relief from their financial necessities by the provision of cathedral dignities. The correspondence of the Duke of Newcastle abounds in embarrassing instances of peers cajoling, threatening, or rebuking his grace for the neglect of their relatives and chaplains in the disposition of Church preferment. The competition for prebends of the churches of Canterbury, St. Paul's, Westminster, and Windsor was so great that Newcastle confessed in 1757 that they were 'sometimes more difficult to be had than a deanery', whilst Archbishop Herring teased him in 1755 by the observation that 'he could not help smiling to see with how much more ease his grace filled up a bishopric than a prebend'. The chief cause of the zeal for the office of prebendary was that, whilst at Windsor the prebends were worth £450, at Canterbury £350, and at Westminster £300, according to George III's list, in the great majority of cases their duties were nominal, the discharge of the obligation to preach twice each year in the cathedral *aut per se aut per alium*.

To the aspiring cleric the way to preferment was clear, by the means of the favour of some influential patron. Prelates of noble birth such as Archbishop Cornwallis, and Bishops Trevor, Keppel, Barrington, and North supplied the condition in their own families. But clergy lacking this initial advantage strove to recommend themselves to the notice of some temporal peer or bishop, either by dedicating to them the literary fruits of their genius or by rendering some political service to their family in elections or otherwise. Despite the aristocratic character of eighteenth-century society several divines of humble birth rose to the highest offices of the Church. Archbishop Potter, the son of a Wakefield linen-draper, dedicated one of his early works of classical scholarship to Robert Harley, but being appointed two years later a chaplain to Tenison, he laid the foundations of his future preferment upon a Whig basis, securing the support of the Duke of Marlborough for his candidature for the Regius Professorship of Divinity at Oxford. His successor at Canterbury, Thomas Herring, was the friend of Lord Chancellor Hardwicke, whose influence had paved the way for his elevation to the primacy through the sees of Bangor and York. Archbishop Secker entered into Anglican Orders upon a promise of Bishop Talbot to provide for him in his family, and after the Bishop's death his son, Lord Chancellor Talbot, made Secker his chaplain, thereby bringing him into closer contact with the Queen and Court circles. Archbishop John Moore became tutor to Lord Blandford, son of the Duke of Marlborough, and made a prudent second marriage with the sister of Sir William Eden, first Lord Auckland, by whose influence he rose to the primacy. Very few clergy lacking influence or money at the outset of their career would have achieved the distinction of Richard Watson, who, being offered at the age of twenty-three by the Vice-Chancellor of Cambridge University 'the curacy of Clermont, and advised to accept it, as it would give him an opportunity of recommending himself to the Duke of Newcastle', the arch-dispenser of patronage, refused because he prized 'his independence above all prospects'. The surest road to success lay through the office of royal chaplain, and the number of candidates for that duty was inexhaustible because of the prospects of preferment. George III, indeed, created consternation amongst the ranks of the clerical body by appointing at his accession an entirely new rota of royal chaplains, from which he might replenish the sees and cathedral dignities as occasion arose. Tradition has recognized fully his personal interest in the distribution of the ecclesiastical patronage of the Crown, from the first year of his reign when he translated Bishop Hayter to London, despite the protests of Newcastle, and nominated Dr. Thomas Newton to Bristol; and throughout the period of his friendship with Warburton and with Hurd, whom he offered the primacy in 1783, down to the famous incident of 1805 when in order to forestall the intention of Pitt to recommend Bishop Pretyman to Canterbury, the King took horse himself to secure Bishop Manners Sutton's acceptance of that see.

The determination of George III to assert his will in the bestowal of preferments differed from that of his predecessor rather in the personnel of his clerical entourage than in the strength of resolve not to be ignored. The Duke of Newcastle not infrequently found that even his most longstanding promises and his closest dependants were put aside by the fidelity of George II to his own chaplains. The rewards of chaplains, both of the King and of temporal lords, were indeed regarded by Bishop Hurd as necessary satisfactions for services rendered; for he argued that 'preferments, when conferred by the great on their dependants, are not so properly favours as debts; that a course of years spent in servitude is the price they pay for such things; and that when promotion comes at last, it comes in the way of recompense and not of obligation'. Notwithstanding, it must be allowed that in many cases the renumeration was adequate to the duty done. Dr. Edmund Pyle, whose *Memoirs of a Royal Chaplain* illustrate the lighter side of Georgian divinity and churchcraft, received ample returns for his moderate abilities and services. Introduced into the royal favour by his friendship with Bishop Hoadly, he received in addition to his preferments at Lynn and Gedney, cathedral dignities. In 1751 he became Archdeacon of York, where he nearly lost his heart to the ladies of that city. 'Nothing but ladies by dozens (and very pretty ones) on the right hand or the left or in front of my stall,' he wrote in his account of his installation; 'but through mercy, having the service to read I was forced to look at least as much on the rubric of the book as upon that of their cheeks.' In 1752 he settled in the household of Hoadly at Chelsea as companion, and in 1756 was made prebendary of the first stall at Winchester. There he learned that 'the life of a prebendary is a pretty easy way of dawdling away one's time: praying, walking, and visiting; and as little study as your heart would wish'; whilst in anticipation that he would outlive his patron, he proposed thereafter to spend of each year, 'May, June, July, August at York and his living: thence to the end of January at Winchester, and the other three months at London'. Greater rewards might be expected by the chaplain chosen for the duty of accompanying George II on his visits to Hanover. When that King wished to find preferment for Dr. John Thomas, chaplain at Hamburg, he resolved to make him one of his chaplains; 'and the next time I come to Hanover,' he promised, 'you shall come over with me, and then if a prebend or deanery should happen to fall, you will have a good chance of succeeding to it.' The royal word was a faithful bond; for in 1740 Dr. Thomas, already a chaplain, accompanied his master to Hanover, where fortune so favoured him that, the deanery of Peterborough falling vacant during his attendance, he was nominated straightaway to it. His case became a precedent quoted by the Duke of Newcastle in 1748, that 'the king's chaplain at Hanover has always set aside at all times all other promises', when he wished to secure the nomination of his friend Dr. James Johnson, then in attendance upon the King abroad, to a residentiaryship of St. Paul's, and again in 1752 when Johnson, now on his third visit to Hanover in the company of Newcastle and their sovereign, was rewarded by the see of Gloucester.

The multiplication of preferments bestowed upon royal and other chaplains led to the widespread pluralism which became the butt of all satirists. In painful contrast also to the wealth of the pluralists was the miserable lot of the inferior clergy whose merits had failed to attract the attention of some powerful patron. To the over-large number of poor scholars of the universities who entered into Orders, their choice of the clerical profession was of the nature of a lottery. The few achieved the prizes, as did Bishop Hurd, born the second son of parents whom he described as 'very plain people, for they were farmers'; but the many continued in poverty. Not only was there a wide disparity between the value of the several benefices with cure of souls, but the number of ordinations was in no wise related to the prospects of promotion to a benefice. From the prevalence of pluralism there followed the natural consequence of non-residence. The cleric without influence or friends, ordained to the diaconate and licensed to serve the cure of a non-resident incumbent, languished often for a long period of years in the obscurity of his country parish. Not infrequently he served an equally prolonged diaconate, for the expenses attendant upon ordination to the priesthood discouraged him from receiving that further status until the presentation to a benefice provided both the occasion and the means for taking this step. Nor even when the hopeful curate added the qualification of priesthood did promotion to a vicarage or rectory follow with any rapidity. The circumstances of Mr. Robert Robson, son of a yeoman farmer of Sebergham in Cumberland and a graduate of Queen's College, Oxford, were typical of many clergy of his time. He received deacon's orders at the hands of Bishop Mawson of Chichester in September 1745, a licence to serve the curacy of Pulborough, and ordination to the priesthood from the same bishop in October 1748. In 1751 he married and removed to act as curate of Cocking, whose rector, Dr. Thomas Hutchinson, was also vicar of Horsham. Thus he continued for a full quarter of a century despite the efforts of relatives to rescue him from what they feared might be the perpetual inferiority of an unbeneficed clergyman. In 1767 his brother John Robson, steward to the Bishop of Durham, wrote that 'it would give him inexpressible satisfaction to hear of his better success at that time of life after the toil of so many years in the curatical state: nothing but drudgery and patience for many in his situation, while many a worthless rector was as hard put to it to live on £5 or £600 per annum as his honest worthy curate upon £50'. Not until 1778 did the influence of another brother with Sir James Peachey secure for him the presentation to the living of Stedham, which he enjoyed until his death in 1783.

Of the conditions of service of the numberless army of curates no alluring picture can be drawn. The general salary varied between £30 and £40 per year, the latter figure being attained in large towns or in wealthy parishes. In 1763 Parson Woodforde had the option of two curacies worth £28 plus surplice fees and £40 respectively at Newton Purcell in Oxon. and Thurloxton in Somerset; having chosen the latter he left Oxford for Somerset, transferring shortly to the curacy of Babcary for £30 plus 'the house, stable, gardens and Easter offerings'. After a further brief interval he added to this the curacy of Castle Cary for £20 a year, which meant that he could serve Babcary only once per Sunday. Upon the death of his father new arrangements had to be made, which resulted in his serving Castle Cary for £30 a year plus surplice fees and combining with it the curacy of Ansford. Thirty years earlier, in 1730, John Wesley had informed his mother of his acceptance of a curacy, possibly that of Stanton Harcourt, eight miles from Oxford, and 'the salary £30 per year'. In 1782 Woodforde, in discharging the financial business of his friend Dr. Bathurst, recorded the payment of his curate at the rate of £50 per annum; and throughout the greater part of the age of Johnson the salaries of curates averaged between £30 and £40 per annum, though in the later years of the eighteenth century the standard showed a steady rise towards double that sum. In addition to the meagre stipend the office of curate involved other difficulties. In most cases it was attended by insecurity of tenure, and curates were often dismissed with the shortest of notice, as when Woodforde himself on July 19, 1773, being a Monday, was informed by the incumbent of Ansford 'that he intended serving Ansford next Sunday himself, which notice of his leaving the curacy' the diarist thought 'not only very unkind but very ungentlemanlike'. Such insecurity led to the existence of a class of vagabond clergy, whose habits of frequent change of curacy and consequent itinerancy presented to contemporary bishops an insoluble problem of clerical discipline. In many villages also no proper accommodation for the lodging of a curate could be found, if the non-residence of the incumbent had been occasioned or followed by the dilapidation of the parsonage. Woodforde himself on arrival at Thurloxton found no house suitable to receive him, until good fortune secured his admission to the squire's house on the terms: 'that I should live as he does, (which is very well I am sure), that I should have my linnen washed by him, and that he should keep my horse (corn excepted): £21; and that for every day that I was absent I should be allowed each day 1s. 1½d.'

In estimating the status of curates, however, the extreme poverty of many benefices should be remembered, for in several cases the transition from the position of unbeneficed to that of beneficed cleric brought little financial advantage. On the establishment of Queen Anne's Bounty at the beginning of the century, there were 5,597 livings, amounting to more than half of the total number, whose income did not exceed £50 per annum; whilst after the lapse of a full century with its changes in the value of money, the diocesan returns of 1809 reckoned 3,998 benefices still under £150 per annum. The practice of pluralism spread, therefore, not only among the wealthy clergy of the Court and cathedrals, but among the poor incumbents of small livings, whose necessities compelled the addition of more than one benefice to furnish means of subsistence. Non-residence also was allowed for other reasons than plurality of cures, for example the ruinous condition of many vicarage houses, the unhealthiness of the locality (a misfortune which had to be borne by the unhappy curate), and the urgent avocation elsewhere of the incumbent. The returns to the Articles of Visitation of Archbishop Herring in the large diocese of York in 1743 revealed that of the 836 parishes making replies to the queries, 393 had non-resident incumbents, and of the 711 clergy officiating in the diocese 335 were pluralists; and in these respects York was typical generally of the dioceses of the kingdom. The existence of such wide disparity between the emoluments and services of the higher and lower clergy afforded both a ready target for the wit of anti-clerical writers and a constant provocation to reforming prelates of the calibre of Richard Watson. To the majority of churchmen, however, it afforded no occasion of scandal. Twice Boswell complained to Johnson of the inequality of livings and the poverty of curates. On the first mention of the subject Johnson replied: 'Why yes, Sir; but it cannot be helped. You must consider, that the revenues of the clergy are not at the disposal of the State, like the pay of the army. Different men have founded different churches; and some are better endowed, some worse. The State cannot interfere and make an equal division of what has been particularly appropriated.' Boswell returned to the attack with the contention that no vicar or rector should be allowed to have a curate unless he paid a salary of £100 a year, but Johnson again rejoined:

> To be sure, Sir, it is wrong that any clergyman should be without a reasonable income; but as the church revenues were sadly diminished at the Reformation, the clergy who have livings cannot afford, in many instances, to give good salaries to curates, without leaving themselves too little; and, if no curate were to be permitted unless he had a hundred pounds a year, their number would be very small, which would be a disadvantage, as then there would not be such choice in the nursery for the church, curates being candidates for the higher ecclesiastical offices, according to their merit and good behaviour.... It is not thought fit to trust a man with the care of a parish, till he has given proof as a curate that he shall deserve such a trust.

Upon which comfortable defence of the régime of privilege and inequality, the faithful biographer made the apt comment: 'This is an excellent *theory*; and if the *practice* were according to it, the Church of England would be admirable indeed'.

That practice should lag far behind the virtues of such theory was inevitable in the unreformed state of the Georgian Church. The survival of many obsolete medieval elements in its constitution made difficult the problem of administration even to the most energetic prelates. The obstacles in the way of episcopal oversight were indeed virtually insuperable, and from the lack of careful supervision on the part of the episcopate followed many of the shortcomings of parochial organization. At the outset, the convention requiring the residence of bishops in London for the greater part of the year, to fulfil their attendance upon the Court and Parliament, withdrew them from the active work of their dioceses except during the interval of the summer recess of Parliament. Viscount Perceval represented contemporary opinion in his commendation of Bishop Wilcocks of Gloucester in 1730 that 'he resides as much as any bishop in his diocese, at least four months in the year, and keeps a very generous and hospitable table, which makes amends for the learning he is deficient in'. To this shortness of time available for diocesan duties, there were added the problems of distance and of the large size of some dioceses. The Reformation had contributed comparatively little to the efficient administration of the *Ecclesia Anglicana* apart from the abolition of the protracted commerce with Rome; for, though it added five permanent bishoprics to the Church, only one of these, Chester, fell in the northern province; that of Bristol presented the difficult problem of the isolation of the episcopal city from its diocese, the county of Dorset; and the creation of Oxford and Peterborough while reducing the extent of the old diocese of Lincoln, had added to the difficulty of its administration by severing it into two isolated parts. Furthermore, by an unhappy accident the provision of suffragan bishops was discontinued after the reign of Mary Tudor, so that the post-Reformation bishops inherited most of the administrative problems of their medieval predecessors without that agency which had made possible the provision of episcopal offices for their dioceses. The largest diocese of Georgian England was that of Lincoln with 1,312 parishes, whilst in the northern province the diocese of York, albeit relieved of a large extent of its jurisdiction by the new and straggling diocese of Chester, yet retained 903 parishes, in striking contrast to the small border diocese of Carlisle with only four deaneries and about 100 parishes, where Bishop Nicolson had made it his boast that his visitation 'seldom kept him above two nights from his own bed'. In the majority of dioceses it was manifestly impossible for prelates resident in the capital during the greater part of each year to exercise an efficient supervision. The episcopal offices of ordination and institution of incumbents to benefices might, indeed, be discharged generally by requiring the candidates to wait upon the bishop in London, as Woodforde did for his institution to Weston rectory, or, alternatively, in the case of ordinands, by the issue of letters dimissory to neighbouring bishops holding an ordination in their diocese. Even so the intercourse of prelates with their clergy was occasional and infrequent, as the diary of Woodforde testifies, for the appearances of the bishop were generally confined to formal visitations with the attendant office of confirmation of the laity.

In regard to confirmation, the 60th canon of the Canons of 1604, reciting the tradition by which 'this holy action hath been accustomed in the church in former ages to be performed in the bishop's visitation every third year', required every prelate in his own person to observe the said custom in his visitation. Accordingly, the bishops held triennial visitations and confirmations in their dioceses, usually during the summer months when Parliament was not sitting, and conditions of weather and daylight facilitated travel. Having mapped out, in consultation with their archdeacons, the centres at which they proposed to call, their lordships customarily held the visitation of their clergy in the morning and the confirmation of the laity in the afternoon. To modern eyes the numbers of persons confirmed triennially are almost incredibly large. Thus Archbishop Drummond of York during the years 1768–71 confirmed in his diocese no fewer than 41,600 candidates, whilst in the diocese of Exeter Bishop Keppel confirmed in 1764 in Devon and in 1765 in Cornwall a total of 41,642, and his successor Bishop Ross confirmed at his triennial visitations of 1779, 1782, and 1785–6, the gross numbers of 26,671, 14,938, and 22,289 persons respectively. The figures of Keppel and Ross are particularly noteworthy as a caution against inferring from the large returns of one bishop any remissness on the part of his predecessor. The task of the laying of hands upon so many people was one involving severe physical exhaustion, and the office of bishop was no easy one in such cases as that of Bishop Benson of Gloucester who confirmed for Archbishop Blackburne of York on 9, 10, and 11 September 1737 at Halifax and Ripponden. At the latter place on the first day he consecrated a new church, following that by the confirmation of about 1,500 persons, whilst on the succeeding days at Halifax 'he was in church from about nine in the morning till near seven at night'. It was noted especially of him that he confirmed in all 8,922 candidates 'by only two at a time, with great devotion and solemnity'. The discovery of the best method of discharging the office of confirmation with so many persons was itself a problem of difficulty to bishops; and Archbishop Gilbert of York gained the credit of introducing a new solution. 'This was, instead of going round the rail of the Communion table and laying his hands upon the heads of two or four persons held close together, and in a low voice repeating the form of prayer over them, he went round the whole rail at once, laid his hand upon the head of every person severally, and when he had gone through the whole, then he drew back to the Communion table, and in as audible and solemn a manner as he could, pronounced the prayer over them all.' Dr. Newton, afterwards Bishop of Bristol, who accompanied his grace on many of his tours, since he had received from him the precentorship of York, averred that 'the clergy and people were struck with the decency as much as with the novelty of the ceremony. The confirmations were performed in less time and with less trouble, with more silence and solemnity, and with more regularity and order'. Throughout the century there are evidences of quiet improvement in the administration of the rite. At the confirmation by Bishop Manners Sutton which Parson Woodforde attended at Reepham church on October 7, 1794, only 200 candidates were presented, but three clergy 'were with the bishop in the church, arranging the people in order as they came, and the chaplain received the tickets at the church gates'.

Similar difficulties to those besetting the bishops in the discharge of the spiritual duties of their office hindered the parish clergy from fulfilling the ideal of a pastoral ministry. Of these the chief were the results of pluralism and non-residence, for a vicar charged with the cure of two small livings the stipends of which were insufficient to maintain a curate, or a curate struggling to serve the parishes of a non-resident incumbent, could not give full services and attention to each of his churches. In parishes where the incumbent was resident and had no other duty, divine service was celebrated twice each Sunday, with one sermon, often delivered alternately in the morning and afternoon. Such, manifestly, was the case with Parson Woodforde, whose diary affords evidence of the alteration of his discourses, whilst the Blecheley Diary of William Cole takes note of one particular September Sunday as 'the only time when there are two sermons'. Not unnaturally the congregation gathered to hear the sermon; and when prayers only were read few parishioners troubled to attend. It was, therefore, a mark of unusual piety in Johnson that 'he went more frequently to church when there were prayers only, than when there was also a sermon, as the people required more an example for one than the other; it being much easier for them to hear a sermon than to fix their minds on prayer'. Where the incumbent or curate had to serve more than one parish divine service was performed only once a Sunday in each of his churches. Thus of the 836 churches represented in the York Visitation Returns of 1743 only 383 maintained two services on Sunday all the year round; whilst in similar returns for the diocese of London in 1741–2, of 436 churches only 236 held divine service twice. Practical considerations compelled the episcopate to acquiesce in this state of affairs, and to limit their prohibitions to the undertaking of services in as many as three different churches by any of their clergy. The Holy Communion was celebrated with varying frequency in different parishes. In large towns some churches attained the standard of a monthly sacrament, and in certain London parishes even weekly; but the great majority of country parishes, as in the days of Woodforde at Weston and also of the High Churchman Cole at Blecheley, had three or four sacraments each year, at Easter, Christmas, Whit-Sunday, and at Michaelmas.

The infrequency of the celebration of the Communion, however, should not be interpreted as a sign of neglect or irregularity of religious life on the part of either clergy or laity. George Herbert had written in the preceding century, 'touching the frequency of the Communion, the parson celebrates it, if not duly once a month, yet at least five or six times in the year'; and before the effects of the Methodist revival were felt on the Established Church the proportion of communicants to the adult population of parishes was remarkably high in most parts of the kingdom. The diocese of York in 1743 was characterized by the large number of communicants which were 'often startling in their size', whilst in the remote diocese of Bangor, the visitation returns of Bishop Pearce in 1749 indicated that 'the number of communicants at Easter was very remarkable,... and seemed to show that... the main body of adults were communicants'. Preparation for the Easter Communion appears to have been a serious exercise both with clergy and laity; for on Good Friday 1777 Woodforde fasted 'till five in the afternoon and then eat only a few apple fritters and some bread and cheese', whilst Johnson on that day in 1775 'fasted so very strictly that he did not even taste bread, and took no milk with his tea'. The Doctor attended church twice, remarking that the holy day 'was upon the whole very well observed, even in London', and after the departure of Boswell he directed his servant's preparation for communion, and spent the eve of Easter Day in private meditation to that end. His diary contains several references to his careful preparation for and reception of the Easter Eucharist, especially in 1773 when he attended Matins and Litany followed by the Communion, at which he recited his special prayer, and again in 1777; whilst the importance which he attached to that preparation was testified further when on June 3, 1781, at Southill church, 'it being the first Sunday of the month, the holy sacrament was administered', and Boswell stayed to partake, whereon Johnson observed afterwards, 'You did right to stay and receive the communion; I had not thought of it'. No estimate of English piety in the eighteenth century is adequate which fails to take account of the religious exercises of such devout laity as Johnson, who was zealous for the proper observance of Sunday, believed that 'the holydays observed by our church are of great use in religion', commended Law's *Serious Call* as 'the finest piece of hortatory theology in any language', and stoutly defended the English clergy as having 'produced the most valuable books in support of religion both in theory and practice'.

Apart from the performance of divine service on Sundays and the quarterly Sacrament, the generality of the clergy fulfilled their other duties as special occasions demanded. Public prayers on weekdays were maintained in large town churches, but not in the majority of country parishes, though Mr. Cole read public prayers on the holydays and saints' days; the clergy catechized the youth in the season of Lent, with additional attention to the instruction of children upon receipt of notice of the bishop's triennial visitation and confirmation. The diary of Woodforde contains a pleasing and homely picture in the autumn of 1794 of his activities in such circumstance; his preaching 'on the benefits and use of confirmation', and the receiving of companies of young people 'come to be examined against confirmation', to whom after due instruction he gave 'cake and a glass of wine'.

Of the ordinary divine service performed on Sundays many accounts have been given; but perhaps that of a hostile witness, whose criticism was sharpened by religious rivalry, may be relied upon to afford the maximum of unfavourable comment. In 1757 John Wesley wrote to a correspondent setting forth the superiority of Methodist public worship to that of the Church.

It is no small advantage that the person who reads prayers, though not always the same, yet is one who may be supposed to speak from his heart, one whose life is no reproach to his profession, and one who performs that solemn part of divine service, not in a careless, hurrying, slovenly manner, but seriously and slowly, as becomes him who is transacting so high an affair between God and man. Nor are their solemn addresses to God interrupted by the formal drawl of a parish clerk, the screaming of boys who bawl out what they neither feel nor understand, or the unseasonable and unmeaning impertinence of a voluntary on the organ. When it is seasonable to sing praise to God, they do it with the spirit and with the understanding also; not in the miserable, scandalous doggerel of Hopkins and Sternhold, but in psalms and hymns which are both sense and poetry.... What they sing is therefore a proper continuation of the spiritual and reasonable service; being selected for that end, not by a poor humdrum wretch who can scarce read what he drones out with such an air of importance, but by one who knows what he is about and how to connect the preceding with the following part of the service.

This caricature touches upon the familiar features of the Anglican service: the metrical psalms, the regular and unvarying form of prayers, the intonation of parish clerk and rustic choir; but the same combination of ingredients produced in many churches an office no less worthy in content and devout in utterance than the less restrained and formal inventions of extemporaneous lay preachers.

The survival of obsolete medieval machinery in the constitution of the Established Church may explain many of the anomalies which hindered the efficient discharge of episcopal and parochial duties in Johnson's England; but to account for the particular kind of religious belief and practice characteristic of that age recourse must be had rather to the intellectual temper of the time. Until the effect of the Methodist revival produced a resuscitation of Calvinist preaching amongst Evangelical clergy within the Church, the prevailing tradition of theology and of preaching was strongly Latitudinarian. Partly in reaction against the theological disputes of the seventeenth century upon abstruse points of divine election and reprobation, and partly under the influence of the new scientific movement which was devoted in particular to the study of astronomy, the intellectual temper of the Hanoverian age was indifferent to matters of church government and to confessional creeds which severed church from church. Revelation even in the discourses of orthodox divines passed imperceptibly into the fashionable vogue of natural religion; sermons were sparing of emotional appeal and dogmatic claims; and the generality of preachers desired to inculcate lessons of morality or to establish belief in Christianity upon the grounds of reasonable evidences. When in 1771 Richard Watson was elected to the Regius Professorship of Divinity in the University of Cambridge, he declared the principles of his religious persuasion.

I reduced the study of divinity into as narrow a compass as I could, for I determined to study nothing but my Bible, being much unconcerned about the opinions of councils, fathers, churches, bishops and other men as little inspired as myself.... My mind was wholly unbiassed; I had no prejudice against, no predilection for, the Church of England; but a sincere regard for the Church of Christ, and an insuperable objection to every degree of dogmatical intolerance. I never troubled myself with answering any arguments which the opponents in the divinity school brought against the articles of the church, nor ever admitted their authority as decisive of a difficulty; but I used on such occasions to say to them, holding the New Testament in my hand, *En sacrum codicem*.

Such a scheme of divinity tended naturally to the dissolution of the differences alike of creed and polity which divided churches from each other. In its positive tenets Latitudinarian theology laid much stress upon the Fatherhood of God and upon the consequent necessity of benevolence in men. Parish clergy even in country cures ... delivered courses of sermons upon Christian evidences, the Apostles' Creed, and the Lord's Prayer, and endeavoured to expound Christianity in a rational manner against the extremes of superstition and fanaticism. The one criticism which Johnson allowed against Anglican sermons was that 'the established clergy in general did not preach plain enough; and that polished periods and glittering sentences flew over the heads of the common people, without any impression upon their hearts. Something might be necessary,' he observed, 'to excite the affections of the common people, who were sunk in languor and lethargy, and therefore he supposed that the new concomitants of Methodism might probably produce so desirable an effect.' In the sphere of practice the Latitudinarian tradition emphasized the importance of good works of charity and benevolence. The Georgian period was the age of hospitals alike in London, in the university towns, and in the widespread foundation of county hospitals; and in the rural life of the parish this solicitude found its counterpart in such ubiquitous charitable gifts as those of Parson Woodforde. That there could be found clergy of scandalous life was true in the eighteenth as in all centuries; that there were also devout parish clergy of the type of Johnson's ideal, Prebendary Zachariah Mudge, vicar of St. Andrew's, Plymouth, and prebendary of Exeter, is evident; and between them stood the host of ordinary country clergy of whom James Woodforde is probably a typical example. The verdict of the editors of Archbishop Herring's Visitation Returns upon the clergy of the York diocese, that they were 'a body of dutiful and conscientious men, trying to do their work according to the standards of their day', may be accepted as true of the majority of their brethren in other parts of the kingdom.

7

REASON AND FEELING IN THE EIGHTEENTH CENTURY

A. R. Humphreys

The traditional stereotype of eighteenth-century English thought and literature as an Augustan age of dispassionate reason has undergone extensive revision in mid-twentieth-century scholarship. In A. R. Humphreys' The Augustan World *the complexity of eighteenth-century English rationalism is carefully examined in its literary and philosophical contexts, and the powerful undercurrent of feeling is given a central place in Enlightenment culture.*

THE EIGHTEENTH century, everyone knows, was 'The Age of Reason'. This deplorably simple formula creates the impression, still strong in undergraduate essays, that by some psychological freak three or four generations of Britons grew up colour-blind to the emotions: a common greyness sobered everything. The world was all before them yet they retired to garrets to write 'rational' essays and couplets on practical matters of town life.

Those who think of the century as phlegmatic must presumably be surprised when they find evidence of feelings not only frequent but effusive. 'At many public solemnities', as sensible a man as Addison informs us, 'I cannot forbear expressing my joy with tears that have stolen down my cheeks' (*The Spectator*, No. 69). The admission would sound sentimental in a modern essayist, and it suggests that if the Augustans spoke so much of reason it was not because their emotions were weak but because on the contrary they were strong. The effusions of sensibility were never far away, and many Augustan thoughts did not by any means lie too deep for tears. It is true that literary fashion required moderation in the expression of feeling, and philosophical fashion required the importance of reason to be asserted. But there is still abundant feeling in Augustan life, though in literature sometimes it must be detected by smaller signs than in 'romantic' work and sometimes (as with Thomson's or Akenside's raptures for science) it has lost its appeal. The relations between reason and feeling need tactful definition.

FROM A. R. Humphreys, *The Augustan World* (London: Methuen & Co. Ltd., 1954), pp. 189-202. By permission of the publishers.

If we start with reason, it is because that faculty recommended itself first, chronologically speaking, to the Augustan attention. Reason had produced the seventeenth century's intellectual triumphs, though reason not as abstract intellect but as a measuring-rod of the 'real' world. The seventeenth century was of course not the first to see the universe as order; classical and oriental antiquity, the Middle Ages and the Renaissance had observed the working of a macrocosmic plan. Hooker for instance has a magnificent paragraph on the 'obedience of creatures unto the law of nature' which guarantees the harmony of things (*Ecclesiastical Politie*, I. iii. 2). Nor was it true that God's existence and ways had hitherto been thought inscrutable and were now found demonstrable by reason; the schoolmen had held that reason could prove the existence of God and deduce therefrom an elaborate theology, and Locke's 'rational' religion was within the tradition. What did impress the Augustans was that after the sectarian violences of the Reformation, with their terrible stress on damnation, predestination and a vengeful Deity, Christianity seemed to become reasonable and 'not mysterious', and that after ages in which the mind grappled with but did not understand the universe science had found, through one type of reason, a method of study which yielded satisfying fruit. Reason, then, had produced the triumphs of Newton and Boyle, and the quieter temper of politics and religion after years of tumult.

Leaving until later the question of science, let us consider how reason worked for the Augustans in the sphere of moral philosophy. Its prestige, in the first place, produced an enviable air of confidence; the dawn was dispelling the mists of night and error. In the second place it evolved a curious kind of moral geometry which generated what is called the 'intellectualist' school of ethics, and this is so characteristic that we may respectfully disinter it for a moment from its resting-place among dead-and-gone philosophical fashions, though all we may notice is the rattle of dry bones.

When in Fielding's *Tom Jones* the hypocritical Deist Square (significant name) champions virtue against the equally hypocritical Churchman Thwackum, he does so by invoking 'the unalterable rule of right and the eternal fitness of things'. This curious phrase was then familiar as the slogan of the thorough-going rationalists. It meant that just as there was a perfectly co-ordinated physical order, which scientific reason could understand, so too there was a similar moral order which moral reason could understand. There was in fact a science of morality, and good behaviour meant the exact concordance of one's actions to this moral order, the nature and details of which were discoverable by pure reason. With their insistence on duty and obedience to moral imperatives the 'intellectualists' (as they came later to be called) were virtually Stoics, though their first representatives were the Cambridge Platonists, whose noble religious spirit was far better than mere rationalism. In their view we perceive by spiritual insight such qualities as Goodness, Truth and Beauty (which really exist and are not subjective or relative), and should harmonise with them through our noblest faculty, reason. Man is by nature good, not sinful, and his reason can keep him so. Vice, said Benjamin Whichcote,

> is contrary to the Nature of Man, *as Man*; for it is contrary to the order of Reason, the peculiar and highest Principle in Man; nor is any thing *in itself* more unnatural or of greater Deformity, in the whole world, than that an Intelligent Agent should have the Truth of Things in his *Mind*, and that it should not give Law and Rule to his *Temper, Life* and *Actions*.
>
> *Moral and Religious Aphorisms,* No. 212

By his best spiritual and intellectual perceptions man understands what his moral duties are, and by reason working on his normally virtuous disposition he obeys them.

This faith, optimistic about man's nature and originally spiritual in its quality, retained its optimism in the eighteenth century but became more coolly rational and therefore more rigidly theoretical—which is why Fielding satirised it in the pedantry of Square. Spirituality dwindled into argumentation. The impoverishment is obvious in Samuel Clarke, a devoted Newtonian and the leading English metaphysician of the early eighteenth century. He would have become Archbishop of Canterbury, Voltaire relates, had not Bishop Gibson of London told Queen Anne that his great intelligence and honesty were marred by one thing: he was not a Christian. He was in fact all but an Arian—not a strong qualification for the episcopate. His fame depended largely on two sets of Boyle lectures—*A Demonstration of the Being and Attributes of God* (1704) and *The Unchangeable Obligations of Natural Religion* (1705)—in which the Platonists' spiritual reason degenerates into Square's chop-logic.

His argument would hardly need outlining were it not that it is the kind of thing that gained the 'Age of Reason' its name and was influential up to the time of Godwin. The universe to Clarke is a moral jigsaw (as to the scientists it was a physical jigsaw), in which, if everyone performs exactly those duties which 'the nature of things' requires, the harmony of moral law will be attained and God's intention fulfilled. The great evidences of God's goodness are the exquisite interdependence and regularity of natural processes, and since this is so in physical law a similar interdependence must obtain in moral law. As a general doctrine this is acceptable enough; what is not acceptable is Clarke's drily demonstrative manner. Voltaire called him 'une vraie machine à raisonnements', and that is precisely his character: his arguments are not false so much as innutrient, with their methodical deductions quite lacking in the inspiration of poetry.

Other 'intellectualists', despite their good intentions, are no more palatable. Tindal's *Christianity as Old as the Creation* (1730) is characteristic in its lack of succulence, and its second chapter heading is an adequate sample of its manner. It runs:

> *That the Religion of Nature consists in observing those things which our Reason, by considering the Nature of God and Man, and the Relation we stand in to him*

and one another, demonstrates to be our Duty: and that those Things are plain: and likewise what they are.

Other men prolonged the same strain and it is not surprising that Hume was soon to reject the supremacy of reason altogether, that the main stream of ethics soon abandoned this flat and dusty bed for the deeper channel of 'moral sentiment', and that the torrent of Evangelicalism with its tumbling life-giving waters was soon to wash into men's minds the idea that there was more to life than this thin grasshopperlike scratching.

Yet the sovereignty of reason had a sudden restoration before the end of the century in the thought of the radicals and above all in Richard Price and William Godwin. Price's *Review of the Principal Questions and Difficulties in Morals* (1757) foreshadowed Kant in establishing absolute moral imperatives to which reason must impel us. Moral rectitude is 'a universal law; the whole creation is ruled by it; under it men and all rational beings subsist' (p. 178). Price is an absolutist with his imperatives understood by reason and conformed to by will; the occasion for passions and appetites, he avers (p. 124),

arises entirely from our deficiencies and weaknesses. Reason alone (did we possess it in a higher degree) would answer all the ends of them. Thus there would be no need of the parental affections were all parents sufficiently acquainted with the reasons for taking upon them the guidance and support of those whom nature has placed under their care, and were they virtuous enough to be always determined by those reasons.

In Godwin such uncompromising rationalism achieved its fullest expression, seeking to make reason supply the place of passion and instinct. Virtue is to him—at least in his early rigorous phase—entirely a matter of right reason and will, whereas vice 'depends for its existence upon the existence of error' (*Political Justice*, 1793, i. 4). The vicious man, that is, has either worked out his moral sum wrongly or has not squarely faced the result of his calculation. Life's true governor, in thought and action, must be the mind; all action must be voluntary, deliberate, and based on reasoning from first principles. Truth, the 'real' state of things, wins allegiance if it is properly understood, for man cannot stand against the conviction of reason. So did the century's confidence reach its peak, in a challenge to man to conquer error and become perfect. It is true that Godwin himself came to see that he had underrated feeling: prefacing *St. Leon* (1799) he admitted that 'for more than four years' (that is, we may assume, since he was first attracted by Mary Wollstonecraft) he had regretted dismissing 'domestic and private affections inseparable from the nature of man and from what may be called the culture of the heart'. But it was *Political Justice* (particularly its uncompromising first edition) rather than *St. Leon* that braced the young radicals with the sense that the dawn was breaking, and transmitted not only to politics but to ethics also the clarifying objectivity of (moral) science. This dramatic culmination of eighteenth-century rationalism in nineteenth-century radicalism is one of the outstanding events of intellectual evolution.

Reason did not however rule unchallenged.... The theme which was fundamental even in the eighteenth century [was] 'the passions'. Godwin himself, as we have seen, came to admit 'the culture of the heart', and Wordsworth after 'Dragging all precepts, judgments, maxims, creeds, Like culprits to the bar' (*The Prelude,* xi. 294–5) under Godwin's influence found his spirit breaking and turned for salvation to the life of feeling. But long before Wordsworth there were protests against too much reason, and fortunately it was not only the rationalists who could invoke great names. If Newton and Locke showed reason's triumphs, Shakespeare showed those of inspired unreason—indeed, it was critical orthodoxy to elevate the impassioned creators like Homer and Shakespeare over the men of judgment like Virgil and Jonson. The Augustans were not so blind to life as not to know that feeling is the major and reason the minor component of man. Only the strictest rationalists could hold that men live by unimpassioned thought: the general and natural conclusion was that 'the passions' are the force of life and that reason, far from impelling life on its course, can at most guide it. Pope wrote a remarkable *Spectator* (No. 408) arguing that men's actions 'can never proceed immediately from Reason', and that the Passions 'are to the Mind as the Winds to a Ship', which may perhaps destroy it but without which it cannot move at all. To extinguish the passions in the supposed cause of virtue would be, he said, 'putting out the light of the Soul', and the attempt to do so by means of education 'certainly destroys more good Genius's than it can possibly improve'. In the *Essay on Man* he put these ideas more pithily (ii. 101–10):

> *In lazy Apathy let Stoics boast*
> *Their Virtue fix'd: 'tis fix'd as in a frost;*
> *Contracted all, retiring to the breast;*
> *But strength of mind is Exercise, not Rest;*
> *The rising Tempest puts in act the soul,*
> *Parts it may ravage, but preserves the Whole.*
> *On life's vast ocean diversely we sail,*
> *Reason the card, but Passion is the gale;*
> *Nor God alone in the still calm we find,*
> *He mounts the storm, and walks upon the wind.*

It is Hume, however, not Pope, who most brilliantly reduces the prestige of reason. He does not scorn reason as an instrument of discussion—indeed his greatest work, the *Treatise of Human Nature* (1739), is a most intently-conducted piece of argument. But he denies the almost divine efficacy attributed to reason by the intellectualists; he points out how fallible it is and how mistaken even the simplest deductions may be, and he argues the theoretical necessity of scepticism about all the evidence of sense or mind (though he candidly agrees that in practice one takes life as it seems to be and deals effectively with it). He admits a dilemma—to distrust reason is to incur fantasy and unreality; to rely on reason is to find nothing ultimately certain and to fall into an abyss of scepticism.

This dilemma makes him alternately desert philosophy in despair and resume it from irresistible curiosity.

Having shown reason to be a pretender, Hume prepares to enthrone passion. Philosophic convention may hold that virtue lies in obedience to reason but, he says (*Treatise*, bk. ii, pt. iii. sec. iii),

> I shall endeavour to prove *first*, that reason alone can never be a motive to any action of the will; and *secondly*, that it can never oppose passion in the direction of the will.

Reason deals with logic and moves in a different sphere from passion; it compares and judges but cannot initiate feeling or action. We think it capable of restraining us, when restraint is necessary, but what does restrain us is something we mistake for reason because it is of a quiet and temperate nature—in other words, passion of a subdued kind, 'certain calm desires and tendencies'. To take a modern parallel, reason no more makes a man embark on or desist from action than his reading of a road-map makes his car start or stop. From the map he judges the route to his destination: the motive power comes from the engine, and the brakes which provide control are only a negative form of that power.

As for moral judgments, they are a kind of feeling. Virtue arouses an agreeable, vice a disagreeable sensation. We like beneficent actions because we feel for the good of men in general, and it is sentiment not reason that prompts us to such liking (*Treatise*, bk. iii, pt. iii, sec. i):

> The approbation of moral qualities most certainly is not derived from reason, or any comparison of ideas; but proceeds entirely from a moral taste, and from certain sentiments of pleasure and disgust, which arise from the contemplation and view of particular qualities or characters.

'To have the sense of virtue', Hume says elsewhere, 'is nothing but to feel a satisfaction of a particular kind from the contemplation of a character'.

The argument is an intricate and brilliant one and penetrates much deeper into the springs of behaviour than did the intellectualists. The *Treatise of Human Nature*, it is true, made no stir at first. But others also were undermining reason: Hutcheson as well as Pope had spoken up for 'passion', and in his posthumous *System of Moral Philosophy* (1755) he maintained like Hume that reason judges the means but not the ends of action, which are what the emotions desire. Adam Smith's *Theory of Moral Sentiments* (1759) holds the same view of moral judgments (VII. iii. 1):

> If virtue therefore pleases for its own sake, and if vice as certainly displeases the mind, it cannot be by reason, but immediate sense and feeling, which reconciles us to the one and alienates us from the other.

Burke in politics was soon to show himself as distrustful of reason, and as devoted to instinct and emotion, as any philosopher of 'sentiment'. It is time to consider the deposition of reason less negatively, less as the demotion of reason and more as the promotion of feeling....

Augustan philosophy is often mellower in tone and more benevolent in mood than we might expect, and the predominant reason for this is the influence of Shaftesbury. Of his elder contemporaries Locke (whose pupil he was) had preached a benevolent God and the duty of benevolence among men; the Platonists, whom he admired, had thought well of human nature; and Latitudinarian divines were holding forth from the pulpit on Christian charity and the social virtues. From such roots, from an ardent love of classical philosophy, and from his sanguine temperament, sprang Shaftesbury's trust in man's natural goodness; he had a generous quality of mind and feeling which was ready to credit mankind with instincts for good. If Locke set 'clear and distinct ideas' ringing down the century, Shaftesbury bequeathed it that no less important concept 'the moral sense', together with his engaging air of urbane humanism.

The *Characteristicks* (1711) has been called a landmark in English thought because it studies man not in his rational nature but by introspection into his mind and feelings (*Encyclopedia Britannica*, 'Shaftesbury'). Seventeenth-century moralists and physiologists had dissected the emotions, but Shaftesbury was the first to base his ethics entirely on good feeling. Against Hobbist and Puritan disparagements he upheld a benevolent enlightenment, enriching English ethics with a benign current of Greek thought more potent than that Christianized by the Platonists, in a style tempered by cool reason and warm emotion, popularising 'moral sentiment' as the basis of social relationships. The certainties in man are his feelings (*Inquiry Concerning Virtue*, ii. 2 *ad fin.*):

we cannot doubt of what passes within ourselves. Our passions and affections are known to us. *They* are certain, whatever the objects may be on which they are employed.

Wordsworth could not speak more clearly. These passions and affections are generous and social; human nature tends towards sympathy, expanding outward from the family by wider and wider circles throughout humanity. As Pope was to write,

> *Self-love but serves the virtuous mind to wake,*
> *As the small pebble stirs the peaceful lake.*
> *The centre mov'd, a circle strait succeeds,*
> *Another still, and still another spreads;*
> *Friend, parent, neighbour first it will embrace,*
> *His country next, and next all human race:*
> *Wide and more wide, th' o'erflowings of the mind*
> *Take ev'ry creature in, of ev'ry kind.*
>   Essay on Man, iv. 363–70

Man fulfils the law of his being in exercising the social virtues and benevolent emotions. Descartes' *Cogito ergo sum* [I think, therefore I am] yields in Shaftesbury to a self-awareness of feeling, though the good life imposes its own discipline in a selection of impulses, the cultivation of charity and elevation of mind, and the suppression of their opposites. Shaftesbury as a champion of feeling has a benevolently patrician air not shared by Blake or D. H. Lawrence.

He gave his time what, on the whole, was good for it. The new spirit of warm and effusive emotion spread through life and letters and became still more popular through those 'overflowing feelings of a tender compassionate heart' which Patrick Murdock signalised in prefacing Thomson's poems in 1762. For Thomson was the most distinguished poetic disciple of Shaftesbury, whose name he joins with those of Bacon, Boyle, Newton and Locke as his favourite philosophers: he praises the 'inward rapture, only to be felt', evoked by benevolence (*Summer*, line 1646), and in *Spring* (556ff.—'Hail, Source of Being!') he versifies Shaftesbury's remarkable Nature rhapsody in *The Moralists*. Gradually the intellectual climate becomes milder and sunnier; literature glows with moral sentiment; the sharpness of satire and the chill of sovereign reason yield before the claims of feeling, as country gardens forsake geometry and soften into the outlines of natural grace. No book represents this better than Hutcheson's *Inquiry into the Original of our Ideas of Beauty and Virtue* (1725), which plays variations on the 'moral sense' (that is, the instincts of moral approval or disapproval). Why, Hutcheson asks, do we feel for or against others even in remote times and places, who cannot affect us personally? Why rate virtue higher than success? Why lose with honour rather than win with dishonour? Such preferences are not reasonable—they arise from moral sense or sentiment, an intuition untrammelled by calculations of advantage.

Human feelings, of course, are more numerous than the qualities (whether rational or instinctive) involved in the special task of moral judgment. But as philosophy begins to consider even moral judgment to be a matter of feeling or sentiment, as it stresses the fraternal emotions which should link mankind, so there unfolds a willingness in ways unconnected with moral behaviour to admit the primacy of feeling, to value the intuitive and indeed irrational impulses, to feel sympathy for living things and awe at the strangeness of Nature. Hutcheson increases the senses far beyond the traditional five, to include 'Public Sense' or sympathy, the 'Moral Sense', the sense of honour, and imagination—'the pleasant perceptions arising from regular, harmonious, and uniform objects'. Burke's *Inquiry into the Origin of our Ideas of the Sublime and Beautiful* (1757) enriches aesthetics as Shaftesbury had enriched moral philosophy. 'The influence of reason in producing our passions', it asserts, 'is nothing near so extensive as it is commonly believed' (I. xiii), and it examines such emotions as sympathy, and the awe aroused by sublimity (Burke is here under the strong influence of Longinus). Sublimity itself is a notable theme, for it transcends the region of the clear and comprehensible for that of mystery and dread. The beautiful, Burke says, implies delicacy, clear colour, and moderate size: the sublime implies great scale (the ocean, or starry skies), obscurity and mystery, dramatic illumination (lightning), majesty and difficulty of achievement (Stonehenge), and above all great power and the thought of infinity, which fill the mind with 'delightful horror' (II. viii). Burke's sense of these qualities, so alien to the classical code, marks an epoch in the analysis of moods. By such introspection many subtle and unaccountable instincts found their way into the forefront of attention, and both prose and poetry turned to a more sensitive consciousness of them.

The vogue of feeling shows itself in philosophy. With Hume and Adam Smith we enter the realm of expansive good nature: as with Shaftesbury and Hutcheson the tone of their writing is almost as significant as the sense. Virtue, fixed as in a frost by the intellectualists, is to be thawed out: the springs of human nature are to be freed from the clear but icy crust of reason and are to flow and bubble from their inmost source. Since philosophy is linking moral qualities to feeling the consequence seems to be that the deeper one's virtue the stronger one's emotions. There is a novel degree of fervour in Hume and Adam Smith as they write on such subjects: 'the sentiments of humanity', Hume declares, are so agreeable that they

> brighten up the very face of sorrow and operate like the sun, which shining on a dusky cloud or falling rain paints on them the most glorious colours which are to be found in the whole circle of nature.
> *Essays Moral, Political and Literary:* 'The Stoic'

Such enthusiasm over sorrow and sympathy is typical. Hutcheson had already imagined a benevolence coextensive with humanity and even with astral space—if, he said, we knew of rational beings 'in the most distant planets' we should wish them well. For Hume, benevolence is no less unbounded; he describes our sensibility as analogous to the sympathetically-vibrating strings of violins, and a glowing sense of public spirit as being almost the summit of human nature:

> No qualities are more readily intituled to the general goodwill and approbation of mankind than beneficence and humanity, friendship and gratitude, natural affection and public spirit, ... and a generous concern for our kind and species.
> *Enquiries Concerning the Human Understanding,* ed. Selby-Bigge (1902), 299–300

Hume's ideal man, in all the delightful complacency of his rich, harmonious and sentimental feelings, can be portrayed only in the words of his creator's essay 'The Stoic', already cited:

> The softest benevolence, the most undaunted resolution, the tenderest sentiments, the most sublime love of virtue, all these animate successively his transported bosom. What satisfaction when he looks within, to find the most turbulent passions tuned to just harmony and concord, and every jarring sound banished from this enchanting music!

Adam Smith's *Theory of Moral Sentiments* (1759) breathes the same intoxicating air—intoxicating not because good sense has been forgotten but because the feelings are indulged and inhibitions relaxed. His panegyrics on sympathy, 'the amiable virtue of humanity', recall the novels of sensibility in their transports and tears. The unfortunate, we learn (I. i. 2),

by relating their misfortunes ... in some measure renew their grief. Their tears accordingly flow faster than before.... They take pleasure, however, in all this, and it is evident are sensibly relieved by it, because the sweetness of the bystander's sympathy more than compensates the bitterness of their sorrow.

Sufferer and sympathiser harmonise with each other, the former moderating his anguish, the latter sharing his situation with all the delicacy of the generous heart. As in Hume, these impulses are the outcome not of reason but of 'immediate sense and feeling'.

As such sympathy spread, Fielding was able to praise the vogue of charity—'this virtue hath shone brighter in our time than at any period which I remember in our annals' (*The Champion*, 16 February, 1740)— and to mention 'a vast number of schemes' for helping the poor (*Covent-Garden Journal*, 5 May, 1752). In 1755 the public contributed £100,000 for the victims of the Lisbon earthquake, and this disinterested generosity for those of another nation and faith was widely approved. Johnson's *Idler* (6 May, 1758) said that whenever the public was asked to help in a good cause,

every hand is open to contribute something, every tongue is busied in solicitation, and every art of pleasure is employed for a time in the interest of virtue.

Smollett observed an 'extraordinary growth' of benevolence; John Brown's *Estimate of the Manners and Principles of the Times* (1757) avowed that 'the spirit of Humanity is natural to our nation', and Goldsmith's Chinese sage in *The Citizen of the World* remarked England's 'exalted virtue' in the cause of charity.

The century's moral evolution was a complicated general trend in which, far from being sacrificed to reason, 'the passions' received abundant honour and even at times an adulation which at last brought sensibility into disrepute. If the literary moods of the late Augustans are in general warmer and more indulgent than those of the early, the credit must go in a marked degree to the philosophers whose thought had given prestige to feeling and the encouragement of psychological theory to the promptings of emotion.

8

THE PLANTER ARISTOCRACY
Richard Pares

A deeper understanding of the qualities of eighteenth-century British imperialism has been gained by the growing number of scholars who have concerned themselves with the modes of existence in British colonial society. The most eminent of this group is Richard Pares, whose premature death at the height of his powers deprived modern English historical scholarship of one of its most original and creative minds. Pares had a comprehensive knowledge of eighteenth-century political and economic institutions, but he sought to give a more compelling evocation of the achievements and limitations of the First British Empire by concentrating much of his research on the family histories of the great plantation patrimonies in the West Indies. A West-India Fortune, from which the following selection is taken, is Pares' masterpiece. Making use of the private papers of the Pinney family of West-India sugar magnates, he was able to depict these Hanoverian frontier lords in a series of detailed sketches.

There are two portraits of John Pinney. They were painted at the beginning and the end of his career, and they might be representations of two different men. That, of course, might happen to anybody who had his portrait painted twice; but there is some significance in the great transformation which took place from the young man to the old. The young Pinney is personable, though his eyes are set a little close together; he looks as if he were more immediately intent upon his social position and his beautiful flowered waistcoat than upon the money which paid for these satisfactions. The old Pinney looks somewhat formidable. Outwardly calm and benign, he has an air of tension, as if he might at any moment be going to jump himself or to make somebody else jump. It was, in fact, this inexhaustible nervous energy, this unremitting nervous tension, that made John Pinney, without any original or creative genius, one of the most successful planters and West-India merchants of his time.

His success appears to vindicate the truth of those copy-book maxims which are associated in most people's minds with Samuel Smiles and his

---

FROM Richard Pares, *A West-India Fortune* (London: Longmans, Green & Co. Limited, 1950), pp. 64-80. By permission of the publishers.

Self Help, but really go back at least as far as Defoe and were the commonplaces of all eighteenth-century merchants. John Pinney bandied about, with the best of them, such platitudes as 'Never put off till tomorrow what can be done to-day,' or 'Let me entreat you not to buoy yourself up with improper or too sanguine expectations, for believe me, nothing but a strict application to business united to an unexceptionable conduct, in every department, will ever induce the rational part of mankind to countenance you.' But there is no inherent efficacy in these frigid commonplaces; it was the emotional intensity with which he felt and lived them that distinguished John Pinney from less successful men. He could not bear having nothing to do: 'Idleness and dissipation,' he once wrote, 'will never suit my disposition.' Above all, he feared and hated debt as other people fear and hate weeds, or dirt, or mortal sin. He once wrote of 'the inexpressible comfort of being free of debt,' and on another occasion told his brother-in-law 'You ought to shudder at the idea of debt. Interest money is like a moth in a man's garment, never asleep.'

In this and similar contexts 'shudder' and 'tremble' were two of his favourite words. He 'shudders' at the thought of what will become of a son who will not cut down his expenditure; 'trembles' at the sight of a bill of exchange drawn upon him by his plantation manager; is 'electrified' by an unfavourable report upon the condition of his slaves, and even has to put off examining some unsatisfactory plantation accounts, 'not feeling pleasant whenever I attempted it.' There is no reason to suspect that all this is mere intimidating cant. When he tells a correspondent that he could not sleep all night for thinking of a bad piece of business, or of the chimneys which have been wrongly placed in the rebuilding of his house, he is obviously speaking the truth. He was a man who made tireless efforts to avoid mistakes himself, and took very hard the mistakes which others made at his expense. That is why his two closest and longest friendships both ended with dreadful and irreparable quarrels; why he treated his father-in-law with a mixture of patronizing contempt and frantic irritation, and turned his brother-in-law out of the plantation. Yet in all these transactions he was never unjust—only hard and implacable. He could even forgive on occasions, but only when misfortune overtook his adversary and his resentment was changed by pity.

He was not a miser; that is too simple a description of him. He certainly did some stingy things, but very few that were merely stingy without some rational justification. There was a particular reason why the owner of a well-managed plantation should dislike spending money on goods or services which his slaves could quite well perform for him without any additional cost. There was also a reason why owners of slaves should lock up their stores, and count the tools and materials they issued (as John Pinney counted the planks he gave out to his carpenters for a particular job); it was the only way to prevent pilfering. Again, he would often withhold money out of deference for a financial principle and confer the same thing in the next breath as a personal favour. For example, when his brother-in-law, who was a qualified doctor, was living on his plantation as manager, John Pinney refused to pay him a separate fee for medical attention to the negroes, proclaiming: 'I never suffer an extra charge for the abilities of my manager in any branch of plantation industry, be it the care of my slaves when sick, stock or anything else, but consider the whole as included in his salary.' This looks mean, but as he immediately increased the salary of his doctor-manager he was, in this instance, only a purist, not a miser. He was often liberal to employees and to slaves, though his liberality sometimes took a curiously commercial form (as when, instead of sending a present to one of his negresses, he sent her some soap to sell for her own profit, charging her for it at something less than the standard rate of advance, but exacting repayment to the last penny). In fact, he was not generally mean, but he was precise. He once wrote to one of his agents, 'Do let me prevail upon you to be very particular in matters of business—admitting I am more so than the generality of people, I flatter myself, as it gives me pleasure, you will indulge me.'

This precision of mind showed itself, above all, in his accounts. It is hardly too much to say that John Pinney made a religion of his accounts; certainly he expressed his most passionate feelings in them, in long vehement comments on particular items, or in marginal rubrics. For example, when he debited the plantation accounts of 1780 with the money spent on an unsatisfactory overseer, he relieved his feelings by adding 'after his arrival he proved so great a drunkard that I was obliged to send him home by the first opportunity.' Again, he inserted in the plantation account for 1790–1 the remark 'Note—the clear profit this year is larger than it would have been, owing to my being on the spot the latter end of the crop.... The shortness of this crop and the preceding ones were caused by the vile management of William Coker, who I discharged the 1st of August, 1790, and placed Doctor Thomas Pym Weekes as manager in his room.' Dr. Weekes's own accounts were soon subjected to the same commentary, and after several bitter notes on particular items, his transgressions too were summed up in red ink on the accounts for 1792–3: 'Doctor Thomas Pym Weekes is an expensive manager, and part of his conduct is reprehensible. If there is not a considerable amendment he must be removed. Mem. Sick of gentlemen managers.'

It is not surprising that a man who made his accounts the vehicle of his feelings in this way should have taken an interest in their form and demanded absolute exactness in their presentation. John Pinney's plantation accounts ... present, from the first, a very clear picture of every aspect of his financial position. He once or twice reformed his accounting procedure, so as to express some new idea or elicit some new fact.... He would sometimes charge imaginary sums in these accounts so as to express some personal relation in financial terms—as when, being without a plantation manager, he charged an annual sum for his own services in that capacity. There may have been some point in this: John Pinney was a tenant for life and the estate was entailed on his sons; it was therefore important to distinguish between his personal property and the plantation. But some of his accounting seems unnecessarily meticulous: for instance, he opened an account with each of his children from the moment of its birth; the child was charged with its midwife, its christening fee, its share of the nurse, and so forth. It is hard to see what could be the use of this. It is true that a particular fund—the income from a certain mortgage—was appropriated to the children's keep; but if the income had failed, it could hardly have made any difference to the treatment of the children. Their father, however, thus satisfied his passion for knowing where everything stood in his finances.

It was this passion which made him harass his attorneys, managers and overseers into weekly or even daily compliance with the elaborate ritual of book-keeping which he had imposed upon them. Very often there was a solid reason for it. For example, a planter or a manager who ran up a number of unpaid debts in the island would have to pay for the credit in the enhanced price of his supplies, whereas, if he cleared all the local accounts and transferred the debit to his sterling account (even if it meant drawing bills on England or lessening the remittances to England), he would actually save money by getting his supplies in the island at cash prices. But some of the satisfaction which John Pinney derived from his book-keeping must have been purely intellectual or emotional.

The same precision showed itself in his legal transactions. The deeds which he signed covered everything. When, for example, he and his son sold the plantation in 1808, they did so in a terrific deed which occupies nearly half a close-roll, with eight parties all indemnifying each other against every conceivable contingency. Sometimes his precautions bordered on the ludicrous. . . .

Yet this meticulousness often stood him in good stead; and if his sons finally got much of their money out of the West Indies in the collapse of the 1830's and 40's, it was chiefly because their father had generally shown caution in investing, and still greater caution in getting an unimpeachable legal security for his investments.

This somewhat formidable character only developed gradually. John Pinney first arrived in the West Indies a little callow and sentimental, though he had already shown, before he left England, some traces of the caution, or timorousness, which became his ruling passion. When first he came into the estate he was tempted, as any other young man would have been, to enjoy the sunshine of youth and prosperity. He served as High Sheriff of the county—an expensive honour for a young man. But he began to retrench as soon as he could, and removed from Bettiscombe, where Azariah and John Frederick had lived in a rather leisurely and expensive manner, to Racedown, which must have been a very small house for a gentleman before the later additions were made. He flirted—indeed he fell in love with an exciseman's daughter, who had no fortune and was by no means his equal in society. He wanted her very badly, and seems to have come perilously near to proposing. But something within him drew him back. His estate was not clear of debt, and if he should die before his son was of age to break the entail, he might leave her penniless. He would have to go out to Nevis and get his affairs in order. In short, he was not free to marry. It was a lucky escape, for the girl was a minx, as she showed by threatening him with a suit for breach of promise. As soon as he could, he fled to Nevis, intent upon plantership and rigid frugality.

He did not mean to live there very long; indeed he still, like his cousin, thought of the plantation as a convenient source of income for a Dorset country gentleman. But he knew it could not be neglected; he meant 'to get master of plantation industry,' and to clear off his cousin's debts as soon as he could. These debts oppressed him more than they need have done. They may not have amounted to more than seven thousand pounds, and the Lowland plantation alone must have been worth nearly twenty thousand. But even in his early twenties, John Pinney could never look debt coolly in the face; perhaps the disclosure of the encumbrances had shocked him violently by blasting a prospect which he had believed to be all ease and dignity.

When John Pinney arrived in the West Indies at the end of 1764 people lived there very much as they had done in his great-great-uncle's time. The white governing class was smaller; but it had developed its own way of living, and a feeble sort of local patriotism. Even the absentees in Bath and London sometimes thought tenderly of the splendours and absurdities of their Creole homelands, though they had little intention of returning to them. Society appeared to have lost some of its turbulence and attained to some stability. This stability, however, was endangered by absenteeism and incipient economic decline. It was occasionally broken by atavistic violence—to say nothing of the hurricanes and the periodical French wars, which added so much to the uncertainty of life. In the midst of the picturesque embellishments of life which charmed Miss Schaw and other transient visitors—the hedges of pomegranate and cape-jasmine, of lime and logwood; the negresses all in white muslin, singing and capering on their way to Sunday market; the round of feasts, with turtle on the table at every meal and thirty-two different kinds of fruit at dessert; the languishing eloquence with which Governors Woodley and Payne billed and cooed at their legislatures; even the enlightened sentiments and up-to-date agricultural methods of the best planters—in the midst of all this, much that was crude was still mingled with the elegance and the seeming prosperity was hollow. Yet, taking all things together, West-Indian Society probably reached its highest point in the decade between the Peace of Paris and the outbreak of the American War.

John Pinney did not much like what he first saw of this society. The climate, indeed, was better than he expected. He could keep cool enough in his 'mountain house' two miles from the town, and he saw no reason why a sober and temperate man should not enjoy his health as well in Nevis as in England. But he never liked the people, in the lump, though he came to recognize that there were good and sensible men among them. 'The Creoles in general,' he wrote after a year's residence, 'are a set of lazy indolent people and some of them will not scruple to go any length to save appearances and serve a turn. In short, interest and self-preservation are their only objects, but there are a few really sensible and good men.' A little later he wrote again: 'The little time I have resided in this part of the world has given me more knowledge into the artifice and cunning of mankind, than ever I experienced before, and will teach me how to value (if ever I am so happy as to live to return) the inestimable blessings I enjoyed the other side of the water.' He never felt himself at one with the Creoles, nor varied from his intention to return home to England as soon as he well could; but perhaps he felt in later years that his first judgment had been too harsh, for he told a newcomer to the West Indies, long afterwards, that 'the customs and manners of our West-India Islands are not, in general, approved of by new settlers, until they become acquainted with the respectable part of the inhabitants.'

The sordid pursuit of material advantage, which first struck John Pinney in the Creoles, resulted from their circumstances. Most of them were there, like himself, to make money or to keep it. There was little to distract them from it. Culture and religion, with little in the way of institutions to support them, were very feeble in the West Indies. Political interest was usually languid. . . . Probably John Pinney found that (as his son complained many years later) nobody in Nevis thought about anything but the price of sugar. He certainly found that politics and personal relations turned, above all, on questions of property and debt, and that these questions themselves became so violently personal as to threaten both peace and justice. An unpopular creditor had little hope of justice, whatever the merits of his cause. John Pinney's letters are full of the fallibility and uncertainty of juries, and he once even had to ask his counsel to begin his speech by admonishing the jury 'to remove every unfavourable impression they might have imbibed out of doors' against Messrs. Mills and Swanston, a much-hated merchant house whose interests he was defending. Indeed he was so much tormented by his experiences as their attorney that he was quite glad to give it up. . . .

Money matters were the commonest cause of quarrels and violence, but they were not the only ones. There were some political vendettas, but they did not run to duels, and the early eighteenth-century habit of murdering governors and lieutenant-governors had been given up. The island was divided from top to bottom in 1781 over the professional conduct of Chief Justice Dasent in a revolting case of incest and murder; but here too, though his fellow-judges refused to sit with him on the bench, there was no positive violence. But certain crimes of passion are reported in John Pinney's letters; for example, the horrid affair of Mr. Higgins who, warned by the 'sable gentry' of his wife's infidelity, found her in an inner room with her lover and shot him dead. A jury acquitted him of murder, but a certain Mr. Reid, 'conceiving that Mr. Higgins had butchered his friend, in a dastardly manner, was determined to provoke him to fight, that he might have the opportunity of sacrificing him (according to the rules of honour) to the manes of his friend.' This he succeeded in doing, by calling him a poltroon (a somewhat random epithet, it would seem) and Mr. Higgins shot him in the belly, of which he died the next day.

If some of the serious business of life was violent, so were some of its amusements. John Pinney seems to have arranged a cockfight, at which he paid £3 6s. for the tea served to the ladies.... John Pinney's accounts show that he betted mildly, but generally on such prosaic subjects as the size of his friends' crops. Once or twice he took part in a raffle. There were some amusements of a higher kind: Baker's diary shows that Shakespeare and modern plays were acted in the islands, apparently by amateurs (for he speaks of rehearsing Lear 'au logis,' which may mean a Freemasons' lodge). Miss Schaw found a professional company of English actors at Antigua in 1774. Plays and concerts, however, were rare. The commonest pastime was drinking. In this the ladies usually took no part; according to Miss Schaw they generally confined themselves to lime-juice and water, which accounted, in the opinion of some of the men, for their general insipidity. The men, released from the restraints of feminine companionship, drank heavily, even to death, or at least to sore legs.... John Pinney attached a proper value, throughout his life, to old rum and best London particular Madeira; but a man of his temperament is not likely to have drunk heavily, though he excused the 'set entertainments' of Nevis by the sound economic argument that 'as there is no market to supply us with necessaries as we want them, therefore when we kill the fatted calf, we ask our neighbours to come and partake thereof.' The planters welcomed all occasions for a banquet. They disputed with each other the opportunity of feasting visitors from England. The arrival of the governor-general at one of the islands within his government was usually celebrated by a 'handsome entertainment,' for which the public treasury paid unless the legislature was on bad terms with him and refused to vote the money. When Prince William Henry (afterwards King William IV) came out in 1787 as a young sailor upon the Leeward Islands station the island of Nevis excelled itself: £800 was voted for the festivities, a hundred gentlemen sat down at the public dinner with him, there were seventy ladies at the ball (where he danced with 'the widow Nisbet,' soon to be more celebrated as Lady Nelson), and he was entertained for a week with horse-racing and cockfighting. No wonder John Pinney congratulated a friend who had had the good fortune to consign some claret to the Nevis market at that moment. There was only one disappointment: 'a remarkable fat beef reserved for the entertainment of his Highness was, a few nights before his arrival, killed by some runaway negroes.'

John Pinney came into the midst of this society as a bachelor, still impressed by tender thoughts of the ladies of Dorset. At first he declared against any idea of marrying a West-Indian wife. 'I entertain,' he wrote, 'too great an opinion of my own country ladies, for to give the preference to Creoles, for they are in general an indolent set of people.' He overcame this prejudice, and married Miss Jane Weekes, daughter of an island busybody of small property and less judgment, who held the offices of treasurer, port-major, and any others he could pick up. But his strictures on the Creole ladies were generally just. They seem, for the most part, to have led extremely limited lives and to have been uninteresting and unenterprising people. Miss Schaw, indeed, thought them uncommonly amiable and intelligent; but as she did not even stay in the islands long enough to hear them talk scandal, she cannot have known very much about them. She noted their 'stewed' look, which she attributed to the excessive use of masks to keep off the tropical sun; and their figures, too thin before thirty and too plump after it. They liked show, and were good-natured in a lazy way.

They generally married young: Christopher Jeaffreson thought fifteen the usual age, and Baker reports the marriage of a child of thirteen, which he disapproved. John Pinney's bride was at least twenty. Many of them were as lazy after marriage as before. They hated walking—Miss Schaw did not think any of the ladies of St. Kitts would have walked two miles. John Pinney, when he got his wife home to England, reported that she had become a great walker but feared that she would lose the habit as soon as she got a carriage again. Some of these ladies may have been diligent housekeepers, but few had anything to do with the plantations. 'As mistresses of families,' wrote Luffman in 1786, 'they are unimportant, almost every domestic concern being left to the management of their negroes and mulattoes.' (Miss Schaw's friend Lady Isabella Hamilton, though no Creole, visited her husband's boiling-house so seldom that when she did so, all the negroes condemned to the lash were automatically reprieved, as if by the prerogative of a travelling queen.) They spent much time in visiting and chatting with each other informally and openheartedly: Miss Schaw was surprised by the freedom with which the people of St. Johns, Antigua, leant in at each other's windows during meals or even came in and sat down if they felt like it. When John Pinney went to Bath in 1784 he reported that 'Mrs. P. likes this place much better than London, as we visit a good deal in the West-Indian style.' Presumably it was upon other West-Indians that she paid these casual calls....

The children of these marriages were nearly always spoilt by their mothers. (Mrs. Pinney, it seems, was no exception to this rule; in later life her eldest son spoke of 'having a West-India mother myself, and knowing from experience how unwisely they act towards their children.') The babies might have a white nurse, but they were sure to have negroes to attend them when they grew a little older, and the indulgence of their attendants could hardly fail to corrupt their characters as well as teach them the unmistakable sing-song intonation of the Creoles which still varies from island to island. There were very few schools on the small island, and the children had to be sent quite young to Europe. If they arrived too old and 'mannish,' it was difficult, according to John Pinney, to do anything with them.

Creole children in England were tempted to play the young millionaire, as the first John Pinney had done at the beginning of the century. Their mothers often unsettled them with too fond letters, full of affecting reminiscences of West-Indian childhood. Their fathers were sometimes even more injudicious: John Frederick Pinney had to expostulate with a friend in Nevis for his folly in enabling his son to purchase other boys to do his sums for him. (Whether a specific subsidy was paid for this purpose, or John Frederick only meant to reflect generally on the excessive pocket-money which the boy received, is not clear.) The excessive expectations of these little Creoles in England, and their romantic ideas of plantation life, might be dissipated by a trip to the islands; one exceptionally sensible father proposed this as a remedy for his son's restlessness. But if they were not cured by this or some other means, they might find, when they returned home as young men and women, that they could not stand West-Indian society, or they might even refuse altogether to try it. Thus the lack of proper schools and colleges in the islands, which might have attached the Creoles to their own society, was one of the causes which further impoverished that society by perpetuating and increasing absenteeism.

Such were the pure-blooded Creoles of the islands. Side by side with them there flourished another society, coloured every shade of brown. Even Miss Schaw, who wished to see the gentlemen of Antigua as paragons of gallantry and sentiment, could not shut her eyes to the fact that miscegenation had been going on, right and left, for generations. But only a minority of the half-castes were descended from the great planters. James Tobin may have heard of a French planter who boasted that a third of his field gang was 'the produce of his own loins,' but this was an exception. The fathers of most, if not all, the mulattoes and quadroons on John Pinney's plantations were the managers, overseers, and other white employees. Almost every man who ever served there left behind him one or two mulattoes who went by his name. Few or none of these children were born in wedlock.

It is easy to blame the fathers; but what else could be expected of the poor boys? Many of them came out from Europe very young and unmarried (a few came to escape from their wives), and there were not many white girls of humble station to be picked up as wives in the islands. The plantations afforded hardly any other means of procuring a semblance of home life, or even domestic service.

John Pinney himself does not seem to have fathered any of these half-castes. One Billy Jones, the mulatto child of Black Polly, who was brought up as a playmate with the little Pinneys, suddenly claimed many years later to be John Pinney's own son. John Pinney was deeply indignant: 'I am very sorry,' he wrote to his manager, 'to find that Black Polly upholds her son Billy in the idea of what you say respecting of me; when she knows the whole is untrue—she never once hinted it whilst I was in the West Indies, but on the contrary applied to Robt. Jones for assistance. I desire you will do all in your power to suppress such an infamous falsehood.' If this does not read like a wholly convincing disclaimer, it is fair to add that John Pinney always treated Robert Jones as Billy's father, and from other things he wrote, much earlier and in a quite different context, about that highly irreverend candidate for Holy Orders, there is no difficulty in believing the charge. Unless we are to treat every evidence of special favour shown to any of his mulatto slaves as an underhand acknowledgement of paternity—which would be very unreasonable—we may suppose that John Pinney himself, both before marriage and after, was an exception to the general libertinism. So, no doubt, were some others of the sober married planters; the half-caste population sprang, for the most part, from other loins. Whatever its origin, it was considered at the time, by other people besides Miss Janet Schaw, to be a dark shadow on the resplendent surface of Creole society. This shadow was further deepened by the revolution in French Hayti, where the mulattoes played an active part—in the end, even for themselves a somewhat unfortunate part—in politics. Yet it can be argued that after the inevitable collapse of white plutocracy in the British West Indies, the mulattoes helped to save what was left of society and western civilization.

John Pinney never meant to stay in the West Indies longer than he could help. At first he said he should return in a few months if the climate did not suit him. He had no difficulty with the climate, but he soon found, like many another proprietor just out from England, that he would need more time, money and trouble than he had supposed, to put his estates in such good running order that he could direct them thenceforth as an absentee. 'I am determined,' he wrote in April 1766, 'to settle my estates completely before I return; for no manager (let him be ever so assiduous) can have it in his power to settle them as well and as fast as myself.' He contrived to go home for a short visit in 1767, but was soon out again, in the hope of winding up the plantations like a clock which should run for the rest of his life. He wrote of himself in November 1769 as 'determined when once I leave this island to reside in my native country the remaining part of my life.' He intended, however, to marry a young lady of nineteen—a Creole lady, after all his good resolutions—of a good family but her fortune not large; this, he thought, might delay him still longer. In 1772, in fact, he was married to Miss Jane Weekes; she was probably, though not certainly, the same lady he had in view in 1769. Three years was a long time for a West-India courtship; a fact which shows John Pinney at his most prudent.

He took his honeymoon in Pennsylvania. He considered it a fine country, and was so much attracted by the prospect of a rise in land values that he thought of buying some property there, to which he could retire, instead of going back to Dorset, when the time came to resume the life of an absentee. It would be 'a proper place for the retirement of West-India gentlemen who are possessed of small estates, as they can have a constant communication with them from hence.' This was quite true: there were several colonial families, such as the Redwoods of Newport and the Dickinsons of Philadelphia, who owned sugar-plantations in the

West Indies and managed them from North America. This prospect, however, was cut short by the hurricane of 31 August 1772, which did £3,000 worth of damage to John Pinney's plantations, though it let him off lighter than most. He rushed back to Nevis, and began once more the treadmill of clearing his affairs. The United States may thus have lost a highly useful citizen, or perhaps only a very stubborn loyalist: we do not know enough of his politics to say.

He still designed to get away to England as soon as he could, and his growing family of children gave him a new motive. He made up his mind that they should not stay in the island to be corrupted by the conversation of slaves. His little boys must go home to Dorset. John Frederick, the eldest, was put under the care of Coker (now Mrs. Pinney's uncle by marriage) in 1778; Azariah followed soon after. For the little girls he made an arrangement designed to keep them from spending their time with negroes: a Mrs. Murray (probably a schoolmistress) was induced to live at the Pinneys' 'mountain house' and board them for £40 a year, paying particular attention to their morals. But all this was impermanent and unsatisfactory. Their father doubtless knew what became of little Creole boys in England without their parents. He implored Coker to counteract his son's vanity as well as he could: 'Only permit me earnestly to request the favour of you never to suffer him to wear any other apparel than such as your son wore of his age—to make him the same allowance of pocket money &ca. and to continue invariably on the same plan as your son.' But it would be far better to have them under his own eye; and almost every year he made up his mind afresh to take his whole family back to England by one of the next homeward convoys.

Every year it seemed that the moment was going to arrive when he could 'wind up all his pecuniary concerns' and fix his family in his native land. He would be content with a very moderate establishment, without waiting to pile up a really large fortune: 'From the many repeated proofs of infidelity I have experienced in this island,' he wrote to Mills and Swanston on 28 September 1778, 'united with dishonourable actions frequently exhibited in the dealings between man and man, it is no wonder I should be heartily tired of residing here, and of my endeavouring to contract my concerns and wind up my affairs as soon as possible, so as to enable me to live in my native land and superintend the education of my children, though it may prove injurious to my fortune.'

West-Indian affairs, however, were not easily 'wound up,' and John Pinney, like many other planters, must have felt like Sisyphus rolling his stone up the mountain again and again, only to have it slip from his hands and rumble back to the bottom. He achieved a most remarkable success, as the account of his plantation affairs will show. But just when he was near the top of the mountain a hurricane, or the American revolution, or the French war, bore the stone down again.

9
ECONOMIC GROWTH IN THE EIGHTEENTH CENTURY
P. Deane and W. A. Cole

The historiography of the Industrial Revolution of the eighteenth century in England has gone through three definable stages. The first, during the late nineteenth and early twentieth centuries, was marked principally by left-wing moral indignation at the sufferings of the industrial worker. The second stage, which prevailed during the second quarter of the twentieth century, was distinguished by the valuable research of J. H. Clapham and T. S. Ashton into the institutional foundations and patterns of industrial growth in England. The third and most recent stage reflects the insight gained by mid–twentieth-century economists' consideration of the experience of economic growth in underdeveloped areas since the Second World War. In the following study two of the ablest of the younger generation of English economic historians draw upon current theories of the causes of economic growth to illuminate the demographic, industrial, and commercial components of the unprecedented entrepreneurial progress after 1750.

It used to be held that in contrast with the slow pace of economic change in other periods, the decades after 1760 brought with them a far-reaching and comparatively sudden transformation in both the organisation of industry and the scale of output which amounted to an industrial revolution. Since the publication of Arnold Toynbee's *Lectures on the Industrial Revolution* in 1884, the discoveries of 'industrial revolutions' in practically every century from the thirteenth to the twentieth, and the extension of the boundaries of the classical revolution backwards and forwards in time, have certainly deprived the concept of some of its significance. But it has never been seriously denied that there was some acceleration in the tempo of economic change in eighteenth-century Britain. Moreover, the contemporary interest in economic growth has tended to encourage a return to something like the classical view of the changes which occurred during that period. For although there is plenty of evidence of economic *change* in other places at other times, it is clear

---

FROM P. Deane and W. A. Cole, *British Economic Growth, 1688–1959* (Cambridge: Cambridge University Press, 1962), pp. 40, 82–86, 88–95. By permission of the publishers.

that for most of human history the pace of economic *progress*—whatever meaning we may attach to that somewhat elusive term—has been painfully slow, and it is only since the eighteenth century that the regular expansion of the total output of goods and services, in both absolute and per capita terms, has become characteristic of the economic order....

...What explanations can we offer for the pattern of growth [in the eighteenth century]? We [do not] wish to over-simplify what was clearly a highly complex process. But we shall comment on certain aspects of that process, and in particular on the part played by three of the major variables—population, harvest, and overseas trade.

There can, of course, be no doubt of the central importance of overseas trade in the expansion of the economy during this period. Apart from the intangible, but nonetheless vital, part which commercial contacts played in widening man's economic horizons, the possession of extensive overseas markets and the comparatively low costs of sea transport in the early stages of economic growth enabled Britain's export industries to enjoy economics of scale, and, at the same time, provided the home economy with supplies of the imported foodstuffs and raw materials on which it increasingly depended. We cannot verify our assumption that the growth of the industries producing exportable products kept pace with the expansion of international trade, which more than quintupled in volume during the century. But it is clear that the major export industries, and those domestic industries which supplied them with some of their raw materials, such as coal-mining and soap-making, enjoyed higher rates of growth than most other branches of economic activity.

This does not necessarily mean that the quickening tempo of economic expansion in the second half of the eighteenth century can be directly attributed to the accelerated growth of foreign trade during that period. Indeed, an examination of the evidence suggests that, if there was a causal relationship between the growth of foreign trade and the growth of national income, it was of a more complex character and operated in a different direction than has usually been supposed. We shall argue here that the expansion of the British export trade was limited by the purchasing power of Britain's customers, and that this in its turn was limited by what they could earn from exports to Britain.

There are two obvious ways in which a largely autonomous growth of foreign trade might be expected to stimulate expansion at home. If the demand for British exports increased, either as a result of expanding demand in existing markets, or the acquisition of new ones, the income of British exporters would tend to increase and ultimately to communicate itself to other sections of the community. Alternatively, if the world supply of goods which Britain imported increased, their prices would tend to fall, and in this way, too, British real incomes might rise. In either case, the terms of trade would tend to move in Britain's favour. In fact it looks as if the accelerated growth of foreign trade in the second half of the eighteenth century was associated with an *adverse* movement of the terms of trade. It is true that over the period from 1745 to 1800 as a whole, the gross barter terms of trade seem to have moved somewhat in Britain's favour, whereas between 1700 and 1745 they had gone strongly against her. But in neither period was the movement continuous, and for most of the years when trade was expanding relatively rapidly—in the late forties and late fifties, and again in the last twenty years of the century—the terms of trade were generally adverse, the only marked exception being the years immediately following the American War of Independence. Of course, the gross barter terms of trade constitute an unreliable guide to changes in relative prices, unless it is possible to assume that the balance of trade was constant. But such price data as we have do not permit a satisfactory index of the commodity terms of trade.... Some of the data are of doubtful value, and the series for broadcloth and linens—which are indicators of average values, not prices—are included here only as a first approximation. Nevertheless, the movements of the individual series are sufficiently clear and well synchronised to justify a few preliminary hypotheses about the probable trends of relative prices.

For most of the century, export prices were comparatively stable, and movements in the terms of trade were largely determined by fluctuations in the prices of imports. The latter tended to rise during war and to fall back to more normal levels when peace was concluded. During the War of the Spanish Succession, for example, import prices were high, but fell rapidly for about twenty years after the Treaty of Utrecht. In the mid-thirties they began to rise, and this movement, combined with a fall in the prices of major exports, such as woollens, non-ferrous metals and iron, which seems to have begun in the 1720's, produced an adverse movement in the terms of trade in the thirties and forties. When the War of the Austrian Succession ended in 1748, import prices fell again, and the terms of trade began to turn in Britain's favour. This movement was again reversed during the Seven Years War, but became more marked in the 1760's, when a fall in import prices was accompanied by a significant rise in the prices of exports. During the American War of Independence, import prices again soared, only to plummet with the return of peace. Finally, in the late eighties and nineties, there was a marked increase in the prices of both imports and exports, but the former rose faster than the latter.

Thus, excluding the period of the American war and its aftermath, it appears that the years of most rapid expansion after 1745 were years in which the terms of trade were adverse, whereas in periods when the rate of growth of foreign trade sank to the low levels prevailing in the earlier part of the century, the terms of trade were moving in Britain's favour. In the light of this evidence, it is difficult to see the expansion of trade as a largely exogenous factor which quickened the pace of industrial growth. The dramatic recovery of foreign trade after the American War no doubt gave a temporary fillip to the home economy which helps to explain the general boom in the 1780's. More generally, however, it seems that the explanation of the higher average rate of growth in the second half of the century should be sought at home rather than abroad.

The explanation may lie in the character of Britain's overseas markets during this period. An outstanding feature of British trade during the eighteenth century was its increasing reliance on colonial markets. In 1700, over four-fifths of English exports went to Europe, and only a fifth to the rest of the world. By the end of the century, on the other hand, this relationship was almost exactly reversed. Even in absolute terms, British goods made little headway in the protected markets of her European rivals. Some progress was made in the first half of the century, but in the last fifty years an extension of trade with Russia and the Baltic was more than offset by the decline in exports to North-West Europe and the Mediterranean. Hence the increase in British exports in the course of the century was almost entirely due to the expansion of trade with the new, colonial markets in Ireland, America, Africa and the Far East.

The most important of these markets from the standpoint of the British manufacturer were North America and the West Indies. Britain's trade with these areas formed a virtually closed system from which competitors were rigorously excluded, and in consequence she was able to increase her exports to America more than twentyfold in the course of the century. But for the same reason the colonists' demand for British goods was largely dependent on the value of the goods which they in turn could sell to her. This was particularly true of the West Indian islands and the tobacco colonies on the American mainland, since, under the Navigation Acts, the staple crops of these plantations could be sold only in other colonial markets or to the mother country. Similar restrictions were not extended to the grain, furs and naval stores of the northern colonies until 1766, and Britain's direct imports from them were relatively small. But in practice the northerners seem to have paid for a large part of their heavy imports of British manufactures by selling their own produce in the southern colonies and West Indian islands. Thus, directly and indirectly, the fortunes of the most rapidly growing section of Britain's export trade were closely bound up with the fortunes of the southern planters. And since it was a cardinal objective of Britain's commercial policy to obtain her imports of primary products on the terms most favourable to the mother country, the chief limiting factor to the growth of her exports was the restricted purchasing power of her colonial customers. The only occasions in the eighteenth century when exports increased and the terms of trade were favourable to the mother country were in the years immediately following the major wars in which she was engaged. This was most obviously true after the Spanish Succession and American Wars, during which the total volume of trade, and in particular imports, had fallen sharply. The prices of imports rose in war time, but this was probably mainly due to the increased costs of freight and insurance, and so was of little benefit to the producers. With the return of peace, Britain's customers were able to clear their accumulated stocks, and though the prices of imports fell in the mother country, the volume of imports and exports rose together. But these were recovery booms, and as soon as the immediate effects of the wars had passed, the normal relationship between the terms of trade and the volume of exports reasserted itself.

The association between the growth of exports and the terms of trade does not mean, however, that the *total* volume of trade always tended to grow faster when the movement of relative prices was unfavourable to the mother country. Until technical change began to exert a decisive influence on manufacturing costs, the rate of expansion of the combined totals of imports and exports mainly depended on Britain's demand for imports, which seems to have been fairly elastic in the eighteenth century. In the first half of the century, both exports and imports tended to fluctuate with the price of imports, therefore, but in opposite directions. Hence it made little difference to the overall rate of commercial expansion which way the terms of trade happened to move. From 1715 to 1730, when the supply of imports outstripped the growth of home demand, Britain enjoyed the benefits of cheap colonial produce at the expense of her export trades. In the thirties and early forties, when the supply of imports dwindled, mainly, it appears, as a result of crop failures and restrictions on output in the West Indian islands, exports increased; but until the outbreak of war in 1739 the overall rate of commercial growth was almost exactly the same as before. It was only after 1745, when the volume and prices of imported goods rose together, that the pace of commercial expansion began to quicken. It seems clear that at the end of the century this increased demand for imports was stimulated by Pitt's reform of the customs duties, and we know, for example, that tariff reductions resulted in a prodigious expansion of the Jamaica coffee plantations, and in the rapid growth of legal imports of tea, in the last twenty years of the century. But for most of the century, the burden of import duties was rising, and if we want to understand the growing import demand, we must look for the factors which were promoting the economic expansion at home.

As we have already observed, it is impossible not to be struck by the close connection between the pattern of growth at home and the course of population change, and it is natural to inquire how far the two were casually related. Recent research has done much to emphasise the part played by population increase in easing the labour scarcity which seems to have been an outstanding feature of the British economy in the late seventeenth and early eighteenth centuries, and in providing the labour force on which the industrial system rested. But at first sight the correlation seems too close to fit this explanation. For an increase in population might be expected to have a significant effect on the supply of labour only after an interval of sixteen or eighteen years; even when all allowances have been made for the uncertainty of the statistics and the possible influence of child labour, it does not seem possible for the acceleration in the rate of economic growth in the 1740's and again in the 1780's to have been directly due to an increase in the size of the labour force, at any rate as a result of population increase. Nor is it obvious that an increase in population would have promoted an acceleration in the rate of economic growth through its effect on demand. For although an increase in the number of mouths to be fed and bodies to be clothed may enlarge wants, will it necessarily increase effective demand? Clearly, therefore, if we are to understand the significance of the population changes, we must consider some of the other factors in the situation.

A good deal of recent discussion has been devoted to the effects of variations in harvests on agricultural prices and the distribution of incomes. In an economy still so largely dominated by agriculture, it is, of course, natural to ascribe a major role to changes in the fortunes of the farming community, and the debate on the consequences of high and low agricultural prices is probably as old as the English Corn Laws. Professor Ashton, following Adam Smith, has suggested that in the eighteenth century good harvests meant, not only an increased return to human effort in the agricultural sector, but also an increased demand for labour to gather the harvest, higher real wages, and hence an increase in the demand for the products of industry. As an explanation of short-run fluctuations, this theory is plausible enough, although the evidence at our disposal makes it difficult to check. Certainly the influence of harvests can be detected in fluctuations in output in many of the industries for which production data are directly available, but since these were mainly industries which, in the short run at least, depend on agriculture for their supply of raw materials, it does not follow that this was entirely due to the income effects of good harvests.

Here, however, we are mainly concerned with long-term trends, and several students have argued that the effects of a series of good harvests may have been very different. For owing to the inelastic demand for foodstuffs—and especially cereals—good harvests meant, not only a rise in real wages, but a fall in agricultural incomes. In the short run this might not be important, since the losses in one year could be made good in the next. But the combination of a succession of good harvests with a stationary population may well have had such a depressing effect on the demand from the agricultural sector as to offset the stimulus which the industrial economy derived from high or rising real wages. It is true, of course, that over a period of years it may be difficult to distinguish improvements in agricultural productivity due to favourable climatic conditions from those due to technical change. The suggestion here, however, is simply that variations in the internal terms of trade between workshop and farm may have had a similar effect on the home demand for industrial goods as did changes in import and export prices on the fortunes of the export trade. And since it is probably fair to assume that the demand for cereals was less elastic than that for sugar and tobacco, it is possible that the economy as a whole may have lost more from sagging demand for industrial goods than it gained from abundant supplies of agricultural products. As Professor Habakkuk puts it: 'The low or stationary agricultural prices of the earlier decades of the century had a depressing effect on agricultural investment and indirectly on the demand for industrial goods. The rising prices over most of the second half of the century stimulated agricultural investment and led to increased demand for industrial goods; they led not so much to a shift of income between the industrial and agricultural sectors as to an increase in the income of both.'

For the first six decades of the eighteenth century there is a good deal of evidence in support of at least the first part of this hypothesis. It is difficult to measure changes in relative prices, but it appears... that at the end of the seventeenth century, and for the first two decades of the eighteenth, the prices of cereals were, on the average, higher, both absolutely and in relation to those of producer goods and other consumer goods, than they were to be at any time in the next thirty or forty years.... Money wages rose little, if at all, at this time, and real wages may even have fallen slightly; and it is possible that the modest industrial expansion suggested by the scanty evidence for the period may have owed something at least to agricultural prosperity. It is true that prices were not consistently high throughout this period, and for most of the first decade of the century they were a good deal lower than in the years immediately before or after. It is significant, however, that in the second decade nearly all the statistical series indicate a definite advance in output which coincides, not only with the foreign-trade boom which marked the end of the long wars with Louis XIV, but with the period of generally high agricultural prices from 1708 to 1717. In the next twenty-five years, on the other hand, when the output of industrial goods seems to have been virtually stationary, agricultural prices were low and tended to fall even in relation to a generally sagging price-level. During the early part of this period, the export trade was also in the doldrums, and it would seem that the production of goods for the home market was at any rate maintained. It should be noted, however, that the fall in agricultural prices was temporarily arrested in the late twenties, with the result that the average price-level of the twenties was not much below that for the previous decade. In the thirties and early forties, on the other hand, when the export trade revived, there was no corresponding increase in the total volume of industrial output, and in some sectors, notably the mining and metal industries, the supply of goods to the home market seems to have dropped sharply. It is significant, therefore, that it was precisely in this period that agricultural prices reached their lowest point, and, while money and real wages were exceptionally high, that there are signs of a sharp depression amongst the farming community, marked by the accumulation of large arrears of rent and, in some cases, even the appearance of vacant holdings. It was not till after 1743, when agricultural prices started their long climb and rent arrears began to disappear, that the home market for industrial goods revived, and, at the same time, the rising demand for imports helped to produce a further expansion of the export trade.

Whether it is also true... that the national income as a whole tended to grow more rapidly when agricultural prices were relatively high, it is difficult to say in the absence of reliable statistics of grain output. In so far as prices rose as a result of increasing demand for agricultural produce, this is, of course, likely to have been the case. But when prices rose simply as a result of bad harvests, there is no reason to assume that the increased demand for industrial goods more than offset the loss in agricultural output. There appears, however, to be a strong prima-facie case for the view that the growth of the home market for industrial goods was closely bound up with the fortunes of the agricultural community, in much the same way as the growth of the export trade depended on the prosperity of the primary producers overseas.

Two obvious explanations may be suggested. In the first place, it should be noted that until 1750 periods of comparatively high agricultural prices were not only periods of population expansion at home, but of growing overseas demand for grain. Corn exports rose in the first quarter of the century, and again in the late forties; from the early twenties until the early forties they were virtually stationary. Exports of corn were encouraged by bounty during this period, but for the most part, the increase in the incomes of farmers, landlords and middlemen exporters associated with an increase in grain exports represented a net addition to incomes at home.

Second, and more important, however, the expectation that the redistribution of incomes arising from low corn prices should have stimulated industrial demand assumes that the marginal propensity of wage-earners and the non-agricultural sector as a whole to consume manufactured goods was in fact higher than that of farmers and landlords. If England had been a society in which the market and taste for manufactured goods was highly developed, and in which, at the same time, the agricultural community tended to hoard its gains, such an assumption might be warranted. But it was not. For centuries English agriculture had had extensive ties of varying strength with the market, and by the eighteenth century it was largely organised on a capitalist basis: the typical farmer was not a peasant toiling for his own subsistence, but an employer of wage-labour holding his land at an economic rent from men who not infrequently ploughed their profits back into agriculture, or into transport, industry and trade. Much industrial output was produced by agricultural wage-earners or their families on a domestic basis. On the other hand, it is probably true that in England, as in any other largely pre-industrial economy, the economic horizons of the mass of the population tended to be narrow, and the range of consumer goods small. Hence the demand for manufactured goods may have been relatively inelastic, and a rise in real wages may have led, not to an increase in their consumption, but to an increase in leisure—or, as contemporaries unanimously complained, to 'idleness'. Probably rising real wages did stimulate an increase in the consumption of some goods, and it is significant that the thirties and early forties witnessed the height of the gin mania. But evidently the demand for gin was not sufficient either to arrest the fall of agricultural prices or to provide the basis for rapid industrial growth.

When prices rose, on the other hand, agricultural incomes also rose and, at the same time, industrial artisans and the wage-earning population as a whole had to work harder to maintain their traditional standard of life. It is not surprising, therefore, that the rise in prices after 1743 seems to have been associated with a modest rise in total output per head. Moreover, it is important to note that the rise in the price of foodstuffs was brought about, not by a decline in agricultural output—indeed the evidence suggests that the yield of the soil in the decades after 1745 must have been substantially greater than it had been before—but mainly by an increase in the number of mouths to be fed. For a growing population and the increase in the size of families which it brought tended to transform the position of the labouring population. Not only did it give an immediate stimulus to wants, but it also meant that, as families grew up and population too continued to expand at an increasing rate, competition in the labour market began to replace the traditional scarcity. From about the middle of the eighteenth century it is possible to discern a significant change in the attitude of contemporaries towards the labouring population. Complaints of the recalcitrance of labourers diminished and some writers began to argue that high, not low, wages provided the greater incentive to industry. By 1776 Adam Smith could assert that the problem among piece-workers, at least, was not that they were idle, but that overwork tended to 'ruin their health and constitution in a few years'.

In these circumstances, food would necessarily constitute the first claim on available incomes, and since the agricultural community was thus assured of an expanding market for its produce, the significance of harvest variations began to change. Provided that farmers and landlords continued to spend or invest their additional incomes, it might make little difference to industrial demand whether the prices of food were low or high. And if the addition to total output resulting from favourable harvests was no longer offset by losses in the industrial sector we might expect the national income as a whole to rise most rapidly when the prices of food were comparatively low. This, indeed, is what the data suggest. As we have seen, it appears that the period from the mid-forties until the early sixties was one of all-round expansion in both industry and agriculture. Despite the very heavy exports of grain in the ten years after 1745 and the unprecedented expansion of population in that and the ensuing decades, the rise in agricultural prices was at first comparatively modest, and their average level rose no higher than in the first two decades of the century. Gradually, however, the growing population began to press against the available resources: exports of corn dwindled, and, with the poor harvests of the late sixties and early seventies, prices rose much more steeply, and Britain was for the first time compelled to import substantial quantities of grain. This brought a sharp increase in agricultural investment. Until the late fifties, the farming community evidently had little incentive to indulge in ambitious schemes of agricultural improvement. From 1730 to 1744, the number of enclosure bills presented in Parliament had averaged about forty per decade, and in the ten years ending in 1754 the total was only forty-nine. In the next ten years, however, the number jumped to 283, and in the following decade to 531. There is no evidence that this wave of investment directly stimulated industrial demand, but it does not seem to have been accompanied by any contraction of the home market for industrial goods. High agricultural prices may have contributed to the trade recession of the early seventies, which appears to have been particularly severe in the linen trade, but in the ten years ending in 1774, the volume of industrial goods consumed at home seems to have risen more than in previous decades. At the same time, however, the rise in the internal price-level no doubt contributed to the favourable swing in the external terms of trade during this period, and hence to the stagnation in the export trade; and since the output of agriculture and of the industries dependent on the land was almost stationary, it is not surprising that our estimates suggest a fall in the overall rate of expansion in both the major sectors of the economy, certainly in relation to the rapidly growing population, and possibly also in absolute terms.

In the late seventies, the effects of enclosures began to make themselves felt. The price of corn was stabilised and, as other prices probably continued to rise as a result of the high cost of imports during the American War, its 'real' price dropped. After 1777, the wave of enclosures ebbed, and for a time, at least, arrears of rent testify to comparatively depressed conditions for the farming community. But again there seems to have been a steady growth in the home market. Despite the virtual collapse of foreign trade in the war years, the available indicators suggest that the rate of growth of even those industries which were normally most dependent on overseas markets was only slightly lower than in the previous decade. And when the return of peace brought with it a great revival of foreign trade, while prices of agricultural produce remained comparatively low, the economy experienced a new wave of expansion which was checked only by the combined effects of commercial difficulties, population pressure and bad harvests during the Napoleonic Wars.

Thus it appears that the importance which economic historians have recently ascribed to demographic factors—or, more precisely, the balance between population and other resources, and particularly land—in shaping the pattern of eighteenth-century economic growth is justified.

10

THE POLITICAL TRAGEDY OF GEORGE III

Herbert Butterfield

The severely functional and anti-intellectual tone of Namier's work on eighteenth-century government and politics has been significantly modified and challenged in the studies of the earlier part of George III's reign made by Herbert Butterfield, the Master of Peterhouse, Cambridge. Butterfield's Christian sensibilities and his perception into the cross currents of ideas in the later eighteenth century led him to emphasize the impact of ideas and personalities, as can be seen in this judgment on George III as a political leader.

AMONGST the private papers of George III at Windsor Castle—and lying in the neighbourhood of such of these as belong to the year 1772—is an undated document which begins as follows:

> It has been my lot to change so frequently Administrations & those out of place have ever laid the blame on Me, that I owe it to myself to write an exact narrative of the principal transactions of my Reign without making any Reflection on them ... I mean them chiefly for the instruction of my son.

Only a little over a page of this autobiographical fragment exists, and its last sentence is a note on George's policy at the very opening of his reign:

> The only difference of conduct I adopted was to put an end to those unhappy distinctions of party called Whigs and Torys, by declaring I would countenance every Man that supported my Administration and concurred in that form of Government which had been so wisely established by the Revolution.

The title of "whig" could still be taken—and indeed often was taken—to denote the men who swore by the revolution of 1688 and favoured the importation of the Hanoverian dynasty into England. On this view both George III and Lord North could legitimately take pride in the fact that they themselves belonged to the whig tradition. George, when he came to the throne in 1760, could regard the "Glorious" revolution and the Hanoverian succession as closed issues—no longer the peculiar fighting-

---

FROM Herbert Butterfield, *George III, Lord North and the People, 1779–1780* (London: G. Bell & Sons, Ltd., 1949), pp. 3–9. By permission of the author. Reprinted by permission of A. D. Peters & Co.

creed of those whig connections which had so long profited from them, no longer the symbols of the achievement or the victory of a mere party. Both had become the heritage of the British people everywhere, and he accepted them fully, as a monarch of his dynasty was bound to do in any case. Great alterations in the manner of governing the country, however —great changes in the distribution of power—had been taking place in the generation before his accession; and these had occurred not by virtue of anything in the Bill of Rights or the Act of Settlement, for example, but partly as a result of the fact that the whig connections had made the revolution their own property—had established a monopoly in the Hanoverian régime. So it came about that George III found it necessary to combat what both he and his grandfather regarded as the unauthorized political and constitutional developments which had been allowed to occur in Great Britain since 1714. Neither he nor the great body of his subjects was yet prepared to accept as recognized "conventions of the constitution" those political practices, those anomalies and usurpations, by means of which under the first two Georges a combination of whig aristocrats had been able to engross political power. George III might well feel himself the champion of a popular purpose and a public cause when he set out to break the power of these whig oligarchs and to recapture for the crown that authority which had been enjoyed by William III. He hoped to rid the country of a division which had now become meaningless and abolish party-names, which had been allowed to continue too long merely to provide the excuse for a policy of proscription. Coming to the throne at the age of twenty-two, and thinking perhaps too much in terms of the ideas of a previous generation, he counted on being the benevolent father of his country, the pattern of a "Patriot King".

The whig aristocrats—besides the tremendous patronage which they enjoyed as territorial magnates—had captured for their use that rich fund of offices, sinecures, pensions, and the like, which constituted the patronage and the bounty of the crown. It was to be a question whether a bishop who in fact had been promoted by the Duke of Newcastle would ever be brought to remember that the real source of the favour he enjoyed—the real fountain of honour in the state—was still the monarch himself. Combining the two sources of "influence"—the aristocratic and the governmental—the whig leaders had made themselves formidable, and had been able to stand as an independent power in the face of the king. It was this usurpation that George III attacked, as he was bound to do if he was to keep to his initial intention, that is to say, if he was to prevent office and favour from being confined to the adherents of a single party. Furthermore, George, who would have found his opinion echoed by many independent people in the country, objected to the way in which this natural system of patronage had been screwed up and made taut— and turned into too direct a mode of control over parties and votes—in the course of the century. He knew that if he could command the system he could destroy its evils—he was the only person who could rid the country of corruption. Then, as he once wrote to Bute, "our memories" would be "respected and esteemed to the end of time".

Never was a youthful dream so turned to ashes. Never was a noble purpose so twisted and torn as it began to move and assert itself in the world of concrete things—began to struggle in a universe of tricks and chances. When we study the reign of George III it is always necessary to remember that this is not what he intended it to be—what we see is not what he wanted to happen, and what he himself did is not at all what he set out to do. We imagine too often that a single man's purposes can make history, and the righteous are often deceived because they think that a good intent gives an individual a claim to exercise a certain kind of sovereignty over the affairs of human beings. It is easy to forget that in the world one human will must mix and mingle with countless other wills; and the result—the piece of tapestry actually produced by the processes of history—is a compounding and a composition between these; like the music of an orchestra, it is a complicated result that depends on inter-actions and harmonies. At the same time, those who are obstinately well-intentioned—the men like George III—are too prone to overlook the fact that other individuals, equally valid, equally self-acting, equally well-intentioned, have their own view of what is "the good", or what is the next turn that ought to be given to human history. He who sets out to achieve a good purpose regardless of these other people—and *coûte qui coûte*—must take care of his soul, for he sins by self-righteousness. He must be prepared to find that, even if only in the conflict with other people's good intentions, he may do more harm than any of the abuses he has had it in mind to remove.

From the earliest years of the reign, George's policy had the effect of multiplying and enlarging the very evils which it had been his dream to see annihilated. Precisely because he was so conscious of his rectitude he could not bear to be beaten, and he was willing, when it came to the point, even to fight corruption with more corruption. Having embarked upon this course, he was bound perhaps to remain a prisoner of the system so long as the whig oligarchy remained in a position to challenge his policy and his régime. Henceforward, in any case, we see George III not as he meant to rule, not as he had set out to be; and the system which he came to personify would never even have presented itself in his mind to be chosen as the next-best-thing. What we have to observe is the plan of government to which he was compelled to resort in order to fight the whig oligarchy—a poor, make-shift interim system, a necessary evil, to be borne until the whig magnates had decided to abandon the struggle. It was hardly even a plan of government, but rather a plan of campaign —a chain of emergency-measures and desperation-policies on the part of a king who could not have what he wanted and had to clutch at anything within reach if he was to keep head above water at all. The dice were loaded in his favour for the purpose of the particular game that he had to play against the main body of the whigs, because he controlled his own patronage now, and because the men who were politically effective in the country were biassed in favor of order and government in any case. Fortunately for the King the course of events during the century since 1660 had brought additional weight to monarchical authority, and had even helped to undo some of the effects of the revolution of 1688, by adding to that "influence" of the crown which was now said to be more dangerous than the ancient "prerogative". The growth of commerce and industry and the spread of empire had multiplied the exchequer officials, the custom-house officers, the colonial places, the government contracts, so that the patronage at the disposal of a ministry had expanded more than the whigs of 1688 would ever have dreamed to be possible. These reasons, rather than any particular viciousness in George III, explain the increasing significance of the problem of corruption during his reign.

Henceforward, also, George was so hemmed in by the opponents of his system—reduced to such desperate straits by the clamour of parties and by the coalition of his enemies—that time after time, though he was able to form ministries and keep his head above water, he found it impossible to establish the multi-party government he had hoped for, or to put into office the trusted first minister he so desired to have. No one needed advice and hungered for counsel so much as George III—no one so cast about to find at each moment the person who would tell him what to do, or confirm his own judgment, or at least hold his hand in the darkness. No king was prepared to do more and to suffer more—as we shall see—provided it was for a first minister in whose loyalty he could really have confidence; and at the beginning of his reign nothing could have been more pathetic than his childish faith in Bute. It was perhaps not an unreasonable claim that he made in these days when kings were not at all supposed to be mere figureheads—the claim that the chief minister should be a man in whom he could trust, a man who would be faithful to him personally. As it was, he might defeat his enemies on particular issues, but he could not choose his first minister where he wanted—could not select a government freely in the free air. He had to take anybody who was willing to fight the hostile whig combination, and once for a moment, in 1765-66, he had to allow his enemies—now under the leadership of Rockingham—to establish themselves in office. From the time of George Grenville in 1763 the first minister might have to be a man not of the first rank in ability, even a man not at all after George III's heart. This being the case, George, still needing counsel—still needing to be told how he must handle even his first minister—would resort to one man here or another one there, seeking the advice on which he could rely, privately consulting people who were not constitutionally responsible for the suggestions they made. On occasion he would even be in the position of conspiring to thwart or to overthrow his own chief minister. So, to the acknowledged abuses of the time, there was added the evil of "closet-influence" and "unconstitutional advice". Now, therefore, his whig enemies had a further article upon which they were able to indict his government.

In this conflict between the King and the main body of the whigs, the supporters of the royal authority thought that they were saving the country from enslavement to a proscriptive aristocratic clique, a Venetian oligarchy. The opponents of George III felt sure that a royal victory at this time would mean, now or later, the establishment of a permanent despotic system. We to-day know that either of these alternatives might have been evil, but, when we resurrect such old quarrels, we ourselves are under a limitation, for we cannot empty our minds of the knowledge that we possess of after-events. We may well be sceptical—may well feel that each party to the struggle was guilty of over-dramatizing the issue to a certain degree. The politician sees contemporary events as too cataclysmic —he thinks that all the future depends on *this* fight; and sometimes he does not discern the deeper kind of history-making that is to transform the whole situation in any case. To see more than George III could see in the minds of his opponents—to know more than politicians consent to learn of the thinking of their political enemies—and to discern those deeper movements which the actors in the story fail to take account of, but which come like the beat of an ocean-wave to deflect and over-ride their purposes—these are the reasons why we study history.

In the reign of George III even the battle between the King and the aristocracy is only the surface-drama, and if we mark it as the ruling theme we do so only at the first level of analysis. It is one of the ironies of the story that in this battle neither of the contestants really defeated the other—neither the King nor the aristocracy was to have the victory—and, though each thought that the whole of the future hung upon his success in this conflict, liberty was saved rather because they fought one another, and because neither of them won, so that a third party could rise and run away with the spoil. Below this surface-drama is a movement long, slow, and deep, and to see something of its progress—to hear its rumbling—is one of the primary objects of the present study. We must conceive it not as a conflict but as a tide—one which throughout the century is bringing wider classes of Englishmen to intellectual awareness and a realization of the part they might play in politics. John Wesley, John Wilkes, and Lord George Gordon are only the most famous examples of those who led this movement, or used it for their purposes, and thereby added to its power. Behind them all the progress in society —all the advance in education, the spread of literature, and the growth of towns—was changing the character of the world itself. Greater masses of people were being brought by various means to a consciousness of their importance, a sense of their public rights, a habit of local self-help and an interest in the destiny of their nation.

11

THE SOCIAL INGREDIENTS OF THE WILKITE MOVEMENT

George Rudé

A new generation of English historians has joined Butterfield in reassessing the significance of ideological pronouncements in the later eighteenth century. In the following original study George Rudé, who has also done important work on popular movements in the French Revolution, attempts to define the groups in English society in the 1760's for whom the cry of "Wilkes and Liberty" was an irresistable summons to political action and agitation.

[Wilkes'] active opponents, though fewer in number, were as dedicated in their hatred as his followers in their devotion. George III, for one, gave 'that devil Wilkes' no quarter and, having vigorously intervened in order to secure his conviction, outlawry, imprisonment, expulsion, exclusion and declaration of 'incapacity', intervened with equal vigour to prevent his election as Lord Mayor of London and his re-election, for the fourth time, as M.P. for Middlesex in September 1774. It was a forlorn and ill-starred venture, in which the King was loyally supported —though with varying degrees of zeal—by a succession of Chief Ministers from George Grenville to Lord North. With few exceptions, the Lords and others of 'the sober, large-acred part of the nation' were equally persistent in their detestation of Wilkes and their support of the numerous measures undertaken by the government to restrain him. This was not true, of course, of the patriarchal brotherhood of peers who, at one stage or another of Wilkes's career, led the opposition groups in Parliament. Their attitude towards Wilkes ranged between genuine or grudging affection, fascinated horror and a sort of malevolent neutrality. Temple alone was a loyal friend—at least until the scandal aroused over the *Essay on Woman*—and his 'warmth' and 'forwardness' in espousing Wilkes's cause that year not only lost him the Lord Lieutenancy of Buckinghamshire but earned him the disapproval of the Duke of Newcastle and the Earl of Hardwicke. But Temple never entirely deserted Wilkes and we find him corresponding with him affectionately after his

FROM George Rudé, *Wilkes and Liberty* (Oxford: The Clarendon Press, 1962), pp. 176–190. By permission of the Clarendon Press, Oxford.

return from exile, offering to visit him in the King's Bench prison, and he appears to have been associated with him in City politics, if only through a third party, as late as the autumn of 1771. Chatham, on the other hand, broke off all personal associations with Wilkes after the publication of No. 45 of *The North Briton,* became one of his most virulent detractors over the affair of the *Essay on Woman,* and refused to intercede on his behalf during his own administration and the latter part of Wilkes's exile. Yet he stoutly defended his right to parliamentary privilege, vigorously opposed and countered the legal arguments used by Administration to justify his exclusion and 'incapacity', and, being as willing as any, when the occasion appeared suitable, to 'play the popular engines', joined with Temple and Rockingham in promoting the petitions of 1769.

The Duke of Grafton, though less given to personal rancour, was far more guarded in his personal associations with Wilkes. After visiting him in the Tower, he rejected a request to stand bail for him. Later, as a Minister and supporter of Administration, he played a rather half-hearted role in the further prosecution and expulsion of Wilkes; but he had doubts about the justice of the decision to recognize Luttrell as Member for Middlesex, though he condoned it on the grounds of political expediency and added lamely: 'How this decision could have been avoided, or better substituted, I cannot well pronounce'. Richmond, like Newcastle, was prepared to recognize Wilkes as a 'Friend (or would-be friend) to Liberty' and a victim of Ministerial persecution, yet he took no initiative in promoting his cause or that of the electors of Middlesex. The Marquess of Rockingham, who succeeded Newcastle as the leader of the main opposition group in Parliament, followed a policy in regard to Wilkes that, for being ambivalent, was none the less consistent. The Marquess refused all personal contacts with him, though he maintained a line of communication open through Burke; he ignored his requests for a free pardon and an early return from exile, yet he contributed materially to his upkeep—a subsidy that must have been continued at intervals since, as we find evidence of Wilkes receiving 'gratuities' from Rockingham, as from the Dukes of Portland and Devonshire, in both 1772 and 1773. Rockingham, like his fellow-peers of the opposition, was willing enough to use 'Wilkes's affair' as a stick with which to beat the government, but he was as scared as they were of getting his fingers burned by appearing in any way to further the personal cause of the man rather than the wider political issues with which his name was associated. Burke, who had some regard and affection for Wilkes and understood him better, neatly summed up this distinction in a letter to Charles O'Hara:

> We had not the least desire of taking up that gentleman's cause as personally favourably to him; he is not ours. . . . Had they attempted to attack him . . . we must have defended him, and were resolved to do it; but still as the Cause and not the Person.

Among the gentry, as among the clergy, Wilkes found only occasional and exceptional support. We have noted the zeal displayed for his cause in Middlesex and during his stay in the King's Bench prison by John Sawbridge and James Townsend, who later became two of his bitterest enemies in the politics of the City. There was also Robert Jones, owner of Fonmon Castle in Glamorgan and a devoted Supporter of the Bill of Rights; and we counted among voters of Wilkes and Glynn in Middlesex the Hon. John Scott of Ealing and Sir John Danvers of Hanover Square. Among other early Supporters of the Bill of Rights were Sir Francis Blake Delaval, Bart., of Seaton Delaval, Northumberland, former Member for Andover; and Sir Robert Bernard, Bart., of Brampton, Huntingdonshire, who became M.P. for Westminster in 1770. Yet these were notable exceptions; and among the sixty-five or more M.P.s who promoted, signed, or presented petitions in 1769–70, a mere handful could with any accuracy be termed Wilkites. We have seen the case of such men as Henry Crabb Boulton (Worcester), Sir George Colebrooke (Arundel) and Sir Thomas Frankland (Thirsk), who, while they signed petitions against the declaration of Wilkes's 'incapacity', had previously voted for Proctor or Cooke against Wilkes or Glynn. The same sort of distinction must be made in the case of the great majority of petitioning justices, gentry and clergy, whose signatures in support of the rights of the Middlesex electors cannot be taken as support for the personal cause of John Wilkes.

Far more solid was the body of support that Wilkes was able to command among merchants—particularly those of the 'middling' and lesser sort—in both London and other commercial cities. In July 1763, he had written to Temple that 'the merchants . . . are firms in the cause of liberty' and that it was in them that 'the strength of our cause really lies'. There were always a number of wealthy merchants among his adherents: Richard Oliver and Samuel Vaughan in London; Sir Joseph Mawbey in Southwark; Samuel Peach, banker and East India merchant in Bristol; Sir Ben Trueman, brewer of Brick Lane, Spitalfields, who voted for Wilkes and Glynn in Middlesex; not to mention such City leaders as Sir William Stephenson, hop-merchant and distiller of Bridge Within; William Bridgen of Farringdon Within and Forty Hill, Enfield; and Sir William Baker, Governor of the Hudson's Bay Company and alderman of Bassishaw. And yet, as we have seen, the hard core of the Court of Aldermen and the City's 'monied interest'—large merchants, government contractors, bankers and directors of trading and insurance companies—were, on the whole, hostile to Wilkes and the 'patriot' groups. It was not from them but from the smaller and 'middling' merchants and tradesmen that he drew his main support. We saw that, in Liverpool, it was the 'lower freemen' that prodded Sir William Meredith's and Richard Pennant's friends among 'the higher rank of people' into drawing up a petition on the Middlesex election issue in October 1769. In the Middlesex elections of 1768–69, we noted the solid weight of support for the Wilkite candidates that came from the commercial parishes lying to the east and north of the City—and from coal-merchants, brewers, warehousemen, shipbuilders and timber-merchants such as Thomas Allen and John

Curteis of Wapping, James Minestone and David Trinder of Shadwell, and Allen Spenceley of Aldermanbury and Islington. Again, in Westminster, among a score of Wilkes's most active associates of 1770 were three apothecaries, two carpenters, a prosperous poulterer, a stable-keeper, an engraver, a bookseller, an upholsterer, a coach-maker and a working jeweller. On the Common Council of the City of London during the years 1768–74, he found his most stalwart supporters among men of the typical City crafts and trades—men like Joseph Partridge, packer, of 112 Fenchurch Street; John Webb, upholder, of Gracechurch Street; Henry George, haberdasher, of Bishopsgate; James Cotterell, chinaman, of Mansion House Street; Samuel Baughan, hatter, of Fish Street Hill; Stephen Camm, linen-draper, of Cheapside; William Bishop, saddler, of 27 Coleman Street; Joseph Stevenson, cooper, of Upper Thames Street; Stanley Crowder, bookseller, of Paternoster Row; Ingham Foster, ironmonger, of Lombard Street; Samuel Freeman, lead-merchant, of Mark Lane; James Stracey, cider-merchant, of Dowgate Hill; and Thomas Axford, broker, of Walbrook. Yet the main bulwark of Wilkes's electoral strength and political authority in the City remained the Common Hall, composed of the 8,000 liveried freemen of the Companies; and it was from them, as we have seen, that he was able to draw a considerable vote even in his first City contest, before he had had time to build up a position within the Courts of Aldermen and Common Council.

And, outside the City, there were the freeholders of Middlesex, whose obstinate and continuous support in the face of every obstacle and discouragement sustained Wilkes in his political battles of this period and, eventually, in the General Election of 1774, assured him of a secure and uncontested seat in Parliament. Some of these freeholders belonged to social groups that have already been mentioned: a handful of gentry and considerable numbers of tradesmen and manufacturers. But the great bulk of Wilkite voters and supporters in Middlesex were formed, as we saw in an earlier chapter, by the lesser freeholders of both urban and rural districts, who owned or occupied freeholds of a value ranging from 40s. to £10 a year. These, then, form a distinctive social category, and one as essential to the strength of the 'Wilkes and Liberty' movement in the metropolis as they were to the success (in point of numbers, at least) of the county petitions of 1769.

Yet these by no means exhaust the number of social ingredients of which the Wilkite movement was compounded. Most active and vociferous of all Wilkes's supporters were those who demonstrated in St. George's Fields, at Hyde Park Corner, at the Mansion House, in Parliament Square and at St. James's Palace; who shouted, or chalked up, 'Wilkes and Liberty' in the streets of the City, Westminster and Southwark; who pelted Sheriff Harley and the common hangman at the Royal Exchange when they attempted to burn No. 45 of *The North Briton;* who smashed the windows of Lords Bute and Egmont and daubed the boots of the Austrian Ambassador; who paraded the Boot and Petticoat in the City streets, and burned Colonel Luttrell and Lords Sandwich and Barrington in effigy outside the Tower of London. These are the elements whom contemporaries and later historians have—either from indolence, prejudice or lack of more certain knowledge—called 'the mob', and, though the evidence on this point is slight, they are not likely to have been composed to any considerable degree of City merchants or of freeholders or manufacturers of the 'middling sort'. Yet there were exceptions: the judicial records tell us that, in the riots of March 1768, Robert Chandler, a City tea-broker, was believed to have 'headed a Mob in Westminster'; that, on the same occasion, one Matthew Christian, 'a gentleman of character and fortune', filled demonstrators with beer and drank with them to 'Wilkes and Liberty'; and that, in Southwark in the following May, Justice Capel was 'insulted' by Richard Gilbert, who stood in a group with 'several well-dressed persons'. Again, eyewitnesses tell us that those who, on an historic occasion, noisily escorted the triumphant Wilkes from Westminster Hall to his house in Great George Street were 'of a higher rank than Common Mob'; that the 'people who gave Lord Mayor Crosby a rousing send-off from the Mansion House on 19 March 1771 were 'of the better sort'; and that crowds demonstrating in Parliament Square a week later appeared to be composed largely of 'respectable tradesmen'. But, even if we take all these reports at their face value, they do not amount to very much. More typical, perhaps, were the Spitalfields weavers who (so Horace Walpole assures us) pelted Proctor and his supporters in Piccadilly in March 1768; or the coal-heavers of East London who, a few weeks later, were drawn, if only briefly, into the Wilkite movement. In the following year, it was observed that,

at the last two Middlesex elections, that part of the mob who behaved most riotously have been chiefly composed of gentlemen's servants, especially at Hyde Park Corner.

Again, to Mrs. Harris (possibly not a reliable witness in such matters) the rioters who blocked the entrance to St. Stephen's Chapel to Members of Parliament on the day that Oliver was committed to the Tower appeared to be 'a most blackguard set of shabby fellows'—a term not dissimilar to that used by her husband, James Harris, M.P., in describing to the Earl of Hardwicke the 'dirty people' that crowded the Lobby in protest against Luttrell's adoption on 15 April 1769. Yet all such descriptions tend to be coloured by the prejudices of their authors. To obtain a more objective, though more limited, picture of these rioters we have to rely on the meagre sample afforded by those who were arrested, committed, brought to trial, released on bail, or against whom 'informations' were preferred in London, Westminster, Southwark and Middlesex, for being implicated in Wilkite riots and demonstrations. Of a total of sixty-four such persons, the occupation or social status of forty-four appears in the records. These include two gentlemen, three merchants or dealers, thirteen tradesmen (who may have been small masters, journeymen or independent craftsmen), four vaguely classified as 'labourers', and twenty-two who were probably wage-earners. The great majority were, in fact, labourers, servants, journeymen, small craftsmen, or petty traders, and we must assume that nearly all lived in lodgings, as not one of those whose addresses appear in the records—not even the two 'gentlemen'—are to be found in the Poor Rate books of Land Tax registers of their parishes. So, in spite of the occasional report of 'well-dressed persons' or 'tradesmen of the better sort' among the rioters, we must conclude, for lack of further evidence, that these formed but a small minority and that the most active elements in Wilkite street-demonstrations and riots, while by no means drawn exclusively from the wage-earners, were overwhelmingly composed of 'the lower orders of the people'.

Yet these, it must be insisted, formed but one of the social elements—however important in point of numbers—of which Wilkes's following was composed. It is misleading to contend, as one of his biographers has done, that, in London, 'Wilkes's supporters were notoriously overwhelmingly of the working class'. It was, in fact, one of the most significant of Wilkes's achievements that he was able to tap the loyalties and political energies of such varying and distinctive social groups as City merchants, the 'middling' and lesser freeholders of Middlesex, and the small craftsmen, petty traders and wage-earners of the capital.

This phenomenon does require some explanation. What prompted so many people, drawn from so wide a range of social classes, to centre their political hopes, loyalties and aspirations over so long a period on a man whose reputation was consistently blackened by those in authority, who was no orator, who offered no social panacea, whose political ideas were without originality, who never attained public office outside the City of London, and whose career within Parliament had, up to 1774, been brief, undistinguished and uneventful? Wilkes's biographers have not failed to stress his charm, his wit, his ready pen and colourful personality, the consistency of his political principles and of the 'image' that he presented to his public, his brazen defiance of authority and considerable courage in the face of adversity, qualities that could not but win him a martyr's crown whether deserved or not. He knew, too, on occasion, how to address himself to, or to solicit the support of, those 'middling and inferior set of people who stand most in need of protection', and whom he declared to be his particular concern; and he understood better than most that Liberty and freedom from subservience to foreigners—even those from north of the Border—were catch-words that, if manipulated with skill and persistence, could yield political dividends both among Londoners and among the county gentry and freeholders. Such qualities must certainly have played their part in evoking a more than ephemeral response from the merchants, craftsmen, freeholders and propertyless classes of the capital, of whom many had already, on more than one occasion, in the name of 'Revolution principles', championed the cause of the City magistrates and of the Earl of Chatham—and, as Burke understood, their 'adoption' of Wilkes was, in a sense, but a logical sequel to the former popularity of Chatham. But Wilkes's support in the metropolis was considerably more widespread than that of either Chatham or his lieutenants, or their predecessors, in the City of London: it extended, as we have seen, into Westminster, Southwark and the rural and 'out-parishes' of Middlesex; and here, for the first time, we have a London movement that is metropolitan in scope rather than limited, as hitherto, to the confines of the City, though occasionally 'spilling over' into Westminster and the urban parishes of Surrey and Middlesex. This has, of course, a great deal more to do with the development of London at this time into a unified capital city, the growth and spread of its population, and the stirring of the social aspirations of its citizens than it has with the personal attributes or qualities of John Wilkes.

There were other factors besides, which, while lying outside Wilkes's own control, must have contributed not a little to the impact that he was able to make on the society of his day. The accession of George III, the dismissal of the old Whig 'undertakers', the resignation of Pitt, the promotion of Lord Bute and his friends, and peace preliminaries with France and Spain had caused a ferment not only among Whig peers but among a substantial part of the country gentry and the citizens of London, Bristol and Liverpool. Temple, who had resigned office with Pitt, wrote to Wilkes in September 1762,

that there never was at any period of time so ardent a zeal in the whole body of the country gentlemen, a very few placemen excepted, as at present against the Ministry.

Even allowing for the wishful-thinking natural in a disgruntled ex-Minister, the discontent was genuine enough; and it was further exacerbated, and spread among the larger body of freeholders, by such measures as the application of the Cider Acts to the west country and the attempts by the Ministry in the General Election of 1768 to impose Sir James Lowther, Bute's son-in-law, on the electors of Cumberland in spite of the higher vote won by Henry Curwen contesting in the Duke of Portland's interest. The unrest among freeholders and gentry was matched by that in the great trading cities, where the government's failure to retain intact the conquests in the Caribbean and the imposition of new restrictions on the American trade excited alarm and protracted resentment—often among men who combined a passionate concern for the Englishman's liberties with a vigorous prosecution of the slave-trade with America and the West Indies. Nor was this all. It was widely believed—and it needed no invention by Burke and the Rockingham Whigs—that corruption was more rampant than ever it had been, and that the influence of the Crown was being used to staff the administration with new Favourites and 'King's Friends', who formed a secret Closet party, beyond the control of Parliament and guided behind the scenes by the sinister combination of the Earl of Bute (who had resigned office in 1763) and the Princess Dowager of Wales. Opponents of the new system talked darkly of a repetition of 'the end of King Charles II's reign'—and such talk was not confined to the circles of the Duke of Newcastle and others, who might be inclined to identify the eclipse of their own public authority with that of the national interest. Merchants and tradesmen, too, might suffer the arrogance and resent the slights of courtiers like Lord Pomfret who, in the House of Lords, commented on the City's Remonstrance to the King in May 1770 in the following inelegant and contemptuous terms:

However swaggering and impudent the behaviour of the low Citizens in their own dunghill, when they came into the Royal Presence, their heads hung down like bulrushes and they blinked with their eyes like owls at the rays of the sun.

Small wonder, then, that among such citizens and gentry, alarmed at the whole trend of events since the accession of George III, there should be many to whom Wilkes, who had been persecuted more relentlessly than any other by the new administration and returned blow for blow and insolence for insolence, might appear as an object of sympathy, respect, or even of veneration.

While small freeholders, City craftsmen and wage-earners were touched by similar considerations, they had grievances of their own, besides, that may have inclined them to espouse the cause of Wilkes. Enclosing landlords and turnpike trusts had long since set their stamp on the countryside. In Herefordshire, memories were still fresh of the turnpike riots that had inflamed the west country thirty years before when, owing to strong local feelings of sympathy, rioters arrested at Hereford had been brought to Worcester for trial. Enclosure had aroused resentment among the smaller freeholders and cottagers even in rural parishes adjoining London. In 1767, the villagers of Stanwell in Middlesex had marched to Westminster to protest against an Enclosure Bill; while it did not appear overtly as an issue in the county elections that followed, who can tell how far it stimulated the lesser freeholders to seek the support of new men in Parliament? The payment of tithe in kind was another grievance of the countryside. In December 1766, a west country farmer, in a letter to the *Gloucester Journal*, contrasts the happy condition of one village with the prevailing misery of its neighbour. In the one (he writes), 'all are happy, and no murmurs or discontents, much less mobs and riots are heard of amongst them even in these times. But [he continues] cross the rivulet and the scene is changing; poverty and distress stare you in the face at once ... for tithe is there taken up in kind'. The same year, owing to the shortage and high price of wheat and flour, there had been unprecedentedly widespread riots all over the country: market towns had been invaded by hungry villagers, miners and weavers, who had compelled bakers to sell their bread at a reduced price. At Gloucester alone, ninety-six men and women were brought to trial at the winter Assizes, and nine men were sentenced to death and seven to transportation.

Whether such factors as these played any part in determining small freeholders to ventilate their grievances by signing the county petitions of 1769 it is impossible to say; yet they may be worthy of attention. Far more tangible is the evidence of a concordance between the movement of food-prices and of certain phases of the 'Wilkes and Liberty' movement in the metropolis. The years 1763–64 were years of low and stable prices, the quarter of wheat, quoted monthly at the London Corn Exchange, ranging between a 'mean' of 32s. and 32s. 6d. It rose sharply in the autumn of 1766, reached a peak of 50s. in July and October 1767, fell to 44s. 9d. in December, and rose by stages to a higher peak of 50s. 6d. in May 1768; the price of bread followed a similar, though less erratic course. Not surprisingly, we find the discontent that this aroused reflected in the agitation of the period. In mid-April, for instance, the *Annual Register* reported that

a half-penny loaf, adorned with mourning crepe, was hung up at several parts of the Royal Exchange, with an inscription thereon, containing some reflections touching the high price of bread and other provisions,

and—even more significantly—demonstrators at the House of Lords on 10 May accompanied their chanting of the slogan 'Wilkes and Liberty!' with shouts of: 'It was as well to be hanged as starved!' And it is surely no coincidence that the numerous industrial disputes of that year, prompted by a similar concern at the rising cost of living, should have come to a head at the same time—and thus appearing to be related to the Wilkite political movement. After that, there was a sharp drop in wheat-prices to 31s. 9d. in January 1769, followed by slight rises in July–August and December, yet, generally, the price of wheat and bread in London remained low throughout 1769 and continued to be so in the early months of 1770. In fact, for some time after the early summer of 1768, rising food-prices cease to be a factor for consideration, and the next phases of the Wilkite movement—including the excitement over the Middlesex election of December 1768, the new outbreak of political rioting in London in March 1769, and the petition-campaign that followed—cannot be explained in such terms.

The years 1771–73 were once more years of steeply rising and fluctuating food-prices; they were marked by renewed demands for higher wages, and the movement of prices may have contributed (though not so evidently as in 1768) to the vigour of the Wilkite movement in the City of London. After rising to 46s. in July 1771, the price of the quarter of wheat fell sharply in the autumn and then rose again to new and higher peaks of 52s. in April 1772, of 56s. in November, and of 58s. in July–August 1773, before falling to 42s. 9d. (still a high price) in the autumn of that year. Already in March 1771, the Mayor and principal inhabitants of Norwich, 'being greatly alarmed at the increasing prices of corn and grain in general', petitioned Parliament to import wheat duty-free from the American colonies. London does not appear to have felt these effects so sharply, for it was not until April 1772 that the *Gentleman's Magazine* reported that great numbers of inflammatory hand-bills were dispersed in Spitalfields & the parts adjacent, with a view to excite the populace to rise on account of the high price of provisions.

The same months, angry crowds in Chelmsford and Sudbury besieged flour-mills and food-convoys; while, in London, Lord Mayor William Nash, returning from Church, 'was roughly used by the populace for not lowering the price of bread'; and the press reported that 'letters from almost every part of the Kingdom bring melancholy accounts of the distress of the poor and of their readiness to rise and to do mischief'. At this time, too, the journeymen tailors were petitioning the London magistrates for an increase in wages 'on account of the dearness of provisions'; and, in October of the same year, while the City echoed with the 'tumults' attending Wilkes's first bid for the mayoralty of London, 'a great number' of sailors assembled at Tower Hill to demand a restoration of wage-cuts imposed by their employers. A few weeks later, shortly after the great riot in Guildhall Yard provoked by Townsend's election in preference to Wilkes, Sheriff Watkin Lewes presented a petition to the Commons on behalf of the City 'relative to the high price of provisions'. Shortly after, ten journeymen curriers were tried (and acquitted) at the Old Bailey for conspiring to raise their wages. A lull followed until March 1773, when the Commons rejected a request by the Lord Mayor and sheriffs of London to impose a bounty of 4s. a quarter on imported wheat; the same day, it was reported that the artificers and labourers in H.M. dockyards had petitioned Parliament for 'a trifling increase of wages'. And, a month later, we find Wilkes, in the course of a perennial letter to the Speaker demanding his right to be seated in the Commons, taxing Parliament with 'indulging in supine ease and luxury amidst the cries of the starving poor'.

While, then, rising food-prices can be seen as the immediate cause of the wages demands and industrial disputes of the period they can only serve as a partial explanation of certain phases of the 'Wilkes and Liberty' movement. Besides contributing substantially to 'a general dissatisfaction [that] unhappily prevailed among several of the lower orders of the people', they no doubt had the effect of adding something to the volume and the vigour of the riots and disturbances of 1768 and 1771–73. Beyond that, we must look to a complex of political, social and economic factors, in which the underlying social changes of the age, the political crisis of 1761, the traditional devotion to 'Revolution principles', and Wilkes's own astuteness, experiences and personality all played their part.

12

THE FIRST REFORM MOVEMENT
Eugene C. Black

The first great movement for parliamentary reform has come to be regarded by many historians as the most significant political development of the early decades of George III's reign. The central role played in this agitation by Christopher Wyvill and the Yorkshire and National Associations, the short-term failure and long-term impact of this extraparliamentary reform movement, are precisely described in this evaluation by the American scholar Eugene Black.

IF THERE IS a cause, there is a committee. Where there are objectives, there are petitions. Narrow interests and broad, negative goals and positive—all are reflected in organizations which seek to convince the public and through public pressure to win legislative endorsement of their programs. The development of parliamentary organization, the modern political party, runs parallel to and interacts with the growth of extraparliamentary political organization. The passage of Fox's Libel Act in 1792, leaving public opinion to determine the fact of libel, meant that Pitt's administration had to organize a political association to convince the public to accept a narrow definition of seditious activity. As one position after another was defined, it was less and less possible to have rule for the sake of rule without at least lip service to program on a hitherto unprecedented scale. The years of war and reaction suspended this development, but only in part. In 1807 the anti-slave trade agitators won their battle.

Consider the evolution of political association even in a narrow political sense. Wilkite agitation lured the great magnates into a field they ill understood. Grenville and Rockingham intended no more than an occasional gesture, expecting in return the support of the commons of England. Such token nods were in the best tradition of eighteenth-century politics. Had not a cleverly contrived storm of misinformed protest over excise threatened to blow the sagacious Walpole out of office? But the little old England of Walpole's time could survive no better in political than in social and economic terms against the forces of change

---

REPRINTED by permission of the publishers from Eugene Charlton Black, *The Association: British Extraparliamentary Political Organization 1769–1793*, Cambridge, Mass.: Harvard University Press, Copyright, 1963, by the President and Fellows of Harvard College, pp. 275–282.

in the late eighteenth century. The Rockinghamites half-grasped one truth: only the public could provide the political strength to stand against the crown. But extraparliamentary organizations and political factions found themselves working at cross-purposes. The Society for the Supporters of the Bill of Rights served narrow political ends in the metropolis, and Rockinghamite or Chathamite aldermen recognized that, however much they might sympathize with its objects, the Society was a Wilkite machine. John Horne attempted unsuccessfully to segregate politics and principles with unfortunate results for both himself and the agitation. The Society threatened to engross metropolitan politics. Sometimes, as in the Westminster by-election of 1770, opposition politicians had no choice but to endorse the Society candidate, if only to hide their own essential weakness. The Society was even invoked in the provinces to swing the balance in a dispute over control of the Bedford corporation. Bedford, however, was an exception. The Society for the Supporters of the Bill of Rights was rarely more powerful in the provinces than the local magnates and gentry wished it to be. Once opposition unity on "the rights of electors" collapsed, Society agitation meant little outside of London. Opposition politicians, finding that extraparliamentary agitation might challenge rather than serve them, disowned the cause.

A decade of continued political exile finally brought Rockingham and his allies back to popular agitation. By this time everyone had learned something. Those whom Rockingham had raised and deserted a decade before would provide their own leaders. Radical ideologues had tasted brief success. With more refined and perfect doctrine they prepared to deflect or destroy the new movement. A misconducted war coupled with social and economic dislocation offered fertile ground for agitation. Country gentlemen and stout forty-shilling freeholders believed that they had counted for much and were now denied their rightful place.

Christopher Wyvill, educated in the political tradition of radical dissent, attempted to rally old and new elements not only against a currently mismanaged government but against the hegemony of those under whom the situation had developed, in fact against the territorial magnates. His Yorkshire movement was a revolution in local politics; but success could only be won in those areas where a new leadership evolved to challenge the old. Outside of Yorkshire and the metropolis, with occasional glimmerings in the home counties, the story of 1769–1770 was repeated on an expanded scale. Reform agitation was a weapon in local politics, although rarely an end in itself. It served to unseat two ministerial members of parliament at Gloucester, but reform, as an issue, proved to have little staying power in the county. The Wyvill program was the basis of unsuccessful parliamentary challenges at Portsmouth and Plymouth, and parliamentary reform continued to be the program of the "outs" of Portsmouth for several years. Wyvillite and radical agitation were used and abused in Cambridge and Cambridgeshire only to be discarded after the election of 1780.

Wyvillites and London radicals could find no common ground. Rhetorical legerdemain could not conceal the basic divergence of aim. Wyvill's country gentlemen would settle for power. They did. The associates of Dr. Jebb and Major Cartwright, with higher ends in view, fumbled away their brief metropolitan political position to Fox. The radicals would have nothing less than a root and branch program—impossible without a revolution. They devoted as much attention to undercutting Wyvill in the metropolis and provinces as to working for a "general reformation." Cartwright thought of petitions as "articles of instruction" in pedagogical terms; Wyvill considered them instruments of policy.

The threat of violence implicit in association sanctions broke through in the agitation of the Protestant Association. While this worked against Wyvill or the metropolitan radicals in terms of immediate results, the Edinburgh and London riots added a further dimension to extraparliamentary activity. They demonstrated that popular prejudice was the best rallying ground for mass support, a point not lost on John Reeves and his colleagues. In 1779 and 1780 Protestantism was in danger; in 1792 not only the constitution but property was threatened by any spread of the revolution from France. Violence or the threat of violence carried some weight. Riot was the last and ultimate sanction of a discontented public. No government would attempt to carry Roman Catholic relief legislation for Scotland for more than a decade after the Edinburgh riots. Even in England perfectly rational men were ready to reconsider the merits of Protestant Association claims during and after the London disorders. Only the most extreme among the leaders of popular clubs during the 1790's advocated violence as a political sanction; rather the lunatic right used this weapon as a final sanction in Church and King clubs.

Wyvill sought to win the enfranchised voter to the cause of moderate parliamentary reform. Reeves attempted to move public opinion convincingly behind the government campaign of persecution. Jebb, Cartwright, and Horne Tooke looked for a broader consensus, although they were not certain exactly what it should be. There was an anonymous and amorphous quality to the "people" they invoked to restore the purity of the Anglo-Saxon constitution. The Rockinghamites asked only for the occasional popular endorsement of their position and opposed any attempt of the extraparliamentary world to dictate policy or principle. Every organization summoned the "public" or some segment of it to participate in the political life of the nation. By 1784 swinging public opinion had registered dramatically in election returns. Pitt recognized what Wyvill had done, allied with him, and then captured Wyvill's political following. Constitutional radicalism proved unnecessary. Peace, retrenchment, and reform—those principles which would make possible the Victorian Whig-Liberal hegemony—proved sufficient when executed on a modest scale.

The old Whig connection lost the most heavily, being the least willing to make concessions to the new forms of political organization. Neither

Fox in 1780 nor Grey in 1792, both of whom saw the potential of political association, could carry more than a small portion of the aristocratic clique with him. Not so William Pitt. He had learned, as the Portlands and Cavendishes had not, that public opinion was counting for more and more in the political equation. Pitt seems to have used Wyvill's 1785 agitation as a counterweight for the hostility to governmental commercial and economic measures. And Pitt had some eye for growing and waning popularity of issues, as seen not merely in his views on parliamentary reform but on such problems as repeal of the Test and Corporation Acts. Burke could verbalize principles, but John Reeves backed by the power of the administration translated those principles into effective political force.

By 1792 political association had arrived. The discerning read the future in organization. Even as association was the hallmark of growing national political maturity, the political expression of popular interests, so political association educated the public, both enfranchised and unenfranchised, on questions of moment. Mysteries of state became less mysterious. As the Commons slowly discovered its own political power in parliament, the public began to intervene in a manner which would prove decisive through political association. Organizations educated men and focused their attention on specific issues. Politicians were forced to respond in kind.

Association made possible the extension of the politically effective public. Discomfited country gentlemen could move against the increasing power of the territorial magnates (which concerned them as much as the increasing power of the crown) with Christopher Wyvill through political association. In the same way powerful, discontented manufacturers and merchants were ready to join Joseph Parkes, even Francis Place, in the Political unions and the struggle for the great reform bill. Modern extra-parliamentary political organization is a product of the late eighteenth century. The history of the age of reform cannot be written without it. The Anti-Slave Trade Association won its battle in 1807; the Abolition Society carried the British conscience in 1833. Daniel O'Connell's Catholic Association wrested Roman Catholic emancipation from a hostile government and parliament in 1829. Who could conceive of the Reform Act of 1832 without the Political unions? The inexorable pressure of the Anti-Corn Law League won such a compelling victory that the myth of free trade survived its usefulness. Even failures or partial failures are of paramount importance. The anti-poor-law organization succeeded in mitigating harsh, utilitarian legislation, although it never secured repeal. Owenite idealism confronted harsh reality with the failure of the Grand National Consolidated Trades Union, but the idea of using the mass strength of organized labor for social and political ends was not lost. Short time committees bounced back from repeated defeats to see victory with Fielden's Factory Act. All three of these organizations contributed to one of the most dramatic, if futile, nineteenth-century associations—the Chartist movement. Few who assembled on the Yorkshire moors to hear Feargus O'Connor and Bronterre O'Brien would live to see five of the six points of the Charter carried into law.

Political association touched every aspect of life. Organized legions of protectors cared for chimney sweeps, the insane, and even dumb animals. The Society for the Suppression of Vice sought to impose its code of Sabbatarianism. Temperance Leagues enforced licensing regulations. Education Leagues brought Britons free elementary and secondary schools. The Church Missionary Society imparted some measure of humanity to imperialism. The Fabians, a small band of intellectuals, not unlike the Society for Constitutional Information in some respects, have left their indelible mark on the annals of our times.

Political association seems the natural concomitant of growing public participation in the life of the nation. The strength of union is a cliché; it is also a fact. It applied equally to those substantial gentlemen who supported Wyvill and to the gaunt handloom weavers, casualties of modern economics, who listened to another clergyman, the Reverend Joseph Raynor Stephens, preach the holy war which would be the Chartist movement. Association made possible the extension of the politically effective public. It was a necessity of the modern age. The limited electorate of the eighteenth century, while representative of much more than landed property, was overweighted in that direction. The least representative parts of the unreformed constitution made possible the representation of new interests and social elements. Wealth or plutocracy could buy its place through rotten boroughs. Wyvill's reform program ironically would have rendered the constitution less rather than more representative. There were elements coming to political consciousness as well as social and economic significance, elements which lacked the means required to make their will felt within the traditional system. Lacking a place within the structure of politics, they turned outside of it.

They could be politically effective. Election implies consent—whether by the seven burgages of Old Sarum or the more than seven thousand electors of Westminster. But only in combination could new elements—rising industrialists, businessmen, or industrial workers—or, for that matter, old elements—displaced gentry or handicraft workers—pit their strength against that of their traditional governors. Program was the matrix of combination, although ties of personal relationship and influence played their part in the extraparliamentary as in the parliamentary world. Political association carried sanctions ranging from reason, negotiation, and the vote to riot and revolution. The casualty of the collectivization of politics was eighteenth-century political individuality. The "Old Whig" connection seemed almost instinctively to recognize this.

Conversion eventually proved more satisfactory than coercion, but political education was a slow process. The most successful early associations were those which appealed to popular prejudices or conditioning as seen in the victory of the Scottish Protestant Association and the near miss of its English counterpart. The Anti-Slave Trade Association, the Society for the Reformation of Manners, the Church Missionary Society, and the Society for the Suppression of Vice capitalized on evangelical fervor in the conscience of the nation. After a century of secular enlightenment, religion was a hallmark of the people.

A negative equation prevailed over the short term. The more idealistic the movement, the less successful. The Society for Constitutional Information reaped a scanty harvest for its plentiful sowing. Its ideas and program slowly touched the skilled workingman and brought his greater participation in political life. The most dramatic response, however, did not come from the London Corresponding Society and its provincial counterparts but from the Association for the Preservation of Liberty and Property against Republicans and Levellers. The long-term assessment would be rather different.

The association educated politicians as well as the public. The Yorkshire Association, the Westminster committee, and the Quintuple Alliance demonstrated new, effective political techniques which embraced an expanding political public. The Whig Club for opposition and the Pitt administration for government anticipated lines of party development. Party developed as a response to growing public awareness of and interest in political principles and the day-to-day conduct of government, and party, sustained by the public, wrought the fundamental revolution in the British constitution. Christopher Wyvill, John Jebb—even Lord George Gordon and John Reeves—led one vital phase of this revolution in their several ways. Even the territorial magnates unwittingly contributed. They made political association, and political association helped to make modern Britain.

13

THE CRISIS OF THE EMPIRE

Vincent Harlow

The disruption of the First British Empire was attributed by Victorian whig-liberal historians to the oppression of the American colonists by George III and his inept ministers. The prodigious researches of twentieth-century American and British scholars and the insight gained from the experience of the fall of great overseas empires in our

---

FROM Vincent Harlow, *The Founding of the Second British Empire* (London: Longmans, Green & Co. Limited, 1952), pp. 146, 156–162. By permission of the publishers.

time has placed the crisis of the eighteenth-century Empire in a much wider perspective. In this passage Vincent Harlow, the Oxford historian, brings together this new knowledge and insight to explain how the burden of Empire loomed as a critical issue by 1760.

WHILE the Empire of the British was being torn apart by revolution, Edward Gibbon sat writing his *Decline and Fall*. The domestic peace and sense of union, observed Gibbon, which characterised the ancient Empire at its height, was the natural consequence of the Roman policy of moderation and comprehensiveness. Unlike the monarchies of Asia, which exibited despotism in the centre and weakness in the extremities, the obedience of the Roman world was uniform and voluntary. The authority of the Emperors was exercised 'with the same facility on the banks of the Thames, or of the Nile, as on those of the Tiber'.

A British Empire, similarly united from Bengal to Massachusetts, founded on domestic peace, had been Chatham's hope; and yet the man whose victories had made such an Empire possible, who had been the hero of the Americans, wrote in grief a few weeks before his death in 1778 that England was engulfed in a war without the virtues, the ministers, or the resources to sustain it. 'We are taken like a covey of birds under a net.' Eleven years earlier Horace Walpole had observed with a disdainful grimace: 'Is not this magnificent? A senate regulating the eastern and western worlds at once! The Romans were triflers to us; and yet our factions and theirs are as alike as two peas.'

The resemblance was, in fact, superficial; but the virulence of English political faction steadily deepened during the later 18th Century, and its causes and consequences are interwoven with the history of Britain overseas.... The contest with Americanism and the confused groping struggle at home were interlaced.

It is against this conditioning background that we must set the problems confronting an Empire that was becoming Asian as well as trans-Atlantic. In the critical years after 1760 Britain faced tremendous issues, not only in the East, but also in the West. At the very time that she was embarking on great enterprises in the Orient she found herself under pressure to sponsor European colonisation on a continental scale. Across the Atlantic the European invasion of North America from the springboard of the Thirteen Colonies was about to begin; and the parent State had to decide between two possible lines of policy. Either she could march westward with the Americans to the Mississippi, and possibly beyond, incurring as she went ever-increasing burdens of administration and defence; or she could adopt the constrictive rôle of the French, try to lock the gates of the West against the colonists and establish a great Indian Reserve where she could monopolise the fur trade.

Under the first alternative she would be promoting the creation of a formidable, unmanageable, and therefore independent Power. In thus opening, peopling, and attempting to govern a continent, patrician England would become less and less able to maintain a controlling influence over 'democratical' Americans. By some Englishmen the growth of a great American State (or States) would be welcomed as the making of a new and staunch friend in international affairs: to men of jealous mind it would be resented as the appearance of a sinister commercial rival and as an encouragement of political ideas dangerous to the *status quo* at home. The alternative course, that of restriction, might be invidious and in the light of subsequent history short-sighted, but it appealed to those who advocated the restraint and subordination of colonies as well as to those who disbelieved in further colonisation as an economic proposition. The multiplication of defiant colonial legislatures across a wide continent was the antithesis of an Empire of Trade. Yet after the French surrender of Canada British Ministers were earnest in their desire that the American colonists should have a square deal and a fair share in the fruits of victory.

The indefinite expansion of British-American settlement across a continent was incompatible with the political and economic rigidity of the old colonial system. Before tracing the course of the controversy, it may be well, therefore, to call to mind the purpose and consequences of the system which new circumstances were requiring the British to revolutionise. One would hesitate to describe American colonial society in the 18th Century as 'democratic'; but, as Lecky puts it—'political power was incomparably more diffused, and the representative system was incomparably less corrupt than at home, and real constitutional liberty was flourishing in the English colonies when nearly all European countries and all other colonies were despotically governed'. The 17th Century builders of the American settlements, whether they were New England farmers and merchants or Virginian planter-squires, were alike the product of a revolutionary age at home. Proprietary as well as 'Royal' Colonies were granted representative institutions, and usually all freeholders qualified as electors of a lower Chamber. The Governor and Council formed an executive, responsible to the Imperial Government in London and separate from the legislative Assembly. This disconnection between the two branches of government has survived to the present day in the constitution of the United States and is frequently productive of disharmony between President and Congress.

The Assemblies in colonial times inevitably regarded the Governor with a jealous eye, for he represented an external authority in which the colonial electorate had no part. He embodied 'Prerogative', which was no less onerously felt because its power emanated from a constitutional monarch. Consequently, colonial Assemblies, instead of being content with the rôle of modern county councils, framing by-laws and implementing the legislation of a supreme authority, assumed to themselves the functions of little Westminsters. Colonial politicians imitated the great parliamentarians—Hampden, Eliot and Pym—and waged war against the Crown's representative with the time-honoured weapon of the power of the purse. The voting of supplies for essential services (often including the Governor's own salary) was made conditional upon the redress of 'grievances'. Not only did the Assemblies insist on initiating money bills and making a detailed allocation of public funds, but they also established the practice of themselves controlling expenditure at every stage—a clear invasion of the responsibility of the Governor. Gradually, by a system of Assembly committees and boards the colonial legislatures absorbed a very large part of the functions of the executive. While theoretically subordinate to the Imperial Government, the Colonies had achieved in a substantial degree *de facto* internal self-government.

This unacknowledged political devolution was co-existent with a highly centralised system of commerce. A group of virtually independent colonies were confined by the authority of the parent State within strictly defined limits as regards economic function; and these limits became less and less adequate as the colonies became larger and more complex societies. The British Empire of the 19th Century did not explode like its predecessor, because political devolution was then accompanied by economic self-determination. Yet that saving elasticity would scarcely have been achieved but for a social-industrial revolution in the parent State which obliged her to reject a unified system of Imperial commerce as inadequate for her own needs.

In the traditional view the *raison d'être* of colonies and plantations was to supplement the stock-in-trade of the national shop by furnishing products which the Mother Country could not herself produce. Thus fortified, the latter could sell more to foreign rivals and buy less from them. The 'balance of trade' would thus move in her favour, and the foreigner would be obliged to remit the difference in hard cash, which was regarded as real wealth.

Under the famous Navigation Acts and other supplementary statutes England confined to her own ports the exportation of certain colonial products. These were of two kinds: first, exotic commodities not produced at home, such as tobacco, molasses, cotton, furs and indigo, and secondly, commodities for which she was dependent (dangerously it was thought) on foreign countries, such as naval stores of all kinds and pig and bar iron. Other colonial products, and particularly those which might compete with home production, could be exported to any part of the world except to European ports north of Cape Finisterre. This proviso was designed to prevent the colonies from exchanging their 'non-enumerated' commodities for European manufactures, since the parts of Europe south of Cape Finisterre were not manufacturing countries. Colonial products on the free list were important, including all kinds of grain, fish, timber, and eventually sugar and rum. The supply of manufactured goods to the colonies was the preserve of the Mother Country.

In return for these restrictions upon their commerce the colonies received substantial advantages. Apart from protection by land and sea, they enjoyed a guaranteed market (and in some cases a monopoly) for many of their products. They benefited from the expensive system of bounties or subsidies in regard to primary commodities, the supply of which Britain was anxious to encourage from non-foreign sources. Their merchants and their shipping shared with the British on equal terms the monopoly of all tropical trades, legitimately or illegitimately exploited under the flag. For example, New England slavers had a large part in supplying from West Africa the American and West Indian plantations, taking (quite legally) their sugar and tobacco to the English market. Indeed, from the point of view of London it was a great flaw in the system that colonial merchants could thus share the advantages which ought, it was felt, to have been reserved to Englishmen in recompense for their heavy naval and military expenditure. From the strict mercantilist point of view the North American Colonies were, by and large, a disappointment. Whereas the sub-tropical products of the West Indies fitted admirably into the scheme of things, the produce of American farms and fisheries was not needed by the Mother Country either for domestic consumption or for re-export and was in general excluded from the home market. As suppliers of naval stores the northern Colonies had proved disappointing. With developing manufactures Britain indeed valued them as buyers; but the closed Imperial system did not provide them with sufficient opportunity to earn their purchases. The New England Colonies partially met the situation by feeding the British West Indies and supplying them with timber. The Islands were, however, a limited market; and as American agriculture expanded, the merchants of Boston and Philadelphia looked round for additional customers, and they found them in the foreign islands, where handsome profits were made. The indignation of Englishmen when they discovered that American shippers were bringing French and Spanish goods, such as sugar and indigo, into English ports in the guise of British colonial procedure deepened into fury when American foodstuffs gave aid and comfort to the King's enemies in the West Indies while the Empire was at war.

Even so, the Americans were often hard put to it to find the wherewithal with which to make their multifarious purchases in London. Inevitably there was a growing scarcity of coin. Prices rose steeply and colonial currencies suffered serious depreciation in relation to sterling. Accordingly, pressure of circumstances accentuated the native enterprise of American merchants of the north, and they began to drive their carrying trade as far afield as the Indian Ocean and China. On their side, the British accused the Americans (and with justice) of outrageous misconduct in breaking the rules: and the Americans, in effect, retorted (with equal justice) that the rules were impossible. And yet, as Adam Smith observed, the commercial policy of Great Britain with regard to her colonies, though dictated by the same mercantile spirit as that of other nations, had been on the whole 'less illiberal and oppressive than that of any of them'.

Both sides grumbled; but both were prospering in spite of the rules. The Americans, in fact, by dint of evasion and defiance had very largely adapted the commercial system of the Empire to suit themselves. Having so few of the raw products that were highly valued and therefore privileged in the British market, they used what they had—their foodstuffs, fish, lumber, and even their ships as counters in a far-flung and complicated system of exchange. In the process they far outgrew their allotted function of provision-merchants to West Indian planters and Newfoundland fishing fleets. In effect, they had set up a rival shop.

However disgruntled the British merchant might be at this unlooked-for competition, the British manufacturer was well aware that the American emporium made almost all its final purchases in London. The situation became really ominous from the mercantile point of view when the Americans began to insist on setting up as manufacturers. Dark visions were conjured up of Britain's technicians being persuaded into wholesale emigration and of great industrial centres springing up across the Atlantic. Official policy stiffened. Heavy penalties were imposed for inducing artisans to emigrate. The exportation of all woollen goods even from one colony to another was prohibited, as was the erection of steel furnaces and rolling mills. In 1750 heavier penalties were ordained and every effort was made to induce the Americans to export their bar and pig iron to Britain. Colonial governments frequently responded by flat defiance, officially encouraging local manufactures. They offered bounties and other inducements, such as exemption from militia musters. The making of the simpler types of iron, steel and woollen goods in the American Colonies continued to increase, and British-made tools and nails lost most of their American market; but the fear that the Thirteen Colonies would be able or would wish to develop large scale industrialisation was unjustified. These selfish prohibitions were stigmatised by Adam Smith as 'only impertinent badges of slavery imposed upon them, without any sufficient reason, by the groundless jealousy of the merchants and manufacturers of the Mother Country'. He adds, however, that when the colonies reached a more advanced state, the restraints might then become really oppressive and insupportable.

There was the rub. After the removal of the menace of France in 1760 thoughtful Americans appreciated the gigantic future that lay before them when the frontier began to move to the Mississippi and then onward to the Pacific coast. Loyalty to the Imperial connection was undermined as they contemplated that prospect as it could be, if freed from the un-American restraints and restrictions of declared Imperial policy.

During the 'wonderful year' of 1759 the leadership of Chatham had raised his countrymen to a height of power previously undreamed. Would their stature grow to their new status? Having inherited a doctrine of empire based on subordination and limitation, would they be capable of adjusting their ideas to meet imperial problems of continental dimensions? And could they achieve this feat of adjustment at a time when they themselves, as a society, were experiencing social and economic stresses, giving rise to political confusion?

14

THE APOTHEOSIS OF THE WHIG ARISTOCRACY

David Cecil

Although the Whig lords were to continue to play a central role in English political life well into the later decades of the nineteenth century, after 1760 they had lost their oligarchic control of the royal government. And yet the late eighteenth and early nineteenth century was a golden age for the Whig aristocracy, one in which their way of life achieved its summit of refinement and cultural leadership. This apotheosis of the Whig aristocracy is beautifully described in the first chapter of the biography of the nineteenth-century English statesman Melbourne by the Oxford don and scion of one of the most celebrated aristocratic families, Lord David Cecil.

THE GREAT Whig country houses of the eighteenth and early nineteenth centuries are among the most conspicuous monuments of English history. Ornate and massive, with their pedimented porticoes, their spreading balustraded wings, they dominate the landscape round them with a magnificent self-assurance. Nor are their interiors less imposing. Their colonnaded entrance halls, whence the Adam staircase sweeps up beneath a fluted dome; their cream and gilt libraries piled with sumptuous editions of the classics; their orangeries peopled with casts from the antique; their saloons hung with yellow silk, and with ceiling and doorways painted in delicate arabesque by Angelica Kauffmann—all combine to produce an extraordinary impression of culture and elegance and established power.

Yet, they are not palaces. There is something easy-going and unofficial about them. Between library and saloon one comes on little rooms, full of sporting prints and comfortable untidiness; the bedrooms upstairs are friendly with chintz and flowered wallpaper. Even the great rooms themselves, with their roomy writing-tables, their armchairs, their tables piled with albums and commonplace books, seem designed less for state occasions than for private life—for leisure and lounging, for intimate talk and desultory reading. And the portraits that glow down from the

---

FROM *Melbourne,* copyright © 1939, 1954 by David Cecil, reprinted by permission of the publishers, The Bobbs-Merrill Company, Inc., and of Constable and Company Limited, London, pp. 15–25.

walls exhibit a similar character. The gentlemen lean back in their hunting coats, the ladies stroll in their parks with spaniels snapping at the ribbons that dangle from the garden hats slung on their arms. In big and in detail these houses convey an effect of splendid naturalness. In this they are typical of the society which was their creator.

The Whig aristocracy was a unique product of English civilization. It was before all things a governing class. At a time when economic power was concentrated in the landed interest, the Whigs were among the biggest landowners: their party was in office for the greater part of the eighteenth century; during this period they possessed a large proportion of the seats in the House of Commons; they produced more ambassadors and officers of state than the rest of England put together. And they lived on a scale appropriate to their power. "A man," said one of their latest representatives, "can jog along on £40,000 a year." And jog very well they did. They possessed, most of them, a mansion in London and two or three in the country; they moved through the world attended by a vast retinue of servants, of secretaries and chaplains, of companions, librarians and general hangers-on; they never travelled but in their own carriages; they kept open house to a continuous stream of guests, whom they entertained in the baroque and lavish style approved by their contemporaries.

For the elaboration of their life was increased by the period they lived in. The eighteenth century, that accomplished age, did not believe in the artless and the austere. In its view the good man, or, as they would have phrased it, "the man of sense and taste," was he whose every activity was regulated in the light of a trained judgment and the experience of the wise in his own and former ages. From his earliest years the Whig nobleman was subjected to a careful education. He was grounded in the classics first by a tutor, then at Eton, then at the University. After this he went abroad for two years' grand tour to learn French and good manners in the best society of the Continent. His sisters learnt French and manners equally thoroughly at home; and their demeanor was further improved by a course of deportment. The Whigs' taste was in harmony with the ideal that guided their education. They learnt to admire the grand style in painting, the "correct" in letters, the Latin tradition in oratory. And in everything they paid strict attention to form. Since life to them was so secure and so pleasant, the Whig aristocrats tended to take its fundamental values very much for granted; they concentrated rather on how to live. And here again their ideal was not an artless one. Their customs, their mode of speech, their taste in decoration, their stylish stiff clothes, are alike marked by a character at once polished and precise, disciplined and florid. If one of them writes a note, it is rounded with a graceful phrase, their most extempore speeches are turned with a flourish of rotund rhetoric.

Yet—and here it is that it differs from those of similar societies on the Continent—theirs was not an unreal life, no Watteau-like paradise of exquisite trifling and fastidious idleness. For one thing it had its roots in

THE APOTHEOSIS OF THE WHIG ARISTOCRACY

the earth. Founded as their position was on landed property, the Whig aristocracy was never urban. They passed at least half the year in their country seats, and there they occupied themselves in the ordinary avocations of country life. The ladies interested themselves in their children and visited the poor; the gentlemen looked after their estates, rode to hounds and administered from the local bench justice to poachers and pilferers. Their days went by, active out-of-door, unceremonious; they wore riding-boots as often as silk stockings. Moreover, they were always in touch with the central and serious current of contemporary life. The fact that they were a governing class meant that they had to govern. The Whig lord was as often as not a minister, his eldest son an M.P., his second attached to a foreign embassy, so that their houses were alive with the effort and hurry of politics. Red Foreign Office boxes strewed the library tables; at any time of day or night a courier might come galloping up with critical news, and the minister must post off to London to attend a Cabinet meeting. He had his work in the country too. He was a landlord and magistrate, often a lord lieutenant, while every few years would come a general election when his sons, if not himself, might have to sally forth to stand on the hustings and be pelted with eggs and dead cats by the free and independent electors of the neighbouring borough. Indeed his was not a protected existence. The eighteenth century was the age of clubs; and Whig society itself was a sort of club, exclusive, but in which those who managed to achieve membership lived on equal terms—a rowdy, rough-and-tumble club, full of conflict and plain speaking, where people were expected to stand up for themselves and take and give hard knocks. At Eton the little dukes and earls cuffed and bullied one another like street urchins. As mature persons in their country homes, or in the pillared rooms of Brooks's Club, their intercourse continued more politely, yet with equal familiarity, while their House of Commons life passed in a robust atmosphere of combat and crisis and defeat. The Whigs despised the royal family; and there was certainly none of the hush and punctilio of court existence about them. Within the narrow limits of their world they were equalitarians.

Their life, in fact, was essentially a normal life, compounded of the same elements as those of general humanity, astir with the same clamour and clash and aspiration and competition as filled the streets round their august dwellings. Only, it was normal life played out on a colossal stage and with magnificent scenery and costumes. Their houses were homes, but homes with sixty bedrooms, set in grounds five miles round; they fought to keep their jobs, but the jobs were embassies and prime ministerships; their sons went to the same universities as humbler students, but were distinguished from them there by a nobleman's gold-tasselled mortar-board. When the Duke of Devonshire took up botany, he sent out a special expedition to the East Indies to search for rare plants; Lord Egremont liked pictures, so he filled a gallery with Claudes and Correggios; young Lord Palmerston was offered the Chancellorship of the Exchequer a year or two after entering Parliament.

This curiously blended life produced a curiously blended type of character. With so many opportunities for action, its interests were predominantly active. Most of the men were engaged in politics. And the women —for they lived to please the men—were political too. They listened, they sympathized, they advised; through them two statesmen might make overtures to each other, or effect a reconciliation. But politics then were not the life sentence to hard labour that in our iron age they have become. Parliament sat for only a few months in the year; and even during the session, debates did not start till the late afternoon. The Whigs had the rest of their time to devote to other things. If they were sporting, they raced and hunted; if interested in agriculture, they farmed on an ambitious scale; if artistic, they collected marbles and medals; if intellectual, they read history and philosophy; if literary, they composed compliments in verse and sonorous, platitudinous orations. But the chief of their spare time was given up to social life. They gave balls, they founded clubs, they played cards, they got up private theatricals; they cultivated friendship and every variety, platonic and less platonic, of the art of love. Their ideal was the Renaissance ideal of the whole man, whose aspiration it is to make the most of every advantage, intellectual and sensual, that life has to offer.

In practice, of course, this ideal was not so broad as it sounds. The Whigs could not escape the limitations imposed by the splendour of their circumstances. Like all aristocrats they tended to be amateurs. When life is so free and so pleasant, a man is not likely to endure the drudgery necessary to make himself really expert in any one thing. Even in those affairs of state which took up most of the Whigs' time, they troubled little with the dry details of economic theory or administrative practice. Politics to them meant, first of all, personalities and, secondly, general principles. And general principles to them were an occasion for expression rather than thought. They did not dream of questioning the fundamental canons of Whig orthodoxy. All believed in ordered liberty, low taxation and the enclosure of land; all disbelieved in despotism and democracy. Their only concern was to restate these indisputable truths in a fresh and effective fashion.

Again, their taste was a little philistine. Aristocratic taste nearly always is. Those whose ordinary course of life is splendid and satisfying find it hard to recognize the deeper value of the exercises of the solitary imagination; art to them is not the fulfilment of the soul, but an ornamental appendage to existence. Moreover, the English nobility were too much occupied with practical affairs to achieve the fullest intellectual life. They admired what was elegant, sumptuous and easy to understand: portraits that were good likenesses and pleasing decorations, architecture which appropriately housed a stately life. In books, they appreciated acute, wittily phrased observation of human nature, or noble sentiments expressed in flowing periods: Cicero, Pope, Horace, Burke. The strange and the harsh they dismissed immediately. Among contemporary authors they appreciated Jane Austen, condemned Crabbe, for the most part, as sordid and low, and neglected Blake almost entirely. If they had read him, they would not have liked him. For—it is another of their limitations—they were not spiritual. Their education did not encourage them to be; and, anyway, they found this world too absorbing to concern themselves much with the next. The bolder spirits among them were atheists. The average person accepted Christianity, but in a straightforward spirit, innocent alike of mysticism and theological exactitude.

Further, their circumstances did not encourage the virtues of self-control. Good living gave them zest; wealth gave them opportunity; and they drew themselves into their pleasures with an animal recklessness at once terrifying and exhilarating to a modern reader. The most respectable people often drank themselves under the table without shocking anyone. "Colonel Napier came in to-night as drunk as an owl," remarks Lady Sarah Napier of the staid middle-aged gentleman who was her husband. And their drinking was nothing to their gambling. Night after night they played loo and faro from early evening till the candles guttered pale in the light of the risen sun. Lord Stavordale lamented he had not been playing higher, on a night when he won £11,000 in a single hand at hazard. Georgiana, Duchess of Devonshire, cost her husband nearly £1,000,000 in card debts. Rich as they were, they often ruined themselves. The letters of the time are loud with lamentations about the duns coming in and the furniture going out. Nor was their sexual life of a kind to commend them to an austere morality. "I was afraid I was going to have the gout the other day" writes Lord Carlisle to a friend. "I believe I live too chaste: it is not a common fault with me." It was not a common fault with any of them. In fact, an unmarried man was thought unpleasantly queer if he did not keep under his protection some sprightly full-bosomed Kitty Clive or Mrs. Bellamy, whose embraces he repaid with a house in Montpelier Square, a box at the opera and a smart cabriolet in which to drive her down to Brighthelmstone for a week's amorous relaxation. Nor did he confine himself to professional ladies of pleasure. Even unmarried girls like Lady Hester Stanhope were suspected of having lovers; among married women the practice was too common to stir comment. The historian grows quite giddy as he tries to disentangle the complications of heredity consequent on the free and easy habits of the English aristocracy. The Harley family, children of the Countess of Oxford, were known as the Harleian Miscellany on account of the variety of fathers alleged to be responsible for their existence. The Duke of Devonshire had three children by the Duchess and two by Lady Elizabeth Foster, the Duchess one by Lord Grey; and most of them were brought up together in Devonshire House, each set of children with a surname of its own. "Emily, does it never strike you," writes Miss Pamela Fitzgerald in 1816, "the vices are wonderfully prolific among Whigs? There are such countless illegitimates, such a tribe of children of the mist." It is noteworthy that the author of this lively comment was a carefully brought-up young lady of the highest breeding. The free habits of these days encouraged free speech. "Comfortable girls," remarks a middle-aged lady of her growing nieces, "who like a dirty joke." And the men, as can be imagined, were a great deal freer than the women. For all their polish the Whigs were not refined people in the Victorian sense of the word.

It appears in other aspects of their lives. They could be extremely arrogant, treating their inferiors with a patrician insolence which seems to us the reverse of good breeding. Lady Catherine de Bourgh was not the caricature that an ignorant person might suppose. Fashionable young men of refined upbringing amused themselves by watching fights where the Game Chicken battered the Tutbury Pet into unconsciousness with bare and blood-stained fists. And the pamphlets, the squibs, the appalling political cartoons that lay open in the most elegant drawing-rooms show that the ladies of the day were not squeamish either.

Still, unseemly as some of its manifestations were, one must admit that there is something extremely attractive in this earthy exuberance. And, as a matter of fact, it was the inevitable corollary of their virtues. English society had the merits of its defects. Its wide scope, its strong root in the earth, gave it an astounding, an irresistible vitality. For all their dissipation there was nothing decadent about these eighteenth-century aristocrats. Their excesses came from too much life, not too little. And it was the same vitality that gave them their predominance in public life. They took on the task of directing England's destinies with the same self-confident vigour that they drank and diced. It was this vigour that made Pitt Prime Minister at twenty-four years old, that enabled the Foxites to keep the flag of liberty flying against the united public opinion of a panic-stricken nation. Nor did they let their pleasures interfere with these more serious activities. After eighteen hours of uninterrupted gambling, Charles Fox would arrive at the House of Commons to electrify his fellow members by a brilliant discourse on American taxation. Rakes and ladies of fashion intersperse their narratives of intrigue with discussions on politics, on literature, even on morals. For they were not unmoral. Their lapses came from passion, not from principle; and they are liable at any time to break out in contrite acknowledgements of guilt and artless resolutions for future improvement. Indeed it was one of the paradoxes created by their mixed composition that, though they were worldly, they were not sophisticated. Their elaborate manners masked simple reactions. Like their mode of life their characters were essentially natural: spontaneous, unintrospective, brimming over with normal feelings, love of home and family, loyalty, conviviality, desire for fame, hero-worship, patriotism. And they showed their feelings too. Happy creatures! They lived before the days of the stiff upper lip and the inhibited public-school Englishman. A manly tear stood in their eye at the story of a heroic deed; they declared their loves in a strain of flowery hyperbole. They were the more expressive from their very unself-consciousness. It never struck them that they needed to be inarticulate to appear sincere. They were equally frank about their less elevated sentiments. Eighteenth-century rationalism combined with rural common sense to make them robustly ready to face unedifying facts. And they declared their impressions with a brusque honesty, outstandingly characteristic of them. From Sir Robert Walpole, who encouraged coarse conversation on the ground that it was the only form of talk which everyone enjoyed, down to the Duke of Wellington, who described the army of his triumphs as composed of "the scum of the earth, enlisted for drink," the Augustan aristocracy, Whig and Tory alike, said what they thought with a superb disregard for public opinion. For if they were not original they were independent-minded. The conventions which bounded their lives were conventions of form only. Since they had been kings of their world from birth, they were free from the tiresome inhibitions that are induced by a sense of inferiority. Within the locked garden of their society, individuality flowered riotous and rampant. Their typical figures show up beside the muted introverts of to-day as clear-cut and idiosyncratic as characters in Dickens. They took for granted that you spoke your mind and followed your impulses. If these were odd, they were amused but not disapproving. They enjoyed eccentrics: George Selwyn, who never missed an execution, Beau Brummell, who took three hours to tie his cravat. The firm English soil in which they were rooted, the spacious freedom afforded by their place in the world, allowed personality to flourish in as many bold and fantastic shapes as it pleased.

But it was always a garden plant, a civilized growth. Whatever their eccentricities, the Whig nobles were never provincial and never uncouth. They had that effortless knowledge of the world that comes only to those who from childhood have been accustomed to move in a complex society, that delightful unassertive confidence possible only to people who have never had cause to doubt their social position. And they carried to the finest degree of cultivation those social arts which engaged so much of their time. Here we come to their outstanding distinction. They were the most agreeable society England has ever known. The character of their agreeability was of a piece with the rest of them: mundane, straightforward, a trifle philistine, largely concerned with gossip, not given to subtle analyses or flights of fancy. But it had all their vitality and all their sense of style. It was incomparably racy and spontaneous and accomplished, based solidly on a wide culture and experience, yet free to express itself in bursts of high spirits, in impulses of appreciation, in delicate movements of sentiment, in graceful compliments. For it had its grace—a virile classical grace like that of the Chippendale furniture which adorned its rooms, lending a glittering finish to its shrewd humour, its sharp-eyed observation, its vigorous disquisitions on men and things. Educated without pedantry, informal but not slipshod, polished but not precious, brilliant without fatigue, it combined in an easy perfection the charms of civilization and nature. Indeed the whole social life of the period shines down the perspective of history like some masterpiece of natural art—a prize bloom, nurtured in shelter and sunshine and the richest soil, the result of generations of breeding and blending, that spreads itself to the open sky in strength and beauty.

It was at its most characteristic in the middle of the century; it was at its most dazzling towards its close. By 1780 a new spirit was rising in the world. Ossian had taught people to admire ruins and ravines, Rousseau to examine the processes of the heart; with unpowdered heads and the ladies in simple muslin dresses, they paced the woods meditating, in Cowper-like mood, on the tender influences of nature. Though they kept the style and good sense of their fathers, their sympathies were wider. At the same time their feelings grew more refined. The hardness which had marred the previous age dwindled. Gainsborough, not Hogarth, mirrored the taste of the time; "sensibility" became a fashionable word. For a fleeting moment Whig society had a foot in two worlds and made the best of both of them. The lucid outline of eighteenth-century civilization was softened by the glow of the romantic dawn.

Dawn—but for them it was sunset. The same spirit that tinged them with their culminating glory was also an omen of their dissolution. For the days of aristocratic supremacy were numbered. By the iron laws which condition the social structure of man's existence, it could last only as long as it maintained an economic predominance. With the coming of the Industrial Revolution this predominance began to pass from the landlords to other ranks of the community. Already by the close of the century go-ahead manufacturers in the north were talking of Parliamentary reform; already, in the upper rooms of obscure London alleys, working-men met together to clamour for liberty, equality and fraternity. Within forty years of its zenith the Whig world was completely swept away. Only a few survivors lingered on to illustrate to an uncomprehending generation the charm of the past. Of these the most distinguished was William Lamb, second Viscount Melbourne.

15

BENTHAM AND THE OLD REGIME

Mary Mack

Although the first middle class movement for political reform was halted by the reaction against the French Revolution, modern historians look upon the late eighteenth century as the harbinger of the

FROM Mary Mack, *Jeremy Bentham* (New York: Columbia University Press, 1963), pp. 66, 74–81. By permission of Columbia University Press and Heinemann Educational Books Ltd.

BENTHAM AND THE OLD REGIME

ideas that were to dominate the second wave of reform after 1815. Perhaps the most powerful solvent of the Old Regime in England was the Utilitarian philosophy of Jeremy Bentham. How this Enlightenment intellectual came to be the most influential English radical theorist of his age is brought out in the following selection from Mary Mack's extremely valuable study of Bentham's early career.

EVERY TIME that Bentham walked through the Strand to Westminster Hall, he was faced with an overwhelming irony. He had been taught and he sincerely wanted to believe Dr Johnson's maxim, 'The law is the last result of human wisdom acting upon human experience for the benefit of the public.' Yet wherever he looked he saw experience running far ahead of the courts' efforts to direct it. Law is the overriding instrument of social regulation and 'the grand utility of the law is certainty'. Yet eighteenth-century English society was remaking itself with almost no help from the law. From year to year subordinate areas of social life became more and more regular and certain while the law itself became more irrational and insecure....

A mysterious cabbala, a stronghold of *laissez faire,* a lottery, a mirror of moneyed interests: these were the law. The invention of fictions, the absent-minded multiplication of statute law, the vindictive proliferation of death punishments and consequent refusal to enforce them: by these haphazard means the law met social change. But there was still another way that ruling members of society adjusted to their insecure scene. They turned their faces and pretended that a glowing false portrait was a true one. In 1765 Blackstone published the first volume of his *Commentaries on the Laws of England.* For the first time the law found a golden-tongued panegyrist and almost overnight his 'aggressive optimism' became the standard response of the upper classes. The law as Blackstone described it was remote from the facts, but people eagerly accepted his complacent picture and used it to reject any criticism of the *status quo.* When Bentham died in 1832, the law was essentially the same archaic mass it had been when he was born, for the illusions spread by the *Commentaries* still triumphed.

Blackstone and Dr Johnson upheld the *status quo* in the same way: the fictions of the constitution are very pretty things; if the actual facts are ugly, so much the worse for them. Blackstone disarmingly admitted the gap between the facts and his descriptions. He spoke, for example, of voting qualifications. Almost every free agent in England, he claimed, had a vote. In an age when votes were freely bought and sold, he knew this was nonsense and therefore added that such at least was the *spirit* if not the letter of the constitution.

The candid and intelligent reader will apply this observation to many other parts of the work before him, wherein the constitution of our laws and government are represented as nearly approaching perfection; without descending to the invidious task of pointing out such deviations and corruptions, as length of time and a loose state of national morals have too great a tendency to produce.

These sophistries never deceived Bentham, who had nothing but contempt for them. In a way Blackstone forced Bentham's career as a legal reformer upon him, for the law never had a more eloquent eulogist and therefore never more urgently needed a passionately determined critic. In Bentham it found one. In December 1763 he returned to Oxford to hear Blackstone deliver the lectures that became the *Commentaries*. He tried to take notes but was soon distracted and confused by the many fallacies. Though six years went by before he began to work out a Utilitarian rationale of law, he sensed at once how powerful an ally the enemies of reform had found. The *Commentaries* were an impressive verbal fortress; the most flagrant abuses could be and were defended behind it.

Bentham fought an unending war with Blackstone. Some of his earliest writings were critical attacks, and so were some of his last. His first published book, *A Fragment on Government* (1776), was an exhaustive scathing analysis of a few pages of the *Commentaries,* the section on 'Law Municipal' in the Introduction, where Blackstone digressed on the origin and forms of government. Bentham planned to subject all four books to the same point-by-point denunciation, but his stamina gave out long before he finished.

Nevertheless in hundreds of unpublished pages he kept up a less systematic crossfire. In *Juries,* a long work written in 1790 for the French National Assembly, he condemned Blackstone's defence of them as preventives of aristocratic monopoly in government. In *Church-Influence,* projected in 1812, he showed the unreality of Blackstone's description of governmental checks and balances, borrowed from Montesquieu. At the same time he criticized Blackstone's view of the uses of 'influence', that great eighteenth-century political oil which kept the wheels of government rolling. Finally in 1828 Bentham wrote another unfinished work, *A Familiar View of Blackstone: or say Blackstone Familiarized.* Like Archdeacon Paley, Blackstone hailed what Bentham sought to destroy, 'the glorious uncertainty of the law'.

One question arched over all Bentham's particular dissatisfactions with constitutional eulogies. If the law could be justified only by legal fictions, by deliberate falsehoods, was it worth defending? His hatred of lies, a grand passion animating his whole career, began personally, when he signed the Thirty-nine Articles, but it grew large and impersonal, when he realized that veracity is the moral foundation of good government. In the Court of King's Bench he discovered that every statement depended directly or indirectly on falsehoods and these not furtively concealed but openly flaunted. The structure of law was a tissue of fictions: to Blackstone it was beautiful; to Bentham it was rotten through and through.

As early as *A Fragment on Government* he denounced 'the pestilential breath of Fiction [which] poisons the sense of every instrument it comes near'. In 1809 his cup of disgust ran over:

'Swearing,' says one of the characters in a French drama, 'constitutes the groundwork of English *conversation:*' *lying*, he might have said without any such hyperbola, lying and nonsense compose the groundwork of English judicature. In *Rome-bred* law in general ... *fiction* is a *wart*, which here and there deforms the face of justice: in English law, fiction is a syphillis, which runs in every vein, and carries into every part of the system the principle of rottenness.

Bentham's first demand was a straightforward clear description of facts. He found none, neither in the law nor in any commentaries on it. Though he admitted that Blackstone was the 'first of all institutional writers, [who] has taught Jurisprudence to speak the language of the Scholar and the Gentleman', his very felicities of style were an added evil because they hid the horrors of the law. His merits were great relative only to other writers, for if Bentham thought some parts of the *Commentaries* untrue, he found others completely unintelligible.

A man must catch at words or catch at nothing. If something in point of sense were said, were that something false, one might sit down seriously and quietly to examine: but the great grievance is to find nothing said in so many words, and that vexation occurring at every step: so that the greatest part of what is said is just so much worse than nothing. His definitions strings of identical propositions or explaining *ignotum per ignotius*. His nomenclature like a weather cock: you never meet with the same terms twice together in the same place.

Here was one origin of Bentham's logic of the will, his central and most original gift to the history of thought. For law is an expression of will. If the language it uses is ambiguous or unsettled, it can neither be understood nor obeyed. Bentham's new logic was his response to the chaotic uncertainties of the law, and his first step was to create a dictionary of the legal vocabulary. In his logic the first subordinate end of government, after the general greatest happiness principle, is security. Bentham was dissatisfied with the law as it was and as it was said to be. What, then, ought it to be? It must first of all be made certain. It must become a logic of the will.

As such an instrument of security, what might the law do? Bentham's imagination soared and his starting-point was the contrast he saw every day on his walk to Westminster Hall. In the streets there were signs of progress and growing certainty everywhere; the courts were centres of reaction and uncertainty. The disparity seemed tragic to him. Law had carried man from barbarism and was now itself lapsing into it. There were three ages of law. In the first, law marched with public opinion and inflicted the vengeance that primitive people demanded. In the second, law moved ahead and administered punishment impersonally and impartially while the people still cried for blood. English law had long been in this second stage but now it was reverting as public opinion surged forward. The third age was yet to be, an Age of Prevention when the law should foresee and intercept the conditions that lead to crime.

In the fifty years between 1750 and 1800 the roles of law and public opinion seemed to be reversed. The cruelty of the English mob had been notorious among foreign visitors, who were shocked by the drunkenness, street fights, cock-fighting, bear-baiting, and the eight annual 'hanging holidays' when all London shops closed so that their employees could flock to Tyburn. They were, on the other hand, impressed with the fairness of English trials and the moral authority the courts exercised. By 1800, however, the people had become more civilized and the law more cruel. The law no longer led public opinion. Its authority was sapped by its uncertainty. It was Bentham's ambition to re-establish the leadership of the law over public opinion by making it certain, and to move it forward into the untried and limitless Age of Prevention.

Why is the logic of the will the centre of Bentham's thought? Why did he dedicate his entire life to law reform? It was not only that the law was in fact bad, nor that descriptions of it were so idealized, nor that he went to school for so many years to the Court of King's Bench and learned the lesson of the evils of uncertainty a thousand times over. Added to these was a vastly exalted view of legal possibilities. For Bentham, simply, the law is everything. It regulates all we do, all we can do, and all we shall do. We are what the laws have made us. The law is the human way of arranging group relationships and carrying them into the future. There is no human act that it does not directly or remotely oversee. Each of us has a name and the law guarantees it; babies are fed and the law seconds it; we are born, clothed, housed, educated, employed, married, prayed over, and buried under the eye of the law.

An acute sense of time courses through his definition. Animals live from moment to moment, unable to control their future. Law is the specifically human way of recognizing, using, and subduing time. Its victory is security.

True it is, that all laws, all political institutions, are essentially dispositions for the future; and the professed object of them is to afford a steady and permanent security to the interests of mankind.

Bentham was a radical reformer but he was never an anarchist. On the contrary. His reforms were aimed at making the uncertain more secure. He always preached obedience.

Bad as the law is, and badly as it is made, it is the tie that holds society together. Were it ten times as bad, if possible, it would still be better than none: obey it we must, or everything we hold dear would be at an end.

In an early plan for an Indian legal code, Bentham wrote a glowing exordium, 'On the Excellence of the Laws'.

The law is every man's best friend: to her under God he is indebted for every thing that is dear to him. To her he owes every thing which he enjoys: whatever protection he has for his peace of mind, his person, or his honour. To her the rich man owes his wealth; the poor man his subsistence; every man who is free, his freedom.

Law was central in Bentham's system of ideas. For an empiricist it could not have been otherwise, for eighteenth-century English life revolved in fact around the law. He observed and drew his own conclusions. He saw how intertwined the functions of government were. The judges legislated as well as judged. Not only was the Lord Chancellor Speaker of the House of Lords, but all the judges sat in the Lords. Crown counsel were usually members of Parliament, combining administrative and legislative roles. Though it was unconstitutional, judges were sometimes Cabinet members. In 1757 Lord Mansfield was Chancellor of the Exchequer for three months as well as Lord Chief Justice. Even after he surrendered the seals he remained in the Cabinet. In 1770 after Yorke, the Chancellor, committed suicide, Mansfield became Speaker of the House and the official government spokesman for some months. The large state trials were national pageants. Probably every literate person in the country disputed Warren Hastings' guilt or innocence. The English were moreover a very litigious people. Property was a national religion and the courts were its church. It is significant, too, that the courts and Parliament met in connecting buildings, and public attention focused on them together.

Bentham's political theory began with description of the law as it was. First he defined power and then he tried to locate it. He found it in the courts, exercised by the judges.

In the formation of the English system of judicature, the judicial has ever been the active,—the ordinarily-operative power; that of the monarch, with the rest of the parliament, the controuling only;...

And so it was in fact. His political theory has often been dismissed as inadequate under twentieth-century conditions. It is—but not for the faults assigned to it. To men like Schumpeter, his theory of democracy is doomed for its superficial psychology: Bentham knew nothing of the depths of mass irrationality. But his political theory did not depend on an independent psychology. It grew out of his observations in the King's Bench. If his analyses are no longer so relevant as they once were, it is because the nature and location of political power have changed. In our society the 'ordinarily-operative power' is where Bentham wanted to see it—in the legislature. The courts are no longer so active as they were when he wrote. Nor did he live in our modern administrative state where so much power is exercised quasi-judicially. He was working with facts, and they have changed. He is therefore in some ways outmoded.

In the same way, and it cannot be said often enough, most of Bentham's theories arose from his criticism of the law. Because he was appalled by the terrible practical effects of legal fictions, he developed a theory of language. Because the law tacitly assumed many propositions about human behaviour that seemed to him superficial or false, he drew up an alternative psychology and theory of ethics. The law, for example, knew little about motives. Bentham borrowed his vocabulary from Blackstone himself. Even his religious opinions were legally oriented. He was disturbed by the political control exercised by the Establishment in Doctors' Commons and the House of Lords. This is fundamental. No one who does not recognize that Bentham's thought grew out of his legal preoccupations will ever see him whole.

Even his discussions of more strictly philosophical questions were legally oriented. Sometimes they were cavalier and superficial; at other times they were profoundly interesting; but he never began them for their own sake. They always arose in a legal context. His explanations of causation, freedom of the will, belief, and probability followed upon his analysis of circumstantial evidence. How should we estimate improbability and impossibility?

We see that some events conform. Calling this conformity an 'effect', we look for a 'cause', and this we name a 'law of nature'. Laws are indeed causes of conformity. They are commands, man-made instruments of security that guarantee expectations. But they refer to certain kinds of human actions and not to the course of nature in general. By pointing out this misapplied analogy from legislation, Bentham thought he had neatly exposed some conventional philosophical issues as mere linguistic confusions.

He wrote for the judge, who must learn to evaluate intangible psychological facts as well as concrete physical ones. May a judge, he asked, rule out any psychological facts as impossible? In answer, he defined 'freedom of the will'. He admitted that the consciousness of it was something most of us feel. Therefore it is the judge's business to account for it. According to Bentham, it is the same kind of verbal cover for ignorance about psychological events as 'law of nature' is for physical events. In the same way we reify other psychological attributes: necessity, impossibility, certainty, uncertainty, probability. They are all instances:

> of a false conception of power, growing out of impotence.... The only sort of fact of which they are really and truly indicative, is the disposition of our mind ... to be persuaded, with a greater or less degree of assurance, concerning their existence or non-existence.

Bentham became a radical reformer reluctantly and conservatively. Until about 1781 he clung to the remote hope that the courts would reform themselves. As each year passed he became more and more discouraged. He first discovered the principle of utility in 1768. Until then he had been a silent rebel, for though he knew what was wrong with the law, he had as yet no better alternative to offer. Now he had an exhilarating vision and he was eager to persuade others to share it. If the first condition of happiness is security, law must fix the grounds of expectation. The vocabulary must be defined. Its expressions of will must be written and codified. All common or judge-made law must be converted into statute law. Fees should be abolished. Judgments should be made swiftly. Punishments must be certain and proportionate to crime.

16

THE HERITAGE OF WESLEY

Élie Halévy

The celebrated historian of late eighteenth- and nineteenth-century England during the second and third decades of the twentieth century was the French scholar Élie Halévy. A fervent liberal and Anglophile, Halévy sought to account for the transformation of the England of the Old Regime into the liberal society of the Victorian era, which he greatly but not uncritically admired. The first volume of his multi-volume history of nineteenth-century Britain, England in 1815, is generally regarded as his masterpiece, and a half century after its publication it remains a work of powerful insight and deep humanity. Halévy, as befitted a French philosopher, passionately believed in the determining role of ideas in modern history. He saw nineteenth-century England shaped by the critical and radical philosophy of Benthamism and by the humanitarian and puritanical spirit of Evangelical nonconformity. The following selection is Halévy's classic statement of his thesis on the far-reaching impact of the Wesleyan movement on English society. His claim that the political conservatism of the Methodists played the indispensable role in inhibiting a working-class revolution in early nineteenth-century England is a subject of historical controversy to the present day.

JOHN WESLEY, whose genius for organization equalled his genius for preaching, had founded under his despotic rule a skilfully organized "society." This society did not propose to break with the Established Church, and had no objection of principle either to her doctrine or to her discipline. In its founder's intention it constituted a species of lay third order whose mission was to complete the work of the clergy and to inspire the Church with the devotion of a genuine Christianity. Nevertheless, the Methodist societies found it an impracticable task to remain in the position Wesley had desired—persistent in fidelity to a Church which repudiated them. Methodism stimulated the growth of new sects, and the first of these was the Wesleyan body itself.

The Methodist preachers were conscious of the influential position they occupied in their local groups. Why should they resign themselves

---

FROM Élie Halévy, *England in 1815* (New York: Harcourt, Brace & World, Inc., 1924), pp. 359–372. By permission of Ernest Benn Limited, London.

to accept a position of humiliating inferiority to the Anglican clergymen who ignored or insulted them? Why should they not claim the same ecclesiastical privileges as were enjoyed by the Presbyterian, Independent and Baptist ministers around them? Why should they bind themselves never to administer the Sacraments to the faithful, never to hold their meetings during the hours when the vicar was gabbling through the Anglican service in the parish church? And around and beneath the preachers their lay adherents made their complaints heard. In the same village they saw Baptists or Independents treat their ministers as their agents and exercise a constant control over their ministers? Why should they accept in the Methodist body the strictly subordinate position that had been imposed upon them by John Wesley, who was personally inclined to the principle of authority and sincerely attached to the hierarchical tenets of Anglicanism? The leaders of the movement hesitated. Disturbed by the violence and persistence of these demands they were nevertheless unable to arrive at an immediate conclusion as to the degree to which the interests of Methodism demanded concessions to the wishes whether of the ministers or of the laity.

To renounce their undecided attitude and to break openly with the Establishment was to sacrifice numerous advantages. The Wesleyan preacher did not demand from his convert a change of creed or church, but merely that he should learn under his spiritual direction a heartier love and a more faithful practice of the religion which he had professed from childhood. He did not, therefore, arouse at the outset of his work the suspicions which would have been excited had he been a minister of one of the old historic sects. But, on the other hand, to refuse the breach was to incur another danger. Nothing would then prevent Methodists determined to sever connexion with Anglicanism from leaving the Wesleyan body and joining the Independents or Baptists. Indeed this was actually happening, and if it became general would reduce Methodism to a recruiting ground for Dissent. First John Wesley himself, then his successors, were driven to adopt a policy of opportunism. They yielded to the advocates of rupture where concession was inevitable, in principle as little as possible, but every day more and more. The rules continued to lay down "that the Sacrament of the Supper shall not be administered in the chapels." But they admitted exceptions in cases where the central or local authorities of the "Society" should sanction it by a majority. It was only in certain cases clearly defined that the rules permitted the Methodist service during church hours, in direct rivalry with the service of the Establishment. But these cases were numerous. To render concurrent services licit it was enough that the parson was a man of notoriously immoral life, that he preached Arianism, Socinianism or any other doctrine equally pernicious, that the number of churches in the neighbourhood was insufficient for the population, that there was no church within a radius of two or three miles; or even that the authorities of the local group had decided by a majority of votes that such was the will of the people and would not result in a split within the society.

A constantly increasing number of societies availed themselves of the permissions granted by the rules. Wesleyan Methodism formed itself into a sect, and with this new sect a new principle of organization made its appearance in the history of English Dissent. The Wesleyans expressly rejected the congregational system. To employ the formula of their own devising, they were connexionalists. They did not hold that each local society could be considered an independent church. All the local societies formed together one single "connexion" strongly centralized. Neither did they hold—for indeed the two principles are mutually inseparable—that the ministers are merely the elected servants of their congregations. The Wesleyan minister has received from God the gift of converting souls, and his preaching has proved his effective possession of that gift. The faithful cannot, therefore, by their votes for or against him confer or take away this miraculous endowment. And if, to discriminate between the truly inspired and the imposter, preachers must be subject to a controlling authority, that control can only be exercised by other inspired preachers, by those possessed of the mission to direct souls, not by those who have themselves need of direction.

The true unit of the Wesleyan organization was not the society but the circuit constituted by the union of a number of societies. At the head of the circuit were placed under the authority of a superintendent two or three travelling or itinerant preachers who within the circuit journeyed from one society to another, detached from any, supervising all and preaching as the representatives of a higher authority. They were not even allowed to remain attached for any length of time to the same circuit. They could be moved yearly, they must be moved at least every second year. Thus the foundation-stone of the Wesleyan organization was the systematic denial of local autonomy. To be sure, if a local society built a chapel, it must inevitably possess the appointment of the lay trustees. But every precaution was taken to preclude the possibility that these trustees would make themselves owners of the chapel and revolt against the corporation which had entrusted it to them. And further, every local society possessed its special preachers, the local preachers, laymen who after their Sunday sermons devoted the remainder of the week to their professional occupations in field, shop or factory. It possessed also its lay treasurers, the stewards. And it was divided into little groups for the mutual edification of their members called classes, and each class had its head, the leader. But the class leaders, stewards and local preachers were chosen not by the congregation but by the superintendent of the circuit, and only after a long series of tests could a local preacher be promoted to the rank of a professional preacher. When every three months the circuit meeting was held, only the stewards and the itinerant preachers took part in it. Neither class leaders nor local preachers were admitted. Nor was the individual congregation or circuit free to fix the stipend of the preacher. In virtue of his position as a preacher of the Methodist connexion, he had the right to £12 a year for himself, £12 for the support of his wife, £4 for each of his children, £6 for the board and wages of a servant. If a circuit were too poor to pay its preachers the connexion must make up the deficiency. To conclude, the entire system represented the sacrifice of freedom to organization. Of all the Free Churches the Wesleyan was the least free.

Several circuits constituted a district, and the totality of districts was the connexion. How, then, was the central government of the sect organized? The central government was John Wesley himself, who, while he lived, exercised an undivided and despotic rule. He had thus created in the Methodist connexion a tradition of clerical authority not to be easily destroyed. He had even desired, when he established his first societies, to debar his lay helpers from preaching and from the administration of the Sacraments. The force of circumstances was too strong for these scruples of Anglican clericalism. In the end he had claimed for himself the episcopal power of Ordination. He had consecrated ministers to work in Scotland, in America, even in England itself. He had actually carried his pretensions so far as to consecrate Methodist bishops in America, though himself only a priest. But who after his death would succeed to his authority? In 1784 he drew up a list of a hundred preachers who became the legal representatives of the entire body, in whose name the trustees held the buildings of the sect. Henceforward these men constituted as of right the Conference summoned every year by Wesley to deliberate on Wesleyan affairs. After Wesley's death what form of government would this senate of preachers, the Legal Hundred, establish?

They could have replaced Wesley by the government of a few preachers permanently invested with superior authority, and thus have instituted a Methodist episcopate. Dr. Coke, an Anglican clergyman on whom Wesley had conferred authority to exercise episcopal functions in America, and Mather, whom Wesley had ordained priest, were advocates of this policy. It satisfied their personal ambition, for they hoped to become the heads of the new hierarchy. But the jealousy of their colleagues proved an insurmountable obstacle. Neither was chosen president of the Conference for the year following Wesley's death, and lest the president should degenerate into a dictator his office was made annual. On the proposal of Mather and Coke the Conference agreed to organize under the name of districts administrative areas comprising several circuits, but it refused to place these districts under superintendents. Methodism should have no bishops. At the same time loud protests were raised against the composition of the Conference. The choice of the original hundred members had already been a source of bitter resentment among the excluded preachers, although Conference then exercised merely advisory functions, all authority being in the hands of Wesley. Now, however, when Conference had assumed all the power, executive and judicial, formerly exercised by Wesley their discontent came to a head. Concessions were made. Henceforward deceased members would no longer be replaced by cooptation, but vacant seats would belong of right to the older ministers in order of seniority. The year 1814 witnessed a further innovation. Election by the body of preachers would henceforward be a factor in the composition of the Conference. To this extent the equalitarian principle of the collective pastorate triumphed over the principle of episcopacy or of government by a coopted assembly. But Conference continued to exercise an uncontrolled authority, and the laity were permanently excluded from all share either in its deliberations or in the choice of its members.

Thus the rude and fanatical preachers that Wesley had enlisted beneath his banner, not only continued to make converts after his death—there were 231,000 Wesleyan Methodists in 1813—but created a skilful organization whose hierarchic character was in some respects almost Anglican, and had been previously unknown among the Dissenting bodies. In matters of ritual also the Wesleyans were far less prejudiced against the practices of the Established Church than the members of the older denominations. They encouraged hymn singing against which the long-rooted prejudice of the Dissenters had persisted throughout the previous half-century. They would soon introduce organs into their chapels. Wesley had prescribed for use in their services either the Anglican liturgy or an abridgment of it drawn up by himself. In short, the Methodist connexion adopted a position intermediate between the Establishment and the older Nonconformist bodies. It thus constituted a transition between the former and the latter, which became the more insensible when new sects arose in turn from Wesleyanism and occupied the space between the Connexion and the original sects.

It was on doctrinal grounds that a section of the Methodists broke with the Wesleyan body. Wesley had adopted the paradoxical position of preaching justification by faith while rejecting the complementary doctrine of predestination. Whitefield had refused to divorce the two doctrines, and the Calvinism of his followers opposed the Arminianism of the Wesleyans. In 1811 in Wales Thomas Charles severed the last links connecting the Calvinistic Methodists with the Anglican Church. This secession possesses a peculiar importance in the religious history of Britain; for it has been estimated that only one-third of the inhabitants of Wales remained in the Establishment.

But more usually it was a question of organization that gave rise to quarrels among the Methodists. On Wesley's death a preacher named Alexander Kilham demanded a democratic reform of the Wesleyan constitution. Expelled from the society, he founded in 1797 the New Methodist Connexion, in which the lay members of the local congregations played an active part in the conduct of worship and in the choice of ministers. In all the assemblies of the sect—Circuit Meeting, District Meeting, Annual Conference—ministers and laymen sat in equal numbers.

In 1806, and the years following, two Staffordshire local preachers—William Clowes, a potter, and Hugh Bourne, a carpenter—organized in imitation of the American Methodists large religious meetings in the open air, known as camp meetings. These lasted for several days and inflamed to the highest pitch the imagination of the pious crowds which frequented them. The new Wesleyan bureaucracy met these camp meetings with the same opposition which the Church of England had formerly displayed to the open-air preaching of Wesley and Whitefield. The "Cloweses" formed themselves into a separate sect which in 1812 adopted the official title of Primitive Methodists. It continued to be governed by a central Conference; but the Conference was elected by the laity, and two-thirds of its members were laymen. Unlike the Wesleyan Conference, it did not assure a fixed stipend to all its ministers. Each circuit might fix what stipend it pleased. Nor did the conference hold itself responsible for debts contracted by a circuit for the construction of chapels. Yet another Methodist sect, the Bible Christians, was formed in 1818 on lines practically identical with Kilham's New Connexion. These three new groups were examples of a type of constitution intermediate between the connexionalism of the Wesleyans and the congregationalism of the Independents and Baptists, and akin to the federal and representative Presbyterian system, as it had been devised by Calvin.

The very existence of these new Methodist sects is a proof that the influence of Wesleyan ideas was not confined to the 200,000 members of official Wesleyanism. Wesleyan influence spread, in fact, even further than these sects, and penetrated all the Dissenting bodies; and everywhere it was a spirit of reaction against the rationalism and republicanism of the old Nonconformity. The dissenting sects of rationalistic tendency were decaying. When the French Revolution broke out, they were swamped by doctrines frankly anti-Christian. Paine, whose *Rights of Man* enjoyed an amazing popularity, was a Deist. The orthodox Utilitarian school, which from 1807 grew up in London around Bentham and James Mill, was radically irreligious, and endeavoured to prove that belief in God was not only a childish superstition but a dangerous error. Carlisle and Hone had inaugurated, or were on the verge of inaugurating, an atheistic propaganda of a more popular and more vulgar type. Orthodox Protestants accused liberal Dissent, Wide Dissent as it was called, of paving the way to irreligion pure and simple; and they regained lost ground among the sects.

The history of the Dissenting bodies at the opening of the 19th century is the relation of an uninterrupted series of victories won by the Independents and Baptists who had remained orthodox over the Presbyterians who had gone over to Unitarianism. A century earlier the Presbyterians had been the most important of the three old denominations. According to some calculations their numbers even equalled the combined total of Independents and Baptists. According to another reckoning they composed by themselves two-thirds of Dissent. Now they barely amounted to a twentieth part. In every county the same spectacle was witnessed. The Arian or Socinian chapels are empty, often no longer used for worship; then the Independents appear on the scene, obtain from the negligent trustees possession of the buildings, preach orthodox Christianity; and once more large congregations fill the chapels. Thus it came about that in London where formerly the Presbyterians had been particularly numerous, in 1796 there were only fifteen Presbyterian congregations as against thirty-three Independent and eighteen Baptist, not to mention thirty Methodist congregations. In Devonshire, the cradle of Arianism, twenty Presbyterian meeting-houses had been closed. In Hampshire, which had contained forty Presbyterian chapels in 1729, only two were left in 1812, and even these two were destined to disappear within the next fifteen years.

The doom which befell the chapels where the liberal ministers preached befell also the seminaries, the Academies, which had been the boast of Latitudinarian Nonconformity. One by one they disappeared, and their place was taken by new schools of another type, orthodox and pietist. Two heterodox teachers, Dr. Kippis and Dr. Rees, taught at the Hoxton Academy. In consequence the school was compelled to close in 1785. It was united with the Academy at Daventry, where Belsham taught. But in 1789 Belsham went over to Unitarianism and resigned his position. Then the Daventry Academy was united with the Academy at Northampton, which the presence of Doddridge had once rendered famous. But this too was infected by Socinianism and in turn was closed in 1798 by the trustees. During these years Kippis and Rees were teaching at Hackney College, founded in 1786, where Belsham shortly joined them. After an existence of only ten years the College was closed. The unpopularity of French ideas, lack of discipline, financial mismanagement had combined to destroy it. The year 1811 witnessed a new attempt to found a Unitarian Academy. After seven years' existence the new school also disappeared. Meanwhile at Hoxton, Hackney and Hitchin liberal Academies were replaced by new foundations where the education was orthodox and Evangelical, and these flourished. The same thing happened in the South-West of England. The Arian Academies of Exeter and Taunton were closed. Rival schools, founded by the Independents at Ottery St. Mary, by the Baptists at Bristol, prospered. In the North the Warrington Academy founded by Priestley, after moving in succession to Manchester and York, was finally closed.

Meanwhile the Baptists founded in Bradford, in 1804, the Northern Baptist Education Society. In twenty years' time its premises needed to be enlarged. In Wales, when the Caermarthen Academy went over to Arianism, the Independents withdrew their support and founded an Academy at Abergavenny. But the new impetus which was pushing Independents and Baptists into victory had been imparted to them by the Methodists. The Methodist sects sent them a constant flow of recruits, and if they did not, like Wesley, repudiate Calvinism, and if it was from Whitefield's Calvinist connexion that they drew the majority of their converts, nevertheless their Protestantism was as remote from the cut-and-dried Calvinism of old-fashioned orthodoxy as from the semi-rationalism of a Priestley. There was no systematical theology, no discussion of doctrinal niceties. The Dissenters drew their members from the lower classes of the population; they were small shopkeepers, small farmers, artisans, agricultural labourers. The example of Methodism had led to the growth of private religious gatherings for the mutual edification of their members. In these a young man could distinguish himself by the fervour of his exhortation, or by the charm of his eloquence. More often than the others he would be called upon to pray or to preach. Admirers and friends would urge him to abandon his trade and enter the professional ministry. He might perhaps scarcely know how to read or write, and would enter one of the Academies of his denomination. This pompous designation concealed a very modest reality. For a low fee a minister took a few boarders, and taught them in the intervals of his preaching. His pupils assisted him and went out to preach in the neighbourhood. In their spare time they learnt Grammar and Spelling. Greek, Hebrew and Theology were out of the question. Dissenters of the old school sorrowfully admitted the intellectual deterioration of their ministers and congregations. "Now, when a vacancy happens, the great object is to find a man of popular talents, who will bring an increase of hearers to their meeting houses" ... "a man who can make the most noise, or tell the most entertaining stories, or talk the most fluently without notes and without study."

The new preachers were illiterate enthusiasts, versed only in the methods of that popular oratory which was best fitted to awaken in the assembled crowd a "revival" of religious feeling, an emotional or "experimental" Christianity. Man bears in the depths of his soul a primitive superstition, which neither science nor abstract theology can satisfy. The notorious Joanna Southcott would be the talk of London for months, because she had promised at the age of sixty-five to become the mother of a son of God. Evangelical Nonconformity provided this appetite for the marvellous with a more spiritual food. They had no desire to overawe their hearers by physical miracles. Their aim was to convert souls. Nevertheless, among the most ignorant classes and in the wilder districts their preaching often produced strange effects. In Wales the members of the sect of "Jumpers," an offspring of Methodist revivalism, threw themselves flat on the ground when the sermon began. Soon they felt themselves inspired from Above, rose to their feet and jumped in time. An outbreak of collective hysteria had begun which might continue for hours on end.

The influence exerted by the religious revival of the 18th century on the outlook of the old Nonconformist sects was manifested in yet other ways. From the beginning the Independent churches had made attempts to form local associations of greater or less extent without violating the principle of autonomy proper to their constitution. But these associations were loose in the extreme and never included all the churches of the denomination even in the district where they had been formed. They possessed no permanent character and amounted to nothing more than annual meetings for prayer in common and the exchange of religious "experiences" between the ministers. They had possessed no power to legislate for their constituent churches; indeed the statutes of the associations expressly prohibited any attempt of this kind. And among the Congregationalists even these Associations had practically ceased to exist by the middle of the 18th century. Among the Baptists, where they had continued to be a regular feature of the organization of the sect, they were viewed with suspicion, even by those who consented to take part in them. Nor did their distrust tend to disappear. "We confess, brethren, we entered this association with great jealousy and caution; for although we clearly saw the practice of associating, consulting and mutually assisting in the purest ages of Christianity, yet we could not but recollect that such associations were in the end productive of the great anti-christian apostasy, an apostasy so fatal to the civil and religious liberties of mankind, and particularly to those of the brave old Puritans and Nonconformists, that the very words synod and session, council and canon, yet make both the ears of a sound Protestant Dissenter to tingle."

But under the influence of Methodism this spirit of almost anarchic autonomy was soon to lose much of its primitive power. If Methodism made such rapid strides, if at each of their Annual Conferences the Wesleyans could publish statistics proving the enormous growth of their sects, this was obviously to a large extent the result of their superior organization. The itinerant preacher was obliged to a continual journey between the towns and villages of his circuit, and must visit not those places only in which congregations had already been established, but also, and indeed it was his first duty, those places where no Methodist had as yet preached. The Independent minister was, on the other hand, the representative of the congregation which had appointed him. To that congregation he belonged. Only with its authorization might he occasionally preach elsewhere. Thus the principle of absolute autonomy was a barrier to the progress of the sects which had adopted it. If missions were to be organized for the conversion of unbelievers, it was indispensable that the congregations should combine and send out the missionaries at their joint expense. And again, if the precarious financial position of the Nonconformist ministers was only too evident, here also the Methodist practice suggested the remedy. Why should not several congregations combine to form a common fund for the assistance of superannuated ministers, their widows and their children? Why should they not form associations which should do more than merely provide opportunities for mutual edification, which should centralize the finances of the sect?

The Congregationalists were the first to give way. In Lancashire in 1786 they founded a county association whose objects were to organize a system of itinerant ministers, and to secure their local ministers against indigence. The association prospered, and its statutes served as a model to the associations which within a few years had sprung up in all or almost all the counties of England. The Baptists followed the example of the Congregationalists. In June 1796 they organized an itinerant tour in Cornwall, in September of the same year a permanent system of itinerancy in Essex, and in the following year they established in London a central society for the encouragement and support of itinerant preaching. Already in 1784 they had created a central committee, the Baptist Case Committee, to assist the construction of chapels in every part of the kingdom. In 1816 they would found a Beneficiary Society for the Relief of Superannuated Baptist Ministers. A more momentous step followed in 1812. After a series of difficult negotiations sixty churches united to form a Baptist Union which embraced the entire kingdom, and although eighteen years had yet to pass before the Congregationalists would form a similar federation, the preliminary negotiations had already been set on foot. To be sure these associations preserved a voluntary character, individual churches were always free to join or to refuse adherence, and the Associations had no power to bind by their majority vote the local congregations. But this leaves unaffected the fact that the necessity of meeting Methodist competition had won Congregationalists and Baptists to the warm support of a systematic organization hitherto unknown among them. They were not, indeed, converted to the connexionalist type of organization which prevailed among the Wesleyans; but they were tending towards a system akin to the old Presbyterian or Calvinist model, and to the system of those dissident Wesleyan sects described above.

Finally, for the reasons already mentioned, the progress of Methodism was tending to render the Protestant Dissenters political conservatives. As their interest in theological polemics had cooled, they had lost their old taste for discussion, their former love of argument. And as their prejudices in favour of ecclesiastical autonomy weakened, their individualism in politics weakened simultaneously. Intermediate between the sects in the strict sense of the word and the Established Church, Methodism filled the gap between these rival bodies. The Methodists, and especially the Wesleyan Methodists, although in fact Nonconformists, refused to regard themselves as entirely cut off from the Anglican Church. The members of the connexion admitted an obligation to communicate according to the Anglican rite when unable to communicate in one of their chapels; and their ministry claimed to be not the enemy but the assistant or the locum tenens of a clergy which neglected its duties. And the other sects were infected with the same spirit. During the first fifteen years of the 19th century only isolated and eccentric individuals among the Nonconformists demanded either a reform of the constitution of the national Church in conformity with their ideas, or disestablishment and equal rights for all denominations.

But for all this the division was not less clearly marked than formerly between the social classes from which the Establishment and the sects respectively derived their adherents. In some respects we might even say that the line of demarcation was drawn more rigidly than ever before. From the beginning Nonconformity had been the religion of the middle class and particularly of the lower middle class. Nevertheless, in the 18th century Dissenters sat in the House of Lords, and on occasion boys of noble family had received their education in the seminaries conducted by Nonconformist ministers. Now both these things had become an impossibility. Nor was the number of wealthy Nonconformist merchants on the increase. In the normal course the more wealthy Dissenters went over to the Church of England. If a successful man of business wished to enter the governing class, to entertain at his country seat the clergy or the gentry of the neighbourhood, to obtain a title or a position in the Civil Service, he must not be a Dissenter. The wealthy Dissenter, therefore, was only too ready to yield to the entreaties of his wife, herself perhaps the daughter of an "episcopalian" family, or of his sons, who were eager to see the family enjoy a social position in keeping with its wealth and with the education they had received. He would seize the first opportunity to pick a quarrel with his pastor or with one of the influential members of the congregation. He thus escaped the moral supervision exercised by the fellow members of his congregation, and which he had so often found galling, and attended the worship of the Established Church where there was no obligation of religious zeal, and where the squire was his fellow worshipper. Puritan nonconformity thus tended to become a transitional creed, a stage in the history of an English family. The unskilled labourer becomes in turn a skilled workman, an artisan, the head of a small business, a business man possessed of a modest capital, and as he rises out of the barbarism in which the working class was plunged, he becomes a Nonconformist. If he himself rises still higher on the social ladder, or if his children rise after his death, he or they go over to the Church of England.

Nor was there the slightest difficulty in effecting the transition from one form of religion to another. The constitution of the Wesleyan body rendered the transition imperceptible. And what is more characteristic of the new spirit in Dissent is its acceptance of this subordinate position. The middle-class Nonconformist was content to be despised by the members of a Church which his own family might some day enter. He compensated himself by indulging an even deeper contempt for the common people of the fields or factories from whom his family had emerged.

Why was it that of all the countries of Europe England has been the most free from revolutions, violent crises and sudden changes? We have sought in vain to find the explanation by an analysis of her political institutions and economic organization. Her political institutions were such that society might easily have lapsed into anarchy had there existed in England a bourgeoisie animated by the spirit of revolution. And a system of economic production that was in fact totally without organization of any kind would have plunged the kingdom into violent revolution had the working classes found in the middle class leaders to provide it with a definite ideal, a creed, a practical programme. But the élite of the working class, the hard-working and capable bourgeois, had been imbued by the Evangelical movement with a spirit from which the established order had nothing to fear.

No doubt the English Nonconformists continued to oppose any movement towards bureaucracy. Without freedom of association they could not exist. But for all their freedom of theological difference the sects agreed among themselves and with the national authorities to impose on the nation a rigorous ethical conformity and at least an outward respect for the Christian social order. With their passion for liberty they united a devotion to order, and the latter finally predominated. Hence freedom of association proved in the end the restriction of individual freedom and the authority of custom replaced and almost superseded the authority of law. And this is modern England. On the Continent the leaders of the English labour movement are sometimes blamed for their middle-class morality and want of imagination, at others praised for their solid virtue and capacity for organization. Perhaps these qualities and defects are inseparable; in any case they derive from a common origin. The majority of the leaders of the great trade-union movement that would arise in England within a few years of 1815 will belong to the Nonconformist sects. They will often be local preachers, that is practically speaking ministers. Their spiritual ancestors were the founders of Methodism. In the vast work of social organization which is one of the dominant characteristics of nineteenth-century England, it would be difficult to overestimate the part played by the Wesleyan revival.

17

THE FORMING OF WORKING CLASS CONSCIOUSNESS

E. P. Thompson

The most remarkable achievement of the new generation of neo-Marxist scholars of the 1960's is E. P. Thompson's study of revolutionary movements among English industrial workers in the era of the French Revolution and the consequences of this class struggle for modern British society. The following selection presents the general thesis of Thompson's angry and persuasive book.

WE MUST... break down the Chinese walls which divide the 18th from the 19th century, and the history of working-class agitation from the cultural and intellectual history of the rest of the nation. Too often events in England in the 1790s are seen only as a reflected glow from the storming of the Bastille. But the elements precipitated by the

---

FROM *The Making of the English Working Class*, by E. P. Thompson. © Copyright 1963 by E. P. Thompson. Reprinted by permission of Pantheon Books, A Division of Random House, Inc. By permission of Victor Gollancz, Ltd., London.

French example—the Dissenting and libertarian traditions—reach far back into English history. And the agitation of the 1790s, although it lasted only five years (1792-6) was extraordinarily intensive and far-reaching. It altered the sub-political attitudes of the people, affected class alignments, and initiated traditions which stretch forward into the present century. It was not an agitation about France, although French events both inspired and bedevilled it. It was an English agitation, of impressive dimensions, for an English democracy....

In the 1790s something like an "English Revolution" took place, of profound importance in shaping the consciousness of the post-war working class. It is true that the revolutionary impulse was strangled in its infancy; and the first consequence was that of bitterness and despair. The counter-revolutionary panic of the ruling classes expressed itself in every part of social life; in attitudes to trade unionism, to the education of the people, to their sports and manners, to their publications and societies, and their political rights. And the reflex of despair among the common people can be seen, during the war years, in the inverted chiliasm of the Southcottians and the new Methodist revival. In the decades after 1795 there was a profound alienation between classes in Britain, and working people were thrust into a state of *apartheid* whose effects—in the niceties of social and educational discrimination—can be felt to this day. England differed from other European nations in this, that the flood-tide of counter-revolutionary feeling and discipline coincided with the flood-tide of the Industrial Revolution; as new techniques and forms of industrial organisation advanced, so political and social rights receded. The "natural" alliance between an impatient radically-minded industrial bourgeoisie and a formative proletariat was broken as soon as it was formed. The ferment among the industrialists and the wealthy Dissenting tradesmen of Birmingham and the northern industrial towns belongs in the main to 1791 and 1792; the peak of "disaffection" among artisans and wage-earners in London, Norwich and Sheffield —whether caused by Jacobin agitation or by starvation—belongs to 1795. Only for a few months in 1792 do the two coincide; and after the September massacres all but a small minority of the manufacturers had been frightened from the cause of reform. If there was no revolution in England in the 1790s it was not because of Methodism but because the only alliance strong enough to effect it fell apart; after 1792 there were no Girondins to open the doors through which the Jacobins might come. If men like Wedgwood, Boulton and Wilkinson had acted together with men like Hardy, Place and Binns—and if Wyvill's small gentry had acted with *them*—then Pitt (or Fox) would have been forced to grant a large instalment of reform. But the French Revolution *consolidated* Old Corruption by uniting landowners and manufacturers in a common panic; and the popular societies were too weak and too inexperienced to effect either revolution or reform on their own.

Something of this was felt even by Thelwall, when he visited Sheffield in 1796. He rejoiced at the intelligence and political awareness of the

Sheffield *"Sanscullotterie"*. "But it is a body without a head. They have unfortunately no leader." While several people "of considerable property and influence... *think* with them", none had the courage to take their part:

> If any three or four persons of weight and pecuniary consequence in that place, would but take these honest, intelligent manufacturers and their cause fairly and publicly by the hand (as persons of that description... have done in Norwich), in Sheffield, as in Norwich, the petty tyranny of provincial persecution would presently be at an end....

Nor was this a symptom of Jacobin apostasy on Thelwall's part. He was faced, in 1796, with a real dilemma: on the one hand, the reformist paternalism which when he met it in practice—as in the case of Gurney at Norwich—he disliked; on the other hand, the exposure of plebeian reformers to victimisation on a scale which was destroying the movement or driving it underground.

Moreover, the movement badly needed the intellectual resources of those men of the educated middle class, some of whom had been most afflicted by revolutionary disenchantment. It had early lost, through forcible and voluntary emigration, two of its most able propagandists and organisers, Gerrald and Cooper. It could not survive for ever on *Rights of Man*, and the imitation of French forms, or in Roman togas and Saxon smocks. But at its peak, in 1795, the movement was scarcely of four years' growth; its thinking had to be done in the press of organisation, amongst alarms and accusations of treason, with supporters defaulting and with Robespierre punctuating the florid periods of their Addresses with the more taciturn guillotine. Thelwall's lectures were thought out on his feet, to an audience which always included one of His Majesty's informers. His best work (significantly) was not done until the comparative calm of 1796 when the movement began to fall apart. It is scarcely surprising that the English Jacobins were guilty of immaturities and suffered through their inexperience, and that many of their speakers made themselves look foolish by their exaggerated postures.

So far, it would seem, it is a record of frustration and of failure. But the experience had another, and an altogether more positive side. Not one, but many, traditions find their origin in these years. There is the intellectual tradition of Godwin and of Mary Wollstonecraft, which Shelley was to reaffirm. There is the tradition of Deism and of free-thought; the Wars had scarcely ended before Richard Carlile commenced the re-publication of all of Paine's works. There is the tradition of the advanced Unitarians and "free-thinking Christians", carried forward by such men as Benjamin Flower and William Frend, to the *Monthly Depository* of W. J. Fox. There is the tradition of Place, and of the sober, constitutionally-minded tradesmen and artisans (some of whom, like Hardy, Galloway and Place himself later prospered as small or large employers) who re-emerged in the Westminster Election of 1807, in support of Tooke's disciple Sir Francis Burdett, and who from that time remained in active association.

These traditions are embodied not only in ideas but in persons. While some Jacobins retired and others—John Gales, Thomas Cooper, "Citizen Lee", John Binns, Daniel Isaac Eaton and many others—emigrated to America, others watched for every new opportunity to re-open the propaganda. John Gale Jones and John Frost were members of London debating clubs during the Wars, where they influenced a younger Radical generation; and Jones remained prominent in London Radical circles until the 1820s. And in many provincial centres the same continuity can be witnessed. Few centres can boast a record as long as that of George Bown of Leicester, who was Secretary of its Constitutional Society in 1792, was arrested in 1794, and who was still writing as an advocate of "physical force" Chartism in 1848. But in many towns like-minded tradesmen and artisans, opponents of the Wars, continued to meet together. The great engraver, Thomas Bewick, recalls the "set of staunch advocates for the liberties of mankind", who met in Newcastle at the "Blue Bell", the "Unicorn", and the News Room. These were "men of sense and consequence", "tradesmen of the genteel sort", "bankers' clerks, artisans, and agents". Bewick's particular associates included a shoemaker, a builder, a founder, a white-smith, an editor, a fencing-master, a radical gentleman, and several actors. All were united in condemnation of the war and of its social consequences:

The shipping interest wallowed in riches; the gentry whirled about in aristocratic pomposity, they forgot what their demeanour and good, kind, behaviour used to be to those in inferior stations of life; and seemed now far too often to look upon them like dirt. The character of the farmers was also changed. They acted the gentleman very awkwardly, and could not, in these times, drink anything but wine.... When these upstart gentlemen left the market, they were ready to ride over all they met... on the way; but this was as nothing compared to the pride and folly which took possession of their empty or fume-charged heads, when they got dressed in scarlet... and were called "yeomanry cavalry".... Not so with the industrious labourer. His privations were great....

If many among the small masters, clerks, and tradesmen felt hostility to the gentry, capitalists, and large farmers, and sympathy with the "industrious labourer" (and this is an extremely important feature of Radical consciousness for fifty years after 1795), nevertheless they were, like the Leeds tradesmen, intimidated by "Aristocratic influence". Even Bewick, with his puritanical zeal, was careful during the Wars to associate only with those who might "set the example of propriety of conduct to those of a more violent turn of mind", and whose indignation with "the political enormities of the times" was kept "within bounds". Hence, the plebeian Jacobins were isolated and driven back upon themselves, and forced to discover means of independent quasi-legal or underground organisation. (In Bewick's Newcastle, scores of tavern friendly societies were formed during the Wars, many of which were undoubtedly covers for trade union activity, in which former Jacobins contributed to the "warm debate and violent language" of club meetings.) Isolated from other classes, radical mechanics, artisans and labourers had perforce to nourish traditions and forms of organisation of their own. So that, while the years 1791–5 provided the democratic impulse, it was in the repression years that we can speak of a distinct "working-class consciousness" maturing.

Even in the darkest war years the democratic impulse can still be felt at work beneath the surface. It contributed an affirmation of *rights,* a glimpse of a plebeian Millennium, which was never extinguished. The Combination Acts (1799–1800) served only to bring illegal Jacobin and trade union strands closer together. Even beneath the fever of the "invasion" years, new ideas and new forms of organisation continue to ferment. There is a radical alteration in the sub-political attitudes of the people to which the experiences of tens of thousands of unwilling soldiers contributed. By 1811 we can witness the simultaneous emergence of a new popular Radicalism and of a newly-militant trade unionism. In part, this was the product of new experiences, in part it was the inevitable response to the years of reaction: "*I have not forgot the English Reign of Terror*; there you have the source of my political tendencies," wrote Ebeneezer Elliott, the "Corn-Law Rhymer", whose father was a Jacobin clerk at an ironworks near Sheffield, with whom "the yeomanry used to amuse themselves periodically by backing their horses through his windows".

The history of reform agitation between 1792 and 1796 was (in general terms) the story of the simultaneous default of the middle-class reformers and the rapid "leftwards" movement of the plebeian Radicals. The experience marked the popular consciousness for fifty years, and throughout this time the dynamic of Radicalism came not from the middle class but from the artisans and labourers. The men of the popular societies are rightly designated Jacobins. Several of their leaders, including Thelwall, were willing to accept the term:

> I adopt the term *Jacobinism* without hesitation—1. Because it is fixed upon us, as a stigma, by our enemies. ... 2. Because, though I abhor the sanguinary ferocity of the late Jacobins in France, yet their principles ... are the most consonant with my ideas of reason, and the nature of man, of any that I have met with ... I use the term Jacobinism simply to indicate *a large and comprehensive system of reform, not professing to be built upon the authorities and principles of the Gothic customary*.

The particular quality of their Jacobinism is to be felt in their emphasis on *égalité*. "Equality" is too negative a term (in its usual English connotations) for the sharp, positive doctrines as to the erasure of all distinctions of status which informed their proceedings. The working-class movement of later years was to continue and enrich the traditions of fraternity and liberty. But the very existence of its organisations, and the protection of its funds, required the fostering of a cadre of experienced officials, as well as a certain deference or exaggerated loyalty towards its leadership, which proved to be a source of bureaucratic forms and controls. The English Jacobins of the 1790s initiated quite different traditions. There was a piquancy in *égalité*, in the outrage to 18th-century forms, as when the Jacobin Lord Daer sat with artisans and weavers as plain "Citizen Daer". But the belief that "a man's a man, for a' that" found expression in other ways which may still be recalled in criticism of the practices of our own day. *Every* citizen on a committee was expected to perform some part, the chairmanship of committees was often taken in rotation, the pretentions of leaders were watched, proceedings were based on the deliberate belief that every man was capable of reason and of a growth in his abilities, and that deference and distinctions of status were an offence to human dignity. These Jacobin strengths, which contributed much to Chartism, declined in the movement of the late 19th century, when the new Socialism shifted emphasis from political to economic rights. The strength of distinctions of class and status in 20th-century England is in part a consequence of the lack, in the 20th-century labour movement, of Jacobin virtues.

It is unnecessary to stress the evident importance of other aspects of the Jacobin tradition; the tradition of self-education and of the rational criticism of political and religious institutions; the tradition of conscious republicanism; above all, the tradition of internationalism. It is extraordinary that so brief an agitation should have diffused its ideas into so many corners of Britain. Perhaps the consequence of English Jacobinism which was most profound, although least easy to define, was the breaking-down of taboos upon agitation among "members unlimited". Wherever Jacobin ideas persisted, and wherever hidden copies of *Rights of Man* were cherished, men were no longer disposed to wait upon the example of a Wilkes or a Wyvill before they commenced a democratic agitation. Throughout the war years there were Thomas Hardys in every town and in many villages throughout England, with a kist or shelf full of Radical books, biding their time, putting in a word at the tavern, the chapel, the smithy, the shoemaker's shop, waiting for the movement to revive. And the movement for which they waited did not belong to gentlemen, manufacturers, or rate-payers; it was *their own.*

As late as 1849 a shrewd Yorkshire satirist published a sketch of such a "Village Politician" which has the feel of authenticity. He is, typically, a cobbler, an old man and the sage of his industrial village:

He has a library that he rather prides himself upon. It is a strange collection.... There is the "Pearl of Great Price" and "Cobbett's Twopenny Trash." The "Pilgrim's Progress"... and "The Go-ahead Journal." "The Wrongs of Labour" and "The Rights of Man." "The History of the French Revolution" and Bunyan's "Holy War"... "The Age of Reason" and a superannuated Bible.

He is "of course a great admirer of Bonaparte". "It warms his old heart like a quart of mulled ale, when he hears of a successful revolution,—a throne tumbled, kings flying, and princes scattered abroad. He thinks the dreams of his youth are about their fulfilment." He indulges in grandiloquent metaphors about the "sun of freedom" rising above "the horizontal atmosphere", and professes knowledge of Russian affairs.

He recollects the day when he durst scarcely walk the streets. He can tell how he was hooted, pelted and spurned ... and people told him he might be thankful if he was not burned alive some night, along with an effigy of Tom Paine.... He makes younkers stare when he tells them about a time when there was no Habeas Corpus ... and the Attorney General went up and down the country like a raging lion.... He tells of a man who said ... that the king was born without shirt, and was in consequence transported for sedition....

The Revolution of which he had dreamed never took place, but there was a revolution of a sort, none the less. It was the loyalists, James Watt the younger complained in 1793, who—by stirring up the mob against reformers—had "tampered" with the "lower order of people:"

They little think how dangerous it is to let the people know their power and that the day will come when they shall curse the senseless cry of Church & King, & feel their own weapons turned upon themselves.

After the near-famine year of 1795, the change can be sensed in a score of places. In Nottingham, where Jacobins had been ducked in 1794, they were strong enough to meet and defeat their opponents in open combat in the election of 1796. "At most of the entrances into this town, wrote a scandalised loyalist in 1798, "a post is set up with a board fixed upon it, on which is written 'All Vagrants will be apprehended and punished as the Law directs'." Now, over the word "Vagrants" the word "Tyrants" had been pasted, and no-one stirred to take it down. "Long have we been endeavouring to find ourselves men," declared the mutineers of the fleet in 1797: "We now find ourselves so. We will be treated as such."

In 1812, looking round him in dismay at the power of Scottish trade unionism and of Luddism in England, Scott wrote to Southey: "The country is mined below our feet." It was Pitt who had driven the "miners" underground. Men like our "Village Politician" were scarcely to be found in the villages of 1789. Jacobin ideas driven into weaving villages, the shops of the Nottingham framework-knitters and the Yorkshire croppers, the Lancashire cotton-mills, were propagated in every phase of rising prices and of hardship. It was not Pitt but John Thelwall who had the last word. "A sort of Socratic spirit will necessarily grow up, wherever large bodies of men assemble":

... Monopoly, and the hideous accumulation of capital in a few hands ... carry in their own enormity, the seeds of cure.... Whatever presses men together ... though it may generate some vices, is favourable to the diffusion of knowledge, and ultimately promotive of human liberty. Hence every large workshop and manufactory is a sort of political society, which no act of parliament can silence, and no magistrate disperse.

PART II
1815-1906

18

THE DEBATE ON THE FIRST REFORM BILL

Norman Gash

The biographer of Sir Robert Peel, Norman Gash, here discusses the attitudes held by the Whig government and the Tory opposition in the crisis of 1831–1832, bringing to bear his wide knowledge of the realities of politics in the era of the First Reform Bill. Gash's work follows the methods and aims of L. B. Namier in trying to establish the degree of correspondence between the pronouncements of early nineteenth-century politicians and the actual conditions of political life.

WHEN whigs, tories, and radicals opened the grand national debate on the reform bill in 1831, it was an occasion for which it would have been necessary to go back to the Revolution of 1688 to find a parallel. Many constitutional changes had taken place since that time; but they had been for the most part gradual changes of administrative habit and convention rather than explicit and fundamental alterations in the legal conception of the constitution. Indeed, so long had the fabric of the constitution stood without formal change that it had acquired in the eyes of men like Eldon a kind of sacrosanctity; as though a prescriptive right against change could be gained by the mere passage of time. The crisis of 1831 was therefore all the more effective in revealing the attitudes of contemporary Englishmen to their most characteristic political institution. Nevertheless, as in 1689, it was a discussion not primarily of abstract principles, nor even of the application of principles to an actual situation, but of certain practical proposals from which principles might perhaps be deduced, though they were not in themselves essential to the work that was done. Had it been a question of abstract principles, the ground of difference between Grey's ministry and the opposition would have been narrow. It was because the controversy was over detail that room for a full-pitched battle was secured.

The parliamentary debate on the reform bill began in March 1831 and continued intermittently until the summer of 1832. Looking back now on that involved and protracted discussion, on the three successive English bills, the two Irish and the two Scottish bills, on the vehement

---

FROM Norman Gash, *Politics in the Age of Peel* (London: Longmans, Green & Co. Limited, 1963), pp. 3–28. By permission of the publishers.

argument in parliament, and the even more vehement participation of the public in that argument, it is clear that given the contemporary political assumptions accepted by both sides the tories were in the right. Almost every point that they made, every fear that they expressed, were good points and well founded fears, even though the whig majority rejected their validity and denied their justification. Sooner or later all the major prophecies of the opposition came true. In some cases it took a century where they had anticipated a few decades; in others their predictions were vindicated within fifteen years where they themselves could scarcely have foreseen so sudden an onset of disaster. But taken as a whole the tory case against the reform bill was an accurate analysis of the real consequences of reform. That in itself, had it been accepted by their opponents, might have been sufficient to destroy the bill; since these consequences were so obnoxious, even in anticipation, to the majority of both parties in parliament, that it was imperative for the whigs to deny the accuracy of the opposition forecasts if they wished to retain the support of their own followers. For except on the specific measure before them there was a substantial amount of agreement between the parliamentary reformers and anti-reformers on political fundamentals; and conversely, therefore, agreement on what were political undesirabilities. Neither party was democratic; indeed, that adjective was still a term of abuse or condemnation among the ruling classes, and whigs as well as tories carefully dissociated themselves from its implications. Neither party was royalist in the sense of being a party pledged to the person of the monarch. Both were monarchical, in the sense of being a party anxious for the maintenance of the crown as an integral part of the constitution. Both were oligarchic and aristocratic; and though sensitive to public opinion both were opposed to demagogy. They were therefore in the position of two physicians, working according to the same science, but differing in their interpretation of a particular case. If the whigs had accepted the tory prognosis, they could scarcely have prescribed the remedy they did. Nevertheless, the tory prognosis was the correct one.

The case of the opposition was clear enough. Whether expressed confusedly by Wetherell, intemperately by Croker, or moderately by Peel, the common attitude can easily be distinguished among the intricate and laborious details of minor argument over schedule and franchise. In the first place the bill would inevitably destroy the existing balance of the constitution. Already the influence of the crown based on the control of patronage had been so diminished during the two preceding generations that it now scarcely counted in the scales. Under the new system the last major prerogative of the crown—the choice of ministers—would be confined within such narrow limits that in effect ministers would henceforth be imposed on the crown by the popular assembly.

> He saw no prospect [Peel told the House] that the King would hereafter be enabled to exercise an unpopular prerogative, however necessary that prerogative might be to the permanent interests of the country.... How could the King

hereafter change a Ministry? How could he make a partial change in the Administration in times of public excitement with any prospect that the Ministers of his choice, unpopular, perhaps, from the strict performance of necessary duties, would be returned to Parliament?

What was true of the position of the Crown applied also to the House of Lords. The strengthening of the popular part of the legislature meant a corresponding decline in the influence of the non-elective house. Every diminution of aristocratic influence in the representative system would widen the difference between the two houses of parliament and deprive the constitution of checks and balances implicit in the character of the House of Lords. So much emphasis was laid by the reform bill on the popular aspect of the legislature that even while the fate of the measure was still undetermined, the power of the House of Lords seemed to be visibly shrinking. Who asked, observed Peel on another occasion, what the House of Lords would do should the reform bill pass the House of Commons. 'It seems taken for granted that it must pass the House of Lords—that it would be vain to oppose a measure that extends popular privileges, and is said to be in conformity with the wishes of the majority of the people.' In such circumstances, with both Crown and House of Lords weakened, if not actually paralysed, as independent working features of the constitution, nothing would remain to challenge the power of the elected branch of the legislature based on the sovereignty of the people. The name and form of the monarchy and peerage would be retained; but their significance would have vanished and the whole balance of the constitution destroyed. 'When you have once established the overpowering influence of the people over this House; when you have made this House the express organ of the public voice; what other authority in the State can—nay more, what other authority in the State ought—to control its will, or reject its decisions?' And so, ultimately, on the basis of the sovereign democratic legislature would be erected the omnipotent and omnicompetent state.

These were the most important, but not the only consequences of reform. It was Peel once more who pointed out that the bill would go far towards creating a division in the legislature between rural and industrial interests, divided geographically by a line of demarcation traceable across the face of England from the Wash to the mouth of the Severn. Of the fifty-six boroughs doomed by Schedule A, five were north and fifty-one south of that line. On the other hand, the great majority of the new boroughs were situated north of the line, and (excluding London) only a mere half-dozen south of it. The stage was thus set for a struggle not of parties but of classes and economic interests. Alexander Baring, M.P. for Thetford, constituted himself the chief spokesman of those who feared that in a reformed parliament, the country interest would be swamped by the town interest. 'The field of coal', he told the house, 'would beat the field of barley; the population of the manufacturing districts was more condensed, and would act with more energy, backed by clubs and large assemblages of people, than the population of the agricultural districts. They would act with such force in the House that the more divided agriculturalists would be unable to withstand it, and the latter would be overwhelmed.' A few days later he renewed his warnings. 'In a Reformed Parliament, when the day of battle came, the country Squires would not be able to stand against the active, pushing, intelligent people who would be sent from the manufacturing districts.'

Should indeed such an opposition of interests arise, there could hardly be any question which would prevail. Already before the Reform Act the Duke of Wellington had doubted the ability of the county representatives to maintain and protect the landed interests of the country without the assistance provided by the members sitting for the close boroughs. It was the latter, he thought, which were the 'true protectors of the landed interest'. The act certainly increased the county representation of the kingdom; but the gain was, in the opinion of the opposition, far outweighed by the loss of the small boroughs, the weighting of the county franchise by tenants and leaseholders from urban areas, and the enfranchisement of the large industrial towns. It needed therefore no special perspicacity to foresee the coming onslaught on the Corn Laws. Even in 1830 and 1831 innumerable petitions to the House of Commons had coupled the repeal of the Corn Laws with reform of the legislature, the ballot, and annual parliaments, in their list of political requirements. Across the narrow gap of fifteen years the tories could already look with apprehension to the time when the sacred cause of agricultural protection would go down before the influence of the inspired bagmen of Lancashire and the industrial north. Lord Wharncliffe was neither a reactionary nor an alarmist; but he told the peers in 1831 that 'he believed that when once this Bill was passed, the landed interest would find, when it was too late, that an opening was made for the total repeal of the Corn Laws'. Behind this immediate threat there loomed even more menacing, if vaguer, vistas of destruction: the decline of property as the basis of society and of the constitution, and the surrender of the State to the confiscatory designs of the non-possessing classes. 'Take away', said Sadler, 'the influence thus possessed by the great masses of property.... The consequences are then certain... Prepare... for similar spoliations to those which have recently been witnessed in a neighbouring country, where property bereft of its political influence lost its rights, and only served to mark out its possessors to certain destruction.' This was perhaps extravagant language; and yet in less than a lifetime an ex-minister of the Crown was to demand in public what ransom would property pay for the security it enjoyed.

Against all this the reformers might argue that in point of fact the extension of the franchise under the reform bill was extremely moderate. At the most it would be a mere half-million of the educated and prosperous middle classes that would join the 'electoral nation'. But the brooding imagination of the opposition was impatient of these schoolroom arguments. Once admit the principle of breaking down the traditional structure of government in deference to popular demand, it then mattered little if on the first occasion a decent moderation confined the additions to the electorate within the half-million mark. It was the first step which marred all. Unlock the door and not only could it never be closed again but inexorably it would be shifted more and more open as the pressure from without increased. Exactly this metaphor was used by Peel himself. 'I was unwilling to open a door', he said in explanation of his opposition to reform, 'which I saw no prospect of being able to close.' It was not necessary that the first generation of politicians bred by the new system should themselves be anxious to introduce fresh measures of democratization. It was enough that they had proclaimed the principle that government must follow the popular voice. On what was the reform bill based fundamentally except that it was desired by the people? But did the people always know what was right? And must statesmen look always to the passions and never to the interests of those that they governed? If so, the Reform Act could only be the first of a long series of changes, the end of which could not be foreseen. Even if those who wielded power immediately after the passing of the act were averse to further developments, they could not restrain the forces they had themselves unleashed. No doubt they would secure a temporary popularity from the mere passing of the measure and the enfranchisement of half a million voters. 'But these are vulgar arts of government; others will outbid you; not now but at no remote period; they will offer votes and power to a million of men, will quote your precedent for the concession, and will carry your principles to their legitimate and natural consequences.' If room or pretext should in future be needed for criticizing the first Reform Act and substituting a second or a third, the whigs themselves had made ample provision for the contingency. The illogicalities of the reformed system were admitted on all sides; but the very men who applied rational criticism to the traditional structure had themselves produced a system crammed with anomalies, complexities, and absurdities, and displaying as illogical and arbitrary a set of arrangements as any that had preceded them. All the arguments used against the old system of representation could be advanced against the new. 'Your own arguments', as Peel rightly told the whigs, 'are conclusive against the stability and permanence of the arrangement you are about to make.' It was less than twenty years later that Lord John Russell began to urge in a whig cabinet the need for a fresh instalment of parliamentary reform.

No doubt fear sharpened the imagination, and a natural desire to score in debate exaggerated the pessimism of the tory opposition. But it is clear that the debate over the reform bill of 1831 went to the roots of political philosophy; and that when stripped of ephemeral argument and selfish motive there remained at the core of the tory position a genuine body of principles ranged against the whole spirit of the Reform Act. Certainly the succeeding century was to vindicate in an impressive fashion the correctness of their prophecies. On this high historic and philosophical plane, therefore, the tory case against reform was irrefutable.

Politics, however, are rarely fought out in such a rarefied atmosphere. A party enjoying the freedom of opposition may be able to indulge in speculative refinements and look to the ultimate consequences of governmental actions. Politicians in office work within a much narrower and more practical context. If the tories were the better historians, philosophers, and prophets, the whigs were the better politicians. What counted for them was not the verdict of posterity but the force of contemporary society. The whigs could not afford, and perhaps had no right, to look too far ahead. 'Distant and eventual', had pronounced the greatest of all whigs, Sir Robert Walpole, 'must yield to present dangers.' Moreover in the long run the politician is the servant of the forces he directs. The deliberations of the cabinet committee on reform, and the Reform Act itself, were only symptoms of a much wider movement in the country. To ascribe solely to the decisions of a handful of ministers or to a single statute the immense political developments after 1832 is scarcely a tenable proposition. The whigs must bear responsibility for the Reform Act of 1832, but as instruments rather than as creators. The whole flank of the powerful intellectual position of the tories could be turned by one short question. What alternative was there to the whig proposals?

At the beginning of the parliamentary struggle Inglis had described the reform agitation as a 'state of diseased and feverish excitement' caused by the examples of France and Belgium, and denied that there was any general demand for reform in the country. But support for that opinion gradually waned in the succeeding twelve months. It was significant that Peel in his first contribution to the long series of reform debates in 1831 and 1832 stated that he did not object to all reform, but merely to the particular bill brought forward by the whigs. Circumstances would have debarred him when last in office from bringing forward a motion for parliamentary reform. But out of office and as a private individual, he continued, 'I do not hesitate to avow, that there might have been proposed certain alterations in our representative system, founded on safe principles, abjuring all confiscation, and limited in their degree, to which I would have assented.' Indeed, when Wellington's tory government went out of office in 1830, all the ministers except the duke himself had told the king that some reform of parliament would be necessary. The incoming whigs therefore did not so much create as merely recognize the situation which confronted them when Grey first formed his cabinet in November 1830. From the start this argument of necessity was consistently upheld. 'The perilous question is that of Parliamentary Reform,' wrote the prime minister to Sir Herbert Taylor, the king's secretary, in January 1831, 'and as I approach it, the more I feel all its difficulty. With the universal feeling that prevails on this subject, it is impossible to avoid doing something; and not to do enough to satisfy public expectation (I mean the satisfaction of the rational public) would be worse than to do nothing.' The whigs, then, took their stand on the fundamental principle of an irresistible demand in the country for parliamentary reform; and on its logical corollary, the futility of piecemeal or half-hearted legislation in answer to that demand. The report which Grey himself received from his committee of four took this argument as the criterion of their reform proposals. 'The plan of Reform proposed by His Majesty's Ministers', they wrote, 'ought to be of such a scope and description as to satisfy all reasonable demands, and remove at once, and for ever, all rational grounds for complaint from the minds of the intelligent and independent portion of the community.'

The question narrowed itself therefore not to the principle but the degree of reform. Here the whig scheme, arbitrary and illogical as it was, represented with rough accuracy the most that could be pushed through parliament and the least that would satisfy the country at large. That the tories regarded it as revolutionary and the more extreme radicals as a betrayal was a reasonable indication of its value as a national solution. But that sooner or later something in the way of parliamentary reform must take place was apparent to most. With all its merits, the unreformed system had by 1830 one gross demerit. It was not regarded as satisfactory by the bulk of informed and influential opinion in the country. It was this practical consideration that was the strength of the whig case. It was never better expressed than by Melbourne in the House of Lords on the occasion of the second reading of the reform bill in 1831. He acknowledged frankly that he had previously resisted reform.

But [he added] all experience proves, when the wishes of the people are founded on reason and justice and when they are consistent with the fundamental principles of the constitution, that there must come a time when both the legislative and executive powers must yield to the popular voice or be annihilated.... When your lordships see, that on every occasion of public calamity and distress, from whatever cause arising, the people call for an alteration in the representation, and that the call is accompanied with a deep, rankling sense of injustice suffered, and of rights withheld, can your lordships suppose that an opinion so continually revived has not some deep-seated foundation, and can you be insensible to the danger of continuing a permanent cause for angry and discontented feelings to be revived and renewed at every period of public distress and public calamity?

Indeed, reading this speech, suffused as it is with a kind of melancholy eloquence, one is reminded of the calm considered presentation of the case against reform put forward by Peel. Despite differences of background and temperament, Peel and Melbourne were together perhaps the truest diagnosticians of the reform crisis; the one opposing without hope, the other assisting without desire.

The defence of the whigs therefore is that they offered a practical remedy for a felt grievance. What the tories said was true; but what the whigs did was necessary. They satisfied in a rough but substantial fashion the immediate demand in the country for parliamentary reform. 'They have done', said Macaulay in vindication of his leaders, 'all that was necessary for the removing of a great practical evil, and no more than was necessary.' Practical remedies, however, can only be applied to practical abuses. What was it that the Reform Act, in the opinion of its creators, was designed to do? In his speech introducing the first reform bill, Lord John Russell went some way to answering that question. The chief grievances of which the people complained, he observed, were three in number. They were the nomination of members of parliament by private individuals; the election of members of parliament by close corporations; and the expense of elections. The first grievance was to be met by the abolition of all boroughs with electorates too small to preserve their independence and too isolated to be easily enlarged. The second was to be met by the institution in all boroughs of a uniform £10 householder franchise. The third was to be met by a variety of measures: the registration of voters, the reduction in the duration of elections, the erection of separate polling stations in large constituencies; and the splitting of large counties into divisions each returning their own members. Stated thus, the project of the ministers was moderate to a degree; and indeed on Russell's own showing was scarcely an adequate account of what the bill intended. In particular, it left almost out of account the question of the creation of new constituencies.

Nevertheless it is clear that the emphasis of the first draft of the reform bill was on the purification rather than on the enlargement of the representative system. It is true that in Grey's opinion, frequently expressed to the king, the essence of the bill lay in three measures: the disfranchisement of the nomination boroughs, the enfranchisement of the large towns, and the £10 householder suffrage. But Grey, like most of the ministerial reformers, including the king himself, was also anxious for a reduction in the total number of M.P.s. He wished to end a gross anomaly but he had no desire to produce a rigid equality in borough representation. Enfranchisement of new boroughs was doled out sparingly. As originally proposed it was to be confined to towns with a population of over 10,000, of which there were reckoned to be about thirty in England. The question of new constituencies thus took up only a minor part in Russell's speech and from its place in the argument seemed almost to result from the *embarras de richesses* in the form of spare seats in the house made available by the abolition of borough seats in Schedules A and B. The initial plan of disfranchisement left 168 vacancies at the disposal of the ministry. But it was not proposed to fill them all up. Forty-two seats were to be allotted to the new boroughs (including eight to the new London boroughs) which by their population, wealth, and importance seemed to deserve representation. But this was to be balanced by additional seats for county members. 'As county members have unquestionably the most excellent class of constituents, they form of themselves a most valuable class of representation.' So Yorkshire, the only county with four members, was now to have six for its three ridings; twenty-six other counties were to be given two additional members; and the Isle of Wight was to be given one. Fifty-five seats, therefore, as compared with the forty-two new borough seats, were to be assigned to the counties. This of course was in England only. But nine additional members for Scotland, Ireland, and Wales, scarcely made a heavy inroad in the ministry's stock of empty seats and as originally calculated the House of Commons would have been reduced by sixty-two members under the first reform bill. Even then, if to Russell's three explicit points is added a fourth, the question of new constituencies, it is obvious that no revolutionary expansion of the representative system was envisaged and that the counties were intended to receive as much if not more consideration than the towns.

Another statement of the basic objects of the reform bill was given by Palmerston two days later. According to his analysis the existing system of representation suffered from five great blemishes. These were nomination by patrons, gross corruption among the lower classes of voters, inadequate representation of the larger manufacturing and commercial towns, the expense of elections, and finally the unequal and inequitable distribution of voting power between the middle and lower classes. The bill before the House, he claimed, would remedy all these defects. Apart from that the object of the government in framing the bill was threefold: firstly to give representation to the big manufacturing towns; secondly to add to the respectability of the electorate; and thirdly to increase the number of those enjoying the right of choosing their representatives in parliament. Both in his list of defects and in his analysis of objectives, therefore, Palmerston was more comprehensive than the first great spokesman on the ministerial side. Nevertheless he too followed Russell's example in stressing the importance of the additional county representatives. The great virtue of the bill, he concluded, was that it would provide a real national representation in the House of Commons, not only by reason of the enlarged representation of the industrial areas, but also—and even more importantly—by enlarging the representation of the county constituencies. 'For without meaning to disparage the manufacturing or commercial interests, he must say that he considered the soil to be the country itself.' There was thus ample agreement between the two speakers. Palmerston perhaps laid a shade more emphasis on the corruption of the electoral system and the importance of the new boroughs. On the question of elections, for example, he attributed much of the previous misgovernment and disregard of public opinion to the bribery and influence exercised at elections whereby 'parties came into parliament without constituents, or only with those whom they had purchased, and might sell again'; and he spoke with unwonted feeling of the existing mode of elections as 'the most offensive and disgusting that could be imagined'. But these were differences of stress rather than divergences of principle. In these two speeches, if anywhere, were contained the explicit declarations of the ministry on the purpose of the Reform Act. What they were is clear enough. It was to be seen later how justified were the hopes and calculations of the authors of the bill.

Apart from these specific observations on the part of two of the most prominent ministers in the House of Commons, a number of general points emerged in the course of the long discussions that dragged on for the next seventeen months. The most recurrent of these concerned the need to bring the middle classes within the orbit of the constitution. In explaining to the House why in 1822 he had championed the cause of reform which he had deprecated in 1819, Lord John Russell placed his whole case upon his awareness in the interval of the power and importance of this new social order. His motives, he said, were the great advance of the middle classes in wealth, intelligence, knowledge, and influence; the insufficient representation of that class in the House of Commons; and the obvious disinclination of parliament in its enacted measures to take that middle-class opinion into account. This was said in public; but in private the whig leaders held the same view. Writing to a ministerial colleague in October 1831 Grey made a remarkable reference to 'the middle classes who form the real and efficient mass of public opinion, and without whom the power of the gentry is nothing'. The middle classes deserved political recognition on their own merits. But the whig argument went deeper than this. From a profoundly conservative point of view, they asserted, it was expedient to enfranchise the middle classes because of the social and political considerations which such a measure would have. Not only did the exclusion of the middle classes from the constitution weaken the power of the government but it also strengthened popular discontent and disorder because the middle classes were inevitably forced thereby into an alliance with the lower classes. If on the other hand the middle classes, those 'vast masses of property and intelligence' as Macaulay termed them, were brought into an alliance with the old governing classes, the balance of the constitution would be restored. It was a significant proof of how widespread this feeling was in the minds of the reformers that an identical attitude was set out in the independent memorandum on Scottish reform submitted to Russell in November 1830 by Kennedy of Dunure.

> The object of an extension of the Elective franchise in the Counties, Cities, and Burghs of Scotland [began the memorandum] must be to give satisfaction to the people of that country; and it is conceived that this may be done by extending the Elective Franchise to those classes, who possess property and knowledge. Much more is demanded by many, but it is hoped that it is not yet too late to make a change in the Franchise, the limit of which shall be the possession of property and intelligence; but any plan must be objectionable which, by keeping the Franchise very high and exclusive, fails to give satisfaction to the middle and respectable ranks of society, and drives them to a union founded on dissatisfaction, with the lower orders. It is of the utmost importance to associate the middle with the higher orders of society in the love and support of the institutions and government of the country.

It was accordingly an essential purpose of the bill to reconcile to the constitution an influential part of the nation which until then had seemed to stand outside it; and, in so doing, to restore to the government that broad basis of national confidence which it had previously lacked and without which it could not efficiently exist. 'To property and good order', proclaimed Durham in the House of Lords, 'we attach numbers.' Once the bill was passed, he argued, the middle classes would be the friends and allies of the government. Then, if the poorer classes rose in discontent, they would find that their natural leaders had been taken from them and the forces of law and order immensely strengthened. Durham was careful to add that he had no reason to believe that the lower orders were disaffected. Nevertheless he had made his point and the history of chartism in the next two decades was to prove its accuracy. In this light, therefore, the whigs appeared as the saviours of society, consolidating, pacifying, and uniting a much divided nation. It was a subtle and not entirely ungrounded argument.

It was at this point that the enfranchisement of the new boroughs assumed its real importance—one far greater than that indicated by Russell in his introductory speech of 1 March 1831. Indeed, at a later stage, he developed a more elaborate theory with regard to the fresh borough creations which followed logically from the main doctrine of the importance of the middle classes. There were, he said, three main principles on which the ministry had acted in the enfranchisement of new boroughs. They thought it desirable in the first place to give representation to important centres of trade and manufacture. They thought it desirable to bind a large class of people to the institutions of the country and to teach them to look to the House of Commons as the political tribunal where their grievances would be discussed and remedied. Lastly they believed that the House of Commons as the representative body of the nation would be improved by the addition of men qualified to take part in the discussions of all the new problems that might come before the legislature. The £10 franchise and the new boroughs were thus the technical means of infusing fresh life into the narrow and unpopular governing system. The method itself involved the admission to the aristocratic *pays légal* not of the people but of the class most akin to the aristocracy in its wealth and education, whose alliance was most to be valued, whose enmity was most to be feared. Even if that brought with it the risk of collision inside the ruling classes of the opposed interests of agriculture and industry, it was better that such a collision should take place within the parliamentary field, where its worst effects would be subdued by the responsibilities of office and the ties of party, than that it should take the form of a landowning parliament set against an unenfranchised industrial population of employers and employed. The essential point was to attach the middle classes to the aristocratic constitution. In all their references to 'the people' and to 'popular representation', the whigs clearly had this implication in mind. When Russell ended his introductory speech with a peroration stressing the need for a new political body which 'representing the people, springing from the people, and sympathising with the people, can fairly call on the people to support the future burthens of the country,' he was using whig and not Lincolnian vocabulary. On the same evening Althorp made the assertion that the bill would give the 'people' of England an overpowering influence in the choice of representatives. This being greeted with ironic applause by Peel, he hastened to add that 'by the people he meant the great majority of the respectable middle classes of the country'. Brougham in the House of Lords made an even sharper definition of the term. In speaking of the people's support, he informed the peers, he did not refer to the mob, or populace. 'But if there is the mob, there is the people also. I speak now of the middle classes ... the most numerous and by far the most wealthy order in the community.'

The last phrase in Brougham's explanation provides another approach to the problem. What the middle classes were in social terms, industrial and commercial property were in economic terms. It was wealth that gave the middle classes their status and it was wealth that the whigs wished to enfranchise. The object of the £10 householder vote, said Russell, was to give representation 'to the real property and to the real respectability' of the cities and towns. When all the changes contemplated by the reform bill had taken effect, the electorate would be fortified by 'about half a million of persons, and these all connected with the property of the country, having a valuable stake amongst us, and deeply interested in our institutions'. The use of the possessive pronoun was revealing. In effect privileged wealth was being asked to admit unprivileged wealth to the close circle of the ruling class; and property was to be the certificate of probity and good behaviour. The principle commonly accepted in the eighteenth century, that the constitution was founded on property, was thus carried over into the Reform Act. 'There is no principle of our constitution,' said Lord Durham, 'there is no principle affecting the representative system, that has not property for its basis, and I am warranted in saying that the plan of the ministers is of this nature.' The only difference was the realization by the whigs that a new type of property had arisen by the side of the traditional landed interest that was powerful enough to demand and deserve recognition. The qualifications of the new voters in both town and country therefore were made dependent on their relationship, whether direct or indirect, with property. The dispute was not on the principle of property qualification but on the details. With regard to the borough franchise it had at one point been decided to choose the £20 householder as the level of qualification. Only later realization that the result would be to transform many substantial towns into close boroughs induced the ministry to lower the standard. The £10 franchise was selected as a practical compromise between the desire to rest the franchise on an unassailable basis of property and the fear of creating narrow constituencies amenable to bribery and intimidation.

To state the case in the bare terms of economic dominance, however, would be to falsify the position. There were various intellectual and ethical arguments for requiring a minimum standard of wealth from the electorate which cannot be dismissed as mere pretexts. It was the social as much as the economic significance of property that counted. Hawkins, the whig member for Tavistock, put the matter concisely in the course of a speech which in print remains one of the ablest and most eloquent passages of the reform debates, though it was badly received by the House and criticized by the opposition as frigid and sarcastic. 'In a country', said Hawkins, 'where no public provision was made for the education of the people, it necessarily happened that a certain amount of income was the only general and practical criterion of a required degree of intelligence.' Macaulay had earlier made the same point when he argued that in view of the distressed and ill-educated condition of the labouring classes, universal suffrage at that juncture was impractical and inadvisable, and indeed could only produce 'a destructive revolution'. A more balanced statement of the ministerial position came from Jeffrey, the Scottish Lord-Advocate, who drew up the reform bill for Scotland and was thus an informed and authoritative spokesman. On the matter of property qualification, he said, it was generally agreed by all parties that the only reasons for requiring the electors to have property were firstly, that it was a kind of test or presumption that they had more intelligence and information than were usually to be found in persons of the very lowest condition; and secondly, it was a pledge of their interest in and consequent disposition to maintain that respect for property in general which all thinking men must feel to be at the bottom of civil institutions. As a test of fitness and as a pledge of legality, therefore, the property qualification was indispensable. It was a blend of the Hanoverian sense of property with the Victorian instinct for education; and however incongruous the two arguments, they formed a powerful alliance in debate. Nobody in parliament advocated a franchise divorced from property or special responsibility. Even Hunt the radical, who constituted himself the champion of the under-privileged classes, contented himself with putting forward the claims of the tax-payers, the men liable to service in the militia, and all who fought in the army or navy, to have a share in the choice of representatives. His specific proposal was that householders paying an annual rent of £3 or more should be added to the electorate but he admitted that he was not in favour of universal suffrage.

It was this conception of the electorate, or as it was more frequently styled in contemporary speech the constituency, that provided the real intellectual opposition to the ballot. If the constituency which literally created the House of Commons was itself to consist of a chosen body of electors, a special responsibility rested on them as spokesmen for the nation. In his first speech Russell spent some time in defending the decision of the government to omit the ballot from provisions of the bill. He argued that under any circumstances it would be impossible to eliminate all influence and that while the ballot would prevent an improper influence on the good voter, it would also prevent a beneficial influence being exerted on the bad voter. It was inadvisable that any class of persons should be left 'wholly irresponsible in the discharge of a great public duty'. No branch of the constitution was infallible, not even the electorate; and the public exercise of the voting function was a kind of constitutional check on the people to whom that function was entrusted.

Of course other and less intellectual considerations affected the issue. To those radical purists who believed that the majority of the electorate were impelled by sinister forces, the ballot seemed to be the only immediate efficacious remedy. Conversely there was a strong desire on the part of the older governing classes to preserve public voting as the indispensable factor in maintaining their influence over the electors. But if the radicals identified themselves with the demand for the ballot, they had no copyright in electoral morality. The introduction of the ballot was seriously considered by the whigs when drawing up the reform bill and Althorp confessed in the House of Commons that he personally was in favour of it, although he did not think that its absence ruined the only chance of effectual reform. After the elections of 1835 and 1837 more and more whigs were inclined to agree that the ballot, while not necessarily acceptable as a principle, might be a valuable barrier against the conservative revival. The tendency to ascribe electoral defeat to anything but the genuine will of the electorate was human; and even for some conservatives the ballot was not without its attractions. If radicals desired the ballot primarily to end land-owning intimidation in the counties, conservatives could hope that it would give them an advantage in the towns. 'It seemed to me', wrote Disraeli of his earlier career, 'that the borough constituency of Lord Grey was essentially, and purposely, a dissenting and low Whig constituency, consisting of the principal employers of labour—and that the ballot was the only instrument to extricate us from these difficulties.' This eccentric strain in tory thought did not escape the cynical eye of Lord Palmerston. 'I should not be surprised', he wrote to Russell in 1835, 'to find some of these days Tories and Radicals combining to become Balloters, each hoping by such means to steal a march upon the others. For certainly the Radicals would lose power by ballot in many towns where they at present lord it over all.'

Among both whigs and tories, however, there existed a strong objection to the ballot, founded on something more principled than a mere apprehension of defeat and loss of influence. Here, as elsewhere, the conflict of opinion over a radical proposal revealed fundamental divergences. The radicals, instinctively and unconsciously perhaps, were moving towards universal suffrage as the only method of discovering the national popular will. When the electorate was equated with the adult population, each voter would represent merely himself and his personal interests, and it would be a legitimate precaution to guard him against the malign influence of others by ensuring the secrecy of his vote. The opponents of the ballot, on the other hand, based their view on the limited electorate, in which the vote was literally a franchise—a liberty and a privilege to be exercised by the elector with deliberation and foresight, and a proper sense of his own position. Where, in the whole United Kingdom, only one man in every seven had the vote, it was absurd to treat the electorate as the British people, the ultimate source of power.

Just as the members of parliament represented their constituents, so did the electors represent the mass of unenfranchised population. Against men in such a responsible position, publicity was the necessary safeguard. Open voting was as imperative for the elector on the hustings as for the member in the lobbies of Westminster. The ballot meant the evasion of responsibility.

It would in my opinion be quite inefficacious as a remedy against bribery and intimidation [wrote Lord William Russell to John Russell in 1838] and would destroy the characters of Englishmen, certainly of the liberal party. What pitiful figures we should cut, sneaking up to the ballot box, looking with fear to the right and the left and dropping in our paper, the contents of which we are afraid or ashamed to acknowledge. Whilst the Tory comes forward like a man, and like an Englishman, and says openly and fearlessly who he votes for. I would rather never give a vote than give a concealed vote—the desire to conceal the votes is a bad sign of the times.

This dislike of secrecy as a kind of stigma on the character of the individual whom it covered was not simply an ingenious argument. Nor was the feeling confined to the aristocratic classes, who conceivably had little to fear themselves from the publicity of their votes. W. E. Forster, for all his humble Quaker background and many radical impulses, shared in his youth the sentiments of William Russell. At a meeting at Bradford in 1848, held in connexion with the chartist movement, he told his audience that he hated secrecy and that he thought if they obtained universal suffrage they would not require the protection of the ballot. There was room for a variety of opinions on the advantages of the ballot at the beginning of Victoria's reign; and the opponents of the device could be as sincere and disinterested as its advocates. Indeed to some people the passage of the Reform Act made the ballot appear not more but less indispensable. In a brief discussion on the ballot in the House of Commons during December 1830, some months before the introduction of the first reform bill, Hobhouse had argued that few of the English electors were men of property and that for such a class the ballot was their only defence. About seven years later, however, in February 1838, he noted that:

at the House of Commons today Sir Robert Peel speaking on the question of the Ballot, made what I considered the true objection to that measure—namely, that it would take away that influence over the vote which preserves the representative system, in our country, from being of too democratic a character. To this opinion I incline. I think the Ballot before the Reform Bill, and without it, would have been a good measure; but I am not prepared to say the same of it after, and with the Reform Bill.

However contradictory, both the main arguments against the ballot were logical deductions from a political theory which postulated property as the basis of the political constitution. If the electorate was regarded as a representative body, for whom publicity was a necessary aspect of their functions, the reason why they were singled out from the mass of the unenfranchised was their property qualification. If on the other hand it was considered that the necessity of maintaining influence over the electorate was the effective argument against the ballot, it was because of the underlying conviction that property must be secured in its predominant position in the constitution as against mere numbers. The fluctuations in the deliberations of the whigs when drafting the reform bill admirably illustrated the direct relationship between property and the ballot. When the drafting committee decided to include the ballot, they raised the borough franchise from £10 to £20. When the cabinet rejected the ballot, the lower £10 franchise was restored. Grey indeed told Sir Herbert Taylor that the ballot had not been proposed by the framers of the original report as good in itself but merely as a concession which would facilitate the raising of the elective franchise in the boroughs and the consequent diminution of popular influence. However, there was little enthusiasm for the £20 franchise, which appeared (without the ballot) in the first draft of reform submitted to the king. William himself offered no objection to a reduction of the borough qualification to £10, though he asserted that he would never consent to the ballot. The omission of the latter therefore was naturally followed by the reintroduction of the lower borough franchise.

An extension of this fundamental principle is to be discerned in the attention paid to those organized and influential forms of property that had become socially distinct interests. In selecting the new boroughs for enfranchisement the criterion was not mere population; and only partially the size of the new electorate. The motive which operated as powerfully as any was the desire to secure representation for 'interests'. In a sense the whole commercial and manufacturing community was an interest which the ministry felt should be more equitably represented in parliament. But beyond that primary objective was the view that specific towns should be chosen for enfranchisement so that they could act as representatives for specific interests of various kinds. When the House of Commons went into committee on the first reform bill, Lord John Russell explained that on the question of enfranchisement the ministers did not look solely to population; they also took into account commercial capital and enterprise. Hence the population test was not a rigid rule. Indeed the ministers proposed 'as a counterbalance to the pure principle of population, to give representation to large towns possessed of manufacturing capital and skill'. A few months later, when introducing the second reform bill in June 1831, Russell elaborated this simple proposition ·by arguing that under the new scheme the members for England and Wales would be composed of about 150 county and 280 borough representatives. The borough members fell into two categories: those representing great cities and towns, including all the big manufacturing interests, such as wool, cotton, coal, and the potteries; and the remainder who numbered about a hundred, drawn from boroughs with a population of from three to six thousand, not immediately representing any interest, but perhaps in consequence 'better qualified to speak and inform the House on great questions of general interest to the community'. Even if this latter class did not represent the commercial interests, it is clear that they were designed to represent interests of a social or political type. At a later stage in committee Russell said that it was imperative to give representation to the populous industrial areas of the north but that the ministry had deliberately retained a class of small boroughs in order to ensure the representation of certain elements in the population that would otherwise be unrepresented. Here he was specifically referring to the forty boroughs of Schedule B (deprived of one member) and the additional thirty boroughs left intact although they did not possess a large constituency. The argument, however, is still relevant. It was a fundamental point of the bill not to produce uniformity but to ensure that a mass of interests great and small, industrial and social, were adequately represented in the House of Commons. The great argument against the unreformed system was not its anomalous structure but the fact that it left unrepresented or insufficiently represented certain important interests and gave representation on a lavish scale not to interests but to individuals.

It resulted from this attitude that the new boroughs formed a practical selection rather than a category capable of statistical definition on a basis of population or electorate. Thus Frome was enfranchised, in spite of its relatively small population of 12,000, because it had a woollen industry and would represent the southwest of England as against the north. Whitby and Sunderland came in to reinforce the interests of the shipping industry. Walsall with a population of about 15,000 and some 800 £10 houses, justified its inclusion on the score of its iron and leather industries. The ministry consented to take Merthyr Tydfil out of its group of Welsh contributory boroughs and give it individual representation after powerful advocates in the House of Commons had dilated upon its four large ironworks, its thirty-three blast-furnaces, its population of 22,000, and its 4,000 houses. It is true that, along with a special interest, the ministry felt bound to insist on the presence of what Russell called the elements of a good constituency. But it is also apparent that an electorate of six or seven hundred was regarded as sufficient if the other factors were there. Conversely one of the major arguments of the opposition in connexion with proposed new boroughs was that some of them did not represent any tangible interest. Those that incurred this condemnation were on the whole of two kinds. The first were the subdivisions of the overgrown and unwieldy metropolis. Thus, Peel, while admitting that he did not oppose a moderate measure of enfranchisement for such large, separate industrial towns as Birmingham, Manchester, and Leeds, criticized the creation of the new London boroughs. He argued that London was already sufficiently represented as an entity and that the further increase in the number of the London members was only justified on the principle of basing representation on population and wealth—a principle which the government had specifically rejected. The second kind was composed of certain towns which formed an entity in the sense of having an identifiable area and character, and possessed a wealthy and numerous population, but seemed to the jaundiced eye of the opposition to represent no special interest other than the sum of the diverse interests of its electors. Such towns, to use the phrase applied by the Earl of Haddington to Brighton, were simply 'an example of an unmeaning mass of population'. The phrase is illuminating for the concept of collective identity as opposed to numbers and aggregates of individuals. Cheltenham and Brighton, the two fashionable watering-places enfranchised by the act, were the chief objects of condemnation under this heading, and tory speakers vied with each other in finding insulting epithets to apply to these two new boroughs. Trevor spoke of the 'petty interests of the keepers of circulating libraries and vendors of oranges and lemonade at Cheltenham and Brighton'; and Baring, in defending the Cornish boroughs as representative of the mining and fishing industries, argued that it was of more consequence to leave some Cornish representation for those interests than to give members to Cheltenham and Brighton and 'such mushroom places as these which derived importance only from the migratory shoals which annually resorted to them'.

Obviously what appeared to the ministry to be a judicious selection of new boroughs might be regarded by the opposition as arbitrary and haphazard decisions. The way was thus left open for an endless succession of arguments conducted on a basis of comparison with selected and unselected towns. But the essential feature was the principle of selecting substantial interests and real communities for enfranchisement rather than attempting to build up a uniform structure on a numerical basis. The actual anomalies which the tories criticized at the time and which were to provide ground for rational objection thirty-five years later, were claimed by the whigs in 1831 as a decided merit in their scheme. In his reply during the opening debate on the first reform bill in March 1831 Russell acknowledged that the bill left anomalies in the representative system but firmly declared that this had been considered by the ministry and was a deliberate act on their part. 'Anomalies they found and anomalies, though not such glaring ones as now existed, they meant to leave. A regular distribution of an equal proportion of members to equal population might be a wise and great scheme, but the proposers of this measure had not thought fit to bring such a plan before Parliament.'

There remains one final point to be considered. Behind the electoral structure as it was left by the Reform Act, with its retention of old practices and old anomalies, its guarded introduction of new forces, its essentially aristocratic and conservative nature, lay a factor not easily susceptible of translation into institutional terms—the power of public opinion. Of the consciousness within the House of Commons of its strength there can be little doubt, for both sides cited it as evidence for their opposed arguments. In particular the power of opinion as expressed through the medium of the press was generally acknowledged. Inglis, for example, when replying to Russell in the opening debate on the first reform bill, pointed out that in fact during recent years the House of Commons had grown steadily more independent. The influence of the crown and the peerage had waned; the House was corrupted neither by money, since no member took money for his vote; nor by place, since patronage had been rigidly circumscribed; nor by party, since the old party divisions and the control of party leaders had disappeared. On the other hand, by means of public agitation and petitions, above all by means of the press, public opinion had secured immense weight in the House. 'This', he said, 'is the real control, to which we all look more or less.' At a subsequent period in the debate Sir James Scarlett, another tory, made a similar observation. 'At present', he remarked, 'no man can rise to deliver his sentiments in this House without exposing himself to the certainty of a comment upon those sentiments, by some public journal.' The whigs claimed this force of public opinion as a virtue, and indeed as a necessary feature of the constitution. Only a government on which an enlightened and informed public opinion was constantly playing could be relied on to carry out its functions correctly. This did not mean mob-rule or ceaseless radical demands; but what the people wanted, said Russell, was a change in the character of the representation of the country on which they could henceforth rely to reform, retrench, and economize when necessary. Hence one of the major whig arguments in favour of their bill was that it would result in a more constant and rapid action of public opinion on the legislature.

Both ministerialists and the opposition therefore were agreed on the strength of public opinion. The difference between them was that the tories believed that government had become so weak that it could not stand up to the weight of public opinion; the whigs believed that government had become so weak that it must have the reinforcement provided by public opinion. This latter aspect was most clearly put by Hawkins in the speech already referred to delivered in September 1831. With Inglis he agreed that the work of government had become increasingly difficult in recent years owing to the disappearance of various methods of influencing the House of Commons which had produced the majorities of the eighteenth century. He described the dilemma of the contemporary minister who, he said, was usually more liberal than his party—'slave, on the one hand, of that handful of dealers in parliamentary power whose zealous and faithful support he had no longer the adequate means of purchasing—hated, on the other hand, by the people, whose rights he would fain have granted, perhaps even at the sacrifice of his own interest, could such sacrifice have availed'. Nevertheless, the abolition of patronage had been the real cause of putting power into the hands of men prepared 'to try that newest and noblest of political experiments, a government by public opinion. And to this complexion must we come at last.' Matters had gone beyond the control of either tory or whig. 'The narrow resting place, on which the old system yet stood, which the current of passing events had long been loosening, was pushed from its base by last winter's torrent.'

19
THE ESSENTIALS OF CHARTISM
Asa Briggs

The radical commitment of a great many twentieth-century English historians has led to an almost continuous re-examination of the left-wing movements of the nineteenth century. Of these movements Chartism has been the most elusive for the modern historian and the most difficult to view in a clear perspective. These difficulties are overcome, however, in Asa Briggs' brilliant essays on Chartism, from which the following selection is taken. Briggs, a Sussex University scholar, is a prolific writer on Victorian cultural and social history; his work is celebrated for a keen appreciation of personality, a vivacious style, and strong powers of synthesis and generalization.

A STUDY of Chartism must begin with a proper appreciation of regional and local diversity. Some of the elements of diversity are measurable, and although adequate statistics do not always and did not exist, contemporaries were beginning to take an increasing interest in their measurement—rents, wages, prices, the incidence of unemployment, the degree of dependence on foreign markets. It is impossible to understand either the birth of Chartism or its fluctuating fortunes between the date of the publication of the Charter on 8 May 1838 and the withering away of the agitation in the 1850's without examining the movement of the relevant economic indices. Historians of Chartism have always recognised the importance of relating Chartism as a social and political force to the general economic history of the period, but recent refinements in the analysis of the changing structure and the cyclical fluctuations of the early nineteenth-century British economy make possible a deeper understanding both of the chronology and the geography of Chartism.

Some of the elements of diversity, however, cannot be measured quantitatively. Variations in local class structure, in the content of local grievances, in the traditions of political leadership and mass agitation, and in the adaptability and persistence of the Chartists themselves and of their opponents, require detailed investigation.... Chartism was a snowball movement which gathered together local grievances and sought

FROM Asa Briggs, *Chartist Studies* (London: Macmillan & Co. Ltd., 1959), pp. 2-15, 289-303. By permission of The Macmillan Company of Canada Limited, St. Martin's Press, Inc., and Macmillan & Co. Ltd.

to give them common expression in a nation-wide agitation. Many of the internal conflicts which divided it had their origins in the differences of background and outlook in what the Chartists called 'the localities'. The differences ante-dated both the publication of the Charter and the onset of the business depression which gave the new movement its greatest momentum. Some of them—like the differences between English and Scottish Chartism—had deep roots in pre-industrial history: others were associated with the growth of machine industry.

The pull of early Chartism seems to have been strongest in two kinds of place—first, in old centres of decaying or contracting industry, like Trowbridge in Wiltshire or Carmarthen in Wales, and second, in the new or expanding single-industry towns like Stockport, described by Engels as 'one of the darkest and smokiest holes in the whole industrial area'. Big cities, which served as regional capitals, had large numbers of Chartists, but were sometimes less militant than adjacent industrial areas. Manchester and Birmingham, for example, were less active in the middle years of Chartism than the textile and metal-working districts nearby: Leeds was quieter than Halifax. In the big cities, where political radicalism had established itself long before the drafting of the Charter, there were more attempts at political accommodation between Chartists and other reformers, although most of them were unsuccessful. Chartism was not strong—and in some cases it was almost nonexistent—in completely agricultural villages, those of Kent or Dorset, for example, in old market towns like Ripon or Bedford, and in new industrial centres with a mixed economy, like St Helens.

Such differences in appeal cannot be attributed to the accident of the presence or absence of active Chartist personalities, however significant was the influence of personality in particular cases. Nor can they be evaluated, however, within a framework of geographical determinism. It is dangerous to personify Manchester and Birmingham or to rely on broad generalisations about North and South or London and the provinces. Local differences need to be related to economic and social structure—to the composition of the labour force, the conditions of work, including relations between 'masters' and 'men', and the timing and extent of local unemployment. Other social factors, including the influence of religion, may also be relevant. In many places Nonconformity figures prominently in the local Chartist story.

There were three main groups within the heterogeneous labour force which played a special part in the development of Chartism—a section of the superior craftsmen, including printers, cobblers, tailors, cabinet-makers, booksellers and small shopkeepers; factory operatives, concentrated in the textiles districts, and familiarly referred to in the current vulgar political economy of the times as 'hands'; and domestic outworkers, including not only handloom weavers but such producers as framework knitters and nailmakers. The economic interests and fortunes of these three groups were not always the same. W. T. Thornton, the economist, remarked in 1846 that 'the labouring population has...been spoken of as if it formed only one class, but it is really divided into several, among which the rates of remuneration are far from being uniform ... so that, in order to represent with perfect fidelity the state of the labouring population, it would be necessary to describe each class separately'. It was not only rates of remuneration which diverged, but the extent of social security, regularity of earnings, the climate of industrial relations, status in the local community, and prospects of future advancement, both for the individual and for members of the family.

A main theme in Chartist history was the attempt to create a sense of class unity which would bind together these three groups. The attempt was never completely successful, however, and differences not only between one Chartist 'locality' and another but within Chartist 'localities' can be explained in part by differences in the balance of the three groups.

Not all the superior craftsmen were drawn into Chartism. New-style craftsmen, like machine-builders, for example, were never prominent. On the other hand, a minority of superior craftsmen, those described by William Lovett and the London Working Men's Association as 'the *intelligent* and *influential* portion of the working classes in town and country', were the leaven of the early Chartist movement, and many of them remained faithful to it until the end. Their belief in the Six Points of the Charter was not conditioned by the movements of the trade cycle, and many of them had been converted to belief in reform—if they needed to be converted—before the Charter was drafted. Although the most articulate of them often misunderstood those of their 'fellow workmen' who 'croaked over their grievances with maudlin brains' and were themselves misunderstood by those militant operatives who dismissed them as 'a middle-class set of agitators', they sought to foster a 'union of sentiment' among the working classes, 'which is essential to the prosecution of any great object.' They refused to look to 'great men' or to 'idols' and endeavoured to create working-class 'discrimination and independent spirit in the management of their political affairs'. Scattered about the country, they were the pillars of the Working Men's Associations. They included men like Henry Lovewell, the Ipswich journeyman tailor who already possessed the franchise in 1837 and had been a foundation member of the Mechanics Institute. Their very respectability, often associated with Nonconformity, which served as an asset to them in dealing with the 'middle classes', usually hindered them in dealing with 'fustian jackets, unshorn chins and blistered hands'.

The factory operatives were concentrated in particular parts of the country—Lancashire, described by Engels as 'the mainspring of all the workers' movements', the scene of the great industrial transformation of the late eighteenth and early nineteenth centuries, 'the cotton kingdom'; the West Riding of Yorkshire, where the woollen industry was in course of transformation, in what Faucher called 'a regime of transition' between old and new methods of production; parts of Cumberland, Derbyshire, Wales and the West of England; and West Scotland. In 1839 there were 192 cotton mills in Scotland employing 31,000 workers. All but 17 of these were located in Lanark and Renfrew. There was a further concentration within these counties as there was in Lancashire and the West Riding.

Work in factories entailed a new discipline and an enforced subordination, but it also stimulated an enhanced sense of solidarity and a quest for social and political independence. In the words of Ernest Jones, who wrote vigorously and eloquently about the implications of steam power:

> Up in factory! Up in mill!
> Freedom's mighty phalanx swell...
> Fear ye not your masters' power;
> Men are strong when men unite...
> And flowers will grow in blooming-time,
> Where prison-doors their jarring cease:
> For liberty will banish crime—
> *Contentment* is the best *Police*.

Both the myth of a pre-factory golden age and the dream of a new social order in the future influenced the thinking—and, equally important, the feeling—of the factory operatives, while both their means of action and their objectives shifted during the course of the 1830's and 40's. The pendulum swung between economic action through the trade unions and political action through Chartism. 'Good times' favoured the former: 'bad times' the latter. The rhythms of what the Leeds Socialist John Francis Bray called 'inordinate idleness and incessant toil' influenced the timing and the intensity of all forms of organisation. At different times 'the equalisation of wages' through 'general union', the Six Points of the Charter, the battle for the Ten Hours' working day, the slogan of 'a fair day's wages for a fair day's work', turn-outs and plug drawing, the repeal of the corn laws, and O'Connor's Land Plan appealed to all or some groups of factory operatives. The Charter was thus one objective among several, and the extent to which it figured as the main objective depended not only on the forcefulness and skill of Chartist leadership but on the state of the domestic and overseas market for textile goods. Some factory operatives remained faithful to Chartism through all its vicissitudes, but the crowds ebbed and flowed with the economic tides.

The absence of a factory system not only in London but in Birmingham is important in explaining local differences. In Birmingham the most important economic unit was not the factory, but the small workshop, and within the workshop small masters rather than industrial capitalists worked in close contact with skilled artisans. Economic development in Birmingham in the first half of the nineteenth century multiplied the number of producing units rather than added to the scale of existing enterprise. Labour-saving machinery, driven by steam power, was far less important than in Manchester. 'The operation of mechanism in this town', wrote a Birmingham man in 1836, 'is to effect that alone, which requires more *force* than the *arm* and the tools of the workman could yield, still leaving his skill and experience of head, hand and eye in full exercise; so that Birmingham has suffered infinitely less from the introduction of machinery than those towns where it is in marked degree, an actual substitute for human labour'. Another feature of Birmingham society was marked social mobility which blurred sharp class distinctions. Small masters might fail in their enterprises and become journeymen again: journeymen had chances of rising when times were good. 'It is easy to see', Faucher said of the city, 'that the *bourgeoisie,* which in all urban centres is the basis of society, scarcely rises in Birmingham above the inferior groups in society'. Engels and Cobden were agreed about the political consequences of this social system, and Engels quoted Faucher's phrase 'industrial democracy' and described the city as 'Radical rather than Chartist'. In fact, as we shall see, Birmingham played an important part in the birth of the Chartist movement as an organised national force, although it had lost much of its importance by the time that Engels wrote.

The third labour group, which was generally recognised by contemporaries to be a key group in Chartist politics, consisted of domestic outworkers. In the Black Country, adjacent to Birmingham, there were large numbers of nailmakers living near the starvation level. In Lancashire, the West Riding of Yorkshire, the West Country, Wales and Scotland there were handloom weavers fighting a grim losing battle against the machine. In the West Midlands there were framework knitters employed in an over-stocked occupation where there was not enough work to go round. It was because all other attempts at betterment broke down that most of these outworkers turned towards Chartism. Many of them had had the reputation in the 1820's of being a quiet, hard working, non-political section of the population, and certainly their first reaction to the privation and distress which followed the end of the Napoleonic Wars was to appeal to the local justices of the peace and to the government for economic protection. The failure of this appeal, which ran counter to the interests of factory owners and the ideas of the newly powerful political economists, led them direct into politics along a road of despair. How little they could expect to get from government was clearly brought out in the *Report of the Royal Commission on Handloom Weavers,* appointed in 1838 'to report whether any, and, if so, what measures could be devised for their relief'. Nassau Senior, the economist, was the chief draftsman of the Report, which has recently been described as an 'admirable' exercise in economic logic. 'The power of the Czar of Russia', the Commissioners concluded, 'could not raise the wages of men so situate. He might indeed order a scale of prices to be paid them for the work which they did, but in such cases the manufacturer would soon cease to give out work, as it would be against his interest to do it. The Czar of Russia, either by fixing on a high scale of wages, or by a direct command, might put an end to the occupation altogether, and such would be a most merciful exercise of his unlimited power; but the authority of the Government of a free country cannot thus control the subjects even for their own good; and all that remains, therefore, is to enlighten the handloom weavers as to their real situation, warn them to flee from the trade, and to beware of leading their children into it, as they would beware of the commission of the most atrocious of crimes'. Such advice, backed up as it was by economic as well as political authority, in considerable measure justifies Thomas Carlyle's emphasis on 'lack of due guidance' besides lack of food and shelter as the cause of the growth of the *isms* of his age. And long before the Commissioners reported nationally, handloom weavers had been told locally that their request for public help was 'absolute folly', 'founded in utter ignorance of the circumstances which regulate the wages of labour which it is impossible for Parliament to control'. It is not surprising that after suffering severely even when times were 'good', the weavers looked when times were bad not to the authority of a Czar of Russia but to the authority of local and national Chartist leaders. The leaders they preferred were those who knew how to use and were willing to use militant headstrong language, who painted bright pictures of the past—a past which had certainly provided handloom weavers not only with bigger wages but with an assured and recognised position in society—and who related the political demand for universal suffrage to the demand for food and shelter. The language of hunger was common to all those parts of the country where outworkers were concentrated. In Lancashire J. R. Stephens defined universal suffrage as the means to secure every working man's 'right' to a good coat on his back, a good roof over his head and a good dinner on his table. In the West Riding Richard Oastler, who never committed himself to support of the Chartist political programme, attacked the factory system as a 'slaughterhouse system' and added that he did not 'think that the Government can claim on any ground the allegiance of the operatives when they see that capital and property are protected and their labour is left to chance'. In the East Midlands, the editor of the *Leicester Chronicle* declared that, since the framework knitters could not hope to achieve genuine social independence, it was not surprising that they turned to a social Chartism, which offered the prospect of 'better wages, limited hours of labour, comfort, independence, happiness . . . all that the fond heart of suffering man pictures to him of joy and prosperity in his happiest moments'. In Wiltshire, a Trowbridge Chartist put the matter even more plainly. He promised his audience 'plenty of roast beef, plum pudding and strong beer by working three hours a day'.

There is a wide gap between language of this kind and the more sophisticated language of skilled artisans and craftsmen. It was the strength of O'Connor that he knew how to talk effectively to despairing domestic workers who were more interested during 1837 in the threat of the New Poor Law of 1834 than in political panaceas. The Poor Law Commissioners turned their attention in January 1837 to the industrial districts which hitherto they had left alone. They had met with some earlier resistance in the South—in Suffolk, for instance, and in small market towns like Bishop's Stortford and Saffron Walden—but in the north they were welcomed with what J. R. Stephens called 'the tocsin of revolt'. Oastler, the revered local leader, and O'Connor, who was beginning to fascinate angry audiences everywhere, both addressed a mass meeting in Huddersfield one week after the arrival of Alfred Power, the Assistant Poor Law Commissioner: it was Oastler who coined the phrase of the moment 'Damnation, eternal damnation to the fiend-begotten, coarser-food New Poor Law', the title he gave to the pamphlet version of his speech. O'Connor was shrewd enough to encourage the proliferation of grievances rather than to canalise them. Later on he told Lovett in 1842, 'I don't lead; I am driven by the people. The people gave the lead to the agitation and we followed.' The *Northern Star*, the first number of which appeared in Leeds on 18 November 1837, reported all local protest meetings with equal enthusiasm. It was not until the winter of 1837–8 that O'Connor turned decisively to the suffrage agitation, and it was not until the spring of 1838, on the eve of the drafting of the Charter, that the Anti-Poor Law movement was merged into the political agitation for parliamentary reform. . . .

The fact that the Poor Law Commissioners set out to put the 1834 Act into operation in the North of England just at the moment that business depression was leading to unemployment of factory operatives as well as starvation among the handloom weavers created the broadest possible front of local opposition. The Act had been intended not to solve the problems of an industrial society but to establish a free labour market in the pauperised agricultural counties. In the north a free labour market already existed. The principle of less eligibility, the cornerstone of the 1834 Act, had no relevance to conditions of involuntary mass industrial unemployment. The attempt to herd together inside the workhouses those people in receipt of poor relief was pointless as well as dangerous. 'It imposed a disgraceful stigma on the genuinely unemployed and their families, it was actuarially far more costly than out-relief, and finally it was tantamount to waging social war'. The language of the opponents of the Act was as violent as any of the later language employed by the militant Chartists. The workhouses were universally known as 'Bastilles', orders were given by local leaders to destroy them, rioting was widespread, and memories of resistance influenced not only Chartist history but the later history of working-class movements in the nineteenth century. The attempt to apply the New Poor Law 'did more to sour the hearts of the labouring population than did the privations consequent on all the actual poverty of the land'.

Before the Anti-Poor Law movement could merge into Chartism it had to shed many of its 'Tory' sympathisers, men who hated 'centralisation', looked to the restoration of an old form of society, deemed 'Whiggery' and 'the march of improvement' as the real curses of the country, and far from wanting further parliamentary reform intensely disliked the measure of 'middle-class' reform which had been passed in 1832. In August 1837 the Whig whip E. J. Stanley wrote to Edwin Chadwick, the most fervent and logical advocate of the principles of 1834, that 'North of

Trent the law is as unpopular as it is possible with all classes—Justices and Guardians for political purposes—overseers, now discontinued, from interested motives.... The whole of the manufacturing population vehemently against it, the agricultural population stubbornly against it'. Before Chartism swallowed up the Anti-Poor Law agitation, some of these critics had to be left by the wayside. Oastler was one of the first to be left, Parson Bull of Bradford a second. There were to be many flirtations between Tories and Chartists in the future, but from the spring of 1838 onwards it was abundantly clear that Chartism would depend on its own leaders and not on alliances with people outside its ranks.

There was a final complication. Although the 1834 Act was detested by popular leaders in all parts of the country, its principles were supported by many Radical members of Parliament, including Joseph Hume, Daniel O'Connell and some of the closest friends of the London Working Men's Association. Some of the members of the L.W.M.A. themselves believed in 'Malthusian principles'. It was within a circle of men not basically unfriendly to the Act of 1834 that the Charter itself was being drafted. Bitterness between O'Connell and O'Connor had an ideological twist to it, and differences between the L.W.M.A. and other working-class groups in London included differences of approach as well as of background. Before the Charter was published, some of the main conflicts within Chartism were clear for the world to see. Julian Harney, for example, one of the most interesting and articulate London Jacobins, attacked the L.W.M.A. not only on the platform but in the correspondence columns of *The Times*. Almost all the later divisions in Chartism can be studied in microcosm in the London disputes of 1835, 1836 and 1837. Men like Harney were just as bitterly opposed to the New Poor Law as the handloom weavers in the north, and while missionaries of the L.W.M.A. were spreading their propaganda quietly and effectively in the provinces, links were being forged between the enemies of the L.W.M.A. in the East End of London and the leaders of discontent outside. The defeat of a considerable number of Radical members of Parliament at the general election of July 1837 redirected Radical energies back into public agitation, but the Radicals were unable to direct provincial discontents because of their equivocal or even hostile attitude towards the views of some of the Chartists of the future. Just as those Tories, like Earl Stanhope, who dreamed of a national federation of Anti-Poor Law societies, pledged to repeal of the Act of 1834, could not take the lead in the years of increasing discontent, so those Radicals who believed in a substantial measure of parliamentary reform were doomed to play a restricted and limited part in popular agitation. Their ideas were written into the Charter, but ideas were not the most important elements in the political equation.

The business depression was more significant than any other factor in setting the tone of national agitation. In the years of relative prosperity, good harvests and expanding trade between 1832 and 1836 most working-class energies had been absorbed in trade-unionism. The Grand National

Consolidated Trades Union was only one example of a number of attempts to form large unions designed not only to raise wages but, in a phrase of Bronterre O'Brien, to bring about 'an entire change in society —a change amounting to a complete subversion of the existing order of the world. The working classes aspire to be at the top instead of at the bottom of society—or rather that there should be no top or bottom at all'. The architects of the new unions dreamed of a new kind of social organisation where Parliament would be replaced by a 'House of Trades', and they put forward ambitious claims for the Grand Council of the G.N.C.T.U. 'There are two Parliaments in London at present sitting', wrote J. E. Smith, the editor of the *Crisis* in 1834, 'and we have no hesitation in saying that the Trades Parliament is by far the most important, and will in the course of a year or two be the more influential.' Although Robert Owen explicitly repudiated universal suffrage, James Morrison, the editor of the *Pioneer,* related this objective to trade-union growth and talked of an 'ascendant scale' by which universal suffrage would be realised. 'With us universal suffrage will begin in our lodges, extend to the general union, embrace the management of trade, and finally swallow up the political power.'

The reasons for the failure of trade-unionism lay not so much in the pricking of these giant bubbles—they fairly quickly pricked themselves —but in the resistance both of employers and local authorities to specific local trade-union claims. Before the prosperous years drew to a close, trade-unionism had been almost completely destroyed as a nation-wide force. Owen himself, who had never agreed with the views of many of the unionists and had failed to understand the nature of the agitation he had helped to inspire, retreated without regret into sectarianism, to a renewed emphasis on 'the principles of the New Moral World in all their extent and purity'. 'I am termed a visionary', he had told Ricardo years before, 'because my principles have originated in experiences too comprehensive for the limited locality in which people have hitherto been interested.' The origins of Chartism as a national movement are to be discovered, as we have seen, in the 'localities'. Before another movement with large claims could be constructed, there first had to be a breaking down of utopian hopes as well as of vast organisations, for Chartism grew not only out of hunger and anger but out of disillusionment, disillusionment both with the Reform Bill of 1832, widely regarded as a 'sham', and with the ambitious trades-unionism of the 'good years'. When Henry Hetherington, the close friend and collaborator of William Lovett, visited Leeds in 1834 after the collapse of local trade-union efforts he drew the moral that nothing less than universal suffrage would break the workers' chains. It was a moral which the *Poor Man's Guardian* preached on every available occasion, and it was a moral which the Chartists took up in 1838. By that time many grievances had accumulated in all parts of the country, and the snowball metaphor which Morrison first applied to trade-unionism was even more applicable to Chartism.

There were links between trade-unionism and Chartism as well as differences of approach. Some local trade-union leaders, but by no means all, were Chartists a few years later. When the Dorchester labourers were sentenced to transportation, it was Lovett who was secretary of the national committee of protest set up in 1834. The committee included many of the men who later drew up the Charter, and collected subscriptions from all the trades which contributed most to the L.W.M.A.—tailors, shoemakers, joiners, cordwainers and coachpainters. It summoned protest meetings in all parts of the country—in factory districts, country towns and large cities as well as the metropolis. Three years later when the 'new Tolpuddle martyrs', the leaders of the Glasgow cotton spinners, were sentenced in January 1838 to seven years' transportation there was a further outburst of working-class indignation. On this occasion, however, some of the differences which were to dog Chartism were again openly demonstrated. Daniel O'Connell was an outspoken critic of the trade unions, as were some of the other Radical members of Parliament, and when he successfully moved in the House of Commons for the setting up of a select committee to inquire into workingmen's combinations, O'Connor, Harney and the *Northern Star* launched a direct attack on the L.W.M.A. for supporting this manoeuvre. The ensuing quarrel between O'Connor and the L.W.M.A. exceeded in bitterness any that had arisen before, and in a sharp letter Lovett not only denied the charges but accused O'Connor of seeking to pose as 'the great I AM of politics'. 'You would have it believed, to our prejudice,' the letter concluded, 'that we have been neglectful of the interests of working men, because we choose another path from yours. But time will show, and circumstances soon determine, who are their real friends; whether they are "the leaders of the people" who make furious appeals to their passions, threatening with fire and sword, or those who seek to unite them upon principles of knowledge and temperance, and the management of their own affairs.'

Within a few months of the writing of this letter the Charter had been published and the first steps were being taken to organise the election of delegates to the 'General Convention of the Industrious Classes'. It was clear from the start that there would be dramatic differences. The local materials out of which nation-wide Chartism was forged were many and various, and the founders of the movement were in disagreement about both tactics and social objectives....

In turning from local factors in the history of Chartism to its national bearings and significance, a new set of perspectives is necessary.

Historians in the past have tended to study it exclusively as a dramatic episode in the history of the labour movement—'the first independent movement of the workers' or in Lenin's words 'the first broad and politically organized proletarian-revolutionary movement of the masses' —and to relate it not only to what came before but to what came afterwards as the labour movement 'matured'. This familiar approach is useful and fruitful, for there were many interesting Chartist pointers to the future even in the early years of the agitation—the emphasis on mutual help and the refusal to lean on other sections of the community;

the attempt to establish friendly relations with other working-class organisations overseas; and the sense that though there might be many defeats in the short run, in the long run history was 'on their side'. During the last years of the agitation there was an unmistakable shift in emphasis from the demand for political reform within the framework of a parliamentary ideal, a demand which grew naturally out of eighteenth-century radicalism, to the search for social democracy, a search which led some Chartists—notably Jones and Harney—into socialism. 'Chartism in 1850', wrote 'Howard Morton' in the first issue of Harney's *Red Republican*, 'is a different thing from Chartism in 1840. The leaders of the English Proletarians have proved that they are true Democrats, and no shams, by going ahead so rapidly within the last few years. They have progressed from the idea of a simple *political reform* to the idea of a *Social Revolution.*' The progression was associated with a further shift in emphasis from local parochialism to international commitment and action. Both Jones and Harney looked beyond the Channel and across the Atlantic to social movements abroad: they were prepared not only to analyse foreign social situations, but to propound a foreign policy of their own.

The changing outlook of Chartist leaders after 1848 was not necessarily shared, however, by the old Chartist rank-and-file. There was a growing popular interest in foreign issues, which led up naturally to the popular excitement just before and during the Crimean War, and there was a limited interest in further reform of the franchise, but the vision of a new society lost much of its appeal. The shift of emphasis, therefore, was a portent of things to come rather than an effective adaptation to new circumstances. The more eclectic Chartism had been, the more it retained its vigour as a mass movement. The more it had drawn on material discontents and local grievances as well as on ideological inspirations, the more it prospered. The more it had attracted those people who looked back to the past as well as those who looked forward to the future, the more it spread. There was, of course, a heavy price to pay, the heaviest price of all, for the kind of challenge Chartists made when they were part of a nation-wide movement—failure. The price of eclecticism was disunity —local differences, faction fights and quarrels about tactics. The price of dependence on 'hunger politics' was the corroding influence even of limited 'prosperity'. The price of a double, or rather a multiple, appeal was inconsistency and inadequate leadership. The Chartist failure was inevitable, but it robs the movement neither of its interest nor of its importance. The Radical demand for the Six Points survived the failure of the Chartist attempt to secure them: the dream of social democracy lost much of its appeal, but it did not disappear. Taken by itself simply as an episode in working-class history, the story of Chartism has many parallels in more recent periods of history in other parts of the world. Most of the differences in outlook, tactics and even principles, which it reflected, and the basic problem it posed, that of 'independent' action (free from the 'contaminating' influence of well-wishers as much as the 'machinations' of opponents), continue to be relevant in colonial nationalist movements. Even the name 'Charter' has been employed by protest movements in South Africa. Both the psychology and sociology of Chartism are of abiding interest.

In every Chartist centre there seem to have been at least four groups of Chartists—a hard core of Radical reformers, whose association with Chartism was one phase, sometimes a formative phase, in a career devoted to political protest movements of one kind and another; a group of new recruits to working-class politics, often consisting of young men; a body of 'loyal supporters', eager not only to sign petitions and to attend meetings but to participate in the social activities which provided the 'fellowship' of Chartism—the procession, the Institute, the Chartist Church or the education class; and a fluctuating rank-and-file, capable of being stirred to enthusiastic activity, but just as capable of remaining silent and apathetic.

The first and second groups did not disappear from local or national politics after 1848. Many of them, like the Leeds Chartists, took up local government. James Sweet, for example, a Nottingham bookseller, gave good service as a Nottingham councillor, and as late as 1872 still proclaimed his Chartist beliefs and rejoiced that so many of the Chartist demands had been granted. Others turned to co-operation, trade-unionism, temperance and education. In Colchester, for example, John Howe, who had been an active Chartist at Thetford and Braintree, founded a branch of the Amalgamated Society of Carpenters and Joiners in 1861 and for over thirty years acted as its secretary, while at Halstead James Hunt and Thomas Ready helped to start the local co-operative society, took an active part in the life of the working men's club and became officials of Joseph Arch's Agricultural Labourers' Union. Other Chartists had more colourful experiences, joining Garibaldi's army, for example, or battling for reform in Australia. At Ballarat in 1854 a Reform League was founded which put forward most of the main Chartist demands and was clearly inspired by ex-Chartists. In the United States many ex-Chartists were completely assimilated, but a few continued to urge Radical causes in a new setting. Most important of all, many ex-Chartists continued to press for parliamentary reform at home.

During the quiet late 1850's, when it was difficult to summon enthusiasm for further parliamentary reform, some 'veterans of former times' were still prominent, as they still were ten years later in the agitation that led up to the passing of the Reform Bill of 1867, which gave the vote to the working classes of the towns. In Halifax in 1885 Benjamin Wilson, an old Chartist, called together a group of Chartist veterans to a dinner at which those present voted thanks to Gladstone for the further extension of the parliamentary franchise. The full story of the 'Chartist aftermath' will never be written, for it depends on the accumulation of a large mass of local material. Chartist organisation disappeared in the 1850's, but 'the old Chartist spirit' often lingered on. It was still being talked about in the North of England when the Independent Labour Party was founded in 1893.

The history of the third and fourth groups is even more difficult to write, for they consisted of men with 'no names, no individuality... anonymous fractions of the multitude'. It is quite misleading, however, to view them as objects rather than as subjects of history, to describe their movements as if they were akin to movements in natural history, or to speak only of 'symbols' and 'myths'. The tendency of some historians to discuss them in these terms produces a parody of social history. Behind the demand for the Charter was a demand for human dignity as well as for material objectives. 'The Chartists were called ugly names, the swinish multitude, unwashed and levellers... What they wanted was a voice in making the laws which they were called upon to obey.' Some of the Chartist rank-and-file, it was claimed, had 'more political knowledge than was possessed by any class of men' forty or fifty years before: it could be argued also that the lack of knowledge in the rest was the result of the lack of an educational system, long hours of work, and a social system which rested on an incomplete conception of citizenship.

The ability of the first and second groups of Chartists to appeal to the third and fourth depended not only on the choice of the right language and the requisite degree of understanding but on social and economic conditions, the strength and persuasiveness of other voices (including the voices of Church and Chapel) and the responsiveness of government and employers to their needs. 'It is a terrible fact', wrote Harney in 1849, 'that after so many years of "Reform" and "Chartist" agitation, multitudes of men whose every interest would benefit by the triumph of Chartism are yet ignorant of or indifferent to the Charter. This is true not only of agricultural workers, but of a considerable portion of the local population.' After the collapse of Chartism as a mass movement there was much retrospective stock-taking of this kind. 'Even in 1848,' one writer remarked three years after the event, 'when European endeavours lent us a sort of shamed impulse, what were our numbers? Some three or four hundreds ... paid their tolerably regular pence for a few months.... Some four or five thousands, appreciating the eloquence of Ernest Jones, etc., thought it tyranny to be called upon for any regular payment. I cannot count the thousands, or say millions, who made noises at monster meetings. Indeed they were never counted. Why should they have been? They were no part of our party.' But they were a part while the 'party' was a genuine national organisation. They gave it its colour, its force, its power of threat to the established order. 'They felt great disappointment at being abandoned by those whom they said they had supported to the utmost of their power.... The consequence of this was the total abandonment of all reliance upon the middle class.' They looked eagerly and hopefully to the Chartist leaders, and the most important of the Chartist leaders, O'Connor, looked to them.

All the groups talked the language of 'class' in a frank and uninhibited manner. 'If they whose interests are (so) identified', the L.W.M.A. had stated, 'do not investigate the causes of the evils that oppress them, how can they expect others to do it for them?' This conception of mutual self help was associated with the view that 'union of sentiment is essential to the prosecution of any great object'. The 'division of classes', treated by the *Northern Star* as a law of nature and of history, made it essential, it was claimed, for the working classes to preserve and develop an intense feeling of emotional identification. In the North there was no need to dwell on the reasons for 'union of sentiment'. Engels, who compared the outlook of the Chartists and the 'Socialists', remarked that while 'the Chartists are theoretically the more backward, the less developed ... they are genuine proletarians all over, the representatives of their class.'

Any full investigation of the Chartist approach to 'class' must take account not only of the demand for 'union of sentiment' but of the impact of recent working-class history and the diffusion of a number of basic economic propositions on different sections of the labour force. The history may be disposed of briefly. It went back to the rise of steam power, the Luddite disturbances, Peterloo and the agitation for Reform. The interests of 'middle classes' and 'working classes' were held to have diverged, and the Reform Bill of 1832 was treated, as the N.U.W.C. had treated it at the time, as a sham. In terms of old-fashioned Radical objectives alone, it had accomplished nothing. 'Not only in the old, but in the Whig mock-Reform-created boroughs as well, were those disgusting practices going on which the Reform Bill was supposed to have abolished'. In terms of social objectives, the Reform Parliaments were worse than the old. 'They had united all *property* against all *poverty*.' They had introduced the New Poor Law, widely regarded as 'a murderer's death-blow to the operative classes'. 'One sole recipe', thundered Carlyle, 'seems to have been needful for the woes of England, refusal of outdoor relief. England lay in sick discontent, writhing powerless on its fever-bed, dark, nigh desperate in wastefulness, want, improvidence and eating care, till like Hyperion down the eastern steeps, the Poor Law Commissioners arose and said, "Let there be workhouses and bread of affliction and water of affliction there".' ...

The economic propositions used to support the case for separate class action were three in number, and they were being stated, apparently often quite independently, in several parts of the country—first, that labour was the source of all value, and its rights could only be defended by the workers themselves; second, that manufacturers were forcing labour to work over-long hours and robbing it of a portion of its proper reward; and third, that exploitation was being assisted by the existence of a 'reserve army' of labour which forced down wages and worsened working conditions. These three propositions were part of the regular oratorical equipment of many platform speakers and working-class journalists as well as of social theorists like J. F. Bray and Bronterre O'Brien who stated the propositions in analytical form. The *Poor Man's Guardian* and the *Northern Star* often went further in directly associating economic exploitation and governmental authority. 'The middle classes', remarked the former, 'are the real tyrants of the country. Disguise it as they may, they are the authors of our slavery for without their connivance and secret support no tyranny could exist. Government is but a tool in their hands to execute their nefarious purposes.'

Although Chartist grievances were by no means always couched in such sophisticated language, Chartists almost everywhere were suspicious of alliances with the middle classes. Many of the detailed local studies have qualified this general statement and the study of the relations between Chartists and Leaguers which follows examines it more closely. It was only after 1848, when corn law repeal had been achieved and working-class objectives had still not been secured, that some of the leading members of the Chartist rump came round to the view that a broader Radical front could be created once more. O'Connor, twisting and turning, talked of an alliance between 'mental labour on the one hand and manual labour on the other': Harney, who by that time was attacking O'Connor, was himself working with middle-class reformers in 1851 and 1852: five years later, Jones who had written earlier that 'an amalgamation of classes is impossible where an amalgamation of interests is impossible also', had come round to the view that 'there can be no doubt as to the wisdom of allying with the middle classes and their leaders if they offer such a measure of reform as we can be justified in accepting'. This declaration was in a very real sense a Chartist epitaph.

It is impossible to understand Chartist arguments about class without fitting Chartism into British history as a whole. In concentrating on Chartism as an episode in working-class history—with international as well as national implications—too little attention has been paid by social and political historians to class relations in the Britain of the 1830's and 40's. Chartism can only be understood, however, if it is related to social history as well as to socialism.

During the late 1830's and 40's two forms of class consciousness were being forged in Britain, not one—middle-class consciousness and working-class consciousness. Each manifestation of class consciousness assisted the articulation of the other. It was fear of working-class numbers as well as hatred of the handful of landlords which buttressed middle-class consciousness. It was irritation with and frustration engendered by the Anti-Corn Law League, itself a child of the business depression, which was set up after the Chartist movement had been inaugurated, that provoked the Chartists to their most violent class declarations. The *Annual Register* described Chartism in 1839 as 'an insurrection which is expressly directed against the middle classes'.

The League prided itself on being a *middle-class* body, and on the wealth, organisation and moral power which were associated with the adjective. On more than one occasion Cobden acknowledged that its manoeuvres and its artifices, its fervour and its efficiency depended upon middle-class opinions and methods. 'We have carried it on by those means by which the middle class usually carries on its movements. We have had our meetings of Dissenting Ministers: we have obtained the co-operation of the ladies; we have resorted to tea parties and have taken those specific means for carrying out our views which mark us as rather a middle-class set of agitators.' When the League secured its objective Cobden was even more precise. In a famous letter to Peel he wrote, 'Do you shrink from governing through the bona fide representatives of the middle class?

Look at the facts and can the country be otherwise ruled at all? There must be an end of the juggle of parties, the mere representatives of traditions, and some man must of necessity rule the state through its governing class. The Reform Bill decreed it: the passing of the Corn Bill has realised it.' This, as much else in Cobden's writings, was a kind of middle-class Marxism, and Peel put it completely on one side. The Chartists could not ignore it, however, nor the attempts which the leaders of the League made to 'use' the operatives in their agitation. They had no desire merely to serve as 'something in our rear to frighten the aristocracy'. At the same time, it is not surprising, considering differences not only of economic interest but of education, outlook and behaviour, that a large section of the middle classes disliked the thought of working men taking on any more active role. The strength of class feelings is well brought out in a casual remark by Sturge's mid-nineteenth-century biographer. After describing the breakdown in 1842 of the negotiations between the Complete Suffrage Union and the Chartists, he adds, 'Mr Sturge's friends felt thankful that this result left him at liberty honourably to withdraw from much uncongenial fellowship.'

The class attitudes of the Chartists and their unwillingness to draw on any outside support doomed them, if did nothing else, to political failure from the start. If problems relating to the development of labour history are put on one side, it can be plausibly argued that the most important historical feature of the Chartist movement in its contemporary British setting was that it demonstrated not the weaknesses of the working classes, which were obvious, but the strength of the middle classes. It may in fact be regarded as one episode in the development of middle-class consciousness. The Kennington Common incident of 1848 certainly reveals more about middle-class than about working-class attitudes, for the real strength of Chartism in 1848 lay not in London but in the industrial provinces, and if there was a fiasco it lay as much in the exaggerated fears of the middle classes of the metropolis as in the ignominious failure of the Chartists. Perhaps as H. M. Hyndman, the late nineteenth-century socialist put it, 'the worst mistake the Chartist leaders made was that they neglected London until too late'. There was more militant middle-class consciousness than militant working-class consciousness in London in 1848. When Russell made it known that he was willing to allow the Chartists to march to the House of Commons with their petition, the London shopkeepers protested against the 'apathy and inaction' of the Government. When the whole incident was closed and the sandbags had been removed from the Bank of England, Lady Palmerston wrote to Mrs Huskisson about what had occurred. 'Your letter reminded me', she explained, 'that I ought to give you private details of our "revolution" as the papers, though very full, could only give the public ones. Our terrace was divided into districts and all the servants made special constables.... I am sure that it is very fortunate that the whole thing has occurred, as it has shown the good spirit of our middle classes.' An American visitor to England shared this assessment of relative power but drew a very different conclusion. 'The middle classes in England, who took up arms against the humbler classes (who, much as we may disapprove the manner in which they seek it, have certainly in view altogether, and only, the benefit of the middle classes, the mitigation of national burdens, and the general cause of liberty), have now, with their hands tied behind them, thrown themselves into the power of the government, and all hopes of reform are extinguished, for at least the next quarter of a century.'

20

FROM EMPIRE TO COMMONWEALTH

W. K. Hancock

The impact of liberalism on the Second British Empire, the achievement of self-government and dominion status in colonies with a preponderance of European settlers, and the development of the ideals and institutions of the British Commonwealth are subjects thoroughly explored in modern scholarship, particularly by historians in the dominions, for whom this aspect of modern English history is fundamental to their national experience. W. K. Hancock, a brilliant Australian scholar, was for many years a professor in England before returning to his native country. In the following remarkable essay he summarizes the whole course of transition from Empire to Commonwealth in a succinct and trenchant manner.

THERE OCCURRED, after the American Revolution, no repudiation or mitigation of the juristic theory which asserted that there was nothing which parliament could not do. On the contrary, the notions of law as a command, and of parliament as the omnipotent commanding authority, entrenched themselves almost impregnably in English minds through crude popularizations of Jeremy Bentham and John Austin. It followed inevitably from these notions—assuming them to be true and immutable—that new disruptions of Empire must some day succeed the

---

FROM W. K. Hancock, *Problems of Nationality, 1918–1936*, Vol. I of *Survey of British Commonwealth Affairs* (London: Oxford University Press [under the auspices of the Royal Institute of International Affairs], 1939, 1964), pp. 13–27. By permission of the publishers.

American disruption. For the unlimited supremacy of a parliament chosen by British constituencies condemned to perpetual inequality and insecurity the British communities overseas, unless they should take the extreme step of separation. And this step, surely, they would one day take. For experience had shown that emigrant Englishmen possessed a craving for liberty no less obstinate than that of the Englishmen who had stayed at home.

All those people, therefore, whose view of the imperial problem was determined by the accepted theory, were convinced that there was no solution of the problem short of imperial disruption. 'There cannot be two imperial legislatures in one Empire.' 'A self-governing dependency is a contradiction in terms.' Emancipation is as natural an event in the history of the colonies as death to an individual.' 'Does anybody believe that a population of twenty millions in Australia would remain subject to a population of forty millions in the British Isles?' These are typical pronouncements from the lips of nineteenth-century statesmen, public servants, and publicists. The mood in which one doctrinaire or another pronounced judgment depended upon his individual temperament and standard of values. If he had thought of the Empire as profit, he could cheerfully contemplate its dissolution, because new and revered teachers were making it quite obvious that 'economics of sovereignty' were fallacious and expensive economics. It became fashionable among Englishmen to wish themselves good riddance of the colonies because there was nothing to be made out of them. 'The monopoly', Adam Smith had said, 'is the chief badge of their dependency, and it is the sole fruit which has hitherto been gathered from that dependency.' During the nineteenth century the majority of Englishmen came to the conclusion that the fruit was not worth the cost of collection. There were better ways of growing rich. Why struggle, why protest, against the inevitable disruption? ... But the Empire might have military and strategic advantages. There were other Englishmen who thought of it in terms of power politics. From this point of view the Indian and tropical dependencies certainly seemed to be worth while. They supported military establishments, they were 'a nursery of our statesmen and warriors', their vast populations were obedient to the word of command. The colonies of British settlers were another matter. Emigrant Englishmen were intractable. 'What is the use of these colonial deadweights which we cannot govern?' They might even get us into expensive trouble. To Disraeli, India was a great British interest and a great British pride: Canada was a liability. There were many who agreed with him. 'Our relations with North America are of a very delicate character,' wrote Lord Granville. 'The best solution of them would probably be that in the course of time and in the most friendly spirit the Dominion should find itself strong enough to proclaim her independence.' Obviously, the 'inevitable day' of a second imperial disruption, when it dawned, would dawn not unwelcome to a considerable section of influential Englishmen.

There was, however, another section of thoughtful Englishmen who contemplated this same inevitable day with different feelings. Theirs was an attitude towards the colonies which expressed itself not in 'good riddance' but in 'good luck'. Accepting regretfully the proposition that a self-governing dependency was a contradiction in terms, they resigned themselves to colonial independence because they believed in colonial self-government. Taking it on trust from established theory that empire and liberty were irreconcilable, they declared themselves for liberty. Liberty without disruption, full liberty as the foundation of empire, would have been their choice, had it occurred to them as a possible one. But the orthodoxies of the theory of sovereignty made it impossible for them to conceive of bonds of empire which were not in some degree a bondage of subjection. Their dream, of which they were but half conscious, was a refashioning of the Empire upon the principle of equal liberty of the parts and free association of the whole; but such a refashioning could not happen by quiet growth, and the gradual diffusion of the living principle of liberty throughout the old structure, and its ultimate transformation. The necessities of imperial command and colonial subjection could not be evaded in this way. There must, therefore, be a moment of disruption. It was the only possible way of achieving unfettered freedom. But it might be followed by a moment of re-integration. Within the space of three years three notable books advocated this neat but rather perilous manœuvre. The colonies were to assume full freedom by assuming sovereignty. Thereafter they were to accept a treaty with Great Britain; as free communities they would join a free association. This was the proposal of Lord Thring in 1865, of Viscount Bury in 1866, of Sir Charles Dilke in 1867. It is in all essentials the proposal on which Mr. De Valera took his stand in 1921. The Articles of Agreement for a Treaty between Great Britain and Ireland are a half-way house between these ingenious mid-nineteenth-century suggestions and the actual experience of the Dominions, which, between 1867 and 1921, was solving the problem of liberty and unity, by the method of pushing to one side its impressive theoretical impossibilities.

Until the end of the nineteenth century there were still in the overseas Empire many thoughtful individuals who, like their English contemporaries, judged more by theory than by their unfolding experience. And their judgement tended to coincide with that of the English doctrinaires. In so far as they remained emigrant British, they were not content with an inferior measure of British liberty. In so far as they were becoming aware of their own environment and their peculiar destiny as members of individual communities, their impatience with legal frustrations of their freedom was sharpened. The new nationalisms which were becoming self-conscious in Australia and Canada could not submit to an empire which meant dependence. If freedom meant separation, they must demand separation. If self-government and empire were contradictories, they must repudiate empire. But there was an underlying reluctance to accept the dilemma. And so, from Australia as from Great Britain, there came voices which preached 'Separation and Nationalism with a subsequent Anglo-Saxon alliance'. An independent federated Australia, they argued, would, under wise councils, be only preliminary to a Union with England. To men of this stamp separation was desirable because it was the only road to mature freedom. Freedom, they hoped, would mean free association. By 1900 the majority of them had realized that free association could be achieved without the moment of disintegration. In the first year of the Australian Commonwealth, one of their leaders confessed that experience had disproved preconceived theory. His speech was valedictory to those idealists, 'of whom I was one', who had believed that Australia could realize her national destiny 'only by establishing an independent entity as the preliminary to a closer alliance with Great Britain'.

Looking back upon these fumblings with the problem of *imperium et libertas,* we now see clearly that their awkwardness was due to the existence of a theoretical obstacle which interfered with the natural disposition of Englishmen and colonists to trust their own experience. Experience was demonstrating with increasing emphasis that liberty was the cement of empire, that each extension of it mitigated irritations, removed frustrations, and liberated an active will for partnership in a common way of life. Experience was progressively refuting the maxim that in sovereignty there are no gradations. This demonstration and this refutation did not, it is true, possess any inherent and eternal doctrinal validity; but they were valid under the existing conditions of time and circumstance. It was the error of the established juristic doctrine, or at least of the current political translations of it, to rule out dogmatically any mitigating possibilities of circumstance. Theory continued to demonstrate that some time, at some point, sovereignty must inevitably operate as a check upon liberty, expressing intolerably in outward relationships its inner nature of command and obedience, superiority and inferiority. It was intellectual subservience to this theory, together with an emotional repudiation of it, which stimulated the doctrinaires to their Humpty Dumpty performances of pulling down the Empire, which meant sovereignty, as a preliminary to putting it up again in the form of a perpetual alliance. The doctrinaires, had they been consistent, would have been forced to confess that all the King's horses and all the King's men could do nothing with the Empire's broken pieces. For, if law inevitably meant merely the command of a superior—and it was this assumption which necessitated the imperial disruption—the refashioning upon a basis of equality could not be binding: unless, indeed, the disrupted Empire reformed itself as a vast state with a single sovereignty. Failing this heroic solution, which was not contemplated by the advocates of an 'alliance', the separated units of a disrupted constitutional structure must henceforth face each other in a state of nature. The moment of independence could not possibly introduce a moment of reunion. The separation must be perpetual.

There was only one sensible attitude for statesmen to take towards political distortion of legal theory which so muddled their heads and thwarted their intentions. The intelligent thing to do with this doctrine was to forget about it, following the lessons of experience until there should emerge a new theory which would help rather than hinder the interpretation of experience. For such an attitude there was good precedent. Burke had advised it. Leave theories to the schools, he had said; 'for there only they may be discussed with safety'. Burke's own theory of sovereignty was no more helpful than that of his contemporaries; it was enshrined in the Declaratory Act; it raised a formal barrier to the principle of equality which we have now accepted as a necessary complement to the principle of liberty. But Burke was not greatly interested in this theory: his thought had a different starting-point. 'I am not determining a point of law; I am restoring tranquillity; and the general character and situation of a people must determine what sort of government is fitted for them.' What sort of government was fitted for colonists of British stock? Surely a free government, a government in accord with 'the antient policy of this Kingdom'.

When this child of ours wishes to assimilate to its parent, and to reflect with a true filial resemblance the beauteous countenance of British liberty; are we to turn to them the shameful parts of our Constitution? are we to give them our weakness for their strength? our opprobrium for their glory? and the slough of slavery, which we are not able to work off, to serve them for their freedom?

The British Commonwealth of to-day, it has been said, is a remarkable product of the political philosophy of Burke. If we are content to ignore Burke's legalistic theory and emphasize, as he emphasized, the unimportance of theory in comparison with experience, we may accept this statement as true. It is indeed tempting to imagine a kind of apostolic succession of magnanimous Whig statesmen who hand on from one to another the virtue which has recreated the Empire upon the principle of broadening freedom. Burke uses the blessed word, 'assimilation'. 'This child of ours', he says, 'wishes to assimilate to its parent, and to reflect with a true filial resemblance the beauteous countenance of British liberty.' Fox reechoes Burke's phrase. 'The principle laid down', he says in 1774, '... has been this, that the government of the colony ought to be assimilated, as much as possible, with that of the mother country.' And in 1791 he repeats the word and gives it the widest possible interpretation. Canada is capable of enjoying liberty in its fullest extent, and—'Canada must be preserved to Great Britain by the choice of its inhabitants'. In Fox's view, empire and liberty are not contradictories: empire is achieved through liberty. Nearly half a century later, Lord Durham, holding the same faith, convinces his doubting countrymen that the Canadians must have a constitution assimilated in the essential matter of executive government to the English model.... From one liberal Englishman to another the torch of colonial freedom is handed on. Reactionary Tories dash in to snatch at it and hurl it to the ground. There is, for example, Thurlow, the formidable antagonist of Fox, both in 1774 and in 1791. Assimilation, he grumbles, cannot be applied to the constitution of a colony. 'It is a

grossness—it is making two allied kingdoms, totally out of our power ...'
'If political liberty, the governing principle of our constitution, be established in a colony, the sovereignty will be established there—and consequently independence.' Liberty by this argument is proper for Englishmen, not for colonists.

Nevertheless, it is quite false to think of the refashioning of the Empire on the principle of liberty as the methodical working-out by English Whigs of a kind of hundred years' plan of liberal imperialism. The historical reality is far more complicated. Pitt, a Tory, is responsible for the instalment of 'assimilation' which is contained in the Act of 1791. Russell, a Whig, resists the further instalment proposed by Lord Durham in 1839. Thurlow's statement of theory is almost universally accepted by Whig and Tory alike, though varying deductions are made from it. The doctrine of assimilation is given a reactionary twist by English governors on Canadian soil, who interpret it in the sense of establishing there the conservative elements of English social and political life as a counterpoise to the equalitarian spirit of American democracy. Its more liberal interpretation is rejected by the loyalist emigrants from the revolted colonies to Canada, although it had in 1791 been asserted primarily for their benefit. These loyalists, like Ulster Protestants, ground their own ascendancy in the community upon its political subordination, which is challenged by the majority of their countrymen. They persuade themselves that this subordination constitutes the essential part of the imperial connexion; they make its acceptance the test of 'loyalty'. Assimilation to British practice by the institution of parliamentary executives would in one Canadian province give the power of government to a majority composed largely of dissenters and democrats of American origin: in the other province it would put it in the hands of French Catholics.

The stubborn fact of French-Canadian nationality cuts right across the constitutional problem and makes it impossible to study the doctrine of assimilation merely as a proposition of governmental theory. The doctrine may be shown, in its origins, to have had emphatic racial connotations. 'Do you propose to take away liberty from the Englishman', cried Burke, 'because you will not give it to the French? I would give it to the Englishman, although ten thousand Frenchmen should take it against their will.' To Fox, a constitutional assimilation of Canada to Great Britain was bound up with a racial assimilation of French Canadians to the dominant British. He wished them to 'unite and coalesce, as it were, into one body'. The early governors of Canada—from motives which, it is true, were mixed—had resisted claims to British freedom which would have given power to a tiny British minority to legislate against French nationality. These military reactionaries had a vision of freedom as national tolerance; they formulated on behalf of the French-Canadians a doctrine of trusteeship. But the governors after 1800 joined with English Whigs and Canadian loyalists in a campaign of racial imperialism. The French element must be swamped by a British immigration. 'The Province must be converted into an English Colony, or it will ultimately be lost to England.' The Canadian population must be 'overwhelmed' with English Protestants. Lord Durham himself failed to disentangle the constitutional and racial implications of assimilation. He had no tolerance for 'the miserable spirit of nationality', for 'the idle and petty notion of a visionary nationality'. He wished Canada to be free in the English way; but he thought it indispensable to put a majority of British race in control of this freedom. Would it then be freedom for the French? Perhaps it would, when they had been taught not to be French.... British constitutional principle was still interwoven with British racial prejudice. The most liberal Englishmen had not yet learnt that the liberty which they valued might be a wholesome diet for people of another nationality.

It is therefore utterly surprising to find French-Canadians asserting, less than forty years after the Durham Report, that they desire the federated Canada which they are helping to make, to remain 'a British colony'. The French want to remain 'British' in order that they may remain French. This means that somehow, between 1839 and 1865, the doctrine of assimilation has shed its racial implications. It has been discovered that Frenchmen need not cease to be Frenchmen in order to share with Englishmen the difficult privileges of self-government. The discovery is perhaps hardly less significant, achieved as it was in an age of bitter national antagonisms, than the principle of 'liberty for tender consciences' towards which men of goodwill struggled in the age of religious wars. Both in seventeenth-century England and in nineteenth-century Canada, the new principle to which society ultimately rallied was discovered and applied in despite of preconceived theory and prejudice. It was wrested out of conflict; it was seized upon and proclaimed by creative leaders whose imaginations were quicker and more generous than those of the majority of men; but it was also in the end achieved by the plain common sense of ordinary individuals honestly learning the lessons of experience. It was a synthesis hammered out by the contrasted ideals, interests, and wills of English Whigs and Tories, of Canadian-British and Canadian-French, of Canadian rebels and Canadian reactionaries, of conflicting creeds and classes and localities. The bitterness of conflict was moderated by old traditions of British constitutional method, of local autonomy, of respect for individual conscience and a rooted dislike of force. Amidst the disorder of interests and beliefs there was one unifying principle, the principle of liberty. At the beginning it had been assumed that the constitutional liberty which the English valued, and the national liberty which the French valued, were contradictories. Searching their experience, British and French came to understand that they could achieve neither, except in a free federated community where both values were ultimately shared.

Lord Durham and his disciples set out to solve a problem of constitutional freedom, and, in solving it, achieved a triumph greater than the one which they had at first imagined. They appeased warring nations. Moreover, they raised a standard which in other countries and other circumstances would encourage those who came after them to face courageously the inescapable and intractable issues of race and nationality which constitute the supreme challenge to the British Commonwealth. Race and nationality will be recurring themes in this book. For the present, however, it will be profitable to keep to the central problem raised in this chapter, the formal problem of *imperium et libertas,* of reconciling the equal freedom of the parts of an association with the unity of the whole.

British statesmanship chose to leave difficult theories to the schools, and to follow the path of liberty, walking rather by faith than by sight. But there were moments when the theoretical reason of statesmen uttered emphatic protests. Such a moment occurred during the thirties and forties of the last century. Here was the turning-point of imperial constitutional history. Lord Durham had carried the principle of assimilation into the sphere of executive government; Canada, like Great Britain, was to be ruled by ministers responsible to parliament. This raised in a new and even more acute form the dilemma which had wrecked the first British Empire. Imagination which had boggled at the vision of co-ordinate parliaments in the same empire must boggle still more at the vision of co-ordinate parliamentary executives in the same empire. Responsible government, said Lord John Russell, was 'a condition which can exist only in one place, namely the seat of empire'. Logically, the existence of separate parliamentary executives involved the acceptance by the Crown of separate advice. The advice might be conflicting. The unity of the Crown, and of the Empire, would then be at an end. Durham and the Canadian reformers thought that they could evade the dilemma by drawing a line between matters which were local and matters which were imperial. In the former, the governor would act on the advice of his Canadian ministers: in the latter, he would follow the instructions of Her Majesty's government. The legislative competence of the Canadian parliament would also be limited to this local field. Russell denied that a line of demarcation could be drawn. Obviously the Canadian constitution could not be assimilated to the British in the sphere of external relations, for nobody would recommend separate executive decision in 'the questions of foreign war and international relations, whether of trade or diplomacy'. According to Russell, assimilation was equally impossible in internal government. 'There are some cases of internal government', he said, 'in which the honour of the Crown, or the faith of Parliament, or the safety of the state, are so seriously involved, that it would not be possible for Her Majesty to delegate her authority to a ministry in a colony'. The reformers of the North American provinces nevertheless argued that a line could be drawn. Doctrinaires in England and in Australia, later on, desired the line to be rigidly defined. But on this matter Russell was right. Experience proved that self-government, to be effective, must be free to expand indefinitely with the expansion of interests and strength in the new communities. The spheres of land policy, constitutions, tariffs, which Durham would have reserved to imperial authority, were soon occupied. More slowly, but definitely, self-government began to expand into the sphere of foreign relations, where, so Russell had said—and there was nobody who ventured to contradict him—unity of control was indispensable.

Lord Russell was extremely far-sighted, but it may sometimes happen that the wisest statesmanship is content not to see too far. The immediate and pressing problem at the time was to extend liberty; the extensions of liberty would create new problems which must be solved in their turn. Astute reasonings might be framed, declared the Canadian reformer Baldwin, and fine distinctions might be drawn; 'but the plain common sense and practical view' of Canadians resented a system which, in the name of imperial unity, subjected the colonial majority to rule by a colonial minority. The remedy, the only remedy, was assimilation of Canadian to British practice. 'Your Lordship', wrote Baldwin to Durham, 'must adapt the Government to the genius of the people upon whom it is to act. It is the genius of the English race in both hemispheres to be concerned in the government of themselves.' The Nova Scotian reformer, Joseph Howe, demanded nothing which was not 'extremely simple and eminently British'.

'It seems strange', he wrote to Russell, 'that those who live within the British Empire should be governed by other principles than those of the British Constitution; and yet it is true, notwithstanding.... Why should we run counter to the whole stream of British experience; and seek, for no object worthy of the sacrifice, to govern on one side of the Atlantic by principles the very reverse of those found to work so admirably on the other?'

In dealing with the thirteen colonies, the British, so Burke had complained, practised 'too much logick and too little sense': in dealing with the Canadians they were persuaded to follow 'the plain common sense and practical view' of the matter. Lord John Russell himself, as Colonial Secretary, played a notable part in evading his own dilemma. Honest rigid men were appalled at the experiment in which they found themselves called upon to take part. The Empire was being wrecked, Canada was being surrendered to republicans and disloyalists; and the governor was expected to assist at the surrender. But there were other statesmen, British and Canadian, who followed their experience with an expanding enthusiasm. In their speeches and dispatches we feel a stir of excitement. They feel that their faith is visibly working miracles. Liberty, instead of disrupting the Empire, is re-creating it. Lord Elgin, Durham's son-in-law, beholds an empire 'growing, expanding, strengthening itself from age to age, striking its roots deep in fresh earth and drawing new supplies of vitality from its virgin soils'. He writes to Earl Grey—'I have been possessed with the idea that it is possible to maintain on this soil of North America and in the face of Republican America, British connexion and British institutions, if you give the latter freely and trustingly.'

In Canada, New Zealand, Australia, and South Africa, colonies and provinces joined with each other in federations or unions under the

British Crown. They assumed the new style of 'self-governing Dominions'; they emphasized their awareness of deepening national individuality; their expanding interests and vitality pushed them forwards in the direction of unfettered and complete national self-government. There remained, it is true, imposing limitations on their power. In their capital cities there was a governor-general, appointed by the Sovereign on the advice of his British ministers, and performing in the Dominions not only the tasks of constitutional headship which the Sovereign himself performed in the United Kingdom, but also special duties enjoined upon him as an imperial officer. The governor-general was the channel through which His Majesty's government sent such communications as it saw fit to make to dominion governments on matters of foreign policy, which, except in the more local and less formal matters, remained outside dominion competence. Over the legislative power of dominion parliaments there lay a 'triple veto'. The governor-general might refuse his assent to a Bill passed by both houses of parliament; or he might reserve the Bill for the Sovereign's pleasure; or—even if the governor-general did neither of these things—the Sovereign, advised by his ministers in the United Kingdom, might himself within one year of the final passing of the act in the dominion disallow it and thereby annul it as law. There was in addition the overriding legislative power of the imperial parliament elected by the constituencies of the United Kingdom. The Colonial Laws Validity Act of 1865, although it removed doubts as to the powers of colonial legislatures within their own sphere, emphasized the fact of their subordination. In legal theory, there were still no gradations in sovereignty. The dominion constitutions were themselves derived from acts of the imperial parliament, and the power which conferred right could also revoke it. The imperial parliament could, if it chose, annihilate the whole constitutional structure of dominion freedom.

This imposing legal system has been described in many books. The point which it is necessary to make now is that theory had very little relation to practice. In practice, none of the formidable restrictions which have been mentioned interfered with dominion freedom in the spheres marked out by dominion constitutions. They operated only in the field where co-ordination of legislation and policy were deemed essential in the interests of imperial unity. In matters of merchant shipping and the extradition of criminals, for example, there were effective legal barriers to dominion action. Yet even within the field deemed to be imperial, many of the weapons of imperial restriction were rusting through disuse. The 'triple veto' is a phrase with repressive implications which, one can imagine, might provoke the most extreme revolutionary fury: a single veto, in the early stages of the French Revolution, was a godsend to demagogic agitators playing upon the emotions of the mob. But in Australia and Canada, where self-assertive nationalism certainly did not lack its uncompromising champions, nobody thought of making play with the phrase. The triple veto was in fact attenuated by the obsolescence of the governor-general's power to reject bills and the Sovereign's power to disallow acts. Even the power of reservation tended to become a device for securing consultation upon matters of common imperial interest; in Canada the practice was to find a substitute for it in suspending clauses inserted in acts of the dominion parliament, providing that they should not come into effect unless by proclamation. This gave to the imperial government opportunity to consider their bearing upon imperial interests. Similarly, the British parliament, which once had been accustomed to legislate in its imperial capacity without paying particular attention to colonial susceptibilities, gradually fell into the practice of choosing 'a form of legislation enacted to secure the co-operation of Dominion legislation for the common end'.

Facts and forms did not correspond with each other. The facts were facts of a liberty which was growing towards equality and seeking a new form of unity through voluntary co-operation. The forms were forms of subordination. They still, in a narrowing field, performed a useful function; but in 1917 General Smuts in effect gave notice that some other way would have to be found of performing that function. 'Too much, if I may say so, of the old ideas still clings to the new organism which is growing. I think that although in practice there is great freedom, yet in actual theory the status of the Dominions is of a subject character.' General Smuts demanded that the forms of the constitution should be brought into correspondence with its facts—a demand which was repeated at later imperial conferences and which produced radical changes in the legal structure.

Sir Robert Borden in 1917 replied to General Smuts by enunciating a principle which did not deny, but which effectively mitigated, the rigours of juristic theory. The principle was a restatement, in a slightly novel way, of constitutional experience. It had long been the fashion to distinguish between the strict law of the constitution and its conventions or customs. In the former were included obsolete procedures such as the Royal Veto and the Act of Attainder; from the latter had grown the cabinet system. In the actual working of the constitution, each had an essential part to play. Sir Robert Borden had in mind this distinction between the law and the custom of the constitution; but his statement enunciated a further distinction between things which—whether legal or customary—were constitutional, and could be done; and other things which—though legal—were unconstitutional, and therefore could not be done.

It is to be observed [he said] ... that constitutional writers draw a distinction between legal power and constitutional right. The British parliament has technically the legal power to repeal the British North America Act—taking our Dominion as an illustration. But there is no constitutional right to do so without our assent, and therefore, while there is the theory of predominance, there is not the constitutional right of predominance in practice, even at present.

This is precisely the doctrine which, according to the joint committee of the House of Lords and the House of Commons quoted at the conclusion of the previous section, is enshrined in the Statute of Westminster. It is a sufficiently effective amendment to the doctrine of the sovereignty of the British parliament. A sovereignty which carries with it no inherent constitutional right need have no terrors for those who live under constitutions assimilated to the constitution of Great Britain. Sir Robert Borden's principle—which in 1917 was a convention of the constitution and is now constitutional law—illustrates the persistence of a peculiar technique which dominion statesmen inherited from seven or eight centuries of English practice. Just as Englishmen had safeguarded themselves against the power of the Crown, not by denying it, but by 'tying the instruments it was to act by'; so now the Canadians set out, not to destroy, but—a subtler task—to harness the sovereign parliament. They led their captivity captive. They so bound imperial sovereignty—a dangerous monster once, but now an amiable, complaisant creature—that it could move, in their business, only at their bidding.

21

THE VICTORIAN MIDDLE CLASS
S. J. Checkland

By the second half of the twentieth century, scholars of the younger generation were far enough away from the Victorian age to stand apart from its culture and society and to examine the structure and character of the nineteenth-century middle class in a dispassionate and sociological way, free alike from the compulsions of nostalgia and hatred. Characteristic of this newly scientific approach to an understanding of the Victorian bourgeoisie is the following careful and incisive analysis by the economic historian S. J. Checkland.

THE DIFFERENCE between the English and the continental aristocracies was to many people in England a point of self-conscious pride —how that the former had always had connections with other orders of society whereas the latter was a closed caste, a true *noblesse*. Just as the upper reaches of the middle class in England could lap over into aristoc-

---

FROM S. J. Checkland, *The Rise of Industrial Society in England, 1815–1885* (New York: St. Martin's Press, Inc., 1964), pp. 290–304. By permission of the publisher and Longmans, Green & Co. Limited.

racy, so too within the middle class itself there was no rigid distinction. Indeed the heir to a dukedom essaying a marriage with a lady high in the middle class might discover that her relations ran a frightening way down the scale. But there could be plenty of bad feeling when the pace of social preferment appeared to be hurried; this was discovered by both the spouses of the railway giants, Mrs Hudson and Mrs Brassey, as they were conveyed by their husbands without preparation or intermediate halts to the upper reaches of society. For such rapid ascents could do damage to the extraordinarily refined distinctions that had come to operate at the margin of each social group. Precedence at an ordinary London dinner-table had become very complex and very rigid by the eighties, so that ludicrous and sometimes insoluble problems might arise in getting the company into the posture for eating. Indeed one contemporary observer found the principal explanation of the reserve of Englishmen, proverbial by the eighties but new in the twenties, in the social pitfalls thus created.

This curious system whereby society was open, yet divided by a great number of delicate though fiercely guarded barriers, had roots running back to the later Middle Ages when the new entrepreneurship in trade and commerce began to appear, and the charms of the alderman's daughter were enhanced by her dowry. In Britain, in contrast to the Continent, the system of primogeniture had long operated to confine the family inheritance to the eldest son, obliging all the others to seek their own fortunes, thus pushing them not only into the professions, but into commerce as well. This had many curious side effects. Such a son kept for long periods in strict subordination to his father's will might well look forward without excessive grief to being orphaned. He would then suddenly find himself in charge of the entire expendable portion of the family fortune, and so with power over all its indigent members. If the heir was sensible all might be well, but if not, like the frantic Duke of Buckingham, he might involve even the wealthiest family in great difficulties. The mania for establishing a line through an eldest son proved contagious, as newly arrived men of business sought to perpetuate their names.

The nineteenth century saw the elaboration of a system of raising children that went back at least to Tudor times. It was now to serve not merely as a means of unifying the élite under a common outlook, but also of allowing new recruitment and the spread of the system downward. The upper classes, in fact, largely delegated the upbringing of their children, putting them in the care of others, rather like Plato's guardians. The nursery was the centre of a system approaching foster-parentage, under which the children were raised not by the woodcutter and his wife in the heart of the forest as in the story books, but by the family servants in another part of the house. It is hardly surprising that the nursery could be a place where weaklings fared ill, with swaddling, the professional wet-nurse, heavy diet, inappropriate clothes, insensitive discipline and purgative medicaments. Parents were on visiting terms with their children, a relationship that could produce uncritical idealization as the respect conveyed by local servants went uncorrected by more intimate contact. The heirs of wealth and power were thus in a state of semi-isolation, a condition that continued at the subsequent stages of prep school, public school, and university, punctuated by visits home that could be almost idyllic, with parents seldom caught off guard or challenged to come to terms with their children under conditions of stress or *ennui*.

So close could such early contacts with gardeners, stable boys, and the rest of the outdoor servants become that the young scion throughout life could enjoy the comfortable feeling of being intimate with the lower orders, and understanding them. Governesses aimed at preparation for school. There a code of attitudes, with strong institutional custodians, was available. The public schools, like the nurseries, dated from earlier generations, but with Thomas Arnold's great work a new synthesis was available, authoritatively dispensed. Through Arnold, in a sense, the middle class took the educational initiative, for he, at the town Grammar School of Rugby from 1828 to 1842, provided boarding education for the sons of the higher professionals and of the larger business men, resting his system upon a concept of the Christian gentleman, of reasonable cultural sensitivity, with a high moral code and a developed sense of social responsibility. This last was induced by entrusting much of the school discipline to prefects. Gradually the old barbarities of Winchester, Harrow, and Eton were diminished as teaching ceased to be a mixture of indifference and arbitrary action, and teachers sought to aid their pupils positively rather than by relying upon the formation of strong character as the only means of survival. Aristocrats and plutocrats could thus mix and merge in the post-Arnoldian public schools, and so in after life. 'Look at the bottle-merchant's son and the Plantagenet being brought up side by side', said Matthew Arnold in an imaginary conversation with a Prussian visitor to Eton in the seventies. 'None of your absurd separations and seventy-two quarterings here. Very likely young Bottles will end up by being a lord himself.' But the 'godliness and good learning' of Arnold's ideal were challenged in the seventies and eighties by the new and more extroverted combination of 'godliness and manliness', with Charles Kingsley as the leading exponent of 'muscular Christianity'. Attempts to use public inquiries or legislation to bring in general reform of the public schools dissolved in the innocuous Act of 1868.

Earlier in the century the wealthier Nonconformists had maintained their separate academies, or had sent their children to the Scottish universities, but from the mid-century there was an increasing tendency for the two elements to come to terms within the same system. Lesser Etons multiplied to meet this need as the middle class grew.

University life continued the process, but in the direction of relaxing supervision, leaving the young man to be tested by his own devices, rather than subjecting him to a final course of training that capped in vigour and comprehension his former education. The new cult of sport was an obsession at the universities by the sixties, with elaborate rites and conventions for the men of brawn; the debates at the Unions allowed prematurely portly youngsters to anticipate the graces of the Chambers of Westminster. The main function of the universities, in short, was social, not intellectual, permitting graduation by the pass degree, an almost derisory requirement.

On the whole those to whom the upper classes entrusted the forming of their children served them well, both in the immediate task and, almost as a by-product, in providing for a somewhat extroverted and inarticulate aristocracy a satisfying concept of itself. There could be further mingling and merging in later life in the privacy of clubs where the loyalties and ethos of school could be renewed.

But there were signs that as the universities began to rediscover a positive identity they were rather less appropriate as the crown of the aristocratic and upper middle-class child-raising process. The University of London, founded in 1826, provided alternative criteria of higher education, unfettered by the dogmatic principles and assumptions that had been so closely woven into the older universities as to have become imperceptible to their products. Pusey, Newman, and others of the Oxford Movement in the thirties, began the long process of disturbing the easy consciences upon which the system rested; Matthew Arnold continued to do so in the sixties, and Pater was leading a movement for aesthetic appreciation in the seventies. The thoughts of all of these men were likely to cause disturbance of the erstwhile healthily extroverted states of mind of young undergraduates. From the great headmasters of the public schools, Henry Montagu Butler (1833–1918), John Percival (1834–1918), E. W. Benson (1829–96), and Edward Thring (1821–87), came new ideas and new pressure upon the universities. The ending of religious tests in 1871, the admission of women to degrees in 1878 by the University of London, followed by Oxford and Cambridge in the eighties, and the removal of the celibacy requirement upon fellows of colleges in 1882, meant that the universities were altering themselves to meet new needs. Mark Pattison and others called for university leadership in research in the new disciplines and in the renovation of the old; Jowett on the other hand sought to reinvigorate the teaching of the universities.

Yet in spite of incipient elements of disruption, the system was still capable in the eighties of producing men of immense self-assurance, able to confront anyone in the world, however high or low, with the steady gaze to which all English boys were to aspire. The type of the upper-class English gentleman was firmly established—a man robust, conservative, somewhat opaque in intellect, closely bound by a code that took no account of those who were afflicted by internal uncertainties or flights of emotion. Those who could gain entry to the system, however dubious the status of their forebears, could acquire the same outlook, at least to some degree, with all its power and limitations. Not least in importance came the assurance to deal with the continuously elaborating *punctilio* of society. There were, however, dangers. The aristocratic proclivity to use others and then discard them may have been strengthened by such conditioning. The highly peculiar background of boyhood could hardly fail to induce a superbly unconscious arrogance and insensitivity toward servants and other inferiors.

Relatively few who had come from trade or industry reverted to it for their adult career, except perhaps among the merchant bankers. Such middle-class men were now ready to enter the esteemed professions: the church, the law, the universities, the army or navy, or the higher civil service. Where there was an insufficiency of such posts at home, they might be found in the Empire, especially in the Indian Civil Service or judiciary, providing a professional class to alien societies. Where a profession might seem too binding, such young men might join the ranks of leisure, either as ornaments to grace the London season, or as cultured amateurs willing to play their part in politics, local government, and the magistracy, or in the various attempts at improving the lives of the less fortunate.

But though aristocrats and plutocrats could find much common ground in the upper reaches of education, it must not be thought that all differences were smoothed away or that all members of the higher bourgeoisie thus lost that distinctive identity that had been so conspicuous in the early years of northern industrialism. John Cobden and Bright called, not without effect, upon their class to resist the urge to aristocratic pretensions. 'The insatiable love of caste that in England, as in Hindostan, devours all hearts', wrote Cobden with some exaggeration, 'is confined to no walks of society, but pervades every degree, from the highest to the lowest.' For many it was religion that stopped assimilation. The old Nonconformity that had given identity and security to so many rising families was not so easily dissolved. Very often it had provided the framework of family life, with the chapel, the Christian Sunday, the Bible, and family prayers. Evangelicalism and Methodism had breathed new life into dissent in the early years of the century. Some of the more respectable Methodists came to terms with the Established Church, but the Oxford Movement, in seeking to renew the soul of the Church of England, was vehement against the Methodists, pushing most of them into a confirmed dissent. Soon they were the largest of such groups. Many of the great industrial families of the north clung to Nonconformity throughout the century. It was from it that the erstwhile screw manufacturer, Joseph Chamberlain, came (retired from business with a comfortable fortune, aged thirty-eight) to demonstrate a new radicalism in civic politics, and to assert in pointed fashion radical hostility to the landed men and their institutions. His ally John Morley, son of cotton manufacturers on one side and of shipowners on the other, had much the same background. It was probably among the lesser families that radical zeal was greatest, for the prospect of assimilation to the culture forming in higher society was sufficiently remote as to have no great effect upon their minds. So was strengthened the famous Nonconformist conscience, formed in earlier generations and still nurtured by its great ministers.

standing for private and public integrity, a court of opinion separate and distinct from the Established Church, to which the great issues of the day must be referred, the sensibilities of which no politician could afford to ignore, and upon which many learned to play.

In retrospect and to many contemporaries the emergent middle orders were the hero-villains of the nineteenth-century scene. They were heroic in renovating society, in sponsoring new wealth, in increasing man's capacity to manipulate his physical surroundings, in filling the ancient gap between workers and owners of land, in sponsoring a political system with an ever-broadening franchise, and in constituting themselves an element of society sensitive to new possibilities, yet remaining robustly pragmatic. As villains they were responsible for embarking themselves and everyone else on an irreversible course leading no one knew where, the unperceiving liberators of forces that could be neither understood nor controlled, creating a society maturing toward an unprecedented vulnerability to manipulation, consolidating in their own hands the elements of wealth and power, seemingly indifferent to the effects of their actions in bringing pain and even destruction, and too often philistines or imitators, unable to develop their own cultural expression to fill the gap left by the destruction of agrarian society.

That each of these often mutually inconsistent views should express a truth, is indicative of the complexity of the groups concerned and the changes they manifested over the decades. When Taine visited England in the sixties bewilderment overtook him as he sought order in this confusion. Some observers could sense a kind of pattern and feeling among the middle class: Disraeli, with his taste for paradox and practicality went to the Queen herself for perceptive judgements about them. It is possible, however, to over-estimate what the Queen may really have known of the new business baronage. It was composed of families that were complex in themselves, and were involved in a continuously elaborating relationship with other families.

The middle class included the new regional oligarchs whose position was consolidating by the later sixties—the small group of men and families in control of the great industrial complexes, constituting, with the great merchant bankers the *haute bourgeoisie*: the families of Peases, Backhouses, Lambtons and Bells on the north-east coast, the Guests and Crawshays in South Wales, Tennants, Dixons, Bairds in Scotland, the merchant princes and the shipowners of the outposts—Rathbones, Forwards, Booths, Holts, the textile families of Manchester, Illingworths of Bradford and Halifax, Forsters, Baineses, and Kitsons of Leeds.

These provincial élites and their London counterparts often contained a considerable foreign element attracted to Britain by greater opportunities. These contributed not only to business expansion, but to the pressure for better technical education and to the mitigation of cultural philistinism in the northern cities. Among these men of alien origins the Jewish community played a very important part, especially in finance and trade. There were really two such Jewish groups: the old, established, and wealthy families of Anglo-Jewry headed by the Rothschilds and recruited by newcomers like the Sassoons, and the submerged new Jewry expelled from Europe and consumed by the need for acceptance. This complicating element of the English middle class was no less anxious than the denizens to acquire landed status.

In some cases the vitality of the first generation might be carried to the second and beyond, but very often the sons and especially the grandsons of pioneers showed a decline of energy or interest. This might not be serious, but it might occur when new difficulties were challenging the family enterprises; there were not a few cases in which the business difficulties of the seventies coincided with just such a family decline. There were cases too where older members of the family persisted in the control of policy well after their vitality had faded, sometimes because they wanted to, and sometimes because they had no confidence in the new generation. Industrial dynasties were beginning to encounter the problem that had so long haunted the landed aristocracy—how to ensure continuity both of blood and assets.

Not all of those who continued in business were innovators nor sought to be titans. By the fifties if not earlier the industrial sector of the economy was producing its 'worthies'—men conducting enterprises that were in the main repetitive or imitative. As an industry approached its phase of maturity, with the potential for new inventiveness declining, as in textiles, an increasing number of those in charge of firms found that though they had occasional minor challenges to meet, the mode in which business was conducted was largely settled. These were not necessarily small men, but were often in charge of large concerns which, once launched, could continue to grow with the general expansion of the economy.

As older lines of output encountered these limitations, new elements of commerce and industry were coming forward, producing new men and families. The great age of the Victorian steamship owner was just dawning in the sixties. Metallurgy was making immense strides with steel replacing iron. So too with engineering. The chemical industry was assuming new proportions and a new versatility producing Muspratts, Albrights, Brunners, Monds. And all the while new men of parts were seeking new opportunities. From these came new draughts of vitality, by which the position of the great business families in the life of society was continuously renewed. But in spite of these new injections the world of business was probably producing an increasing proportion of less aggressive men.

In the heroic phase of the family, while its founders were establishing their great enterprises, there was no great tendency for incoherence of outlook to appear. For the members of the new race of tycoons had much in common. It has been argued that in the early phase of industrialization there were profound forces at work, of a psychological kind, inducing an aggressive spirit of commercial and industrial enterprise and generating an ethos that inspired and even obsessed men with the urge to launch new ventures and to extend old ones. There can be little doubt that the new individualist approach to religion and social life gathering momentum after the Reformation was far more favourable to the emergence of a class of entrepreneurs than the continued acceptance of ancient authority and the relegation of the pursuit of wealth to an inferior and even contemptible role in society. The entrepreneurs of the nineteenth century, great and small, had managed to find a formula that justified the vigorous pursuit of market gain.

In the case of the first half of the nineteenth century the idea of a British business class dominated by a cult of working and saving must be treated with caution. Indeed, entrepreneurs seem to have fallen into two main categories. There were those who, once having placed their capital in an enterprise, took very little interest in its workings beyond the receipt of profits, delegating responsibility to managers and foremen, and who were the targets of bitter working-class criticism for their failure to do more. There was also the other and more typical kind—the men who did, indeed, take a close interest in their undertakings, but did so, not as a form of self-discipline, but in eager enjoyment. Nor was there much morbid addiction to saving. Foreign observers were amazed and sometimes disgusted at the level of spending they saw among the new tycoons of Britain. The notorious contrast between the French and the British was frequently drawn in these terms: the French got rich by saving, the British by heavy toil and lavish spending. 'Extravagance', said Smiles, addressing himself to all classes of society in the seventies 'is the pervading sin of modern society'. The fact that there might be drastic cutting of the family budget in times of depression was indeed a form of thrift, but this could as well be construed as an act of propitiation for a fall from grace. Nor must we believe too easily that the urging of thrift upon the impecunious working class implied a belief that it should be practised by all.

The second half of the century may well have seen in Britain a greater emphasis upon the virtues of disciplined work and thrift. But it remains doubtful how far this was due to a deeply rooted set of 'puritanical' ideas. The later Victorian business man may have produced or at least induced a view of himself that was something of a retrospective self-justification. As, in the second half of the century, he began to perceive that his role in society must eventually become dominant, and that it would become subject to scrutiny, he might well, in a kind of instinctive collaboration with his fellows, begin to elaborate the lines of a group apology. What better than to stress the work-ethic, of such great antiquity, and of such immense justificatory power? From the fifties onward the concept of men who during most of their waking hours were wholly preoccupied with business gained much greater acceptance. With the migration out of the cities by the business class, the old connection with the life of the community within which they worked was much weakened; in its place came the distinct and regularized habit of attendance at the office. In this way it was made more obvious that the business man was 'working', and often for very long periods.

For the most part, the vigorous men of business were notoriously unintellectual. They had little use for the idea of sitting and reflecting, or of the elaboration of abstract concepts. Their mental processes were the business analogues of the engineering thinking of Stephenson; just as his mind was organized like a workshop, so theirs were organized in terms of business relationships. In both cases, reflective leisure seemed to have no place in the important business of life, and certainly could offer no basis for self-justification. Indeed, it was necessary to place the vigour of things done and decisions taken against the passivity of savouring and assessing.

But this limitation of outlook had its dangers, both economically and politically. Men of business by the sixties had discovered that to hold a seat in Parliament was to increase one's eligibility for directorships. Their unwillingness to face the growing importance of science and its fundamental significance from the point of view of their own activities, was part of their businessmen's blindness. As they assumed their places in Parliament the new men were a source of worry to observers: 'They have excellent ideas as to their own business to which they have been accustomed', wrote *The Economist,* 'but they have very few, and those bad, ideas as to the subtle and new political business to which they have not been accustomed.'

It would seem that these business executants were possessed of a very high level of physical energy. The new kind of opportunity situation had allowed a new kind of self-selection within society to operate; out of it came the new captains of industry, free, in their phase of vigour, from pseudo-aristocratic conventions, motivated by drives that were highly personal, intensely obscure, enormously powerful, and sustained by the will to dominate. But the mellowing process among the families of the more successful men of business, like recruitment, was continuous. Many, perhaps most of those who gave the great lead in matters of conscience and social amelioration in the first half of the century, and who then and subsequently constituted a kind of intellectual aristocracy, lived upon wealth gained in the later eighteenth and very early nineteenth centuries.

But not all men of business could operate on the grand scale. A new order of lesser bourgeoisie developed rapidly from the mid-century or earlier, composed of those men whose character and opportunities precluded them from major ventures. Among these were many smaller manufacturers, struggling against the trend toward greater scale, together with shopkeepers, dealers, milliners, tailors, local brewers, millers, coal merchants, in short the 'third rate men of business', forming a growing lower adjunct to the middle class.

They were tainted with the stain of trade, involved in a triple opprobrium. Dealing in small quantities, being in intimate contact with, and even touching, the goods themselves, and directly receiving money payments from hand to hand, constituted the trinity of shameful acts. These criteria, derived from an agrarian aristocracy, however devoid of ethical content, were a sufficient basis of judgement for those whose opinions determined who was on the right side of the prestige gap that separated tradesmen from others. To those engaged in minor trade and industry there should be added the rapidly expanding army of office workers in both business and government, school-teachers, railway officials, the emergent managerial class, and the 'lesser' professions of accountancy, pharmacy, and the various branches of engineering.

But even those of the lower middle class found compensations. They too maintained a conceptual distinction, no less arbitrary, separating themselves from their inferiors—the workers by hand. Moreover, as pressure to extend the franchise became irresistible after the mid-century, the upper middle class and some of the nobility sought, through the principle of property qualification, to limit the extension of the franchise in such a way as to embrace mainly men unlikely to be infected by revolutionary ideas or to respond to inflammatory appeals. Indeed the importance for the operation of the political system of these men was much stressed by the eighties.

This judgement contained much truth. Many members of the lower middle class, as they sought income and identity in their task of distributing the growing flood of goods and services, were without strategic advantage of any kind. Yet they were exposed to chance and to engineered pressures, doing a large part of the stock-holding of the community, though in small parcels. The natural consequence was a conservative disposition. This attitude might well extend beyond business to an obsessive conventionality, necessary both to reassure their customers as to their business soundness and themselves as to their own station. So indeed the lesser men of business might become custodians of stability, a kind of drag-chain on hasty political action.

But by the same token such attitudes could be destructive of imagination and of zest. It was among this order of society, rather than among the greater traders and manufacturers, that English puritanism cast its most powerful blight over self-expression and the exploration of temporal pleasures. The Nonconformist tradesman who became a pillar of his chapel and a custodian of morality among fellow members of the congregation, could join with other like-minded men to become censors over a large part of society. Moreover it was very easy for these attitudes to induce a sense of loneliness and isolation in those who held and preached them, so that an Englishman's home, though his castle, might also be, at least to some degree, his prison.

According to Marx this lower middle class could not survive. The *grande bourgeoisie* would simplify the national scene in two directions, ousting the landed class from its long-held dominance as the owning element in society, and thrusting the *petite bourgeoisie* down into the wage-earning proletariat. But, though anxious to make a recognized place for themselves in the nation, the greater men of business did not wish to destroy either aristocracy or the lesser traders. For the first could only be disposed of in measurable time by penal taxation, which by the third quarter of the century would hit profits as hard as rents; the destruction of the second would mean the eclipse of an order of men who, for many reasons, including the stability of the nation, there was no desire to destroy.

It was true enough that many groups of smaller men could not maintain themselves indefinitely. Their chief enemy was the improvement in technology, causing the economies of scale to oust the small producer from one industry after another. In textiles the trend had become clear as early as the forties; by the seventies and eighties it was spreading to other industries, including the metal trades, and was about to overtake even traditional local industries—milling, brewing, tailoring, and retailing. But there were considerable time lags in many industries, new products came forward to provide new opportunities for small beginners, and the economy as a whole was growing, so that the small producer and petty trader was still very important in the eighties.

Some elements of the lesser bourgeoisie were not to languish but to thrive. The growth in the scale of enterprises, and the spread of the limited liability company brought new status and new incomes to the men who had served as managers in concerns formerly run by partners. So too with professional men providing services, especially accountants, surveyors, notaries, and engineers. As such elements began to perceive where their future lay they aspired to provide better education and professional training for their sons. To master their continuously elaborating professions, these men had to develop a steadiness and self-discipline that would carry them past severe academic and professional examinations; this they were prepared to do for there was no other way to advancement. Such close application to closely construed problems could not but leave its mark. Out of the lower middle class there was coming by the eighties an order of society that, far from being thrust down among the wage-earners, was eventually to offer its own challenge for supremacy.

The lesser bourgeoisie had, however, no real access to the system of education shared by those above them. Some might enter the older public schools as Scholars or Town Boys, and thus find themselves embarked upon a rapid ascent once they had purged their stigma of social inferiority. But these fortunates were few. It was to the local grammar school that the son of the tradesman looked for his education. By the mid-century there was strong feeling at Oxford that the university should take more men of modest income, but there was considerable shock in 1858 when Oxford examiners in seeking for talent from provincial schools had to reject a high proportion of the candidates; the middle classes were rebuked for failure to produce a better result, and for their lack of interest in Owen's College, Manchester. But the grammar schools, some 1,000 in all, were not really aided by their endowments, for these were not applied with vigour and imagination, but were largely monopolized by the

Church of England and were rather a cause of complacency. The revelations of the inquiry of 1868 prompted the belief that education would positively benefit from the loss of these monies, for then constructive thinking could take place. Improvement was on the way, especially after the Endowed Schools Acts of 1869 and 1874. Yet the immense disparity of educational opportunity, with the consequent differences in outlook, was only slightly modified by the eighties.

The changing condition of the middle class affected their behaviour at a most important point—the size of their families; it was among them that the tendency to smaller households was strongest. Lengthy periods of education, the desire to achieve a standard of living that was satisfactory both in real and in prestige terms, reduced the number of children. As the death rate fell, middle-class couples, as well as those of the skilled artisan class, finding their homes filling more rapidly than had been the case with their parents, might well consider whether, in the interests of a higher standard of living for the family and better prospects for the children, numbers might be curtailed.

22

INDIVIDUALISM AND COLLECTIVISM IN MID-VICTORIAN ENGLAND

W. L. Burn

Once in a while a historical work is published that is so overpowering in its learning, so profound in its thought, and so eloquent in its exposition as immediately to be hailed as a classic. Such is justifiably the reputation of W. L. Burn's Age of Equipoise, *published in 1964, from which the following discussion is taken. In this passage Burn shows how the well-known trend toward individualism in the mid-Victorian period was counterbalanced by the entrenchment of communal institutions that continued to enforce against aggressive middle-class individualism a tradition of collectivist social action.*

REPRINTED FROM *The Age of Equipoise* by W. L. Burn. By permission of W. W. Norton & Company, Inc. Copyright © 1964 by George Allen & Unwin, Ltd. By permission of George Allen & Unwin, Ltd., publishers.

THE PICTURE which has... emerged may well seem that of a society fragmented and reduced to social and political incoherence by its excess of vitality. Our next task, therefore, is to notice some of the forces which regulated and disciplined society. It will not be possible to say exactly where the balance between regulation and liberty was struck; it may be possible to see that a balance *was* struck, however fortuitously.

But the difficulties in the way of achieving even this are exceptionally formidable. If one talks very much about individualists and collectivists (or anti-individualists) one is in danger of producing a travesty of events. It is almost as though one sought to assess the proportion of dark-haired to fair-haired men pouring into Victoria Station or Liverpool Street in the London rush-hour. For some purposes the assessment might be important but it could never be as important as the fact that the stations were crowded. In mid-Victorian England people had certain matters to deal with which they deemed urgent, they had certain problems to solve. These are more important than the labels which these people attached to themselves or which posterity has attached to them. Admittedly the labels are not to be ignored but they indicate the way in which particular people sought the answers to questions rather than the answers they found.

In saying this one is impliedly but inevitably criticizing Dicey's *Law and Opinion*. It would be easy and pleasant to repeat the commendations lavished on that book and to invent new ones; for example, that it places every historian of nineteenth-century England under obligations to the author. That is literally true: Dicey's work in analysing some of the forces which resulted in legislative measures and of the effect of those measures, in their turn, upon public opinion, was that of a pioneer. Much useful work which has subsequently been done could not have been done so easily or perhaps at all but for him. Yet, as with every pioneering book, there comes a moment when one is bound to ask oneself whether *Law and Opinion* has not become a barrier rather than an aid to further investigation.... While Dicey in one passage spoke of "that faith in *laissez-faire* which is of the very essence of legislative Benthamism" he declared in another that "this dogma of *laissez-faire* is not from a logical point of view an essential article of the Utilitarian creed". Again, Dicey could commit himself to the opinion that what he called "Benthamite liberalism" suffered "its earliest and severest defeat" in the matter of factory legislation and yet maintain that there was nothing in the early factory movement "which was opposed either to Bentham or to the doctrines of the most rigid political economy". Confusion was made worse by Dicey's use of a number of terms, "Benthamism", "Utilitarianism", "Individualism" and "Benthamite Liberalism" which he regarded or allowed his readers to regard as synonymous.

Dicey was a lawyer, a university teacher and an enthusiastic amateur politician; he was not a political philosopher or an historian. But historians could make their own mistakes. Thus, Halévy argued that "the new and simplified form of the Utilitarian philosophy" which grew up in

England during the twenty years after Bentham's death owed less to him than to Adam Smith and that its exponents had abandoned the principle of the artificial identification of interests (that is, the governmental or administrative idea) for that of the spontaneous identification of interests, itself coupled with the doctrine of free trade. In saying this, Halévy was guilty of over-simplification. If the essence of the governmental or administrative idea is the conscious preference for one set of values over another and the deliberate use of governmental power to make the first effective, there are enough examples in the late 'forties, the 'fifties and the 'sixties to rebut Halévy's argument that it had been by that time abandoned: the Encumbered Estates Acts, the Police Act of 1856, the Medical Act of 1858 and the Contagious Diseases Acts of 1864, 1866 and 1869 will serve for the moment. Halévy was certainly more careful than Dicey to avoid the confusion inherent in allowing several different meanings to the same word or term but this statement that "the new doctrinaires" (that is, the post-Bentham Utilitarians) "were hostile to any kind of regulation or law" has only to be quoted for its absurdity to be manifest; and, even apart from such exaggerations, he was content to regard the period we are examining as one of *laissez-faire*. We are more cautious today and an opposite contrast to the assurance of Dicey and Halévy is provided in a recent work by Mr R. Prouty. "*Laissez-faire* in early nineteenth-century Britain was never a system.... While...as a general principle or an argument against a particular measure it might continue to receive wide publicity, it was persistently defeated in practice.... State intervention... was the growing reality."

It may be permissible to regard *laissez-faire*, so viewed, as corresponding to the legal rule that the Crown, in a criminal case, must satisfy the jury beyond reasonable doubt of the guilt of the accused before it is entitled to a verdict. The burden of proof is thus thrown upon the prosecution as, arguably, it was thrown upon those who advocated measures irreconcilable with *laissez-faire* principles. The comparison is not exact because (as we shall see) there were occasions on which the exponents of intervention had little or no burden of proof to discharge; but it may serve as a working hypothesis.

If one discards the idea of a *laissez-faire* system, can one continue with that of *laissez-faire* principles? The answer is a rather dubious, yes. The dubiety arises from several causes. The same man could be an "individualist" in one sphere of policy and a "collectivist" in another, critical perhaps of any amelioration of the Poor Law but interested in preventing the adulteration of food. He was not sworn to one "side", as a player is engaged for a particular season to appear for a particular football team; and it is enough to mention Edwin Chadwick to show that a "collectivist" could be as much of an individualist as the most besotted adherent of *laissez-faire*. Such men as the Revd John Allen, inspector of Church schools, and H. S. Tremenheere were no lickspittle servants of the State. We have seen, too, that what passed as *laissez-faire* principles might be no more than reflections of social or religious prejudice, or might easily be discarded (as by imperialist free-traders) in order to secure some advantage through the aid of the State; conversely, a devotion to the "principle" of State intervention might mean no more than an ambition to find paid and pensionable employment under Government. But even if one admits that there were principles at stake it is difficult to resist the argument that Dicey (though not, of course, Dicey alone) saw them in unrealistically sharp contrast. He wrote, "It is hard for the man of 1905 to realize how earnest eighty years ago was the faith of the best Englishmen in individual energy and in *the wisdom of leaving everyone free to pursue his own courses of action, so long as he did not trench on the like liberty or the rights of his fellows.*" The words which I have italicized show one of the major defects of vision or of analysis from which those born and brought up in mid-Victorian Liberalism suffered. They believed that a fairly clear line divided the liberty of the individual from the coercive power of the State. No one pretended that the line ran straight and there was constant argument between those who wanted to move it in one direction or another or to keep it where it was. But there was general agreement that the line existed and J. S. Mill pointed out that, "The struggle between Liberty and Authority is the most conspicuous feature in the portions of history with which we are earliest familiar."

Over-simplified notions derived from a study of the classics were not necessarily the best guides to problems arising in a very different society but, be that as it may, two things were little understood. One was that the liberty of X to do something might well be incompatible, and be intended to be incompatible, with the liberty of Y to do the same thing at the same time or place. The right which X enjoyed to walk through his own field might be incompatible with the right of Y and of everyone else to do so; in that event, Y's obligation to respect the right of X diminished the area in which he could exercise his liberty; if X owned all the fields in the neighbourhood Y's liberty was still further contracted; the right to privacy and "quiet enjoyment" could have the effect of depriving someone else of both. The other consideration, which so many people found it difficult to understand, was that liberty, in many senses and aspects, was the creation of authority and depended on authority for its maintenance: as a result, there was a tendency to exaggerate the amount of liberty actually enjoyed and to regard it as having an independent existence of its own.

A simple, if hypothetical, illustration will suffice. Mr Brown is taking the air on the terrace of his house on a fine summer morning in the late 'fifties. He has finished reading his letters and is contemplating improvements in his gardens. His household is running like clockwork; his park and, beyond it, his compact little estate are spread out before him; he has no need to sell timber or to save money on labour, indoors or out; he appears to enjoy liberty in the highest possible degree, to be as nearly isolated from coercive forces or authority as a civilized man living in a civilized community can be. But, in fact, the liberty which he so happily enjoys is dependent to a large extent on the existence of coercive power, his own or that of the State. His butler and his maids and his gardeners do their work well, partly because they would be dismissed if they did not. His house and estate were purchased by power in the form of money and, indeed, the vendor seeking to repudiate the contract, Mr Brown was obliged to obtain an order for specific performance. He can depend on the State protecting him in the quiet enjoyment of his property by coercing such persons as seek to disturb him. It provides him with facilities for suing trespassers and intruders and for detecting and prosecuting poachers and burglars. His handsome gold watch is the safer because anyone convicted of stealing it is likely, if convicted, to be sent to gaol. The value of his money is the more secure because the State punishes coiners and forgers and utterers whose activities, if unchecked, would depreciate the currency. The very letters which he is reading have come to him through a jealously monopolistic channel, the Post Office, which will not brook competition in the carriage of the mail or allow stamps to be sold by persons unlicensed to do so. One of the letters is a bookseller's catalogue and Mr Brown has been so much shocked by the apparently scabrous nature of its contents that he is meditating handing it over to the police. The coercive powers are not, of course, only on one side. His cigars, his wines and spirits, his tea, coffee and sugar would cost him less but for customs or excise duties. He has to pay the inhabited house duty, land tax and income tax; when his aunt died a few years ago and left him a sizeable legacy he had to pay probate duty and legacy duty; he has to pay the assessed taxes on his male servants, his dogs and his horses. Much as he would like to, he cannot close a public footpath which runs through his park and, only last year, a hot-tempered refusal to pay what he regarded as an inflated bill resulted in the ignominy of his receiving a county court summons. No doubt as compared with his great-grandson, crippled by penal taxation, threatened by compulsory purchase schemes and planning restrictions, burdened with tenants protected by an elaborate set of rights, Mr Brown, on balance, enjoys a notable amount of liberty. But he is in part dependent on and in part subjected to the exercise of coercive powers. The same was true of his predecessors in title. The estate he owns was formerly monastic land, acquired by a favourite of Henry VIII. In the next century it changed hands to meet a heavy fine imposed on a royalist owner. In the eighteenth century it changed hands again when an East Indian "nabob" mortgagee foreclosed on a gambler mortgagor. Mr Brown is the beneficiary of coercion, but of coercion which in his day and for him has come to be so quietly and decorously applied that he, and Mill, and Dicey could almost ignore its existence. This made it the easier to suppose that a hard-and-fast line could be drawn between individualism and collectivism. One of the few mid-Victorians who was fully conscious of the role of coercion in history and in contemporary society was Fitzjames Stephen but his *Liberty, Equality and Fraternity* (1873) was not a success....

... The fact that certain things can be done in one generation which were not done in another is one of those which gives a generation its particular character. When men were willing to establish the Civil Service Commission, to make the establishment of county police forces and the registration of medical practitioners obligatory they were, in certain important respects, different from the men who had not done so. To say this is not to say very much but if it is accepted it makes an attempt at an appraisal justifiable.

It would be possible, if one wanted to prove that the administrative structure was defective, to find evidence for this conclusion in any generation and in any sphere of action. It is currently being said that the structure of local government is defective and that there are still too many small, separate police forces. Whatever the truth of these statements it is incontestable that local government is less confused than it was a century ago and that there were far more small, separate police forces then. *Something* has been done in the interval, the amount of confusion has been reduced.

Various factors combined to make the mid-century a particularly confused period, one in which it is difficult to trace coherent lines of policy. As "evils" came to light they were dealt with, as we have seen. But it is not easy to see why, for instance, lace factories became a subject for legislation before bleachfields, or bleachfields before agricultural gangs. There was no lack of people capable of taking wide and sweeping views. There was, indeed, rather a superfluity of them than otherwise; the men who wrote the leaders for *The Times* and the articles for the *Saturday Review* had no hesitation about taking wide and sweeping views on anything. But neither the political nor the administrative structure allowed of the easy translation of ideas into action. The importance of the political fluctuations of the years 1852-9 is largely negative, in the sense that they created conditions which made drastic action, not indeed impossible but not to be lightly embarked on. Napier's "code" on Irish land which might (if it could have passed the Lords) have made a great difference to subsequent Anglo-Irish relations, did not survive the Conservative defeat of December 1852. The motion which brought about Chadwick's retirement was only carried by a majority of nine votes in a very thin House but Palmerston, much as he disapproved of it, did not try to reverse it. The Public Health Act of 1858 which put an end to the General Board of Health and transferred its medical functions to the Privy Council was only passed for one year. Dr (later Sir John) Simon, who had been Chief Medical Officer of the Board since 1855, explained that this was a compromise to pacify the chief opponent of the Bill, T. S. Duncombe. That a government should be afraid of Duncombe was a sure sign of its weakness. But, wrote Simon, "The Bill was of Ministerial promotion but Ministers did not pretend that it represented any strong conviction of theirs; and in the House of Commons, in the summer of 1858, the state of parties was eminently not that in which Ministers are expected to stand to their proposals." It was Palmerston's government which introduced the Bill which became the Public Health Act of 1859 (22 and 23 Vict. c.3), giving permanence to the provisions of the 1858 Act.

Duncombe renewed his attack and it was chiefly due to the resolution of Lowe, who was in charge of it, that the third reading was carried by the narrow majority of 101 votes to 93. Admittedly Palmerston's government was stronger than either of Derby's had been and the political fluctuations of the 'sixties were less violent than those of the 'fifties. But Palmerston's government was very far from being omnipotent and, moreover, in this period of "conservative reaction", certain "causes" (such as the campaign for the abolition of the purchase of commissions) lost the impetus which they had once possessed.

The administrative structure, too, was defective, so that both the formation and the implementation of policy suffered from a lack of adequate means. It was not surprising that in these circumstances governments should be inclined to follow the initiative of private individuals and societies and to concentrate their energies on such subjects as public indignation and public fear forced on them. The dogmatism which comes to one so easily a hundred years later would allow it to be said that quite inadequate attention was given to the structure and methods of administration. Was an ordinary department of government, or a board, or a commission the best agency? Was it desirable that the Privy Council should be made a sort of maid-of-all-work? What were the proper relations between departments when "Treasury control" was only in the course of establishment? Treasury control, in any event, was no infallible nostrum. Chadwick, about 1851, accused the Treasury of deliberate obstructionism and hinted at even more sinister possibilities. No doubt the Treasury was jealous of the General Board but, as Professor Finer has pointed out, it was also understaffed and overworked and had been frightened into excessive caution by the clamour for financial reform.

The passion for public economy lay very near the root of many difficulties and administrative shortcomings. The Northcote-Trevelyan report, with its emphasis on open competition and promotion by merit, offered what were in one sense red herrings which diverted attention from the real trail. At that moment it probably mattered less how civil servants were recruited than that they should be recruited in adequate numbers and should be adequately paid. It is easy, of course, to make these general and critical observations, whose validity could only be established by a highly detailed "time-and-motion" study of particular departments; which it may be impossible, now, to carry out. All the same, there are omissions which have to be explained somehow. Why had so many municipal corporations been allowed to default in respect of their police obligations under the 1835 Act? Why had not the Home Office seen to it that these obligations were discharged? Why were the London vestries allowed so much latitude in the matter of public health? Professor Finer notes that the Adulteration of Food Act of 1860 gave them power to appoint public analysts, that the Act remained a dead letter and that the power had to be made a statutory obligation in 1872 and 1873. The Public Health Act of 1866 had not merely given local authorities very considerable powers to inspect dwelling-houses and make by-laws to promote their cleanliness and sanitation but had also provided the central government with a means of obliging the local authorities to act. Yet, ten years later, it was found that only seven of the London parishes had made and enforced by-laws; that six had made them but not enforced them; and that twenty-five had done nothing.

Another question which must be asked here, though it cannot be answered, is that of the quality of local government administration. How competent and how active were the clerks to the several local authorities, the medical officers, the sanitary inspectors, the public analysts? What type of man was predominant among the elected representatives? An overworked and understaffed department of the central government in conjunction with timid and apathetic administrators at the local level could account for a good deal. For when the execution of national policy was in the hands of strong and energetic men, with power in the last resort to override local opposition, the results could be startling: within four years of the passing of the Endowed Schools Act of 1869 the three commissioners with their seven assistants had published schemes for 317 schools, had had ninety-seven of them laid before Parliament and were engaged in formulating many others. This energy, in many instances ruthless and unpopular, was in marked contrast with the attitude often displayed towards public health; just as the tolerance shown towards railway companies was in contrast with the intolerance shown towards the emigrant passenger trade.

A further possible explanation of the "patchiness" of legislation and administration may lie in the fact that the State was disinclined to formulate long-term plans and policies. Usually it waited to be jogged into action, and that along paths which private initiative had marked out for it. This was not unreasonable in an age when governments were preoccupied with the problem of remaining in power. But there was also the fact, or the accident, that no Prime Minister or Leader of the House had the comprehensive intellectual capacity of Peel or Gladstone. Gladstone's drafting of the Irish Land Bill of 1870, with the assistance of information provided through Chichester Fortescue, was to be one of the most remarkable feats of the century, beyond the powers of Russell, Derby, Aberdeen, Palmerston or Disraeli: compared in this respect with him, the others, even Palmerston, were like poor swimmers, content to cling to a floating plank without much attention to spare for the direction it was carrying them in.

One thing which has perhaps become evident in the course of this long chapter is that an investigation along the strict lines of individualism *versus* collectivism is not likely to yield a great deal of benefit, or avoid a great deal of confusion. On the one hand there were certain obvious extensions of the sphere of individual liberty. The Oxford University Act of 1854 and the Cambridge University Act of 1856 abolished religious tests as a condition of matriculation or the taking of the bachelor's degree. The Matrimonial Causes Act of 1857 (20 and 21 Vict. c. 85) superseded the jurisdiction of the ecclesiastical courts in matrimonial matters by that of the new Court for Divorce and Matrimonial Causes which was enabled to grant a decree of divorce to a husband on the grounds of his wife's adultery and to a wife on the grounds of her husband's adultery, aggravated in certain ways (for instance, by cruelty or by desertion of upwards of two years), and to grant an order of judicial separation to husband or wife on the ground of desertion for upwards of two years. The Oaths Act of 1858 (21 and 22 Vict. c. 49) allowed each House of Parliament to determine the form of oath which it required to be administered to a Jew and the Parliamentary Oaths Act of 1866 (29 and 30 Vict. c. 19) provided for both Houses a new and simplified form of oath from which the words "on the true faith of a Christian" were omitted. Between 1858 and 1868 the right to affirm instead of taking the oath was extended, piecemeal, to persons who had a religious objection to taking the oath which appearance as a witness in legal proceedings had hitherto necessitated. And in 1869 (by 31 and 32 Vict. c. 72) a qualified right to make "a promise and declaration" was given to persons who, because of their lack of religious belief, had not come within the scope of the previous legislation. On the other hand, certain types of people found their liberty of action much curtailed by new or increased penalties for certain kinds of conduct. These, as we have seen, included the purveyors of obscene publications, parents who refused to have their children vaccinated, husbands who assaulted their wives or assaulted or starved their servants, diseased prostitutes operating in specific areas, criminal or disreputable doctors. On the whole these restrictions on individual liberty were moralistic and the morality which they tended to promote was, more or less, that of the religious, fairly well-educated middle class; but they did not all fall within this description.

Yet another limit to the usefulness of the individualist *versus* collectivist argument is the extreme difficulty, in certain instances, of using it at all. In respect of two subjects in particular Dicey evidently felt this, for he treated them shortly and with commendable caution. One was that of property in land in relation to the increased powers gradually secured to tenants for life and others to deal with land of which they were not the absolute owners. Is the act of one man who seeks to "tie up" his land to be regarded as more or less consistent with individual liberty than that of another who seeks to escape from the consequences of previous attempts to ensure this? It raised an issue which Dicey saw clearly.

It is here worth noting that individualism in legislation, since it has for its object to free from unnecessary trammels the action of individuals who, at any given moment, are in existence, will tend, on the one hand, to liberate each generation from the control of the past, and, on the other hand, to restrain the attempt of each generation to fix the devolution of property in the future, and thus diminish the individual liberty of its successors.

He was equally cautious and judicious in considering the creation of the limited liability company. He saw it as a Benthamite effort to widen the area of contractual freedom but he realized that "at this point individualistic and collectivist currents of opinion blend together". His caution was justified. Robert Lowe, in moving the 1856 Bill, represented it as an extension of liberty.

The principle is the freedom of contract, and the right of unlimited association —the right of people to make what contracts they please on behalf of themselves, whether those contracts may appear to the Legislature beneficial or not, as long as they themselves do not commit fraud or otherwise act contrary to the general policy of the law.

But Lord Overstone, the banker, and Lord Mounteagle in their protest in the Lords argued against the principle of limited liability on individualistic grounds. It was, they said,

Antagonistic to, and will probably prove seriously destructive of, the sober and substantial virtues of the merchantile character. By weakening in the mind of the trader the sense of full responsibility for the consequences of all his actions, and limiting the obligation which now rests on him to return in full all that he has borrowed from others, the general tone of commercial morality must be deteriorated.

They were, in fact, seeing liberty in depth rather than in mere area; they believed that it ought to be judged by its success in promoting honesty; just as Trollope associated it with "manliness". It is very interesting that people insisted on discussing company legislation in such terms and not surprising that the discussions were confused. To describe the 1855 Act as a "rogues' charter" (as the *Law Times* did) was to take too gloomy a view of the future; the tribute of the Manchester Chamber of Commerce to "that high moral responsibility which has hitherto distinguished our Partnership Law" implied too rosy a view of the past. The Acts of 1855 and 1856 were not a device to allow the capitalist to rob his poorer fellow-countrymen: half of the wealthier witnesses who gave evidence before the Commission of 1854 and six of its eight members were opposed to the extension of limited liability. And it is worth observing that, just as divorce was not invented in 1857, so limited liability was not invented in 1855 and 1856. The Chartered Companies Act of 1837 (7 Will. IV, 1 Vict. 1 c. 73) had provided that the letters patent granted to a company in lieu of a charter might limit the personal liability of the members to so much a share; and in theory it was open to a company, in making a contract, to stipulate that only its own funds should be liable. Moreover, the much more extensive use of limited liability did not bring to an end an era of commercial blamelessness. There had never been such an era. No doubt the small, intimate group of merchants, each of them imbued with a direct, personal responsibility, each aware that he was liable to the full extent of his possessions for the debts of the partnership, each watchful of his partners and of himself, presented an impressive tableau. But to the unscrupulous one of the great advantages of the unincorporated company had been that while it was possible, in law, to sue and levy execution on all its members it was very difficult to do so in the case of companies with a large and fluctuating membership, particularly if some of the members had been carefully "planted" outside the jurisdiction; indeed, companies of the Anglo-Bengalee sort had been careful not to take advantage of the facilities for a greater measure of incorporation offered by the Trading Companies Act of 1834 and the Chartered Companies Act.

The conflict between centralization and localism offers a somewhat straighter and wider path. "Localism", for this purpose, is more than a geographical expression; it includes local authorities, from vestries upwards, but it also includes a wide range of bodies, whether incorporated or not, from the Oxford and Cambridge colleges and the chapters of Cathedrals down to the trustees of the most obscure and poverty-stricken of endowed schools. Even here, as we noticed long ago, arguments which could be and were set out like answers to an examination paper in political science had, in fact, a very different origin. What could be paraded as opposition to centralization *per se* might well be no more than the resentment felt by a self-made nonconformist manufacturer to "centralization" as represented by an inspector or other administrator who was a gentleman and an Anglican, who held a degree of Oxford or Cambridge and who had connections with the aristocracy or the landed gentry. Conversely, acceptance of centralization might mean little more than a sense that the central government was comfortably in the hands of one's own kind of people or that one was going to receive some kind of benefit in return: the agricultural interest... as it demonstrated in the matter of the Cattle Plague, had (and has) no stupid, *doctrinaire* opposition to centralization accompanied by grants or subsidies.

The State, about 1867, was working on rules of policy which affected local authorities, and what may be loosely termed corporations, differently. It was more tolerant towards local authorities; the localism of contemporary politics left it no alternative. There were variations of policy in different fields but it is safe to say that, increasingly, the central government was coming to insist on its ultimate supremacy, making certain duties obligatory instead of merely permissive, insisting on compliance with its own rules and regulations and giving its grant (if it did so) only when it was satisfied with the degree of compliance. But where no grant was given and the initiative rested with the local authority the enforcement of the law and the implementation of policy were, in many spheres, slack. Towards corporations (including within that term analogous bodies which were not incorporated) the State was almost ruthless and it is notable that such a man as Lowe, a strong, almost a typical, "individualist", had little mercy for them.

There were, however, a number of factors which, for the moment, made the action of the State much less stringent in practice than in theory. We have already, at one stage or another, noticed most of these: the doctrine of the "free choice"; the political fluctuations and the disposition of the Commons to set itself up as a sort of court of appeal from the executive, the attitude of the Courts. And there were others. No settled policy had been worked out in respect of the delegation of legislative and executive powers. Such a measure as the Diseases Prevention Act of 1855 (18 and 19 Vict. c. 116) is a perfect example of the delegation of legislative power, in this instance to the Privy Council. On the other hand, Mr MacDonagh has concluded, from his investigations into the emigrant passenger trade, that the Government preferred, almost as a matter of course, to give very wide discretionary powers to the individual officers it employed. In some instances it had given its officers powers so wide that they had later to be narrowed. The Act of 1833 (3 and 4 Will. IV. c. 103) provided for the appointment of four inspectors with power to enter factories, take evidence on oath, make regulations having the force of law and impose penalties for the breach of them: not surprisingly they lost, in the course of time, some of these powers: in 1836, for example, they were deprived of their legislative authority.

The character of the inspectorate is another matter of some importance. For the most part its members did not interest themselves in certain things simply because they were servants of the State; rather, they were servants of the State because they were interested in those things, because they had formed opinions which an official position allowed them to translate into action. However good the case might be for open competition for all civil service appointments it could not produce men more dedicated than Tremenheere and Crawford, John Allen or Matthew Arnold, Rowland Hill or, in his own way, Trollope. Paradoxically, the State acted through men who were themselves highly individualistic; the factory inspectors strongly resented the idea of having an inspector-general over them and declined even to appoint one of their own number to preside at their meetings.

At a time when the civil service was ill-paid in most of its branches and looked upon with a good deal of contempt it was necessary to look outside its ranks when the State undertook new and unexpected duties. What the country would have done without the services of naval and military officers, especially of the Corps of Royal Engineers, it is difficult to imagine. Half-pay officers of both services formed the majority of the Special Magistrates sent out to the West Indies to administer the apprenticeship system and half-pay naval officers were entrusted with the enforcement of the Emigrant Passenger Act. At a higher level there were such men as Sir William Reid (1791–1858), who had served in the Peninsula and at New Orleans, carried out the ordnance survey of Ireland, held various West Indian governorships with credit and acted as chairman of the executive committee of the Great Exhibition; Sir Edward Sabine (1788–1883), the astronomer; Sir Roderick Murchison (1792–1871), the geologist and Director-General of the Geological Survey; Sir Thomas Larcom (1801–79), who served on the Ordnance Survey, became a commissioner of public works in Ireland and ultimately under-secretary; Sir John Bateman-Champain (1835–87), a pioneer in electric telegraphy; and as we have already noticed, Sir Edward Du Cane. All these men had served in the Royal Engineers which provided a fruitful field, also, for the recruitment of railway managers; as the army at large did for the recruitment of chief constables of counties. But the fact that it was necessary to employ so many officers pointed to a serious shortage of civilian administrators, both technical and non-technical: a good many of the results which have been ascribed to a deliberate "policy" of *laissez-faire* may well have been due to a lack of competent administrators and that, in its turn, partly to the lack of facilities for training them (as in the sphere of public health) and partly to a reluctance to pay them.

In a courageous and helpful article on "The Nineteenth Century Revolution in Government" Mr MacDonagh has delineated the course of action which usually followed upon the discovery that something existed which was "intolerable" ("No wall of either doctrine or interest could permanently withstand that single trumpet cry"). The first impulse was to legislate the evil out of existence, to get rid of it once and for all by Act of Parliament. This rarely proved possible. The next stage was to provide summary processes and appoint special officers to execute them. The powers of these officers scarcely admitted of and rarely received precise definition; they used a mixture of legal, moral and social authority, bluffed and bullied and cajoled. In the third stage there came into being some superior ("centralizing") authority to which the officers were directly responsible, which sifted and checked and pooled the first-hand information they provided. As this body of information and practice grew, the belief in the final efficacy of some great legislative sweep, of rough-and-ready, "damn 'em, ram 'em" methods of enforcement, gave way to a soberer approach. It was no longer assumed that the "evil" would be suppressed simply by appointing more officers and giving them still wider powers. Scientific techniques and foreign practices were studied and in time, on the basis of experience, a *corpus* of regulations was built up which could be passed, almost effortlessly, into law.

Mr MacDonagh, of course, does not suppose that all these stages followed in a regular and invariable procession and as a sort of natural law in every sphere of governmental activity. The variations in timing and in methods were wide enough to give the mid-century an appearance not, indeed, of purposelessness but of extreme confusion; the old belief in the possibility of the permanent extinction of an "evil" flared up on the Contagious Diseases Acts. Excessive reliance on the efforts of private philanthropists and philanthropic associations, and a belief in the capacity of society to improve itself almost automatically, allowed evils and abuses to proliferate until they threatened to become intractable; then, in a moment of reaction, there was a clamour for decisive action and in some instances action was taken too brusquely.

It is worth remarking, however, that what appears to the historian hopelessly confused may not necessarily have so impressed contemporaries: an immigrant from Jamaica who has to make his way by public transport from Tilbury to Brixton is likely to encounter difficulties which a Londoner would make light of. And even the historian searching for "patterns" and "trends" has something to reward him in the mid-

Victorian generation. For one thing, a body of knowledge and experience was being built up for the use of government, knowledge of what could be done and of what could not be done, of the agencies to be used, of methods of enforcement and methods of persuasion. Occasionally the very fact of a pause in action allowed of investigations being made at leisure: the precarious position and uncertain future of the General Board of Health between his appointment in 1855 and the Act of 1859, though it embarrassed Dr Simon, gave him the chance of compiling valuable reports on vaccination and on London's water supplies in relation to cholera. It had come to be accepted, too, that the enforcement of what may be called social legislation could not be left to the justices but must be entrusted to special officers; just as the maintenance of law and order could not be left to parish and special constables. Centralization was gaining ground at various levels; in the relations between the central government and local authorities, in the co-ordination of the activities of the several branches of the inspectorate. And we can remember, without setting them all out again, the proofs of that hardening of opinion, that inclination towards comprehensive action on a national scale instead of limited *ad hoc* measures, which the report of the Taunton Commission so well illustrates. Not only was knowledge being accumulated, the will to use it was gathering force. And this was, in the main, the will of the upper middle class, of men conscious of their capabilities, often intolerant of their social superiors and inferiors, with a sharp, cutting edge to their Liberalism, not remarkable for sympathy towards what they regarded as unsystematic or disreputable. Opposed to them was a heterogeneous mass of people who had, somehow or other, got in the way: lifefellows of colleges, trustees and masters of decayed grammar schools, the vendors and purchasers of army commissions, parish vestrymen, the men who bribed and took bribes at elections, the convicts, the prostitutes, the habitual criminals.

It was a formidable as well as a heterogeneous mass and in dealing with it the mere accumulation of information and the will to use it were not enough. There had also to be a decisive change in the political situation. So long as governments were weak and consequently on the defensive there was bound to be a reservoir of knowledge and will which could not be used. The substitution of Gladstone for Palmerston, the steady growth of national party organizations which could supply the government of the day with a stable majority, the admission to the Cabinet of a higher proportion of men of a rank of life below the aristocracy—these were the essential conditions for the reforms which were to distinguish the Liberal ministry of 1868–74.

It is easy, however, to anticipate the parting of the ways before one comes to it. And in 1867 or 1868 England had not quite come to it. The country at large, and within it the counties, was governed by the upper and not by the middle classes. Most Englishmen had some particular interest which they were prepared to use the action of the State to forward but, in general, they were suspicious of the State and of centralization

They were still reluctant to believe that individual energy, initiative and philanthropy would not, given time, accomplish all that had to be accomplished. They accepted the truth that society must be subjected to discipline and we have seen that, in particular instances, they did not shrink from imposing rigorous legal disciplines. There was more positive action on the part of the State than is sometimes realized, perhaps almost as much as the State, with its existing resources, was capable of. What was more open to criticism was not the amount but the timing of that action, the failure to prevent rather than the failure to repress. But before that criticism can be pressed there are to be taken into account the other disciplines, social and domestic, upon which the country confidently relied.

23

THE VICTORIAN MIND
W. E. Houghton

General accounts of Victorian thought are legion, but none can equal the learning and subtlety of The Victorian Frame of Mind *by the American literary scholar W. E. Houghton. What is especially significant in Houghton's work is his keen perception of the ambiguities of Victorian thought, of the tension between the countervailing attitudes of optimism and confidence on the one side and anxiety and doubt on the other. Houghton's work, of which the following selection comprises the Introduction, demolishes once and for all the myth of the smug and self-satisfied Victorian middle class.*

BY THE LATE nineteenth century it was clear that the feudal and agrarian order of the past had been replaced by a democratic and industrial society. The emergence of democracy meant not only the transference of political power from the aristocracy to the people, mainly by the successive Reform Bills of 1832, 1867, and 1884, but also the arrival of what is often called a democratic society. The latter, indeed, was so striking that Mill once called the distinguishing feature of modern institutions and of modern life itself the fact "that human beings are no

---

FROM W. E. Houghton, *The Victorian Frame of Mind, 1830–1870* (New Haven: Yale University Press [for Wellesley College], and London: Oxford University Press, 1957), pp. 4–23. By permission of the publishers.

longer born to their place in life ... but are free to employ their faculties, and such favourable chances as offer, to achieve the lot which may appear to them most desirable." This breakdown of the old conception of status owed something to democratic ideas about the rights of man, but its primary cause was economic. The development of commerce, drawing men off from the land and opening new and independent careers to talent, had been the main instrument in dissolving the feudal nexus of society. In politics, too, the Industrial Revolution underlay the democratic revolution. What Thomas Arnold had in mind when he remarked, on seeing the first train pass through the Rugby countryside, that "feudality is gone for ever," is made explicit by a passage in *Sartor Resartus*, written on the eve of the Reform Bill of 1832: "Cannot the dullest hear Steam-Engines clanking around him? Has he not seen the Scottish Brassmith's IDEA (and this but a mechanical one) travelling on fire-wings round the Cape, and across two Oceans; and stronger than any other Enchanter's Familiar, on all hands unweariedly fetching and carrying: at home, not only weaving Cloth; but rapidly enough overturning the whole old system of Society; and, for Feudalism and Preservation of the Game, preparing us, by indirect but sure methods, Industrialism and the Government of the Wisest?"

Whether wisest or not, the bankers and manufacturers who rose to political power through the revolutionary legislation of 1828–1835—the repeal of the Test and Corporation Acts, the Municipal Reform Act, and above all, the Reform Bill—owed their victory to the financial and psychological power they acquired from the Industrial Revolution. Both factors are seen in Disraeli's analysis of the capitalist mind in *Coningsby*. Mr. Millbank is discussing the English peerage: "I have yet to learn they are richer than we are, better informed, wiser, or more distinguished for public or private virtue. Is it not monstrous, then, that a small number of men, several of whom take the titles of Duke and Earl from towns in this very neighbourhood, towns which they never saw, which never heard of them, which they did not form, or build, or establish,—I say, is it not monstrous that individuals so circumstanced should be invested with the highest of conceivable privileges, the privilege of making laws?" Those are the social forces, wealth and outraged pride, which demanded the Reform Bill. And once the middle class attained political as well as financial eminence, their social influence became decisive. The Victorian frame of mind is largely composed of their characteristic modes of thought and feeling.

But far more striking at the time than democracy was the tremendous industrial development that came with the use of new machines for manufacturing and communication. The great inventions date from the later eighteenth century; and in the early decades of the nineteenth the introduction of more canals, macadam roads, railways, and steamboats hastened the growth of large-scale production by making possible a vast expansion of commerce. This development revolutionized the economic life of England. The old system of fixed regulations, which paralleled that in fixed social relations, was abandoned for the new principle of laissez-faire, on which the manufacturer bought his materials in the cheapest market and sold them in the highest, and hired his labor wherever he liked, for as long as he pleased, at the lowest wages he could pay. In Southey's *Colloquies on the Progress and Prospects of Society* (1829) and Macaulay's fighting review of it (1830), the world of big business and unlimited competition was debated by the old conservatism and the new liberalism.

To live in this dynamic, free-wheeling society was to feel the enormous pressure of work, far beyond anything known before. When new and more distant sources of supply and demand were constantly being opened up by the railroad and the steamship, the battle for new markets became intense. To neglect them could mean ruin. So could failure to take advantage of the latest invention or adapt one's business methods to the most recent developments. Disraeli's *Coningsby* is startled to learn from Mr. Head, who is building a new mill at Staleybridge, that Manchester is already gone by. "If you want to see life," he says, "go to Staley-bridge or Bolton. There's high-pressure." Only the Manchester Bank has kept up with the times: "That's a noble institution, full of commercial enterprise; understands the age, sir; high-pressure to the backbone." The masters had to work almost as long hours as their hands—the Messrs. Carson, for example, who did not become acquainted with their agreeable daughters until their mill was burned down: "There were happy family evenings now that the men of business had time for domestic enjoyments." The same pressure was felt in the professions. "The eminent lawyer, the physician in full practice, the minister, and the politician who aspires to be a minister—even the literary workman, or the eager man of science—are one and all condemned to an amount and continued severity of exertion of which our grandfathers knew little." That was due as much to the social system as to business conditions. When class lines broke down and it became possible as never before to rise in the world by one's own strenuous efforts, the struggle for success was complemented by the struggle for rank. Even apart from personal ambitions, the very existence of hundreds of objects, once unknown or within the reach of few, now made widely available and therefore desirable, increased the size of one's expenses and the load of his work. Moreover, the growing wealth of the wealthy advanced the style of living in the middle and upper classes to a point where the Victorian had to struggle for things his father had been able to ignore. George Eliot remarked that £3,000 a year had seemed wealth to provincial families in 1830, "innocent of future goldfields, and of that gorgeous plutocracy which has so nobly exalted the necessities of genteel life."

Not only the tempo of work but the tempo of living had increased with striking impact, so much so that one observer thought that "the most salient characteristic of life in this latter portion of the 19th century is its SPEED." Until the Victorian period the rate of locomotion and communication had remained almost what it had been for centuries. The horse and the sailing vessel were still the fastest things on earth. But within a few years the speed of travel by land increased from twelve to fifty miles an hour on the new railroads (over 400 per cent) and the new steamships were doing fifteen knots "with wonderful regularity, in spite of wind and tide." But it was less the mechanical speed of the new inventions than the speed of living they produced which impressed the Victorians. Faster locomotion, of goods and letters and people, simply increased the number of things one crowded into a day, and the rush from one to another. Once upon a time "people did not run about the town or the land as we do." They traveled less often, did not hurry to catch trains, wrote one letter a morning instead of ten. Now "we are whirled about, and hooted around, and rung up as if we were all parcels, booking clerks, or office boys." It seems far more modern than Victorian. But if the speed of life has increased in the twentieth century, the sense of speed has declined, for what has become commonplace today was then a startling novelty. Our great-grandfathers may have had more leisure than we do but it seemed less. Even more than ourselves they felt they were living "without leisure and without pause—a life of *haste*—above all a life of excitement, such as haste inevitably involves—a life filled so full ... that we have no time to reflect where we have been and whither we intend to go ... still less what is the value, and the purpose, and *the price* of what we have seen, and done, and visited."

This sense of faster and more crowded living had its intellectual as well as its mechanical basis. The spread of education coupled with the enormous expansion of knowledge and the corresponding increase of publication, books and periodicals and newspapers, gave "every man ... a hundred means of rational occupation and amusement which were closed to his grandfather," and led George Eliot, in a threnody on the death of leisure ("gone where the spinning-wheels are gone, and the pack-horses, and the slow wagons, and the peddlers, who brought bargains to the door on sunny afternoons") to say that "even idleness is eager now, —eager for amusement; prone to excursion-trains, art-museums, periodical literature, and exciting novels; prone even to scientific theorizing, and cursory peeps through microscopes." By the sixties Frances Cobbe was comparing her own generation with that of 1800–30 in words which sound exactly like someone today comparing the generation of 1950 with that of 1850: "That constant sense of being driven—not precisely like 'dumb' cattle, but cattle who must read, write, and talk more in twenty-four hours than twenty-four hours will permit, can never have been known to them."

The radical transition in the human mind was less apparent at first than that in society, but sensitive observers were soon aware that the traditional framework of thought was breaking down. By 1838 Thomas Arnold had noticed a new "atmosphere of unrest and paradox hanging around many of our ablest young men of the present day." He was speaking not merely of religious doubts but "of questions as to great points in moral and intellectual matters; where things which have been settled for centuries seem to be again brought into discussion." This is the atmosphere reflected in the early essays of Macaulay and Carlyle, in *Sartor Resartus* and Mill's *Spirit of the Age,* and the novels of Sterling and Maurice. All of them, written between 1825 and 1834, show that the old certitudes are certain no longer and that a reconstruction of thought is now a prime necessity. "The Old has passed away," wrote Carlyle in 1831, "but, alas, the New appears not in its stead; the Time is still in pangs of travail with the New." There was, of course, more destruction to come, for the old was by no means gone (traditional Christianity, indeed, under Wesleyan and presently Tractarian influence was reviving). And there had been earlier efforts to bring forth the new, most notably by Bentham and Coleridge, the respective heirs of the French *philosophes* and the German transcendentalists, "the two great seminal minds of England in their age." But *the New* had not yet appeared by the thirties. All that was then clear to the intellectuals was that their task was precisely what Carlyle found attempted in the two books he had under review in the essay "Characteristics": "Both these Philosophies are of the Dogmatic or Constructive sort: each in its way is...an endeavour to bring the Phenomena of man's Universe once more under some theoretic Scheme ...they strive after a result which shall be positive; their aim is not to question, but to establish."

That is the starting point. What was the situation a generation later? What corresponds in the intellectual world to the establishment of bourgeois industrial society? The answer is—nothing. In 1850 the age is still one "of fusion and transition.... Old formula, old opinions, hoary systems are being thrown into the smelting-pan; they are fusing—they must be cast anew: who can tell under what new shapes...they will come forth from the moulds?" In the seventies men are still searching—"amid that break-up of traditional and conventional notions respecting our life, its conduct, and its sanctions, which is undeniably befalling our age,— for some clear light and some sure stay." By the eighties "the disintegration of opinion is so rapid that wise men and foolish are equally ignorant where the close of this waning century will find us." Though the Victorians never ceased to look forward to a new period of firm convictions and established beliefs, they had to live in the meantime between two worlds, one dead or dying, one struggling but powerless to be born, in an age of doubt.

The phrase is ambiguous—and at first glance dubious. When one thinks of Macaulay, Spencer, and Huxley, or of Browning, even of Mill and Ruskin, let alone thousands of pious Evangelicals and Anglicans, one is ready to deny it. Indeed, it was still common until very recently to draw a radical contrast between the Victorians and ourselves. One modern critic thought that "a spirit of certitude, wonderful to us who live in an age which has taken the note of interrogation as its emblem, impregnated the great Victorians." Another has claimed that it was only after 1900 that "the old certainties were certainties no longer," and "everything was held to be open to question"; and that "the Victorians seemed to themselves to be living in a house built on unshakable foundations and established in perpetuity... the Home, the Constitution, the Empire, the Christian religion—each of these... was accepted as a final revelation." From such assumptions we could predict the reversal, under the powerful incitement of nostalgia, of the anti-Victorian movement represented by Lytton Strachey:

> If, after the first World War, we were all debunking the nineteenth century, after the second we are deferring to it, and even yearning nostalgically after it... In our own unpleasant century we are mostly displaced persons, and many feel tempted to take flight into the nineteenth as into a promised land... In that distant mountain country, all that we now lack seems present in abundance: not only peace, prosperity, plenty and freedom, but faith, purpose and buoyancy.

Though this contrast of the Victorian period with our own has its element of truth, the tendency to invest the past with the virtues one finds lacking in the present has led to a serious misconception. The fact is, while moral values were firm until about 1870, all intellectual theories, including those of morality, were insecure. What John Morley said of the fifties and sixties applies to the entire period, though with greater intensity and wider repercussions as the years passed: "It was the age of science, new knowledge, searching criticism, followed by multiplied doubts and shaken beliefs." The very effort to resolve the situation made it worse. New solutions raised new controversies, which raised new questions. "Intellectually," wrote J. A. Froude—with religion in mind, but his remark has broader relevance—"the controversies to which I had listened had unsettled me. Difficulties had been suggested which I need not have heard of, but out of which some road or other had now to be looked for." But which road? The choice was baffling. "None of the ways in which... mental regeneration is sought," Mill recognized in 1842, "Bible Societies, Tract Societies, Puseyism, Socialism, Chartism, Benthamism, etc.—will *do*, though doubtless they have all some elements of truth and good in them"; with the result that he was finding it very hard to make up his mind "as to the course which must be taken by the present great transitional movement of opinion and society."

The range of discussion reflected by Mill's list is significant. It was not only in religion that one faced a series of alternatives: is there a God or is there not, and if so, is he a person or an impersonal force? Is there a heaven and a hell? or a heaven but no hell? or neither? If there *is* a true religion, is it Theism or Christianity? And what is Christianity? Roman Catholicism or Protestantism? Is it Church or Chapel? High Church? Broad Church? Low Church? Similar questions, if not so pressing or so widespread, invaded ethical theory and the conception of man: have we free-will or are we human automatons? and if we have the power of moral choice, what is its basis? a God-given voice of conscience? or rational calculation deciding which of two actions will promote the greatest happiness of the greatest number? Is man a man or simply a higher ape? Even the political-economic order of bourgeois capitalism, if an established fact of the outer environment in 1850, held no unquestioned supremacy in the world of ideas. The sanctity and blessings of private property, laissez-faire, and unlimited competition were challenged, in one aspect or another, by Owen and Mill, Carlyle and Ruskin, the Chartists and the Christian Socialists. The abortive "communism" of 1848 in France further opened Victorian eyes to the possibility that the old political economy was limited and temporary. And the provisional character of middle-class government, suggested by the Chartist agitation of the forties, was confirmed by the Reform Bill of 1867. By 1870 the uncertain future seemed to belong to the unpredictable populace.

It was not, however, the mere existence of competing philosophies which called all in doubt. It was also the prevailing atmosphere. As one prophet after another stepped forward with his program of reconstruction, the hubbub of contending theories, gaining in number as the century advanced, and spreading out from the intellectuals to the large audience of the periodicals, created a climate of opinion in which, quite apart from any specific doubts, the habit of doubt was unconsciously bred. One had an uneasy feeling, perhaps only half-conscious, that his beliefs were no longer quite secure. Nor should we forget the complementary effect of the vast increase of knowledge, scientific and historical, that almost inundated the Victorians and left them often baffled by the sheer number and complexity of its implications. The yeasty state of mind which Kingsley ascribed to the young men of 1851 was not only one in which "the various stereotyped systems which they have received by tradition [are] breaking up under them like ice in a thaw"; it was also one in which "a thousand facts and notions, which they know not how to classify, [are] pouring in on them like a flood." Three years later Mill's diary for January 13, 1854, contains what is perhaps the best single statement on Victorian doubt:

Scarcely any one, in the more educated classes, seems to have any opinions, or to place any real faith in those which he professes to have.... It requires in these times much more intellect to marshal so much greater a stock of ideas and observations. This has not yet been done, or has been done only by very few: and hence the multitude of thoughts only breeds increase of uncertainty. Those who should be the guides of the rest, see too many sides to every question. They hear so much said, or find that so much can be said, about everything, that they feel no assurance of the truth of anything.

Without contrary evidence, who would be surprised if the passage were dated *1954*?

This evidence—and much more could be given—suggests that continuity rather than contrast is the conclusion to be drawn from comparing the Victorians with ourselves. And yet, if both periods can be called ages of doubt, it is certainly with a difference. Neither the kind of doubt nor the strength of its hold was the same in 1850 as it is today.

In the four decades under inspection, doubt never reached the point of positive or terminal skepticism. It never involved a denial of the mind as a valid instrument of truth. No mid-Victorian ever described his age as Dobrée described the 1930's: "All the previous ages ... had something they could take for granted.... We can be sure of nothing; our civilization is threatened, even the simplest things we live by.... In our present confusion our only hope is to be scrupulously honest with ourselves, so honest as to doubt our own minds and the conclusions they arrive at. Most of us have ceased to believe, except provisionally, in truths, and we feel that what is important is not so much truth as the way our minds move towards truths." Though the seeds of that radical doubt were planted by the 1870's, as we shall see in a moment, they did not grow up until the dissolving influences of modern sociology, anthropology, and psychology had done their work, and mined the old confidence with relativism and rationalism. The Victorians might be, and often were, uncertain about what theory to accept or what faculty of the mind to rely on; but it never occurred to them to doubt their capacity to arrive at truth. When Mill thought of his age as one of intellectual anarchy, his reaction to such a condition was quite different from ours. He could see it as a momentary and necessary stage in a process of growth: "So long as this intellectual anarchy shall endure, we may be warranted in believing that we are in a fair way to become wiser than our forefathers; but ... we have not yet advanced beyond the unsettled state, in which the mind is, when it has recently found itself out in a grievous error, and has not yet satisfied itself of the truth." Not yet but soon! "If your opinions, or mine, are right," he told Sterling, "they will in time be unanimously adopted by the instructed classes." It is this faith in the existence of ultimate truths in religion and ethics, in politics, economics, and aesthetics (as well as in the natural sciences), and in the capacity of the human mind to discover them, by some form of reason or of intuition, which unites the partisans of every school. That, one is tempted to say, is the one intellectual certitude in Victorian England. But it is a great one, for on such a foundation the universe can be held together: it can remain rational. That is why Chesterton could claim that the Victorian period was "orderly compared with what came after." (But not, he added, "compared with the centuries that came before.") On that foundation it was still possible, as it no longer is, to find comfort in the thought

> That, though I perish, Truth is so:
> That, howsoe'er I stray and range,
> Whate'er I do, Thou dost not change.

It was still possible to adopt this or that theory of Church or State with full confidence that it might well be true—though not that it *was*.

But less possible after 1870. For about that time a number of things converged to suggest the relativity of knowledge and the subjective character of thought. This radical change, bounding the mid-Victorian temper, is documented in the popular work of Walter Pater.

The historical method, as it was formulated under the influences of Romantic and scientific conceptions of development, meant the study of social phenomena of all kinds, institutions, customs, beliefs, as the natural product of a given time and place; with the result that the type of question one put to the past underwent a crucial change. One no longer asked, What do I think of this? is it good? is it true? For once everything was thought relative, good or true only for a particular society at a particular stage in its cultural evolution, the right questions became: How shall I account for it? Why did men believe that it was good or true?

In the intellectual as in the organic world the given product, its normal or abnormal characteristics, are determined, as people say, by the "environment." The business of the young scholar therefore, in reading Plato, is not to take his side in a controversy, to adopt or refute Plato's opinions... still less, to furnish himself with arguments on behalf of some theory or conviction of his own. His duty is rather to follow intelligently, *but with strict indifference,* the mental process there, as he might witness a game of skill.... To put Plato into his natural place, as a result from antecedent and contemporary movements of Greek speculation, of Greek life generally: such is the proper aim of the historic, that is to say, of the really critical study of him.

The phrase I have italicized adds the final touch: nothing could be less Victorian. Though recognized earlier, the awareness that the historical attitude could issue in skepticism did not reach general consciousness, I think, until after 1870 when it came to be debated in the periodicals by men like John Morley, Edward Dowden, and Henry Sidgwick.

At the same time the scientific view that all things, material and human, were in constant flux, changing under the inevitable influences of many and complex factors, could make all truths seem relative only to a particular moment. In the opening paragraphs of the "Coleridge" (1866) and the "Conclusion" to *The Renaissance* (1873), Pater revived the skepticism of Hume and reduced all knowledge to a series of "impressions unstable, flickering, inconsistent," each of which "is the impression of the individual in his isolation, each mind keeping as a solitary prisoner its own dream of a world." On such assumptions the intellectual life was ridiculous. Only the aesthetic life of delicate perceptions and sensitive response had any importance. Not that philosophy or "speculative culture" was ruled out. It still had value for the human spirit—but only "to rouse, to startle it into sharp and eager observation." By suggesting "points of view" it could "help us to gather up what might otherwise pass unregarded by us."

To turn back from Pater to Arnold is to return to the Victorian world. For Arnold threw his whole weight against relativism. Not, it is true, with reference to historical or scientific theories, but to the liberal dogma of individualism and its assertion of private judgment, which in society as a whole was the major force that undermined the belief in absolute truths. By 1864 Arnold was aware of a "baneful notion that there is no such thing as a high, correct standard in intellectual matters; that every one may as well take his own way." To the contemporary boast that every Englishman could believe what he liked, what was true for him, Arnold kept asking whether it was not important that what people were free to believe should be worth believing; whether, in short, the anarchy of individualism should not be checked by the authority of Culture, with its inherent power of discovering truth. For Culture, "bent on seeing things as they are," can dissipate delusions like the worship of freedom for its own sake, and fix "standards of perfection that are real!" What is meant here by things as they are or standards that are real is the very absolutes which Plato affirmed and Pater denied. "To see things as they are" is "to draw towards a knowledge of the universal order which seems to be intended and aimed at in the world ... to learn, in short, the will of God"; and this insight comes from the use of right reason, meaning intuitive judgment, by a man of wide learning and flexible intelligence. Indeed, Arnold cites Plato by name as explicitly denying to the mere man of virtue the Greek instinct for what he (Plato) calls "the true, firm, intelligible law of things." "He reserves it for the lover of pure knowledge, of seeing things as they really are...."

The contrast of Pater with Arnold is pointed by their respective conceptions of the "modern spirit." To Pater, of course, it is the relative spirit, which considers that "truth itself is but a possibility, realisable not as a general conclusion, but rather as the elusive effect of a particular personal experience"; and which "must needs content itself with suspension of judgment, at the end of the intellectual journey, to the very last asking: *Que scais-je?* Who knows?" For Arnold the modern spirit is the awareness that traditional beliefs and institutions are no longer adequate to embody contemporary life; and the representatives of the modern spirit, "the would-be remodellers of the old traditional European order," are "the invokers of reason against custom." For them the end of the intellectual journey is not doubt but reconstruction.

Pater and Arnold face each other across the gulf between two basic conceptions of the human mind that opened up between 1865 and 1875. By 1877, at the house party given by W. H. Mallock where "culture, faith, and philosophy" are discussed in a new "Republic," the Paters have become a society, still small but destined to rise to fame, or notoriety, in the nineties. Mr. Herbert, who speaks for the mid-Victorians (he is Ruskin) berates the younger generation because, in the face of conflicting opinions, they persuade themselves "that neither opinion is of much moment—that the question cannot be decided absolutely—that it should not be decided absolutely." This is as true of morality as of everything else. "There is no recognised rule of life anywhere," comments Mr. Leslie. "Every one who does right at all only does what is right in his own eyes. All society, it seems, is going to pieces." To which another guest replies:

"I," said Mr. Rose, "look upon social dissolution as the true condition of the most perfect life. For the centre of life is the individual, and it is only through dissolution that the individual can re-emerge. All the warrings of endless doubts, all the questionings of matter and of spirit, which I have myself known, I value only because, remembering the weariness of them, I take a profounder and more exquisite pleasure in the colour of a crocus, the pulsations of a chord of music, or a picture of Sandro Botticelli's.

Mr. Rose, I need hardly say, is Pater—a caricature of Pater. A decade later Canon Liddon, who like Arnold and Ruskin was a mid-Victorian, observed that "a morbidly active imagination which cannot acquiesce in the idea of fixed and unalterable truth" had become a malady of modern society.

Though the Victorians were certain that truth existed and the mind could discover it, they found themselves involved in two forms of doubt: either what is sometimes called negative skepticism, when the judgment is suspended between alternate conclusions, one of which is considered true; or the affirmation of a belief which they only half believed—and half doubted. Both types of insecurity are present in the important passage from Mill's diary quoted earlier: "Scarcely any one, in the more educated classes seems to have any opinions [because he sees "too many sides to every question"] or to place any real faith in those which he professes to have."

When Alfred North Whitehead spoke of the nineteenth century as being disturbed by the conflicting claims of incompatible doctrines, he pointed out that Cardinal Newman in his *Apologia pro Vita Sua* found it a peculiarity of Pusey, the great Anglican ecclesiastic, that "he was haunted by no intellectual perplexities." "In this respect," Whitehead continued, "Pusey recalls Milton, Pope, Wordsworth, as in contrast with Tennyson, Clough, Matthew Arnold, and Newman himself." A letter of George Eliot's, written in 1839, gives a characteristic illustration of this new state of mind, and with reference to a topic which for Newman was especially baffling:

I think no one feels more difficulty in coming to a decision on controverted matters than myself.... The other day Montaigne's motto came to my mind (it is mentioned by Pascal) as an appropriate one for me,—"Que sais-je?"—beneath a pair of balances, though, by the by, it is an ambiguous one, and may be taken in a sense that I desire to reprobate.... I use it in a limited sense as a representation of my oscillating judgment. On no subject do I veer to all points of the compass more frequently than on the nature of the visible Church. I am powerfully attracted in a certain direction, but when I am about to settle there, counterassertions shake me from my position.

Nothing could better describe the negative skepticism of the time, including, as it does, the rejection of the positive skepticism which Pater drew from the same passage in Montaigne. It was not, of course, limited to religion. In the forties Disraeli found society "in the midst of a convulsion in which the very principles of our political and social systems are called in question," and created a hero in its image—"confused, perplexed," his mind "a chaos"; but his spirit sustained "by a profound, however vague, conviction, that there are still great truths, if we could but work them out." In the same years, worried because the condition-of-England problem was "shaking many old beliefs, and leading him whither he knew not," Tom Brown at Oxford plunged into works on political economy, then consulted an Anglo-Catholic friend about High Church teaching on social questions, and finally read *Past and Present*—

and so filled his head "full of a set of contradictory notions and beliefs." By the time he graduated, reading and discussion had combined to drag him into "perplexities, and doubts, and dreams, and struggles." The Victorian plight was summed up by Clough in a poem which deals with still another area of doubt, the nature of man: *Is* he a human automaton?

> Oh say it, all who think it,
> Look straight, and never blink it!
> If it is so, let it be so,
> And we will all agree so;
> But the plot has counterplot,
> It may be, and yet be not.

It must not be supposed, however, that the normal state of the Victorian mind was one of indecision or suspended judgment. The confidence in reason or intuition and the powerful will to believe made doubt itself unstable. It came and went. Individuals passed through it. Mill confessed in 1833 that "I am often in a state almost of scepticism, and have no theory of Human Life at all, or seem to have conflicting theories, or a theory which does not amount to a belief"; but he added at once, "This is only a *recent* state, and, as I well know, a passing one, and my convictions will be firmer." Passing but recurrent. What he says of his own transition (from his early Benthamism through doubt to his later liberalism) applies in general to all the mid-Victorian intellectuals. For reasons we shall have to consider, Carlyle, Newman, Disraeli, Froude, Eliot, Arnold—none was any more content than Mill to remain "confused and unsettled." All like him succeeded in weaving new ideas and old dogmas into a fresh pattern of thought.

Not until the sixties does a settled state of baffled judgment and a mind empty of beliefs begin to appear. It was then, when the *Origin of Species* and *Essays and Reviews* intensified the difficulties of decision, especially in religion, while at the same time positive skepticism was emerging, that Frances Cobbe was struck by a new disposition "to accept as a finality that condition of hesitation and uncertainty which in the nature of things should be one of transition." Such a condition, as we might expect, is habitual in the society of Mallock's *New Republic,* where "nobody knows what to believe, and most people believe nothing," but it did not exist a generation earlier. It had only afflicted individuals for shorter or longer intervals. Most of the time the Victorian mind contained beliefs and not doubts—but the beliefs were shaky.

What *is* constantly present, therefore, is the fear or suspicion, or simply the vague uneasy feeling, that one was not sure he believed what he believed. I do not mean that no one had any strong beliefs. The traditional morality was firmly held by almost everyone until the seventies and by a vast majority until after World War I; and there were certainly many people whose religious or political convictions remained unshaken. But the more one studies the period, the more certain he is that most Victorians were aptly described by Mill himself in *The Spirit of the Age:*

"The men of the present day rather incline to an opinion than embrace it; few ... have full confidence in their own convictions"; or, in a variant phrase, people "have no strong or deep-rooted convictions at all." How could it have been otherwise in a period of dissolving creeds and clashing theories? If one's formal doubts were sooner or later discarded for one creed or another, the taint of doubt remained. A prayer attributed to the Victorians is a witty distortion of the truth: "O God—if there is a God—save my soul—if I have a soul." Like Spencer in later life (and the example is significant, since no one could seem more certain or dogmatic), one clung to his dogmas, old or new or a mixture of both, "but without confident faith." Or like Tennyson. In the representative poem of the age, the key words are "trust," "hope," "guess":

> Behold, we know not anything;
> I can but trust that good shall fall
> At last—far off—at last, to all.
>
> I trust I have not wasted breath:
> I think we are not wholly brain,
> Magnetic mockeries.
>
> The Power in darkness whom we guess.

In Memoriam is not a poem of belief or of unbelief. It is a poem of doubt, that is, of doubtful beliefs. In our generation, Kingsley noted, "few of us deeply believe anything."

The two outstanding features of their world which most impressed the Victorians are now before us. No one could escape them. No one could take them, as we can take them now, with the indifference or the neutrality adopted toward the customary. Everyone in all classes to some degree felt their impact. We might well expect, therefore, that the major Victorian attitudes would have been mainly determined by the powerful influence (as much from the reaction they provoked as from their positive effect) of these two things, one or both of which are implicit in every reference to "the age of transition"—bourgeois industrial society and widespread doubt about the nature of man, society, and the universe. In the analysis that follows this is the central thread in a pattern planned to include, in due relation to it, other important influences, especially that of the so-called Puritan or Evangelical revival.

At the threshold stand two emotional attitudes, in the broad sense of pleasure-pain responses, which were bound to occur in a period of conscious and radical change, and which were nourished by many of the same social and intellectual developments. The Victorians reacted to their age with hope and dismay, optimism and anxiety.

24

THE SOCIAL HISTORY OF NINETEENTH-CENTURY EDUCATION

Raymond Williams

A left-wing literary critic and scholar of enormous influence on the younger generation of English intellectuals, Raymond Williams has published several works dealing with the question of the forms a good society ought to take in the industrial era. The following account of Victorian education—a subject that more and more appears to be a key to understanding the social and intellectual development of modern England—demonstrates Williams' great ability as a social historian and at the same time reveals his devotion to a philosophy of egalitarianism and rational social planning.

IN THE seventy years between 1751 and 1821, the population of the British mainland doubled, from seven to fourteen millions, and by 1871, at twenty-six millions, it had nearly doubled again. In addition to this remarkable expansion, the proportion of the population living in towns, including the new industrial towns, and also the proportion of children in the population as a whole, again remarkably increased. These changes would have been enough to disorganize a much better system of education than the eighteenth century actually had, and the first half of the nineteenth century is full of reports showing the utter inadequacy, in part revealed, in part created, by the social and economic transformation. The desire to reorganize education, on a fuller basis than hitherto, was the motive of many of these reports, but at the same time the forces opposed to any general reform were very strong. In 1816, of 12,000 parishes examined, 3,500 had no school, 3,000 had endowed schools of a varying quality, and 5,500 had unendowed schools, of a quality even more variable. But to do anything about this the reformers had to get past the representative opinion of a Justice of the Peace in 1807:

It is doubtless desirable that the poor should be generally instructed in *reading*, if it were only for the best of purposes—that they may read the Scriptures. As to

FROM Raymond Williams, *The Long Revolution* (New York: Columbia University Press, and London: Chatto & Windus Ltd., 1961), pp. 135-144. By permission of the publishers.

writing and *arithmetic,* it may be apprehended that such a degree of knowledge would produce in them a disrelish for the laborious occupations of life.

It is true that at no previous period had the poor, as a whole, been educated, although in exceptional parishes the attempt was made. But there had been provision, again and again, for the exceptional poor boy to get to the university. Under the new dispensation, education was organized on a more rigid class basis.

> To every class we have a school assign'd
> Rules for all ranks and food for every mind.
> (Crabbe.)

Only the last clause was untrue.

But the process of change from a system of social orders, based on localities, to a national system of social classes—a change extending from the fifteenth to the late eighteenth centuries—was now virtually complete, and its result was a new kind of class-determined education. Higher education became a virtual monopoly, excluding the new working class, and the idea of universal education, except within the narrow limits of 'moral rescue', was widely opposed as a matter of principle.

The first new educational institutions of the Industrial Revolution were the industrial schools, providing manual training and elementary instruction, and, much more important, the Sunday schools, available to adults as well as children, and, while varying in methods, mainly organized on the principle noted: that for moral reasons the poor must learn to read the Bible, but that writing and arithmetic, to say nothing of more dangerous subjects, were less necessary or even harmful. In the new kinds of day school, under the rival systems of Lancaster and Bell, teaching was similarly based on the Bible, but by a new method—what Bell called 'the STEAM ENGINE of the MORAL WORLD'—which by the use of monitors and standard repetitive exercises allowed one master to teach many hundreds of children simultaneously in one room. It has been estimated that with the development of Sunday schools and the new day schools, and with the surviving parish and adventure schools, some 875,000 children, out of a possible 1,500,000, attended a school of some kind for some period in 1816, and that in 1835 the figure was 1,450,000 out of 1,750,000. To assess these figures adequately, we must remember that the same inquiries showed an average duration of school attendance, in 1835, of one year. From the eighteenth century some assistance to schools from the rates had been empowered in a few places, and from the 1830s there was a beginning of national assistance in school building. By 1851, the average duration of school attendance had been raised to two years, and by 1861 an estimated 2,500,000 children, out of a possible 2,750,000 may have been in some form of school attendance, though still of very mixed quality and with the majority leaving before they were eleven. The curriculum was broadening a little, usually now including writing and arithmetic, and in some schools other general subjects. The

Revised Code of 1862 instituted a system of payment by results in relation to definite standards in reading, writing, and arithmetic (reading a short paragraph in a newspaper; writing similar matter from dictation; working sums in practice and fractions). Increasing public aid to the schools was thus tied to the old criterion of a minimum standard. In 1870, school boards were established, to complete the network of schools and bring them under a clearer kind of supervision, and in 1876 and 1880 this extension was confirmed by making universal elementary schooling compulsory. In 1893, the leaving age was raised to 11, in 1899 to 12, and in 1900 to a permissive 14. Thus by the end of the century a national system of elementary schooling, still largely confined to the provision of a minimum standard, had been set going.

Meanwhile, the old grammar schools had been widely developed, as the institutions of a largely separate class, served mainly, at the primary stage, by an extended network of preparatory schools. Attendances at the old schools, particularly at the leading nine, had begun to revive in the period 1790–1830, and in their different ways Butler at Shrewsbury, from 1798, and Arnold at Rugby, from 1824, had begun to change their character. Arnold's influence was not mainly on the curriculum, but on the re-establishment of social purpose, the education of Christian gentlemen. Butler's influence is perhaps even more significant, for his emphasis on examination-passing marks the beginning of a major trend. By the 1830s, the examination system between these schools and the universities was firmly established, and this, while raising educational standards within the institutions, had the effect of reinforcing the now marked limitation of the universities to entrants from a narrow social class. In the curriculum, classics were 'business' and other subjects were extras, but the establishment of the Civil Service Commission and the Board of Military Education, from mid-century, had the effect of promoting mathematics and modern languages, and of further organizing the schools in terms of examinations. In the 1840s, there were altogether some 700 grammar schools, and more than 2,000 nonclassical endowed schools, but an inquiry showed in 1868 that in two-thirds of the towns of England there were no secondary schools of any kind, and in the remaining third there were marked differences of quality. In the late 1860s, through two commissions and the Public Schools Act of 1868, the reorganization of secondary education, still on a narrow class basis, was conceived and in part carried through. The Act of 1868 broke many of the old foundation statutes, and instituted new governing bodies. From this date, the new curriculum (classics, mathematics, one modern language, two natural sciences, history, geography, drawing, and music) and the confirmation of a separate class of 'public schools', were established. The Headmasters' Conference, embracing the many new nineteenth-century schools of this type, and some of the old foundations, was begun in 1869. The Taunton Commission of 1867 envisaged three grades of secondary school: those for the upper and upper-middle classes, keeping their boys till 18 and giving a 'liberal education' in preparation for the universities and the old professions; those for the middle classes, keeping their boys till 16 and preparing them for the Army, the newer professions, and many departments of the Civil Service; and those for the lower middle classes, keeping their boys until 14, and fitting them for living as 'small tenant farmers, small tradesmen, and superior artisans'. Where possible, minorities should be enabled to pass to a higher grade, and in particular there might be a connection between third-grade secondary schools and the elementary schools, enabling some sons of labourers to go on to secondary education. Secondary education, in these three grades, should be made available to 10 children for every 1,000 of the population, and of these 8 would be in the third grade. In practice this would mean a national total of 64,000 children in the first and second grades, and 256,000 in the third grade, out of some 4,000,000 children. 'It is obvious', the Commission commented, in relation to its tripartite grading, 'that these distinctions correspond roughly, but by no means exactly, to the gradations of society.'

In practice, while secondary education was not yet a public responsibility, the effect of this suggested organization was uneven. From the 1850s, a system of University Local Examinations, first called 'Middle-Class Examinations', had enabled endowed and proprietary schools of the first and second grades to aim at some recognized national standard of secondary education, and the extension of the examination system by official and professional bodies had the same rationalizing effect. The campaign for the secondary education of girls was beginning to show results, and then in 1889 Wales took the lead, with an Intermediate Education Act which succeeded in establishing an organized secondary system linking the board and voluntary elementary schools with the universities, and providing for both boys and girls. In 1902 the creation of Local Education Authorities, with responsibility for the full educational needs of their areas, laid the basis for a national system of secondary education. The third-grade school had been overtaken by the raising of the elementary school-leaving age, and it was to the creation of first- and second-grade secondary schools that the new authorities, with varying energy, applied themselves. The Board of Education had come into existence in 1899, and in 1904 it defined a four-year secondary course, leading to a certificate, in English language and literature, geography, history, a language other than English, mathematics, science, drawing, manual work, physical training, and household crafts for girls. If we look back from this to the eighteenth-century curriculum of the Dissenting Academies, we shall see where the main line of the tradition lies.

Meanwhile, in the course of the century, university education had been radically changed. The institution of public examinations, in Cambridge from the eighteenth century, in Oxford from the early years of the nineteenth, had an important effect on teaching, which did not pass without protest that the examination system was making education mechanical. At the same time, the religious exclusiveness of the two ancient universities, and the effective restriction of their curriculum to classics and mathematics, led to the foundation of London University (1828–1836), while the new University of Durham (1832), though governed by the Church, had a notably broader curriculum. Reforming movements at Oxford and Cambridge led to substantial statutory changes in the 1850s, with the dual aim of broadening the range of subjects offered, and ensuring a social representation wider than that of 'prospective parsons, prospective lawyers, (and) young men of rank and fortune'. Further legislative changes in the 1870s and 1880s, and the reorganization and extension of faculties, led to the achievement of modern university status. Meanwhile, university colleges were springing up, and the foundations of Manchester, Nottingham, Reading, Southampton, Leeds, Liverpool, Sheffield, and Birmingham, together with the three Welsh colleges, were being laid.

The nineteenth-century achievement is evidently a major reorganization of elementary, secondary, and university education, along lines which in general we still follow. Both in kinds of institution, and in the matter and manner of education, it shows the reorganization of learning by a radically changed society, in which the growth of industry and of democracy were the leading elements, and in terms of change both in the dominant social character and in types of adult work. At no time in England have the effects of these influences on the very concept of education been clearer, but, precisely because this was so, a fundamental argument about the purposes of education was the century's most interesting contribution. Two strands of this argument can be separated: the idea of education for all, and the definition of a liberal education. The former, as we have seen, was fiercely argued, and the history of the century represents the victory of those who, in the early decades, had been a minority. Two major factors can be distinguished: the rise of an organized working class, which demanded education, and the needs of an expanding and changing economy. In practice, these were closely interwoven, in the long debate, and the victory of the reformers rested on three elements: genuine response to the growth of democracy, as in men like Mill, Carlyle, Ruskin, and Arnold; protective response, the new version of 'moral rescue', very evident in the arguments for the 1870 Education Act in relation to the franchise extensions of 1867—'our future masters ... should at least learn their letters'; and the practical response, perhaps decisive, which led Forster in 1870 to use as his principal argument: 'upon the speedy provision of elementary education depends our industrial prosperity'. In the growth of secondary education this economic argument was even more central.

The democratic and the industrial arguments are both sound, but the great persuasiveness of the latter led to the definition of education in terms of future adult work, with the parallel clause of teaching the required social character—habits of regularity, 'self-discipline', obedience, and trained effort. Such a definition was challenged from two sides, by those with wider sympathies with the general growth of democracy, and by those with an older conception of liberal education, in relation to man's health as a spiritual being. This interesting alliance is broadly that which I traced as a tradition in *Culture and Society,* and the educational argument was always near the centre of this continuing tradition. On the one hand it was argued, by men with widely differing attitudes to the rise of democracy and of working-class organization, that men had a natural human right to be educated, and that any good society depended on governments accepting this principle as their duty. On the other hand, often by men deeply opposed to democracy, it was argued that man's spiritual health depended on a kind of education which was more than a training for some specialized work, a kind variously described as 'liberal', 'humane', or 'cultural'. The great complexity of the general argument, which is still unfinished, can be seen from the fact that the public educators, as we may call the first group, were frequently in alliance with the powerful group which promoted education in terms of training and disciplining the poor, as workers and citizens, while the defenders of 'liberal education' were commonly against both: against the former because liberal education would be vulgarized by extension to the 'masses'; against the latter because liberal education would be destroyed by being turned into a system of specialized and technical training. Yet the public educators inevitably drew on the arguments of the defenders of the old 'liberal' education, as a way of preventing universal education being narrowed to a system of pre-industrial instruction. These three groups —the public educators, the industrial trainers, and the old humanists— are still to be distinguished in our own time, and we shall see, later, their influence in twentieth-century developments. In general, the curriculum which the nineteenth century evolved can be seen as a compromise between all three groups, but with the industrial trainers predominant. The significant case is the long controversy over science and technical education. If we look at the range of scientific discovery between the seventeenth and the end of the nineteenth centuries, it is clear that its importance lies only in part in its transformation of the techniques of production and communication; indeed lies equally in its transformation of man's view of himself and of his world. Yet the decisive educational interpretation of this new knowledge was not in terms of its essential contribution to liberal studies, but in terms of technical training for a particular class of men. The old humanists muddled the issue by claiming a fundamental distinction between their traditional learning and that of the new disciplines, and it was from this kind of thinking that there developed the absurd defensive reaction that all real learning was undertaken without thought of practical advantage. In fact, as the educational history shows, the classical linguistic disciplines were primarily vocational, but these particular vocations had acquired a separate traditional dignity, which was refused to vocations now of equal human relevance. Thus, instead of the new learning broadening a general curriculum, it was neglected, and in the end reluctantly admitted on the grounds that it was of a purely technical kind. The pressure of the industrial trainers eventually prevailed, though not with any general adequacy until the

Technical Instruction Act of 1889, and even here, significantly, it was 'instruction' rather than 'education'. This history was damaging both to general education and to the new kinds of vocational training, and yet it was only an exceptional man, such as Huxley, who could see this at the time and consequently argue in the only adequate way: that science must become a part of general education and of liberal culture, and that, as a further provision, there must be an adequate system of specific professional training, in all kinds of scientific and technical work, on the same principle as the further professional training of doctors, lawyers, teachers, artists, and clergy. We can take only a limited satisfaction in the knowledge that the industrial trainers won, inert and stupid as the old humanists were and have continued to be. Huxley was a public educator, in the full sense, and it was only in this tradition that the problem might have been solved.

The shadow of class thinking lies over this as over so much other nineteenth-century educational thinking. The continued relegation of trade and industry to lower social classes, and the desire of successful industrialists that their sons should move into the now largely irrelevant class of gentry, were alike extremely damaging to English education and English life. As at the Reformation, a period of major reconstruction of institutions was undertaken largely without reference to the best learning of the age, and without any successful redefinition of the purposes of education and of the content of a contemporary liberal culture. The beginnings of technical instruction in the Mechanics' Institutes might have developed into a successful redefinition, but again it was the training of a specific class, whereas in fact the new sciences were radical elements in the society as a whole: a society which had changed its economy, which under pressure was changing its institutions, but which, at the centres of power, was refusing to change its ways of thinking. And then to the new working class, the offered isolation of science and technical instruction was largely unacceptable, for it was precisely in the interaction between techniques and their general living that this class was coming to its new consciousness. Politics, in the wide sense of discussing the quality and direction of their living, was excluded from these Institutes, as it was to remain largely excluded from the whole of nineteenth-century education. It was only very slowly, and then only in the sphere of adult education, that the working class, drawing indeed on very old intellectual traditions and on important dissenting elements in the English educational tradition, made its contribution to the modern educational debate. This contribution—the students' choice of subject, the relation of disciplines to actual contemporary living, and the parity of general discussion with expert instruction—remains important, but made little headway in the general educational organization. Like the individual public educators, their time was not yet.

In the twentieth century, the framework inherited from the nineteenth century has been greatly expanded and improved. Elementary education has been redefined as primary education, ending at eleven, and from this definition, since 1944, it has been possible to provide secondary education for all. A greatly expanded system of combined first-grade and second-grade secondary schools has been brought into being, and arrangements for a substantial minority to pass from primary schools into this system, and for a much smaller minority to pass on to higher education, have been if not completely at least effectively established. A large number of third-grade secondary schools, with limited connections to the minority system, are in process of creation, and vary considerably in quality. In primary education, a notable expansion of the curriculum is perhaps the century's major achievement; it is mainly here that the influence of the public educators has been effective. The universities, if unevenly and at times without clear definition, have expanded their curricula in vitally important ways. It is at the level of secondary education, whether 'grammar' or 'modern', that the essential argument continues, in terms that reveal again the close relationship between curriculum and organization.

25

BENTHAMITE DOCTRINE AND THE VICTORIAN STATE

O. MacDonagh and H. Parris

The late nineteenth-century publicist A. V. Dicey regarded Benthamite teaching as the blueprint of the Victorian state, and Élie Halévy also stressed the powerful influence of Utilitarian philosophy in the shaping of Victorian government. In recent years this thesis has been challenged by scholars who are suspicious of attributing such great importance to rather abstract theory and who envision the Victorian political institutions as developing in response to the stress of social and economic pressures. The assessment of Benthamite influence on nineteenth-century government is further complicated by the fact that Benthamism can be regarded as the theoretical source of laissez faire and yet also as tending toward the modern welfare state. The opposing arguments in this historiographical controversy are effectively outlined

FROM O. MacDonagh, "The 19th Century Revolution in Government, A Reappraisal," *Historical Journal*, I (1958), 57–61, and H. Parris, "The 19th Century Revolution in Government: A Reappraisal Reappraised," *Historical Journal*, III (1960), 28, 33–37. By permission of the authors and of the publishers, Cambridge University Press.

in the following debate between two young English historians, O. MacDonagh and H. Parris. MacDonagh presents a model of the making of Victorian government without direct Benthamite inspiration; in reply Parris argues for the retention of the Dicey-Halévy thesis, with some appropriate modifications.

I

IN VERY general terms, the change with which we are concerned is the transformation, scarcely glimpsed till it was well secured, of the operations and functions of the state within society, which destroyed belief in the possibility that society did or should consist, essentially or for the most part, of a mere accumulation of contractual relationships between persons, albeit enforced so far as need be by the sovereign power. Now our first proposition is that very powerful impulses towards such a change were generated by a peculiar concatenation of circumstances in the nineteenth century. Again in very general terms, these circumstances were as follows: the unprecedented scale and intensity and the other novelties of the social problems arising from steam-powered industrialization, and from the vast increase, and the new concentrations and mobility, of population; the simultaneous generation of potential solutions, or partial solutions, to these problems by the developments in mass production and cheap and rapid transport, by the new possibilities of assembling great bodies of labour, skills and capital, and by the progress of the technical and scientific discovery associated with this economic growth; the widespread and ever-growing influence of humanitarian sentiment and of stricter views of sexual morality and 'decency'; the increasing sensitivity of politics to public pressures, and the extraordinary growth in both the volume of legislation and the degree to which its introduction became the responsibility of governments, with the corollaries of changes in parliamentary practice and of the rapid development of parliament's investigatory instruments.

The legislative-cum-administrative process which this concatenation of circumstances set in motion may perhaps best be described by constructing a 'model' of its operation. Very simply, the most common origin of this sort of process was the exposure of a social evil. Sometimes, the exposure was sudden and catastrophic, the consequence of an epidemic, a mine explosion, a railway calamity; sometimes, dramatic in another sense, the revelation of a private philanthropist or of an altogether fortuitous observer. On the whole, exposures were, so to speak, exogenous. Rarely were they, in this first instance, the fruit of the practice of administration or regular inquiry. Nor was sensationalism unimportant, for exposures were effective in so far as they directed public or parliamentary attention to particular dangers, suffering, sexual immorality or injustice. Once this was done sufficiently, the ensuing demand for remedy at any price set an irresistible engine of change in motion. Once it was publicized sufficiently that, say, women on their hands and knees dragged trucks of coal through subterranean tunnels, or that emigrants had starved to death at sea, or that children had been mutilated by unfenced machinery, these evils became 'intolerable'; and throughout and even before the Victorian years 'intolerability' was the master card. No wall of either doctrine or interest could permanently withstand that single trumpet cry, all the more so as governments grew ever more responsive to public sentiment, and public sentiment ever more humane. The demand for remedies was also, in the contemporary context, a demand for prohibitory enactments. Men's instinctive reaction was to legislate the evil out of existence. But at this point the reaction was usually itself resisted. As the threat to legislate took shape, the endangered interests, whatever they might be, brought their political influence into action, and the various forces of inertia, material and immaterial, came into play. Almost invariably, there was compromise. Both in the course of the drafting of the bill, when trade interests often 'made representations' or were consulted, and in the committee stage in parliament, the restrictive clauses of the proposed legislation were relaxed, the penalties for their defiance whittled down and the machinery for their enforcement weakened. None the less the measure, however emasculated, became law. A precedent was established, a responsibility assumed: the first stage of the process was complete.

The second stage began when it was disclosed, sooner or later, gradually or catastrophically, that the prohibitory legislation had left the original evils largely or perhaps even altogether untouched. For, generally speaking, first statutes tended to be ineffective even beyond the concessions yielded to trade and theory in the course of their drafting and passage. This was so because the draftsmen and the politicians (preliminary parliamentary inquiry in some cases notwithstanding) knew little or nothing of the real conditions which they were attempting to regulate, and paid little or no attention to the actual *enforcement* of penalties and achievement of objects. In consequence, the first act was commonly but an amateur expression of good intentions. Of what value was it, for example, to offer remote (and, incidentally, irrelevant and insufficient) remedies at common law to very poor and often illiterate men? As James Stephen, with characteristic fatalism, observed of one such case, 'These [men] are not the first, nor will they be the last to make the discovery that a man may starve and yet have the best right of action that a special pleader could wish for'. Simply, the answer was to provide summary processes at law and the like, and special officers to see that they were carried into action; and sooner or later, in one form or other, this was done where mere statute making of the older sort was seen to have been insufficient.

Like the original legislation, the appointment of executive officers was a step of immense, if unforeseen, consequence. Indeed we might almost say that it was this which brought the process into life. There was now for the first time a body of persons, however few, professionally charged with carrying the statute into effect. As a rule, this meant some measure of regulation where before there had been none. It also meant a much fuller and more concrete revelation, through hard experience and manifold failures, of the very grave deficiencies in both the restrictive and executive clauses of the statute; and this quickly led to demands for legislative amendments in a large number of particulars. These demands were made moreover with a new and ultimately irresistible authority. For (once again for the first time) incontrovertible first-hand evidence of the extent and nature of the evils was accumulating in the officers' occasional and regular reports; and there was both a large measure of unanimity in their common-sense recommendations for improvements, and complete unanimity in their insistence upon the urgency of the problems. Finally, side by side with the imperative demand for further legislation, there came an equivalent demand for centralization. This, too, arose as a matter of obvious necessity from the practical day-to-day difficulties of their office. For, without a clearly defined superior authority, the executive officers tended towards exorbitance or timid inactivity or an erratic veering between the two. Usually the original appointment had left their powers and discretions undefined, and usually the original statute was both imprecise and framed before an executive was contemplated. In consequence, the officers' efforts to secure 'substantial justice' often led to miserable wrangling, partiality, 'despotism' and bad relations with the parties with whose conduct they were concerned. On occasion it even led to counter-prosecution. Thus the officers themselves soon came to recognize the need for an authoritative superior both for the definition of law and status and for protection and support against the anarchic 'public'. Moreover, centralization was quickly seen to be required for two other purposes, the systematic collection and collation of evidence and proposals for reform and the establishment of an intermediary or link between parliament and the executive in the field. Sooner or later, the pressures born of experience succeeded in securing both fresh legislation and a superintending central body. The point at which they did may be taken as the culmination of our third phase.

The fourth stage in the process consisted of a change of attitude on the part of the administrators. Gradually it was borne in upon the executive officers, and through them upon the central authority, that even the new amending, and perhaps consolidating, legislation did not provide a fully satisfactory solution. Doubtless, it embodied many or most of their recommendations and effected substantial improvements in the field concerned. But experience soon showed that it was possible, endlessly possible, to devise means of evading some at least of the new requirements, and equally that the practical effects and judicial interpretations of statutory restrictions could not be always or altogether foreseen. Experience also showed, though less rapidly and clearly, that the original concept of the field of regulation—we might almost say the very concept that there were definite boundaries to such a field at all—was much too narrow. Finally, the appetite for regulation (not in the pejorative sense of regulation for regulation's sake but in the sense of a deepening understanding of what might and should be done) tended to grow with every partial success. All this subtly wrought a *volte face* in the outlook of the administrators. Gradually they ceased to regard their problems as resolvable once for all by some grand piece of legislation or by the multiplication of their own number. Instead, they began to see improvement as a slow, uncertain process of closing loopholes and tightening the screw ring by ring, in the light of continuing experience and experiment. In short, the fourth stage of the process witnessed the substitution of a dynamic for a static concept of administration and the gradual crystallization of an *expertise* or notion of the principles of government of the field in question.

In the fifth and final stage, this new and more or less conscious Fabianism worked itself out into modes of government which seem to us peculiarly modern. The executive officers and their superiors now demanded, and to some extent secured, legislation which awarded them discretions not merely in the application of its clauses but even in imposing penalties and framing regulations. They began to undertake more systematic and truly statistical and experimental investigations. They strove to get and to keep in touch with the inventions, new techniques and foreign practices relevant to their field. Later, they even called directly upon medicine and engineering, and the infant professions of research chemistry and biology, to find answers to intractable difficulties in composing and enforcing particular preventive measures; and once, say, ventilation mechanisms or azimuth compasses for ocean-going vessels, or safety devices for mines or railways, or the presence of arsenic in certain foods or drinks, had been clearly proved, the corresponding regulations passed effortlessly into law, and, unperceived, the ripples of government circled ever wider. In the course of these latest pressures towards autonomy and delegated legislation, towards fluidity and experimentation in regulations, towards a division and a specialization of administrative labour, and towards a dynamic role for government within society, a new sort of state was being born. It was modern in a much fuller and truer sense than even Edwin Chadwick's bureaucracy.

Let us repeat that the development outlined above is but a 'model', and a 'model' moreover which, with a few important exceptions such as slavery reform, applies peculiarly to the half century 1825–75. It does not necessarily correspond in detail with any specific departmental growth. Even in the fields of social reform where it was most likely to operate 'purely', it was not always present. In an exact form, in an unbroken adherence to the pattern, it was perhaps rarely present. Nor are the stages into which the process has been divided to be regarded as sacrosanct or necessarily equal in duration or indeed anything more than the most logical and usual type of development; and it is true, of course, that minor variants and elements have been omitted from the structure for purposes of simplification. To sum up, what has been attempted in the preceding section is simply a description, in convenient general terms, of a very powerful impulse or tendency, always immanent in the middle quarters of the nineteenth century, and extraordinarily often, though by no means invariably, realized in substance.

II

IF IT IS wrong to assume that men were influenced by Bentham's ideas, it is equally wrong to assume, as Dr MacDonagh does, that they were not. ... In any case, Dr MacDonagh makes no allowance for the unconscious influence of ideas on men's minds....

Why should anyone seek to eliminate Benthamism as a factor of importance in nineteenth-century history? A possible answer is that it is one way of resolving an apparent contradiction which has puzzled many students of the subject. Some have discerned contradiction within the theory itself. Halévy, for example, contrasted the principle of artificial identification of interests, on which Bentham founded his theory of politics and law, with the principle of natural identity of interests, which appeared fundamental to his view of economics. Sir Cecil Carr has remarked, 'How the Benthamites could reconcile [their theory of law] with their natural addiction to the doctrines of *laissez faire* is one of the puzzles of political science'. Others have perceived contradictions between theory on the one hand, and the course of events, on the other. Professor Prouty, for example, has written:

Laissez faire in early nineteenth century Britain was never a system.... While ...as a general principle or as an argument against a particular measure [it] might continue to receive wide publicity, it was persistently defeated in practice.... The most determined liberal could not consistently argue for laissez faire; he sooner or later found himself advocating a measure which involved the Government in the regulation of some part of industry. State intervention may not have been the policy but it was the growing reality.

Dr MacDonagh is similarly puzzled; he begins one of his valuable papers by saying that it 'is concerned with the extraordinary contrast between this appearance of a "free society" and the realities of the situation'; and ends, 'We have seen how a "despotic" form of administrative discretion came into being almost casually in the very hey-day of liberal individualism and *laissez-faire*'.

An extreme solution to this problem was propounded by the late Professor Brebner. His attitude to Dicey resembles that of Marx towards Hegel. Dissatisfied with his argument, he sought to correct it by turning it the other way up. Dicey had assumed that the consequences of Benthamism were limited, in practice, to the promotion of *laissez-faire*. Brebner suggests, on the other hand, that 'laissez faire was a political and economic myth in the sense formulated by Georges Sorel'. But 'although laissez faire never prevailed in Great Britain or in any other modern state, many men today have been led to believe that it did. In this matter ... Dicey ... seems to have been the principal maintainer of the myth for others.' *Law and Opinion* 'amounted to an argument against increasing collectivism. The lectures were so passionately motivated as to be a sincere, despairing, and warped reassertion of the myth in terms of legal and constitutional history.... In using Bentham as the archetype of British individualism he was conveying the exact opposite of the truth. Jeremy Bentham was the archetype of British collectivism.' Developments of *laissez-faire* did of course take place; but these Brebner attributes to a separate current of opinion, deriving ultimately from Adam Smith, and though often working in alliance with Benthamism, never assimilated to it.

Valuable as a corrective to Dicey, Brebner's argument is too violent a reaction against it. The twin themes of his paper—*laissez-faire* and state intervention—were equally characteristic developments of the middle quarters of the nineteenth century, and it is not necessary to assume that they were in contradiction to one another. Professor Robbins has shown how they were reconciled in the field of economic theory. He denies Halévy's argument that there was a contradiction between the assumptions underlying Bentham's theory of law, on the one hand, and classical economics, on the other. The latter was not based on an assumed identity of interests. 'If [the classical economists] assumed anywhere a harmony, it was never a harmony arising in a vacuum but always very definitely within a framework of law ... they regarded the appropriate legal framework and the system of economic freedom as two aspects of one and the same social process.' They advocated free enterprise as the general rule in economic affairs on the grounds that it was the system most likely to benefit the consumer. But they recognized no natural right of free enterprise. Like any other claim to freedom, it had to be justified by the principle of utility. As a rule, it was so justified; but there were many situations (e.g. where producers enjoyed a monopoly) where the State should intervene.

Following this lead, it is possible to suggest a model which avoids the difficulties inherent in those discussed above, while taking into account all the facts enumerated. Its stages are as follows:

1. The nineteenth-century revolution in government, though a response to social and economic change, cannot be understood without allowing for the part played in it by contemporary thought about political and social organization; to adopt Dicey's terminology, there was a close connexion between law and opinion.

2. In the relationship between law and opinion, the nineteenth century falls into two periods only, with the dividing line about 1830.

3. Throughout the second of these periods, the dominant current of opinion was Utilitarianism.

4. The main principle of Utilitarianism was what its supporters themselves believed and asserted—the principle of utility. The application of this principle led to considerable extensions both of *laissez-faire* and of State intervention simultaneously.

5. Once special officers had been appointed to administer the law, they themselves played a leading role in legislation, including the development of their own powers.

... The first stage (as also the last) incorporates factors which Dicey ignored, and to which Dr MacDonagh rightly calls attention. But there is nothing inevitable about the process by which institutions respond to changes in the society around them. The nineteenth-century revolution in government was one example of such a response; the French Revolution, and the Hitler regime, were others. One essential factor differentiating the three situations is the nature and quality of current thought about society, its problems, and their solution. It would be absurd to argue that Bentham revolutionized the British system of government by power of abstract thought alone. His ideas were influential because they derived from the processes of change going on around him. He was working with the grain. But it does not follow that the same solutions would have been reached had he never lived.

The second point does not deny that there was a change in the tone of legislation after about 1870. But it resulted from such factors as the Great Depression, the extension of the franchise, and pressure from the administration itself, rather than from the adoption of a hypothetical philosophy of collectivism. Utilitarianism was at work throughout—'that current of thought which arises in Bentham at the beginning of the century and flows into Fabianism at its end'.

The fourth point may appear something of a paradox. Yet at the time, there were those who believed in both principles simultaneously. Nassau Senior, for example, believed in *laissez faire,* but not in the 'nightwatchman' conception of the State. . . . So celebrated an advocate of State intervention as Chadwick still allocated a large, though limited, area to private enterprise:

He had great faith in self-interest. He commended it as the spring of individual vigour and efficiency; and it figures prominently in his thought as the most persistent and calculable element in human character. But he saw no evidence at all that social benefits resulted of necessity from its pursuit, and much which persuaded him that without the barriers erected by the law its undirected energies might disrupt society. He put his trust, therefore, not in the rule of some 'invisible hand' blending the interests of the individual and society in a mystic reconciliation, but in the secular authority of the State which, abandoning the superstitions of *laissez-faire,* should intervene to guide the activities of individuals towards the desirable goals of communal welfare.

When, therefore, existing institutions were subjected to the test of utility the result might be either more free enterprise or less. When it was asked 'Do the Corn Laws tend to the greatest happiness of the greatest number?' the answer (in 1846) was 'No'. When it was asked 'Since free competition does not work in the field of railway enterprise, would public regulation tend to the greatest happiness of the greatest number?' the answer (in 1840) was 'Yes'. The question was then, as indeed it is today, not *laissez-faire* or State intervention, but where, in the light of constantly changing circumstances, the line between them should be drawn.

Dr MacDonagh has done well to draw the attention of administrative historians to the importance of factors which Dicey did not take into account. Some of these were external, such as economic and technical change; others were internal, for example, the influence of the administrators on legislation. Few would deny the importance of these factors, although little has been done so far to work out their implications in detail. In this respect, his studies of the regulation of emigrant traffic are important pioneer work. He has shown that it is possible to account for the development of one minor branch of central administration without considering the influence of Benthamism. But he has not shown that other branches developed in a similar way, as would be necessary to sustain his thesis that Benthamism was a factor of, at most, very minor importance. The accepted view holds the field; namely, that the nineteenth-century revolution in government, though not attributable to Benthamism as sole cause, cannot be understood without allotting a major part to the operation of that doctrine.

26

GLADSTONE AS A CHRISTIAN STATESMAN

Philip Magnus

William Gladstone, the most dynamic and idealistic of Victorian prime ministers, has been rescued from the tedious obfuscation of his official biographer and given a new and strongly dramatic portrait by Sir Philip Magnus. In the following general evaluation of Gladstone's career and personality, Magnus emphasizes the high religious cause that inspired Gladstone's life and his unparalleled contribution to the moral and spiritual emancipation of the English masses. At the same time, Magnus implies that this paragon of a Christian statesman in some ways paradoxically prefigures the totalitarian ideologues of the twentieth century who represent the antithesis of Liberalism.

FROM *Gladstone: A Biography* by Philip Magnus, pp. 440–445. Published 1964 by E. P. Dutton & Co., Inc., and reprinted with their permission. By permission of John Murray (Publishers) Ltd., London.

As the great congregation filed out of Westminster Abbey to the organ notes of Schubert's *Marche Solennelle* in E flat, many of its members must have asked themselves upon what foundation Gladstone's title to enduring fame would ultimately be found to rest. He had dominated the political world for as long as most of them could remember, and had rendered splendid service to his country and to the world. Yet the office of Prime Minister, which he held, in all, for twelve years, was not one for which he was temperamentally well fitted.

Gladstone's heart was not in politics, which he had chosen early as his field of action from motives with which he was never wholly satisfied. He had resolved, as far as possible, to make politics conform with the highest Christian ethic. He was conscious of the possession of great gifts, and he loved power for the opportunities which it gives; but all his affections were centred upon the universal Christian society, and not upon any local temporal kingdom. After he had abandoned his exalted theory of a union between Church and State, he was content to see the Church become a voluntary body. But the problem of the right relationship between two societies—the one, eternal and divine; the other, mortal and mundane—which has troubled the conscience of Europe for two thousand years, continued to torment Gladstone and to plunge his mind into a seething ferment of restlessness. Throughout the ages, the parties to that ancient dispute have constantly shifted their positions, and Gladstone also shifted his own position. The increasing secularization of nineteenth-century thought made him desist from the intellectual search for a unifying principle. He continued, however, to thirst for it emotionally, pending the full conversion of the leading nations of mankind to the Christian way of life.

Many, perhaps at first a majority, of Gladstone's contemporaries saw as clearly as he did the hand of God at work, behind all the transient phenomena of history, to propel mankind towards some transcendent and, as yet, imperfectly apprehended goal. No statesman in modern times, however, has made so little concession to human weakness; and none has been in a position to dedicate such an extraordinary combination of qualities so unreservedly and effectively, on so grand a scale and for so long a period, to the task of giving affect in politics to the Christian religion. In that respect Gladstone's record is unique, and his approach to politics was as different from that of his colleagues as it was from that of his opponents.

Gladstone regarded Party as an alliance of enlightened individuals formed to serve a series of high moral causes, such as his mission to pacify Ireland. He conceived that it was his duty, as leader, to devise such missions, and he was convinced that the electors could be taught to respond to the voice of God appealing directly to their consciences. When his own class rejected him as a prophet he called the masses to his aid by extending the franchise. The study of Homer had helped him to persuade himself that the spirit of justice in its purest form had its habita tion in the hearts and minds of the untutored masses; and he argued with simple faith that the masses were less exposed than the classes to motives of self-interest.

Gladstone understood from the outset that Party ties—despite the practice of Lord Chatham, the theory of Edmund Burke, and the inchoate aspirations of many warm-hearted and self-respecting individuals—had seldom represented more than a tangle of alliances between groups of politicians competing for material satisfactions. Nevertheless, Gladstone indulged the noble hope that the evangelical spirit would prove as potent in purifying the nation's political life as it did in fact prove in restoring the religious life of the Church of England.

Gladstone was not interested in bread-and-butter problems, except when, as in the early part of his career, they were related directly to his transcendental purpose of setting individuals free. He left the details of Party organization and election programmes as far as possible in the hands of others, while he concerned himself with the task of creating, rather than merely inspiring, the unity and enthusiasm which held the Liberal Party together. The campaigns against Turkish misrule in the Balkans and English misrule in Ireland were products of the irrestrainable energy of a single dæmonic individual.

Gladstone would not have been able to remain in politics if he had not been successful in finding a series of high moral causes to serve. He was always intensely in earnest, and he discovered them usually after prolonged periods of self-absorbed concentration, and of partly subconscious brooding. He considered that his instinct for 'right-timing' was his most striking political gift, and his high-mindedness led him to suppose that others would attach as great a weight to ethical considerations and as small a weight to considerations of expediency as he normally did himself. He was, however, constantly liable to overlook the need for nursing and preparing public opinion; he was capable of self-deception; he did, quite unconsciously, persuade himself occasionally that an expedient course had become a moral duty. Once he had found a compelling cause he was willing, if necessary, to incur martyrdom on its behalf for himself and his Party. In that way he eventually wrecked the Liberal Party which was his instrument. He tore and wrenched its roots so violently that at the end of his life they were left exposed and dry, and no longer sunk securely in the life-giving soil of public opinion.

The seismic quality of Gladstone's mind bewildered his contemporaries, and caused a majority of them to believe that his methods concealed a greed for power and office. He seemed to be bent upon playing a heroic rôle against an Olympian background, and upon plunging the country into an enervating ferment of excitement. Many statesmen throughout the ages have drawn expertly upon the reserves of elemental passion which drive men and nations on their courses; few, if any, during an epoch of comparative tranquillity, have generated so much heat themselves. In periods of danger, a Chatham, a Pitt, a Lloyd George, or a

Churchill has hitherto always been at hand to summon the spirit of the nation from its depths. That spirit is, however, apt to sulk when it is summoned in counterfeit emergencies.

Many of Gladstone's colleagues and most of his principal opponents thought that his approach to politics was liable to make the best cause become the enemy of the good. It seemed to them that the nation was being made bilious on a diet of caviare and champagne, when cheese and beer would have suited it better. Lord Beaconsfield and Lord Salisbury, Lord Hartington and Lord Rosebery, did not share Gladstone's belief that the masses would prove more politically disinterested than the classes. They regarded the advent of democracy as inevitable, and they considered that it had become necessary, in consequence, to conciliate and serve a vast new range of varied and interlocking group-interests. In such conditions, as Disraeli was the first to discern, the possession of an efficient Party machine was of more practical importance than a transcendental purpose; furthermore, an ability to compromise, and to act as the chairman of a board, was more valuable in a Prime Minister than a mission. It would often have been possible to apply to Gladstone words which Oliver Goldsmith had once used about Edmund Burke—'too fond of the right to pursue the expedient'. If others were of the earth, commonplace and practical, Gladstone seemed to be of the heavens, nebulous and incalculable.

At the apex of Great Britain's moral and material ascendancy during the nineteenth century, liberalism was the operative political creed of most Englishmen. Gladstone was gradually converted to it as a result of his experiences at the Board of Trade and at the Exchequer. Throughout his life those were the only great departments of State in which he took a deep and constant interest. He was excited sometimes by foreign affairs, when great moral issues were involved; he disliked the Army and Navy; he was bored by education; and he seldom thought about India.

Liberalism, in Gladstone's hands, became a fiery sword which was used, at first with superlative success, to set the individual free. It was used later, with considerable success, to extend the ideal of chartered liberty throughout the world. That ideal was concerned with means; the ends were never clearly formulated; and the sword itself became rusted when, towards the end of the century, the economic and intellectual climates changed.

The means which liberalism had used were freedom of worship and expression, and freedom of enterprise and trade. Those means were found, in the end, to be inadequate, after the decline of religious faith had removed powerful restraints which had once seemed almost strong enough to hold aggressive nationalism in check, and to set a limit to the cultivation of material standards. In the absence of those restraints human society was menaced by anarchy. It became increasingly apparent that welfare had been recklessly sacrificed to wealth; and wealth itself began to appear increasingly insecure as other nations challenged Great

Britain's commercial and industrial lead, and adopted protective practices in defiance of free trade doctrines.

It had become evident, before Gladstone died, that a new set of moral values was needed; and Gladstone's appeal to the consciences of individuals led to results utterly at variance with anything that he had intended. He had told the masses to forget their fears and to curb their wants; and the first incoherent attempts to formulate the modern ideals of freedom from fear and freedom from want released two new currents of opinion from both of which he averted his head in disgust.

The first of those currents was imperialism, which sprang, in England, from the uneasiness caused by foreign economic competition, and by the growth of militarism among the great European powers, after the hopes of the organizers of the Great Exhibition of 1851 had been blasted by the Crimean War. Confronted by swollen conscript continental armies it was natural that Great Britain should seek to redress the changing balance of power in the old world by extending and consolidating her ties with the new.

The second of those currents was social reform, which sprang, in England, from evangelical philanthropy. Prince Bismarck's example in Germany helped to convince some thoughtful sections of British opinion that there might be a case for embarking upon constructive action to remove the causes of distress, instead of concentrating, as heretofore, upon individual action to relieve its symptoms. During the late 1870s, and the 1880s, slumps, unemployment, riots, and strikes stirred the conscience of the classes and aroused the anger of the masses.

Gladstone coupled imperialism with militarism and called the compound 'jingoism'. He argued that jingoism would enslave the masses to mean passions, and that it would disqualify them from fulfilling the rôle for which he had cast them, of acting as a supreme tribunal on earth to which men and nations could appeal. He coupled social reform with socialism and called the compound 'construction'. He argued that construction would ruin the national character, sap individual initiative, and overturn the strict principles of economy on which British prosperity had been founded.

Gladstone had seen the power and wealth of the State expand during his lifetime beyond all precedent, and he was more afraid of misusing both than he was of neglecting problems. He considered that politics would be debauched, and divorced from the service of God, if policy were to be auctioned by Party leaders ambitious to buy votes from selfish and, possibly, unscrupulous pressure-groups. Behind the luxury and pride which capitalist industry had generated, behind Bismarck's ruthless concentration and use of force, behind the growing and almost universal demand for increased material satisfactions, Gladstone glimpsed monstrous shadow-shapes which danced convulsively in the fiery furnace of his imagination. The full measure of the twentieth century's shame was concealed from him. He did not foresee extermination camps; he did not foresee the enslavement of a vast portion of the human race to a non-Christian creed which denies integrity to the individual conscience and personality; but he fought to the last against the tendency to replace the worship of God by that of Cæser on any species of idolatry.

Gladstone was no mystic who lived withdrawn from the world. His genius ripened slowly in the mart and exchange of everyday human affairs, but he lived his life deliberately and consistently upon a higher plane than that of others who were similarly, if less conspicuously, employed. He was often compelled as a statesman to use a politician's arts, but he did so with visible reluctance, as when, in 1891, he propounded the 'Newcastle programme' of social reform. Gladstone was a man of peace who loathed war as the greatest of human calamities; but his boyish glee at the victory of Tel-el-Kebir in 1882 and the stand which he took against Russia during the Penjdeh crisis of 1885, showed that he could be as fierce and uncompromising as anyone when confronted by a challenge to his conscience.

In the last analysis what Gladstone was is of vastly greater significance than what he did. Mortal men are condemned to see mortal events 'through a glass darkly' and the echo of dead political controversy sounds ever more faintly down the ages until it is barely distinguishable from that of the mythical war between the kites and the crows. Gladstone may be judged as a statesman; few would venture to judge him as a man. He dedicated his life to the task of teaching men and nations to govern themselves by schooling their passions, and thereby to realize on earth the spirit of the Christian ethic.

By this radiant example, Gladstone did more than any statesman since the Reformation to give effect in politics to that ideal. In its service he started as the foe, became the agent, and ended as the prophet of the Liberal experiment.

27

PALMERSTON AND DISRAELI

A. J. P. Taylor

A. J. P. Taylor, an Oxford scholar who works on both modern German and English history, has gained a very wide audience because of his broad erudition and skill in describing traits of character. The

FROM A. J. P. Taylor, *Englishmen and Others* (London: Hamish Hamilton Ltd., 1956), pp. 36–44, 66–69. By permission of the publishers.

following account of the Victorian Prime Ministers Lord Palmerston and Benjamin Disraeli, in which the former is depicted as an old-line Whig and the latter as a selfish but charming trickster, reveals very clearly how Taylor is able to suggest whole facets of experience and character in a few intuitive and ironic phrases.

I

Palmerston

AMONG the surprising careers of British Prime Ministers, none has contained more surprises than that of Lord Palmerston. For twenty years junior minister in a Tory government, he became the most successful of Whig Foreign Secretaries; though always a Conservative, he ended his life by presiding over the transition from Whiggism to Liberalism. He was the exponent of British strength, yet he was driven from office for truckling to a foreign despot; he preached the Balance of Power, yet helped to inaugurate the policy of isolation and of British withdrawal from Europe. Irresponsible and flippant, he became the first hero of the serious middle-class electorate. He reached high office solely through an irregular family connection; he retained it through skilful use of the press—the only Prime Minister to become an accomplished leader-writer.

Palmerston was not a member of one of the great Whig families or even connected with them. He was an Irish peer, moderately rich, who naturally entered politics to supplement his income. For a peer, he was an educated man. He went to Cambridge, which—even at the worst time—provided a solid grounding in mathematics; and he early absorbed the principles of political economy. Hence, he was not staggered, as Peel and Gladstone were, by the sudden impact of the Free Trade case; this had been a commonplace of his thought for thirty years. Born in 1784, he entered the House of Commons at the age of twenty-three, without either strong convictions or defined party ties; simply a young man of the fashionable world who wanted a good appointment and—rarity enough—was qualified to hold one. Having a reasonable grasp of figures and of economics, he was offered his choice among the junior financial offices; he chose that of Secretary at War and retained it for twenty years. This was the equivalent of the present-day Financial Secretary to the War Office; a post strictly administrative and financial, without a seat in the Cabinet. Though Palmerston ran his office competently, he did not trouble much with politics and seemed to care only for life in society. Good-looking and fickle, he established himself as 'Lord Cupid', a name which tells everything. But the years of obscurity were not wasted: he served a more prolonged apprenticeship in administration than any other Prime Minister has ever done and, when he came to sit in Whig Cabinets, was distinguished from his colleagues by his ability to run an office. It was this ability, not his policy or his personality, which finally made him Prime Minister in 1855.

Though Palmerston served a Tory ministry, it would be wrong to describe him as a Tory; he was simply a 'government man'. Nor was he a Canningite until late in the day; what brought him over to the Canningites was his support for Catholic emancipation. With his gaiety of spirit and his easygoing morals, he hated tyranny and oppression wherever it occurred. After twenty years of comfortable office, he left it for the sake of the Catholics; just as, at the end of his life, he threatened to resign as Prime Minister rather than relax the struggle against the slave trade. In 1828 Palmerston, out of office, found himself associated with Melbourne and Huskisson, the Canningite remnant who had broken with Wellington and were drifting over to the Whigs. There were also personal grounds for this tie. After a good many adventures, Palmerston had settled down with Lady Cowper, Melbourne's married sister. He lived with her more or less openly; had children by her; and married her in the late eighteen-thirties after Lord Cowper's death. Melbourne was a more important man than Palmerston, more influential and better connected; when he joined the Whig Cabinet in 1830, he carried his illegitimate brother-in-law with him. Without the Melbourne connection, Palmerston would hardly have reached the Cabinet rank which started him on the path to the premiership; and Melbourne was to sustain him against the criticism of the orthodox Whigs at the end of the 'thirties. In the last resort, Palmerston owed his position as Prime Minister to the odd chance that the sister of one of his predecessors had become his mistress.

Palmerston was to make his name at the Foreign Office; but this was neither intended nor expected. Lord Grey, Prime Minister in 1830, had been Foreign Secretary in a remote era and meant to conduct foreign policy himself; all he wanted was a competent underling in the House of Commons. Lady Cowper was again of service. Princess Lieven, her closest friend, recommended Palmerston to Grey as presentable and well-mannered. For some time it was believed that Grey supplied the policy; Palmerston was held to be 'frivolous' and failed to establish his hold over the House of Commons. The peaceful solution of the Belgian question was primarily a triumph for Grey. When Melbourne became Prime Minister, Palmerston had things more his own way; and his conduct of British policy during the eastern crisis of 1839–41 was brilliant, perhaps the most perfect in the records of the Foreign Office. But it was a performance for experts. It did not make him popular with the general public; and it made him much disliked by many of the great Whigs, such as Holland and Durham. In 1841, when the Whig government declined into collapse, Palmerston was still a relatively little-known figure. His frequent evocation of Canning, whose policy he neither understood nor followed, was an implied confession that he could not stand on his own feet.

The five years between 1841 and 1846, when Peel was in office with a Conservative government, were decisive for Palmerston's future. The succession to Melbourne as Whig leader was open. Lord John Russell assumed that it would automatically be his as political representative of the greatest Whig family; and he thought he had done all that was necessary when he secured the allegiance of such Whig managers as 'Bear' Ellice. Palmerston could hardly play his family connection against Russell's, even if it had counted for anything; he therefore decided to play the British public. He built himself up deliberately as a public figure: established relations with the Press, and himself wrote leading articles in his forthright, unmistakable style. At the end of 1845, when Peel first resigned, the third Earl Grey made it a condition of his taking office under Russell that Palmerston should be excluded: the condition wrecked Russell's Cabinet-making. The episode was at once an unconscious recognition by the great Whigs that they had taken a cuckoo in the nest, and a sign that the cuckoo was now too strong to be ejected. Later, in 1846, Russell formed the last Whig government of our history; and Palmerston went undisputed to the Foreign Office. This feeble government had a record of failure, broken only by Palmerston's dazzling display in foreign policy. His policy had its serious side and can be defended, as it were, on technical grounds; but there was a flamboyant touch as well—Palmerston was deliberately playing Russell off the centre of the stage. His triumph came in 1850 with the Don Pacifico debate, when he held his own against the greatest speakers of the age—Peel, Gladstone, and Cobden; held his own and worsted them. The triumph was not one of oratory in the conventional sense. Palmerston was always a bad speaker; full of 'hums' and 'haws', his voice trailing away before the end of the sentence, and the pause filled up by a flourish of his handkerchief. Rather it was a triumph of character. With his dyed whiskers and his red face, Palmerston exemplified British self-confidence and bounce.

Still, it needed the impact of war to finish the job for him. At the end of 1851 Russell finally got rid of Palmerston; early in 1852 the Russell government fell in its turn. Then, at the end of the year, Russell and Palmerston found themselves together again in the coalition of Whigs and Peelites, brought into being by Prince Albert and presided over by Aberdeen. Palmerston was relegated to the Home Office. He was rescued from it by the disasters of the Crimean War. Though he shared the common responsibility of the Cabinet, public opinion seized on him as the man of destiny, the man who would win the war. This was the moment of crisis in Palmerston's life and, for the historian, the most interesting point in his career. Again and again in modern history, Great Britain has drifted unprepared into war; then, after early failures, has discovered an inspired war-leader. How does public opinion make its choice? And what is it that Palmerston had in common with the elder Pitt, Lloyd George, and Winston Churchill? It was not done merely by advertisement, though all four made skilful use of publicity; it was not even done by brilliant speeches in the House of Commons or outside. It turned rather on the impression of resolution and courage laid down in the House of Commons over a period of years. During a crisis the members of parliament broke away from the conventional pattern—whether of family connection or party organization—and acted according to their patriotic duty. Curiously enough, the popular choice has always been right: on all four occasions it hit on a leader who was not only more colourful or more dramatic than his peace-time predecessor but who was also more efficient technically. This is puzzling. The general public or even the members of the House of Commons could hardly deduce from Palmerston's speeches that he was an administrator of the first quality, who could challenge the Peelites on their own ground of efficient government without any of the high moral tone which they found necessary to accompany it.

The government which Palmerston formed in 1855 was neither a party government nor a coalition; it was an association of individuals, united only to win the war. The old system of family connections was in decay; the new system of defined parties had hardly begun. The Conservatives were on the way to becoming a party in the modern sense; but they were doomed to perpetual minority so long as there was a middle-class electorate. Those acceptable as ministers were in confusion. The Peelites broke with Palmerston and disintegrated; when Russell bungled the conference at Vienna shortly afterwards, Whig solidarity also dissolved. Palmerston's personality was the only stable point in a fluid political system. It would be absurd to claim that his government was a war-cabinet of the highest order. Though it began the reform of the British military system, these reforms stopped half-way like the Crimean War itself. Opportunity had come to Palmerston too late in life: he was seventy-one when he became Prime Minister. More important, opportunity came at the wrong time: Great Britain could not be turned into a military nation only four years after the Exhibition of 1851. Still, in one way, Palmerston did better than his peers, those other great men who have saved their country. He not only won the war that he had been called on to win, he actually survived his success. The elder Pitt, Lloyd George, Churchill, were all ruined by victory. All three were ejected from office before the end of the war or shortly after it. Palmerston stayed safely in office; and, even more remarkable, won a general election a year after the war was over.

The general election of 1857 is unique in our history: the only election ever conducted as a simple plebiscite in favour of an individual. Even the 'coupon' election of 1918 claimed to be more than a plebiscite for Lloyd George; even Disraeli and Gladstone offered a clash of policies as well as of personalities. In 1857 there was no issue before the electorate except whether Palmerston should be Prime Minister; and no one could pretent that Palmerston had any policy except to be himself. Of course, we know very little about the general election of 1857 (or for that matter about any other in the nineteenth century); and it may turn out on detailed examination that the result of it was really determined by less obvious factors. Still, there was in it, at the least, a plebiscitary element: as though even the British had to be in the fashion and had caught the taste from Louis Napoléon. In the same way, Neville Chamberlain in the nineteen-thirties got as near the *Führerprinzip* as an Englishman could.

The political victory of 1857 was not the end of Palmerston's career. He had presided over, and in part caused, the end of the old political order; he was destined to inaugurate the new. His period of personal government lasted only a few months after the general election of 1857. The rather cantankerous patriotism which had sustained him against the Peelites and the pacifists turned on him when he tried, sensibly enough, to appease Louis Napoleon after the Orsino plot. Since no one could form a government with majority support, the Conservatives—as in 1852—formed a government without one; this in turn was bound to be followed, again as in 1852, by a coalition. But the government which Palmerston organized in June 1859 was a coalition of a different kind: not a coalition of groups which looked back to the past, but a coalition which anticipated the future. Had it not been for Palmerston himself— too individual, too full of personality to be fitted into a party-pattern— it would have been the first Liberal government in our history. Everything that was important in it was Liberal—finance, administrative reform, its very composition: the first government with unmistakable middle-class Free Traders as members. Palmerston would even have included Cobden, if he could have got him. It was Cobden who had scruples against tolerating the irresponsible survivor from an older world; and not the other way round. Of course, tolerance and good-nature had always been Palmerston's strong points; not virtues for which Radicals are usually distinguished.

Palmerston was too strong a character to be swamped by Liberalism even in old age. It was not so much that he resisted reforms; he himself had welcomed and often promoted the administrative reforms of the preceding thirty years. It was rather that he thought a government had other tasks than to be always reforming: it should conduct a forceful foreign policy and strengthen the national defences. Palmerston is one of the few Prime Ministers who has literally left his mark on the face of the country: all those odd-looking brick fortifications behind Portsmouth are his doing—they are still useful and effective, which is more than can be said for Gladstonian finance. But Palmerston in his last ministry was fighting, and winning, the wrong battle. For nearly a hundred years—ever since Dunning's famous motion in 1780—self-confident British aristocrats had aimed to reduce the powers of the Crown—to prevent its interference in the course of government and of policy. Melbourne and Palmerston had had four blissful years on the accession of Queen Victoria when the Crown seemed on the point of becoming politically null. The process had been reversed by Prince Albert; and when Palmerston was at the Foreign Office between 1846 and 1851 he had to contend with ceaseless royal interference—the more galling for being justified by every historical precedent. The years of the Crimean War had been too serious to allow of constitutional squabbles; but these began again in 1859. Between 1859 and 1861 the Crown fought persistently the policy of Palmerston and of Russell, now Foreign Secretary; intrigued, as George III had intrigued, with members of the Cabinet behind the Prime Minister's back; dreamt of ejecting Palmerston as the Fox-North coalition had been ejected in 1784.

Then, in 1861, the Prince Consort suddenly died. Victoria was both unwilling and unable to carry on the contest; she became again and remained the political nonentity that she had been before her marriage. Palmerston had fulfilled the highest Whig ambition, though after the death of the Whig party: the Crown had been eliminated from politics. It turned out almost at once that the victory was of no use at all. The Whigs had evoked public opinion against the Crown; Palmerston had played off public opinion against his Whig rivals. Now public opinion interfered more effectively than the Crown had ever done. Though Palmerston had been much harassed by the Crown when he was at the Foreign Office, he had always got his way in the end; and this was equally true of Palmerston and Russell in the severe disputes between 1859 and 1861. Despite the Prince Consort's Germanic enthusiasm for Austria, they managed to back up Italian unification from start to finish. Things were very different between 1862 and 1865. Russell, for instance, would have liked to recognize the southern states in the American Civil War and go to war for the sake of Poland in 1863; Palmerston would have threatened war for the sake of Denmark in 1864. They were overruled by the majority of the Cabinet, itself reflecting the opinion of the majority of members in the House of Commons, and they in their turn accurately voicing the opinion of the middle-class electorate. It is often said that Palmerston's foreign policy was a failure at the end of his life; it would be much truer to say that he was not allowed to have a foreign policy. Public opinion had pulled off the feat that was beyond the Prince Consort or even George III. Palmerston, the first—perhaps the only—Prime Minister to owe his success solely to public opinion, ended his life its prisoner.

Yet he was very near hitting on the method by which public opinion would be tamed. At the time of the general election of 1859, party organization meant nothing at all except perhaps among the Conservatives. Whig grandees put up money to fight a few constituencies, from a mixture of family and party motives; all the rest still depended on local initiative. By 1868 the Liberal Whips were handling a party fund, and were seeking subscriptions much more widely than at Brooks's. The transition took place when Palmerston was Prime Minister. He it must have been who decided to leave these matters to the Whips, and to keep the Prime Minister out of the financial side of the party-system; it may even have been Palmerston who first, though unwittingly, recommended men to honours in return for their contributions to the party chest. Gladstone found the system settled when he took over the leadership of the Liberal party in 1868. After all, it was the only way to run a party once the moneyed men pushed aside the members of the great families; and Palmerston no doubt acquiesced in it more easily since he had never belonged to these select Whig circles. Thus, without knowing it, he invented both the Liberal party and the modern party-system; no mean achievement for an individualist adventurer.

This is the essential point about him, the secret of his failures as of his success. He was never dependent on connection or on party, and rather disliked both; he was self-made. Men have written many books about his foreign policy; and will write more. Very little has been written, or ever will be, about his place in British political life; for it is an empty one. The British political system has no room for the rogue elephant. Though he may ruin others—as Palmerston ruined the Whigs, or as Lloyd George wrecked the Liberal party sixty years afterwards—he will certainly ruin himself. He will be barren as Prime Minister; he will not create. Our system is admirably suited to represent interests and to voice general ideas; it does not like independent characters, except as an eccentric adornment. In war both interests and ideas are pushed aside; hence, as an exception to the rule, the great individuals then triumph. Once peace comes, their power is ended, even if they cling to office as Palmerston managed to do. The steady men of solid principle and mind are the ones who achieve effective success; but the adventurers are more fun. Palmerston was not the spokesman of a class, though he defended the Irish landowners towards the end of his life; and he did not voice any great principle or idea. He was simply an individual of strong personality—resolute, self-confident, and with great powers of physical endurance. As Foreign Secretary he was always too independent of the Prime Minister and of the Cabinet; as Prime Minister, though he stood loyally by his colleagues, he failed to dominate the Cabinet or even to lead it.

He was not an Irish peer and an Irish landowner for nothing. He had the Irish jauntiness which always wins English hearts. He could never rein in his irrepressible high spirits; even his best speeches have here and there a touch of flippancy. He would rather make a good joke than win a debate. He was not, as is sometimes alleged, a survivor from the eighteenth century. Rather he had 'Regency' written all over him—in his clothes, his morals, even in his way of talking and his metallic laugh. Nor did he 'represent' the electorate of the Reform Bill, if this means that he resembled the middle-class voter. The men of the time delighted in Palmerston just as Churchill is now admired by millions who would never vote for him; but their serious taste was for Peel and Gladstone— these were the truly 'representative men'. Palmerston was certainly the most entertaining of Queen Victoria's Prime Ministers. Though there have been greater Prime Ministers, there has been none more genial; and, for that matter, none so good-looking....

II

Disraeli

DISRAELI... was the oddest great man in our public life by a long chalk. Nothing connected him with the Tory party of the early nineteenth century—nothing, that is, except his calculation that its leadership would be easier to attain than that of the Whigs. He owned no land; he was not English in blood; he was lucky to be even a nominal member of the Anglican Church. In temperament he was even less conservative than in origin. He had a flighty mind, which drifted from smart triviality to adolescent day-dreaming and back again. He held nothing sacred except perhaps some Hebrew phrases vaguely remembered. He despised the members of the aristocracy even more than he disliked the poor. He did not even enjoy power when he achieved it. It was not merely that, in his own phrase, 'it came too late'. Power was too practical an affair to interest him. He relished the trappings of power, not the reality—the drama of great debates, the high-sounding titles, his name echoing through history. Yet in appearance he was least conservative of all. Thick black ringlets, fancy waistcoats, powder and scent were not the marks of a gentleman or even of a politician; and his affected voice—half-drawl, half-lisp—completed the foreign impression. Disraeli increased the obstacles in his path for the pleasure of overcoming them.

He was first and last a great actor, watching his own performance and that of others with ironic detachment. He cared for causes only as a means of combat. Having ousted Peel from the leadership of the Conservative party by defending the Corn Laws, he cheerfully proposed the next year that Protection should be dropped; and he did nothing to aid agriculture when the great depression hit it at the end of the eighteen-seventies. He attacked Palmerston's irresponsible support of Turkey during the Crimean War; yet repeated this support even more irresponsibly twenty years later. He foresaw the independence of the wretched colonies—'a millstone round our necks'—and welcomed this dissolution of the British Empire; a few years later he claimed a great stroke by making Queen Victoria Empress of India—the biggest piece of tushery even in his career. *Sybil* is supposed to contain a profound social analysis. In fact, it says no more than that the rich are very rich and the poor very poor—by no means a new discovery. His own social policy, when he came to power, turned out to be nothing more startling than municipal wash-houses. He took one step of real importance when he placed the trade unions above the law; but this was a matter of electoral calculation, not of social justice. His only genuine emotion in politics sprang from personal dislike—of Peel in his early career, of Gladstone even more strongly towards the end. What these two men had in common was a readiness to put their convictions above their ambition—the worst of offences in Disraeli's eyes.

In his novels Disraeli invented an interpretation of political history which is sometimes still taken seriously, and was repeated in the twentieth century by our only anti-Semitic writer, Hilaire Belloc. This was the myth of the Venetian oligarchy which was supposed to have taken the Crown prisoner at the time of the Glorious Revolution and from which the Crown should rescue itself by an alliance with the people. This myth had no glimmer of truth. Though eighteenth-century England had indeed a rich and powerful aristocracy, the Crown was always the head of the executive and the ministers were its servants. The Whigs certainly talked of 'forcing the closet', but they never succeeded in doing so effectively until after the great Reform Bill, and then only for a decade. The Crown was still of great weight in politics at the time of the Crimean War. By a wild irony, it was Disraeli himself who finally excluded the Crown from politics and turned it into a decorative figurehead. When he introduced household suffrage in 1867 in order to dish the Whigs, he made mass-parties inevitable, and these could not be swayed, as the old aristocratic politicians had been, by personal loyalty to the Crown. Disraeli disguised this, perhaps even to himself, by the flattery which he gave to Queen Victoria, as to many other distinguished ladies; but this was play-acting, not politics.

The two-party system does not figure much in Disraeli's writings, but it was the real basis of his political life and his legacy to posterity. The Whigs had had a theory of party conflict; but they regarded this as a conflict between the party of the Crown and the party of the people, by which, of course, they meant themselves. Even when Peel recognized after the Reform Act that the Crown could not sustain a party of its own and therefore built up the Conservative party, he did not acknowledge any loyalty, as leader, to his own followers, and said firmly in 1846: 'I am not under any obligation to any man or to any body of men.' This was his unforgivable sin in Disraeli's eyes. Disraeli hounded Peel out of the party leadership and seized the vacant place. He was the first politician to put loyalty to party above loyalty to country; and his example has been universally admired, though not always followed. Disraeli, and Disraeli alone, riveted on our political life the conception that politics consist entirely in two parties fighting for office. These two parties were to represent not programmes but interests. What interests Disraeli did not much mind. Sometimes he talked of the Conservative party as 'the landed interest'; sometimes he appealed to all who had 'a stake in the country'; in practice his party was an alliance between the City and the mob. None of this mattered. The important thing was the struggle for power—a tradition which the Conservative party has faithfully observed to this day. It is true also to Disraeli's tradition in not knowing what to do with power when it has got it. To catch the other side bathing and make off with their clothes is still its only resource.

One can understand how Disraeli achieved the leadership of the party by offering the prospect of unremitting combat. The field always prefers a huntsman who halloos them on. But Disraeli knew better tricks. His novels, his speeches, his casual remarks, all held out the promise of a mystery which he never revealed, which was not, in fact, there to reveal. He, not Napoleon III, was the true Sphinx without a secret. Or, rather, his secret was the absence of moral earnestness. A rarefied mountain-air becomes intolerable in time, and the holiday-maker is glad to escape to Monte Carlo. So it was with the Victorians. No age has been more high-minded; and the strain often became unendurable. Gladstone was the Victorian conscience; Disraeli the release from it.

28

COUNTY POLITICS IN THE AGE OF DISRAELI AND GLADSTONE

H. J. Hanham

Applying the methods and concepts of L. B. Namier and J. E. Neale to the structure of politics in the 1870's and 1880's, H. J. Hanham has revealed, as the following selection demonstrates, how persistent was the hold of aristocratic families on the party machines in their counties and how much of the old England of lordship and habitual deference survived into the modern industrial world.

BECAUSE estates voted as a unit, county electioneering was a simple business. Once the register had been checked for errors and duplicate entries and a list of non-resident voters had been drawn up, little remained to be done. First, the county agent had to discover how each big estate would vote. This he usually did by visiting tenants on the estate whom he knew personally and who habitually supplied him with information. Thus Disraeli's agent in Buckinghamshire reported to him well in advance of the by-election which was caused by his elevation to the peerage in 1876.

> We shall undoubtedly win our County Election... I yesterday made a point of seeing one of the leading tenants on the Ashridge estate, & he told me, nearly to a man, the Brownlow tenantry, & retainers would go for Fremantle [the Conservative], and as your Lordship well knows, that many a time has that division of the County won the election—I also saw a leading tenant on the Mentmore estate [of Baron Meyer de Rothschild], & he told me they are all to do as they like, and that many would not vote at all, as they did not like the Liberal party. Mr. Treadwell, who you know, & who is one of the Tenants on the newly purchased Winchendon Estate of Baron Ferdinand [Rothschild], told be they could do as they liked—& they should probably vote as they had hitherto done—I think the Brill, Ashendon & Wotton division, will be sound as heretofore—The Claydons & part of Buck[ingha]m will be against us—as Sir Harry [Verney] smarts so, at losing his seat for Buck^m.

At this stage it was essential to persuade any landlord who might be friendly, but whose political allegiance was not clear to his tenants, to

---

FROM H. J. Hanham, *Elections and Party Management* (London: Longmans, Green & Co. Limited, 1959), pp. 17–25. By permission of the publishers.

make his views known. Thus Henry Brand, the Chief Liberal Whip, wrote to Gladstone during the 1861 Flintshire by-election asking him to give his support to the Whig cause now that he was a member of a Whig cabinet, and no longer a quasi-Conservative.

> Thanks for your letter about Flintshire, and for your announcement that your agent will vote for Lord Richard Grosvenor. Let me ask you to go a step further, and to tell him to let it be known to your tenants that your wishes are with Lord Richard.

And as a postscript:

> It is important that you should move your Agent to let your wishes be known.

Such an appeal from London was not usual, however. Most landowners acted on their own initiative or were prodded by their friends and relatives to let their wishes be known. Thus in 1868 old Lord Overstone, the Whig banker, informed the prospective Whig candidate for North Northamptonshire that he could not support him because of his views on the disestablishment of the Irish Church. Whereupon the candidate, the Hon. Fitzpatrick Vernon, promptly gave up what had become a hopeless canvass, and published Overstone's letter as a sort of justification. The Duchess of Sutherland (who was Countess of Cromartie in her own right) made a similar announcement in 1880 lest it be thought that she had embraced her husband's Whig politics. She wrote to Lord Beaconsfield, 'I am anxious to tell you that I have, (as I once told you I would) let my tenantry know that I expect them to give their votes according to the principles always held by my house.'

After attending to these essential preliminaries the principal agent in a county division could leave most of the work of preparing for polling day to the local committees in each polling district. The only tasks to be dealt with centrally were the allocation of cabs and other conveyances and the distribution of circulars to non-resident voters. These latter had usually to be sent details of trains and eating places and to be met at the nearest railway station.

There could be no general canvass because it was still thought to be an impertinence to canvass a man's tenants without his permission, and such permission was not readily given. In any case, a general canvass was unnecessary because the politics of an estate depended on its landlord. When the Liberals of Mid-Cheshire came to canvass the country districts of the division in 1868 they could discover only two estates whose proprietors professed to allow their tenants any freedom of choice. But even in these two cases the freedom was illusory: on one the tenants refused to pledge their votes without the written permission of their landlord, which he not unnaturally refused to give, while the other was owned by the Liberal candidate's father, Lord de Tabley.

Even local party committees had little to do. Most squires and agents rather liked to do such canvassing as seemed necessary, with the help of their relations and the local clergy. Indeed, we are told that in North Norfolk in 1868 'the parson of the parish, naturally enough, thinking the Church was in danger, and the squire, naturally enough, thinking that he was the great man, were acting in each particular parish as a sort of committee'. One not untypical squire treated the election as a great family event, providing breakfasts and dinners, and conveyances to the poll for his tenants at his own expense. And although this was before the ballot, this expenditure was regarded by the election judge as perfectly legitimate and in no sense an inducement to vote for one party rather than another.

The general control of each party in a county division was in the hands of a steering committee composed of the largest landowners and most active politicians, assisted by a prominent solicitor such as the clerk of the peace, the county coroner, or the clerk to one of the more active benches of magistrates. In addition, there were subordinate committees in each polling district composed of local squires, clergymen and large farmers, under the direction of a member of the central committee as chairman, and also assisted by a local solicitor. These district committees enjoyed a great deal of independence in the larger counties, and it is quite in character that four of the eight district committees in South-West Lancashire in 1868 took little notice of the central committee in Liverpool, even though Mr. Gladstone was their candidate. Leigh district, we are told, was 'entirely under the management of Mr. Kirkpatrick who for several years has devoted much attention to the subject and who has required very little attention from the centre'. Ormskirk district was 'under the entire control of Mr. Musgrove and Mr. Hill who have declined any assistance whatever and have strongly deprecated any interference'. Warrington district was managed by George Crosfield, a member of a leading local family, who paid all the expenses himself and employed his own solicitor as agent, while at Wigan there were two committees, independent not only of Liverpool but of one another.

Sometimes the central committee in a division was also the executive committee of a formally-constituted party association, but this was by no means always the case. In 1874 there were Conservative associations in only forty-four of the eighty-two English county divisions. There was, moreover, considerable opposition to the promotion of associations. When the Cenéral Committee of the Conservative party tried to reorganise the counties after the defeat of 1880 it encountered much resistance. The Dorset Conservatives, for instance, positively refused to form an association until dragooned into doing so. The county had been shared between the two parties since 1857, the Conservatives taking two seats and the Liberals one, and the Conservative members could not see what good an association would do them, while they could see that it would cost them a lot of money and that it might make contested elections more likely. Earlier a proposal to set up an association in Cambridgeshire had met with a rather different type of hostility. Both the squires and farmers in the county proper and the townsmen of Cambridge opposed the suggestion when it was first mooted by Lord Hardwicke in 1868, because they feared that they would be called upon to pay for an association over which they would have no control. The inaugural meeting had to be abandoned because so few people attended, and to make a second meeting a success Hardwicke had to give an undertaking that he would not use the proposed association as a means of financing his family's election ventures, and that the town should have a voice in its conduct.

When once associations had been formed, however, their officers made the most of them. Thus when the thoroughly unrepresentative Cambridgeshire Conservative Association met to choose a candidate in 1874, it was told by its agent, Major Barlow:

> They had a Central Conservative Association and District Associations. The Central Association was formed of the chairmen and vice-chairmen of the district associations as delegates to this central association. By these means the feeling of all the electors of the various districts was ascertained, and that feeling was represented by these delegates at a public meeting of the central association, so that they were aware of the general feeling throughout the county as to who should be the representative for the county.

Yet at this very time there was an independent Conservative candidate in the field (Hunter Rodwell) with the support of the farmers round Newmarket, whose candidature was certain to be successful in spite of the Association.

In divisions dominated by one great magnate or group of magnates, the fiction that a party association or committee represented the electors was utterly transparent, and even important squires had to be content to leave the management of their party to its hereditary leaders. Thus in North Devon, where Earl Fortescue and the Earl of Portsmouth were the recognised Whig leaders, Sir Thomas Acland, M.P. (who owned 35,000 acres in Devon and Somerset), regarded it as perfectly natural that they should lead the party. He wrote in 1885, when it was necessary to find candidates for the new divisions of the county:

> It is very difficult *for me* to stir a finger between the Houses of Fortescue and Portsmouth. Redvers Buller, son of my predecessor, ought not to be lost sight of —he stands well with farmers generally. I think he is Vice-Chairman of the Liberal Association, which is little more than 'nominis umbra'. The Whig Peers have always settled these things.

This subservience preserved the old custom by which the greatest magnates nominated one of the members in counties where they possessed the preponderant influence. In return for this compliance with his wishes, the magnate paid most of the registration and election expenses and gave his support to a second candidate, who was usually chosen from among the local country gentlemen. He also relinquished the nomination when his family lacked suitable candidates, retaining only an indirect veto in the form of his ability to withhold contributions towards the election expenses and to prevent his tenants from voting for any candidate of whom he disapproved. Sixteen English county seats and a variable number of Welsh, Scottish and Irish seats were in the gift of patrons after 1867, and in addition there were a number of other seats over which great magnates had a more precarious hold.

There had been comparatively little redistribution of power in the counties for fifty years so that the seats which magnates controlled were, for the most part, those which Oldfield had listed in 1816. The attitude of the electors in such counties had also remained virtually unchanged, and it was thought to be part of the natural order of things that the Duke of Bedford should return his heir for Bedfordshire, the Duke of Manchester his for Huntingdonshire, the Duke of Northumberland his for North Northumberland, and the Duke of Rutland his for North Leicestershire. In Gloucestershire, where the Conservative Duke of Beaufort's interest had decayed since 1832, an active Liberal wrote of his part in a by-election in 1867: 'I frequently stated that, had the Marquis of Worcester [the Duke's eldest son] been in the field, I should not have voted against him, as I think it desirable that our future hereditary legislators should have an opportunity of learning their duties in the Lower House.' Some of the greatest magnates were willing to go to extraordinary lengths to keep up their traditional prestige, even in counties where their political opponents had gained a permanent majority. The Liberal committee for South Devon thought that there was nothing odd about a request that they should not start a subscription to help with the cost of Lord Amberley's contest in 1868, on the ground that 'the Bedford family would not like a public subscription to be made for anyone of their name', although it meant asking the Duke for £4,000.

A few counties were almost entirely in the hands of great magnates. Westmorland, once monopolised by the Earl of Lonsdale, had since 1854 been shared between him and the Marquess of Headfort (heir of William Thompson, M.P., of Underley Hall); Huntingdonshire had since 1837 been shared between the Duke of Manchester and the Fellowes family; Rutland was habitually shared among four families, the Finches, the Heathcotes, the Noels, and their Lowther connections, and two of the three seats for Cambridgeshire were controlled until 1874 by the Earl of Hardwicke and the Duke of Rutland. A sixth county, Cheshire, although not a family preserve in the same sense, was also dominated by a small group of Tory families: the Egertons, the Leghs, and the Tollemaches, all of them more or less distantly related.

The tendency of Welsh, Scottish and Irish county politics was so strongly anti-landlord, even in 1868, that the great landowners found it extremely difficult to maintain their traditional interests. In 1868 about twenty seats were in the hands of patrons, but by 1880 the number was less than ten, and by 1885 only three remained firm in their allegiance, all of them in Ulster. The only Welsh county completely dominated by great magnates was the half-English county of Monmouth, whose representation had been shared since 1841 between the Duke of Beaufort and Lord Tredegar. In Wales proper, only Sir Watkin Williams-Wynn, who kept his seat for Denbighshire until 1885, and also controlled Montgomeryshire until 1880, exercised a similar influence. He was, as readers of Borrow's *Wild Wales* will remember, more of a national institution than a Tory magnate, and his influence even survived his death by a few months. When he died early in 1885 the Denbighshire Liberals let it be known that they would not offer any opposition to the return of the new Sir Watkin, but that they would oppose any other Conservative candidate. The young Sir Watkin was reluctant, but he eventually came forward and sat for the county until the dissolution, when he was defeated in the new Eastern Division of Denbighshire and the 182-year tenure of the Wynns was ended. The other Welsh interests were very shadowy compared with this: C. R. M. Talbot, who represented Glamorganshire from 1830 to 1890, had an unrivalled personal influence in the county and could doubtless have chosen a successor if he had wished to retire; the Duke of Westminster, Lord Mostyn, and Lord Hanmer controlled Flintshire between them; Earl Cawdor virtually controlled one seat for Carmarthenshire, and Lord Ormathwaite could usually carry Radnorshire.

In Scotland long-drawn-out contests between rival families continued to be a prominent feature of county politics, but family monopolies were few and growing fewer. The Duke of Buccleuch had lost his preponderance in the border counties by 1868, Buteshire had ceased to acknowledge the rule of the Marquess of Bute and was saved for the Conservatives only by the Duke of Hamilton's control of Arran, and after 1873 the Dundases gradually lost their influence in Orkney and Shetland. As a result, only two 'pocket counties' survived intact to 1885. The Duke of Argyll continued to dominate the county of Argyll in spite of the growth of a formidable Conservative opposition headed by Malcolm of Poltalloch, and the Duke of Sutherland remained master of Sutherland. The latter was, indeed, an almost impregnable interest, since the Duke owned 1,176,343 of the county's 1,299,253 acres (and with them £68,602 of the estimated gross rental of £71,494), and there were only 325 electors.

Ireland shook off its patrons equally decisively. Many of them had with difficulty restored their interests during the fifties after the irruptions which O'Connell had made in them, and they were powerless to resist the Home Rule movement. Twelve or thirteen seats were more or less securely held by great landowning families in 1868, but only five of them were in the same hands by 1880. Patronage was not destroyed, however, for the Ulster reaction against Home Rule in 1885 had the effect of guaranteeing a number of seats (notably Mid Antrim, West Down, and North Tyrone) to their old patrons.

The English counties were the chief strongholds of the Conservative party, which regularly won in them more than twice as many seats as its opponents, and actually won five times as many in 1874. However, the individual county constituencies were not so overwhelmingly Conservative as the election results as a whole seem to suggest. Small majorities were by no means unusual, and in Kent and Essex, where there was a large urban element in the county divisions, very small majorities were the rule: thus in 1880 the Conservative majorities in the three Essex divisions were 192, 402, and 625 in a total electorate (for the three) of 241,000. The Liberals were not so much weak as on the defensive, and, because they acted defensively, not as ardent in the fight as their opponents.

It is difficult to overstress the contribution of Whig landowners to the Liberal cause in the counties even as late as the eighties. There were few agricultural counties in which they could not sometimes win one seat and occasionally two, while in the industrial counties they provided candidates and leaders. The typical Whig was not a small country squire but a county magnate enjoying considerable influence. The three largest estates in Bedfordshire were Whig, the Whig Lords Fitzhardinge and Ducie were two of the three largest landowners in Gloucestershire, and five of the estates over 5,000 acres in Durham (total 92,569 acres) were Whig....

Because there were relatively few Whig landowners, and many of them owned big estates, their individual attitudes mattered far more to the Liberal party than those of individual Conservative magnates mattered to the Conservative party.

29

THE SOCIAL FOUNDATIONS OF LATE VICTORIAN POLITICS

G. Kitson Clark

Several decades of supervising research students at Cambridge and of omnivorous reading in the sources for nineteenth-century history, as well as a keen perception of the relations between social change and political institutions, have gone into G. Kitson Clark's The Making of Victorian England.

The latter part of this work, from which the following selection has been made, clearly reveals how it was possible that the granting of a democratic suffrage in England was contemporaneous with the continued triumphs of the Conservative Party during the last two decades of the nineteenth century.

REPRINTED by permission of the publishers from G. Kitson Clark, *The Making of Victorian England*, Cambridge, Mass.: Harvard University Press, Copyright, 1962, by G. Kitson Clark, pp. 240–253, 255–259, 263–264, 266–267, 270–274. By permission of Methuen & Co., Ltd., London.

WHAT PROBABLY in the long run determines the shape of politics are the social movements, the groupings and regroupings in the mass of the community, which are beyond the reach of politicians; and what happened at this moment has already been suggested. In the second and third quarter of the nineteenth century a mass of industrial and commercial wealth had come together at a central point in the social pyramid. It extended from the great manufacturers and merchants downwards through the shopkeepers and clerks to the upper ranges of the working class, the skilled workmen and craftsmen. The people in this section often differed widely in their ideas, their religion, their way of life and their politics. But enough of them resembled each other closely enough to supply the foundations of the great Liberal party which was the most important political fact in the country between 1865 and 1885. However, as is normally the case with the situations which such forces produce, at the very moment when one social pattern had become marked a close inspection could have shewn that the currents of change were preparing a new social pattern that would succeed it, and that in its turn would at least partially define the politics of the country for the next twenty years and probably for longer.

Speaking in very general terms, two processes seem to have been at work. At one point the increase in wealth, the increase in self-consciousness and confidence in a section of the working class had gradually created a new social group whose centre of gravity so to speak was at a lower point in the economic and social pyramid than in the group on which the Liberals had depended. More people in this group would have more markedly different interests from those who were the natural leaders of the old group than had been the case in the past, and they would want different things. Whether in fact this must necessarily have led to the replacement of the Liberal party by a Labour party it would be impossible to say, but it seems likely that if it had not done so an effective Liberal party in the second quarter of the twentieth century would have been very different in structure and in policy from the one which Gladstone led, or Chamberlain aspired to lead. However, while this was happening at one point in the scale, at another point the currents of social change were depositing another group which was to form the foundation of a new Conservative party.

The effect of this second process became evident before the first process became in any way decisive. It appears in the unexpected renewal of Conservatism at the end of the century; but it was a renewal, not a return. There could be no return to the political conditions that had been normal before 1865. The aristocratic society which had been so firmly planted in rural England could not survive unchanged till the end of time, or even, without any change, till the end of the nineteenth century. Rural England itself was changing and contracting, contracting physically so that the actual acreage in which rural conditions can be said to have existed or to have existed without the intrusion of some urban element had become progressively less, contracting morally so that it became of much less importance to the country.

The town had invaded the countryside in a variety of ways. The growth of industrial cities and towns had meant that areas that had quite recently been farmland had sometimes become covered with densely packed working-class houses, or sometimes had been more loosely and extensively penetrated by suburbs of varying social standing or further out still by the houses of wealthy men whose centre of gravity was the town. Sometimes industry had pushed its fingers directly through the countryside, sometimes creating new towns or sometimes only industrialized villages. This is what had happened with the development of coalfields in Durham or South Wales, or with the railways which introduced alternative employment into districts where previously the background had been completely agricultural and called into existence new urban centres like Swindon and Crewe. Or in some cases there might be the development of small pockets of industry, a brick-field, a brewery, a tannery. But whatever was the process of urbanization it was a threat to the coherence of the countryside. In some cases there might be a flow into the area of people like the Irish who were strangers to past traditions and not by nature amenable. In some cases many of the young men would be diverted into a new form of labour which meant a new way of life, while men of wealth and importance would emerge who would not be subject to the ordinary influences of the country but rather hostile to them.

The first two Reform Bills had in some sort protected the lords of the countryside from the results of this process. The first enfranchised, as boroughs in their own right, the industrial towns whose inhabitants would otherwise have voted in the counties and possibly liberalized a number of them, but because it increased the numbers of county constituencies and retained a large number of country pocket boroughs it did not allow the industrial towns so enfranchised to preponderate in the new electorate. The second emphasized the separation of the county and borough electorate and also permitted the survival of a number of small country constituencies which offset the members of the great centres of population. None of this could, however, reverse the fact that the urban population was in the second half of the nineteenth century continually gaining in size over the rural population and that urban conditions were intruding into the countryside; while the authors of the third Reform Bill of 1884 had no desire at all to protect the country from the influence of the town. The country voter was given a vote on the same terms as the borough voter, there was a drastic redistribution of seats, many of the small pocket boroughs were finally disenfranchised and it was believed that the Liberals intended so to rearrange the constituencies that rural voters would normally be grouped with a majority of urban ones by whom they would be submerged. It was for this reason that the House of Lords demanded to see the heads of the Bill for redistributing seats before they passed the Bill for enfranchising new voters. It seems doubtful whether they did themselves much good by this procedure.

But the Reform Act of 1884 was only the last stage in the process by which the Conservatives in large part lost the battle of the counties. There were two factors in this process. In the first place the agricultural prosperity upon which so much depended first became unstable and then disappeared. As Lord Ernle wrote of this period, 'Since 1862 the tide of agricultural prosperity had ceased to flow; after 1874 it turned and rapidly ebbed.' But at the same time there were signs of increasing independence on the part of farmer and labourer, and growing tension between tenant and landowner.

There seem to have been a variety of domestic reasons for this, and, especially after 1868 there was the disturbing example of Ireland. In Ireland it was clear that the main centre of trouble was the power of landlords, and from 1869 onwards the Liberals started to legislate first timidly then drastically to reduce the power of the landlords and transfer the real control over the land to their tenants. Conditions in England were widely different from those in Ireland and the English landlord could make a case for himself which the Irish landlord could not normally do. Nevertheless, there were uncomfortable analogies, and land reform was in the air. Consequently it is not surprising that the minds of English Radicals turned with ever greater insistence to the position of English landlords and to the law which favoured them so notably. It might not be at all likely that at that moment the matter would be effectively pressed at once as far as the Liberals were prepared to go in Ireland, or as many Radicals desired for England. But the tendencies of the time meant that proposals would be made on such matters as the form of the law affecting compensation for tenants' improvements or of the laws affecting Settled Estates, matters on which many tenants not necessarily Radical urgently desired changes which the Conservatives were reluctant to concede.

In addition to the legal question, there were other sources of tension in these years. As early as 1862 there were signs of trouble between landlord and tenant over the proposals in a Game Preservation Act which many farmers very much disliked. In 1864 an old agricultural grievance emerged again which had on earlier occasions been inconvenient for the Conservatives, the grievance of the Malt Tax. This was a tax for which the farmers had a very great dislike, an exaggerated dislike as it turned out, for when in the end it was repealed they did not gain nearly as much relief as they had hoped for; it was, however, a tax which had for long been considered to be necessary for the country's finances and the Conservative leaders could not risk a promise that they would be able to do without it if they got into power. Unfortunately for them, Gladstone as Chancellor of the Exchequer held the financial initiative in this matter. In any year he might decide that it was now possible for him to modify or abolish the tax, things which the Conservative leaders could not possibly pledge themselves to do in undisclosed circumstances in the future. In 1864, just before the election of 1865, Gladstone modified the tax, which tempted many farmers to try to get the whole tax abolished.

At the general election of 1865 two independent farming candidates took the field to agitate for the repeal of the tax. They were not Anti-Conservative, the men they attacked were Whigs, and one of them, C. S. Read, was prepared to take office for a short time in Disraeli's Government. But their appearance was a serious portent for the Conservatives; they had not been sponsored by the usual landowning influence and the policy they advocated was one which the Conservative leaders could not possibly support.

It might have been possible to counteract these tendencies if the Conservatives could have found a policy which would unite both landlord and tenant in the face of common dangers. But they could not do so. Earlier in the century when the Corn Laws had not yet been repealed tenant and landlord had been united on the common policy of the protection, but even then the Conservative leaders were unable to retain the Corn Laws. Towards the end of the third quarter to have declared for the re-imposition of the Corn Laws would have been to sacrifice all hope of ever gaining a majority in Parliament again. The only moment during these years when circumstances suggested a policy on which landlord and tenant could agree was during the cattle plague of 1865 and 1866. The policy which the agricultural community desired to be adopted to deal with the plague was that of the compensated slaughter of infected animals and the prohibition of suspect imports from abroad. The Government did not wish to adopt this policy, since it appeared to be a kind of protection, but in 1866 the county members united to force the hand of the Government, and were successful. But this was a very narrow bond of union at a time when other matters, sporting rights, compensation for tenants' improvements, the laws concerning settled estates, the wishes of the landowners and the tenants, were splitting the countryside.

Then in the early 'seventies a new source of danger appeared, the formation of Trade Unions by the farm labourers. This was the cause of more disagreement between the tenants and the landlords, for the landowners seem to have to some extent sympathized with the Unions, or at least not to have wished to antagonize men who it now seemed clear would at some time or other have the Parliamentary vote. Therefore the landlords intervened in various instances to prevent the farmers from destroying the Unions, and the farmers on their part took steps to secure that those landowners who were too favourable to the Unions did not stand in the general election of 1874. In spite of this, it was not likely that the labourers would favour the landlords. They had little reason to love the order of the countryside in which the landlords had taken their pleasure. Their leaders were apt to be Primitive Methodists and therefore to include the disestablishment of the Church of England in their programme. Altogether it was not going to be difficult to persuade them that their real enemy was the landowner, that if his influence was removed and the legal trammels which hampered the farmer were destroyed the lot of the labourer would be better.

Nor were there lacking those who were anxious to enlist the farm labourers into a general radical movement, and when the labourers came to form their Unions they gained a very formidable ally. These Unions developed in 1871 and 1872 in various counties, but the beginning of the National Movement is always held to have been the meeting at Wellesbourne in February 1872 which was addressed by Joseph Arch. Wellesbourne is in Warwickshire, the same county as Birmingham, and twelve days later Joseph Chamberlain made a passionate speech there calling attention to the wrongs which the agricultural labourer had suffered and proclaiming his right to have a share in governing the shires in which he lived. Chamberlain's close friend Jesse Collings also became trustee for the National Agricultural Labourers Union of which for a time Joseph Arch was organizing secretary.

The situation therefore in the early 'seventies was full of dangers for landowning interest, but the full extent of them was concealed. At the time of the Franco-Prussian War there was a recovery of prices, if also an increase of rents. The social and political position in the counties seemed to be very strongly held. The landlords still retained their leadership in country business, as the history of the chambers of agriculture seems to show, and except in very rare cases held the elections to Parliament in their hands. In a description of Gorst's work in developing Conservative Constituency Associations before 1874 Gorst's son said that: 'In the counties these associations always remained aristocratic in character and chiefly consisted of country gentlemen and the superior class of farmers.' This was a contrast to the more popular associations which were being developed elsewhere, but the policy seemed to be justified by its results. In the general election of 1874 the Conservatives won 143 of the seats for the English counties, excluding Monmouth, as against only 27 county seats won by Radicals and Whigs.

It was a fatal victory. The years 1874 to 1879 proved to be disastrous for the English corn-grower. There were a series of very bad harvests culminating in the terrible year 1879, but prices did not rise because of the importation of foreign corn and rents did not fall, or at least did not fall fast enough. In previous years when things had gone wrong with agriculture the Conservatives had been able to blame the Government, which was normally Liberal or Whig; now the Government was itself Conservative and did, indeed situated as it was politically was probably able to do, singularly little for the farmers.

At the outset the Conservative Chancellor for the Exchequer was able to make an important concession to the county rate-payer, transferring certain expenses from the rates to the central government and providing increased grants for others. But he was not able to abolish the Malt Tax. With the legal grievances of the farmers the Government dealt ineffectively, making what seemed to be half-hearted efforts which did not get to the roots of the problem. In 1875 they produced an Act to give the tenant compensation for improvement which was held to be ineffective and derisory. In 1877 they produced the Settled Estates Act, which was largely a consolidating Act but allowed tenants for life to apply to the Chancery Division of the High Court for leave to sell the land or to grant leases binding on their successors, though it allowed in certain conditions the granting of leases up to 21 years. This was much less than what was needed. What was needed was to give to the tenant of an estate for life liberty to grant leases or to sell land without referring to a court at all. In 1880 the Tory Government, hard hit by the disasters to agriculture, apparently determined to yield this and a new Bill, the Settled Land Act, was brought forward, but the sands had run out, Parliament was dissolved without anything effective having been done. The snapping-point had come.

During the period of the Conservative ministry discontent among the farmers had been growing. In 1875 there had been indignation at the miserable nature of the Conservative Act for compensation, and C. S. Read, one of the independent farmers' candidates of 1865, retired from the Government. In 1879 a farmers' alliance had been formed by a certain James Howard, with apparently the assistance of O'Donnell, an Irish Home Ruler who was interested in the landlord question in Ireland. In 1880 the farmers' alliance played a part in the contests for the counties at the general election, as did also the National Liberal Federation. Two land reformers were returned, Howard for Bedfordshire and Duckham for Herefordshire, but it is not altogether easy to form an estimate of the influence of either body, since it is difficult to abstract what they did from the results of other factors operating in this election and it is not satisfactory to trust too completely to their own accounts of the matter. Certainly the results of the election were not only damaging to the Conservatives, at that moment they were menacing for the future. The Conservative English county members were reduced from 143 to 116, and it seems probable that the results might quite easily have been worse for the Conservatives. *The Annual Register* for 1880 says that this election was remarkable for the number of seats contested, particularly of county seats, which looks as if the Liberals saw signs that in a good many places the old monopoly was breaking up; but even so it seems that they did not recognize the greatness of their opportunity, for the *Register* adds: 'How slow Liberals were to believe in the possibility of gaining any victories in the counties, may be judged from the fact that in one county, North Lincolnshire, the candidate, Mr Laycock retired from his canvass, came forward again a quarter of an hour before the nomination took place, and was returned at the top of the poll.'

Thereafter new blows were rained in a savage succession on the unfortunate landowning interest; for the Liberals did all those things the Conservatives had been unable to do, and some things they can have only envisaged in nightmares. In 1880 the Ground Game Act was passed which gave the occupier an inalienable right to destroy hares and rabbits on his land. In 1880 the Malt Tax was converted into a beer duty. In 1882 the Settled Land Act was passed two years too late. In 1883 an Act was passed giving a tenant adequate rights to compensation for improvement, in 1883, also, the Corrupt Practices Act was passed which, even more than the Ballot Act of 1872, made old methods of electioneering impossible. In 1884 the farm labourer was enfranchised, the whole country was cut up into equal electoral districts and the small patronage boroughs disappeared. In 1885 another general election was held under the terms of the new Reform Act, during which a concerted attack was made on the landowners and Joseph Chamberlain raged horribly over the whole scene breathing fire from his mouth against the landowning Whigs as much as against the landowning Tories. The result was a curious reversal in politics, for though the Liberals were not nearly as successful as they had hoped to be in the towns, they were saved by the votes in the county constituencies, and so secured in the end 335 votes to the Conservatives' 249. Indeed, in the counties men from completely outside the old landowning caste won seats, such as a townsman like George Newnes the Wesleyan publisher, who was elected for Cambridgeshire, or a labourer like Joseph Arch, who was elected for North-West Norfolk.

Things do not end simply or quickly in England, but this looks like the end of a very long chapter. In many places the old form of political influence had been destroyed, and old political methods seemed to have become obsolete. The agriculture which had seemed so important socially and politically had received a shattering blow, to be followed by others, for the misfortunes of the corn-growing districts were followed after an interval by the threat to British livestock that came from cold storage. The balance of the country had changed, and the agricultural community were now heavily outweighed by the town-bred people who must be provided with food from whatever source it could come most abundantly and cheaply, and that source was not the farmer at home. Commercial and industrial wealth now bulked larger in the country's capital and income than did the landowner's agricultural wealth and the income which was derived from it; and very soon the mechanism of representative government was to be introduced into the administration of the shire itself. In 1888 the County Councils Act took nearly all of their administrative powers from the justices of the peace and gave them to the new elective county councils, and one of the greatest of all historians realized the significance of the occasion. It was the passing of the Act of 1888 that led F. W. Maitland to write his very brilliant paper 'The Shallows and Silences of History' to mark the disappearance of a form of government of very long standing and of great historical significance.

Indeed, to a man with historical imagination the moment might well seem to be a notable one. Those old elements in English society—the landed interest, the gentry, the nobility—had played a very long and very important part in English history. Even if the hereditary connexions were not always so long dated or so continuous as some of their number liked to pretend, as orders of society the body of the nobility and gentry had come confidently out of the mists of time, and now perhaps in the bustling industrial Liberal England of the nineteenth century there was no longer room for them. At length, now that the fourth quarter of that century was well under way, their bright day was done and they were for the dark.

But were they for the dark? If you had taken your stand in Hyde Park on a fine afternoon during the season of some year towards the end of the century and watched the carriages go by it is possible you might have been tempted to believe that several of them had not got very far in that direction. Of course, there was much new wealth in London, but I think it would be found that a good many of the well-dressed people you saw were the bearers of ancient names. That would be certainly true if you went into the House of Commons, and if you penetrated the countryside you would still find many ancient halls and noble palaces in full occupation, if some of the vicarages and rectories were beginning to look a little threadbare, and some of the halls and country houses were let for the summer to rich townspeople.

In fact, much of the life in the countryside might seem in appearance to be the same. Much of the agricultural prosperity had gone, and many of the young men had gone also, which may be part of the reason why agricultural radicalism had not been pressed as far as at one moment seemed probable. But many of the old relationships seemed to have survived, and in many constituencies the habits of the politics of deference seem to have continued but thinly disguised by the forms of a more representative system.

What lay behind many of these survivals was no doubt the fact that so many of the great estates had been able to draw their income largely from non-agricultural resources. As a result some of the great noblemen were still among the richest men in the country; the will of the 3rd Marquis of Bute which was proved in May 1901 shewed an estate valued at £1,864,310 and that of Earl Fitzwilliam in June 1902 one valued at £2,950,000 and there were some other very large noble fortunes at that time. How far this wealth on the old scale continued to be enjoyed by all the nobility or still more by the gentry it would be impossible to say without a good deal of research; no doubt an estate which depended too completely on agricultural rents was very hard hit. But even with the gentry there must have been a fair number with non-agricultural resources and investments, and not a few who had married into non-agricultural fortunes. More than this, to judge by very haphazard impressions, there seem to have been a good many places where a substitution had happened, where the old family had sold out and disappeared and a new family whose wealth had been made elsewhere occupied the big house and kept it up—house, gardens, stables and as much of the rest as they cared to take. This was of course an old process, but it seems possible, at a guess, that as the value of non-agricultural investment increased such new families would put a smaller proportion of their wealth into the land and in fact live to a larger and larger extent on money drawn from other sources of revenue; while in the early twentieth century the advent of the motor car must have made it much easier to live in the country and retain roots in the town. As a result of all this it would seem that a change came over certain areas of the English countryside. They partly ceased to be districts where most of the inhabitants lived on what could be earned from the production and sale of food for the general market and came to depend more largely on the fact that rich men found it pleasant to live in them, or at least to take their sport there.

On the other hand, if men from the town came to live in the country, men from the county families had for long taken up their abode in the town. Possibly there had always been branches of noble families and still more of the families of gentlefolk who had not drawn their livelihood from the land but from the law or Government service, or a sinecure, or some other form of revenue. As a result there was a section of the community who maintained their claim to be gentlefolk but who were not directly connected with any agricultural estate, and probably lived in London. The existence of this section was extremely convenient to others whose origins were more equivocal. As has been said, as wealth became more diffused there were many people who began to assume the trappings of gentility, but for many of the more wealthy the trappings would not be enough; they would want the name, and if they were careful they could gain the name simply by assuming it. They would suddenly emerge like Mr Veneering in *Our Mutual Friend* with a mansion, a coat of arms, Parliamentary ambitions and, as a guest at his dinners, a scion of the real aristocracy who would discover to his bewilderment that he was one of Mr Veneering's oldest friends.

The existence of such aspirations, and the uncertainty of social definition, led however to an agonizing problem which possibly in the nineteenth century caused more trouble and heartburning in well-nourished bosoms than any other secular problem: Who were gentlefolk and who were not? In more antique times this problem may have been a relatively simple one, a gentleman was a man who sprang from an appropriate family, or who had had a grant of arms, or owned an appropriate estate. But in the eighteenth, and still more in the nineteenth century, these relatively simple tests seem to have become ever more difficult to apply. Society was becoming increasingly complex and changing rapidly. Men and women became less certain of the sufficiency of the simple ideas of a hierarchy of birth and began to supplement and confuse the conception of a gentleman with the attribution of mental and moral qualities. A gentleman would naturally have received the education of a gentleman, his manners and his conduct ought to shew a refinement which was one of the attributes of gentility....

One obvious test that came to be of increasing importance was the test of education. If to be a gentleman implied a certain refinement of motive, a certain liberality of spirit which took a larger view of human affairs than the meanness of motive and narrowness of view which were the probable results of experience confined by the walls of the counting house or the factory, then it was right and desirable that the natural instincts of a born gentleman should have been fostered by an appropriately liberal education. Therefore it came to be increasingly assumed that a gentleman would have had the education of a gentleman, a proposition which in time might carry the convenient converse that someone who had had the education of a gentleman was likely to be a gentleman. It was a conception that was going to be of very great importance in the nineteenth century and its development and consolidation was much assisted by the fact that an increasing number of people were receiving what could be considered the education of a gentleman, that it came to be increasingly clear where that education could be received and that there constantly developed more and more facilities for it. In fact, the conception hardened into a belief that the education of a gentleman was likely to have been received at a certain type of school and at one of the older universities.

This is probably reflected in the history of the older universities. One of the most remarkable developments in the early years of the nineteenth century is the increase in the size of Oxford and Cambridge. The admissions at both had fallen to a very low ebb in the eighteenth century, Cambridge had indeed fallen to a lower point than Oxford and had reached its nadir later, that is between 1760 and 1765. After 1800 the numbers at both started to climb. At this point Oxford increased more slowly than Cambridge; Cambridge developed a steady rise in matriculations after 1807 and became larger than Oxford in 1817. Cambridge in fact remained ahead of Oxford till 1870, when Oxford drew ahead to be passed again quite soon, but in fact both Universities remained curiously close together shewing in the line of their development the same major fluctuations. This suggests that what was taking place was under the control of general social considerations and was only to a minor extent influenced by the particular characteristics or standing of either body. In both the rise at the beginning of the century continued till about 1826 when the annual admissions to either ranged between about 300 and 400 men. After that there was a period of fluctuation at about that level which lasted roughly till about 1860, then both Universities started to climb swiftly, the numbers of freshmen for instance admitted each year at Cambridge increasing from 400 in the 'fifties to 800 in 1880.

The numbers, of course, are very small when compared with the numbers of other groups and classes in the country. But this group is an important one, its nature was going to have far-reaching effects on society; it is therefore very desirable, though not very easy, to try to see what factors were causing this growth, and what were likely to be the results of what was happening on the nature and characteristics of Oxford and Cambridge. No doubt in this as in other matters the basic factor in both periods of growth was the increase in the population of the country and the increase in its wealth. Probably the first period of growth was also facilitated by the beginnings of University reform. In both Oxford and Cambridge gross scandals, odd and not very defensible personalities and some very queer institutions and customs persisted till well on into the nineteenth century. But from the beginning of the century an increasing number of University teachers had an eye to their duties and in certain colleges both the teaching and discipline were good. In fact, particular colleges developed characteristics and attracted particular groups. Christchurch became a school for Tory statesmen, first Oriel and then Balliol attracted intellectual men, Trinity College, Cambridge, attracted the sons of Whig noblemen, gradually displacing its neighbour St. John's in that service, first Magdalene, Cambridge, and then Queens', Cambridge, attracted Evangelicals, and so on and so forth.

But all this would only appeal to certain particular sections of the community. Even where it was reasonably taught, the curriculum in both Oxford and Cambridge was exceedingly narrow; if a good University education had been the main object of a student he would in fact have been better advised to go to Glasgow or Edinburgh as many Englishmen did. Moreover, the whole atmosphere of both Oxford and Cambridge was aggressively Anglican; indeed, Dissenters from the Church of England could not take a degree at Cambridge till 1856 and could not matriculate at Oxford till 1854, while the various posts and distinctions in either University were not generally thrown open to them till 1871. Therefore, though no doubt the first period of growth in Cambridge and Oxford was a response to a growth in wealth and numbers it was likely to be at that time mainly a response to the growth in numbers and wealth in certain classes with certain special social values and aspirations, and not in others. To many of the people who were making money and shaping the future of the country Oxford and Cambridge would be as yet forbidden and very foreign ground; places which supplied an education which many of them probably did not as yet much desire.

It is, for this reason, not surprising to find that those who have made analyses of the social structure of Oxford and Cambridge in the nineteenth century have revealed the fact that the classes who were traditionally associated with Oxford and Cambridge, the landowners and the clergy, were still predominant. The increase so far had largely been in the terms of the increase of particular groups and not reflecting the nature of the increase of wealth in the whole country, still less of the increase of numbers in the whole population. This did not mean that there had not been a good deal of infiltration from outside by men whose family traditions had been remote from the Universities, but who desired to share the social values of those who normally went there. There are indeed obvious and very eminent examples of men whose parents had made fortunes in commerce or industry and who passed through Oxford or Cambridge in the first half of the nineteenth century. Many of them entered into the life of the aristocracy, indeed two of their number, Peel and Gladstone, rose to the highest place in the land.

How far such infiltration took place through the Universities it would be hard to say until more extensive research has taken place, nor how effectively in the first half of the century the mere possession of a University degree placed a man above the salt. It must be remembered that social origins at both Oxford and Cambridge were at this time mixed, possibly more mixed in the early years of the century when the locally restricted scholarships and locally restricted fellowships still existed than in the second half in the century when these had been reformed away, as the social origins of the clergy of the Church of England, for whose benefit Oxford and Cambridge so largely existed, were also very mixed. At this point, however, the matter becomes involved in an important question which is slightly different from the question of education as a social test, though related to it. Could it be that a clergyman of the Church of England must be presumed to be a gentleman not only on account of his education but also on account of his profession? The problem is important because it raises the whole question of the claim to gentility by reason of a profession, and therefore the whole problem of the gentility of the professional classes in general.

Certainly not all the clergy had been in the past automatically gentlemen. Everyone is familiar with Macaulay's drastic picture of the country clergy in the reign of Charles II in the third chapter of his history. It is probably oversimplified, as such vivid historical pictures are apt to be, but modern research has suggested that it is substantially true. If so, it would be hard to call many of these people gentlemen, whether you use the ancient test of blood, or the more modern test of refinement of manners. They were a separate caste, narrow and professional in their outlook in life, bucolic in their habits, barbarous in their manners and often plebeian in their origins and associations. In the eighteenth century, however, a gradual change seems to have taken place. Probably country livings had become more valuable and a larger number of well-connected men had condescended to take them. More country clergy came to hold a high position in the countryside and to mix on equal terms with the gentry. More of them became magistrates. Their learning often became more secular and more liberal, they were more often antiquarians rather than theologians, and if refinement of manners was to be the test such refinement was perhaps often more likely to be found in the vicarage than the Hall. Jane Austen was of course a clergyman's daughter and her standards were learnt in the parsonage; but a certain type of early nineteenth-century country clergyman of whom she approves—educated, reasonably well endowed with high principles, if to our mind with a strangely secular outlook—seems to present a good model of what many people in the nineteenth century thought a gentleman probably ought to be like.

...As the century went forward the presumption developed that a clergyman of the Church of England was likely to be a gentleman. It is the presumption behind the great saying of Archdeacon Grantly in Trollope's novel the *Last Chronicle of Barset* published in 1867. When the Archdeacon confronted in his library the battered perpetual Curate of Hogglestock, a graduate of Oxford it is true, but a man bearing in his mind and body, and in his clothes and boots, the scars of the harshest poverty, he still would not agree that their positions were unequal. 'We stand', said he, 'on the only perfect level on which such men can meet each other. We are both gentlemen.'

It was the consolidation of a caste. To those who were traditionally gentlemen had been added men who were gentlemen by education and profession. It was a caste which would obviously include members of another ancient profession, also largely fed from the older Universities, the profession of a barrister. But the matter was to go further. The later eighteenth and the early nineteenth centuries saw the beginning of the development of other organized professions in their modern form. In many walks of life—in medicine, in the army and the navy, in architecture and in engineering—it came to be realized that an increasingly higher standard of technical capacity would be required by anyone who wished to do their work successfully, and at the same time in many of these professions the rewards became greater, and it seemed at least for many of those who practised them that they had a claim to a more assured and distinguished social position than their predecessors might have had in the past. To make good this claim, however, in many cases it was necessary to organize the profession, in order to make sure that its members maintained its standards and that their ranks were not invaded by the unsuitable and the untrained. Something could be done to further these ends by organizing professional societies if the profession as a whole could be made to accept their authority, but in the end if the organization was to be really effective it was in many cases necessary to go to Parliament to gain powers to keep out of practice men who were not properly qualified and to impose a code of behaviour on all those who had been admitted to practice, as a protection both for other professionals and for the public whom they served.

The road to full recognition and effective professional organization was long and arduous, and not all professions in the nineteenth century achieved the full position of an officially organized profession with the sanction of the State to enforce the discipline of its professional institutions. But in the eighteenth century there are a good many signs of what was to come. Several important professions developed a consciousness of their identity in the course of the eighteenth century and produced professional organizations fairly early in the nineteenth. For instance, it was in the late eighteenth century that the architects began fully to realize themselves as a profession, and in 1834–35 the Institute of British Architects was founded; it was Smeaton, who died in 1792, who seems to have conceived the profession of Civil Engineer, and in 1818 the Institution was created to be incorporated in 1828. The Institution of Mechanical Engineers followed in 1847. At the same time two other respectable professions which were going to play a very important part in the making of Victorian England were being created from groups whose calling was by no means new but whose position in the community had not been well established before or in many cases rated very high. From the mass of despised petti fogging attorneys of the eighteenth century there developed the respectable profession of solicitors effectively organized by a succession of Solicitors' Acts, a profession in whose hands an immense amount of confidential business was placed; and from the very mixed and in many cases very rough crowd of surgeons, and apothecaries and physicians evolved the medical profession as we know it controlled by the Medical Act of 1858.

If, however, a profession was to emerge and take shape in this way, two things had to happen. First, inside the profession active members of it had to emerge who were anxious to organize it, to improve its standards of performance and to raise its status; and secondly, members of the public outside the profession had to become prepared to accept it at a new valuation, and perhaps to concede the very considerable legal powers which were conceded to such bodies as the British Medical Council or the Law Society. The second process is very significant because it entailed a partial reconsideration of the values of society. There is reason to believe that such a partial reconsideration was going on from the beginning of the nineteenth century. The increasing complexity of society and the complication of the services it required enhanced the value of the men who could supply the requisite techniques, while the increasing rationality with which all but the stupidest men tended to think about these matters encouraged the belief that men who were trained to perform difficult and responsible services, for which they were likely to be well paid, were at least as socially valuable as men who had done no more than inherit an ancient name with possibly not much money and not much sense to go with it. It was perhaps a convenient way of thinking for those who wished to find jobs for young men who did not wish to forfeit their title to be gentlemen. Certainly there seems to be an example of the change in 1820 when Sir Walter Scott was discussing the occupation to be followed by a nephew of his. If, he said, the boy had the appropriate disposition he might become a soldier, but otherwise 'he cannot follow a better line than that of an accountant. It is highly respectable.'

There is, indeed, a good deal of evidence for the existence in the second quarter of the nineteenth century of a fairly large society of professional men—barristers, civil servants, literary men and others—whose status was assured and to whom the title of gentleman would hardly be denied, except by rather old or very stupid people. There were probably the largest numbers of these people in London, and it seems possible that the foundation of certain important London clubs—the United University founded in 1827, the Athenaeum in 1824, the Oxford and Cambridge in 1830 and the Garrick in 1831—is evidence of the kind of life that they lived and the estimation which they claimed for themselves. If it was the world which Pen entered when he came down from Trinity in Thackeray's novel *Pendennis,* it had its contacts with fashionable society, if one of its exits was also into the Fleet prison. But the ethos and the method of life of professional men were often very different from those of the aristocracy, and not a few people in this stratum came to look on those who might consider themselves to be their social superiors with little interest and some contempt, believing that the real aristocracy of the country was—but perhaps the phrase is late Victorian—'the educated and professional classes'. It was possibly from this group that the non-democratic liberals of the third quarter of the century were drawn.

There is, however, a potential conflict or at least contrast between two of the concepts that were enriching social values. A *professional* man was not necessarily an *educated* man. He was by definition a *trained* man, but from a nineteenth-century point of view a professional training was not necessarily an education, certainly not the education of a gentleman. The most normal form of technical education had been apprenticeship. The barrister had learnt his trade in chambers, the solicitor as an articled clerk, the medical practitioner in the surgery or the hospital, the officer with his regiment, and the clergyman, if at all, in the parish. There is much to be said for this type of training when it is carefully attended to by those in charge, certainly the training received by mechanical engineers at Maudslay's factory in London was of the greatest importance in the development of the British Engineering industry. As, however, technological skill develops and comes to depend more and more on general scientific knowledge, systematic advanced training of some sort, possibly University training, becomes necessary for the technician, either in addition to the period passed as an apprentice, or as a substitute for it. This change is of the greatest importance because it links practice and practical skill with an extended view of more general knowledge in the sphere in which the practitioner is to work, and opens up to the technician the possibility of using the results of general research. It is a change which is reflected in the increasing importance of a University qualification for medical men. In the early years of the nineteenth century many medical practitioners gained their training at Edinburgh or Glasgow, and the importance of such men not simply in medicine but in all spheres of English life was very great indeed.

Such a technical University training, however, could not in the early years of the nineteenth century be obtained at Oxford or Cambridge, where for long any scientific teaching that there was was disjointed and casual; nor would such technical education quite satisfy the conception of the education of a gentleman. The education of a gentleman was supposed to lift him above the narrow bounds of mere professional competence, to teach him about men and life, not to impart one skill but to discipline his mind so that he could grapple with any kind of problem. Such a knowledge of life and of men, and such a mental discipline, could, it was held, be gained most certainly from a training in the Classics possibly stiffened by intensive drill in the old-fashioned type of mathematics which formed the staple of the course at Cambridge. If, therefore, professional men were to be men of liberality of mind with the status of gentlemen, they should accept a general education before they turned to their more professional training....

... The reformers of the public administration had something of the same object in mind. They wished to secure that those admitted to the public service had had the education of a gentleman, and had profited by it and indeed were admitted to the public service by the test of the extent to which they had profited by it and, in the end, by no other test. That is for appointment by nomination by politicians and aristocrats appointment by competitive examination was to be substituted, the examination being directly geared to the courses at the older Universities. The key date in that development is 1853. In that year posts in the Civil Service in India were thrown open to competitive examination. In the same year Gladstone set in hand the famous Northcote-Trevelyan enquiry which in 1854 produced a report which established the principle of government by men who have received a liberal education. It was some time, however, before the full ideal was realized. The Civil Service Commissioners were appointed with the duty of examining candidates in 1855, but at first they could only extend their influence by subjecting nominated candidates to a qualifying examination. It was not till 1870 that Gladstone was able to secure that most posts in the Home Civil Service could be obtained by an open competitive examination. When, however, this was achieved the examination gave the greatest advantage to those who had had a liberal education.

Roughly the same course was being followed with regard to commissions in the Army....

In 1871 purchase was abolished and in 1875 commissions in the cavalry and infantry were thrown open to competitive examination. But before that the Army examinations had had their effect on the educational system of the country, for they were the tests of entry into a profession which was unquestionably gentlemanly, and yet one for which other subjects than Latin and Greek were obviously relevant.

For all this development would obviously have its effect on the educational system of the country. It was increasingly important to have received the education of a gentleman, there were more openings for anyone who had received the education of a gentleman, and there were more gentlemen in circulation, which by a very natural process meant that there were more gentlemen's sons to be educated, particularly if you counted the sons of the clergy. Consequently there was an ever-increasing demand for the education of a gentleman. No doubt this was in part responsible for the increase in the numbers of Oxford and Cambridge after 1860, though this was possibly assisted by the admission of Dissenters to degrees at Oxford in 1854 and at Cambridge in 1856. But before then this demand for the education of a gentleman had been responsible for an even more significant development, the development of what came to be known as the public schools....

... The remarkable fact is not that in a country, which was so rapidly increasing in wealth, new and improved schools should come into existence for the sons of the well-to-do; it is the fact that they should be on the public school model. They were not the schools which might have been expected to develop in a growing commercial and industrial community.

The study of Latin and Greek continued to dominate their curricula to the continued neglect of subjects like modern languages or science which might have been considered to be more useful. They were dominated by the clergy of England to an extent that one would have thought would have made them repugnant to Dissenters, in a period when Dissenters were increasing in importance and wealth. Their institutions and customs looked back to a past remote from the influences of industrialized society and very different in its virtues and in its failings. But it was in those anachronistic virtues that lay the attractive power. The nature of that attraction can best be judged in what the Public School Commissioners have to say in favour of the ancient public schools after they had minutely analysed what was wrong with them, and it is worth while quoting at length and in their own words for it sums up what became one of the most cherished ideals in Victorian England.

'Among the services which they have rendered is undoubtedly the maintenance of classical literature as the staple of English Education, a service which far outweighs the error of having clung to these studies too exclusively. A second, and a greater still, is the creation of a system of government and discipline for boys, the excellence of which has been universally recognized, and which is admitted to have been most important in its effects on national character and social life. It is not easy to estimate the degree in which the English people are indebted to these schools for the qualities on which they pique themselves most—for their capacity to govern others and control themselves, their aptitude for combining freedom with order, their public spirit, their vigour and manliness of character, their strong but not slavish respect for public opinion, their love of healthy sport and exercise. These schools have been the chief nurseries of our statesmen; in them, and in schools modelled after them, men of all the various classes that make up English society, destined for every profession and career, have been brought up on a footing of social equality, and have contracted the most enduring friendships, and some of the ruling habits of their lives; and they have had perhaps the largest share in moulding the character of an English Gentleman.'

That was the lodestone. Its tractive force was not much affected by the problem whether there were decent opportunities at any school for learning French, or arithmetic, or science. The ideal which drew people was this ideal picture of the education of a gentleman, an ideal which had somehow flowered from the rough soil of the ancient schools and more ancient universities. It was an education based on the cultivation of classical literature, the formation of character through the prefectorial system and fortified by a love of exercise and the open air. There was much to be said against it. Its intellectual scope remained very narrow, on the part of the teachers as well as of the taught. Its failure to develop the teaching of science was going to be very serious indeed for the future of Britain, when the leaders of industry began to be drawn into its sphere. It is true that scientific studies had been introduced into both of the older Universities, but the progress was very slow. If the list of the Natural Science Tripos contained in Sir Clifford Allbutt's year, 1860, contained only six names, it was not till 1875 that the Natural Science Tripos contained more than twenty names. No doubt this had its effect on the public schools, for not only did many boys go on to Oxford and Cambridge but most masters came from them. Consequently the range of studies was restricted, and the standard of industry clearly not always very high. The taint of brutality remained even into the twentieth century in spite of the supposed responsibilities of the prefects or monitors, and the love of exercise developed into the cult of organized games which might support the silliest of false values.

Yet it may be the case that the Commissioners made was not wholly nonsense. In that materialistic England there was some value in an education which was not completely utilitarian and which produced at the lowest, particularly after Arnold had done his work, a greater sense of responsibility and a greater sense of freedom than existed in other systems. It was the legacy of the old English aristocratic class to an ever larger class, and it is only fair, when thinking of what the public schools were, to conceive what an aristocratic education based on a strictly military system as in Germany would have been like, or a middle-class education directed strictly to technological and commercial ends. At any rate, whether they deserved to do so or not the public schools exercised a powerful attractive influence over the educational system of the country. Not only were many new public schools founded but a great many boarding schools were built which more or less approximated to them. Schools of other traditions, dissenting schools, Roman Catholic schools were drawn to model themselves upon the public schools and humbler boys who, alas, could not hope for more than an unsatisfactory primary education in due course were given a fairy land remotely based on the public schools in the fifth form at St Dominick's or the adventures of Billy Bunter.

This attraction drew individuals into the social sphere of the public schools from sections of society naturally remote from it. At first no doubt the public schools attracted primarily the sons of the nobility, gentry and professional classes, but at least by the fourth quarter of the century and probably earlier very many of the wealthier people in the industrial districts seem to have been sending their sons to the public schools. Even so stern an opponent of the aristocracy and the old governing classes as Joseph Chamberlain sent his sons to Rugby, and the one, Austen, who was destined for a political career, to Trinity College, Cambridge, where he took his degree in 1885. The next year, 1886, Albert Kitson took his degree from the same College, the son of Sir James Kitson who took the lead in the National Liberal Federation after Chamberlain had left it.

It was the final stage of the consolidation of the caste. First there had been the broadening of the conception of a gentleman by the emphasis on the test of the education of a gentleman, a broadening of which the professional classes had made use. Then there had been the development and multiplication of the institutions which could give that education, and now the sons of the leaders of industry were drawn in also. They were very often drawn to places of education remote from the places where their parents had made or were making their money. They mixed with the sons of men of different traditions. They learnt a new way of talking and of thinking. They were trained in disciplines which often enough had no relation to the scientific side of their work. They were drawn away from the men who must continue to be the rank and file and non-commissioned officers of industry, and they became acclimatized to a life which very often drew them and their money out of industry altogether.

But even before this last stage, what had been happening had in other ways led to the separation of classes and to the denial of privileges to the sons of poor men which they had previously enjoyed. In most of the ancient schools which had been turned into public schools there had been provision in the intention of the founder, or of some other benefactor, for the education of poor children, or at least of local children. In many cases it was for such scholars that in fact the school had been founded; but as the school was developed into a public school their needs were often pressed to one side for the benefit of richer strangers, and these local children were often largely eliminated. This very often caused bitter local feeling and the Public Schools Commission indulged in a good deal of special pleading to justify what had happened. But justifiable or unjustifiable, the process went forward and the division became more marked. The tendency was probably reinforced by the reform of the Oxford and Cambridge scholarships, which ceased often to be attached to particular localities where poor lads had a chance of getting them and were thrown into open competition in which those trained at the public schools were very much more likely to be successful.

Without question this social consolidation had disadvantages for the country; what advantages it may have had would presumably in part depend on the values which were gained from the educational system itself, from the development of freedom, a sense of responsibility and the retention of the conception of a liberal education. These possible merits deserve a fair historical appraisal which they do not always get, and it is possible that the conception of a liberal education, not as the privilege for a few but as a necessity for all, may be an important one. Fortunately, however, such an attempted judgment would be out of place here. The object here is to discover the factors that helped to make Victorian England. One of those factors had been, from the beginning, the aristocratic power in the country. It had presented itself at first in the formidable shape of the old noble and landowning interest which for a remarkably long period dominated the political and social life of the country. The processes of history, in due course, began to shake that domination, though to the very end of what might be called Victorian England remarkably large fragments of it remained. Meanwhile, however, there had been forming in its shadow a new type of aristocracy, a new caste, more extensive, more adaptable, less open to the attacks of economic change or of discriminatory taxation, and that aristocracy certainly remained in full vigour when Victorian England, however defined, came to its end. It is indeed with us still.

30

THE WHITE MAN'S BURDEN

A. P. Thornton

The disintegration and virtual disappearance of the British Empire in Asia and Africa in recent years has inspired historians to go back and reconsider the whole course of aggressive British imperialism from the time it took on new life in the 1870s. Among scholars who are making this re-evaluation the most profound is certainly A. P. Thornton, of the University of Toronto. In the following selection he describes in a few dramatic pages the justificatory imperialist doctrine of civilization, or the white man's burden, that was popular in the late nineteenth century. Thornton also suggests why this doctrine was doomed to failure in practice even when applied with the best of intentions, and he indicates the tragedy for mankind inherent in the inability of great political enterprises to provide for human happiness in face of the conflict between cultures and the misunderstanding between the conquering and conquered races.

LORD Salisbury, a statesman who disliked the noiser style of imperialism which painted the map red, still had no doubts, as a good Christian, that the civilized nations had a mission to perform in the world. Their paternalism was best expressed through an authoritative imperial rule. They had a responsibility to colonial peoples themselves—to protect, equip, and educate them. In doing this, a larger service was also performed, to the idea of civilization itself, since these new recruits to it, properly guided and guarded, would enlarge and enrich the area of the civilized life. Salisbury allowed that the African had a right to law, a right to protection, a right to education. But he did not allow that

---

FROM A. P. Thornton, *Doctrines of Imperialism* (New York: John Wiley & Sons, Inc., 1965), pp. 157–158, 170–181. By permission of the publishers.

the African had a similar right to self-determination, and why? Because the African had not yet found a self to determine. Salisbury's generation had seen what "Africa for the Africans" could mean: pillage, barbarities, slavery. Civilization did not lie at the end of that road. A similar, if less severe, case presented itself in Egypt. There, after the invasion of 1882, it was Britain's task to bring forward the people within the pale of the civilized world, under an ordered government approved of by the public opinion of Europe. And there were always those who said these same things about the Irish, denying them Home Rule because they would abuse it. And they at least were not surprised when the first thing the Irish did when presented with freedom in 1922 was to start a civil war.

But men do not allocate a secondary and subordinate place to other men without developing a contempt for them. They can justify their dominance only on the assumption that these others are not worthy to share it. The subsequent anti-colonialist campaigns have accordingly had as their principal objective the release of whole peoples from this contempt, which is the most searing of all forms of bondage....

... Imperialism ... did not often pause to assess whether it was making a durable impression on those whom it physically controlled: only the missionaries took this issue to heart. So long as energy was abundant, its authority would be secure. Imperialists, the accredited agents of their civilization, intended to promote peace, order, the prevention of crime, the redress of wrong, the enforcement of contracts, the development and concentration of their own military forces, the construction of public works, and the collection and expenditure of the revenue required for all these objects "in such a way as to promote to the utmost the public interest." There were always officials who knew that the imperial coinage, the imperial medals, had their other side. One of them categorized the items listed above as "somewhat grim presents" for one people to make to another—but none the worse for that. Henry Lawrence, like his brother John a faithful servant of the Indian system, who was to die in its defense at Lucknow during the Mutiny of 1857, commented in 1843 how erroneous it was to reckon on the attachment, in any crisis, of the peoples of India:

> ... as if any Hindu or Mohammedan *could* love his Christian lord, who only comes before him as master or tax-gatherer; as if it were not absurd to suppose that the chiefs of Burma, Nepal, Lahore and the like could tolerate the Power that restrains their rapacious desires and habits—that degrades them in their own, and each other's, eyes.

But there were always, too, a great number of imperial officials who saw no need to trouble themselves with this kind of analysis. It was also in 1843 that Sir Charles Napier conquered the province of Sind in northwestern India: and he made a riposte to some brand-new subjects of the Company's *Raj* that became deservedly famous. They came to plead before him for permission to retain certain of their time honored social customs. Be it so, said Napier magnanimously,

This burning of widows is your custom. Prepare the funeral pile. But my nation has also a custom. When men burn women alive, we hang them and confiscate all their property. My carpenters shall therefore erect gibbets on which to hang all concerned when the widow is consumed. Let us all act according to national customs.

This forthright language is a measure of the depth of contempt felt. It was an attitude that the English were sometimes to mute but seldom entirely to lose. In India their eyebrows, from the outset, remained raised. Lord Cornwallis, Bengal's Governor-General in 1792, declared his belief that every native of Hindostan was corrupt. A century later Lord Roberts, on his retirement as England's foremost "sepoy-general," testified in his autobiography *Forty-One Years in India* (1897) that in that country evidence on almost any subject could be had for the buying. He added that, however well-educated and adept a native might be, and however brave he might have proved himself, it was his own belief that no rank that the government could bestow on such a man would cause him to be considered as an equal by the British officer. This opinion died hard. An official committee, examining in 1921 the problem of "Indianizing" the Army, thought the business would take forty years, and considered segregation as a possible solution to the difficulty of getting white officers to serve under Indian officers.

The overriding problem, as seen by India's masters, centered on the matter of "character." By this was meant the qualities of energy and initiative, probity and loyalty, with the self-respect that was their natural accompaniment. Prestige rested upon conduct; and Macaulay had declared that English valor and English intelligence had done less to extend and preserve England's Empire in the East than English veracity. Throughout the nineteenth century public schools were founded in England with no other purpose than to inculcate these qualities in the young. No institution in India was thought likely to do as much for the Hindu, whose character had been formed, and continued to operate, within a very different context. The misappropriation of public funds, remarks one twentieth-century commentator, was generally regarded more as a subject for mirth and envy than reprobation; while another records his discovery that an enlightened ruler of a princely State, the founder of many schools and other useful institutions, a nobleman highly eulogized by Lord Curzon himself, held no greater place in popular memory or esteem than his successor, who had to be deposed for drunkenness and riotous living, having squandered the State's resources on merry-making, fireworks, and colorful debauches.

Earlier observers took a severer tone. James Mill's *History of India,* a six-volume bible which every aspiring Company cadet took with him on his first ship out, describes the natives of India, and the Chinese for good measure, as dissembling, treacherous, mendacious, cowardly, unfeeling, conceited, and unclean, the victims of despotism and priestcraft. (Mill never visited either India or China, and there is no record of his ever having met a native; but Robert Morrison, the London Missionary

Society's solitary representative in China, had written home in 1817 urging his superiors that they should henceforth tell all future missionaries to the Chinese "that of this people it is true—'All men are liars.' ") Young men who arrived in Asia with these preconceptions grew to be old men without having found any occasion for changing them. In 1876 a distinguished senior remarked that executive government posts demanded qualities other than intellectual, such as energy, decision, self-reliance, power of combination and organization, of managing men, "and so on." No Indians qualified under those headings: in 1870, of the 325 candidates who applied for 40 vacancies in the Indian Civil Service, seven were Indians, and one passed.

Sir Walter Scott once commented how the lesser gentry of Scotland sent their younger sons to India, as automatically as they sent their black cattle to market in the south. G. O. Trevelyan's *Letters from a Competition Wallah* (1865) tell how boys brought up in "Anglo-Indian" families looked upon India as their birthright. Here was Tom, for example, at the age of thirty-one in charge of a population as numerous as that of England in the reign of Elizabeth. How could any member of the Service, with so broad a horizon stretching before him, feel any misgiving concerning the dignity and importance of his work?

Few did. But the thought of young Tom, turned loose to dispense high, middle, and low justice in the Deccan or Rajputana with what assistance his character could give him, disturbed some commentators. On the one side an attractive image was presented of the fair-haired Saxon youth opposing his well-trained intellect to the new difficulties which crowded around him. Alternatively, as the same historian points out, this same youth might be assessed as

an ignorant upstart, slenderly acquainted with the native languages, and not at all acquainted with native feelings, laying down the law... and committing errors of the most irritating kind with an incredible amount of assurance and conceit.

But this assurance was in fact the key to any situation; and the system, the machinery of the *Raj,* was reckoned flexible enough to circumvent the consequences of anyone whose assurance turned out to be ill-founded.

The older school of officialdom felt anyway that it was the competition-wallah himself, product of the examination system, who was likelier to make a fool of himself, since his intelligence had been trained without reference to the quality of his instinct. Henry Lawrence's biographer commented, admiringly, on that hero of the Punjab and the Mutiny, that he would have been failed by the examiners for a cadetship in the Indian Army, "a fate which, under the circumstances, must have befallen Nelson himself, and about three-quarters of the heroes to whom England owes her glory." At the turn of the century in the Sudan, its new British masters were still anxious to recruit to the ranks of government not intellectuals but tent-and-saddle men, men who "fitted in," men who had for example the social grace to prefer Turkish to Virginia cigarettes.

A competitive examination was in almost any case an absurd method of selection for administrative personnel, "where character is of the first importance." This dogma lodged itself in far places. When the Japanese set up their National Foundation Training Institute in Java in April 1945, they insisted on character, not scholastic ability, as a prerequisite in their students, and were forever seeking "sincerity" in their relations with the various nationalities of their Co-Prosperity Sphere.

An exported civilization looked for its own reflection where it could find it: not an easy task, but easier than setting up courses in perpetual schoolmastering. The kind of character that the English appreciated was to be found in India, they felt, far oftener among hillmen than among plainsmen, among hostile Muslim tribesmen than among servile Bengali clerks. In the hills could be found, in Lord Curzon's phrase, the common bond of manhood, a type of outdoors comradeship (reminiscent of school playing fields) among men who respected one another. An instinct for recognizing this "was the secret of the success of every great frontier officer that we have ever had." It was a misfortune for both sides that the earliest conquests in India took place in Bengal: for had the English encountered sooner in their imperial career the Hindu warrior-races—Marathas, Rajputs, Sikhs—they would not have formed so harsh a stereotype of the "native character." Much in contrast was their instinctive reaction to the world of Islam. This had a long pedigree. It perhaps began with the eastern odyssey of Lady Hester Stanhope (1810–39). It gained strength from Eliot Warburton's *The Crescent and The Cross* (1848). It borrowed an aura of mystery from Disraeli's *Tancred* (1847). It attracted the satire, even at this early stage, of Thackeray, in his personification of "young Mr. Bedwin Sands." Its principal misconception, one that would have puzzled the medieval Crusaders, Tancred included, was that Christian civilization had a lot in common with that of Islam.

The nature of this sympathetic fallacy (which in popular fiction was to make of the *sheikh*, pre-eminently a tent-and-saddle man, a figure of high romance, and in reality helped to detach T. E. Lawrence from the world of the practicable entirely) was early grasped by the Hindus, who accurately judged the estimate in which their masters held them. It led them to popularize the cry that the British were holding India not by the exercise of justice but by expediency, by means of the old Roman method of "divide and rule." It was also a leaf taken from the book of imperialism in Ireland; for, as that country's first modern nationalist, Wolfe Tone, had discerned, the English maintained their ascendancy there "by perpetuating the spirit of internal dissension grounded on religious distinctions." In Ireland, too, did not the English use the weapon of contempt? Had there not been "a systematic defamation" of the Irish character ever since the Act of Union in 1800?—with the result that few Englishmen took either the Irish or the Irish Question seriously, or saw it as a matter to be discussed between equals?

Whether it was policy or merely instinct, "divide and rule" certainly suited the book of the Indian Muslims, since there was no doubt, if ever they had to choose between a British and a Hindu *Raj*, which could expect their support. They kept in mind the precepts of their first leader, Syed Ahmad Khan. Think for a moment, he had urged in 1887, what the result would be if all government appointments were allocated by competitive examination; "there would remain no part of the country in which we should see at the tables of justice and authority any face except those of Bengalis." It was a thought not then, and not ever, to be borne.

Thus, although the British denied the charge that they were dividing in order to rule, their sympathies in fact lay at no great distance from their policies, as two Viceroys of the same era bear witness. In 1893 Lord Lansdowne's government in India reported on a resolution previously passed by the House of Commons in England, to the effect that examinations for entry into the Indian Civil Service should be held simultaneously in England and in India (and not, as heretofore, in England alone). The report declared that a material reduction of the European staff then employed in India would be incompatible with the safety of British rule, and that any system of unrestricted competition would also practically exclude from the imperial Service

Muhammedans, Sikhs, and other races accustomed to rule by tradition and possessed of exceptional strength of character, but deficient in literary education.

In 1906 another Viceroy, Lord Minto (more tory than his ancestor a century back), cordially welcomed a Muslim delegation led by the Aga Khan. They justly claimed, he said, that their position should be estimated not merely on their numerical strength but in respect to the political importance of their community, and the service it had rendered to the Empire: "I am entirely in accord with you." It is thus not surprising that one of the aims of the All-India Muslim League, founded that year, was to promote feelings of loyalty toward the British *Raj*. This contrasted remarkably with the drive of the Hindu National Congress towards self-government.

To inculcate the principles of one's own civilization in men in whose company was felt at best a deep bewilderment, and at worst as deep an antipathy, was a task always too great for the pragmatic, nonphilosophic rulers of India, who assumed that their own degree of civilization was so self-evident as not to need any propaganda in its behalf. As a result, an English authority on eastern religions doubted that Christianity would ever make much progress in Asia, since what was commonly known by that name was not the teaching of Christ but a rearrangement of it made in Europe and, like most European institutions, practical rather than thoughtful. The British Empire also was practical rather than thoughtful. In it the formulation of policy depended not so much on any philosophy of empire as upon the economic and social conditions that existed in the colonial field, and upon the economic relationship between the colony and the metropolis. But even British pragmatism was hard put to it to accommodate both the doctrine that dependencies should eventually graduate into self-governing status, and the conviction that in the Indian case this would never be practicable.

For the Hindus were simply not to be trusted within the arcana of the *Raj*. Their "character" was too faulty: or the structure of their personality was too different. Whatever the terms of the verdict, the consequences were clear. It was not safe to acquaint men so innately unreliable, so unaware of the Anglo-Saxon codes of civilized behavior, with state secrets on military and foreign affairs: as late as 1942 Stafford Cripps on his mission to India was authorized to accommodate the Congress on many points, but *not* on the immediate creation of a Ministry of Defense, with a Hindu in charge.

It was Lord Lytton, the only Viceroy (1874–80) who was also an intellectual and a poet, who put on record the true nature of the dilemma in which the officers of the *Raj* found themselves. Such phrases as "religious toleration," "liberty of the press," "personal freedom of the subject," "social supremacy of the law," and others, which in England conveniently summarized ideas of long standing and broad appeal, were in India, to the vast mass of the natives there, only the mysterious formulae of a foreign and uncongenial system of administration. They produced bafflement. By enforcing these principles and establishing these institutions,

> We have placed, and must perpetually maintain ourselves, at the head of a gradual but gigantic revolution—the greatest and most momentous social, moral, and religious, as well as political revolution, which, perhaps, the world has ever witnessed.

The western-educated Hindu was putting forward many claims. He was nursing many expectations. But they were claims and expectations of a kind that never could or would be fulfilled. Believing this, the rulers of India

> have had to choose between prohibiting them and cheating them—and we have chosen the least straightforward course.

For what fortune lay before the "babu," the English-educated clerk, who had learned to simulate but had not the capacity to emulate? He represented nothing but the social anomaly of his own position.

What Lytton could discern in 1878 became much plainer to the sharply critical eyes of the next generation. Mary Kingsley deduced from her West African experience that the white race would never "drag the black race up to their own particular summit in the mountain range of civilization." Cecil Rhodes declared that the missionaries were wrong, for they were civilizing in the wrong direction. When they turned out men who were capable of administering the telegraph and postal systems, and of doing carpentry and managing machines, they would be doing their job: for these were the men who would get the franchise without any difficulty. Who wanted Kaffir parsons who knew Latin and Greek? Gilbert Murray, all his long life a liberal, was also a convinced paternalist. White men were superior to black, brown, red, and yellow men; "that is to say, that on the whole the first mentioned colour tends to rule and the other colours to obey." Hobson's *Imperialism* stressed the disappointment that lay at the end of the road, one to confound both the ruler and the ruled:

We are incapable of implanting our civilisation in India by present methods of approach: we are only capable of disturbing their civilisation.

And this civilization, whether disturbed or left to stagnate, still commanded no respect from the aliens in its midst. Very few of the able, energetic officials who administered the British Empire from Downing Street, or in the field, either believed that the populations they ruled were capable of being trained for effective free self-government, or geared their policy to accommodate such a contingency in the near or remote future. They were certainly committed to a policy of educating natives along western lines, but they remained pessimistic as to the results of this process. Men who distrusted intellectual development when they encountered it among their fellow Englishmen were no more inclined to welcome it in their subordinates.

One bad omen was the indolent sophistication of the *effendi* class in Egypt, French in culture but not in action: for here again was emphasized the usual result of a European system of education on the Oriental mind: a mind that absorbed learning quickly but superficially and, of course, "without the stability of character that learning should bring." Egypt accordingly, in the opinion of the imperialist periodical *The Round Table* in December 1918, provided an example of those countries of the Near East for which there was at present "no hope, except in the guardianship of some civilised state." In India the guardians remained resolved to entrench themselves. They neither wished nor hoped that native officials should one day become the servants of a free Indian nation. "We do our humble best," said the Viceroy, Lord Curzon, in 1905, "to retain by justice what we have won by the sword."

The sword might be acceptable: but the humility, the excellence, and the justice were not. In the East the arbitrament of the sword had always been better understood than a concept of justice whose terms of reference belonged to an alien tradition. Similarly with all other forms of action in India, since the context was mysterious, the action was unintelligible.

Englishmen in the East, wrote a distinguished jurist with Indian experience, Sir Henry Maine, came into contact with vast populations of a high natural intelligence, to which the very notion of innovation was loathsome. The very fact that such populations existed suggested that the true difference between the East and the West lay in the fact that in western countries there was a larger minority of exceptional persons who, for good reasons or bad, had a real desire for change. From the English proconsul in Egypt, Lord Cromer, came the same testimony. When the European once stepped outside of the influence acquired by the power of the sword and looked for any common ground of understanding with the subject race, he found that he was, by the elementary facts of the case, debarred from using all those moral influences which in more homogeneous countries bound society together.

The western-educated saw this problem from another angle. They saw it from below. Intelligent aliens could gauge the breadth of the gap that lay between ruler and ruled; but the ruled knew its nature and the humiliation engendered by living a life at secondhand. Gandhi when on trial in March 1922 said that he was satisfied that many English and indeed Indian officials honestly believed that they were administering one of the best systems devised in the world, and that India was making steady, if slow, progress. What they did not know was that a subtle but effective system of terrorism and an organized display of force on the one hand, and the deprivation of all powers of retaliation and self-defense on the other, had emasculated the people and induced in them the habit of simulation. But Cromer, too, had noticed this: "the common oriental habit of endeavouring to say what is pleasant to the interrogator, especially if he occupies some post of authority." And it was with this same diagnosis that Southern Rhodesia's Lord Malvern shocked the more sensitive ears of the 1950's when he said it out loud: "All Africans are liars." There was, therefore, a particularly vicious circle here. The rulers despised the ruled because they lacked character. But the system of government that the rulers imposed was such as to prevent the ruled from expressing any character worth the name. A mutual bewilderment and exasperation thus persisted.

This, it appeared, was the upshot of what a governor of Bombay had called, in 1860, the perilous experiment of continuing to legislate for millions of people, with few means of knowing, except by a rebellion, whether the laws suited them or not.

31

ENTREPRENEURIAL DECLINE IN THE LATE NINETEENTH CENTURY

H. J. Habakkuk

Although in 1900 England still seemed to be the most prosperous nation in the world, her economic sun was in fact beginning to set. Historians of the 1960s are able to look back and point to the fundamental deficiencies in British business that were to become steadily accentuated in the first half of the twentieth century. The distinguished Oxford scholar H. J. Habakkuk in the following selection accounts for the advent of the long autumn of English entrepreneurial enterprise by comparing economic growth and institutions in the late nineteenth-century United States with conditions in England, and by examining social and cultural as well as strictly economic factors.

IN THE United States, there was no long-established class system to impede social mobility. The possibility of rising to the top was believed to be greater than anywhere else in the world, and probably was so in fact. This belief in an open avenue to wealth was one of the main reasons for the amount of ability devoted to entrepreneurship in the United States. Moreover, in the United States, there were few competitors to business success as a source of social prestige. There was no large and powerful bureaucracy, no hereditary aristocracy. There was no professional military class and soldiers were not held in high esteem. Horatio Alger, the hero of the American success story, wanted to be a business man, not a general or a civil servant or a great landowner. The men of ambition and ability turned naturally to business, not only because of the gains which might be made there—though they were sometimes certainly enormous—but because business men, a Rockefeller or a Pierrepont Morgan, were the leading men of the country. Morgan himself, in his early middle age, nearly decided to give up business and become a gentleman; but he did not do so, and later American business men did not even consider the possibility.

FROM H. J. Habakkuk, *American and British Technology in the 19th Century* (Cambridge: Cambridge University Press, 1962), pp. 190–194, 205–207, 212–215. By permission of the publishers.

hand, birth and family, education, behaviour, manners, accent, played the dominant part in determining social standing. The ideal of the 'all-round man', the man of well-developed but non-professional competence in many fields, the ideal of Renaissance Europe, was still strong; and, within the limits left by birth and family, social standing was influenced by the whole range of a man's achievements and abilities, his physical strength or weakness, the way in which he ordered his life, his capacity to paint, or to play instruments, his whole character and personality. A society in which the main emphasis is placed on success in one's job as measured by income is more favourable to the full exercise of business abilities, and for this reason England was less favourably placed than the U.S.A.

These are general characteristics of English society which might militate against English entrepreneurship (and even more against that of continental European countries) at all times. But there are additional reasons which apply with particular force to the later nineteenth century. There are two assertions which need to be distinguished: the first is that English entrepreneurs were apathetic, by comparison with their American and German contemporaries, that is were men of less general capacity and force: the second assertion is that, though still able, they were men of abilities which had ceased to be relevant. Because England industrialised earlier, English entrepreneurs were more likely to be second- and third-generation entrepreneurs; as such they had less need and incentive to exert their full effort, and were more likely to be distracted from concentration on business by the possibilities of social life, which are open to the man who has arrived but not to those who are still climbing. The drive inside the individual entrepreneur to expand his concern, to make the most of opportunities, is greatest in the early stages of industrialisation and loses some of its force once an industrial society has been created. This, it is argued, is true whatever the form of industrial organisation, but it applies with most force to the members of a family concern, which was probably still the principal form of organisation at this time: the impetus in the first generation is very great but it loses force with succeeding generations. Second- and third-generation business men tend to be less energetic (an argument, however, which is rarely applied to second- and third-generation Professors).

The second assertion is that, quite apart from any decline in the quality of the entrepreneurs, their virtues were not the relevant ones in the later nineteenth century. In some industries the course of technical and economic change called for the exercise of qualities different from those by which the entrepreneurs had established themselves. In the iron and steel industry, for example, the founders of the older British firms succeeded by the operation of qualities which were not those most required in the 1880's and '90's. The ability most evidently absent was technical expertise. The later innovations embodied more technical knowledge than the early ones, that is there were fewer within the scope of the ingenious artisan. Furthermore, many more of the later technical innovations consisted in applying the techniques of one industry to another, in the cross-fertilisation of the techniques of different industries. In such cases even an entrepreneur who had acquired from experience considerable technical mastery, was at a disadvantage compared with someone whose technical training had been more formal and so more general. Altogether therefore British industrialists tended to be less well equipped than their rivals, 'to judge the commercial prospects of innovations while these were in their experimental change' and 'to forecast the trend of technical change'. The English employer was, contemporaries said, more of a commercial man and took less interest in the technical part of the work than those of France and Germany. There was, said Siemens, 'more prejudice against innovations'.

That in late nineteenth-century England there were entrepreneurial deficiencies of a social origin few students of the period would be disposed to deny, but exactly how important they were it is very difficult to say. There is no reason to believe that the English business man, though he may have been less well equipped technically than the German, was less well-qualified than the American. Moreover, in general the argument ignores, or at best does not explain, the curious patchiness of English business performance in this period. The rapidity of technical advance in shipbuilding and in the open-hearth sector of the steel industry, for instance, show that the second generation of entrepreneurs in family firms could be conspicuously successful. And many of the deficiencies can be explained in more narrowly economic terms and with less recourse to sociological influences....

... For the first six or seven decades of the nineteenth century market prospects in England were favourable to the creation of new capacity; there were vigorous sources of demand for U.K. goods. This increased demand was not, of course, independent of the technical efficiency of English industry, but given the initial English superiority it proceeded even in the absence of technical progress, and it warranted an increase in capacity which gave English manufacturers excellent opportunities of adopting new methods and gaining experience.

After the 1870's the market prospects for British goods were less favourable to the creation of new capacity. In the first place, once England had become an industrial state, the possibilities of an increase in income from intersectoral shifts within the English economy were much more limited. In the second place, so far as foreign markets were concerned, though the increase in their real income was considerable, particularly in the U.S.A. and Germany, there was a decline in their marginal propensity to import from the U.K. The propensity would in any case have declined as these countries developed their own manufacturing industry, but the speed of the decline was accelerated by the tariffs which these countries imposed, and also by the fortuitous incidence of technical discovery in the key industry of the period—steel....

In Germany and the U.S.A. market prospects were much more favourable in the later decades of the nineteenth century than they were in

England. In both there were large reserves of unexploited natural resources which had been developed rapidly as soon as the areas were supplied with railways. In Germany, too, simply because her industrialisation was late, the possibilities of increasing income by intersectoral shifts were still considerable. And the tariffs, which curtailed British exports of certain goods, concentrated the increase in domestic demand in Germany and America on local production. The fact that their total capacity was growing more rapidly meant that these countries had more opportunity of trying out new ideas, at a time when there were many to be tried out....

Some of the reasons... for England's smaller increments of new investment in the later nineteenth century, compared with America's, arise from England's early and long-sustained start. It is not argued that England was on balance a loser from her early start. Because of this start England's income in the 1870's was higher than it would otherwise have been (and higher than that of other countries except the U.S.A.) and her savings were much larger. Because she had already a large industrial plant she was able to use her savings to build more and better houses and to provide the regions of overseas settlement with their complement of public utilities. But because she already had a large industrial plant which in many branches was adequate to the demands made upon it in the '80's and '90's, the incentive to install new capacity and the opportunity of trying out new methods were circumscribed. And in explaining the different rates of technical progress this fact is of crucial importance.

The same circumstances may also account in large part for the quality of British entrepreneurial performance in the same period. The entrepreneurial deficiencies to which the performance of the British economy is attributed can plausibly be explained as a consequence of that performance. The slow rate of expansion of British industry affected the performance of business men. Great generals are not made in time of peace; great entrepreneurs are not made in non-expanding industries. Because the market was growing slowly, the risks of adventure were much greater than in Germany and America, as may clearly be seen from the fate of those who showed enterprise in the electrical industry in the early '80's, and came croppers as a result.

But the slow expansion must also have affected the recruitment of business men. An Englishman's choice of career was, it is true, very much influenced by tradition, convention and inertia, and no doubt in England these tended to channel talent away from business towards the professions. But it was also responsive to changes in reward, and after the 1870's several purely economic circumstances combined to divert men of ability away from business. The high profits of the 1850's and '60's had attracted an unduly large number of entrants into business so that even had the rate of profit been sustained in the following decades, the rewards of individuals would have fallen. But, over and above this there was a fall in profits, a decline in the ability of firms to offer attractive salaries; in periods of falling prices business was at a disadvantage *vis-à-vis* the professions in competing for talent. The overflooding of an occupation which in any case was becoming less popular meant that business was very much less attractive for men who were making their choice of profession from the 1870's on. Where there was lack of growth there were few new firms, the average age of men at the top of existing firms was high and nepotism was most likely to occur....

But was the difference of entrepreneurial ability all that great? In electricity, the men who developed the industry in England, Swan, Crompton and Siemens, were all men of considerable ability and very little behind the Americans technically. The difference in the development of the internal combustion engine was greater: there was more experiment in America than in Britain. But it may be doubted whether this kind of disparity in 'pure entrepreneurial ability' mattered a great deal in the later nineteenth and early twentieth centuries. Where there were no other impediments, it did not prevent the rapid adoption of methods pioneered elsewhere. The absence of the higher forms of inventive and entrepreneurial ability represented by Brush and Edison in the electrical industry was not a major handicap to the development of the British industry, since the Brush and Edison systems were very rapidly imported. Where advanced technology of foreign origin was not incorporated, the explanation is probably more often the limitations of economic circumstances rather than the inertness of British entrepreneurs.

If, as we have argued, technical progress in England was retarded by the slow growth of demand for British exports in the last three decades of the century which afforded relatively few opportunities for the growth of new capacity, why, it may be asked, did the boom in exports after 1900 not stimulate technical development? In certain industries the answer is probably that the British lag was, by then, too substantial to be made up easily, because of the lack of the know-how which would have been accumulated by keeping more continuously in touch with new methods. Partly also the explanation may be that the increase in export demand was principally for those goods where the possibilities of technical progress were slightest. It was in the new industries that the possibilities were greatest. Their methods were more elaborate than those of the older industries, and the potentialities of these methods had been less fully exploited. They were the industries with the best long-term demand prospects, and the least stereotyped labour-force.

32

THE FORMATION OF THE LABOUR PARTY

Henry Pelling

Of the many accounts of the Labour Party's origins the most circumstantial and judicious is the work of the Cambridge scholar Henry Pelling, whose conclusions are given in the following passage. Pelling makes sense out of the political maneuvering of the late nineteenth and early twentieth centuries, and he is able to define precisely the roles played in the formation of the Labour Party by both socialist intellectuals and the trade union leaders.

THE Socialists were the one active political group interested in bringing the party into being. They alone could provide a programme which would make it distinct and separate from the existing parties. Without a programme, as Engels realised, there could be no such party on a permanent basis, and every attempt to found one would fail. Indeed, the political independence of the Labour Party always seemed to be in doubt until in 1918 it accepted a Socialist constitution. In addition, the Socialists possessed a faith in the righteousness and ultimate victory of their cause which acted as a powerful driving force. This faith was based, ultimately, upon the analysis of society first presented by Marx and Engels in the Communist Manifesto of 1848, and elaborated in their subsequent writings. However much the analysis was modified, as by Hyndman and the Fabians, and simplified for popular consumption, as by Morris and Blatchford, it still had a certain comprehensive reality for those who accepted it. To its working-class adherents it gave a sense of purpose and pride in class consciousness; to others it afforded the consolation that they were working in harmony with the tendencies of social change.

The history of the world has often shown the dynamic qualities of a faith devoutly held, like that of the early Christians, the Ottomans, or the Calvinists. It does not matter if the faith feeds on illusions, for it is capable of conquering reality. Socialism had this quality for the early members of the S.D.F., the Socialist League and the I.L.P. It led them at times into foolish misstatements, such as that of *Justice* in 1885: 'If

FROM Henry Pelling, *The Origins of the Labour Party* (London: Macmillan & Co. Ltd., 1954), pp. 229–241. By permission of the Clarendon Press, Oxford.

Socialism were the law in England every worker would get at least four times his present wages for half his present work. Don't you call that practical politics?' or such as Blatchford's declaration in *Merrie England* that 'this country is capable of feeding more than treble her present population'. But the faith did not stand or fall by the accuracy of facts and figures: it depended much less for its sources and strength upon reason than upon deeper and simpler forces in human nature. 'Socialism', said Shaw in 1897, 'wins its disciples by presenting civilisation as a popular melodrama, or as a Pilgrim's Progress through suffering, trial, and combat against the powers of evil to the bar of poetic justice with paradise beyond.' It was this crusading zeal which drew attention to the Socialists in the eighties, and enabled them, like the Narodniks in Russia with whom Kropotkin compared them, to have an influence in politics far beyond what their numbers justified; it was this again which gave the early I.L.P. the strength to play such an important part in the negotiations for the making of the L.R.C. The Socialists made up in energy and enthusiasm for their lack of numbers: in spite of their eccentricities and discords, they formed, in a real sense, a political *élite*. When it came to fighting elections—speaking at street-corners, canvassing, delivering manifestos—the man with the red tie was worth a score of his more easygoing fellow trade-unionists—a fact that the union leaders were obliged to take into account in drawing up the terms of the alliance in 1900.

Not all the Socialists, however, could claim to have made a valuable contribution to the formation of the new party. The S.D.F. originated in a labour revolt against the middle-class National Liberal Federation: yet in the course of a few years it came to embody an attitude of exclusiveness and hostility to all save the initiates of its own narrow creed. Engels resented the fact that it had 'managed to reduce the Marxist theory of development to a rigid orthodoxy'. Hyndman's was a doctrinaire radicalism, full of echoes of Tom Paine and the Jacobins, but barren of revolutionary technique.

The fact was that the British working class as a whole had no use for the conception of violent revolution. Any leader who failed to recognise this could not expect to win widespread support. Economic grievances could temporarily arouse bitter discontent as they had done in the early years of the industrial revolution: the Norwich shoemakers who joined the Socialist League were, like the Chartist hand-loom weavers, making a protest against the harshness of the extending industrial system, which had no use for their craftsmanship. But dislocations of this type were for the most part transitory: a permanent political organisation of the working class needed to disavow the use of violence. Only those who recognised this could effectively set on foot a movement to form a Labour Party.

The Fabian Society performed the essential service of adapting Marxist theory to a form compatible with British constitutional practice. For this purpose they drew heavily on indigenous Radical ideas, on Mill and the Benthamites, on the Positivists and on the historical economists. All this work of synthesis was a vital contribution to the British Labour movement. But the literary tradition of the past half-century which has favoured the Fabians so strongly should not lead us to conclude that they had much direct part in the establishment of the Labour Representation Committee. For their tactics were too subtle and too compromising for the working class to adopt as its own. In this period, the Fabians were never ready to believe that the time was ripe for the formation of a new party. It was not without reason that Hyndman and later Champion described them as 'the Micawber club'. The failure of permeation, in which they had placed such high hopes, turned their complacency to gloom, and by the end of the century the most prominent members of the Society were falling into that attitude of distrust of democratic processes that is so clearly reflected in Shaw's *Man and Superman* (1903). They thought that the L.R.C. would fail just as they believed the I.L.P. had failed, and in 1906 Shaw had so far despaired of it as to publicly 'apologise to the Universe for my connexion with such a party'.

Apart from the early efforts of Engels and the Marx-Avelings, therefore, it is Champion and his associates who deserve the credit for devoting themselves to propaganda on behalf of a Labour Party. The example of independence to which they constantly pointed was that of the Irish Nationalists, who had held Parliament to ransom in 1885-6. The Irish example held good in the years leading up to the formation of the I.L.P. in 1893, and was repeatedly cited by Champion himself, by Keir Hardie, and by others. But from 1893 onwards the I.L.P. began to provide its own examples of the value of independence. It had the initial support of Engels, and Aveling helped to draw up its programme: yet it was steadfastly constitutional in its attitude, although this was not explicitly stated at its foundation. Within the limits of constitutionalism, however, it seemed to be determined to fight its battles without compromise. It paid for its own politics, and was not afraid to publish its balance-sheet to the world. It was this which made the political scientist Ostrogorski describe it as 'a novel phenomenon in the life of English party organisation'. It governed itself by means of a supreme annual conference—a democratic device inherited from the trade unions, but not at that time accepted by any existing political party, for we must remember that the conferences of the National Liberal Federation had no control over the Liberal Party machinery. Further, the I.L.P. showed that, poor as it was, it could fight elections against both Liberals and Conservatives and yet secure polls that were no discredit to the cause. It was a party with a future; and, given the support of the trade unions, it was obvious that the future would be rich in Parliamentary success.

The greatest achievement of Keir Hardie and his I.L.P. lay in the capture of trade-union support as early as 1900. The whole strategy of the party from its foundation in 1893 was based on the conception of collaboration with trade unionists with the ultimate object of tapping trade-union funds for the attainment of Parliamentary power. It was primarily to defend this strategy that Hardie fought tooth and nail against fusion with the S.D.F. His attitude was justified by the behaviour of the S.D.F. leaders at the critical moment of the formation of the new party—their intransigence at the foundation conference and their decision eighteen months later to secede.

In 1900 Hardie retired from the chairmanship of the I.L.P., which he had held since the post was instituted. He had often previously made a show of wanting to give way to others, and he could no longer expect to be 'drafted' into office now that the immediate object of establishing an alliance with the unions had been achieved. Blatchford was continuing to demand that all officials of the party should be retired after a single year's service. This was a conception of democracy that Hardie believed to be utterly impractical, for he had learned from his own experience in trade unionism and politics that '... for a long time to come democracy—even social democracy—will mean finding the fit person, and loyally and generously trusting him or her in the performance of the allotted task'. He believed, with Carlyle, that history is made by great men, who can provide leadership for others. He was conscious that no one could guide the I.L.P. as well as himself, and in spite of all the principles of 'democracy' he was determined to continue giving it that guidance in the pages of the *Labour Leader,* which remained in his personal control. It was significant that whenever conference time came round he was careful to insert a note in the paper urging the branches not to follow the practice of binding their delegates to strict instructions, but to leave them free to be influenced by the debate, which would of course be dominated by himself and his colleagues.

Now that he had to leave the chairmanship, Hardie retired with good grace. The party was still devoted to his policy, and he was succeeded by a close personal friend, Bruce Glasier, a mild-tempered propagandist who had had a long career of activity since the early days of the Socialist League. Glasier had been a Clarion Van lecturer, and was in the almost unique position of being friendly with Blatchford as well as with Hardie. The I.L.P. was at this time deeply in debt, so deeply that the Council was only saved from bankruptcy by the generosity of wealthy supporters such as George Cadbury, who as a Quaker appreciated their stand against the war, and gave £500 to the election fund. But with Hardie's re-election to Parliament, and, in the following years, the reaction against imperialism, the I.L.P.'s position steadily improved, and it began to build itself up again and to gain fresh recruits. By 1906 it was as strong as it ever had been, even though it had not yet felt the full force of the Socialist revival of that time.

By contrast, the resignation of Hyndman from the leadership of the S.D.F. was pathetically undignified. At the turn of the century the impatient pioneer was in very low spirits, seeing the decline in numbers that the Federation had suffered and the weakening of its members' intransigence towards the Radicals. In September he admitted privately his 'utter disgust with the workers here in general, and with our own party in particular', and he added in a phrase all too typical of his own personal arrogance, 'Neither deserve to have men of ability from the educated class to serve them. . . . Liebknecht at any rate had the satisfaction of feeling the movement going well under him all his life.' In August 1901 he withdrew from the S.D.F. executive, complaining sadly of the lack of 'class consciousness and class antagonism' even among the members, and declaring himself 'deeply discouraged at the results of our long-continued propaganda'. Yet he too had left his closest associates in control of the organisation; at the very time that Hyndman retired, they were withdrawing the Federation from participation in the L.R.C.; and it was not long before he was again in office, flaying the rest of the Socialist movement with his incessant, bitter denunciations.

But the Labour Representation Committee represented an alliance of forces in which the Socialists, organised as such, were only a tiny fraction. ... The Labour Party was in fact not committed to Socialism as a political creed until 1918; and both before and after that date, but especially in the years of its existence, it contained many who were hostile to it.

All along, there is little doubt that most of the non-Socialist trade-union leaders would have been happy to stay in the Liberal Party—which most of them had belonged to in the past—if the Liberals had made arrangements for a larger representation of the working class among their Parliamentary candidates. Again and again, it was the fault of the official Liberal Party constituency caucuses that this did not happen; and it was the behaviour of these caucuses that set many of the leaders of the workers thinking in terms of a separate party. Even Keir Hardie's revolt at Mid-Lanark in 1888 had been directed, not against the policy of Gladstone, but against the system by which the local association chose its candidate. The subsequent success of the I.L.P. was largely due to the failure of its rival, the Labour Electoral Association, to make any satisfactory terms with the Liberal Party for the fuller representation of Labour. Threlfall himself, the trade-union leader who ran the L.E.A. and was responsible for the whole attempt to bargain with the Liberals on behalf of Labour, was forced to confess the complete failure of his policy. He wrote in 1894:

> Theoretically the caucus is a perfect machine, but in practice it is one-sided. ... It is a curious commentary upon this 'ideal system' that of the thirteen Labour members representing England and Wales in the present House, four ran in opposition to or without recognising the existence of the caucus, five represent constituencies where the miners absolutely dominate the position... and only four either captured the caucus or out-generalled it. It is only a waste of time to advise the working classes to attend and make the caucus what they want it to be. The fact is they distrust it—they regard it as a middle-class machine; they have neither the time nor the inclination to compete with the wire-pullers who work it, and they have a decided objection to being made the puppets of anyone. It has served its purpose, and it has carried the people through one state of their development: but as it exists to-day it is too narrow and too much hampered with class prejudice to be a reflex of the expanding democratic and labour sentiment.

It is true that the stubborn attitude of the local caucuses was realised and regretted by the principal leaders of the Liberal Party. Herbert

Gladstone, for instance, later to be Liberal Chief Whip, admitted: 'The long and short of it is that the constituencies, for social, financial, and trade reasons are extremely slow to adopt Labour candidates'. But the leaders could do little, the constitution of the party being what it was. Thomas Burt, himself a Liberal-Labour M.P., testified to their powerlessness in spite of their good-will. They could not force a Labour candidate on to a constituency: all that they could do, as Schnadhorst said, was to 'earnestly bespeak for him the generous support of the Liberal Association'. Further, as the Fabians discovered, the usual type of local association did not respond satisfactorily to attempts to permeate it with 'advanced' men, for, as they had to admit, the moment permeation was carried beyond a certain point it was nullified by 'the bankruptcy of the swamped caucus'—that is to say, the people with the money refused to go on financing it.

The principal reason why money was required was that there existed at this time no system for the payment of Members of Parliament: and here again the Liberal Party was found wanting. This was a reform that the Liberal leaders might well have taken up at a much earlier date than they did. If carried or at least urgently pressed by the 1892–5 Liberal government, it might have removed a main factor in the support given by the smaller unions to the idea of a separate Labour Party. E. Cowey of the Yorkshire Miners, a prominent Liberal-Labour leader, made this clear when he moved a resolution at the 1897 T.U.C. in favour of State payment of M.P.s:

> Mr. Cowey said that money was still the golden key that opened the door to a seat in the House of Commons. Only large and powerful societies could have their own members in the House, for only such societies could afford to keep their representatives in such a responsible and expensive position. For this reason he claimed that the payment of members was absolutely necessary to the success of the Labour movement.

Yet although it had figured in the Newcastle programme of 1891, it was not until 1911, after the Osborne judgment, that the Liberal Party found it desirable to give priority to this reform and to pass it into law; and in the meantime the small unions had wedded themselves to the Labour Party idea.

For these reasons it is not difficult to see why the Liberal Party failed to retain the popularity that it had once had among the responsible leaders of trade unionism. There was justice in Ramsay MacDonald's observation to Herbert Samuel: 'We didn't leave the Liberals. They kicked us out and slammed the door in our faces.' The failure of the Liberals to make any gesture of response to the growing electoral power of Labour was directly responsible for the early demise of the Labour Electoral Association. Founded originally in 1886, it reached the climax of its activities in 1891, when it was claimed that the delegates at its Congress represented an aggregate of 750,000 members of trade unions, of trades councils, and of ten local branches of the Association. The first two points in its political programme were demands for the State payment of M.P.s and the payment of Returning Officers' fees out of the rates. Yet the Liberal Party took almost no notice of it, and the result was that after the ignominy of two General Elections in which it secured no concessions, it faded away in 1895-6. In inverse ratio to the decline of the L.E.A., the I.L.P. steadily established itself in those years as the hope of the working class for a say in Parliament.

The early components of the Labour Party formed a curious mixture of political idealists and hard-headed trade unionists: of convinced Socialists and loyal but disheartened Gladstonians. The great difficulty the L.R.C. had to face was the maintenance of an independent political line by all its members. Richard Bell, one of the only two M.P.s representing the party in the 1900 Parliament, saw no need to hold himself aloof from the Liberals, and in 1904-5, when he refused to sign the Labour Party constitution, he had to be expelled. Similar trouble, though not leading to expulsion, was experienced with the three Labour M.P.s elected at by-elections before 1906: two of them—Shackleton and Arthur Henderson—had to be reprimanded in 1904 for appearing in support of a Liberal by-election candidate. It was only in 1906, with the election of a substantial group of thirty M.P.s who drew a regular salary from the L.R.C. fund, that the Labour Party was put on a firm footing inside Parliament.

Part of the trouble had arisen from the extreme weakness of the Socialist societies both numerically and financially, as compared with the trade unions. The contributions to the party funds were computed on the basis of the membership of the affiliated bodies, and even in 1901, before many trade unions had joined, the Socialist societies numbered less than one-sixteenth of the total affiliated membership. Matters were not improved in this respect by the secession of the S.D.F., for their two seats on the L.R.C. executive were assigned to extra union representatives, which considerably weakened the position of the Socialists. The Fabian Society had lost respect among the trade unionists for its willingness to compromise with jingoism; and the I.L.P. had so little support in the country that it was on the verge of utter bankruptcy. It is true that for reasons of prestige the I.L.P. regularly paid fees to the L.R.C. on a much higher figure of membership than it actually possessed: yet in 1906 this nominal figure was only 16,000, and the Socialist societies' proportion of the total contributing membership of the party had sunk to less than one-fiftieth.

Furthermore, many of the political difficulties of the Labour Party's early years arose from the fact that the I.L.P. itself, for all its insistence on the principles of independence, was frequently inclined to take the Liberal point of view. It was assumed as a matter of course that Free Trade was right and Protection wrong, since the latter was proposed by Joseph Chamberlain; and the strong Nonconformist ties of the party naturally led it to disapprove of the Education Act of 1902, which Sidney Webb had had a hand in designing. The *Manchester Guardian* was able to say of the 1901 I.L.P. conference that: 'What must strike a Liberal...

is, one would say, how much of the proceedings is devoted to the advocacy of traditional Liberal principles'. After Champion was finally discredited, the ex-Liberals had it all their own way in the leadership. Ramsay MacDonald, whom Hardie described as the party's 'greatest intellectual asset', sided with the Liberals against the Fabian 'old gang' on almost every immediate issue of the time; and Hardie, who had been much more friendly to the Radicals since the outbreak of the South African War, in 1903 actually wrote an open letter to John Morley, the great Liberal opponent of State intervention in industry, asking him to act as leader of the Labour Party. It was just at this time that Ramsay MacDonald, with Hardie's connivance, was arranging a secret electoral understanding with the Liberal whips. With the leaders of the Socialist wing acting in this fashion, how could the non-Socialist elements be expected to keep clear of Liberalism?

Still, by 1903 the new party machine was in existence, and whatever the political views of its officers, it soon began to build up among them a vested interest in its maintenance. The officials of the great trade unions had made up their minds in favour of a distinct party of their own, and so long as their industrial strength continued to grow, the strength of the political organisation would also increase. In the years that followed, there were doubts at times about the value of political action; there were personal feuds among the leaders as well as disagreements on policy; there were stresses and strains arising from war and revolution in Europe. Some of the unions, such as the Miners, suffered much in the vicissitudes of the British economy and became more radical; others, such as the new unions of 1889, moved in the opposite direction. But the unity of the party, once established, remained substantially intact, and in the first half-century of its life, every General Election but two that it fought resulted in an increase of the aggregate Labour poll. The association of Socialist faith and trade-union interest, of hope for an ideal future and fear for an endangered present, seemed on the point of disruption at times: yet it survived, for a variety of reasons which lie outside the compass of this book, but also because in the years before the party's birth there had been men and women who believed that the unity of the working-class movement, both in industry and politics, was an object to be striven for, just as now most of their successors regard it as an achievement to be maintained.

PART III
1906 to the Present

33

THE LABOR AND WELFARE POLICIES OF THE LIBERAL GOVERNMENT, 1906–1914

E. H. Phelps-Brown

The Liberal government that took office in 1906 had both an overwhelming majority and as great a collection of talent as any ministry in English history. The greatest expectations were held for this government, and its ultimate failure to stave off world war and to solve the Irish question, its breakup in 1916 under rather sordid conditions of personal feuding (which in turn contributed to the disintegration and decline of the Liberal Party), have led many historians and biographers to judge the last Liberal ministry quite severely. The account, therefore, given by the historical sociologist E. H. Phelps-Brown of the accomplishments of the Liberal government in effecting the full legal emancipation of labor unions and introducing the welfare state into England is particularly salutary and welcome and restores the balance towards a more judicious and sensible estimation of the work of Asquith, Lloyd George, Churchill, and their colleagues before the lights went out in Europe.

WHEN Labour swept the country in 1945, one of its first steps was to repeal lock, stock and barrel an Act restrictive of the unions which had been adopted after the General Strike. One of the first steps of the majority in the Parliament of 1906 was to sweep away the upshot of the Taff Vale judgment.

The Royal Commission that had been appointed to consider this law reported shortly after the election. Informed opinion had been agreed that though the unions should be given some shelter from the risks to which the Taff Vale judgment had exposed them, they could not possibly be exempted from all liability to be sued: that immunity they might long have enjoyed *de facto*, but once the Lords removed it, it was seen as too anomalous to be restored. This was the view taken by three of the Commission, including Sidney Webb; the other two were even less indulgent

---

FROM E. H. Phelps-Brown, *The Growth of British Industrial Relations* (London: Macmillan & Co. Ltd., 1959), pp. 294–311. By permission of St. Martin's Press, Inc., The Macmillan Company of Canada, Ltd., and Macmillan & Co. Ltd.

to the unions. The majority held that the immunity had never been conferred on principle, and had been only the unintended by-product of the rule adopted by the Courts of Common Law that damages could not be recovered from anyone not named as a defendant in the action —since every member of a union was a part owner of its funds, and must be held to have lost something if damages were paid out of them, the Courts would not levy any damages on them unless every man jack in the union had been named as a defendant, and this was impossible. But some Judges had suggested a new procedure: they pointed out that the representative action, by which damages could be claimed from the fund held in common by numerous persons if only certain representative figures among them had been named as defendants, could be extended to cover the trade union. Further, in the Taff Vale case, the House of Lords had found that a trade union could in any case be sued in its registered name. 'In short,' the majority said, 'it turns out that the notion of a Trade Union having been intended to be specially exempted from actions of tort is a mere misconception resting on no other foundation than long practical immunity, which was simply the result of defects in general legal procedure that have now been remedied on general considerations of equity quite irrespective of Trade Unions and Trade Union law. And the Taff Vale case shows that, even if the rules of general legal procedure were not available in the case of Trade Unions, nevertheless under the Act of 1871 registered Trade Unions would be liable to be sued in tort.'

So there was no question of going back on Taff Vale. But a union commonly had many members in many places, and it was hard that the funds of all should suffer for the unauthorized action of some one of them, so the law should furnish means 'whereby the Central Authorities of a Union may protect themselves against unauthorized and immediately disavowed actions of Branch Agents.' Also many unions combined the functions of a trade protection and bargaining agency with those of a benefit society, and damages awarded in respect of the first should not fall on the funds held for the second: these when segregated should be given immunity.

The bill that Campbell-Bannerman's government brought in followed the majority in the main principle of not removing the liability to be sued, and it gave the unions only the first of the two reliefs that the majority had recommended, providing in effect that an action for damages against a union should not lie unless the act complained of was committed with the authority of the union executive. But it also gave those acting on behalf of the unions some relief from the additions that the courts had made to the list of actionable wrongs. It dealt with civil conspiracy by providing that if two or more persons combined to do some act in contemplation or furtherance of a trade dispute, this act would not be actionable unless it would be so if one person did it alone. Peaceful persuasion was recognized as a legal object of picketing. Some actions taken in a trade dispute—applying a sympathetic strike or secondary boycott to an employer, for instance, or securing the dismissal of a non-unionist workman—interfere with a man's business, or his right to dispose of his capital or labour as he wills: the bill said they were not to be actionable on that ground alone. In saying this it did not go beyond what the House of Lords had already laid down in a decision of 1897, but the immunity was now made explicit.

The House accepted these supplementary provisions, and extended the last to cover also inducing the breach of a contract of employment. But on the main issue the majority wanted a cleaner sweep. Taff Vale had not been a dominant issue in the election, but it had been raised everywhere. The Liberals did not depend on Labour votes in the House, but they did in the constituencies, and most of them had given pledges. Campbell-Bannerman himself, it is said, preferred an outright clause. One such was before the House in a labour bill for whose second reading he himself voted. The bill the Government sent up to the Lords provided simply and completely that an action in tort against a trade union, in its own name or by representative action, should not be entertained by any court.

The Lords, preferring to stand on an issue that would not embroil them with the unions, let the bill through.

Something extraordinary had happened. 'That vast and powerful institutions', the majority of the Royal Commission had written, 'should be permanently licensed to apply the funds they possess to do wrong to others, and by that wrong inflict upon others damage perhaps to the amount of many thousand pounds, and yet not be liable to make redress out of those funds would be a state of things opposed to the very idea of law and order and justice.' Precisely that had been done now. Workpeople who have no quarrel with their own employer suddenly walk out, in breach of their own contracts of employment, because their union says they must stop him supplying some other manufacturer with whom it is in dispute; the stoppage is prolonged, and he suffers very heavy losses: he has no remedy against the union. A man who wants to go on working during a strike is knocked down by a picket the union has posted, and is crippled for life: the picket, if identified, may be punished for assault, and may be required to pay to the victim such damages as his own means permit; the funds of the union may be immense: the victim cannot draw a penny from them. Nor is the immunity of the union confined to trade disputes: alone among the press of the country the journals of trade unions can libel a man without his being able to recover damages from the proprietor. The Trade Disputes Act of 1906 declared that the union, like the King, could do no wrong.

The Crown has lost that immunity now, but the union has it still. We may well ask why. Perhaps the ultimate reason cannot be given without exploring the relations between the categories of law and the changing structure of society. But the immediate answer is, this anomaly was the price paid for the right to strike. In practice, if the funds of a union are liable to make good the damage caused by wrongful acts done on its behalf, it will lose heavily from time to time, and can never enter upon a trade dispute, even in ultimate self-defence, without apprehension of losing heavily. The remedy, it may be said, is to make sure that wrongful acts are not done: as the law stood after Taff Vale a union could still conduct a great strike, and so long as no wrongful act was committed the greatest loss suffered by employers or public would not enable anyone to recover a penny from it. But a union with many thousands of members in many places cannot exercise effective control over all the actions they take on its behalf. Especially when so many strikes were partial, or fought by the importation of blacklegs, they were likely to bring some struggle on the picket line. The liability to an action for damages was not inherent in strike and lock-out in principle, but it was in practice. So long as it was there the most conservative and orderly unions would hesitate to enter upon any stoppage. But for eighty years now the principle had been accepted that men might combine to withhold their labour in order to maintain or advance its price.

This case for the settlement of 1906 was reinforced by the knowledge that the new statute was not a leap in the dark, but only restored what had been the state of affairs *de facto* if not *de iure* for thirty years before Taff Vale. Under that dispensation industrial relations had improved, and they had improved most where the unions were strong. The lesson was that industrial peace was in practice most likely to be maintained not by the sanctions of law but by the goodwill of free agents.

To this we may add that discussion had failed to devise any satisfactory halfway house between the liability Taff Vale imposed and complete exemption. The suggested provision, for instance, whereby a union would not be liable for wrongful acts unless they were committed by, or with the authority of, its executive, or without subsequent repudiation by it, would have enabled unions with forethought and ingenuity to cover themselves against most claims: the difference would be only that the position was trickier.

None the less the regime of immunity had brought enough hardship to unoffending men for the Taff Vale judgment to be welcomed by many as the overthrow of an abusive power. Hardship was inflicted especially by the sympathetic strike or secondary boycott against those who were not parties to a dispute, and by the sanctions the unions applied against non-members. The remedy that had been found was to enable the sufferer to sue the union for damage. When that particular remedy was found objectionable, the suffering came to be regarded as irremediable in principle. But this was unnecessary. British law could have done then what American law does today, and safeguarded the right to withhold labour in combination pending agreement on the terms of employment, while forbidding other practices that make oppressive use of union power.

It was the railwaymen who had taken the knock of Taff Vale, and been most hampered by it afterwards: a union in settled relations with the employers could do something even if it had to be chary of striking, but a union refused recognition could do nothing at all. Now the railwaymen had a green light again, and at once they moved forward. In 1907 the country faced the imminent prospect of a stoppage of all its railways. That had never happened yet. It threatened a trial of strength approaching civil war. If it came about, men did not see how life could go on.

A sufficient cause of the railwaymen's discontent was that for twenty years they had been falling behind other wage-earners. Down to the 1880's they had been relatively highly paid, as one would expect in an expanding industry; but in the last twenty years industrial wage-rates generally had risen by a quarter, and theirs by hardly five per cent. Their hours, though somewhat reduced, remained exceptionally long: in 1907 the predominant week was of sixty hours, and not a few worked seventy-two, whereas the engineers and the builders had won the fifty-four-hour week in the 1870's. One reason for this relative recession was that the age of expansion of the railways was over: now they were rationalizing, economizing, and using more powerful engines and heavier trains so as to save labour. An expanding industry is likely to build up a labour force with a high proportion of younger men; when expansion stops these become in time a high proportion of older men, competing with one another for promotion and blocking the way of those who joined after them. So it came about that after the 1880's work on the railways lost the prospects of promotion that had once made it attractive.

But the check to the demand for railwaymen would hardly of itself have brought all the worsening of their comparative position that they actually suffered: they laboured also under a disadvantage that might almost be called accidental. At the end of the 1880's Parliament had taken in hand a general regulation of goods rates. The original object had been to hold them down, and the new schedules only prescribed maxima; but most of them when authorized proved to be higher than actual rates hitherto, and when they came into effect in 1893 most companies put their charges up to them. The indignation of traders at this, coming as it did after nearly twenty years of predominantly falling prices, was very great, and the next year Parliament adopted an extraordinary Act, laying it down that if someone should complain to the Railway Commissioners that any rise made since the end of 1892 was unreasonable, the burden of disproving that lay on the company, even though the rate lay below the maximum that Parliament itself had approved. The effect was to clamp most rates down in perpetuity. But precisely at this point the tide of prices turned, and year by year the railways had to pay more for their coal, their steel, their timber. In the 1880's their working expenses had always been less than 55 per cent of their receipts; by 1900 the ratio was up to 62 per cent. Dividends came down. At a time when a rise in the cost of living made it natural for the wages of railwaymen to go up too, the companies were under mounting pressure to keep them down.

This was a principal reason for the obstinate refusal of all the companies except the North Eastern to recognize the unions. Something was due to the tradition of discipline in the service, and something to the railway directors being an unenterprising lot—Charles Masterman, who was to see something of them from the Home Office in 1911, said they struck him 'as distinctly inferior in capacity and energy to most other big business men they had had to deal with'. But they would hardly have become so different in labour policy from most other big employers if they had not been in a cleft stick: they stuck to their traditional policy of not recognizing the unions because otherwise they thought their costs would be raised against rigid revenues. The remedy might have seemed to be to go to Parliament with the unions' support and ask for permission to raise their charges so far as was necessary to cover higher wages—such permission as was in fact to be given in 1913. But the Taff Vale judgment came, and brought them years of peace, and made them think they could go on as they were.

That was all changed by the Trade Disputes Act. Already in 1905 the members of the Railway Servants had been calling on head office to launch a national all-grades movement. Both terms had pointed meanings. Whereas hitherto each company dealt separately with the pay of its own employees, now the union was to seek a single agreement covering all the railways in the country. Whereas hitherto the pay of different grades had been fixed separately, and the men themselves had been grade-conscious, now they were to stand together and demand improvements for each and every grade. In November 1906 a conference drew the programme up. All its claims depended on one of them: 'the time had arrived when the members of the Society insist upon recognition of Mr Bell and the other head officials by the railway companies to negotiate on their behalf.'

Richard Bell himself was a moderate and cautious man: though he had entered Parliament under the auspices of the Labour Representation Committee in 1900, he had incurred the wrath of the left by supporting the Liberal against the Independent Labour candidate in a by-election. He moved cautiously now. When his request for a meeting, simultaneously submitted to all the companies, was rejected by all except the North Eastern, he did but repeat it. It was rejected again, as was the plea for recognition that the Locomotive Engineers had made quite independently. In the summer of 1907 it became apparent that the resentment of union members was mounting fast and high. The companies stressed what a small part the unionists formed of all railwaymen, and their spokesman Lord Claud Hamilton appealed for the support of the public in 'the stand we are making to preserve for ourselves and the staff we employ the right to continue to enjoy the privileges of free citizens, untrammelled by the coercion and tyranny of an outside, irresponsible body'. In July Bell approached the companies for a third time, with no more success. In October his union voted overwhelmingly for a strike.

There was only one way, Lloyd George as President of the Board of Trade advised the Prime Minister, to avoid catastrophe, if the Directors refused conciliation. 'We must, when Parliament meets, at once introduce a measure making arbitration in railway disputes compulsory in all cases where the Board of Trade consider the nature and magnitude of the dispute warrants such a course being adopted.... The Conciliation Act itself is a poor thing. It is only the knowledge that there is something behind it that will induce the Directors to pay any attention to it.' Against the advice of his officials Lloyd George intervened, and it was the employers he went for. He would put to them a plan for joint boards of conciliation on the pattern of coal, and iron and steel—'failing that, the steamroller,' he told his brother. 'The Companies must give way on that point I am definite.' Ten days later he wrote, 'All day with the Directors. In the morning I had to threaten them. Told them that there must not be a strike on any account.' He brought the union leaders to the Board of Trade, but still the employers would not deal with them. The two parties sat in separate rooms, and even when by going to and fro he got their agreement, the employers would not sign a joint statement, but each side gave its adhesion separately.

Nor did the scheme itself require the companies to recognize the unions. It provided only that company by company, and section by section, boards of conciliation should be set up, in which employees who had been elected by their fellows would meet some of the managers immediately concerned, to discuss wages and hours, so far as these could not be settled in the usual way. If the sectional board could not agree, the issue would go to a central board for each railway, and if this could not agree, it would go to a single arbiter. How he would hear the case was for him to decide: the agreement said nothing; if he chose to hear the men's side from the lips of a union officer, he could.

In fact, it was expected that he would. The companies had saved the form, the union had won something in substance. Its officers could still not deal with management, but in practice they could get management taken to arbitration on any issue of wages and hours, and they were not debarred from themselves appearing before the arbitrator.

The Locomotive Engineers and the General Railway Workers adhered to this agreement the same day. The North Eastern railway was not a party to it, but later set up a scheme of conciliation by direct agreement with the unions, other than the clerks, whose unionization it resented and tried to repress.

Lloyd George's settlement in 1907 was a landmark in more ways than one. Once before, in 1893, the government had been brought in by the shortage of essential supplies consequent upon an industrial dispute, but the stoppage in the coal industry then was by no means complete, and supplies were exhausted only gradually: this time the dislocation was expected to be so swift and overwhelming that the mere threat of it was enough to bring the Government in. And it intervened now not to conciliate but to force a settlement on the employers under threat of special legislation. At a time when most of the institutions of industrial relations were confined to particular districts, it imposed common institutions on virtually a whole industry. Once again an industry-wide agreement on procedure had been reached before there was any industry-wide bargaining.

Save for a notable extension of workmen's compensation, the Government had achieved little as yet for 'the condition of England question': in the next four years it laid the whole foundations of the welfare state. Mostly this was the work of 'the terrible twins'. On the reconstruction of the Government in April 1908, Lloyd George became Chancellor of the Exchequer and Winston Churchill President of the Board of Trade. Experimentally minded, combative, kindled with the thought of a new social order, these two picked up the ideas and improvised the agencies of a nation-wide attack on destitution. By impulse Lloyd George was Labour. His account of one conference has been recorded. ' "There", he said, "were the employers on the one hand, plump, full-fed men, well dressed—men who had never known what it was to go short in their lives. On the other side were the men, great gaunt fellows, pale with working underground, their faces all torn (drawing his own nails down his cheeks) with anxiety and hard work." He made a sort of gesture of dismissal. "I know which side I am on when I see that sort of thing," he said.' Churchill's impulsive sympathies were partly Tory, and he was ambivalent towards labour when it was in revolt and his strategic responsibility for maintaining supplies or deploying the forces of law and order aroused the warhorse in him; but with his humane and venturous imagination he entered into the lot of the poor, and when he met the men's leaders he warmed to them with his outgoing friendliness and his liking for a bonny fighter. 'Slightly bent, hesitant of speech, almost an apologetic manner, youth left in mobile features, ready for boyish fun, the cares of office sitting lightly on a good-sized brow, eyes that sparkle with a wistfulness almost sweet'—that was how Ben Tillett saw him in the dock strike of 1911. 'If patience and courtesy, if anxious effort and sincerity count for respect, then Winston Churchill is entitled as a man to gratitude.'

The measures Lloyd George and Churchill took up were mostly to be found in the stock of proposals assembled by the unions. When the unions recovered their effective freedom to strike in 1906, they turned (save the railwaymen) not to industrial action but to Parliament. The report of the Parliamentary Committee to Congress in 1907 said 'One lesson, at any rate, can be enforced from the Parliamentary work of the past eighteen months, and that is the political power that lies in the hands of labour. It is overwhelmingly within the competence of labour to alter the present unequal state of society.... We urge our members to take up the following social and industrial reforms:

1. Miners' legal eight-hour day, and a reduction in hours in all trades.
2. Old age pensions.
3. Unemployed.
4. Compulsory State insurance.
5. Land nationalization.
6. Amendment of the Poor Laws.
7. Legal restriction of systematic overtime.
8. Housing of the working classes.'

The Government was now to take action under the first four of those heads, thereby effectively doing something under the sixth as well, and the gesture it made under the fifth involved it in a crisis of the constitution.

One reason for its carrying out the unions' programme was the one they vaunted, their own political power. But there was another. The use of governmental agencies to tackle poverty was a leap in the dark in those days, and there were many wise men who believed it a perilous one. Any government intent on doing something would therefore draw as much as possible from the lessons of other people's experience. This was to be found partly overseas, notably in Germany and Australia and New Zealand, and partly in the practice of our own friendly societies and trade unions. We have seen how the trade unions had already worked out provisions against most of the contingencies that caused destitution: the legislative programme they had in mind was only a generalization, with support from the taxpayer, of the means they had long tried and tested within their own societies of meeting what they knew to be the foremost needs. Any government that sought the same end would have taken much the same road as they even without their prodding it.

But they did prod the Liberal Government continually. Soon after the election one of their delegations had waited on Campbell-Bannerman and Asquith to call for old age pensions, and it was here that the attack on poverty opened when Asquith in his budget of 1908 made financial provision for the Old Age Pensions Bill that Lloyd George brought in. The pensions were to be non-contributory, paid for entirely by the taxpayer. They brought five shillings a week—say a quarter of the labourer's wage—to men and women of seventy who had no more than £21 a year coming in already, smaller sums for those with between £21 and £31, and nothing beyond. If husband and wife were both eligible, they got at most 7s. 6d. between them. By 1913 the annual cost was over £12 millions, nearly half as much as that of the army. Of the many schemes that had long been before the public, most were contributory, and Bismarck's Law of 1889 had shared the cost between workpeople, employers, and taxpayers. But the Danes had had a system of non-contributory pensions since 1891, and a Select Committee under high Tory chairmanship had recommended in 1899 that we adopt something very like it; by now too there was a precedent of ten years' standing in New Zealand. Since, moreover, any self-supporting scheme could pay out next to nothing for twenty years and pensions would have to rest on the public purse meanwhile, the Government took the plunge, and laid them on it in perpetuity.

We are told how the pension transformed the world for the old folk living in daily fear of the workhouse in a hamlet of Oxfordshire. 'At first when they went to the Post Office to draw it, tears of gratitude would run down the cheeks of some, and they would say as they picked up their money, "God bless that Lord George! [for they could not believe one so powerful and munificent could be a plain 'Mr'] and God bless *you*, miss!" and there were flowers from their gardens and apples from their trees for the girl who merely handed them the money.'

Unemployment was next to be dealt with. The last Tory Government had already accepted the principle that the taxpayer's money might be spent on helping the unemployed outside the Poor Law, but the problem was how to help effectively. That was up to John Burns at the Local Government Board, but 'the man with the Red Flag' was a stick-in-the-mud minister, hiding fear of his own incapacity behind his officials' reasons for inaction. So a joint board of unions and Labour members drafted their own bill: it followed a traditional approach in taking the problem to be chiefly one of rehabilitation, and its main proposal was to settle the unemployed in farm colonies. There was an echo in that, going back to Charterville and beyond, of a deep longing of the workman whom the growth of population had denied access to the land. But the experiments recently made at Hollesley Bay and Osea Island showed how hard it was to move that way. Meanwhile, however, the boom which had kept jobs plentiful through the first eighteen months of the new government ended abruptly. Some recessions have been gradual, but this one was sharp, and the very rate at which men began to lose their jobs in August 1907 added to the alarm. In 1908 the proportion of wage-earners out of work was bigger than it had been since 1886, the year of Bloody Sunday in Trafalgar Square, and the absolute numbers now were even higher. The resentment was higher still. The Government had to do something.

It would not act, as we should expect a government to do today, to raise the flow of spending on consumption and investment at home: those channels had not been charted yet. But it could do something to help the men who were out of work. Two measures seemed practicable —employment exchanges, and unemployment insurance.

Experiments with 'labour bureaux' went back more than twenty years: in particular, a number of London boroughs had set them up. But they were associated with the relief of distress, so the good workman would not go to them, nor the employer look for him there. Abroad it was very different: Germany was using public labour exchanges extensively, Austria, Belgium, France, Norway and Switzerland had them or were going in for them. The Poor Law Commission set up at the end of 1905 had been instructed to inquire into means outside the Poor Law of meeting distress arising from unemployment, and when its massive majority and minority reports appeared in February 1909 they agreed in recommending a national system of Labour Exchanges. In May Churchill brought a Bill for one before Parliament, it became law in September, and the first exchanges opened the next February. Effective action could be taken swiftly because an exceptional Minister was at the Board of Trade then with two outstanding civil servants, Llewellyn Smith and Beveridge; and also because there was little resistance.

The unions, it is true, had had misgivings. It happened that thereby they first attained the status of an estate of the realm. They had been afraid that the Exchanges would be used to supply blacklegs, or would require men to take jobs below the union rate. Churchill not only worked through these anxieties with the Parliamentary Committee of

Congress, but asked it to set up a sub-committee that he could consult continuously on the administration of the Act, and he made the President of Congress a member of the committee of three to which he handed over the filling of all but the highest posts in the system of Exchanges. In fact, many of those appointed were trade union officers—Richard Bell among them, who had led the railwaymen through the Taff Vale law suits and the crisis of 1907. The unions must have lost much administrative capacity. But they felt they had a new status: delegations they had sent to Ministers in plenty before, but this was something new.

Once the unions' fears were assuaged, at least no one thought the Exchanges would do much harm, but unemployment insurance was a very different matter. It ran the obvious risks of subsidizing underemployment and pampering the ne'er do well. Even Germany had stopped short of it—there had been no instructive experiment overseas, only a fiasco in one Swiss canton. Though both reports of the Poor Law Commission had looked towards it, the majority thought it needed more consideration, the minority preferred subsidizing the out of work donation of the unions. To set out upon it now was, as Beveridge said later, 'a daring adventure'. But Churchill had daring, and Llewellyn Smith and Beveridge brought unrivalled knowledge to bear, and powerful minds fertile in expedients. They designed a scheme that would confine benefit to men who wanted to be and usually were in work, but were sometimes out of a job by reason of industrial fluctuations. Accordingly it was confined to a limited list of industries where that sort of unemployment was most marked, leaving out the steady trades on the one hand and the casual ones on the other: those it covered contained about one in six of all wage-earners. Since its object, within its practicable enclave, was to help the majority who were not supported by trade union benefit already, it had to be made compulsory and general; but its benefit could be paid through the unions within the industries it covered, and there was provision for a subsidy to unions that relieved unemployment outside them. Unlike old age pensions, unemployment insurance could be made contributory from the first, because there was no actuarial principle in the field to make using one man's current subscription to pay another's current benefit seem improper; so contributory it was made, but the taxpayer added a third to the joint contribution of employer and workman.

It took time to work all this out. It came from Parliament only as Part II of the National Insurance Act of 1911, and the first benefit was not paid until January 1913.

The same Act brought health insurance in. It followed a German model already tried for more than twenty years in practice, and it covered virtually all the wage-earners. In practice it was much more than a scheme of insurance, it was an organization of the medical service with a bigger staff of doctors, and wage-earners now began to get medical care in a regular way unknown to many of them before. It was Lloyd George's adroitness and darting energy that made this rearrangement possible. He

In England, as, of course, in other countries of Western Europe conditions were more complicated. There existed a strongly entrenched social system which limited social mobility, a social system inherited from pre-industrial times when landowners were the ruling groups. Moreover, there were sources of power and prestige besides business. Landownership, bureaucracy, the army and the professions were all powerful competitors of business for the services of the able men. There was therefore a haemorrhage of capital and ability from industry and trade into landownership and politics. Robert Peel and Gladstone both came of entrepreneurial familes, but their abilities were devoted to politics not to industry and trade.

In particular the high social standing of the professions drew off a large number of the ablest men. One of the most successful British entrepreneurs of the twentieth century, Lord Nuffield, is said to have entered business only because his father was unable, for economic reasons, to fulfil his original intention of making him a surgeon. In England in the first forty years or so of the century, the professions attracted too many able people and business too few. After 1902, there was a vast increase in educational opportunities in England, but of those who profited from such opportunities up to 1939 many more became teachers or lawyers, doctors or architects than business men. Why were the professions more attractive? Certainly not because they yielded higher incomes; it was partly because, for a person with no personal contacts in business, the professions were more accessible, and partly because business in general lacked the social prestige of the professions. Moreover in the present century a business career and the acquisition of profit became actively disapproved of among the many people who were influenced by socialist ideas about capitalism and the profit motive. In England, therefore, as in Western Europe generally, business has had to face greater competition for the able men than it has had to face in the U.S.A. The wider the circle from which a country draws its business men, the more likely it is to produce great entrepreneurs.

Moreover, much the same circumstances which facilitated the recruitment of entrepreneurs in America were also favourable to the performance of men once they had become entrepreneurs. In the United States, almost from the beginning, birth and hereditary status were of small influence in determining a man's social standing as compared with the highly efficient performance of a specific and limited function. There the man who concentrated his energies on a single goal and achieved success in his occupation was the man who commanded respect; the accepted ideal was that he should rise as far in terms of wealth as his abilities could carry him. A man's success in his occupation was not invariably judged by the amount of money he made. Some occupations were very highly regarded which did not yield very high rewards, for example, membership of the Supreme Court, but income was certainly an important criterion of occupational success. The signs of social standing could more easily be acquired with money. In England, on the other would himself have liked a complete national health service: he advanced towards it now up to the limits of the politically practicable. One of the ideas he took up was that it should not by-pass but utilize the existing friendly societies, including those trade unions that gave friendly benefits. The insured were encouraged to join an approved society. That was a powerful argument for the organizer, and one of the reasons why the unions gained nearly a million members in the next two years.

We saw how a higher proportion of children than of grownups was in poverty: something was done to help the children now. Already in 1906 an Act had provided for the feeding of hungry children at school. One of 1907 provided for the medical inspection of schoolchildren, after the German pattern. At the same time the first step was taken on a path of utmost social consequence: a higher grant was offered to the secondary schools that would give a quarter of their places without fee to boys and girls from the elementary schools. The education of children from middle-class homes was helped when Lloyd George's budget of 1909 first gave income tax relief for children. By 1914 the number of places in grant-aided secondary schools had been nearly doubled: even at that they provided for less than seven per cent of the children aged fourteen to seventeen in Great Britain. In 1908 came the Children's Act, a charter bringing many provisions together against such evils as baby-farming, maltreatment by drunken parents, children smoking and drinking, vermin on children; it stopped the imprisonment of children under fourteen, and regulated the reformatories to which they might be sent instead.

All these measures tackled the poverty that was brought by life's misfortunes and exigencies, but there was also the poverty simply due to low wages. We have seen how the idea had been worked out of boards to arrive at minimal terms and conditions that should then be made legally binding for particular groups of wage-earners; but also how the campaign for them had failed. Now an Anti-Sweating League revived it, and attention was drawn to the boards in Victoria that had actually been working for ten years without any apparent trouble. An investigator sent out by the Home Secretary reported very cautiously that the experience of Victoria had been 'too brief, too simple, and too exclusively connected with an era of prosperous trade' to be conclusive; the distinguishable effects of the boards on wages were slight; but he was clear that the boards were 'greatly valued and widely believed in' because they gave a sense of security and fairness. He also made the point that they were looked on as a natural extension of the Factory Acts. That was taken up by a Select Committee of the Commons which now investigated the most desperate form of sweating, namely home work, and in recommending a limited and experimental use of boards held that it was as legitimate to enforce a minimum standard of pay by law as one of sanitation or hours of work.

What had once seemed a leap in the dark now appeared only as a short step forward on a familiar path. Churchill took it. Under his Trade Boards Act of 1909 three boards were set up—for Black Country chain making, paper box making, and the making of 'ready made and wholesale bespoke male garments'. There were three independent members in each board, including the chairman, and equal numbers of employers, and persons appointed as spokesmen for the workpeople. When the board, by majority if need be, arrived at a recommendation concerning wages or hours, it went to the President of the Board of Trade; he allowed an interval for objections; he might refer the recommendation back to the board, but could not alter it; in due course he would normally embody it in an order, and then any employer who paid less was liable to prosecution by the Crown and to civil action by the employee for recovery of wages underpaid. The fact that the employee had freely agreed to take less would give the employer no defence.

The experiment was being tried on a narrow front, and even there moved slowly—not till February 1913 was the first order issued. The workpeople it affected were at first almost all women: the trade unions thought little of it accordingly, and made no move to extend it into their own fields of interest—many unionists had as unaffected a dislike as any employer of seeing the Government take a hand in fixing men's wages.

Even if some folk had not been so much too poor, it still seemed to many who stood near the Government that some folk were too rich. An attack on the inequality of wealth by making the wealthy pay higher taxes forms a distinct strand in the Government's policy. It was pushed on by the need to raise more revenue to pay for the attack on poverty, but it was an end in itself. Asquith in 1907 first differentiated between earned and unearned income. True, he did it only by giving a reduction of the standard rate of income tax—from a shilling in the £ to ninepence —to the smaller earned incomes, while withholding it from others. It had indeed long been argued, on the strictest principles of proportionality, that an income which would come to an end with the working energies of the earner, and out of which he had to make provision for old age, should pay less while it lasted than an income from property that ran on in perpetuity. But the implication that the unearned income was somehow less deserved and socially justified leapt to the eye when Lloyd George put his land value duties into his budget, and joined them with a super-tax. The land value duties were far from swingeing—twenty per cent on the 'unearned increment', to be paid when the land was sold, and a halfpenny in the £ on the capital value of undeveloped land; the super-tax was only of sixpence in the £ on incomes over £5,000—say £15,000 in the money of the later 1950's. But the fury with which these measures were opposed was aroused by the principles they were felt to rest on—that owning was less reputable than earning; that the budget should be used to make incomes more equal.

There was fury again in an outcry against national health insurance two years later. Twice the Albert Hall was packed with women pledging themselves not to stamp their servants' cards. This sort of reaction is not just the normal human resistance to paying more out: its disproportion suggests not so much the reasoned defence of self-interest as the gnawing of an unacknowledged anxiety. In the human heart much is linked with its opposite, and pride in the power of wealth carries with it an uneasy sense of personal dependence. The rich man is like a baby in that the way he lives depends on other people doing most things for him, and when they turn on him he may be as terror-struck by his own helplessness as a baby that feels itself deserted. But for insecurity nature's remedy is aggression.

Some of the well-to-do will also have felt themselves attacked in their self-respect. National insurance implied that they had failed in their accepted duty of looking after their dependents.

34

RUPERT BROOKE—SYMBOL OF AN AGE

George Dangerfield

Three decades after its publication, by far the most exciting and cogent view of pre-World War I culture, society, and politics is still George Dangerfield's The Strange Death of Liberal England. In the following selection from this beautifully written and imaginative book, Dangerfield uses the personality of the universally admired poet and war martyr Rupert Brooke as a symbol of the sickness in the soul of Liberal England. After the publication of this extremely controversial work Dangerfield moved from England to the United States and has devoted himself exclusively to the writing of prize-winning works on American history. This selection demonstrates that English history's loss was very much American history's gain.

THE LOFTY SHADE, the hastening sound, are not to be discerned nor heard in the poems of Rupert Brooke. And yet, in the opinion of his friends and of a small but increasing public, he was the poet of young England: after his death a larger public reached the same conclusion, and with more enthusiasm. He was then, of course, the poet of

---

FROM George Dangerfield, *The Strange Death of Liberal England, 1910–1914* (New York: Capricorn Books, 1961, Copyright © 1935 by George Dangerfield), pp. 429–442. Reprinted by permission of Ann Elmo Agency, Inc., 545 Fifth Avenue, New York 17, N.Y. By permission of MacGibbon and Kee, Ltd.

a vanished England. But in either case he was considered the representative of all that was best in his times, to have embodied in a curious way the spirit of a lost generation. This may have been true. But it does not mean that he was, even in that vanished England and among that slaughtered generation, a modern poet. Art anticipates. Certain types of human being simply do not exist until a novelist has created them, nature labors to mold herself after the work of a great painter, and truly "contemporary" poetry is engaged with the shape of things to come. Brooke's poetry was sufficiently eager to appear new, but its best effects had already been anticipated and surpassed; it was born old-fashioned. Hopkins (whom unfortunately he had no chance to read) was far more modern than he, so was Housman, and the prosodic enterprise of Robert Bridges has revealed certain lyric qualities which we are only beginning to appreciate today. These men would have seemed to the readers of *Georgian Poetry* the voices of the past: and yet, sad to say, it is *Georgian Poetry* which has slipped soundlessly into the past, while the voices of Hopkins and Housman and Bridges remain.

But to the examiner of pre-war England, its youngest poetry is full of meaning. How faithfully that poetry sought the refuge of the past and found—in the sunlit ruins of the Romantic Revival—a place where the encroaching sounds and fears of the twentieth century were quite unheard and unfelt. There was no Poets' Rebellion. Until the very outbreak of war, the poets stayed unresponsive to the changing times; stubborn, sweet, unreal, they were the last victims and the last heroes of Liberal England. And in the midst of them, a little in front of them, as one who takes his place before an effective background, there stands the engaging figure of Rupert Brooke.

The son of a Rugby master, and grandson of a Canon of Bath, Rupert Brooke was born in 1887 and educated at Rugby and Cambridge, appropriately the University of poets. Of his last term at Rugby he wrote: "As I looked back upon five years I seemed to see almost every hour golden and radiant, and always increasing in beauty as I grew more conscious." It was true that he thereupon became aware of "transience, and parting, and a great many other things," and that he subsequently expressed this awareness both in prose and in verse; but somehow or other it was never very convincing. *Golden and radiant and always increasing in beauty*—this was to be the theme of Brooke's life. It was also, in a time of profound revolution in thought and behavior, the main theme of *Georgian Poetry*, with a gentle counterpoint of formal sorrow and happy despair.

At Cambridge Brooke assumed, imperceptibly, unaffectedly, a leading place—he was sincere, friendly, shy but not modest, astonishing to look at. Nor is it surprising that at Cambridge, "whose cloisters have ever been consecrated to poetry," he should have become a poetical socialist, that he should have fallen under the spell of the Sidney Webbs. Undoubtedly the shape of their arguments—the strong prose, the vigorous thought, the feeling that infuses the whole of lives given up to the betterment of mankind—blinded him to the meager conclusions which might be found at the end of them. As Edward Marsh says, who wrote a Memoir of him, "Rupert wore his socialism with a difference." He did, indeed. Class-consciousness he found "not inspiring"; what he tried to hammer into the heads of his fellow socialists was a faith in the goodness of man. But sometimes even he was forced to doubt. Sometimes it seemed that goodness alone would not bring about the necessary millennium; and then he began to wonder, with infinite reluctance, whether "the best hope isn't in an upheaval of some kind," though speculations like these always gave him pain. Such was the socialism of Rupert Brooke, and it would be unkind to expect more of a young man who once said to a fellow member of the radical *Carbonari*—"There are only three things in the world. One is to read poetry, another is to write poetry, and the best of all is to live poetry."

Yet he was not one of those *dilettante* socialists who, arguing for effect and amusement, and because it was the fashion, were drifting already through the drawing rooms of Mayfair. He pitied the poor man with all the sincerity which springs from an enthusiastic heart and a comfortable income. He genuinely longed for the reform of abuses and the destruction of privilege. If only everyone—rich and poor, worker and capitalist—would just be good! Meanwhile one could live the life of poetry.

It might seem, even when we separate from these sentiments those which rightly belong to the stage-play of youth, that here was a young man who was unconsciously something of a *poseur*. But this was not the case. The memories of all who knew him are filled with affection, love, reverence; and the young poet who emerges from them is not merely a charming but a candid figure. And yet—there is no doubt about it—he was always in flight from reality, not fearfully, but rather as one who exercises for the sake of his figure. He fled from it into the practice of verse and the examination of Elizabethan drama; into Ibsen, and the English countryside, and the Common Room of King's; into America, Honolulu, Samoa, Fiji, and Tahiti. Reality was faint but dauntless. It pursued him into uniform and brought him within sound of the German guns at Antwerp; and when he died at last of blood-poisoning in the Homeric island of Scyros, it might have permitted itself a smile of satisfaction. But even then, one cannot help feeling, it arrived too late: he had escaped into Death, with his illusions and his beauty untarnished, just one jump ahead.

This unreality pervades the pre-war volumes of *Georgian Poetry*, to which Brooke was the most typical and eventually the most admired contributor. As one reads through those volumes again, it is a vision of England which seems to haunt them and to give their long exhausted ecstasies that lingering magic. But what an England!—the rural England of Shakespeare and Milton and Wordsworth and Hopkins, gone very soft at the heart. It is an England surprised at those exceptionally becoming moments when "stars into the twilight steer, Or thrushes build among the may, Or wonder moves between the hills"—*that* kind of an England; an England where passion perspires roses, and the abandoned heart slowly freezes into the sweet complacency of an ice cream; where it is almost always either spring or autumn, or exactly midsummer; where "I go round corners on the roads"—so Brooke wrote one March—"shivering and nearly crying with suspense"; where sorrow dies with sunset and even despair is crowned with new-mown hay. That such a vision could spring from a deep love of the country, a real national pride, is altogether beyond doubt; nor is it by any means, or at its most crepuscular, a fading vision. Writers like H. V. Morton still pursue it with diligence and profit, and there is hardly a man who knows that countryside but has experienced it. The strange thing is that it should have been concentrated, unsupported by theories or philosophies, among a group of highly intelligent young men, and—stranger still—that it should have been crowned with the glittering laurels of critical applause.

Could it be that the Georgian poets were truly representative, in some way, of pre-war England? and if this is the case, what did they represent? Did they, as they flattered themselves, awaken a new spirit—at once subtle and fresh—in the heart of English poetry? or were their poems the effect and not the cause of a less particular, a more public emotion? The more one ponders these questions, the more it seems as if they were in whole what the youth of England was in part; that their romantic unrealities came chiefly up from the immature soul of a doomed generation. Immaturity is infectious. In the memoirs of the time the young people—from such glimpses of them as we are vouchsafed—seem at once to fear and to long for reality, and to increase by some inner confusion that outer violence which has been the subject of this book. When War came they welcomed it with a cry of eagerness, as if they had been rescued from the lavender-scented, the nightmare-haunted embrace of a large feather bed.

To this state of mind the pages of *Georgian Poetry* bear evidence. There are people who say, and they may be right, that poetry is not evidence of anything; but where, then, *are* you to look? The novels of Saki seem to promise, on first sight, a careful picture of the youth of the times: but the novels of Saki actually present us with (1) a portrait of Saki— witty, cruel, childish, with a gift for admiring all the wrong things, and (2) a singular anticipation of the young men of 1925. You may search the contemporary writings of Shaw, Wells, Conrad, Galsworthy, Maugham, and search in vain, for a detailed picture of the pre-war young men. Important writing, strange to say, rarely gives the exact flavor of its period; if it is successful it presents you with the soul of man, undated. Very minor literature, on the other hand, is the Baedeker of the soul, and will guide you through the curious relics, the tumbledown buildings, the flimsy palaces, the false pagodas, the distorted and fantastical and faery vistas which have cluttered the imagination of mankind at this or that brief period of its history. If the soft and ripe countryside of *Georgian Poetry* is insufficient for 1910–1914, one might turn to Compton Mackenzie's *Sinister Street,* a novel which the public devoured with shuddering relish just before the war. There is a great deal of good writing in this book, the characters have life, and the first volume, especially, is haunted with a sense of present changes and calamities to come. And yet —it is really very strange—whenever a scene of great importance is to be played, or a situation of extra subtlery to be explored, it has to take place before the glimmer of ecclesiastical candles, or in summer orchards soaked in moonlight and dew. The youthful characters, in spite of their eagerness, their outward look, are dragged back and smothered in this unreal scenery, and the story, pulled simultaneously backward and forward, collapses. *Sinister Street* is second-rate. But it is also highly significant. It has embodied in a very readable form the confusions of a generation. It was from these confusions that *Georgian Poetry* provided a refuge, both for those who read it and for those who wrote it.

Apart for their craving for the unreal, their romance, their ability to communicate with apparent distinction the most undistinguished of emotions, these pre-war poets seem also to have been blessed—or was it cursed?—with an unusual innocence. (The critic might venture to suggest that this was not so much innocence as childishness; that the Romantic Revival, now senile to a degree, was on its deathbed and babbling o' green fields. But let that pass.) Theirs was a level innocence, easily irritated into ecstasy and easily abashed into despair, and nowhere is it more noticeable than in the work of Rupert Brooke. His poem called *Lust* is particularly striking; it begins "How should I know?" And there are some lines from *The Great Lover* which deserve quotation:

> These I have loved:
>   White plates and cups clean-gleaming,
> Ringed with blue lines; and feathery, faery dust;
> Wet roofs, beneath the lamp-light; the strong crust
> Of friendly bread; and many-tasting food;
> Rainbows; and the blue bitter smoke of wood.
>   .   .   .   .
> Then, the cool kindliness of sheets, that soon
> Smooth away trouble; and the rough male kiss
> Of blankets; grainy wood; live hair that is
> Shining and free; blue-massing clouds; the keen
> Unpassioned beauty of a great machine;
> The benison of hot water; furs to touch;
> The good smell of old clothes and other such—
> The comfortable smell of friendly fingers,
> Hair's fragrance, and the musty reek that lingers
> About dead leaves and last year's ferns....

These are pleasing lines—rather more than pleasing, in a quiet way. Only one is shocked to realize that both poet and public thought them not inconsistent with their title, and that the sentiment at the heart of them was much admired. Yet anything could happen in those days. Harold Monro, as gifted a poet as any and more gifted than most, was able to write some verses in which he berated man for not being more grateful to his furniture and kitchen utensils, those faithful companions which follow life "not far behind." And nobody thought this at all odd. Was it the poet who was to blame? or was it that haunted and bewildered and inexplicable and rather sorry phenomenon—the soul of Liberal England?

The Georgian poets were certainly persuasive. How eager they were, how tremulous, and melancholy, and musical! And who deserved these epithets more than Rupert Brooke? Taste should have made him ridiculous by now; history should have made him tragic: and yet he has escaped both ridicule and tragedy. If he had been born thirty years earlier or later... But one can only see him, poised, in an attitude of highly attractive unawareness, on the cross-roads of history.

> A young Apollo, golden-haired,
> Stands dreaming on the verge of strife,
> Magnificently unprepared
> For the long littleness of life.

This epigram was written about Brooke while still an undergraduate, by Frances Cornford. That it should have been highly thought of at the time need occasion us no surprise when we consider that another poem of hers, beginning

> Oh fat white woman, whom nobody loves,
> Why do you walk through the fields in gloves,
> Missing so much and so much...

was regarded almost with veneration. She was very Georgian. But the epigram, none the less, is an appropriate one, it suits very well with the portraits of Brooke. If a man's destiny is written on his face, then Brooke, you might think, was destined to become a legend. He was beautiful; he composed verses: the combination is irresistible. And yet there is something—some shadow flitting from mouth to eyes, elusive and disturbing—which makes you pause and think again. Is it mockery which you discern there? or inspiration? or challenge? or is it perhaps—uneasiness? "Magnificently unprepared" has a fatal ring. Was he destined to become a legend; or was he doomed, after all, to finish up as nothing more than an epigram?

On May 22, 1913, he set forth on a year of travel. He was to go to America first, and come home by way of the Pacific Ocean. The record of his wanderings will be found, in a series of letters and verses, in Edward Marsh's admirable *Memoir* which prefaces *The Collected Poems of Rupert Brooke*. The verses are fragmentary, and the letters chiefly distinguished for that intimate charm, that gift for offering himself unreservedly to his friends, which their author possessed above almost all the men of his time. They also have the quality of an exclamation mark. American hospitality he loved—"Oh, dear, the tears quite well up into my eyes when I think of a group of young Harvard people I tumbled into—at Harvard." At Lake George he lay naked on the red-gold beach

"and ate cold caribou-heart, and made tea, and had, oh! blueberry pie."
Hawaii was disappointing, but Samoa—"There it is; there it wonderfully is; heaven on earth, the ideal life, little work, dancing, and singing and eating; naked people of incredible loveliness.... Can't you imagine what a fragmentary heart I'm bearing away to Fiji and Tahiti? And, oh dear! I'm afraid they'll be just as bad." They were. At Fiji he was able to say, "I prefer watching the *Siva-Siva* to observing Nijinsky"; and as for Tahiti, he discovered there everything his heart could desire except a lost Gauguin. "It is all—all Papeete—like a Renaissance Italy, with the venom taken out." "This afternoon I go fishing with a native girl on a green and purple reef." These are Pacific commonplaces, no doubt, but they are also a refuge from reality—a refuge even more accommodating than the practice of romantic verse. In the consequent *Tiare Tahiti* people have been known to discover, not merely the immortal youth which belongs to true poetry, but also the tragedy of genius nipped in the bud. And yet such poetry becomes inseparable from his physical memory, it was his background too. He was beautiful, he was 26, he would be dead in little more than a year. Was this so very tragic? There is immortal youth and—youth that is not quite so immortal, the youth of Peter Pan. What would have happened to Brooke's eager spirit when wrinkles devoured the flesh? Would it have been agile enough to escape even *that* reality?

That year of changing scenes and peoples—the naïve Americans, the cannibals in Fiji, the laughing loving children of Polynesia—becomes, in retrospect, no more than a various frieze behind the enchanting person of Rupert Brooke. And when he returned to England, "the friend" wrote Walter de la Mare,

> who placidly appeared from the ends of the earth seemed as little changed as one who gayly and laughingly goes to bed and gayly and laughingly comes down next morning after a perfectly refreshing sleep.

Mr. de la Mare appears to have been surprised. Surely those spell-bound islands should have left some mark upon his versatile and impressionable young friend! Had he not written to say that life was changed for him? And except for a bleaching of the golden hair, there was no mark at all. But should there have been? Never-Never-Land has no geography. Scarcely had Brooke left the "gentleness and beauty and kindliness" of Polynesia than he was beginning to think of Plymouth—"Oh, blessed name, oh, loveliness! Plymouth—was there ever so sweet and droll a sound? Drake's Plymouth, English Western Plymouth, city where men speak softly... and there is love and beauty and old houses...."

He landed at Plymouth on June 6. The year was 1914.

The first news of war alarmed him: "the world seems so dark—and I'm vaguely frightened." In that growing darkness there lurked Reality, licking its lips, preparing for the final leap. But quite suddenly very different sentiments appeared. He was given a commission in the Royal Naval Division, and now "the central purpose of my life, the thing God wants of me, is to get good at beating Germans. But that isn't what it *was*. What it was, I never knew ... I'm the happiest person in the world." The songs, the talks, the Elizabethan dramatists, the English spring, and socialism, and Tahiti—they were nothing. He put them out of his mind. Here was the truth at last—this crouching final illusion, the magical German dragon, crowned and deadly, and breathing fantastical fire.

And so came the last, the most surprising event: for War—that loudest and least amenable of backgrounds—meekly retiring, subdued itself to the personality of Rupert Brooke. Beyond Antwerp, within the reach of shells and death, he slept in a château-garden, "and round corners one saw, faintly, occasional Cupids and Venuses—a scattered company of rather bad statutes—gleaming quietly. The sailors dug their latrines in the various rose gardens...." Above the trench in which at last he found himself, and which the Germans refrained from attacking "seriously," there passed "once or twice a lovely glittering aeroplane." And so home to England—a "remarkable" England. In February, 1915, he left with his Division for the Dardanelles.

Just one month before another Georgian poet, scarcely less characteristic, had died in the winter bleakness of a Swiss health resort. James Elroy Flecker could squeeze color out of words as one squeezes paint out of a tube, and some of his poems—*The Four Gates of Damascus,* for instance—are the literary equivalent of a Bakst *décor*. He too fled from reality, the reality of tuberculosis, into the lighter side of oriental religion. But though the best of his oriental work, it is true, remains so Anglo-Saxon at heart that it has something of the effect of an amateur charade, only a very narrow mind would deny that he was a poet. He spent much of his life in the Near East, and one could wish that it had ended there, if only because such a *mise-en-scène* would have been more appropriate. But it was not to be. As he lay in Switzerland, very near his death, he thought of war as he had once known it, at Beyrout. "Unforgettable the thunder of the guns shaking the golden blue of sky and sea while not a breath stirred the palm-trees, not a cloud moved on the swan-like snows of Lebanon." He opened his eyes, and the kindly vision fled. Before him were the cold mountains, and beyond them the zones of a colorless war, cutting him off even from his friends. Reality had caught up with Flecker.

But not with Brooke. "I had not imagined," he wrote to Miss Asquith, just before he set out for the Dardanelles campaign, "that Fate could be so benign.... But I'm filled with confident and glorious hopes. Do you think *perhaps* the fort on the Asiatic corner will want quelling, and we'll land and come at it from behind, and they'll make a sortie and meet us on the plains of Troy? ... Will Hero's Tower crumble under the 15" guns? Will the sea be polyphloisbic and wine-dark and unvintageable? Shall I loot mosaics from St. Sophia, and Turkish Delight, and carpets? ... I've never been quite so happy in my life, I think. Not quite so pervasively happy...."

The German dragon had almost disappeared, and the old paths

stretched before him, more shining than ever and—more empty. His troop-ship sailed past "the good smell of land—and of Spain, too!"; past the mountains of Africa where the sea was a jewel, "and sunset and dawn divine blazes of color"; past Lemnos "like an Italian town in silverpoint"; through the phosphorescent Aegean. And then—just as they were preparing to make their landing in a warm and green dawn, on a murderous Gallipoli beach, beneath the Turkish guns—as they watched the shore "crammed with Fate and ominously silent"—someone said, "We're going home." It was nearly true. They retired to Egypt.

The path fades in a shining mist. "I know what a campaign is," he wrote; "it is a continual crossing from one place to another, and back, over dreamlike seas." On April 17, they returned to the island of Scyros, from which Achilles went forth against Troy, and where Theseus is buried. In Scyros, Brooke caught blood-poisoning, and died, and was buried there: in Scyros "like one great rock-garden of white, and pinkish-white marble, with small red poppies and every sort of wild-flower; in the gorges ilex, dwarf holly, and occasional groups of olives; and everywhere the smell of thyme (or is it sage? or wild mint?)" (Brigadier-General Arthur Asquith to his sister). The background was faithful to the last. He was buried on St. George's day, by moonlight: and above his head, on the white wooden cross, an interpreter had written in Greek—"Here lies the servant of God, sub-lieutenant in the English Navy, who died for the deliverance of Constantinople from the Turks." "That infinitely lovable soul," a friend wrote to his mother, "that stainless heart..." One would not change any of these words; they were true. As for the legend which seems so profoundly buried in them today—will it perhaps shine again? Will the life of Brooke arouse the curiosity and cupidity of some biographer a hundred or so years from now?

However this may be, with his death one sees the extinction of Liberal England. Standing beside that moonlit grave, one looks back. All the violence of the pre-war world has vanished, and in its place there glow, year into backward year, the diminishing vistas of that other England, the England where the Grantchester church clock stood at ten to three, where there was Beauty and Certainty and Quiet, and where nothing was real. Today we know it for what it was; but there are moments, very human moments, when we could almost find it in our hearts to envy those who saw it, and who never lived to see the new world.

35

AUGUST 1914

Barbara Tuchman

Mrs. Tuchman's best-selling and celebrated account of the outbreak of the First World War, The Guns of August, *demonstrates anew that popular history can be based on the highest kind of professional scholarship. In this selection from her book she evokes the fatal moment when the world turned upside down and the well-meaning English Liberal government stood paralyzed with confusion and doubt, while ignorant armies hastened the destruction of European civilization.*

IN LONDON that thought hung heavily in the room where small, white-bearded M. Cambon [the French ambassador] confronted Sir Edward Grey. When Grey said to him that some "new development" must be awaited because the dispute between Russia, Austria, and Germany concerned a matter "of no interest" to Great Britain, Cambon let a glint of anger penetrate his impeccable tact and polished dignity. Was England "going to wait until French territory was invaded before intervening?" he asked, and suggested that if so her help might be "very belated."

Grey, behind his tight mouth and Roman nose, was in equal anguish. He believed fervently that England's interests required her to support France; he was prepared, in fact, to resign if she did not; he believed events to come would force her hand, but as yet he could say nothing officially to Cambon. Nor had he the knack of expressing himself unofficially. His manner, which the English public, seeing in him the image of the strong, silent man, found comforting, his foreign colleagues found "icy." He managed only to express edgily the thought that was in everyone's mind, that "Belgian neutrality might become a factor." That was the development Grey—and not he alone—was waiting for.

Britain's predicament resulted from a split personality evident both within the Cabinet and between the parties. The Cabinet was divided, in a split that derived from the Boer War, between Liberal Imperialists represented by Asquith, Grey, Haldane, and Churchill, and "Little Englanders" represented by all the rest. Heirs of Gladstone, they, like their late leader, harbored a deep suspicion of foreign entanglements and considered the aiding of oppressed peoples to be the only proper concern

---

FROM Barbara Tuchman, *The Guns of August* (New York: The Macmillan Company, 1962), pp. 90–97, 112–118, 131–133. Reprinted by permission of the author from *The Guns of August,* by Barbara Tuchman. Copyright © 1962 by Barbara W. Tuchman.

of foreign affairs, which were otherwise regarded as a tiresome interference with Reform, Free Trade, Home Rule, and the Lords' Veto. They tended to regard France as the decadent and frivolous grasshopper, and would have liked to regard Germany as the industrious, respectable ant, had not the posturings and roarings of the Kaiser and the Pan-German militarists somehow discouraged this view. They would never have supported a war on behalf of France, although the injection of Belgium, a "little" country with a just call on British protection, might alter the issue.

Grey's group in the Cabinet, on the other hand, shared with the Tories a fundamental premise that Britain's national interest was bound up with the preservation of France. The reasoning was best expressed in the marvelously flat words of Grey himself: "If Germany dominated the Continent it would be disagreeable to us as well as to others, for we should be isolated." In this epic sentence is all of British policy, and from it followed the knowledge that, if the challenge were flung, England would have to fight to prevent that "disagreeable" outcome. But Grey could not say so without provoking a split in the Cabinet and in the country that would be fatal to any war effort before it began.

Alone in Europe Britain had no conscription. In war she would be dependent on voluntary enlistment. A secession from the government over the war issue would mean the formation of an antiwar party led by the dissidents with disastrous effect on recruiting. If it was the prime objective of France to enter war with Britain as an ally, it was a prime necessity for Britain to enter war with a united government.

This was the touchstone of the problem. In Cabinet meetings the group opposed to intervention proved strong. Their leader Lord Morley, Gladstone's old friend and biographer, believed he could count on "eight or nine likely to agree with us" against the solution being openly worked for by Churchill with "daemonic energy" and Grey with "strenuous simplicity." From discussions in the Cabinet it was clear to Morley that the neutrality of Belgium was "secondary to the question of our neutrality in the struggle between Germany and France." It was equally clear to Grey that only violation of Belgium's neutrality would convince the peace party of the German menace and the need to go to war in the national interest.

On August 1 the crack was visible and widening in Cabinet and Parliament. That day twelve out of eighteen members declared themselves opposed to giving France the assurance of Britain's support in war. That afternoon in the lobby of the House of Commons a caucus of Liberal M.P.s voted 19 to 4 (though with many abstentions) for a motion that England should remain neutral "whatever happened in Belgium or elsewhere." That week *Punch* published "Lines designed to represent the views of an average British patriot":

> Why should I follow your fighting line
> For a matter that's no concern of mine? ...
>
> I shall be asked to a general scrap

> All over the European map,
> Dragged into somebody else's war
> For that's what a double entente is for.

The average patriot had already used up his normal supply of excitement and indignation in the current Irish crisis over the Curragh Mutiny. As a result of the Home Rule Bill, Ulster was threatening armed rebellion against autonomy for Ireland and English troops stationed at the Curragh had refused to take up arms against Ulster loyalists. General Gough, the Curragh commander, had resigned with all his officers, whereupon Sir John French, Chief of General Staff, resigned, whereupon Colonel John Seely, Haldane's successor as Secretary of War, resigned. The army seethed, uproar and schism ruled the country, and a Palace Conference of party leaders with the King met in vain. Lloyd George talked ominously of the "gravest issue raised in this country since the days of the Stuarts," the words "civil war" and "rebellion" were mentioned, and a German arms firm hopefully ran a cargo of 40,000 rifles and a million cartridges into Ulster. In the meantime there was no Secretary of War, the office being left to Prime Minister Asquith, who had little time and less inclination for it.

Asquith had, however, a particularly active First Lord of the Admiralty. When he smelled battle afar off, Winston Churchill resembled the war horse in Job who turned not back from the sword but "paweth in the valley and saith among the trumpets, Ha, ha." He was the only British minister to have a perfectly clear conviction of what Britain should do and to act upon it without hesitation. On July 26, the day Austria rejected Serbia's reply and ten days before his own government made up its mind, Churchill issued a crucial order.

On July 26 the British fleet was completing, unconnected with the crisis, a test mobilization and maneuvers with full crews at war strength. At seven o'clock next morning the squadrons were due to disperse, some to various exercises on the high seas, some to home ports where parts of their crews would be discharged back into training schools, some to dock for repairs. That Sunday, July 26, the First Lord remembered later was "a very beautiful day." When he learned the news from Austria he made up his mind to make sure "that the diplomatic situation did not get ahead of the naval situation and that the Grand Fleet should be in its War Station before Germany could know whether or not we should be in the war *and therefore if possible before we had decided ourselves.*" The italics are his own. After consultation with the First Sea Lord, Prince Louis of Battenberg, he gave orders to the fleet not to disperse.

He then informed Grey what he had done and with Grey's assent released the Admiralty order to the newspapers in the hope that the news might have "a sobering effect" on Berlin and Vienna.

Holding the fleet together was not enough; it must be got, as Churchill expressed it in capitals, to its "War Station." The primary duty of a fleet, as Admiral Mahan, the Clausewitz of naval warfare, had decreed, was to remain "a fleet in being." In the event of war the British fleet, upon which an island nation depended for its life, had to establish and maintain mastery of the ocean trade routes; it had to protect the British Isles from invasion; it had to protect the Channel and the French coasts in fulfillment of the pact with France; it had to keep concentrated in sufficient strength to win any engagement if the German fleet sought battle; and above all it had to guard itself against that new and menacing weapon of unknown potential, the torpedo. The fear of a sudden, undeclared torpedo attack haunted the Admiralty.

On July 28 Churchill gave orders for the fleet to sail to its war base at Scapa Flow, far to the north at the tip of mist-shrouded Orkney in the North Sea. It steamed out of Portland on the 29th, and by nightfall eighteen miles of warships had passed northward through the Straits of Dover headed not so much for some rendezvous with glory as for a rendezvous with discretion. "A surprise torpedo attack" wrote the First Lord, "was at any rate one nightmare gone forever."

Having prepared the fleet for action, Churchill turned his abounding energy and sense of urgency upon preparing the country. He persuaded Asquith on July 29 to authorize the Warning Telegram which was the arranged signal sent by War Office and Admiralty to initiate the Precautionary Period. While short of the *Kriegsgefahr* or the French State of Siege which established martial law, the Precautionary Period has been described as a device "invented by a genius ... which permitted certain measures to be taken on the *ipse dixit* of the Secretary of War without reference to the Cabinet ... when time was the only thing that mattered."

Time pressed on the restless Churchill who, expecting the Liberal government to break apart, went off to make overtures to his old party, the Tories. Coalition was not in the least to the taste of the Prime Minister who was bent on keeping his government united. Lord Morley at seventy-six was expected by no one to stay with the government in the event of war. Not Morley but the far more vigorous Chancellor of the Exchequer, Lloyd George, was the key figure whom the government could not afford to lose, both for his proved ability in office and his influence upon the electorate. Shrewd, ambitious, and possessed of a spellbinding Welsh eloquence, Lloyd George leaned to the peace group but might jump either way. He had suffered recent setbacks in public popularity; he saw a new rival for party leadership arising in the individual whom Lord Morley called "that splendid condottierre at the Admiralty"; and he might, some of his colleagues thought, see political advantage in "playing the peace-card" against Churchill. He was altogether an uncertain and dangerous quantity.

Asquith, who had no intention of leading a divided country into war, continued to wait with exasperating patience for events which might convince the peace group. The question of the hour, he recorded in his passionless way in his diary for July 31, was, "Are we to go in or stand aside. Of course everybody longs to stand aside." In a less passive attitude, Grey, during the Cabinet of July 31 almost reached the point-blank. He said Germany's policy was that of a "European aggressor as bad as Napoleon" (a name that for England had only one meaning) and told the Cabinet that the time had come when a decision whether to support the Entente or preserve neutrality could no longer be deferred. He said that if it chose neutrality he was not the man to carry out such a policy. His implied threat to resign echoed as if it had been spoken.

"The Cabinet seemed to heave a sort of sigh," wrote one of them, and sat for several moments in "breathless silence." Its members looked at one another, suddenly realizing that their continued existence as a government was now in doubt. They adjourned without reaching a decision.

That Friday, eve of the August Bank Holiday weekend, the Stock Exchange closed down at 10:00 A.M. in a wave of financial panic that had started in New York when Austria declared war on Serbia and which was closing Exchanges all over Europe. The City trembled, prophesying doom and the collapse of foreign exchange. Bankers and businessmen, according to Lloyd George, were "aghast" at the idea of war which would "break down the whole system of credit with London at its center." The Governor of the Bank of England called on Saturday to inform Lloyd George that the City was "totally opposed to our intervening" in a war.

That same Friday the Tory leaders were being rounded up and called back to London from country houses to confer on the crisis. Dashing from one to the other, pleading, exhorting, expounding Britain's shame if the shilly-shallying Liberals held back now, was Henry Wilson, the heart, soul, spirit, backbone, and legs of the Anglo-French military "conversations." The agreed euphemism for the joint plans of the General Staffs was "conversations." The formula of "no commitment" which Haldane had first established, which had raised misgivings in Campbell-Bannerman, which Lord Esher had rejected, and which Grey had embodied in the 1912 letter to Cambon still represented the official position, even if it did not make sense.

It made very little. If, as Clausewitz justly said, war is a continuation of national policy, so also are war plans. The Anglo-French war plans, worked out in detail over a period of nine years, were not a game, or an exercise in fantasy or a paper practice to keep military minds out of other mischief. They were a continuation of policy or they were nothing. They were no different from France's arrangements with Russia or Germany's with Austria except for the final legal fiction that they did not "commit" Britain to action. Members of the government and Parliament who disliked the policy simply shut their eyes and mesmerized themselves into believing the fiction.

M. Cambon, visiting Opposition leaders after his painful interview with Grey, now dropped diplomatic tact altogether. "All our plans are arranged in common. Our General Staffs have consulted. You have seen all our schemes and precautions. Look at our fleet! Our whole fleet is in the Mediterranean in consequence of our arrangements with you and our coasts are open to the enemy. You have laid us wide open!" He told them that if England did not come in France would never forgive her, and ended with a bitter cry, *"Et l'honneur? Est-ce-que l'Angleterre comprend ce que c'est l'honneur?"*

Honor wears different coats to different eyes, and Grey knew it would have to wear a Belgian coat before the peace group could be persuaded to see it. That same afternoon he dispatched two telegrams asking the French and German governments for a formal assurance that they were prepared to respect Belgian neutrality "so long as no other power violates it." Within an hour of receiving the telegram in the late evening of July 31, France replied in the affirmative. No reply was received from Germany.

Next day, August 1, the matter was put before the Cabinet. Lloyd George traced with his finger on a map what he thought would be the German route through Belgium, just across the near corner, on the shortest straight line to Paris; it would only, he said, be a "little violation." When Churchill asked for authority to mobilize the fleet, that is, call up all the naval reserves, the Cabinet, after a "sharp discussion," refused. When Grey asked for authority to implement the promises made to the French Navy, Lord Morley, John Burns, Sir John Simon, and Lewis Harcourt proposed to resign. Outside the Cabinet, rumors were swirling of the last-minute wrestlings of Kaiser and Czar and of the German ultimatums. Grey left the room to speak to—and be misunderstood by—Lichnowsky on the telephone, and unwittingly to be the cause of havoc in the heart of General Moltke. He also saw Cambon, and told him "France must take her own decision at this moment without reckoning on an assistance we are not now in a position to give." He returned to the Cabinet while Cambon, white and shaking, sank into a chair in the room of his old friend Sir Arthur Nicolson, the Permanent Under-Secretary. *"Ils vont nous lâcher"* (They are going to desert us), he said. To the editor of *The Times* who asked him what he was going to do, he replied, "I am going to wait to learn if the word 'honor' should be erased from the English dictionary."

In the Cabinet no one wanted to burn his bridges. Resignations were bruited, not yet offered. Asquith continued to sit tight, say little, and await developments as that day of crossed wires and complicated frenzy drew to a close.... At the Admiralty the First Lord was entertaining friends from the Opposition, among them the future Lords Beaverbrook and Birkenhead. To keep occupied while waiting out the tension, they played bridge after dinner. During the game a messenger brought in a red dispatch box—it happened to be one of the largest size. Taking a key from his pocket, Churchill opened it, took out the single sheet of paper it contained, and read the single line on the paper: "Germany has declared war on Russia." He informed the company, changed out of his dinner jacket, and "went straight out like a man going to a well-accustomed job."

Churchill walked across the Horse Guards Parade to Downing Street, entered by the garden gate, and found the Prime Minister upstairs with

Grey, Haldane, now Lord Chancellor, and Lord Crewe, Secretary for India. He told them he intended "instantly to mobilize the fleet notwithstanding the Cabinet decision." Asquith said nothing but appeared, Churchill thought, "quite content." Grey, accompanying Churchill on his way out, said to him, "I have just done a very important thing. I have told Cambon that we shall not allow the German fleet to come into the Channel." Or that is what Churchill, experiencing the perils of verbal intercourse with Grey, understood him to say. It meant that the fleet was now committed. Whether Grey said he had given the promise or whether he said, as scholars have since decided, that he was going to give it the next day, is not really relevant, for whichever it was it merely confirmed Churchill in a decision already taken. He returned to the Admiralty and "gave forthwith the order to mobilize."

Both his order and Grey's promise to make good the naval agreement with France were contrary to majority Cabinet sentiment. On the next day the Cabinet would have to ratify these acts or break apart, and by that time Grey expected a "development" to come out of Belgium. Like the French, he felt that he could count on Germany to provide it....

On Sunday afternoon, August 2, a few hours before the German ultimatum was delivered in Brussels, Grey asked the British Cabinet for authority to fulfill the naval engagement to defend the French Channel coast. No more distressing moment can ever face a British government than that which requires it to come to a hard and fast and specific decision. Through the long afternoon the Cabinet squirmed uncomfortably, unready and unwilling to grasp the handle of final commitment.

In France war came and was accepted as a kind of national fate, however deeply a part of the people would have preferred to avoid it. Almost in awe, a foreign observer reported the upsurge of "national devotion" joined with an "entire absence of excitement" in a people of whom it had so often been predicted that anarchical influences had undermined their patriotism and would prove fatal in the event of war. Belgium, where there occurred one of the rare appearances of the hero in history, was lifted above herself by the uncomplicated conscience of her King and, faced with the choice to acquiesce or resist, took less than three hours to make her decision, knowing it might be mortal.

Britain had no Albert and no Alsace. Her weapons were ready but not her will. Over the past ten years she had studied and prepared for the war that was now upon her and had developed, since 1905, a system called the "War Book" which left nothing to the traditional British practice of muddling through. All orders to be issued in the event of war were ready for signature; envelopes were addressed; notices and proclamations were either printed or set up in type, and the King never moved from London without having with him those that required his immediate signature. The method was plain; the muddle was in the British mind.

The appearance of a German fleet in the Channel would have been no less direct a challenge to Britain than the Spanish Armada of long ago, and the Sunday Cabinet reluctantly agreed to Grey's request. The written pledge which that afternoon he handed to Cambon read, "If the German Fleet comes into the Channel or through the North Sea to undertake hostile operations against the French coasts or shipping, the British Fleet will give all protection in its power." Grey added, however, that the pledge "does not bind us to go to war with Germany unless the German fleet took the action indicated." Voicing the real fear of the Cabinet, he said that as England was uncertain of the protection of her own coasts, "it was impossible safely to send our military forces out of the country."

M.Cambon asked whether this meant Britain would never do so. Grey replied that his words "dealt only with the present moment." Cambon suggested sending two divisions for "moral effect." Grey said that to send so small a force or even four divisions "would entail the maximum risk to them and produce the minimum of effect." He added that the naval commitment must not become public until Parliament could be informed on the next day.

Half in despair but yet in hope, Cambon informed his government of the pledge in a "very secret" telegram which reached Paris at 8:30 that night. Though it was but a one-legged commitment, far less than France had counted on, he believed it would lead to full belligerency, for, as he later put it, nations do not wage war "by halves."

But the naval pledge was only wrung from the Cabinet at the cost of the break that Asquith had been trying so hard to prevent. Two ministers, Lord Morley and John Burns, resigned; the formidable Lloyd George was still "doubtful." Morley believed the dissolution of the Cabinet was "in full view that afternoon." Asquith had to confess "we are on the brink of a split."

Churchill, always ready to anticipate events, appointed himself emissary to bring his former party, the Tories, into a coalition government. As soon as the Cabinet was over he hurried off to see Balfour, the former Tory Prime Minister, who like the other leaders of his party believed that Britain must carry through the policy that had created the Entente to its logical, if bitter, end. Churchill told him he expected half the Liberal Cabinet to resign if war were declared. Balfour replied that his party would be prepared to join a coalition, although if it came to that necessity he foresaw the country rent by an antiwar movement led by the seceding Liberals.

Up to this moment the German ultimatum to Belgium was not yet known. The underlying issue in the thinking of men like Churchill and Balfour, Haldane and Grey was the threatened German hegemony of Europe if France were crushed. But the policy that required support of France had developed behind closed doors and had never been fully admitted to the country. The majority of the Liberal government did not accept it. On this issue neither government nor country would have gone to war united. To many, if not to most Englishmen, the crisis was another phase in the old quarrel between Germany and France, and none of England's affair. To make it England's affair in the eyes of the public, the violation of Belgium, child of English policy, where every step of the invaders would trample on a treaty of which England was architect and signatory, was required. Grey determined to ask the Cabinet next morning to regard such invasion as a formal *casus belli*.

That evening as he was at dinner with Haldane, a Foreign Office messenger brought over a dispatch box with a telegram which, according to Haldane's account, warned that "Germany was about to invade Belgium." What this telegram was or from whom it came is not clear, but Grey must have considered it authentic. Passing it to Haldane, Grey asked him what he thought. "Immediate mobilization," Haldane replied.

They at once left the dinner table and drove to Downing Street where they found the Prime Minister with some guests. Taking him into a private room, they showed him the telegram and asked for authority to mobilize. Asquith agreed. Haldane suggested that he be temporarily reappointed to the War Office for the emergency. The Prime Minister would be too busy next day to perform the War Minister's duties. Asquith again agreed, the more readily as he was uncomfortably conscious of the looming autocrat, Field Marshal Lord Kitchener of Khartoum, whom he had already been urged to appoint to the empty chair.

Next morning, Bank Holiday Monday, was a clear and beautiful summer day. London was crammed with holiday crowds drawn to the capital instead of the seashore by the crisis. By midday they were so thick in Whitehall that cars could not get through, and the hum of milling people could be heard inside the Cabinet room where the ministers, meeting again in almost continuous session, were trying to make up their minds whether to fight on the issue of Belgium.

Over at the War Office Lord Haldane was already sending out the mobilization telegrams calling up Reservists and Territorials. At eleven o'clock the Cabinet received news of Belgium's decision to pit her six divisions against the German Empire. Half an hour later they received a declaration from the Conservative leaders, written before the ultimatum to Belgium was known, stating that it would be "fatal to the honor and security of the United Kingdom" to hesitate in support of France and Russia. Russia as an ally already stuck in the throats of most Liberal ministers. Two more of them—Sir John Simon and Lord Beauchamp—resigned, but the events in Belgium decided the pivotal Lloyd George to stay with the government.

At three o'clock that afternoon of August 3, Grey was due in Parliament to make the government's first official and public statement on the crisis. All Europe, as well as all England, was hanging on it. Grey's task was to bring his country into war and bring her in united. He had to carry with him his own, traditionally pacifist, party. He had to explain to the oldest and most practiced parliamentary body in the world how Britain was committed to support France by virtue of something that was not a commitment. He must present Belgium as the cause without hiding France as the basic cause; he must appeal to Britain's honor while making it clear that Britain's interest was the deciding factor; he must stand where a tradition of debate on foreign affairs had flourished for three hundred years and, without the brilliance of Burke or the force of Pitt, without Canning's mastery or Palmerston's jaunty nerve, without the rhetoric of Gladstone or the wit of Disraeli, justify the course of British foreign policy under his stewardship and the war it could not prevent. He must convince the present, measure up to the past, and speak to posterity.

He had had no time to prepare a written speech. In the last hour, as he was trying to compose his notes, the German ambassador was announced. Lichnowsky entered anxiously, asking what had the Cabinet decided? What was Grey going to tell the House? Would it be a declaration of war? Grey answered that it would not be a declaration of war but "a statement of conditions." Was the neutrality of Belgium one of the conditions? Lichnowsky asked. He "implored" Grey not to name it as one. He knew nothing of the plans of the German General Staff, but he could not suppose a "serious" violation was included in them, although German troops might traverse one small corner of Belgium. "If so," Lichnowsky said, voicing the eternal epitaph of man's surrender to events, "that could not be altered now."

They talked standing in the doorway, each oppressed by his own urgency, Grey trying to leave for some last moments of privacy in which to work on his speech, Lichnowsky trying to hold back the moment of the challenge made explicit. They parted and never saw each other officially again.

The House had gathered in total attendance for the first time since Gladstone brought in the Home Rule Bill in 1893. To accommodate all the members extra chairs were set up in the gangway. The Diplomatic Gallery was packed except for two empty seats marking the absence of the German and Austrian ambassadors. Visitors from the Lords filled the Strangers' Gallery, among them Field Marshal Lord Roberts, so long and vainly the advocate of compulsory military service. In the tense hush when, for once, no one bustled, passed notes, or leaned over benches to chat in whispers, there was a sudden clatter as the Chaplain, backing away from the Speaker, stumbled over the extra chairs in the aisle. All eyes were on the government bench where Grey in a light summer suit sat between Asquith whose bland face expressed nothing and Lloyd George whose disheveled hair and cheeks drained of all color made him look years older.

Grey, appearing "pale, haggard and worn," rose to his feet. Though he had been a member of the House for twenty-nine years and on the Government bench for the last eight, members on the whole knew little—and the country much less—of his conduct of foreign policy. Questions put to the Foreign Secretary rarely succeeded in trapping Grey into a clear or definitive answer, yet his evasiveness, which in a more adventurous statesman would have been challenged, was not regarded with suspicion. So noncosmopolitan, so English, so county, so reserved, Grey could not be regarded by anyone as a mettlesome mixer in foreign quarrels. He did not love foreign affairs or enjoy his job but deplored it as a necessary duty. He did not run over to the Continent for weekends but disappeared into the country. He spoke no foreign language beyond a schoolboy French. A widower at fifty-two, childless, nongregarious, he seemed as unattached to ordinary passions as to his office. What passion broke through his walled personality was reserved for trout streams and bird calls.

Speaking slowly but with evident emotion, Grey asked the House to approach the crisis from the point of view of "British interests, British honor and British obligations." He told the history of the military "conversations" with France. He said that no "secret engagement" bound the House or restricted Britain's freedom to decide her own course of action. He said France was involved in the war because of her "obligation of honor" to Russia, but "we are not parties to the Franco-Russian alliance; we do not even know the terms of that alliance." He seemed to be leaning so far over backward to show England to be uncommitted that a worried Tory, Lord Derby, whispered angrily to his neighbor, "By God, they are going to desert Belgium!"

Grey then revealed the naval arrangement with France. He told the House how, as a consequence of agreement with Britain, the French fleet was concentrated in the Mediterranean, leaving the northern and western coasts of France "absolutely undefended." He said it would be his "feeling" that "if the German fleet came down the Channel and bombarded and battered the undefended coasts of France, we could not stand aside and see this going on practically within sight of our eyes, with our arms folded, looking on dispassionately, doing nothing!" Cheers burst from the Opposition benches, while the Liberals listened, "somberly acquiescent."

To explain his having already committed Britain to defend France's Channel coasts, Grey entered into an involved argument about "British interests" and British trade routes in the Mediterranean. It was a tangled skein, and he hurried on to the "more serious consideration, becoming more serious every hour," of Belgian neutrality.

To give the subject all its due, Grey, wisely not relying on his own oratory, borrowed Gladstone's thunder of 1870, "Could this country stand by and witness the direst crime that ever stained the pages of history and thus become participators in the sin?" From Gladstone too, he took a phrase to express the fundamental issue—that England must take her stand "against the unmeasured aggrandizement of any power whatsoever."

In his own words he continued: "I ask the House from the point of view of British interests to consider what may be at stake. If France is beaten to her knees... if Belgium fell under the same dominating influence and then Holland and then Denmark... if, in a crisis like this, we run away from these obligations of honor and interest as regards the Belgian Treaty... I do not believe for a moment that, at the end of this war, even if we stood aside, we should be able to undo what had happened, in the course of the war, to prevent the whole of the West of Europe opposite us from falling under the domination of a single power ... and we should, I believe, sacrifice our respect and good name and reputation before the world and should not escape the most serious and grave economic consequences."

He placed before them the "issue and the choice." The House, which had listened in "painful absorption" for an hour and a quarter, broke into overwhelming applause, signifying its answer. The occasions when an individual is able to harness a nation are memorable, and Grey's speech proved to be one of those junctures by which people afterward date events. Some dissent was still vocal, for, unlike the continental parliaments, the House of Commons was not to be exhorted or persuaded into unanimity. Ramsay MacDonald, speaking for the Laborites, said Britain should have remained neutral; Keir Hardie said he would raise the working classes against the war; and afterward in the lobby, a group of unconvinced Liberals adopted a resolution stating that Grey had failed to make a case for war. But Asquith was convinced that on the whole "our extreme peace lovers are silenced though they will soon find their tongues again." The two ministers who had resigned that morning were persuaded to return that evening, and it was generally felt that Grey had carried the country.

"What happens now?" Churchill asked Grey as they left the House together. "Now," replied Grey, "we shall send them an ultimatum to stop the invasion of Belgium within 24 hours." To Cambon, a few hours later, he said, "If they refuse, there will be war." ...

No sooner had England delivered herself of the ultimatum than fresh disputes broke out in the Cabinet over the question whether to send an Expeditionary Force to France. Having declared themselves in, they began to dispute how far in they should go. Their joint plans with the French were predicated on an Expeditionary Force of six divisions to arrive in France between M-4 and M-12 and to be ready for action on the extreme left of the French line by M-15. Already the schedule was disrupted because the British M-1 (August 5), which had been expected to be two days behind the French, was now three days behind, and further delay would follow.

Mr. Asquith's cabinet was paralyzed by fear of invasion. In 1909 the Committee of Imperial Defence after a special study of the problem had declared that as long as the home army was kept sufficiently strong to make the Germans mount an invasion force of such size that it could not evade the navy, a large-scale invasion was "impractical." Despite its assurance that the defense of the home islands was adequately guaranteed by the navy, Britain's leaders on August 4 could not summon up the courage to denude the islands of the Regular Army. Arguments were put forward for sending fewer than six divisions, for sending them later rather than sooner, even for not sending them at all. Admiral Jellicoe was told his planned escort of the Expeditionary Force across the Channel would not be required "for the present." No button at the War Office automatically put the BEF in motion because the British government could not make up its mind to push it. The War Office itself, without a minister for the last four months, was distracted for lack of a chief. Asquith had progressed as far as inviting Kitchener up to London, but could not yet nerve himself to offer him the post. The impetuous and tempestuous Sir Henry Wilson, whose uninhibited diary was to cause such anguish when published after the war, was "revolted by such a state of things." So was poor M. Cambon who went, armed with a map, to show Grey how vital it was that the French left should be extended by Britain's six divisions. Grey promised to bring the matter to the attention of the Cabinet.

General Wilson, raging at the delay which he ascribed to Grey's "sinful" hesitation, indignantly showed to his friends in the Opposition a copy of the mobilization order which instead of reading "mobilize and embark," read only "mobilize." This alone, he said, would delay the schedule by four days. Balfour [the previous Prime Minister and founder of the Entente] undertook to spur the government. He told them, in a letter addressed to Haldane, that the whole point of the Entente and of the military arrangements which had flowed from it was the preservation of France, for if France were crushed "the whole future of Europe might be changed in a direction we should regard as disastrous." Having adopted that policy, the thing to do, he suggested, was "to strike quickly and strike with your whole strength." When Haldane came to see him to explain the nature of the Cabinet's hesitations, Balfour could not help feeling they were marked by "a certain wooliness of thought and indecision of purpose."

That afternoon of August 4, at about the time when Bethmann was addressing the Reichstag and Viviani the Chambres des Députés, Mr. Asquith announced to the House of Commons a "message from His Majesty signed by his own hand." Mr. Speaker rose from his chair and members uncovered while the Mobilization Proclamation was read. Next, from typewritten copy that trembled slightly in his hand, Asquith read the terms of the ultimatum just telegraphed to Germany. When he came to the words "a satisfactory answer by midnight," a solemn cheer rose from the benches.

All that was left was to wait for midnight (eleven o'clock, British time). At nine o'clock the government learned, through an intercepted but uncoded telegram sent out from Berlin, that Germany had considered itself at war with Britain from the moment when the British ambassador had asked for his passports. Hastily summoned, the Cabinet debated whether to declare war as of that moment or wait for the time limit set by the ultimatum to expire. They decided to wait. In silence, each encased in his private thoughts, they sat around the green table in the ill-lit Cabinet room, conscious of the shadows of those who at other fateful moments had sat there before them. Eyes watched the clock ticking away the time limit. "Boom!" Big Ben struck the first note of eleven, and each note thereafter sounded to Lloyd George, who had a Celtic ear for melodrama, like "Doom, doom, doom!"

Twenty minutes later the War Telegram, "War, Germany, act," was dispatched. Where and when the army was to act was still unsettled, the decision having been left for a War Council called for the following day. The British government went to bed a belligerent, if something less than bellicose.

36

LLOYD GEORGE IN WAR AND PEACE

Lord Beaverbrook

From the time he entered the Liberal Cabinet of 1906 until he lost political office in 1922, David Lloyd George was an enigmatic and fascinating leader. He remains the most controversial figure of twentieth-century British political history. Creator of the welfare state and liberator of the masses, cunning demagogue and charleton, the savior of England and European civilization, betrayer of the Liberal Party, crook and lecher—Lloyd George has been viewed in all these ways by people who knew him. Until Lloyd George's private papers are opened to professional scholars, students of twentieth-century history will have to be satisfied with the more well-informed evaluations of his contemporaries, such as the following one given in his memoirs by press magnate Lord Beaverbrook, who served under Lloyd George in the Cabinet of the First World War.

L LOYD GEORGE led the nation to victory though confronted by desperate perils. He faced a terrible task when full command of the nation came to him. He had special difficulties. There were no road signs on the journey he had to undertake. As Britain had not been engaged in a major war since the Crimea, there were no precedents and there was no experience he could rely on. He had to improvise everything and at the time when one major mistake could have been fatal. Also he had no personal knowledge of war on any scale.

He had the further terrible disability that he was pestered by the King. George V intrigued with the Generals against him, right up to the post-War election. Lloyd George did not have full Conservative support. There were too many rankling memories of his pre-War speeches for that. Nor did he have full Liberal support. The Lloyd George Liberals were much too weak a part of the divided Party, and Asquith Liberals regarded him as something worse than a traitor.

Liberal enmity was actively promoted by McKenna and deeply resented by Lloyd George. An incident was the cause of bitter complaint by both of them.

FROM Lord Beaverbrook, *The Decline and Fall of Lloyd George* (Des Moines: Duell, Sloan and Pearce, 1963, copyright by Lord Beaverbrook, 1963), pp. 301–307. By permission of Meredith Press and The Beaverbrook Foundations.

Readers of my book *Men and Power* will recall the exciting incident of the "Lost Box" containing a revised document, which if disclosed to Parliament might have altered the trend of events. Lloyd George was the beneficiary of the "Lost Box". Another Red Dispatch Box gave him much trouble and tried him to the utmost in devising explanations.

According to his critics he was at that time leading the opposition to Asquith's Administration, though holding second place in that Government. A meeting of several discontented Conservative Coalition Ministers was held. F. E. Smith, as secretary, prepared a minute of the proceedings for Lloyd George's information and forwarded the document in a Red Box addressed to the "Chancellor of the Exchequer" (and of course these Red Box communications go direct to the Minister who holds the key). But Lloyd George had just left the Exchequer for higher and better War employment. Reginald McKenna, who had succeeded him as Chancellor, opened the Box, read the memo., showed it to his political associates. Gross treachery, double dealing and political assassination was McKenna's description of the document. After two days' delay McKenna sent the Box on to Lloyd George. A "rocket", as they say in military circles, was the only possible way out for Lloyd George. He wrote McKenna: "Next time a letter comes into your hands by mistake, put it back into the same Box and send it to the right person at once—*after reading it.*"

Lloyd George and McKenna were never reconciled. McKenna persisted in his charge of "Traitor" and Lloyd George cried "He stole my letter."

He got nothing but hatred from the Generals who in that war fiercely opposed any civilian attempt to interfere with their strategy. Though Lloyd George had a deep and well-founded distrust of the Generals, his political instinct warned him that it would not be safe to go against popular idols such as Haig and Robertson. Consequently he could and would conspire against Haig and seek to undermine him, but he would not assert his authority and insist that campaigns of senseless slaughter must cease. He was and had to be the politician, the man who tried to gauge the current and not to go against it. Failure to heed that same current would have driven him from power.

It is right to say that Lloyd George always had an eye on the newspapers which were mostly under the spell of the Generals. Perhaps to some extent it was for that reason that he made so few changes in the High Command when he knew that he ought to have made many. He had always one eye on victory but he never failed to keep the other eye on the movement of public opinion. He was only too conscious of the glamour of the highly publicised Generals. He feared Haig and his mistrusted Robertson. These two held the support of King and Commons in their keeping and acting in unison could and would have brought Lloyd George down if he had given them the chance.

Nor did Lloyd George have full public support. He was not spared the horror of huge and ever mounting casualty lists which were setting up an unconscious war resistance among the people when he came to power. That war resistance was expressed in the famous Lansdowne Peace Letter and also in much industrial trouble. The people of Britain had no notion of what total war was like. They were quite unaccustomed to doing with too little food, and they were angered by the countless regulations which interfered with their daily lives. The Defence of the Realm Act was intensely unpopular.

There was the further heavy disability that the people could not see a possible defeat in terms of catastrophe. They imagined that defeat would mean the loss of gold from the Bank of England by way of indemnity. They thought they would suffer no more than France had suffered in 1871.

After the 1918 election the Press regarded Lloyd George with increasing hostility. This, strange as it may seem, was the hour when George V at last decided that Lloyd George was indispensable. He gave full support to his Prime Minister at the very time when Lloyd George's fate was sealed.

It was a magnanimous decision. For the King had been annoyed by a certain indifference to Royal favour and indeed a somewhat insolent attitude by Lloyd George on occasion. When offered an audience on a Saturday morning, Lloyd George exclaimed: "Damn the King! Saturday is the only day I have to play golf." He sent a reply: "I was going away for the week-end, but of course if the King wishes an audience of me, I will put it off." The King graciously replied that Monday would do as well. "God bless His Majesty!" said Lloyd George.

As a gesture of good will and confidence George V asked Lloyd George to carry the state sword before the King at the opening of Parliament. Lloyd George dodged the invitation. To his intimates he said: "I won't be a flunkey."

The Lords had supported him in the days of danger but when the sky was clear they were bitterly hostile to him. Their condemnation of Lloyd George was a constant source of debate and discussion in the Gilded Chamber.

Struggling against these obstacles, Lloyd George once threatened to resign. It was in the garden at 10 Downing Street that he said to me, "I am a C_3 character," referring to the lowest medical category for the forces. "I want a C_3 job." He of course had no intention of resigning but Churchill would never have made the suggestion.

I shall not call him George, he hated it. He considered this form of address almost as an insult. Bonar Law was not aware of Lloyd George's attitude and when speaking of him invariably called him George. However when he addressed the Prime Minister he called him at first Lloyd George, and afterwards L.G. When Lloyd George took to himself a title in 1945 he adopted a hyphen and became in fact Earl Lloyd-George of Dwyfor.

He was of course devious. He was inclined to secure his ends by methods of which Bonar Law did not always approve. Lloyd George was not above misrepresenting the character and motives of those who stood in his way. He could be bitter in his public and private attacks on his opponents.

But he took a lenient and charitable view of human frailties. This compassionate nature found practical expression when attempts were made to exclude unmarried mothers from benefits under Government projects. Lloyd George, pointing to a member of a hostile deputation of ladies, said: "Who is she to talk of immorality? Why, her husband lived on immorality! He was President of the Divorce Court."

He did not have many intimate friends. The late Lord Reading was attached to him and also Lord Riddell, but in time he lost both. Riddell was his chosen companion and the relationship was exceedingly close for thirteen years. Several volumes of an interesting and absorbing diary are devoted almost entirely to the sayings and doings of Lloyd George. A column in *News of the World*, Riddell's own paper, was the best informed gossip page and particularly on political subjects. Riddell himself was often the writer.

As an orator Lloyd George was superb. I remember him speaking of a Nonconformist village high up on the hillside when a neighbour rode in the night time to bring the Nonconformist Minister to a dying man, passing the house where the Anglican parson would have been only too willing to go to the death-bed. When he spoke of the hoof beats clattering on the roadside, you could positively hear the passing horse.

He had a marvellous command of imagery and powers of repartee. Before his downfall he dominated the House of Commons. There was none to equal him. And he had a pleasant voice, a very pleasant voice. With sympathetic look and gesture, with a welcoming smile, and with seductive and vibrant voice he could win any man's interest—or woman.

Lloyd George's conversation was entertaining and indeed invariably exciting too. He spoke about the personal idiosyncrasies of those who came in contact with him and with extraordinary insight and understanding. Certainly he was not above discussing the social weaknesses of those who served under him.

It cannot be denied that Lloyd George lived for the day and the hour. He had no thought of history. He often indulged in reminiscence but seldom about the great events with which he was so intimately connected.

There was however a story going back to the First War and of Germany's invasion of Belgium which has always held my interest. The Belgian Government, he said, were on the point of giving way, and allowing the Germans to pass through their territory, when M. Vandervelde, the Socialist leader, came to the Ministry, and taking a letter out of his pocket, said: "Jaurès has been murdered: this is a letter from the French Socialists asking me to go to Paris and lead them. Unless you can tell me that Belgium will resist violation, I will shake the dust of Belgium from my feet, and take my stand among the French—and France shall know the reason why." This came to the ears of the Belgian King, who sent for Vandervelde, and together they turned the tide and Belgium declared war on Germany.

Lloyd George was fond of talking about the great days of Liberal ascendancy before the First World War. He talked frequently about his triumphs in the little community in Wales where he practised law as a solicitor. The memory of his battles in Welsh courtrooms against the pretensions of the Established Church and the aristocracy aroused him, and he of course aroused the simple people of Wales.

I have told of an occasion when, after many days working intimately with Lloyd George, the end was attained: the fall of Asquith. Lloyd George was called upon to form a Government. All day long I sat in my room at the Hyde Park Hotel waiting for the telephone call from him which would have been a confirmation of the pledge he had given me under the trees at Cherkley that I would be his President of the Board of Trade. Silence reigned. The telephone did not ring. I worried over the profound silence. How I longed for the sound of that voice that I knew so well and that I had heard so often during the days when the political upheaval was in the making.

After the election of 1935 Lloyd George returned from his own campaign in high spirits and good humour after having suffered a very severe defeat, and after having held only four seats, including his own.

In the following week-end there was not a single telephone message for Lloyd George from any source, political or otherwise. The telephone was silent. When I heard of this experience I was reminded of my own lonely vigil and for Lloyd George I had deep sympathy.

He had a passion for churches, preachers, hymns and psalms. His devotion did not appear to be religious fervour, but just a deep response of the emotions.

Lloyd George himself of course loved to sing Welsh hymns. On occasional Sundays he and his entire family and Miss Stevenson would go to the service at Castle Street Chapel and on their return would sing together what Lloyd George called "the glorious Welsh hymns". He would discuss Welsh preachers, assessing their preaching, describing their personal appearance and occasionally finding some idiosyncrasy to describe with high good humour.

He was familiar with the New Testament. Saint James was his favourite and he often read aloud with much feeling the chapter denouncing the rich, though by this time he was himself "passing rich": "Go to now, ye rich men, weep and howl for your miseries that shall come upon you."

David Davies, M.P. and one-time Lloyd George's Parliamentary Private Secretary, held his job for long by amusing Lloyd George with stories about Welsh preachers. One of them was about a sermon on the parable of the ten virgins which the preacher concluded with a flourish, "Oh my Brethren! where would you rather be—with the five wise virgins in the light? Or with the five foolish virgins in the dark?"

Lloyd George was of course deeply interested in agriculture. He had a real liking for the farm and devotion to the farming community. He had no talent for managing his own farming property. He did not even have any real understanding of husbandry. However he pretended that his farm paid. He made such a statement on one occasion to Churchill who was also engaging in agriculture. Churchill said, "I am going to make my farm pay, whatever it costs."

I also had a farm. At that time it was a chicken farm. Lloyd George asked me how many chickens I had. I replied that I had about 25,000. "And how many pigs have you got?" I asked. "Perhaps 500," he said. As he drove away from Cherkley where these conversations took place, Lloyd George laughingly enquired of his companion, "How many pigs did I say I had?" On being told "500", he said, "Of course I have not got anywhere near as many at that. But he hasn't got 25,000 chickens either." He was right about his own exaggeration but not about my affairs. I did have 25,000 chickens, and when I disposed of them I made a loss of £8,353.

Lloyd George frequently referred to himself in the words of Robert Louis Stevenson as "a bonnie fighter". Another passage in Stevenson described even more accurately his character and attitude to events. " 'Is it only me they're after, or the pair of us? . . . How many would ye think there would be of them?' I [David Balfour] asked.

" 'That depends,' said Alan [Breck]. 'If it was only you, they would like send two-three lively, brisk young birkies, and if they thought that I was to appear in the employ, I dare say ten or twelve,' said he."

37

JOHN MAYNARD KEYNES AND THE BLOOMSBURY GROUP

Roy Harrod

A far-reaching shift in values and attitudes occurred in English intellectual circles in the 1920s. The leaders of this cultural revolution, which affected social thought, moral values, art, and literature, were the Cambridge-trained Bloomsbury group. The economic theorist John Maynard Keynes and the novelist Virginia Woolf have gained the greatest posthumous reputations among this London elite, but there were several other highly creative avant-garde thinkers and writers at work in the London of the 1920s, all striving to

FROM Roy Harrod, *The Life of John Maynard Keynes* (London: Macmillan & Co. Ltd., 1951), pp. 174–194. By permission of The Macmillan Company of Canada Limited, St. Martin's Press, Inc., and Macmillan & Co. Ltd.

undermine what they considered to be the false values of late Victorian and Edwardian society and to replace them with a freer, more personal sensibility. In his extremely felicitous biography of Keynes, his disciple Roy Harrod gives us a sympathetic and well-informed view of the members of the Bloomsbury group.

CHELSEA is the name of a London postal district. It also has a connotation. Certain famous painters have had their studios there, a multitude of art students have lived there, and been seen in the streets clad unconventionally in a way that struck spectators more forcibly in the early years of the century than it would now. Thus Chelsea means essentially a place of art and of art students. The annual "Chelsea Arts Ball" has nation-wide celebrity.

Bloomsbury also had a connotation, but this was of a different kind. For a number of years, if one used the word "Bloomsbury", otherwise than as a postal address, one referred to a particular group of people. Lexicographers may have their qualms. The question turns on the consequence of the group and on how wide is the currency of the designation used with specific reference to it.

The difference between Chelsea and Bloomsbury was that the former referred to general qualities while the latter referred to particular people and through them to their point of view. One could live in the middle of Bloomsbury and yet say that one was very anti-Bloomsbury.

Who were these people? In this matter of definition an element of snobbery may enter in. Some purists who refined and refined—"X was not quite Bloomsbury because he lacked one quality, nor Y because he lacked another"—and who excluded brothers, sisters, husbands, wives, might reduce the membership so much that the number could be counted upon the fingers of one hand. Taking a more generous view, taking account of those who were on terms of close intimacy with the leading members of Bloomsbury at some time or other within the period from 1907 to 1930 and who partook of their general way of life, one might reach some such figure as twenty or thirty. One could certainly cast the net wider, and by accepting others, who might not have been intimate friends, but who acknowledged the leadership, were in some respects of the same way of thinking, and spoke with a "Bloomsbury voice", one could reach a much larger number. However the argument may go, no one could deny that the Misses Stephen* were part of the central core of Bloomsbury. How did it happen that they became such important figures in an intellectual group?

There may have been qualities which came by heredity and upbringing. There was Stephen's free-thinking and there was the distinguished social position which he achieved in the Victorian period. Thus on the

---

* Virginia and Vanessa, daughters of Sir Leslie Stephen. Virginia married Leonard Woolf, the writer and publisher, and Vanessa married Clive Bell, the art critic.

one hand there were the germs of rebellion, which might sprout into a new kind of free-thinking and a new kind of intellectual ferment. On the other hand there were the traditions of society, which imply certain amenities that are necessary, if a circle is to be held together in harmony, however unconventional and Bohemian that circle may seek to be.

In their own persons, they were beautiful and clever and had also a sense of fun and liveliness. They were very individual people, with complex characters which it was a pleasure to their clever men friends to unravel. Furthermore they had a particular quality which differentiated them from the majority of their sex and was essential for the purpose in hand—intellectual coolness. (One need not imply that in most women the absence of this trait is a deficiency; this turns on the function they are destined to perform.) With Virginia and Vanessa all the subjects under the sun could be equably discussed, all opinions, however outrageous, quietly assessed. The men who frequented their society knew that they were in no danger of hearing those rising, strident tones of emotion which must destroy good talk. They had no tendency, as an argument took this turn or that, to read into its bearing an affront to their class, their set, their sex, or themselves.

Another great asset was that there were two ladies with these notable attributes; and, already by 1907, there were two centres. One lady may by her outstanding attainments draw around her a circle of people; that is a *salon;* it is the Hôtel de Rambouillet. But if there are two centres, they may form the nucleus of a social group.

It may be thought that the characteristics enumerated were not enough by themselves. English society contains many clever, level-headed, witty women, who are good talkers and good friends, who have drawn around them a circle for a time, but none the less have not gone so far as to become the centre of an interesting community, have lost their friends with the passage of the years, are known to be interesting and delightful people, but in the long run become more or less isolated figures, seeing their friends occasionally and giving pleasure, but living rather lonely lives. Were the qualities that I have mentioned sufficient ingredients for the creation of a social nucleus?

The fact of the matter is that there was a third leading figure, who lived at home, with no independent establishment in London, one with tremendous resources of inner vitality, with a point of view to assert, with absurd mockery always lurking and awaiting its moment, with a zest for life and friendship, exclusive in the highest degree, cruelly crushing to alien intruders, galvanic, temperamental, dominating, even terrific. This was Lytton Strachey. By a most happy harmony the Misses Stephen and Lytton Strachey, whose families had been on cordial terms and had had common friends among distinguished Victorians, found themselves in great sympathy on many matters of discourse, serious or gay. Between them, these three sufficed to make the coterie.

It was a piece of the greatest good luck for Strachey. We have seen how much "the Society" and his group of Trinity friends meant to him at

Cambridge, and how he tended to remain there after his proper period. These friends had lived together, pooling their ideas, impressions and experiences, building up a community of taste and of philosophy, and sharing their private jokes, whose meaning depended on their common experiences. It is very rare for such groups, formed at a University, to hold together. There some young men may seem to themselves to have constructed, out of the views they share on life and on art and out of their common idioms and interpretations, durable, spiritual habitations, in which they will be able to meet together for the rest of their days. They are but summer-houses, destined to be deserted and to fall into rapid disrepair. The man, when he has to face the battle of life, usually finds that he has to advance alone. He is always tending to fall away from his friends, to be pushed about hither and thither, moving in and out of different circles, in accordance with his shifting interests and fortune. Then, if he marries, it is the wife who builds anew for him, decides what is to be done, who is to be seen and what the pattern of life is to be. He may pay a visit to his old college, he may attend an annual reunion of his friends, reviving the old anecdotes, rehearsing the old jokes, living in the old atmosphere for a pleasant evening; but it is all a mere echo; the next day's work will go forward as usual.

With Lytton it was to be different. In Vanessa and Virginia he found two women who were Apostles to the finger-tips—no less so for having had no university education. With their aid the old summer-houses could be kept in being, and enlarged into great mansions, into palaces. The old thoughts could continue to flow, the new impressions be shared and the jokes kept green and living.

To these we must add Duncan Grant. He was an important element. It may well be that he was a necessary element, not only on account of those qualities which had made him so much beloved, but on account of his steady intelligence and balanced judgment. After all, Strachey often let his imagination run away with him, adopting extreme and untenable positions. Duncan Grant had the brains to understand him, but could maintain his own view. He had the painter's intelligence, which has a peculiar quality of level-headedness. For an imaginative writer, a new idea, albeit fundamentally unsound and in fact false, may none the less have some ingredient which will be an indispensable aid to the work of creation. For the time being and provisionally, he must cling to it, and assert it. But the painter creates with his brush. In the world of ideas he has no axe to grind. And he can thus preserve his balance.

With these aids Strachey was to be able to keep his community alive. It was by a further piece of good fortune that the two young ladies elected to marry two of his intimate friends from Trinity. We have seen already Vanessa marrying Mr. Clive Bell. Six years later Virginia married Mr. Leonard Woolf, after his return fom Ceylon. Thus the Trinity party was kept together, gaining strength from its new adherents.

When Maynard returned to Cambridge he retained a London *pied-à-terre* in Belgrave Road; a year later he took rooms in Fitzroy Square with

Duncan Grant. In 1911 he made a change, taking a share in a house at 38 Brunswick Square, his fellow-tenants being Adrian and Virginia Stephen, Duncan Grant and, on his return from Ceylon, Leonard Woolf. (When Leonard and Virginia married in 1913 they went off to Clifford's Inn.) The act of leaving London for Cambridge made the whole question of London much more important to Maynard. When residing there he had been busy at the office and with his pen; the whole future lay before him. But when the future lay in Cambridge, he had to be careful not to let his connections with London decay. In due course, sharing houses, sometimes here, sometimes there, he became a member of the Bloomsbury family. He lived as a bachelor in college for part of the time; but Bloomsbury was in a very real sense his home, providing the feminine interest and the human interest which were the background of his daily work.

The question has been raised whether he can be considered as part of the innermost circle of Bloomsbury. Some high authorities would like to raise a doubt and stress certain differences. There were inevitably certain differences. Most of the others were devoting their lives to writing or to some form of artistic endeavour. Maynard was a don; his work in economics was more in the nature of science than of literature; in due course he became a man of business; and in part of the period he was in public life. The nature of the influence he strove to exert implied a difference in outlook. His friends sought to influence the world—in so far as they could be said to do that at all—through the perfection of their artistic achievement. He sought to exert a more direct influence, namely by persuasion and personal intervention. Thus his life was bound to be more littered up with the transaction of business and he had at times fairly close contacts with the great, whom Bloomsbury despised. In no other way could he have achieved his object.

What is so remarkable is that, despite the pressure of worldly interests which were the interests inherent in his profession, he preserved his inner self so untainted that he was always welcomed by the Bloomsbury friends as one of themselves. They felt that at heart he was their unqualified supporter. And so indeed he was. There is no doubt that in his own mind he believed that the work and the personalities of these friends mattered more than the eminent and famous persons with whom he came in contact. It was the friends who provided him with the specific image of what is meant by the idea of a good life. And it was their good opinion of him that he valued most.

It must not be supposed that there was a self-conscious attempt to form a group or that its members wished to be known by a collective name. The group grew up naturally and spontaneously. In the early days there were a number of young people, who were on friendly terms with the others; some of these eventually drifted away, and new friends were added. It turned out that a certain number desired to remain intimate and maintained continuous contact for a long period. With the passage of years these friendships became deep-rooted. To the emotional sympathy, which is present at the inception of a deep friendship, there was added something less usual, namely, the growing familiarity of daily intercourse, so that the friends became almost a family or clan.

What were the leading characteristics of this group? ... There is no authoritative record, and it is to be feared that there may never be one; the student of this episode in the history of British culture will have to glean his information from bits and pieces. A few fragmentary notes must suffice in this place. They are necessary, since what so filled the mind of Keynes and furnished forth his idea of the kind of society which it was the economist's task to make possible must be of relevance to his history and to his economics.

As philosophical background, G. E. Moore's theories were translated from Cambridge to London and became *de rigueur* in Bloomsbury. The supreme values of live were the states of consciousness involved in human relations and in the appreciation of beauty. In a certain sense it may be said that Bloomsbury was a prolongation in London of that phase in the life of "the Society" which was reached in the years immediately following 1900.

At Cambridge Strachey had laid an emphasis, unusual at a university, on the importance of the visual arts, in this ably supported by Clive Bell. This doctrine remained a central one. Maynard was infected by the enthusiasm, and, in due course, became a buyer of pictures as well as books. His flair for the subject is testified by the value of his collection of modern pictures (£30,000 at his death), which he bought, for the most part, at very modest prices. Some hold, perhaps correctly, that his success in this field was due to some uncanny extension of his intellectual power into the world of aesthetics, and that he was never deeply moved by visual, as he undoubtedly was by literary, beauty. Strachey, indeed, is said to have remarked when in a peevish mood, "What irritates me so about Pozzo is that he has no aesthetic sense". Whatever may be the true view about his independent aesthetic judgment, there is no doubt that he shared the sentiment that the painter and the sculptor should be the most highly honoured among men. It must be mentioned that Roger Fry was from early days a great friend.

Much had been done, before Bloomsbury, to redeem English society from the deep philistinism of the mid-Victorian period. Indeed movement succeeded movement. Bloomsbury in turn made its contribution, notably at the period of the first French post-Impressionist Exhibition in London, towards the wider education of public opinion. We shall see that later in his life Maynard endeavoured to carry this education further, by devising practical arrangements for making modern work better known to the general public.

Then there was the other ultimate good defined by G. E. Moore, the good to be found in personal relations. This raises wide questions. Conclusions might be reached which disturbed age-old moral conventions and codes. Leslie Stephen raised the banner of agnosticism concerning the date of the creation of the world. If the Misses Stephen disregarded established codes of everyday behaviour, this would be a revolution even more significant for ordinary people. They too would become pioneers in their day, no longer the daughters of the veteran rebel, going to conventional dances, but rebels on their own account, leaders in a new movement for emancipation.

It may well be said that Bloomsbury was but an eddy in a mighty stream carrying world-wide opinion far from the tenets of the Victorian era. None the less it had its specific characteristics. The first answer of many, in reply to the question who in England had been most responsible for a change of sentiment in these matters, would be Mr. George Bernard Shaw. There is, however, considerable difference between his tone and temper on these subjects and that of Bloomsbury. The lessons to which the writings of Shaw appeared—to the young in the early years of this century—to point were that the Victorian codes were harsh and brutal and replete with hypocrisy, and that, if we brushed those cobwebs away, natural instinct, which was sound and healthy, could be trusted to secure the right arrangements. Shaw in this, as in other matters, seems to suggest that the final answer to these vexed questions is really simple and under our noses. If only we would all think with the clarity and boldness with which he seems to write, our affairs would fall into proper shape.

Bloomsbury cordially agreed that the Victorian codes were harsh and brutal and replete with hypocrisy, and that the cobwebs must be brushed away. But the answer did not seem so simple. When one examines with integrity and disinterestedness the phenomenon of love, taking Nature as we actually find her, we shall discover many curious and unexpected deviations, many twists and quirks. Nature must be examined fearlessly, without prejudice or inhibition. The human heart will be found to have many strange complexities. Bloomsbury would not presume to think that the problems were simple or that the solutions could be written into a modern text-book. Rather they felt that they were on the eve of a great awakening. But much would have to be thought, much tried, much experienced, before we should understand how to arrange affairs so that human relations could be harmonious and happy, and fulfil Moore's ideal of the good.

The debate which proceeded in this society, over the years, covered many matters which it was unusual at that time for women to discuss, matters that are dealt with in treatises on psychoanalysis. They were not discussed in the language of the clinic, but in the language of humanity and charity. Science might take many ages before it reached precise conclusions or formulated them in an intelligible way. Meanwhile these were human problems, demanding an answer if we were to advance to a better way of life. They were discussed in a spirit of humanity and charity, but also, when the occasion was suitable, in one of levity and frivolity. This was a very important point. In problems concerning sexual impulses, whether straightforward or abnormal, one was not likely to reach a sane and balanced judgment if the discussion was always in hushed tones and with solemn faces. What this subject needed, above all others, was far greater frankness and sincerity. And if the ice was really to be broken, laughter and jest must be introduced into the consideration of the matter. In politics or business it would be obvious enough that one could not achieve a realistic view of what was happening if one was debarred from discussing principles or acts save in terms of respectful solemnity. Fun and ridicule must be allowed to play their part in the analysis of the motives or characters or doings of the principal actors; otherwise political discussion would remain at an unrealistic level, and those who discussed them would have a sense of servitude. And so in these questions of sex.

At that time there were many who were shocked at these proceedings. But in this matter of being shocked it is expedient to demand the credentials of those who are shocked and of those at whom they are shocked. I suggest that there did not exist in England at that time any persons who had a moral claim to be shocked at the discussions in which these ladies thought fit to engage. Since this is but an opinion, it is proper to bring as evidence to the court of posterity the writings of Virginia Woolf. These contain passages showing the finest delicacy and sensitivity, deep psychology, great humanity. I suggest that the opposition will not be able to bring forward contemporary writings of greater spiritual quality, whether from pens of reverend persons, professors, philosophers or any other class of society, which would entitle their authors to censure the conversation of the author of *The Waves;* and what applies to Virginia applies to her sister also.

It may be that these controversies are dead and done with now, and that all these problems are freely and openly discussed, save, perhaps, in some very restricted circles. Has the Bloomsbury point of view in fact triumphed? The matter is not so certain. It may be that in the last resort what is important is not merely that certain matters shall be discussed fearlessly, but also the quality of mind and intention that is brought to the discussion, the high elevation of Moore, or the great tradition of "the Society". Has true emancipation even triumphed in what might be called "highbrow" circles? One may go to a party of a younger generation in London. On the walls are pictures by Duncan Grant, Matisse, Chagall, on the tables books from the press embodying the current creative effort. The setting seems similar. And what of the conversation? Yes; these problems of human relations are being discussed in a spirit of frankness; the Bloomsbury emancipation has held its ground. But listen again. What is being said sounds, surely, very crude and callow. Surely one ought not to be allowed to say such things in public. One may imagine at this party a young man fresh from school, mature beyond his years, with his secret experiences and visions. He may resolve that when he goes to Cambridge, or it may be to Oxford, he will found a society whose main principle shall be that the tender and delicate affairs of the heart shall only be allowed, by a strict convention, to be discussed with a sole confidant, and that all this crude gossip and unfeeling comment should be most strictly ostracised. If such a man got, Strachey-wise, astride public opinion in the university, and later in a wider circle, the wheel might come full circle back to the Victorian conventions.... The situation is perhaps not quite so parlous. The steady progress of professional psychology is a safeguard.

But there is another point that strikes us when we ask whether the humanising influence of the Bloomsbury coterie is being more widely diffused in our society. If circumstances rivet the attention of thinking people upon the problems of Hitler, atomic warfare or the Police State, will they find a residue of intellectual energy to direct towards the problems of personal relationships? Do not these aspirations require those old presuppositions of Harvey Road—a stable British Empire and assured material progress? May we have to face a period in which civilisation slips back for a while, and the deeper human questions which intoxicated the mind of young Bloomsbury are neglected? Yet in the long run that period too will pass. It is a misfortune that the thoughts of these friends have not been better recorded for the consideration of coming generations.

Bloomsbury was something more than a discussion group, conducting its deliberations over a number of years. It also set out to achieve a way of life. The Cambridge ideals of unworldliness, pursuit of truth and other absolute values, were carried forward, and the group of friends attempted, in ways admittedly imperfect, to pursue them. In the past, idealists have gone forth to outlandish places to establish communities based on the principles of Robert Owen, Fourier, etc. Here was a village community, living in our midst, using the same shops, post-offices, omnibuses as other people. It was sustained, no doubt, by certain elements of unearned income, and Maynard's un-Apostolic activities in financial speculation often led to his purchase of an object of visual art at a convenient moment. Bloomsbury would not presume to be proud of this achievement and was conscious of its own imperfections as well as those of the wider society within which it lived. Despite all these imperfections, it remained an experiment very sincere in its intentions, which is worthy of study as an episode in the history of culture.

The Waves gives a picture of certain elements of Bloomsbury. It is also coloured by the very individual personality of the authoress; and it is suffused with a certain melancholy. Bloomsbury consisted of sensitive people, who had their fair share of sadness and distress. But in its social aspect the keynote of Bloomsbury was its perpetual gaiety. How could it be otherwise, with Lytton Strachey setting the pace? Maynard's sparkling spirits and his impishness made their contribution. He might go forth into the grave world of high finance and politics; but he came back full of stories of how ludicrously and comically people were behaving, often parodying them, and exaggerating shamelessly. And the others too, plying their daily affairs, returned to the fold full of absurd anecdotes. If one listened to Bloomsbury conversation, one envied these people for finding in the course of what might seem to be a dull day's work so many incidents, which were fantastic in the telling. Why was one's own life not filled with diverting interludes of this kind? They had the seeing eye. Furthermore, if one rejects the presuppositions upon which ordinary people talk and act, and puts in their place other, perhaps juster, presuppositions, that serves to make ordinary sayings and doings seem highly ridiculous. It was impossible to be bored for a moment in Bloomsbury society. Each utterance was pointed.

The Bloomsbury voice was a distinct contribution. It was based on Lytton Strachey's, consisting not so much in a special pronunciation of words as in the cadences of sentences. These cadences could be used to express implications, additional to the formal meaning of the sentences. Many distinguished persons adopted these mannerisms, probably without knowing it. They were infectious. Maynard alone, among the men in the inner circle, was altogether immune; his soft, distinctive manner of speech remained unchanged from early years.

The voice was emphatic, but restrained. Certain syllables, or even letters, were rather strongly stressed, but not at all in the manner of a drawl. The presupposition of the cadence was that everything one said mattered. Emphasis had to be applied. In a subtle way this maintained the standard of conversation. For if one was on the verge of uttering something silly or flat, one perceived in advance that it would not bear the emphasis that the Bloomsbury manner required, and so it would be left unsaid, to the benefit of all.

The cadence was a trick by which one could produce various effects. A favourite word was "really". In ordinary speech the stress is on the first two vowels. In Bloomsbury speech it fell upon the ll's, which were rolled luxuriously and followed by a sharp diminuendo. A stranger might utter a bromide. "Really"—with great interest and surprise. The stranger felt flattered at the interest taken. These clever people evidently paid special attention to everything that was said. It was nice to have this considerate reception. After all, what he had said had not been so particularly interesting. But why the surprise? Surely his remark had expressed quite a commonplace truth. Its truth could not presumably be questioned. But wait! Could it be? Was it conceivable that these clever people took a different view? Was it really true? Then an abyss would open. Pausing to reflect, he realised that this old truism was in fact a piece of consummate balderdash. He had been horribly crushed by one word.

Another trick could be played with this "really". A philistine might say that X "liked", "was fond of", or "was devoted to" Y, meaning little more than that if X and Y were placed next to one another at a dinner-party, they would get on very well together. He was confronted with "Really", spoken again with great interest and surprise, the implication being that his harmless words referred to a scandalous intrigue or to a desperate and forlorn love. There were two distinct "reallys" in this connection; one with a rising note on the "..all.", suggested that it was delightful news that a friend should be involved in this happy affair; the other, with a diminuendo on the "..all.", suggested disgust. This might be a mere tease. Or it might be a joke, if the idea of these two people being in love with one another was particularly incongruous. Or there might be a more subtle implication. Bloomsbury was deeply interested in all questions of love and wished to make it plain that in their view, if one could apply such a word as "devotion" to X's attitude towards Y, that was a matter which must be taken seriously and had weighty implications. They were determined to maintain a heightened interest in human beings, and sustain an active-minded commentary; they were not content to have dry, colourless words applied to the motions of the heart; if people were so dull as to have no deep feelings, then at least these should be attributed to them.

Some reference should be made to the achievements of the group. One may cite examples, without claiming to provide an exhaustive list. Although Keynes drew spiritual sustenance from these friends, the main part of his work has, of course, quite different sources of inspiration. There are occasional traces of Bloomsbury influence in points of style and illustration. Monsieur Étienne Mantoux ... accuses him of dragging into his *Economic Consequences of the Peace* (1919) a mention of Freud in order to titillate the reader by this reference to a recent finding of psychology. The criticism is extremely wide of the mark. The kind of analysis which Keynes gives of President Wilson's character had been common form in his discussions with his friends for more than a dozen years. Of greater importance was his persistent tendency to ridicule those in authority. This was in part a native strain, but we may believe that it was encouraged—some may think unduly—by the persistently mocking vein of those among whom he spent his happiest hours. And then there was that vision of the good life, which animated his endeavours, of which his readers catch glimpses all through his works.

The achievements of those whose names I have mentioned are well known—Lytton Strachey, Virginia Woolf, Vanessa Bell, Duncan Grant, Clive Bell, Leonard Woolf, Roger Fry. To these we must add E. M. Forster and David (Bunny) Garnett. The latter was younger than the others; he became an intimate and devoted friend of them all, and of Maynard in particular. When the group was established, containing so many whom Lowes Dickinson had known as undergraduates, he was inevitably in some sense of it. Sheppard retained his links. There was another younger member, whose work may possibly survive that of all the others—Arthur Waley. Whatever the beauties of Lady Murasaki's novel in her native tongue, Waley's exquisite translation must long remain a classic, giving English readers their chance of comparing this great masterpiece with the finest products of Greece or France or Russia. James Strachey and W. J. H. ("Sebastian") Sprott have produced work in psychology. Gerald Shove, the economist, had close contact at a certain period. After the First World War, marvellous to relate, a very small infiltration of Oxford men was permitted. Of these first mention should be made of Raymond Mortimer, a literary critic of great distinction, who has done much to kindle and sustain British appreciation of the civilisation of France. He was fully adopted by Bloomsbury. With the advantage of years on his side, he has carried forward some of its traditions into a generation that knew it not. May it yet fall to this Oxford man to compose for posterity some record of what was in essence a Cambridge movement? Other Oxford figures were Stephen Tomlin, Philip Ritchie, Roger Senhouse and Edward Sackville-West. The future will not have the chance of hearing Sackville-West's superb execution on the piano as a young man, but the novel entitled *Simpson* and the biography of De Quincey, entitled *A Flame in Sunlight,* will surely long be treasured. What strikes the eye, when it inspects this catalogue of work, is the great dissimilarity between the items. There is no case here of a literary school self-consciously imitating its master. It is quite a different kind of phenomenon—a grouping together of men of individual genius or talent, finding stimulus in the society of the others, finding a congenial way of life, but each pursuing his own bent and striving after his own unique form of expression.

It has been erroneously held that Bloomsbury was in the nature of a mutual admiration society. This is very far from the truth. No doubt as friends they would give each other a helping hand towards material advancement. But within the circle they were keenly critical of one another. There was no question of mollycoddling. A sharp, biting wind of criticism blew through all the recesses of their habitations. They did not give mercy nor expect it. Indeed, if you chanced to hear one member of Bloomsbury pull another to pieces, not leaving a shred, destroying him utterly, you might wonder what form their criticism would take when directed against an outsider. The fact of the matter is that, broadly, outsiders were neglected. It was a world within a world. By concentrating on the criticism of their friends, they focused their thoughts.

This concentration was not a device for self-advancement but for protection against all the irrelevant, distracting and disintegrating forces at play in our rather loosely connected modern society. It was a return to the Greek City State. No doubt there was a consciousness that other men of talent were also writing or painting. This might occasionally be denied in conversation—"Really, you know, there isn't anyone else"—but this pleasant, whimsical conceit was not to be taken too seriously. Many other distinguished people were living in London at the time, and many of them were very anti-Bloomsbury. Action and reaction are said to be equal. . . .

Such were Keynes' associates for more than a dozen years. Later, the pattern was to change somewhat. He found in a happy marriage the ideal background for the prolonged creative work that he had then to do. Meanwhile he profited much from the constant stimulus and affection of his Bloomsbury friends. And of course he gave much. They on their side were stimulated by his delightful company, his vitality and the impact of his abounding interests. And they gained, too, from his resources of knowledge and worldly contact. He was their main pillar of strength, their sage, their financial adviser, their patron. He was always ready to help, in one way or another, to promote their material interests. They also drew intellectual sustenance from him. Was he not a logician, a mathematician, a philosopher, an economist and an expert on many aspects of public affairs? They valued his judgment on all these topics.

They were not flimsy *littérateurs,* content to take up philosophical or scientific ideas by hearsay or from inferior sources. One and all, they wished their work to be well based, if only it were possible, on a sound philosophy. "Is it right, Maynard?" "Is it sound?" "Is it logically tenable?" "Are these really the facts?"

They were all people of strong individuality, and were strongly individualist in creed. And so was Maynard. He was an individualist to the finger-tips. For him those concerned with government were a lesser breed of men, whose rôle was essentially a subordinate one. The idea that a government, however popularly elected, should be entrusted to make certain value judgments on behalf of the community was anathema to him. He had no sympathy with the project of limiting consumers' freedom of choice for the sake of greater efficiency, mass production or standardisation.

On the other hand, he was violently opposed to *laissez-faire*. Mr. Sheppard recalls a speech which he made at a Liberal meeting when an undergraduate. He defined Conservatives and Liberals in this way: let there be a village whose inhabitants were living in conditions of penury and distress; the typical Conservative, when shown this village, said, "It is very distressing, but, unfortunately, it cannot be helped;" the Liberal said, "Something must be done about this." That was why he was a Liberal. Sheppard was impressed with this simple statement of creed. Whether or not it can be regarded as an adequate and comprehensive definition of the philosophies of the two parties at that time, the view asserted to be Liberal was assuredly Maynard's throughout his life. He believed that distress in all its forms should not go unheeded. He believed that, by care and pains, all our social evils, distressed areas, unemployment and the rest, could be abolished. He believed in planning and contriving. A way could be found. That was his experience in his private life and in the affairs of his college, and the same maxim should be applied in public affairs. He always had a scheme. His mental energy and resources were limitless. If a thing could not be done in this way, it could be done in that.

How can one reconcile the adamant and uncompromising individualism which was at the centre of his being and his fervent belief in planning? Did he resolve what might seem on the surface to be a contradiction?—a question of no little interest, since its successful resolution may be the prerequisite for the maintenance of the kind of civilisation we have known. In Keynes' economic writings is to be found his solution of this dilemma. It is one of the problems to which he applied his whole mind, a not inconsiderable one, and deep study of his conclusions will long remain worth while.

This problem is tied up with another, to which he gave less explicit thought. We have seen that he was strongly imbued with what I have called the presuppositions of Harvey Road. One of these presuppositions may perhaps be summarised in the idea that the government of Britain was and would continue to be in the hands of an intellectual aristocracy using the method of persuasion. If, owing to the needs of planning, the functions of government became very far-reaching and multifarious, would it be possible for the intellectual aristocracy to remain in essential control? Keynes tended till the end to think of the really important decisions being reached by a small group of intelligent people, like the group that fashioned the Bretton Woods plan. But would not a democratic government having a wide multiplicity of duties tend to get out of control and act in a way of which the intelligent would not approve? This is another dilemma—how to reconcile the functioning of a planning and interfering democracy with the requirement that in the last resort the best considered judgment should prevail. It may be that the presuppositions of Harvey Road were so much of a second nature to Keynes that he did not give this dilemma the full consideration which it deserves.

There is also the eternal question in economics of the relation of means to ends. Conscientious economists usually stress the point that their science is concerned with means only, and that it is for others to prescribe the ends. None the less it is hard to draw the line, especially when the economist concerns himself with practical issues. An idea as to what the appropriate ends are may lurk implicit in his recommendation. Some economists are felt to have had too narrow a view of the ends of society. Not so Keynes. His writings are instinct with broad and generous views. We need not attribute this to the influence of Bloomsbury; but we can associate it with his being the kind of man who would enjoy Bloomsbury society.

While he had his own inner vision, he was none the less aware that economists as such must not overstep the mark. He once defined his position in some words very carefully chosen. It was at the end of his speech at a dinner given him by the Council of the Royal Economic Society in 1945 on his retirement from the Editorship of the *Economic Journal* after thirty-three years. It had been a wonderful speech, easy, pleasantly flowing, mellow, full of amusing anecdotes and fascinating character sketches of Balfour, Haldane and other eminent people, with whom he had had contact as secretary of the Society. Finally he came to the toast. "I give you the toast of the Royal Economic Society, of economics and economists, who are the trustees..." It would have been easy to say "the trustees of civilisation", and to have sat down amid appropriate applause. "... who are the trustees, not..." One could not help having the idea—"Why this pedantic 'not'?" Surely this was not the moment for academic qualifications, for ifs and buts. It was true that he was addressing the members of the Council of the Royal Economic Society, professors, men of learning. But still, we were also human. It was a golden hour; our hearts had been touched; we had drunk champagne. We had in fact each had one modest glass of champagne, but had arranged that Maynard should have champagne only, from the soup onwards through the evening. Really there was something intolerable about the donnish "not" coming at this hour and place. It was so unlike Maynard not to say a thing simply and boldly. But he was choosing his words: "... and to economists, who are the trustees, not of civilisation, but of the possibility of civilisation." He had said what he wanted to say.

And what he had said was true, not something slipshod, which might pass muster on such an occasion, but an accurate description, which would bear the test of close scrutiny in the clear light of day. And it did full justice to economics. When he came to the "not", did there flit through his mind a vision of Lytton, of Duncan, of Virginia? They were the trustees of civilisation. Economists had the humbler, but still quite indispensable, rôle; it was that to which he had devoted his own life.

38

A JUDGMENT ON MUNICH

J. W. Wheeler-Bennett

The British public's acclamation of Neville Chamberlain in 1938 as a statesman who had provided "peace in our time" turned a few months later, when Hitler's aims became fully apparent, to a sense of great betrayal and a condemnation of Chamberlain as the leader of "the guilty men" whose appeasement policy had brought England to her darkest hour. After three decades the nature and quality of Chamberlain's foreign policy is still a matter of historical controversy. Among the more balanced judgments on Munich is the following made by the diplomatic and military historian J. W. Wheeler-Bennett in 1948.

... The story of Munich ... is a story in which the human frailties and virtues are inextricably commingled. Vacillation and tenacity; faith and suspicion; trust and betrayal; over-confidence and under-estimation; conduct courageous and conduct ignoble—they are all there. It is a gloomy story.

Let us say of the Munich Agreement that it was inescapable; that, faced with the lack of preparedness in Britain's armaments and defences, with the lack of unity at home and in the Commonwealth, with the collapse of French morale, and with the uncertainty of Russia's capacity to fight, Mr.

FROM J. W. Wheeler-Bennett, *Munich: Prologue to Tragedy* (Des Moines: Duell, Sloan and Pearce, 1948), pp. 433-437. By permission of Macmillan & Co. Ltd.

Chamberlain had no alternative to do other than he did; let us pay tribute to his persistence in carrying out a policy which he honestly believed to be right. Let us accept and admit all these things, but in so doing let us not omit the shame and humiliation which were ours; let us not forget that, in order to save our own skins—that because we were too weak to protect ourselves—we were forced to sacrifice a small Power to slavery. It is of no avail to say that we saved Czechoslovakia from that fate which was later suffered by our ally Poland, that, but for Munich, Bohemia and Moravia would have been devastated as were the provinces of Cracow and Lodz and Warsaw. In reality it was the Czechs who saved us, for, had President Beneš elected to fight with Russian support and thus precipitate an Eastern European war, it is impossible to believe that Britain and France could have kept aloof, however reluctantly they might have been dragged into participation.

In fairness to Mr. Chamberlain it must be said that he was the victim of circumstances which he had previously foreseen and had striven to prevent. The blame for the delay in British rearmament lies not so much at Mr. Chamberlain's door as at those of Mr. Baldwin and Mr. MacDonald, and the credit for the fact that Britain began to rearm even in 1936 is due in great measure to their Chancellor of the Exchequer. But, because of these sins of omission between 1933 and 1937, Britain was forced to other sins of commission in 1938; because she was too weak to do otherwise, she was compelled to condone chicanery, aggression and injustice and to become an accessory to these outrages. There is nothing for pride or congratulation in the story of this whole period; British statesmanship has never been so humbled by a foreign Power since the Dutch burned the British Fleet in the Medway. In that time Britain attempted to play the part of a Great Power "on the cheap". She assumed obligations which she had not the will to carry out. From the original violations of the Treaty of Locarno in 1936, when Britain was forced to admit that she had put her name to a treaty which she could no longer maintain, to the Munich Agreement, when Germany achieved the full measure of her demands, there was a fundamental failure of leadership which resulted in the complete lack on the part of the British public, at any time between the wars, to realize how far their vital interests lay in Europe. It is true that Mr. Baldwin had declared in 1934 that "our frontier is on the Rhine", but he had never followed up this statement.

The apologists for Munich cannot have it both ways. Either Britain was so ill-armed and undefended that she was, with great reluctance, forced to a certain course of action in order to ensure peace, or else she *was* in a position to fight, and, of her own free will, chose not to do so. In neither case is there cause for self-approbation, but there is less ground for contrition in the first than the second. It may be true that we could not "stand up to Hitler and damn the consequences", but if so we should not be proud of it.

Moreover, it must not be forgotten that the whole basis of the defence of Munich shifted midway between October 1938 and March 1939. The original argument of Mr. Chamberlain, Sir John Simon, Sir Samuel Hoare, and Sir Thomas Inskip was that the Prime Minister had saved the world from war and had brought back "Peace for Our Time". Later, however, when the international situation began to deteriorate, the Munich Agreement began to be hailed by its supporters not so much as a great act of statesmanship which had preserved anew the palladium of peace, as an astute act of diplomacy by which Britain had "bought time" in order to complete her rearmament and build up her defences. Of this last argument there was no sign in October 1938, and, in any case, whichever claim is made for Munich, it was a failure. It brought neither peace with honour nor for our time, and not until it had been destroyed by the march into Prague did His Majesty's Government take the crucial decision to introduce conscription.

Should we have fought in October 1938? On this point the military authorities on the highest level are divided. There are those who believe that, considering our lack of preparation, that Germany was from two to three years ahead of us in armaments, that France was in little better state than ourselves and Russia an unknown quantity, we were not only more than justified in not fighting in 1938, but were guilty, in Lord Trenchard's phrase, of "sheer audacity in going to war in 1939". Others maintain that, although our essential weakness must be admitted, it would have been better to have fought in 1938, since war with Germany was inevitable, with the military forces of Czechoslovakia and Russia on our side than later when Germany had been able to destroy the one and neutralize the other. They point out, in addition, that the German defences in the West were not completed in 1938 and that, in obtaining at Munich the necessary time for this, Germany profited more from the breathing-space than did Britain and France, since for her it represented a year's work at full speed, and to them only seven months' work at a varying tempo.

It is true that the interval between September 1938 and September 1939 enabled Mr. Chamberlain to meet the Polish crisis with the support of a united Britain and a united Commonwealth, and that the British Government no longer felt that it was useless to go to war if the immediate object of their assistance was to be at once overwhelmed by Germany. This had been the argument employed with Czechoslovakia in 1938, but by 1939 it had been realized that Hitler must be fought and beaten even with the certainty of initial reverses.

Yet it is equally true that if, in 1939, it was the hope of British statesmanship to avoid war, the chances of so doing had been materially diminished by the events of 1938, since Hitler can hardly be blamed for thinking that those Powers who had abandoned an unassailably strong moral and political position in respect of Czechoslovakia, would not proceed to extremes in the case of Poland. Just as Mr. Chamberlain had failed to comprehend the depths of German infamy, so, in his turn, Hitler under-estimated the capacity of the British for illogical virtue.

In the United States of America great harm was done to British prestige by the policy of Munich, harm of which the full degree was not to be realized until after the outbreak of the Second World War. France and Britain lost more friends in America, and the forces of Isolationism gained more recruits, by reason of the Munich Agreement than by almost any other event in the years between the wars. Though there was no great body of American opinion which would have favoured intervention on the side of Britain had she gone to war in 1938, the fact remains that the hands of those who bitterly opposed the granting of American aid in 1939–41 were substantially strengthened by the suspicion and mistrust of British policy which was engendered by her surrender at Munich, and the protagonists of the "all-aid-short-of-war" movement before Pearl Harbour numbered among them many former friends of Britain, who openly proclaimed that their motives were opposition to Hitler and not friendship for Britain. Those supporters of outright intervention, such as Miss Dorothy Thompson, found difficulty in undoing in 1939 and 1940 the harm which their own vituperation against Britain had effected in 1938, and the American public, ever prone to adopt an anti-British attitude, were more deeply moved by the writings of Professor Frederick Schuman and Mr. Louis Bromfield after Munich than by the eloquent appeals of Mr. Herbert Agar after Dunkirk. The ill-effects of the Munich policy were only partially obliterated by the appearance of Mr. Churchill as Prime Minister of Britain, and it cannot yet be said that the seeds of suspicion then implanted have been completely eradicated.

There remains the enigma of Russia, ever a sphinx, ever a mystery. Had Britain and France made in 1938 the advances to Moscow which they made a year later, would the result have been different? That Russia was prepared to fight at the time of Munich is more than a strong probability; it is only the effectiveness and capacity of her intervention which are in doubt. If Mr. Chamberlain had not deemed "premature" the Soviet proposals for consultation put forward after the annexation of Austria and the occupation of Prague, would Russia to-day be the object of the world's suspicion and concern? These questions can only be pondered. Their answer is unknown. The fact, however, remains that, with the Munich Agreement, Soviet policy was radically reorientated, and that to-day we are confronted with a parallel in history of which the possibilities are terrible in the extreme.

But, above all, the salient point of the story of Munich is not so much its immediate importance as its significance as an analysis of a case-history in the disease of political myopia which afflicted the leaders and the peoples of the world in the years between the wars. For the problem posed then is the same which confronts us now—and remains unsolved. It is not, fundamentally, a political or a technical problem; it is psychological and spiritual.

39
THE PARTY STRUCTURE IN THE TWENTIETH CENTURY
Robert McKenzie

Perhaps the most carefully explored field of twentieth-century British history has been the history of political parties. This work has been undertaken partly under the inspiration of Namier, partly under the influence of the concepts of the behavioral sciences, and partly in response to the fact that party organization and discipline have come to replace the House of Commons as the operative focus of political life, including decision-making by the government of the day. The most widely acclaimed effort to establish a sociology of British political parties in the twentieth century has been the work of Robert McKenzie, a professor at the London School of Economics. This selection comprises the conclusion to the first edition of his book, published in 1955, and presents the provocative thesis that the parliamentary Labour Party does not differ in any fundamental way from the parliamentary Conservative Party.

AFTER he had examined the Conservative and Liberal Party organizations almost half a century ago, A. L. Lowell wrote: "Both are shams, but with this difference, that the Conservative organization is a transparent, and the Liberal an opaque, sham." It can be argued that if the word "Labour" is substituted for "Liberal," there is a sense in which Lowell's remark is equally appropriate to-day. Some might dissent from the use of the word "sham" since it suggests, perhaps unfairly, that the two major parties operate in an atmosphere of conscious duplicity and deceit. Such of course is not the case; but it can hardly be denied that party conflict, by its very nature, requires that the rival party organizations should exaggerate their own virtues and misrepresent their opponents. They do so in their discussion of the policy differences between them and also in their comments on their respective party organizations. This study has not been concerned with party ideologies and programmes; in the matter of policy differences, therefore, one need only note that, in the thirty years in which the Labour and Conservative Par-

---

FROM *British Political Parties: The Distribution of Power Within the Conservative and Labour Parties*, Revised Edition, by R. T. McKenzie, London, Heinemann Educational Books Ltd., 1963, New York, Frederick A. Praeger, Inc., Publishers, 1964. By permission of the publishers.

ties have faced each other as the principal rivals in the House of Commons and in the country, the *real* gulf between them has never widened to the point where the parliamentary system threatened to become unworkable. Balfour argued that the prerequisite for the successful operation of the British parliamentary system was that the parties which contend for office must be so thoroughly in agreement on fundamentals that they could safely afford to bicker about details. Certainly in the course of the last thirty years the Labour and Conservative Parties have debated issues of major importance which cannot be dismissed as "details." But neither great party at any point has threatened to disrupt the parliamentary system in order either to impose its own policies or to prevent its opponents from implementing theirs. The "agreement on fundamentals" is to-day very nearly as great as it has ever been in the modern history of British politics.

But the second element in the process of exaggeration and misrepresentation is of greater importance for this study. There has been a persistent tendency ... for the two major parties to exaggerate the differences between their party organizations with a view to proving that their own is democratic and that of their opponents is not. The Labour Party customarily argues that the Conservative Leader rules his party with the iron hand of an autocrat; that he is not subject to the effective control either of his followers in Parliament or of the mass organization of the party outside Parliament. Labour spokesmen claim that, in contrast, their own party is fully democratic because their party leaders are subject to annual re-election (at least when the party is in opposition) and both the Leader and the parliamentary party, they claim, are ultimately responsible to the annual conference of the party. The Conservatives habitually reply that the Labour Party in Parliament is in fact subject to the control of a tight-knit clique of party managers at the party head office at Transport House; and these party "bosses," the Conservatives charge, manipulate the affairs of the party in their own interest and are in no way responsible to the electorate. The Conservative spokesmen draw a sharp contrast between this state of affairs and the position in their own party, where the parliamentary leaders (who *are* subject to the control of the electorate) are assigned full responsibility for the affairs of the party, although (the Conservatives add) they give due weight to the views of their party followers both inside and outside Parliament.

It should be clear from the analysis in the preceding chapters that the most nearly accurate of these interpretations of party organization is the Conservative statement of the position within their own party; although it must be added, that in their anxiety to keep the mass organization in its place, the Conservatives have tended (in the formal explanations of their party organization) to exaggerate the authority of their Leader. But the Conservative view of the Labour Party and the Labour Party's own picture both of itself and of its opponents are highly misleading.... In reality the distribution of power within the two parties is overwhelmingly similar.

Some part of the confusion arises... from a careless use of terms and a failure to distinguish between several autonomous organizations which are loosely associated together for common political purposes. Two parliamentary parties face each other in the House of Commons: they are correctly called "the Conservative Party" and "the Parliamentary Labour Party." Each is an autonomous organization and is aided for electoral purposes by a mass organization of its supporters: the Conservatives by "the National Union of Conservative and Unionist Associations," the Parliamentary Labour Party by a body properly known as "The Labour Party." At the regional and national level each of these mass organizations is sustained by a professional staff, the Conservative Central Office and the Labour Party head office. These mass organizations are best understood as voluntary associations of the politically-active section of the population who are prepared to work for the return to office of one or other of the parliamentary parties. Each mass organization represents a vast reservoir of largely voluntary and unpaid labour of the sort which is indispensable in the era of the mass electorate. All other functions of the mass organization are, and must remain, subsidiary to their primary task as vote-getting agencies. The mass organizations can and do exact a certain price for their labour; they expect to be listened to by their leaders. Like Bagehot's constitutional monarch, the annual party conference has the right to be consulted, the right to encourage, and the right to warn. But this is not to say that the members of the mass organization have the right under the British parliamentary system to control or direct the actions of their parliamentary leaders.

The evolution of the British political parties in the era of the mass electorate has witnessed two striking developments, both of which reflect the ascendancy and the primacy of Parliament. Until well into the nineteenth century the Conservative Party was no more than a grouping of a few hundred Members of Parliament and Peers who were associated together for sustaining (whenever it proved feasible) a Conservative Cabinet. They had neither a professional staff of any size nor a mass organization of voluntary supporters in the country; nor did they need them. They were able to rely for the most part on the allegiance and authority of the squirearchy and the generous financial contributions of a section of the business community to provide the very considerable financial resources which were required to win elections in the days of great political corruption. But two developments forced the Conservative Party to transform itself. The first was the rapid expansion of the electorate especially in 1867 and afterwards; and the second, the drastic tightening of the electoral laws against corruption. Even if the Conservatives had not themselves become aware that these developments would force a transformation of the party, the initiative of the Liberals under Joseph Chamberlain would certainly have forced them to do so. In any event, a combination of pressures forced the Conservative Party to devise a mass organization of voluntary supporters to sustain the Conservative cause and to secure votes at elections. Disraeli and Lord Randolph Churchill provided a new statement of Toryism which succeeded in attracting a wide range of popular support and a number of hard working party managers did the job of building the National Union as the co-ordinating agency of Conservative activity in the country.

It was by no means certain (when Ostrogorski wrote at the end of the century) that the National Union or the Central Office (or both) might not manage ultimately to become the controlling influence in the affairs of the Conservative Party. Parliament might, as Ostrogorski feared, ultimately be supplanted by the caucus. But... this has not happened. Effective control of the affairs of the Conservative Party remains in the hands of the Leader thrown up by the parliamentary party and those he chooses as his associates; they retain their authority as long as they retain the support of their followers in Parliament. The National Union remains what it was declared to be in its earliest beginnings, "a handmaid" to the party in Parliament, although, as befits a more democratic age, it has fairly frequently talked to its masters in a way that no Victorian domestic servant would ever have dared to do. The Conservative Party has been transformed since the mid-nineteenth century; it now has a vast appendage of voluntary supporters who labour on its behalf between and during elections; but the working of the parliamentary party has been remarkably little affected.

The transformation of the Labour Party in the half century of its existence has been in one sense diametrically different from that of the Conservatives, although the end product is strangely similar. A gathering representing some hundreds of thousands of organized trade unionists and a few thousand members of socialist societies decided in 1900 to co-operate together to secure increased working class representation in the House of Commons. They soon found it necessary to instruct their representatives in Parliament to form themselves into what amounted to a parliamentary party. That parliamentary party began increasingly to resemble the other great parliamentary parties as it came to rival them in size and strength. By the time the Parliamentary Labour Party had taken office in 1924 its transformation was almost complete. By accepting all the conventions with respect to the office of Prime Minister and of Cabinet government, it ensured that the Labour Party outside Parliament would be relegated to a status not unlike that of the National Union. The Labour Party's devices for ensuring the ascendancy of its parliamentary leaders are infinitely more complex than those which obtain in the Conservative Party. One must comb Labour literature with care to find the occasional forthright declaration of the autonomy of the Parliamentary Labour Party. But the working relationship between the Parliamentary Labour Party and its mass organization is in essence very similar indeed to the equivalent relationship on the Conservative side.

The essential function of the two mass organizations is to sustain two competing teams of parliamentary leaders between whom the electorate as a whole may periodically choose. When the electorate has made its choice the leaders of the successful team don the garments of authority which are provided under the Cabinet system and they retain this authority so long as they retain the confidence of their followers in Parliament (and, of course, of the electorate). Their followers outside Parliament become little more than a highly organized pressure group with a special channel of communication directly to the Leader, the Cabinet and the parliamentary party. Any disposition to take advantage of this special relationship is normally more than neutralized by feelings of pride and loyalty to their leaders and by an anxiety not to embarrass them in the execution of their duties, or to provide aid and comfort to the rival team, who are eagerly preparing to overthrow them at the forthcoming election. Most governments at one time or another find it advisable to make concessions on some issue of policy to the clearly expressed views of their followers outside Parliament. But they make such concessions much more frequently to their followers *in* Parliament on whose day to day support in the division lobbies the government depends, than they do to their followers in the country whose allegiance is tested normally only at five-yearly intervals. While the parliamentary party is in opposition it tends to listen more readily to the voices of its supporters in the country; but even while in opposition no major parliamentary party in the modern period has allowed itself to be relegated to the rôle of spokesman or servant of its mass organization.

Ostrogorski's fears notwithstanding, the institution of Parliament has survived almost unimpaired into the age of mass electorates and of mass parties. One of the few significant developments has been the decline of the independent Member of Parliament (although this has been a much less spectacular process than some have maintained) and in addition, the diminishing freedom of action accorded to the independently-minded members of both of the great parties. As each parliamentary party has developed a vast, cumbersome, but highly organized appendage outside Parliament, the flexibility of parliamentary parties has undoubtedly declined. The parliamentary leaders can be virtually certain that the withdrawal of the whip by the parliamentary party or expulsion from the mass organization will result in the political death of the apostate concerned. In addition, the two great machines between them have almost ground out of existence the minor political parties, and it is now difficult to see how a third party of any importance could emerge again unless one of the two great parties broke cleanly in two and each of the sections carried with it some part of the mass organization outside Parliament. In these respects it may be argued that the growth of the mass party has greatly increased the rigidity of party relationships in the House of Commons. Two great monolithic structures now face each other and conduct furious arguments about the comparatively minor issues that separate them.

In such circumstances it would appear to be more than ever important that minority groups within each of the great parties should be given reasonable scope for expression of their views and for an opportunity to convert their fellow party members both in the House of Commons and in the mass party outside to their own point of view. Admittedly no party can tolerate a fully organized "party within a party"; this was shown conclusively by Labour's experience during the period 1929–31 ... which culminated in the break with the ILP. It is largely because of this experience that the Labour Party has viewed all attempts to organize minority opinion within the party as an intolerable threat to its own survival. There are clearly defined limits beyond which organized minorities cannot be permitted to go if the parent party is to function as a coherent contender for office. But the Labour Party appears to lean towards a dangerously rigorous conception of party discipline which sometimes appears to resemble the Communist conception of democratic centralism. If both major parties become too grimly intolerant of honest differences of opinion among their followers on major matters of policy then there are real grounds for concern in a period in which the prospects for minor parties and independent candidates are so poor. The danger has been more evident in the case of the Labour Party; but in another form it is no less real in the case of the Conservatives. They have found it less necessary to rely on rigid codes of discipline; this may be in part a reflection of the fact that ideological disputes culminating in threatened party splits are rare. The Conservative Party may be in more danger of sinking into a drab uniformity of opinion through lack of internal intellectual vitality. If the two great parties together are to dominate the whole political life of the community, then it is essential that every encouragement should be given to the expression of honest political differences within each. These differences become a source of concern only if they threaten the ability of a party to form and sustain a government. Short of this, intra-party differences must be welcomed as an indispensable means of preventing the sort of intellectual sclerosis which appears at times to threaten the two great parties of this country.

Apart from these particular sources of concern, one must face the more fundamental question as to whether the present system of party organization in Great Britain deserves the label "democratic." Because the party leaders in Parliament do not hold themselves directly responsible to the members of the party outside Parliament it is sometimes alleged that this proves that both great parties are "undemocratic." Or, as some would argue, it provides a triumphant vindication of the "iron law of oligarchy" associated with the name of Robert Michels. Certainly ... there is ample evidence of the working of what Michels calls the "technical" and "psychological" factors which tend to ensure the emergence of, and the retention of power by, a small group of leaders in each party. But evidence has also been provided (it is perhaps more extensive in the history of the Conservative Party than in the Labour Party) of revolts against the party leaders which have culminated in their overthrow. The "law of oligarchy" is certainly not an "iron" law. Parties are usually content to be led; but this is largely because there is no other way in which they can operate. This does not mean, however, that party leaders can ignore with impunity the moods and aspirations of their followers; they must carry their followers (and above all their followers in their parliamentary party) with them. And to do so, they have to take into account at every stage the clearly defined currents of opinion within their party. Blind appeals to loyalty (either to the person of the Leader or to the party itself) are frequently resorted to, and often they achieve their purpose. But they are rarely successful in bridging a real gulf when one does develop between the leaders and their followers.

Another factor must be taken into account in assessing the relevance of Michels' theories. Largely no doubt as a result of his own continental background, Michels appeared to assume that a "democratic" political party ought ideally to be under the direction and control of its mass membership. Michels suggested that this relationship never proves feasible in practice because of the operation of his law of oligarchy. But in the British context there is another reason of greater importance: the conventions of the parliamentary system (which have been accepted by all parties, including the Labour Party) require that Members of Parliament, and therefore parliamentary parties also, must hold themselves responsible solely to the electorate and not to the mass organization of their supporters outside Parliament. In other words, a crude application of Michels' theories would ignore what might be termed the division of labour within British political parties. It would ignore the fact that the primary function of the mass organizations is to sustain competing teams of potential leaders in the House of Commons in order that the electorate as a whole may choose between them. All other functions (involving attempts by the mass organizations to influence the formulation of policy and the emergence of leaders within the parliamentary parties) are, and must remain, subsidiary. The mass organizations may be permitted to play a small part in these respects; but if they attempted to arrogate to themselves a determining influence with respect to policy or leadership they would be cutting across the chain of responsibility from Cabinet, to Parliament, to electorate, which is a fundamental feature of the British parliamentary system.

But Michels apart, many of the other criticisms of the alleged undemocratic nature of party organization reflect a persistent belief in what might be termed the classical conception of the democratic process. In a penetrating analysis of the shortcomings of this classical conception, Joseph Schumpeter has shown how little relation it bears to the democratic process as it has evolved in Britain and most other political democracies. In the late eighteenth century it was assumed that the democratic process would ensure the triumph of the common good by permitting the people themselves to decide issues through the election of representatives who assembled to carry out "the people's will." The electorate, it was assumed, might be called on to pronounce on certain major issues (perhaps by means of referenda); all other issues would be decided by a committee (Parliament) elected by the whole adult population. The function of the members of this committee would be to voice, reflect or represent the will of the electorate. Lip service is still paid to this classical conception of democracy even by many who are aware of the extent to which it has proved unworkable. The study of the psychology of political processes has revealed the importance of the extra-rational and the irrational elements in social behaviour. The parallel development of the arts of political propaganda has enabled political leaders to exploit the irrational element in human behaviour and to manufacture what is often a purely synthetic "general will." So much so that some are prepared to argue, with Schumpeter, that the will of the people is the product and not the motive power of the political process.

It has also become increasingly evident that the classical theory attributed to the electorate an altogether unrealistic degree of initiative; it came near to ignoring completely the importance of leadership in the political process. It is no doubt more realistic to argue that the essence of the democratic process is that it should provide a free competition for political leadership. The essential rôle of the electorate is not to reach decisions on specific issues of policy but to decide which of two or more competing teams of potential leaders shall make the decisions. The democratic process ensures that there will be a periodic opportunity for the electorate to review the record of the decision-makers who currently hold office; and, if the electorate wishes, it may replace them with an alternative team. The competing teams usually offer broad declarations of policy respecting their long range goals; they may also promise to introduce specific items of legislation; or alternatively they may, like the National Government formed in 1931, ask only for a "Doctor's Mandate" to do whatever they may subsequently decide to be necessary in the national interest. In the formulation of declarations of policy and of electoral programmes the membership of the mass party usually plays some part, although in both the Conservative and Labour Parties final decisions in this regard rest with the parliamentary leaders. These leaders are bound to be concerned mainly with their own conception of the national interest and with the competing demands of various interest groups which may or may not be adequately reflected within their party organizations. But one thing is certain: initiative in the formulation of policy cannot possibly come primarily from the several millions of party supporters or from the electorate as a whole. The active party workers must devote themselves primarily to sustaining the teams of candidates for leadership and the electorate in turn must content itself with choosing between these competing teams.

The mass organizations of the Conservative and Labour Parties have, of course, additional functions which have been examined in some detail in the course of this study. They serve as a two-way channel of communication between the leaders of the parliamentary parties and their supporters in the country; when the parliamentary party is in office its mass organization plays a vital rôle in explaining and defending the work of the government and in keeping it informed of currents of opinion in the country. A further function of the mass political organizations is to provide a means whereby the politically active individuals in the community can play some part, however limited, in influencing both the formulation of party policy and the emergence of party leaders. And for those citizens who seek to play a more influential part in the political life of the community, participation in the mass organizations provides an excellent preliminary training for parliamentary candidature and eventual entry into Parliament.

Seen from the viewpoint of society as a whole, mass political parties of the kind that have emerged in Britain fulfil an invaluable set of functions. By exposing the electorate to a cross-fire of political argument and debate they stimulate public interest in the essential business of "attending to the arrangements of society." The mass parties also fulfil an important integrating function. They are one of the main channels through which interest groups and both organized and unorganized bodies of opinion can bring their views to the attention of parliamentarians. The parliamentary leaders in turn must sift, weigh, analyse and evaluate the views that are conveyed through the party organizations. Inevitably these views are taken into account in the formulation of parliamentary policy. Lord Bryce saw American parties as "brokers" whose primary business it was to serve various interests and to reconcile them. In the much more homogeneous society of Britain the mass parties are inevitably less preoccupied with this task; they do nevertheless play an important rôle in integrating the diverse and sometimes conflicting interests and opinions in the community. But this study has been concerned not with the broad social function of parties but with their internal structure and the distribution of power within each. And no emphasis on the auxiliary functions of the mass organizations outside Parliament can be allowed to obscure the basic proposition that the mass parties are primarily the servants of their respective parliamentary parties; that their principal function is to sustain teams of parliamentary leaders between whom the electorate is periodically invited to choose.

If this is a fair description of the realities of the democratic process then it should be evident that the two major British political parties are well suited to play an appropriate rôle in this process. They have managed to avoid most of the serious pitfalls into which party organizations in many other countries have fallen. The ideological conflict between the parties is not so great as to threaten the survival of the democratic process itself; yet it is great enough to ensure that the members of the mass organizations of the two main parties will work willingly for the victory of their cause without seeking illicit material rewards for their efforts. The autonomy of the two great parliamentary parties is almost completely unimpaired, although each of them has devised a system of consultation with its mass organization which ensures that the latter will not be so exasperated with its impotence as to refuse to fulfil its function as a vote-getting agency. Each major party has organized a professional machine which works alongside the mass organization and ensures the latter's efficiency without appearing too obviously to dominate it. Neither of these machines has in any way threatened to become the real centre of power within its respective party organization. Both great parties have tapped large scale financial resources without becoming completely beholden to those who provide the funds; neither party in office has sacrificed its conception of the national interest in order to serve the purposes of those sections of the community which provide its funds.

Reference has been made throughout this study to serious shortcomings in each of the major party organizations; there is plenty of scope for the reformer in both the Conservative and Labour Parties. There may also be scope for those who seek to modify or to transform other aspects of British parliamentary democracy. But an extensive review of the working of British party organizations inspires neither alarm nor gloom; half a century after Ostrogorski wrote there appears to be no reason to conclude that events have justified his pessimistic expectation that the parliamentary system was unlikely to survive the emergence of the mass party. It might be argued, indeed, that the parliamentary system gives every appearance of outliving the age of the mass party; there is much evidence to support the view that the traditional electoral activities of the mass party, including the conduct of public meetings, canvassing and the rest, are now of declining importance in influencing the outcome of elections. It seems likely that the really effective electioneering of the future will rely increasingly on the newer mass media of radio and, above all, on television. Perhaps in retrospect it will be evident that the mass party saw its heyday during the period when the extension of the franchise had created a mass electorate, but there was as yet no effective means of reaching the voters in their own homes. But meanwhile, there can be no doubt that despite the many problems it created, the mass party did not fulfil the gloomy expectations of its early chroniclers. Perhaps the most apt conclusion for this study can be borrowed from Lord Bryce's foreword (written in 1902) to the first edition of Ostrogorski's *Democracy and the Organization of Political Parties*. Bryce had praised Ostrogorski's work very highly, but he questioned his preoccupation with "the pathology of party government." Bryce concluded: "In England, happily for England, the (party) organizations have not ceased to be controlled by men occupying a position which makes them amenable to public opinion, nor have they as yet departed far from the traditions in which the strength of English free government lies." Bryce's observation is equally valid to-day.

40

THE LABOUR PARTY AS A POLITICAL INSTITUTION

S. H. Beer

A decade after McKenzie's study appeared, the Harvard political scientist Samuel Beer published another major analysis of party structure and function in "the collectivist age." As the following selection from Beer's book indicates, he strongly dissents from McKenzie's categories and sees in the development of the Labour Party a consistent pattern of devotion to an ideological program.

WHEN THE Labour Party came on the scene, British constitutional practice had already endowed a Prime Minister with certain well-understood elements of authority and these, in turn, strengthened the position of a party Leader who, although in Opposition, was a potential Prime Minister. When, for instance, a party Leader was summoned by the monarch to accept the commission to form a Government, the Leader made his own decision whether to accept and, if he accepted, what persons to select for his Cabinet. In Cabinet meetings, while he might "take the voices" on a controverted question, he was not bound to accept the majority view: after all, he had the authority to secure the dismissal of any minister. Similarly, the decision on the resignation of the Government or a request for the dissolution of Parliament was his sole decision. In all these cases, of course, the Leader faced certain realities—the existence, for example, of colleagues with strong personal followings or with helpful executive skills. And in his decisions to accept office, form a Cabinet, resign, or dissolve he would usually choose to consult informally with colleagues. Constitutional norms, however, left him free to take these decisions by his sole authority and without consulting anyone (except the monarch), and certainly without seeking instructions from his party organization.

During the interwar period efforts were made from time to time in the Labour Party to restrict the Leader's exercise of these traditional prerogatives. This aim could well be considered a logical deduction from the plain words of the party constitution, which could be taken to legitimize arrangements such as those that prevailed under the "caucus" system

---

FROM *British Politics in the Collectivist Age*, by S. H. Beer. © Copyright 1965 by Samuel H. Beer. Reprinted by permission of Alfred A. Knopf, Inc.

in the Australian Labour Party. On the whole, however, these efforts failed, and on the three occasions between 1924 and 1945 when a Labour Leader took office as Prime Minister his procedure in accepting the King's commission, making a Cabinet, presiding over it, and deciding on a dissolution was in accord with the usual practice.

These are not unimportant decisions and the authority to make them endowed the Leader of the Labour Party with powers well beyond what he gained from the party constitution and Labour's official theory of its structure of authority. Yet a party Leader could exercise these powers and still not exert a decisive influence on his party's goals or strategy. British constitutional norms leave a great deal to circumstance and can fit quite different structures of effective power and influence. In assessing the effective power of the Leader of the Labour Party during the Socialist generation the case of MacDonald is crucial, as it is obvious that his influence over the party greatly exceeded that of any of his successors—Henderson, Lansbury, and Attlee. If we can find limits on his scope of decision, we shall have located the outer boundaries of the Leader's power in that period.

On what questions of party purpose did MacDonald exercise a determining influence? A major question that divided the party in the 1920's and 1930's will illustrate both the extent and the limits of his effective power. This was a question inherent in the position of an ideological and programmatic party confronted with the prospect of taking office while still in a minority. Should it introduce "some bold Socialist measures" which would lead to its defeat, but which could then be made the basis of an appeal to the country? Or should it attempt only those ameliorative reforms which might be expected to win the support of Parliament and which would also help the party to show that it was "fit to govern"? MacDonald's preference was clearly for the latter alternative, and throughout his period of leadership he had his way in spite of opposition from sections of the parliamentary and extra-parliamentary parties.

In 1924 this choice was weighed by the inner core of the parliamentary leadership—MacDonald, Snowden, Thomas, Henderson, and Webb—who decided against the "extreme policy." Criticism of their choice was voiced while the party was in office and in later years merged with the initiative taken by the I.L.P. for *Socialism in Our Time*, the title of its 1927 policy statement the principal proposal of which was for a "Living Wage." What the I.L.P. demanded was not only that the party adopt these proposals, but also that any future Labour Government, even though in a minority, should base its immediate policy upon them, deliberately inviting defeat in order to make a further appeal to the country. MacDonald and the parliamentary leaders continued to prefer the tactic of 1924, which was implied by the less restrictive program offered by them in *Labour and the Nation*. At the conference of 1928, when this program was adopted, they easily beat down the I.L.P. challenge and again the 1929 Government embarked on the more prudent course.

Although in the long run the MacDonald tactic was designed to promote Labour's pursuit of supreme power, in the short run it qualified the policy of political independence by entailing, in effect, that the Government would introduce only those measures which a substantial body of Liberals would support. During MacDonald's day this choice of tactics involved the parliamentary leaders in a sharp, running controversy with important sections of the party in which the views of the leaders, whether in or out of office, were upheld by conference and accepted by the parliamentary party. For the sake of argument, let us grant the elitist case and agree that the Leader "imposed" his answer to this question upon the party. The essential point remains, however, that the controversy was over tactics and did not bring into question the fundamentals of Labour's orthodoxy. For all its militant language, the I.L.P. accepted the strategy of winning power and achieving Socialism by democratic, parliamentary means. Moreover, in the context of Labour's received doctrine and program, there was nothing particularly radical about the content of the "Living Wage" proposals. If, therefore, we wish to cite this controversy as an example of the influence of the parliamentary elite, we must also recognize that it did not involve the fundamentals of the party's purpose and that the alternatives the leadership chose among fell well within the boundaries of the consensus on ends and means. Even in the era of MacDonaldism, and with regard to its major controversy, elitism in the Labour Party extended only to questions of tactics, not strategy, and involved variations on an agreed design in program, not fundamental alterations.

The limits imposed on the elite by the party consensus are seen even more clearly if we turn to the major instance when the Leader overstepped those limits. This was, of course, MacDonald's agreement to form a National Government in 1931. He and Snowden had not been able to carry the Cabinet with them in accepting the 10 per cent cut in employment benefits that the New York banks had made a condition of a loan to support sterling. For although a majority of the Cabinet favored acceptance, the minority who would resign was so substantial that MacDonald concluded that he could no longer carry on the Government. A measure such as the proposed cuts struck at the party's ancient commitment to the "interests of labour." The General Council of the T.U.C. had firmly informed Snowden of its opposition and the parliamentary party had on the whole been strongly against.

The party's ability to resist its Leader on this question of social policy, however, was exceeded by the virtual unanimity of its negative when MacDonald attempted to lead it into coalition. In the Cabinet, for instance, while MacDonald was able to find eleven of its twenty-one members who would follow him on the unemployment cuts, he could bring along only three in support of the National Government. This is understandable. For if the party had gone into a National Government, it would have meant not only supporting an attack on the "interests of labour," but also a major reversal of the basic commitment of 1918 to a strategy of political independence.

"Evidence of practical unanimity in the Party is growing," wrote Hugh Dalton the day after MacDonald had informed his astonished Cabinet of his decision to lead a National Government. "Press estimates of J. R. M.'s Parliamentary following rapidly falling. How ignorant of our Movement the enemy Press is!" The Press, and perhaps even the King, had expected a large defection to MacDonald, who himself had thought that about half the parliamentary party would follow him. In the ensuing general election MacDonald did attract many who otherwise would have voted Labour, and the party's poll fell by two million as compared with 1929. But the organized party remained solid. Only three ministers—Snowden, Thomas, and Sankey—and a tiny handful of M.P.'s followed the leader, all of whom the N.E.C. duly expelled. Not a single constituency organization or trade union budged.

Judging by the previous behavior of other British parties, such solidarity was unprecedented. For a decade MacDonald had enjoyed a vast ascendancy over the party in Parliament and in the country and Snowden and Thomas, his principal associates in the decision of 1931, had for years belonged to the innermost circle of the political elite. It is hard to believe that either of the older parties could have suffered such a defection among its leaders without being split from top to bottom. Indeed, the National Government tactic of which Neville Chamberlain was the "constructive engineer" is reminiscent of a similar maneuver in which the Conservatives, by accepting the leadership of Lloyd George for a short while after World War I, helped enormously to widen the schism among Liberals and hasten the decline of that party. If a similar effect was indeed intended in 1931 by the Conservatives, like the "enemy Press" they showed themselves gravely ignorant of the "Movement."

The similarity of response among the various sections of the Movement—parliamentary party, General Council, and N.E.C., constituency organizations and trade unions—can be understood only in the light of Labour's deep-running commitment to the strategy of political independence. But the original organizing force, the trade unions, also came into play. During the days of crisis the General Council, and especially its dominating personality, Ernest Bevin, took critical initiatives in the disavowal of MacDonald and the settlement of a new political line. Moreover, in succeeding years the center of leadership moved away from the small and weakened parliamentary party toward the trade unions. "The General Council of the T.U.C. under the leadership of Bevin and Citrine," writes Pelling, "abandoned its usual role of being the sheet-anchor of the party and instead moved in to take the helm." The National Council of Labour, which represented the party and the unions, but on which the unions had a majority, laid down the outlines of policy. Within these outlines the National Executive worked out detailed programs for a Labour Government. Under this new balance in the party elite, all elements of the party accepted without controversy the new statements of party program set forth in *For Socialism and Peace* (1934) and *Labour's Immediate Programme* (1937). These, however, although more precise and definite than *Labour and The Nation,* involved no fundamental innovations.

In the 1930's another threat to Labour's orthodoxy was raised, when members of the intellectual elite of the party attempted, particularly through the Socialist League, to commit the party to a United Front with the Communists or to a Popular Front with a broad range of representatives of other parties as well as the Communists. These efforts, however, which again endangered the strategy of political independence and at times also had strong anti-parliamentary overtones, were easily defeated, with the union leadership playing a major role.

In the same period, the menace to peace of the Fascist powers raised the issue of sanctions. This prospect of a use of force in which Britain might take part created problems that were difficult for the party's anti-militarists and impossible for its pacifists. Again the unions, and especially Bevin, exerted a weighty influence on the major decisions, such as the repudiation of Lansbury's pacifism at the conference of 1935 and the acceptance of rearmament by the parliamentary party in 1937, by which the party adjusted to the new international situation. Important as these adaptations were, they fell within the boundaries of Labour's internationalism, in particular its long-standing commitment to collective security under the League.

In short, although the union leadership "moved in to take the helm" after 1931, it used its influence to keep the party on the same broad course in domestic and foreign affairs on which it had embarked in 1918. The scope of the union elite in MacDonald's day was limited by the consensus on Labour's orthodoxy. Bevin himself enjoyed great personal influence thanks to his remarkable personal capacities as well as his position as head of one of the largest trade unions. But he was able to push the party only in directions in which it was already committed to move by long-standing commitments. His power was by no means dictatorial. In spite of his best efforts, we should recall, he was unable to secure the election of Arthur Greenwood as Leader in 1935.

Pluralism Within Consensus

TO SPEAK of "pluralism within consensus" may seem curious, if not self-contradictory. If the various groups in the party were agreed on program and purpose, their activity in favor of some goal would be in harmony with the intentions of others: hence, whoever the spokesmen, the ends pursued were common to all and an apparent pluralism is swallowed up in an actual monism. Such indeed was very generally the case with the flourishing pluralistic democracy of Labour during the Socialist generation. Vast numbers of resolutions were moved at party conferences in these years and normally were voted with unanimity. This was quite natural, since they were for the most part restatements of familiar declarations.

Yet the agreement on purpose was not wholly clear, detailed, and unchanging. Occasionally new items were added to the received program and old proposals were developed and adapted. Sometimes new proposals were raised, briefly accepted, then discarded. In these interactions the activity of groups was often important. Even where an item of program was commonly accepted in the party, pressure from a group might greatly help maintain it in a position of high priority. As with the elites, groups within the party were limited and guided by the party consensus. But in the maintenance of that consensus and in such development as it underwent, group activity was a significant force....

Early in 1945 the N.E.C. appointed a small campaign committee to take charge of preparations for the coming election. Morrison was put in the chair, his primary duty being to draft a policy declaration. "This I did," he recalls, "and gave it the title of 'Let Us Face The Future.' " The committee gave Morrison "plenty of elbow room," but on April 11th, according to Dalton, there was "a row."

> Morrison proposed, supported by Greenwood, to back down on iron and steel, and leave it out of the Policy Declaration. He had been lunching, he said, with some friends of ours in the City, who had told him that it was too ambitious to talk of any Public Board "owning" this complicated and troublesome industry. I strongly resisted this, and won. I said that, if iron and steel was dropped, I should refuse to speak in support of the Policy Declaration at Conference, and then Morrison and Greenwood could explain to the delegates why this item, which had been enthusiastically adopted by Conference only last December, had now vanished.

The threat to appeal to the forthcoming conference was Dalton's weapon; the fact that conference had strongly and recently made its mind known put this weapon in his hand. In short, the insurgency of conference in December was very probably responsible for the heavy commitment that the manifesto's declaration in favor of "public ownership of iron and steel" imposed on the Labour Government. Yet, we must immediately observe, conference had this influence only with regard to an item that had long since gone through the mill of trade union and party inquiry and approval. Formally, the Mikardo amendment also made nationalization of building and banking items of the party "program." Operationally, this aspect of the conference decision was meaningless. Conference exerted influence only with regard to an item which, although not enjoying a high priority, had been at least on the margin of Labour's orthodoxy.

Moreover, the decision of conference had influence only on the condition that it find a weighty advocate among the party elite. Once the draft had gone through the N.E.C. and had been published, there was little real opportunity to change it. Having been sent out to unions, local parties, and other affiliated organizations in April, the statement was the basis for a three-day discussion at the conference which met at Blackpool, May 21–25. Conference debated and approved the statement section by section, but its procedure did not permit amendments to be offered. To be sure, resolutions were moved and some were passed against the advice of the platform. But, although the Executive said that it would "take account of" any resolutions passed, they were not considered to be amendments to the manifesto, which emerged from conference and went to the public in exactly the form given it by the N.E.C. The crucial and only moment for bringing to bear the influence of conference had been seized and utilized by Dalton in February.

Conference took seriously the ultimate authority over program with which the party constitution endowed it. Leaders and rank and file delegates alike accepted this premise of party action. Over the years, however, the constitution had acquired a complex gloss, a system of expectations that defined and legitimized the role of conference and other elements of the party in the making of policy. As the history of the iron and steel proposal illustrates, this gloss legitimized a degree of pluralism not specified in the constitution. In particular, it included great deference to the wishes of a trade union in matters concerning its industry. The initiative in bringing the proposal for public ownership of iron and steel before the movement was exercised by I.S.T.C. But this special role of the union was not simply the product of group pressure. It was clearly part of the accepted protocol of decision-making in the party. Once, however, the proposal had been included in Labour's orthodoxy, it could be legitimately advocated by party members in general.

The previous analysis of party decisions does not by any means suffice as a complete description of this complex system of expectations with which the constitution had been glossed. One must attempt to ascertain some of these premises of party action, however, if one is to say when conflict did or did not arise between conference and leadership. The plain words of the Mikardo amendment, for instance, stipulated that the election manifesto was to include the building industry and all banks as candidates for public ownership. Yet it is quite clear that conference did not feel that it had been "defeated" or "overridden" when they were omitted. At the 1945 conference, during the debate on that section of the manifesto pertaining to nationalization, a resolution in almost the same terms as the Mikardo amendment was moved. After the reply by Shinwell, speaking for the N.E.C., however, the resolution was withdrawn without fuss or objection. More interesting is the reaction of Mikardo himself to the omission of these two items. Immediately after Morrison introduced the draft, Mikardo welcomed it as "a good and workmanlike job," the result of "a successful partnership between the decisions of the last Conference and the results of studying just how much work is involved in controlling Britain's economy and nationalising Britain's industry and just how much of that work we can expect to do in our first five years of power." Mikardo's opinion expressed in a letter to the author also shows his lack of concern over the omissions. "Of course, I wasn't ... much disturbed by the fact that some points covered by my resolution were not included in *Let Us Face The Future*. When one defeats the N.E.C. one is quite happy with a 90 per cent victory!"

A Programmatic Party in Power

ELITIST and pluralist theory direct attention to important features of the structure of power of the Labour Party between 1918 and 1945. The roles of leaders and of groups, however, were limited and guided by a consensus within the party on both broad principles and items of program. In this sense the behavior of the party was a function not of the independent decisions of leaders or of the pressure of groups and balancing of interests, but of a widely shared programmatic commitment.

What shall we say of the party after the election of 1945, when for the first time it won a majority in Parliament and a full five-year lease on office? One can readily see different possibilities. The attempt to plan the economy might well intensify group pressures that ran contrary to the party's programmatic commitments. Similarly, the complex and changing actualities of home and foreign affairs, one might think, would often oblige Labour ministers to make decisions on major matters that were not anticipated by the party program and which could not sensibly be referred for decision to the party conference. In view of these highly plausible questions, does the model of the programmatic party give us much help in understanding the behavior of the Atlee Governments of 1945–51? Does program explain the basic decisions of these years?

When we examine the legislative record of the Government, the answer is emphatically "yes." The statutes in which it embodied its purposes of social and economic reconstruction were derived directly and by deliberate intent from the party program. The framing and carrying out of these statutes were, of course, affected by the advice of experts, the suggestions of civil servants, the demands of interest groups, and the personal preferences of ministers. But the main fact remains: to an extent unprecedented in British political history the legislation of a Government was dictated by a party program.

In the first place, the legislation of the Government was deliberately based upon the pledges of the manifesto of 1945. "It was on the basis of this policy document," Herbert Morrison has written, "that the majority Labour Government set about shaping both its legislative programme and its work of administration." The Future Legislation Committee, of which he was chairman, had the task of deciding what bills would be introduced during each session. It acted on the assumption, Morrison relates, "that subject to unforeseen circumstances we would seek to implement the legislative aspects of *Let Us Face The Future* within the lifetime of a single Parliament."

How well the Government succeeded one can readily see by going through the Public General Acts of 1945–50 and comparing the promises of the manifesto with the major statutes put on the books. It is no great exaggeration to say that for every paragraph of pledges one finds a corresponding statute. The items are familiar, but it is well briefly to recall the principal ones in order to have a sense of the magnitude of the accomplishment.

In the manifesto Labour promised to bring under public ownership the Bank of England, the fuel and power industries, inland transport (by road, rail, air, and canal), and the iron and steel industry. This it did in seven statutes: the Bank of England Act of 1946, the Coal Industry Nationalisation Act of 1946, the Civil Aviation Act of 1946, the Electricity Act of 1947, the Transport Act of 1947, the Gas Act of 1948, and the Iron and Steel Act of 1949.

In fulfilling the pledge of "great national programmes" of social services, the Government consolidated and extended the social insurance scheme by the National Insurance Act of 1946, which provided sickness, unemployment, and retirement benefits as well as maternity grants, widows' pensions, and death grants, and by the Industrial Injuries Act of the same year. The National Assistance Act of 1946 covered the destitute not provided for, or not adequately provided for, by national insurance. The National Health Service Act of 1946 nationalized almost all hospitals and set up a free and comprehensive medical service. In seeking to carry out its promises with regard to housing—the goal was "a good standard of accommodation for every family in this island"—the Government enacted important legislation, such as the Rent Control Act of 1949 and the Housing Acts of 1946 and 1949. The Children Act of 1948 helped fulfill the pledge of "better child welfare services."

Corresponding to the party's pledge of a "radical solution" to the problems of land acquisition and land use, the Town and Country Planning Act of 1947 nationalized development value, restricting the owner's interest in land to its existing use and transferring to the state the exclusive right to financial benefit from the development of land. To the farmers Labour promised "stable markets" and a "fair return": by the Agriculture Act of 1947 it established a system of "assured markets and guaranteed prices." A first step toward the promised "supervision of monopolies and cartels" and prohibition of "anti-social restrictive practices" was taken by the passage of the Monopolies and Restrictive Practices (Inquiry and Control) Act of 1948.

In line with long-standing party policy, the manifesto advocated "taxation which bears less heavily on the lower-income groups" and Labour's Chancellors maintained from wartime, and in some respects sharpened, a steeply progressive scheme of income taxation. To the list of major legislation one should also add the Supplies and Services (Transitional Powers) Act of 1945, which contained many of the wide powers over the economy that the Government had exercised during the war and which gave it, in Morrison's words, "appropriate authority for the economic planning and control which we regarded as essential if we were to achieve a successful transition from war to peace."

Pledges of legislation were not the sole content of the manifesto. Its first and major pledge of full employment—"Jobs For All"—was understood to depend both upon structural reforms achieved through legislation and upon administrative and fiscal policies. The manifesto also gave attention to international affairs. But much as it stressed the importance of keeping the peace, its proposals in foreign policy were few —and its hopes rosy—by far the greater part of the program being concerned with home affairs.

If promises and performance in the field of legislation are compared, Attlee was fully justified in claiming, when he went to the country in February, 1950, that his Government "had carried out the programme which we had put forward at the last General Election." But the Government not only performed what the party pledged; it also did not go substantially beyond those pledges. One can find important statutes that cannot be traced back to the manifesto—for instance, the Criminal Justice Act of 1948—but they are few. With regard to the Government's legislative record, the manifesto was not only imperative, it was also conclusive.

Herbert Morrison called this record "the most extensive and significant legislative programme in the history of our great Parliament." He could also have said that never before had a Government's actual record of law-making been previously laid out before the country in such completeness and detail by a party seeking office at a general election. Even in the days when Radical influence ran strongly in the Liberal Party, its electoral promises were a far less complete and accurate guide to its Government's actual legislative efforts.... The great reforming Government that came to power in 1906 committed itself to a number of important measures—especially those in the field of social reform—which its spokesmen had not anticipated during the election.

Origins of the program. Labour ministers felt that they were entitled, indeed obliged, to carry out the pledges which their party had made at the election and for which the voters, by sending Labour to Westminster with a majority, had given the Government a mandate. But how did these pledges achieve this status? Who or what made them a program that would be binding on a Labour Government? While the party constitution (by Clause V) gave conference the authority to decide what proposals should be included in "the Party Programme," it provided that the N.E.C. and Executive Committee of the P.L.P. should jointly decide which items from that program should be included in the manifesto for a general election. Binding pledges, in short, were to be determined by the parliamentary and extra-parliamentary authorities. If there was conflict between leaders and followers or between conference and P.L.P., this requirement of joint determination would be very important. But in a party as fundamentally at one as Labour in 1945, it was superfluous—and in the actual procedure by which the manifesto was authorized was not followed. The P.L.P. as such was not brought into the process by which the manifesto was prepared and approved, and Labour's election pledges acquired their authority exclusively by the action of the extra-parliamentary party.

As we have seen, it was the N.E.C. and its campaign subcommittee that initially drew up and approved the manifesto. Similarly, the debate at conference made it quite clear that the statement was not merely advisory to the parliamentary leadership, but was to be an authoritative control on their action if they won office. Introducing *Let Us Face The Future* for the N.E.C., Morrison called it "Labour's Five-Year Plan" of legislative and administrative work. That these, but only these, promises would be binding on the party was explicit in his warning to candidates that "the Labour Government is not going to meet promises not authorized by the party program." Closing the debate, the conference chairman, Ellen Wilkinson, asked delegates to vote their approval of the manifesto "as a declaration of policy on which we shall go forward to victory at the General Election."

Drawn up and submitted by the N.E.C. and approved by conference, the statement was called "our Election Manifesto" by Attlee, "an election manifesto and programme" by Morrison, "the document on which we fought the last election" by the N.E.C., and the Labour Party's "main declaration of policy" by the principal students of the election of 1945. Not endorsement by the Leader, by candidates, or by the parliamentary party gave it this status, but the action of the N.E.C. and the annual conference. The point is worth stressing because of the radical difference from Conservative procedure. Moreover, as we have seen, such authority was never claimed or exercised by the representative assembly of the Liberal Party of Victorian and Edwardian days, even at the height of Radical influence. Not only in its Socialist purpose, but in its conception of democratic politics, the Labour Party showed itself to be a distinctive type of political formation.

Party cohesion. As wholeheartedly as their leaders, the parliamentary rank and file accepted the manifesto and the legislative program based on it. Recalling the triumphs of the early days of the Attlee Government, Hugh Dalton exclaimed nostalgically, "Yes, we were all in step then!" With the help of a study of voting in the House during the 1945–6 session, one can put this impression in quantitative terms. Twenty-nine divisions, a sample of one in every ten, were examined. All twenty-nine were party votes in the sense that 90 per cent or more of Labour M.P.s taking part voted on the same side and, since the Government put on the whips in every case, this meant that all votes were party votes for the Government position. The coefficient of cohesion gives a more exact measurement. In twenty-eight divisions, since there was no cross-voting whatsoever by Labour M.P.'s, this coefficient was 100 per cent. For the whole sample the coefficient of cohesion was slightly more than 99.9 per cent. . . .

Throughout the life of Attlee's Governments, party cohesion in the division lobbies continued to be virtually perfect. This does not mean there was no dissension. Even during that "annus mirabilis," as Dalton calls 1946, there were at times rebellious mutterings among some backbenchers. At first centering on foreign and defense policy, dissent was fed during the later years of Attlee's regime by disagreements that raised fundamental questions regarding the meaning of Socialism.... With regard to the massive legislative program proceeding from the manifesto of 1945, and with the exception of Cabinet doubts that delayed the introduction of the bill nationalizing iron and steel, agreement in the party at all levels was monolithic.

No doubt many factors played a part in producing and maintaining such unity. In controlling individuals and small groups of dissidents, the large formal powers of discipline with which the party constitution and standing orders endowed party organs were useful. In five individual cases the N.E.C. exercised its authority to expel members from the party and, although the P.L.P. suspended its standing orders—which among other things required M.P.'s not to vote contrary to the decision of the party meeting—the right to withdraw the whip was retained and exercised in such "extreme cases." Leaders were strengthened by their control over the avenues of advancement toward and up the ministerial ladder and such impulses toward rebellion as might exist were powerfully restrained by the prospect that mutiny might help the Tories. But if one imagines these forces removed from the situation and consults the known wishes of M.P.'s, it is obvious that the great bulk of them would have similarly supported the program of *Let Us Face the Future*.

However one analyzes the party—as leaders and followers, as parliamentary and extra-parliamentary, as trade unions and constituency organizations—one finds the same unity of purpose. During the war the main thrust in preparing a program for postwar reconstruction had come from the leaders, and already in 1943 a policy statement submitted by the N.E.C. to conference, entitled "The Labour Party and the Future," embodied the principal proposals of the manifesto of 1945 and, indeed, under much the same headings. Conference had approved this statement as it did the manifesto, and in its *Interim Report on Post-War Reconstruction* of 1944, the T.U.C. had expressed its support for substantially the same proposals. The cohesion on these basic measures of reconstruction that prevailed in the party within parliament and outside parliament under Attlee's regime was essentially the product of the consensus on purpose which had reigned in the party for many years and had been given comprehensive expression in the election program of 1945. Thanks to this consensus, and within its limits, the party could act effectively, harmoniously, and coherently. In this sense Attlee's Governments were the culmination of the Labour Party of the Socialist generation. It remained to be seen how the party would behave when it could no longer rely upon such consensus.

"This federal hybrid," R. H. S. Crossman has said of the Labour Party's constitution, "with its ambiguous division of powers, is as unworkable as the constitution of the United States; and here, as there, the test of a leader is whether he can make it work." The comment is just, but it attributes too much to the powers of a leader. The Labour Party, as a party both ideological and internally democratic, worked effectively when and because its various, sprawling parts were united by a strong sense of common purpose. The disruption of that consensus produced a decade of crisis.

41

ELECTORAL SOCIOLOGY

D. E. Butler

The science of discovering voting patterns and of drawing profiles of the electorate has been intensely cultivated among contemporary historians in the United States and is just beginning to be pursued in England. The authoritative work of David Butler, whose general conclusions are given in this selection, summarizes the current state of knowledge in England in the new field of electoral sociology.

It is hard to assess what is signified by the individual vote, which constitutes the foundation of all electoral analysis. A vote is too easily taken as a declaration of unwavering faith in the preferred candidate, in his party, and in every item in its programme. But it may, of course, be an expression of anything from a mere whim to a deep-rooted prejudice, or from a reasoned assessment of the lesser evil to a confident assertion of political faith. It may be cast by a person who dislikes all existing parties, by one who has no representative of his own party standing, or by one who votes against his convictions recognizing that his preferred candidate has no chance. It may be influenced by the personality of the candidate or by some local issue quite extraneous to the national struggle. But whatever its motivation, every vote looks alike in a table of figures. Therefore if any meaning is to be drawn from election results certain minimum assumptions have to be made about the behaviour of voters. It has at least to be assumed that wholly irrational voters tend to cancel each other out and that, whether as the fruit of conscientious reflection or of mere prejudice, a vote represents a definite expression of preference between the general outlook of the contending parties.

By and large, these assumptions lead to few difficulties. They are not

FROM D. E. Butler, *The Electoral System in Britain Since 1918*, 2nd ed. (Oxford: The Clarendon Press, 1963), pp. 205–208. By permission of the Clarendon Press, Oxford.

susceptible of proof, but they do not seem unrealistic. However unthinking many electors may be, their votes do seem on balance to represent a general judgement between the merits of the national parties. The most notable lesson offered by a comparison of election results is the similarity of behaviour between different constituencies. In the last five general elections scarcely a single seat has changed hands in a direction opposite to the national trend; if the percentage swings in votes are considered, the differences between neighbouring constituencies were surprisingly small. It would appear that neither the quality of the candidate, nor the efficiency of his organization, nor the special local issues which may have arisen, were capable of affecting the result to anything like the same degree as the national party struggle.

Since elections are so predominantly fought on the merits of the parties as a whole to the exclusion of local issues, the problem of interpreting the results should be much simpler than in a more diverse country, such as the United States. But it is complicated enough and provokes many erroneous statements. The main sources of confusion can be roughly classified.

1. *Votes and seats.* There is a natural tendency in commenting upon elections to focus attention upon victories and defeats to the exclusion of the turnover in votes. This is quite proper if interest is confined to the affairs of the House of Commons, but all too often interpretations of the public mood are also based upon the number of seats which have changed hands rather than upon the losses and gains in votes. After each election it is salutary to remember how many people supported the minority party. In 1945, for example, so much was written about the 'landslide' that it was sometimes forgotten that less than 5 out of every 10 voters had supported the Labour party and that virtually 4 out of every 10 had supported the Conservatives. In both 1950 and 1951, if over the whole country 1 voter in 100 had changed his mind in one direction or 2 voters in 100 in the other, the outcome would have been decisive and 'the clear verdict of the British people' would have been discussed. Overmuch attention to the winning and losing of seats has repeatedly led commentators into wildly excessive generalizations about the meaning of election results as expressions of the public mood.

2. *Candidatures.* Comparisons between the share of the national vote secured by a party in successive elections may be largely vitiated by failure to consider changes in the number of candidates put forward. In individual constituencies too, when a new contestant appears or an old one withdraws, allowance is not always made for the ways in which their supporters may have been distributed between the other parties.

3. *Turnout.* The full electorate never votes. The causes of most non-voting have no direct connexion with political conviction, but a reduction in turnout may none the less affect the fortunes of the parties. There is good reason to believe that the upper classes are more conscientious about exercising their franchise than the lower. This factor is not of such great importance in general elections where a high proportion of the potential

voters has always voted. But in by-elections the turnout fluctuates much more and the apparent swing of opinion may be as much due to this selective apathy as to any change of heart. Therefore those who try to draw conclusions from elections in which the poll has dropped substantially may be misled.

4. *By-elections and general elections.* Variations in turnout are not the only or even the main cause for the misinterpretation of by-election results. Irrespective of turnout there has been a general tendency for by-elections to go more against the Government than general elections. While this tendency continues crude forecasts based upon by-elections may prove most deceptive.

5. *Majorities.* In individual contests excessive attention is often paid to the victor's lead in votes. An increase in the numerical majority is regarded as a triumph and a reduction as a defeat. But the majority may vary in a manner quite opposite to the swing in opinion owing to a fall in turnout or to the intrusion or withdrawal of an extra candidate. By the use of percentages some, though not all, of this confusion can be avoided.

6. *Conclusion.* In addition to these causes for the misunderstanding of election results, which relate to factors partially capable of statistical demonstration, there are other illusions which are largely due to verbal confusion.

The 'personification' of the electorate is perhaps the most outstanding example. Speaking after the results in 1950, Mr. Morrison provided an admirable instance of this almost universal tendency:

> The British electorate has a habit of knowing what it wants and has a habit of overdoing the getting of what it wants ... this time I think it wanted Labour back with a smaller majority but ... it said it in italics instead of roman and the result is that it has got a tighter situation than it meant.

The dangers of presenting the change of mind of a small proportion of the population as though it represented the considered decision of the whole have only to be pointed out to become obvious.

There are several similar and widespread confusions; some, for instance, are fostered by the excessive use of the analogies of war in the description of the electoral process and some by the use of unexamined clichés such as 'the floating voter' or 'the balancing power of the middle class'. But there is no point in pursuing too far this analysis of the errors with which electoral commentaries habitually abound. Many foolish things have been said and will continue to be said about the meaning of elections; they may be traced almost entirely to two causes—the comparison of figures which are not comparable, and the thoughtless acceptance of unsupported generalizations about voting behaviour. Since relatively few election statistics are strictly comparable between one election and the next, and since there has been so little systematic investigation of voting behaviour, commenting on elections is naturally hazardous. But with the aid of research and reflection the hazards can be greatly reduced.